For Reference

Not to be taken from this room

CINEMA,
THE MAGIC VEHICLE:
A Guide to Its Achievement

by
ADAM GARBICZ
and
JACEK KLINOWSKI

Journey One:

The Cinema Through 1949

The Scarecrow Press, Inc.

Metuchen, N. J.   1975

ACKNOWLEDGMENTS

The authors wish to thank the film archives
and libraries in many countries for their assistance,
and especially Mr. Akira Shimizu of the Japan Film
Library Council.

Thanks are also due to Dr. Timothy Burstein
for reading the manuscript and making useful comments.

FRONTISPIECE

The Gold Rush: the lonely Tramp watches his
beloved Georgia amid the New Year celebrations at
the saloon; © The Roy Export Company Establishment.

Library of Congress Cataloging in Publication Data

Garbicz, Adam.
    Cinema, the magic vehicle.

    Includes index.
    CONTENTS: journey 1. The cinema through 1949.
    1. Moving-picture plays--History and criticism--Col-
lections. I. Klinowski, Jacek, joint author. II. Title.
PN1995. G25   791. 43'09   75-2183
ISBN 0-8108-0801-3

Printed in the United States of America

CONTENTS

List of Films Discussed   v

Preface   xix

Technical Notes   xxii

Comparison of Running Times
  for Two Standard Projection Speeds   xxv

Short Outline of the Main Events
  in Cinema History through 1949   29

The Films, by Year   39

Index of Directors   523

Index of Films   537

iii

LIST OF FILMS DISCUSSED*

		page
1913	The Student of Prague (Stellan Rye)	39
	Cabiria (Giovanni Pastrone)	40
1915	+The Birth of a Nation (D. W. Griffith)	42
1916	†Intolerance (D. W. Griffith)	44
	+A Man There Was (Victor Sjöström)	46
1917	†The Outlaw and His Wife (Victor Sjöström)	48
1918	Shoulder Arms (Charles Chaplin)	50
1919	+The Cabinet of Dr. Caligari (Robert Wiene)	52
	+Sir Arne's Treasure (Mauritz Stiller)	53
	+Broken Blossoms (D. W. Griffith)	55
	Polikushka (Alexandr Sanin)	56
1920	+The Phantom Carriage (Victor Sjöström)	58
	+L'Homme du large (Marcel L'Herbier)	59
	The Golem (Paul Wegener and Carl Boese)	60
	The Parson's Widow (Carl Theodor Dreyer)	61
	Way Down East (D. W. Griffith)	62
	Erotikon (Mauritz Stiller)	63
1921	†Destiny (Fritz Lang)	65
	+The Kid (Charles Chaplin)	67
	+Foolish Wives (Erich von Stroheim)	68
	+Souls on the Road (Minoru Murata)	69
	+Witchcraft Through the Ages (Benjamin Christensen)	71

---

*This list is divided, by symbols, into three categories that in the opinion of the authors reflect the relative standards of the films discussed: † indicates a film of the first rank; + indicates one of the second rank; no symbol denotes a work of the third rank.

+Shattered (Lupu Pick)   72
+Seven Years' Bad Luck (Max Linder)   73
+Eldorado (Marcel L'Herbier)   74
Backstairs (Leopold Jessner)   75

1922   +The Pilgrim (Charles Chaplin)   77
+Dr. Mabuse, the Gambler (Fritz Lang)   78
+Nosferatu (F. W. Murnau)   79
+Crainquebille (Jacques Feyder)   81
+L'Auberge rouge (Jean Epstein)   82
+Warning Shadows (Arthur Robison)   83
The Three Must-Get-Theres (Max Linder)   84
Vanina (Arthur von Gerlach)   85

1923   +Coeur fidèle (Jean Epstein)   87
+Our Hospitality (Buster Keaton and Jack G. Blystone)   88
+The Covered Wagon (James Cruze)   89
+A Woman of Paris (Charles Chaplin)   90
+La Belle Nivernaise (Jean Epstein)   92
La Roue (Abel Gance)   92
New Year's Eve (Lupu Pick)   95

1924   †Greed (Erich von Stroheim)   97
†The Last Laugh (F. W. Murnau)   98
†Strike (Sergei Eisenstein)   100
+Sherlock Junior (Buster Keaton)   101
+The Navigator (Buster Keaton and Donald Crisp)   102
+Nibelungen (Fritz Lang)   103
Visages d'enfants (Jacques Feyder)   105
The Iron Horse (John Ford)   106
Waxworks (Paul Leni)   107
He Who Gets Slapped (Victor Sjöström)   108

1925   †Battleship Potemkin (Sergei Eisenstein)   110
†The Gold Rush (Charles Chaplin)   111
+Vaudeville (Ewald André Dupont)   112
+The Big Parade (King Vidor)   113
+Master of the House (Carl Theodor Dreyer)   114

+Seven Chances (Buster Keaton)   115

+The Joyless Street (G. W. Pabst)   116

  Go West (Buster Keaton)   117

1926 †Mother (Vsevolod Pudovkin)   118

+The General (Buster Keaton and Clyde Bruckman)   119

+The Lodger (Alfred Hitchcock)   121

  Metropolis (Fritz Lang)   122

  The Scarlet Letter (Victor Sjöström)   123

  Battling Butler (Buster Keaton)   123

  Wings of a Serf (Yuri Tarich)   124

  Death Bay (Abram Room)   125

1927 †The Passion of Joan of Arc (Carl Theodor Dreyer)   126

†The End of St. Petersburg (Vsevolod Pudovkin)   127

†Sunrise (F. W. Murnau)   128

†October (Sergei Eisenstein)   129

+The Wedding March (Erich von Stroheim)   130

+Thérèse Raquin (Jacques Feyder)   132

+The Italian Straw Hat (René Clair)   133

+Underworld (Josef von Sternberg)   134

+Bed and Sofa (Abram Room)   135

+The Love of Jeanne Ney (G. W. Pabst)   136

+The Circus (Charles Chaplin)   137

+The Firty-First (Yakov Protazanov)   138

  En Rade (Alberto Cavalcanti)   139

  Seventh Heaven (Frank Borzage)   140

1928 †Storm Over Asia (Vsevolod Pudovkin)   141

+The Wind (Victor Sjöström)   142

+The Crowd (King Vidor)   143

+The Fall of the House of Usher (Jean Epstein)   144

+Pandora's Box (G. W. Pabst)   144

+Lonesome (Pál Fejös)   145

+Les Deux timides (René Clair)   146

+Crossways (Teinosuke Kinugasa)   147

+The Docks of New York (Josef von Sternberg)   148

+Steamboat Bill Jr. (Charles F. Reisner)   149

+Queen Kelly (Erich von Stroheim) 150

+Finis Terrae (Jean Epstein) 152

+Les Nouveaux messieurs (Jacques Feyder) 152

+The Spies (Fritz Lang) 153

The Cameraman (Edward Sedgwick) 154

Eliso (Nikolai Shengelaya) 155

The Honeymoon (Erich von Stroheim) 156

White Shadows in the South Seas (Woodbridge S. Van Dyke) 157

The House in Trubnaya Street (Boris Barnet) 158

Our Daily Bread (F. W. Murnau) 158

1929 †Hallelujah! (King Vidor) 160

+Diary of a Lost Girl (G. W. Pabst) 161

+Such Is Life (Karl Junghans) 162

+The Ghost That Will Not Return (Abram Room) 163

+Fragment of an Empire (Friedrich Ermler) 164

+The Blue Express (Ilya Trauberg) 164

+Mother Krause's Journey to Happiness (Phil Jutzi) 165

+Blackmail (Alfred Hitchcock) 166

+Spite Marriage (Edward Sedgwick) 167

Sun (Alessandro Blasetti) 168

Alibi (Roland West) 169

Rails (Mario Camerini) 169

1930 †Earth (Olexandr Dovzhenko) 171

†City Lights (Charles Chaplin) 172

†The Blue Angel (Josef von Sternberg) 173

+Sous les toits de Paris (René Clair) 175

+Westfront 1918 (G. W. Pabst) 176

+All Quiet on the Western Front (Lewis Milestone) 177

+Little Caesar (Mervyn Le Roy) 179

The Big House (George Hill) 180

Murder (Alfred Hitchcock) 181

1931 †Kameradschaft (G. W. Pabst) 182

+M (Fritz Lang) 183

+The Threepenny Opera (G. W. Pabst) 184

+Tabu (Robert Flaherty and F. W. Murnau)   185

+Le Million (René Clair)   187

+Girls in Uniforms (Leontine Sagan)   187

+The Congress Dances (Erik Charell)   188

+A Pass to Life (Nikolai Ekk)   189

+Hotel Paradis (George Schnéevoigt)   190

+Public Enemy (William A. Wellman)   191

+The Front Page (Lewis Milestone)   192

+Marius (Alexander Korda)   193

+Vampyr, ou l'étrange aventure de David Gray
(Carl Theodor Dreyer)   194

City Streets (Rouben Mamoulian)   195

Emil and the Detectives (Gerhard Lamprecht)   196

An American Tragedy (Josef von Sternberg)   197

L'Or des mers (Jean Epstein)   198

Tell England (Anthony Asquith and Geoffrey Barkas)   198

1932   †¡Que Viva Mexico! (Sergei Eisenstein)   200

+I Was Born, but.... (Yasujiro Ozu)   202

+Poil de Carotte (Julien Duvivier)   203

+I am a Fugitive from a Chain Gang (Mervyn Le Roy)   204

+Liebelei (Max Ophüls)   205

+À nous la liberté (René Clair)   206

+Scarface (Howard Hawks)   207

+Counterplan (Friedrich Ermler and Sergei Yutkevich)   209

Arrowsmith (John Ford)   210

Before Matriculation (Vladislav Vančura and
Svatopluk Innemann)   210

Marie, a Hungarian Legend (Pál Fejös)   211

What Rascals Men Are! (Mario Camerini)   212

Fanny (Marc Allégret)   212

1933   +Quatorze Juillet (René Clair)   214

+Le Grand jeu (Jacques Feyder)   215

+Passing Fancy (Yasujiro Ozu)   216

+1860 (Alessandro Blasetti)   217

+The Testament of Dr. Mabuse (Fritz Lang)   218

+The Private Life of Henry VIII (Alexander Korda)   219

ix

	Don Quixote (G. W. Pabst)	220
	The River (Josef Rovenský)	221
1934	+L'Atalante (Jean Vigo)	222
	+Chapayev (Sergei and Georgy Vasiliev)	223
	+Man of Aran (Robert Flaherty)	224
	+It Happened One Night (Frank Capra)	225
	+The Youth of Maxim (Grigori Kozintsev and Leonid Trauberg)	226
	+Toni (Jean Renoir)	227
	+Pension Mimosas (Jacques Feyder)	228
	+The Man Who Knew Too Much (Alfred Hitchcock)	229
	+Revolt of the Fishermen (Erwin Piscator)	230
	+Jolly Fellows (Grigori Alexandrov)	231
	+Our Daily Bread (King Vidor)	232
	+Boule de Suif (Mikhail Romm)	233
	+Maskerade (Willi Forst)	234
	+Crime and Punishment (Pierre Chenal)	235
	The Wave (Fred Zinnemann)	236
	Angèle (Marcel Pagnol)	236
	The Lost Patrol (John Ford)	237
	The Young Trees (Józef Lejtes)	238
1935	+The Informer (John Ford)	239
	+Jánošík (Martin Frič)	240
	+Carnival in Flanders (Jacques Feyder)	241
	+Le Crime de M. Lange (Jean Renoir)	242
	+The Ghost Goes West (René Clair)	243
	+Peter Ibbetson (Henry Hathaway)	244
	+Captain Blood (Michael Curtiz)	245
	Wife, Be Like a Rose (Mikio Naruse)	245
	Maryša (Josef Rovenský)	246
	Peasants (Friedrich Ermler)	247
	I'll Give a Million (Mario Camerini)	248
	The Thirty-Nine Steps (Alfred Hitchcock)	249
1936	†Modern Times (Charles Chaplin)	250
	†Partie de campagne (Jean Renoir)	251

+We from Kronstadt (Yefim Dzigan)   253

+Mr. Deeds Goes to Town (Frank Capra)   254

+Osaka Elegy (Kenji Mizoguchi)   255

+Fury (Fritz Lang)   256

+Sisters of the Gion (Kenji Mizoguchi)   257

+Baltic Deputy (Alexandr Zarkhi and Yosif Kheifits)   258

+Rembrandt (Alexander Korda)   259

+The Secret Agent (Alfred Hitchcock)   260

+César (Marcel Pagnol)   261

Pépé le Moko (Julien Duvivier)   262

The Thirteen (Mikhail Romm)   263

La Belle équipe (Julien Duvivier)   264

The Only Son (Yasujiro Ozu)   265

The Story of Louis Pasteur (William Dieterle)   265

Theatre of Life (Tomu Uchida)   266

Tudor Rose (Robert Stevenson)   267

1937   †La Grande illusion (Jean Renoir)   269

+The Return of Maxim (Grigori Kozintsev and Leonid Trauberg)   271

+Bezhin Meadow (Sergei Eisenstein)   271

+Drôle de drame (Marcel Carné)   273

+They Won't Forget (Mervyn Le Roy)   274

+Snow White and the Seven Dwarfs (Walt Disney)   275

+Un Carnet de bal (Julien Duvivier)   276

+Dead End (William Wyler)   278

+Humanity Like a Paper Balloon (Sadao Yamanaka)   279

+Young and Innocent (Alfred Hitchcock)   280

Lenin in October (Mikhail Romm)   281

The Life of Émile Zola (William Dieterle)   282

Il Signor Max (Mario Camerini)   283

1938   †Alexander Nevsky (Sergei Eisenstein)   284

+The Childhood of Maxim Gorky (Mark Donskoy)   286

+Quai des Brumes (Marcel Carné)   287

+Pygmalion (Anthony Asquith and Leslie Howard)   288

+Jezebel (William Wyler)   289

+Les Disparus de Saint-Agil (Christian-Jaque) 290

+Volga-Volga (Grigori Alexandrov) 291

+The Lady Vanishes (Alfred Hitchcock) 292

+The Guild of the Kutná Hora Maidens (Otakar Vávra) 293

+The Vyborg Side (Grigori Kozintsev and Leonid
Trauberg) 294

+You Can't Take It with You (Frank Capra) 295

+Among People (Mark Donskoy) 295

La Bête humaine (Jean Renoir) 296

The Citadel (King Vidor) 298

Bank Holiday (Carol Reed) 299

Peter the First (Vladimir Petrov) 300

The Adventures of Robin Hood (Michael Curtiz and
William Keighley) 300

1939   †Le Jour se lève (Marcel Carné) 302

†Stagecoach (John Ford) 303

†La Règle du jeu (Jean Renoir) 305

+The Story of the Last Chrysanthemum (Kenji Mizoguchi) 307

+Earth (Tomu Uchida) 308

+His Girl Friday (Howard Hawks) 310

+The Stars Look Down (Carol Reed) 311

+La Fin du jour (Julien Duvivier) 312

+A Great Citizen (Friedrich Ermler) 313

+Of Mice and Men (Lewis Milestone) 314

+The Baker's Wife (Marcel Pagnol) 315

Young Mr. Lincoln (John Ford) 316

Confessions of a Nazi Spy (Anatole Litvak) 317

Wuthering Heights (William Wyler) 318

Gulliver's Travels (Dave Fleischer) 319

Ninotchka (Ernst Lubitsch) 320

1940   +The Grapes of Wrath (John Ford) 321

+The Great Dictator (Charles Chaplin) 322

+Fantasia (Walt Disney) 324

+The Return of Frank James (Fritz Lang) 325

+Foreign Correspondent (Alfred Hitchcock) 326

+Dr. Ehrlich's Magic Bullet (William Dieterle)   327

+Northwest Passage (King Vidor)   328

Major Barbara (Gabriel Pascal)   328

The Philadelphia Story (George Cukor)   329

Gaslight (Thorold Dickinson)   330

1941   †Citizen Kane (Orson Welles)   332

+Us Kids (Louis Daquin)   335

+The Maltese Falcon (John Huston)   336

+Sullivan's Travels (Preston Sturges)   338

+The Murder of Father Christmas (Christian-Jaque)   339

The Little Foxes (William Wyler)   339

Sergeant York (Howard Hawks)   340

How Green Was My Valley (John Ford)   341

The Sea Wolf (Michael Curtiz)   342

Horse (Kajiro Yamamoto)   343

Suspicion (Alfred Hitchcock)   344

49th Parallel (Michael Powell)   345

Western Union (Fritz Lang)   345

1942   +Les Visiteurs du soir (Marcel Carné)   347

+The Magnificent Ambersons (Orson Welles)   348

+Ossessione (Luchino Visconti)   350

+The Road to Heaven (Alf Sjöberg)   351

+In Which We Serve (Noël Coward and David Lean)   352

+The Ox-Bow Incident (William A. Wellman)   353

+I Married a Witch (René Clair)   354

+Goupi Mains Rouges (Jacques Becker)   355

+Four Steps in the Clouds (Alessandro Blasetti)   356

+Mrs. Miniver (William Wyler)   356

+Next of Kin (Thorold Dickinson)   357

+Pontcarral (Jean Delannoy)   358

There Was a Father (Yasujiro Ozu)   359

Strangers in the House (Henri Decoin)   360

Casablanca (Michael Curtiz)   361

1943   +The Crow (Henri-Georges Clouzot)   362

+Day of Wrath (Carl Theodor Dreyer)   363

+Judo Saga (Akira Kurosawa) 365

+Air Force (Howard Hawks) 366

+Les Anges du péché (Robert Bresson) 367

+Lifeboat (Alfred Hitchcock) 368

+The Children Are Watching Us (Vittorio De Sica) 369

+San Demetrio, London (Charles Frend) 370

+Douce (Claude Autant-Lara) 371

+Shadow of a Doubt (Alfred Hitchcock) 372

+Maria Candelaria (Emilio Fernández) 373

+Adémaï, bandit d'honneur (Gilles Grangier) 374

+Nine Men (Harry Watt) 375

Sahara (Zoltan Korda) 376

Le Ciel est à vous (Jean Grémillon) 376

Action in the North Atlantic (Lloyd Bacon) 377

Madame Curie (Mervyn Le Roy) 378

The More the Merrier (George Stevens) 379

1944 †Ivan the Terrible (Sergei Eisenstein) 380

+Henry V (Laurence Olivier) 382

+Frenzy (Alf Sjöberg) 383

+The Woman in the Window (Fritz Lang) 385

+It Happened Tomorrow (René Clair) 385

+The Way Ahead (Carol Reed) 386

+Double Indemnity (Billy Wilder) 387

+Laura (Otto Preminger) 388

+Arsenic and Old Lace (Frank Capra) 389

The Seventh Cross (Fred Zinnemann) 390

Gaslight (George Cukor) 391

Hail the Conquering Hero (Preston Sturges) 392

1945 †Les Enfants du paradis (Marcel Carné) 394

+They Who Step on the Tiger's Tail (Akira Kurosawa) 395

+La Bataille du rail (René Clément) 396

+The Story of G. I. Joe (William A. Wellman) 398

+The Lost Weekend (Billy Wilder) 399

+Brief Encounter (David Lean) 400

+Rome, Open City (Roberto Rossellini) 401

+The Way to the Stars (Anthony Asquith) 402

+Les Dames du Bois de Boulogne (Robert Bresson) 403

+The Great Turning Point (Friedrich Ermler) 404

+The Last Chance (Leopold Lindtberg) 405

+A Tree Grows in Brooklyn (Elia Kazan) 406

+The House on 92nd Street (Henry Hathaway) 407

+Boule de Suif (Christian-Jaque) 408

+The Southerner (Jean Renoir) 409

+A Walk in the Sun (Lewis Milestone) 410

+The Overlanders (Harry Watt) 411

Blithe Spirit (David Lean) 412

Mildred Pierce (Michael Curtiz) 413

1946   †The Boyars' Plot (Sergei Eisenstein) 415

†Paisà (Roberto Rossellini) 417

+Notorious (Alfred Hitchcock) 418

+Le Diable au corps (Claude Autant-Lara) 419

+Great Expectations (David Lean) 420

+The Best Years of Our Lives (William Wyler) 422

+Shoeshine (Vittorio De Sica) 423

+The Big Sleep (Howard Hawks) 424

+Beauty and the Beast (Jean Cocteau) 425

+La Symphonie pastorale (Jean Delannoy) 426

+Vivere in Pace (Luigi Zampa) 427

+My Darling Clementine (John Ford) 428

+Dead Among the Living (Bořivoj Zeman) 429

+The Sun Rises Again (Aldo Vergano) 430

+The Murderers Are Amongst Us (Wolfgang Staudte) 431

+The Killers (Robert Siodmak) 432

No Regrets for My Youth (Akira Kurosawa) 433

The Bandit (Alberto Lattuada) 434

1947   †Odd Man Out (Carol Reed) 435

+Germany Year Zero (Roberto Rossellini) 436

+Le Silence est d'or (René Clair) 437

+Quai des Orfèvres (Henri-Georges Clouzot) 438

+Monsieur Verdoux (Charles Chaplin) 440

xv

+Kiss of Death (Henry Hathaway)   441

+Macbeth (Orson Welles)   442

+Les Jeux sont faits (Jean Delannoy)   443

+Brute Force (Jules Dassin)   444

+Call Northside 777 (Henry Hathaway)   445

+The Tragic Pursuit (Giuseppe De Santis)   446

+Somewhere in Europe (Géza Radványi)   447

+The Treasure of Sierra Madre (John Huston)   448

+Boomerang! (Elia Kazan)   449

+Le Silence de la mer (Jean-Pierre Melville)   450

+Ditta, Child of Man (Astrid and Björne Henning-Jensen)   452

+Antoine et Antoinette (Jacques Becker)   452

+Les Maudits (René Clément)   453

+Dark Passage (Delmer Daves)   455

+La Chartreuse de Parme (Christian-Jaque)   456

+They Live by Night (Nicholas Ray)   457

+The Lady from Shanghai (Orson Welles)   458

+The Strike (Karel Steklý)   458

Jour de fête (Jacques Tati)   459

Pursued (Raoul Walsh)   460

One Wonderful Sunday (Akira Kurosawa)   461

Les Dernières vacances (Roger Leenhardt)   462

Presentiment (Otakar Vávra)   463

No One Knows a Thing (Josef Mach)   463

1948   †Bicycle Thieves (Vittorio De Sica)   465

†Louisiana Story (Robert Flaherty)   466

+The Fallen Idol (Carol Reed)   467

+Hamlet (Laurence Olivier)   468

+The Last Stage (Wanda Jakubowska)   469

+The Naked City (Jules Dassin)   470

+Red River (Howard Hawks)   471

+Letter from an Unknown Woman (Max Ophüls)   472

+Manon (Henri-Georges Clouzot)   473

+Yellow Sky (William A. Wellman)   474

+Drunken Angel (Akira Kurosawa)   475

+La Terra Trema (Luchino Visconti) 476

+The Street Has Many Dreams (Mario Camerini) 478

+The Soil Under Your Feet (Frigyes Bán) 478

+Border Street (Aleksander Ford) 479

+Sorry, Wrong Number (Anatole Litvak) 480

+Criss Cross (Robert Siodmak) 481

+Une si jolie petite plage (Yves Allégret) 482

+Without Pity (Alberto Lattuada) 483

+The Winslow Boy (Anthony Asquith) 484

+The Snake Pit (Anatole Litvak) 484

+L'École buissonnière (Jean-Paul Le Chanois) 485

+Le Mura di Malapaga (René Clément) 486

+Rope (Alfred Hitchcock) 487

+As Others See Us (Jean Dréville) 488

The Quiet One (Sidney Meyers) 488

The Mill on the Po (Alberto Lattuada) 489

Oliver Twist (David Lean) 490

Key Largo (John Huston) 491

Scott of the Antarctic (Charles Frend) 492

Fort Apache (John Ford) 493

Les Parents terribles (Jean Cocteau) 494

Clochemerle (Pierre Chenal) 495

Conscience (Jiři Krejčik) 496

Passport to Pimlico (Henry Cornelius) 496

Maclovia (Emilio Fernández) 497

1949 +Bitter Rice (Giuseppe De Santis) 499

+Late Spring (Yasujiro Ozu) 500

+La Beauté du diable (René Clair) 501

+Stray Dog (Akira Kurosawa) 503

+Intruder in the Dust (Clarence Brown) 504

+Thieves' Highway (Jules Dassin) 504

+Los Olvidados (Luis Buñuel) 506

+The Third Man (Carol Reed) 507

+All the King's Men (Robert Rossen) 508

+The Set-Up (Robert Wise) 509

+The Heiress (William Wyler)   510
+Give Us This Day (Edward Dmytryk)   511
+In the Name of the Law (Pietro Germi)   512
+Champion (Mark Robson)   513
+Les Enfants terribles (Jean-Pierre Melville)   514
+Kind Hearts and Coronets (Robert Hamer)   515
+She Wore a Yellow Ribbon (John Ford)   516
 Under Capricorn (Alfred Hitchcock)   517
 Manèges (Yves Allégret)   518
 Occupe-toi d'Amélie (Claude Autant-Lara)   519
 Knock on Any Door (Nicholas Ray)   519
 Pueblerina (Emilio Fernández)   521
 On the Town (Gene Kelly and Stanley Donen)   521

PREFACE

The purpose of this book is to give a panoramic view of the achievement of the cinema through the "film-by-film" approach. The trouble is that in fact most movies are interesting for one reason or another. A film might attract interest because Greta Garbo appears in it; in a book about this actress it will certainly be considered worthwhile just because of this circumstance alone. There are also scores of pictures whose reputation was based on topicality or curiosity value, but which now seem disappointing.

We do not want to write only about cult-movies or the so-called milestones of the cinema. There are enough books which analyze those in great detail. While not actually trying to make obscure discoveries, we simply feel that people interested in the cinema have the right to know about all movies which are good and exciting to watch, especially if relatively little known. The idea behind the book is completeness: we have tried to include all films which anyone seriously interested in the cinema would consider worth seeing, wherever they come from.

Our main concern is the aesthetic standard of a film. What makes the films of von Stroheim or René Clair works of art? What elements of style and film technique are involved? What is vital to their personal vision and makes their films what they are? It seemed to us that the most natural way to answer such questions would be to analyze their pictures individually, in the form of mini-essays. We have tried not to assume any previous knowledge of the cinema on the part of the reader. This is why a short introduction-synopsis of the most important events in cinema history is included. The text of the critiques always tries to set each film in its historical context and to outline the necessary trends and styles.

The arrangement of the material in the book is chronological.

Titles of films are given according to year of production, which is
more relevant than the sometimes much later release date.   This
arrangement makes it easier to give a coherent account of the development of schools and trends: to show that no work of art is
isolated but must always be treated as a product of its time and to
draw attention to the exchange of ideas and the interaction of film-
makers from different countries.   When read together, the essays
dealing with the films of any director should give an account of his
line of development.   Similarly the critiques of gangster movies, for
instance, are so written as to reflect the development of the genre.

The order in which individual pictures are discussed within
a given year, although subjective, is in our intention an indication
of their relative quality.   Unfortunately it is often difficult to point
out in so many words why a film is good.   After all, literary critics
forever discuss the strange fascination of Shakespeare without actually getting very far.   To give an example, the plot of The Wedding
March is to say the least banal while the formal aspect of the film
gives strong hints of dilettantism.   The greatness of this captivating
picture seems to be derived from the difficult to describe, obsessive
precision of detail and the compelling, realistic mise en scène.

We have tried to give the outline of the plot of each film.
Yet is sometimes happens (the most celebrated example being The
Birth of a Nation) that the plot itself hardly survives print while
being exceedingly complex and simply not very interesting.   The story
is always given when it is important for the sense of the message of
the picture.   Thus, for instance, one has to go into the plot of Battleship Potemkin in some detail.

Each critique is preceded by screen credits.   The relevance
of these for the understanding of a picture is rarely appreciated by
authors of film books.   What is more, they are seldom correct, especially for silent pictures.   Yet screen credits can sometimes give
more idea of a film than scores of words, and are for this reason
of special interest to many students of the cinema.   We can think
of some who collect them straight from the screen.   Thus we have
taken great pains to give credits correctly, to check the spelling

of foreign words and uniformity of transcriptions from Cyrillic and Japanese. Quite simply, this book provides the most correct list of film credits anywhere to be found.

The subject matter of the book is feature cinema, i.e. "fiction" films over 60 minutes in projection time. Because of sheer numbers involved we have not included documentaries with no fictional element. Short experimental films which often exerted great influence on other film-makers (like the words of the French Avantgarde or the Surrealists) are also not discussed separately but only referred to where necessary. Some medium-length films of particularly high standard (as well as one-hour television films in the volume to come) are included.

TECHNICAL NOTES

Screen Credits. The discussion of each film is preceded by its screen credits. These normally include the names of the director, scriptwriter, music composer and all leading actors, with the exception of silent pictures where music credits are not given. The scores often written for silent pictures and performed by an orchestra at the theatre can hardly be considered relevant, quite apart from the fact that they are now almost never used. When silent pictures are nowadays occasionally shown with musical accompaniment this is mostly quite independent of the original score. Incidentally, the fashionable practice of supplying musical illustration sometimes actually does injustice to silent pictures: silence is often a vital component of a silent film. The names of designers are included in the credits only when the designs are either outstanding or particularly characteristic. In ballet films the name of the choreographer is given.

The Spelling of Names. Although Victor Sjöström did make several films in America under the name of Seastrom, he was a Swedish director and must be treated as such. On the other hand, there are directors who lived away from the countries where they were born for most of their creative lives. It is therefore only right to talk about Michael Curtiz and not use the director's real surname, Kertesz. The same applies to the premanently assumed names of film actors: one would not say Greta Gustafsson but Greta Garbo. When however pseudonyms were created whimsically for use in one film only, it was considered better to refer to the person's real name. Finally, in the case of films based on literary works the original title of the book is given in order to make it easier to find, should the reader so wish.

Running Times. This complex problem has never been sorted out properly by film critics and historians who are usually averse to technicalities. Sound films, encompassing very nearly all produced after 1929, must be shown (because of the sound track) at a uniform speed of 24 frames per second, corresponding to 90 feet per minute of running time. If a sound film is shown on television the rate of projection is, for purely technical reasons, 25 frames per second. This difference is too slight to be heard on the soundtrack, but in terms of projection time television films run 4 per cent faster than in the cinema. This difference must be taken into account when applying the running times quoted in the book to films seen on television.

A real problem arises in case of silent pictures. It is generally believed that silent films were shot and projected at a uniform speed of 16 frames per second (60 feet per minute). Unfortunately, this is not the case. Upon looking at many silent pictures it becomes clear that they were not shot at a constant speed. "Film Notes" published by the Museum of Modern Art, New York (edited by Eileen Bowser), gives an interesting account of the situation: "... comedies were usually to be run a little faster than more serious dramatic films; the camera operators began to speed up filming to compensate for too fast projection in the theatres. By the late Twenties a rate near modern sound speed was generally adopted." With most modern cinema equipment only two speeds of projection are available: 16 and 24 frames per second. This is the reason why 16 frames per second became subsequently the generally accepted projection speed for silent films, regardless of the original intentions of their makers. Distribution catalogues quote running times calculated on the above basis. Yet some sophisticated film societies do use discretion in the matter: at the National Film Theatre in London silent films are projected at a speed "which seems most suitable for their individual character." In the text of the book we therefore quote footage and running times only for sound films where the problem of speed of projection does not arise. For silent films we give merely the footage, as the only absolute measure of their lengths.

The actual running time will depend in this case on the speed of projection. The table giving length (in feet and meters) together with the corresponding running times (in minutes) for the speeds of 16 and 24 frames per second can be used for orientation purposes in these cases.

References to titles. Film titles quoted anywhere in the text without the production date in brackets are discussed elsewhere in the book and can be located through the index. Films followed by dates are only mentioned in passing and are generally not enlarged upon. Film titles are underscored and are listed under the names by which they are most commonly known in English-speaking countries. Titles of books are in quotation marks. Sometimes, in fact nearly always in the case of French productions, only the original title of a film is ever used. Finally, since the original title of every picture is given both in the text and in the index (and thus the problem of mistaken identity does not arise) the book sometimes takes no account of the numerous English language titles which some films have acquired over the years.

COMPARISON OF RUNNING TIMES
FOR TWO STANDARD PROJECTION SPEEDS

Mins	16 Frames/Second		24 Frames/Second	
	Meters	Feet	Meters	Feet
58	1060	3480	1591	5220
59	1078	3540	1618	5310
60	1097	3600	1645	5400
61	1115	3660	1673	5490
62	1133	3720	1700	5580
63	1152	3780	1728	5670
64	1170	3840	1755	5760
65	1188	3900	1783	5850
66	1207	3960	1810	5940
67	1225	4020	1837	6030
68	1243	4080	1865	6120
69	1261	4140	1892	6210
70	1280	4200	1920	6300
71	1298	4260	1947	6390
72	1316	4320	1975	6480
73	1335	4380	2002	6570
74	1353	4440	2029	6660
75	1371	4500	2057	6750
76	1389	4560	2084	6840
77	1408	4620	2112	6930
78	1426	4680	2139	7020
79	1444	4740	2167	7110
80	1463	4800	2194	7200
81	1481	4860	2221	7290
82	1499	4920	2249	7380
83	1517	4980	2276	7470
84	1536	5040	2304	7560
85	1554	5100	2331	7650
86	1572	5160	2359	7740
87	1591	5220	2386	7830
88	1609	5280	2414	7920
89	1627	5340	2441	8010
90	1645	5400	2468	8100
91	1664	5460	2496	8190
92	1682	5520	2523	8280
93	1700	5580	2551	8370
94	1719	5640	2578	8460
95	1737	5700	2606	8550

| | 16 Frames/Second | | 24 Frames/Second | |
Mins	Meters	Feet	Meters	Feet
96	1755	5760	2633	8640
97	1773	5820	2660	8730
98	1792	5880	2688	8820
99	1810	5940	2715	8910
100	1828	6000	2743	9000
101	1847	6060	2770	9090
102	1865	6120	2798	9180
103	1883	6180	2825	9270
104	1901	6240	2852	9360
105	1920	6300	2880	9450
106	1938	6360	2907	9540
107	1956	6420	2935	9630
108	1975	6480	2962	9720
109	1993	6540	2990	9810
110	2011	6600	3017	9900
111	2029	6660	3044	9990
112	2048	6720	3072	10080
113	2066	6780	3099	10170
114	2084	6840	3127	10260
115	2103	6900	3154	10350
116	2121	6960	3182	10440
117	2139	7020	3209	10530
118	2157	7080	3236	10620
119	2176	7140	3264	10710
120	2194	7200	3291	10800
121	2212	7260	3319	10890
122	2231	7320	3346	10980
123	2249	7380	3374	11070
124	2267	7440	3401	11160
125	2285	7500	3428	11250
126	2304	7560	3456	11340
127	2322	7620	3483	11430
128	2340	7680	3511	11520
129	2359	7740	3538	11610
130	2377	7800	3566	11700
131	2395	7860	3593	11790
132	2414	7920	3621	11880
133	2432	7980	3648	11970
134	2450	8040	3675	12060
135	2468	8100	3703	12150
136	2487	8160	3730	12240
137	2505	8220	3758	12330
138	2523	8280	3785	12420
139	2542	8340	3813	12510
140	2560	8400	3840	12600
141	2578	8460	2867	12690
142	2596	8520	3895	12780
143	2615	8580	3922	12870
144	2633	8640	3950	12960
145	2651	8700	3977	13050

Mins	16 Frames/Second		24 Frames/Second	
	Meters	Feet	Meters	Feet
146	2670	8760	4005	13140
147	2688	8820	4032	13230
148	2706	8880	4059	13320
149	2724	8940	4087	13410
150	2743	9000	4114	13500
151	2761	9060	4142	13590
152	2779	9120	4169	13680
153	2798	9180	4197	13770
154	2816	9240	4224	13860
155	2834	9300	4251	13950
156	2852	9360	4279	14040
157	2871	9420	4306	14130
158	2889	9480	4334	14220
159	2907	9540	4361	14310
160	2926	9600	4389	14400
161	2944	9660	4416	14490
162	2962	9720	4443	14580
163	2980	9780	4471	14670
164	2999	9840	4498	14760
165	3017	9900	4526	14850
166	3035	9960	4553	14940
167	3054	10020	4581	15030
168	3072	10080	4608	15120
169	3090	10140	4636	15210
170	3108	10200	4663	15300
171	3127	10260	4690	15390
172	3145	10320	4718	15480
173	3163	10380	4745	15570
174	3182	10440	4773	15660
175	3200	10500	4800	15750
176	3218	10560	4828	15840
177	3236	10620	4855	15930
178	3255	10680	4882	16020
179	3273	10740	4910	16110
180	3291	10800	4937	16200

SHORT OUTLINE OF THE MAIN EVENTS
IN CINEMA HISTORY THROUGH 1949

The fact that the human retina preserves images of objects
a little after they have disappeared has been known since antiquity.
Following this principle, a number of instruments were devised during the 19th century which gave the optical illusion of movement.
Since 1893 Edison had showed films on a peep-show machine to one
person at a time. But it was only on 28 December 1895 that the
brothers Auguste and Louis Lumière gave the first film show in the
modern sense of the word in the Grand Café in Paris. The Lumière
brothers despatched their operators on journeys all over Europe to
film sights and important occasions, but did not realize the potential of the new invention (which a certain Léon Bouly called "cine-
matograph"). Their films were mostly chronicles of ordinary
events, but also included L'Arroseur arrosé (1895), the first cinematic comedy sketch.

Films were first considered as a medium by another Frenchman, a popular magician named Georges Méliès, who discovered
double exposure, fast and slow motion, fade-outs, dissolves and
other technical tricks. By stopping the camera in the middle of
the scene and then re-starting it with changed details he could show
for instance Mary Stuart's head being chopped off. Méliès considered cinema as an extension of magic and made literally thousands
of science-fiction films (A Trip to the Moon, 1902), staged "actu-
alities" (The Coronation of Edward VII, 1902), fairy tales (Cinderella, 1900) and "literary adaptations" (The Queen of Hearts, 1905).
While technically primitive, Méliès' activities had a considerable
charm and perfectly captured the essence of the cinema.

By the early 1900's other centers of film activity began to
appear: the Brighton School in England, and Stuart Blackton and

29

Edwin S. Porter in America.   Porter is generally considered to
have discovered, in The Great Train Robbery (1903), the "cinematic"
narrative style.

     For more than ten years, however, cinema remained no more
than an unsophisticated amusement; the screens were full of primitive adaptations of sensational short stories and filmed theatre.   The
quasi-theatrical productions sometimes used famous stage actors, including Asta Nielsen, Sarah Bernhardt and Eleonora Duse.   Exaggerated gesticulation was meant to compensate for the absence of
dialogue, and the immobile camera photographed the whole stature of
the actors.   In America this period is called the "Nickelodeon Age";
in Europe such works are known collectively as "Film d'Art."

     Cinema developed into an art form not by making the content
of films more respectable, but through improving their formal aspects.   The major role in this process was played by D. W. Griffith.   He was the first to change the camera position in the middle
of a scene, to vary its distance from the actors, to use close-ups
with artistic justification and to employ lighting creatively.   By
means of film editing, which he discovered, Griffith achieved a flexible and refined narrative and "codified" his stylistic and technical
achievements in two great pictures, The Birth of a Nation and Intolerance.

     By then cinema had become an industry attracting larger and
larger audiences with its products and paying higher and higher sal-
aries to the performers--the "Star System" was under way.   The
genre to develop first was the comedy, where Mack Sennett, the
pioneer of film burlesque proceeded to caricature the world and its
inhabitants.   Sennett exerted great influence on comedy and was
closely followed by others: Harold Lloyd, whose type was a shrewd
middle-class young American; Max Linder, the immaculate French
dandy; the imperturbable Buster Keaton, huge Mack Swain, and "Fatty" Arbuckle.   The burlesque soon developed, enriched by social
references and by reflections on man and the world he lives in, at
times reaching a near-philosophical dimension.   The man who was
principally responsible for this was Charlie Chaplin, undoubtedly

the greatest film star ever; and the audiences soon discovered that
he was talking about universally important matters. Other pillars
of the Star System were at that time the leading ladies, Mary Pickford, Gloria Swanson and Pola Negri, the swashbuckling Douglas
Fairbanks, and Rudolf Valentino, the Latin-Lover-in-Chief.

By around 1916 the basic principles of film narration were
well enough developed and cinema sufficiently popular around the
world for film-makers in individual countries to try to diversify
their products by making use of national characteristics, customs,
landscape and literary heritage, as well as the prevailing mood and
attitude to life. By doing this, Victor Sjöström and Mauritz Stiller
in Sweden created the first genuine film school, of which the principal works are A Man There Was, The Outlaw and His Wife and Sir
Arne's Treasure.

In Germany, the difficult social and economic situation after
the lost war and the depressed mood which pervaded the newly-
created Weimar Republic resulted in the creation of Expressionism.
The principal directors of this trend, which favored powerful visual
form and stylized content, were F. W. Murnau, G. W. Pabst, Fritz
Lang and Paul Leni; the most outstanding actors were Emil Jannings,
Conrad Veidt, Lil Dagover, Paul Wegener, Rudolf Klein-Rogge and
Greta Garbo, the last named having been imported from Sweden (and
soon exported to the United States). The manifesto of Expression-
ism, Robert Wiene's The Cabinet of Dr. Caligari, was followed by
a series of pictures about tyrants (Vanina), master criminals (Dr.
Mabuse, the Gambler), the subconscious (Warning Shadows), and
"kolossal" super-productions such as Nibelungen and Metropolis.
Development of the intimate version of Expressionism known as the
"Kammerspiel" was led by Lupu Pick (Shattered, New Year's Eve).
Both trends were inspired by the immensely influential scriptwriter,
Carl Mayer, and culminated in The Last Laugh.

In France, the cultivated enthusiasts of the new art of the
visual (L'Herbier, Epstein, Gance) created Impressionism, professing a poetic vision of the world. It was only then, in the early
1920's, that cinema began to attract wide interest among educated
and creative people.

Immediately after the Russian Revolution Lenin declared: "Of all the arts, the cinema is the most important to us"; in 1919 the film industry was nationalized and given state patronage. The new political system called for new themes and new approaches and attracted many young talented people to film-making: Eisenstein directed Battleship Potemkin and October; Pudovkin did Mother and Storm Over Asia; and Dovzhenko, Earth. Appropriately for the system of government, Soviet cinema avoided individual protagonists and thus no stars emerged, at least in the silent period.

In the U.S.A., the Western, which dates from Porter's early The Great Train Robbery (1903), became the first national genre. Although in the early 20's it was not yet mature, it had indisputable achievements, such as Ford's The Iron Horse and Cruze's The Covered Wagon. The greatest of the early Western stars was William S. Hart. Another typically American product is the gangster film. At first it was just a whodunit strip cartoon; but a breakthrough was achieved by Josef von Sternberg, who through his classics, Underworld and The Docks of New York, ennobled gangster cinema by investing it with psychological motivation and analyses of the personalities of the protagonists. Several years later Hawks, Le Roy and Wellman initiated the "gangster series," which placed their main stress on the social causes of gangsterism, blaming society for pushing some of its members onto the path of crime. The best films and stars of this trend were Little Caesar with Edward G. Robinson, Scarface with Paul Muni and Public Enemy with James Cagney. Reactionary political pressures soon brought the "gangster series" to a premature close. The rest of the American cinema, completely overwhelmed by the Star System, served--with the exception of Chaplin and Keaton--as a trivial amusement for the masses. But technical progress did not cease, and led to the development of Technicolor and, more or less simultaneously, to the invention of sound cinema.

On 6 October 1927 Warner Bros. showed in public The Jazz Singer (1927), the first talkie. Barely two years later virtually all the output of American film studios had a soundtrack. The new

invention amused the audiences and thus tended to be used in an endless series of crude film operettas, for its own sake, rather like an
indiscriminately employed circus effect. At first the artistic standard of films deteriorated but soon the novelty effect wore off and
the soundtrack was open for use as a means of artistic expression.
All this meant a collapse of the mature style of silent cinema, characterized by highly developed editing and a fine, purely visual narrative. The silent pantomime came to an end and Keaton and Lloyd
were the first casualties. Chaplin resisted the "sound revolution"
for as long as he could although he ended up, belatedly, by joining
it. Of the famous stars of the silent cinema Greta Garbo was one
of the few survivors, by virtue of her acting talents.

Also in France the first sound films (for example René Clair's
Sous les toits de Paris) belonged to the silent convention from the
formal point of view. Yet the talkies had obvious advantages: by
resorting to dialogues directors could narrate with a greater economy of shots and also tackle a wider variety of themes on the screen,
which amounted to a further refinement of the language of the cinema. The new technical achievements were used in the concrete
social and political conditions of individual countries, causing a rush
of artistic activity. Several new trends were formed which, unlike
those in the silent cinema, differed from each other primarily by
their thematic (rather than formal) content.

In Germany Expressionism gave way to the "New Objectivity"
(Neue Sachlichkeit), which was mainly concerned with social problems and in a fashion close to documentary portrayed ordinary people in the factories, shops and employment agencies of inflation-rid-
den Germany.

Pacifist cinema developed in many countries, producing Westfront 1918 in Germany, All Quiet on the Western Front in the U.S.A.
(where antiwar films started first, with Vidor's silent The Big Parade) and, towards the close of the 30's, Renoir's La Grande illusion.

The Wall Street Crash and the Great Crisis left deep marks
on the cinema; erotic and gangster films were actively discouraged

by the censors, who laid stress on austerity and decency. The difficult economic situation stimulated interest in social problems and
extinguished romantic sentiments. The screen characters were for
once real people; this was reflected by the appearance of a new
type of film star, the best known of which were Spencer Tracy,
James Stewart, Victor McLaglen, Clark Gable, Fredric March, Cary
Grant, Janet Gaynor, Carole Lombard, Claudette Colbert and Jean
Arthur. The three former heroes of the "gangster series" also appeared in this new wave of pictures. It was only natural that the
newly created "socially conscious" cinema scriptwriters, who provided the themes, had a greater influence than before. Thus Fury
and They Won't Forget accused lynch law, I Am a Fugitive from a
Chain Gang, the penal system, and The Front Page criticized the
ruthlessness of the tabloid newspapers. On the other hand, the optimistic films of Frank Capra were pervaded by the sentiments of
the New Deal: Mr. Deeds Goes to Town and You Can't Take It with
You. There was also the always heartening and ardently patriotic
John Ford and his studies of man's encounter with nature. Chaplin
then made City Lights and Modern Times, which saw the Tramp in
the difficult conditions of Industrial Society. Cartoon films developed,
mainly through the efforts of Walt Disney and the Fleischer brothers.

   In England Korda professed an informal portrayal of historical characters (The Private Life of Henry VIII, etc.); Hitchcock, by
making sophisticated thrillers such as The 39 Steps, The Man Who
Knew Too Much and The Lady Vanishes, gave the genre a new lease
on life.

   In the early 30's the cinema in France, a country which has
always had a tradition of individualism in art, was dominated by
René Clair (Le Million, À nous la liberté). Jean Renoir, a great
director unconnected with any movement, gravitated towards social
criticism presented in a refined intellectual form (La Règle du jeu,
La Grande illusion). Another important director was Jacques Feyder (Le Grand jeu, Pension Mimosas). Towards the close of the
decade the director, Marcel Carné, and the scriptwriter, Jacques
Prévert, created the style known as "Poetic Realism," which,

pervaded by the mood of fatalism and hopelessness, expressed the traditional national sentiments of the French in an artistic manner. The works of the trend (Quai des brumes, Le Jour se Lève) talk about individuals defeated by the hostile environment.

Russia witnessed a long series of pictures about the leading personalities of the Revolution and the Civil War (which created a unique "Pantheon of Revolutionary Heroes"). Some of these pictures, namely the "Maxim Trilogy," We from Kronstadt, Chapayev, and the first two parts of the "Trilogy of the Young Gorky," are artistically valuable, but originality and inspiration were soon lost in a flood of crass propaganda. For the next twenty years, the only asset of Soviet cinema was to be the great Eisenstein (Alexander Nevsky, Ivan the Terrible and The Boyars' Plot).

Full-scale film production in Japan started around 1912, when 155 films were made. Two styles which emerged were jidai-geki (historical costume films inspired by the traditional Japanese Kabuki theatre) and gendai-geki (films with contemporary subjects). Several Japanese directors were trained in Hollywood and brought back technical and narrative innovations. The early 20's were the years of the rapid growth of capitalism; the crisis began in 1922. Cinema reacted to this by introducing radical themes which, combined with the mood of desperation, reflected the sharp social conflicts. Souls on the Road was the first outstanding Japanese film; the later Crossways used the favorite motif of a samurai fighting the society that had wronged him. The introduction of sound cinema was foreshadowed by commentators, called benshi, who explained to the audience what happened on the screen.

The 30's witnessed an extremely sharp competition among individual film companies; in 1936 there were as many as 531 films produced in Japan. A new critical approach appeared to the traditional historical samurai themes: contemporaneity was seen through the past. This was the time when outstanding directors appeared in Japan. The specifically Japanese genre which developed, lower middle-class melodrama, is known as shomin-geki; the leading directors were Naruse, Gosho and Ozu. The latter and Mizoguchi were to be

the greatest directors of the national cinema for many years, until
joined in the mid-40's by the third, Kurosawa.   In the face of the
growth of militarism and dictatorship Japanese directors were forced
to use historical, rather than modern, motifs.

The Second World War with its fierceness and totality had a
profound influence on the cinema.   All over the world films became
a way of discussing matters vital to everybody and at the same time
a much-needed medium of recreation.   The temporary isolation from
Hollywood had a stimulating influence on the cinema of countries
which had so far little or no achievement in the field: Switzerland
(The Last Chance), Mexico (Maria Candelaria) and Denmark (Day of
Wrath).   Of course, war itself was the prevalent theme.   Since it
was imperative that it was shown faithfully and honestly, the best
war films were made in the countries which had some tradition of
documentary cinema.   In England, where the starting point was the
documentary school of the 30's (Rotha, Grierson, Wright, Flaherty),
realism prevailed and the best films of the period were In Which We
Serve, Next of Kin, and San Demetrio, London, which so well conveyed the mood of Battle of Britain.   The heyday of British cinema
survived the war by only a few years, but gave rise to the outstanding works of Olivier, Reed, Lean and the series of "Ealing Comedies. "

In collaborationist Vichy France the directors were forced to
resort to "neutral" themes.   Even so, several outstanding pictures
were made: Les Visiteurs du soir, Les Anges du péché and Douce.
Towards the end of the war realist tendencies began to dominate
(The Crow, La Bataille du rail).   As soon as the war was over the
great poetic synthesis, Les Enfants du paradis, was released.

In America war was also the main subject.   It was discussed
with truth and honesty in the para-documentary The Story of G. I.
Joe, Action in the North Atlantic, Confessions of a Nazi Spy and
Air Force.   The same interests, but in a more fictional mood were
in evidence in Casablanca, Foreign Correspondent and Mrs. Miniver.
Of the comedies The Great Dictator ridiculed Fascism and The More
the Merrier humorously exploited the theme of accommodation diffi-

culties in wartime Washington. On the threshold of war Orson
Welles made his momentous Citizen Kane.

The stagnant calligraphy of most of the prewar Italian film
production gave rise to the Italian Neorealism, one of the major
stylistic trends in the cinema, which started during the war with
Visconti's Ossessione and Rossellini's Rome, Open City and continued
for several years afterwards with Paisà and Germany Year Zero,
finally producing its masterpiece in De Sica's Umberto D.

Similarly in Japan: after years of official intervention into
the cinema, the clutches of which only a few pictures managed to
escape, there was a marked return to reality, running parallel to
Neorealism in Italy. The development of a cinema with strong social tendencies in the late 40's was mainly due to Kurosawa (One
Wonderful Sunday, Drunken Angel, Stray Dog).

All over the world, cinema adopted the stock-taking tone and
analyzed the war events and their consequences (The Best Years of
Our Lives and The Seventh Cross in the U.S.A., The Great Turning Point in the U.S.S.R., The Last Chance in Switzerland, Border
Street and The Last Stage in Poland, Somewhere in Europe in Hungary, Vivere in Pace in Italy, The Murderers Are Amongst Us in
Germany and No Regrets for My Youth in Japan).

It was only during the war that Hollywood managed to break
with the "Morality Code" and became able to tackle a variety of
previously forbidden subjects. The genre known as "film noir"
placed much stress on the dense and oppressive atmosphere of evil
and cared less about the moral implications of the films (Double Indemnity, Laura, The Big Sleep, The Treasure of Sierra Madre, The
Maltese Falcon, Monsieur Verdoux, Sorry, Wrong Number, Key
Largo, The Woman in the Window). Another important development
in America was the socially critical films: The Snake Pit examined
the life of mental patients, The Lost Weekend tackled the problem
of alcoholism, and They Live by Night, Thieves' Highway and Brute
Force discussed the ever-present urban gangsterism. The Set-up
and Champion uncovered the ugly side of professional sports, and
All the King's Men showed machinations in local politics. Some of

the films, such as <u>Call Northside 777</u>, were made in a distinctly semi-documentary manner.

Among the film stars of the 40's were Orson Welles, John Wayne, Burt Lancaster, James Stewart, Cary Grant, Henry Fonda, Ray Milland and Humphrey Bogart in America; Gérard Philipe and Pierre Brasseur in France; Laurence Olivier in England. The women in this age of tough male roles were Ingrid Bergman, Bette Davis and the <u>femmes</u> <u>fatales</u>:   Barbara Stanwyck and Rita Hayworth.

1913

THE STUDENT OF PRAGUE (Der Student von Prag)   Stellan Rye

Script: Hanns Heinz Ewers. Photography: Guido Seeber. Art Direction: Klaus Ruchter. Cast: Paul Wegener (Baldwin), John Gottowt (Scapinelli), Lida Salmonová (Lyduschka, country girl), Grete Berger (Margit, Countess Waldis-Schwarzenberg), Lothar Körner (Count Waldis-Schwarzenberg).

Deutsche Bioscop GmbH, Berlin, Germany. 5 reels, 5046 ft., later cut to 4817 ft.

Seventeen years passed from the day the Lumière brothers opened the era of the cinema with their Paris show. In that period, which became known as "fairground," the new medium undertook more or less bold, but unsuccessful, attempts at improving its aesthetic status. But then the first films appeared which, though not necessarily consciously on the part of their creators, were definitely something more than primitive amusement. Among these pictures was The Student of Prague, which not only marked the real beginning of the creative German cinema, but was also a harbinger of the days of its greatest glory, which would follow the development of Expressionism.

Stellan Rye's film is a version of the Faustian legend, presented in the diabolical spirit of the tales of E. T. A. Hoffmann and Edgar Allan Poe. A student called Baldwin sells his mirror image in exchange for immense riches. Scapinelli, a sorcerer, uses the purchase to create Baldwin's double, which will drive the poor student to crime and ruin. Baldwin attempts to destroy his mirror image but the bullet pierces his own heart. Externally, the plot does not go beyond the limitations of a horror story--but it already contains in embryo the fascinating theme of the dualism

39

of human nature, and presents it as a blend of good and evil elements (Baldwin vs. his double). This motif, basic for the German
cinema, would be fully developed in the 20's, especially in the films
of Fritz Lang.

But quite apart from this, The Student of Prague is the first
film in which the personality of the main protagonist is depicted with
such naturalness and conviction--and one of the first in which the
photography has a genuine artistic purpose. Guido Seeber, a veteran
German cameraman, employed all the cinematic attributes pent up
in the theme (for instance Baldwin's mirror image), and used a pattern of deep low-key contrasts of light and shadow which has been
compared to Albrecht Dürer's engravings, and is so characteristic
of the national traditions. This visual style, later developed by the
Expressionists, was to become the most valuable part of their films.

CABIRIA   Giovanni Pastrone

Script: Pastrone and Gabriele D'Annunzio. Photography: Segundo
de Chomon, Giovanni Tomatis, Augusto Batagliotti and Natale Chiu-
sano. Cast: Lidia Quaranta (Cabiria), Umberto Mozzato (Fulvius
Axilla), Bartolomeo Pagano (Maciste), Itala Almirante Mazzini
(Sophonisba), Vitale De Stefano (Massinissa), Enrico Gemmelli
(Archimedes), Luigi Chellini (Scipio).

Itala Film, Italy. Originally approx. 14,746 ft., now approx. 8345
ft.

Appropriately for the character of the newly-created art, Cabiria,
the most famous of the early triumphs of the cinema, was the success of a spectacle. Paradoxically, it is not only the first of the
costume giants attempted on such scale, but also one of the best of
its kind up to the present. Of course, the film does not have ambitions in the field of psychological analysis and its claim to historical fidelity cannot be treated seriously. The reconstruction of
time and place, quite apart from being a secondary consideration
with respect to the final spectacular effect of Cabiria, was still
bringing poor results. In 1913 the cinema quite simply did not yet
enjoy sufficient status and respect and remained a domain of amateur enthusiasts. Nobody yet dreamt of consulting experts and doing
research on the documents of the period. In the final effect this
story, about a young patrician girl kidnapped by Carthaginian pirates
during the Punic Wars and saved by her kind slave friend, has more
in common with a strip cartoon than with historical literature.

Still, this is a strip cartoon of prime quality. Through the
purposeful employment of the sets of temples and palaces, and also

by skillful direction of crowds of extras, Giovanni Pastrone, known
under the pseudonym Piero Fosco, has given considerable charm
and in a sense an artistic expression to the episodes of Roman history presented. Hannibal crossing the Alps, the eruption of Mount
Etna, the sacrifice to Moloch, the market place in Carthage, the
destruction of the enemy fleet by Archimedes with lens-focussed
sun rays and a number of other scenes demonstrate clearly the
power of expression of the cinema, which Pastrone enriched by
many valuable technical innovations. Among them are the tracking
shots of the camera, for the first time mounted on a dolly, and the
employment of arc-lighting in exterior shooting. These are pioneering achievements, but limited only to the technical aspect of film-
making. From the narrative point of view Pastrone's film does not
move one step forward. Individual scenes are only chapters in a
screen book and each of them is explained by specially commissioned captions. The cinema had to wait for D. W. Griffith to give
fluency to the narrative, although Cabiria was a major source of inspiration for him during the making of Intolerance.

1915

THE BIRTH OF A NATION   David Wark Griffith

Script: Griffith and Frank Woods, from the novel, "The Clansman,"
by the Rev. Thomas Dixon, Jr. Photography: G. W. Bitzer.
Cast: Lillian Gish (Elsie Stoneman), Mae Marsh (Flora Cameron),
Henry B. Walthall (Col. Ben Cameron), Miriam Cooper (Margaret
Cameron), Mary Alden (Lydia, Stoneman's housekeeper), Ralph
Lewis (the Hon. Austin Stoneman), George Siegmann (Silas Lynch),
Walter Long (Gus), Robert Harron (Ted Stoneman), Wallace Reid
(Jeff, the blacksmith), Joseph Henabery (Abraham Lincoln), Elmer
Clifton (Phil Stoneman), Josephine Crowell (Mrs. Cameron), Spottis-
woode Aitken (Dr. Cameron), G. A. Beranger (Wade Cameron), Max-
field Stanley (Duke Cameron), Jennie Lee (Cindy), Donald Crisp
(General U. S. Grant), Howard Gaye (General Robert E. Lee), Sam
de Grasse (Senator Sumner), Elmo Lincoln (White Arm Joe), Olga
Grey (Laura Keene), Raoul Walsh (John Wilkes Booth), Eugene
Pallette (Union soldier), Alberta Lee (Mrs. Lincoln), William de
Vaull (Jake), Tom Wilson (Stonemans' servant).

Epoch Producing Corporation (D. W. Griffith), U.S.A. Originally
13,058 ft. Re-issued with sound: 1930 (12,083 ft., 134 mins);
1962 (11,745 ft., 130 mins).

"It is like writing history with lightning," said Woodrow Wilson, referring to the stunning boldness of scope of The Birth of a Nation.
After making nearly 500 short films in the years 1908-1914, D. W.
Griffith, the father of the American cinema, condensed his experiences in his first longer work, a fresco from the time of the American Civil War describing the sufferings of the Southern family of
Camerons brought about by the victory of the Union and the advent
of rule by the Carpetbaggers and Negroes. This is set against the
rich background of the main events of the war (the battle of St.

Petersburg) and its aftermath (the assassination of Lincoln).

Griffith created here an archetypal silent film with an astounding variety of narrative devices and a multitude of pioneering means of expression. He discovered the variety of ways in which to use the film camera--purposeful close-ups, fast overhead traveling shots, pans, panoramas, split screen and change of camera position in the middle of a scene. He discovered and brilliantly demonstrated that films not only can but must be cut. Thus Griffith became the inventor of film editing, and showed this to be the distinguishing element between cinema and theatre.

The action of The Birth of a Nation is masterfully counterpointed with a pulsating and flexible narrative rhythm. The length of each shot was designed to influence the spectator's emotional response (thus tense dramatic scenes are cut faster). Griffith developed editing according to two principles, "contrast" (the quietness of a home opposed to the din of battle) and "parallel development" (scenes from the hut besieged by the Negroes intercut with the triumphant ride of the rescuers). The director employed a variety of stylistic devices which helped him narrate with maximum fluency. The picture is divided into sequences punctuated by fade-ins, fade-outs, and iris. Furthermore, the lighting is used to create the desired atmosphere of a scene. It is amazing that Griffith did all this in a mere nine weeks, using one camera and two lenses, on a budget of $110,000.

Unfortunately the story of The Birth of a Nation is far from the excellence of the form. In the intention of Griffith (who came from the South) it was to be a sentimental defense, in the name of justice, of the dignity of the South humiliated by the lost war. It turned on the screen into an apology for the racialist and jingoistic mentality of the South, a glorification of the Ku-Klux Klan and a libel on the American black community. A further fault is Griffith's Victorian sentimentality (the captions!) and the exaggerated acting. All these things however now seem unimportant: The Birth of a Nation matters because it marked the birth of cinema as a serious concern--the fantastic box-office success of the film forever destroyed the notion that the cinema was only a fairground amusement.

Its tumultuous reception had a marked influence on Griffith's later films; anxious to defend himself from the accusations of chauvinism he took Intolerance as his next topic.

1916

INTOLERANCE   David Wark Griffith

Script: Griffith (modern story based on "The Mother and the Law" and records of the Stielow murder case). Photography: G. W. Bitzer and Karl Brown. Cast: Lillian Gish (Woman who rocks the cradle); and

Modern Story 1914, Mae Marsh (The Dear One), Fred Turner (Her father, a mill worker), Robert Harron (Boy), Sam de Grasse (Jenkins, mill magnate), Vera Lewis (Mary Jenkins, his sister), Monte Blue (Strike leader), Tod Browning, Edward Dillon (Two crooks).

Judean Story A.D. 27, Howard Gaye (The Nazarine), Lillian Langdon (Mary, the mother), Olga Grey (Mary Magdalene), Erich von Stroheim (First Pharisee), Günther von Ritzau (Second Pharisee), Bessie Love (Bride of Cana).

Medieval French Story A.D. 1572, Margery Wilson (Brown Eyes, daughter of a Huguenot family), Eugene Pallette (Prosper Latour, her sweetheart), Frank Bennett (Charles IX, King of France), Josephine Crowell (Catherine de Medici), Constance Talmadge (Marguerite de Valois, sister of Charles IX), Maxfield Stanley (Duc d'Anjou, heir to the throne), Joseph Henabery (Admiral Coligny).

Babylonian Story 539 B.C., Constance Talmadge (Mountain girl), Elmer Clifton (The Rhapsode, her suitor and secret agent of the High Priest of Bel), Alfred Paget (Prince Belshazzar), Seena Owen (Princess Beloved, adored of Belshazzar), Carl Stockdale (King Nabonidus, ancient apostle of religious toleration), Tully Marshall (High Priest of Bel, who conspires against the Throne), George Siegmann (Cyrus, emperor and war lord of the Persians, world-conqueror).

Wark Producing Corporation, U.S.A. 13 reels. British National

Film Archive print: 10, 930 ft.   Originally 12, 598 ft.

Intolerance is the apogee of the early spectacular cinema, a display
which later films could not match even in part.   It is also the most
expensive film ever made, in comparative cost.   Its creation was
made possible by the colossal box-office success of The Birth of a
Nation, Griffith's previous work.   With such considerable means at
his disposal, the director wanted to make a gigantic, quadripartite
fresco as a vehicle for voicing his protest against all kinds of intolerance and injustice.

        The four episodes are set in different historical periods:
the life of Jesus Christ, the St. Bartholomew's Day Massacre, the
fall of Babylon and the events following a strike in a present-day
American factory (partly based on authentic events)   The latter
part, where a working class couple are near-victims of exploitation
and a judicial error, had been filmed earlier as an independent feature, "The Mother and the Law, " but later the director decided to
include it in Intolerance, of which it constitutes the best and the
most expanded component.   There is also an epilogue "prophesying
the ultimate liberation of all men and all nations from every form
of bondage. "

        The stories are developed not one after another, as is usual,
but simultaneously; this narrative method finds similarities in situations people find themselves in throughout history, works as a powerful generalizing symbol and stresses the omnipresence of evil and
man's undying struggle towards a happy world.   According to Griffith's poetic explanation, "The four stories start apart like four
streams seen from the top of a mountain, flow in the beginning
peacefully, but later merge closer and faster, in the end to become
one in the final chord of deep emotion. "   Indeed, the "parallel editing" previously employed by the director in The Birth of a Nation
is here used with even greater perfection and is of tremendous value
for achieving the expressiveness of the whole work.   The four stories related by that method impress with their legibility and fluency,
which is all the more remarkable as the film was made without a
scenario of any kind.

        The beautiful leitmotif cementing the individual parts of In-
tolerance is the shot of a mother rocking a cradle, even though its
introduction interferes at times with the build-up of tension.   The
final chord, perhaps the purest example of Griffith's "last minute
rescue, " comes in the modern story where the innocent convict's
wife chases the train carrying the governor who can grant the stay
of execution.

        It is however not only the editing which is the greatest formal
achievement of Intolerance; here Griffith reiterated, but in a more
balanced and mature form, all his previous narrative devices (the
variation of speed of story-telling, the contrast of situations, the
surprise) and enriched them by new experiments.   One of them is

the attempt at varying the aspect ratio (i.e. the dimensions) of the screen--this eternal, and still unfulfilled, dream of the cinema.

Admittedly, some parts of Intolerance (for instance the Babylonian story) are weaker than others, but it seems that the accusations of lack of taste leveled against Griffith at the time are now of little validity: what was awkwardness before, now has a period flavor. This applies even to the captions, the last of which reads, "And perfect love shall bring peace forevermore." What a naive romantic Griffith was!

The scope of the picture is impressive: for the Babylonian episode a life-size replica of the city of Babylon was built on 254 acres with 200-foot walls around it; 60,000 extras (and scores of famous actors) were used. It was unfortunate that the release of Intolerance (in 1918) coincided with the United States' joining the First World War: the pacifist tone of the film was a discordant note in this context, and was one of the main reasons for the painful defeat the film suffered in its confrontation with the public. Another was that Griffith overestimated the intelligence of the spectators when he presented them with such a demanding and complex picture. For years to come Hollywood expended great efforts not to repeat this miscalculation. But all this does not affect the stature of Intolerance as a great humanist epic and a veritable almanac of the possibilities of the cinema.

The period of experiments was now over: the new art had mastered its tools.

A MAN THERE WAS (Terje Vigen)   Victor Sjöström

Script: Gustaf Molander, based on the poem by Henrik Ibsen. Photography: Julius Jaenzon. Cast: Victor Sjöström (Terje), Bergliot Husberg (His wife), August Falk (English captain), Edith Erastoff (English lady).

Svenska Bio, Sweden. 3929 ft.

In the years 1914-1920, sparsely populated Sweden became the leading influence in world cinema. One of the reasons for this was Sweden's neutrality in the First World War, which allowed her films to conquer world markets. The greatness of the early Swedish cinema rested entirely on two directors, Victor Sjöström and Mauritz Stiller. (It is interesting that the second heyday of the national cinema would be the one-man achievement of Ingmar Bergman.) Sjöström, a returned emigrant to America, started as a stage actor and had already by 1900 achieved a considerable reputation. In

1912 he joined Svenska Bio, the first film company in Sweden, first
as an actor and then as director.

Ingeborg Holm (1913), an exposé of the exploitation of the
poor, was his first film to attract critical attention and A Man
There Was is his first masterpiece. As with all Sjöström's works
this is a tragic picture, a story of loss, resignation and forgiveness.
During the Napoleonic wars a fisherman named Terje defies a naval
blockade in order to take food to his family, thus bringing upon himself the wrath of the English. While he is in prison, his wife and
son die of hunger. After many years Terje rescues in a storm the
English captain who arrested him. The sight of the captain's wife
and small child makes him forget vengeance and let them live.

The two greatest assets of the Swedish cinema were the
great Scandinavian writers, Henrik Ibsen and Selma Lagerlöf, and
the magnificent landscape of the country. Sjöström started off from
a poem, whose lines are used as titles. However, the character
of the picture is to a greater extent the product of his own vision
of the world and his own cinematic style which, in contrast to
Stiller's, gave most prominence to the story and the acting. This
is understandable in view of Sjöström's past career.

In A Man There Was he created a convincing and full screen
character sufficient to make the picture more than just an adventure
story--a film with a clear line of thought, illustrating the change in
a man's character through hardship. But perhaps an even more important actor in the film is the sea; the sea--sometimes placid,
more often violent, but always omnipresent. It generates the drama,
gives the story breadth, serves as a commentator to human action
and feelings, and becomes a modern version of the Greek chorus:
it determines the mood of the picture. Ibsen wrote his poem in the
Norwegian port of Grimstad, and a visit to that town inspired
Sjöström to make it into a film.

The director's creative profile was now fully formed and,
more importantly, the future path of Swedish cinema was charted.

1917

THE OUTLAW AND HIS WIFE (Berg-Ejvind och Hans Hustru)
   Victor Sjöström

Script: Sam Ask and Sjöström, based on the play by Johan Sigur-
jönsson. Photography: Julius Jaenzon. Cast: Victor Sjöström
(Berg-Ejvind), Edith Erastoff (Halla), John Ekman (Mayor).

Svenska Bio, Sweden. 9124 ft.

The Outlaw and His Wife, Sjöström's best picture, is one of the
great tragedies of the silent cinema. The theme of this epic story,
set in Iceland in the 1850's, is the surrender of man, but also the
omnipotence of love. A man proscribed for stealing a sheep takes
a job at a farm and falls in love with the lady owner. The jealous
local bailiff comes to arrest the fugitive and the lovers have to leave
all and seek refuge in the mountains where they live happily for
several years. But the hunt has not ceased; Berg-Ejvind and Halla
are forced to sacrifice their little daughter and escape still further.
Finally, broken and desperate, they voluntarily die in the snow.

      This picture is perhaps the clearest and purest example of
the style of the Swedish film school: nature is used as more than a
background or even a dramatic element--it becomes a symbol of
man's inner states and almost an independent actor. Hills, torrents,
geysers were always important to Sjöström, but here they form an
organic part of the story. The dramatic construction is very simple; the film is divided into three fairly distinctive parts, each set
in a different landscape and dominated by a different mood: idyllic
life on the farm, peaceful refuge into the hills, solitude and despair
in the hostile snowbound mountains. Thus The Outlaw and His Wife
is a profoundly Scandinavian film through its formal restraint and
its view of life dominated by Protestant determinism.

By talking about things that are always important in a manner which never strikes a wrong note Sjöström reached for the heights of Shakespeare. The protagonists are like the proud heroes of ancient Swedish sagas. Curiously (though perhaps necessarily for true art) The Outlaw and His Wife is a film of invincible optimism, of victory through defiance of evil and faith to one's inner self: Berg-Ejvind and Halla die in the end, but love has won.

1918

SHOULDER ARMS   Charles Chaplin

Script: Chaplin. Photography: Rollie Totheroh. Cast: Charles
Chaplin (American soldier), Edna Purviance (French girl), Sydney
Chaplin (American sergeant/the Kaiser), Jack Wilson (German
Crown Prince), Henry Bergman (German sergeant/barman/Field
Marshal von Hindenburg), Albert Austin (American officer/German
soldier/Kaiser's chauffeur), Tom Wilson (Sergeant in the American
camp), John Rand (American soldier).

First National, U.S.A.   Originally 7 reels, cut to 3 reels, 3445 ft.

Charles Spencer Chaplin was born in 1889 in London, the son of a
couple of music-hall actors. He entered the ranks of his parents'
profession as a child; in 1907 the young pantomimist joined "London
Comedians," one of the troupes run by Fred Karno. The company
toured the United States in 1911 and 1912; Chaplin's second visit to
America lasted until 1951 and made him the most famous film-
maker in cinema history. In 1913 Chaplin was invited to join the
Keystone film company.

   The first film in which he appeared (as a Mephistophelean
character) is called Making a Living (1914). Almost immediately
after, he developed his Charlie the Tramp character, firstly in Kid
Auto Races at Venice (1914), but still without his cane, although
the same year saw Between Showers (1914), where the screen personality loved by millions was completed. In 1915 Chaplin signed a
contract with Essanay, in 1916 with Mutual, and in 1917 with First
National. Literally all of his 62 films made up till then, mostly
two-reelers, testify to his profound social sense. Yet it is not until Shoulder Arms that he appears not only as a sensitive comedian,
but as a committed militant artist.

The breakneck plot of the film is set during the First World
War. Charlie, an awkward private, is unhappy in the misery of
the French trenches. Other soldiers receive letters but all he gets
is a parcel of Swiss cheese. Thinking about New York is his only
consolation; his sole amusement is playing with the enemy fire and
striking matches from passing bullets. When the trenches are
flooded with water Charlie sleeps breathing through a gramophone
tube. Strange things happen: he takes scores of German soldiers
into captivity and later crosses enemy lines disguised as a tree.
In a destroyed house Charlie meets a French girl and falls in love
with her. Later, disguised as a German, he captures the Kaiser,
the Crown Prince and Chancellor Hindenburg. Suddenly the hero
wakes up in the mud: all his exploits were but a dream.

When Chaplin made Shoulder Arms his art was as yet far
from mature. But, strangely, this circumstance added wings to
this film, which was not designed as a display of cinematic finesse,
but as a vicious political cartoon; or rather a series of cartoons:
Shoulder Arms is in fact a conglomerate of hilarious and sometimes
extremely ingenuous episodes, each of them with a distinct tinge of
a newspaper caricature, whose near-anarchistic author is not frightened by anyone. When the Allied leaders give a party in Charlie's
honor, the King of England cuts a button off the hero's uniform to
keep as a souvenir. One only wonders which Allied newspaper editor
would have been able to print the scene at the time, if it had been
a cartoon.

Chaplin seems to understand very well that the most useful
propaganda tools are exaggeration and the cartoon-like psychological
simplification of the characters. It would appear that this is the
best language in which to talk about the total absurdity of war, the
army and everything military. It suffices to turn the obviously
primitive film technique and the custard pie-throwing gags into outright advantage and invalidate the complaints that Shoulder Arms
lacks the emotional palette of The Gold Rush.

It is easy to see why Chaplin's attack on the establishment
(President Wilson was not spared either) was not allowed: it was
feared that pacifist ideas might demoralize the army. By the time
the picture was released the war was over. The enemies had
ceased to be enemies; international courtesies were again in force.
Four out of the original seven reels of Shoulder Arms became the
prey of the censor, and the public in effect never saw the whole of
what is one of the best (and surely the funniest) antiwar film ever
made.

But the little tramp tried again. Twenty years later war
was once more in the air and this time he would not be too late:
The Great Dictator settled the long-outstanding account.

1919

THE CABINET OF DR. CALIGARI (Das Kabinett des Dr. Caligari)
 Robert Wiene

Script: Hans Janowitz and Carl Mayer. Photography: Willi Hameister. Art Direction: Hermann Warm, Walter Reimann and
Walter Röhrig. Cast: Werner Krauss (Dr. Caligari /Director of
mental hospital), Conrad Veidt (Cesare), Lil Dagover (Jane Olsen),
Friedrich Fehér (Franz), Hans Heinz von Twardowski (Allan), Rudolf Lettinger (Dr. Olsen), Rudolf Klein-Rogge (Criminal).

Erich Pommer, Decla-Bioscop, Germany. 6 reels, 5587 ft.

The great poet Friedrich Hölderlin's captivating comment about
Germany, "shadow is the country of our soul," finds a fascinating
illustration in The Cabinet of Dr. Caligari, one of the most momentous (which is not to say most nearly perfect) works in the history
of cinema. The importance of the Mayer, Janowitz and Wiene film
is twofold. Firstly, as a considerable artistic achievement, initiat-
ing the domination of Expressionist imagery on the screen; secondly,
as a political metaphor.

 This story of a provincial hypnotist called Dr. Caligari, who
during the day performs as a fairground magician, but at night
sends his medium Cesare on sinister missions during which mysterious crimes are inflicted on the local inhabitants, was to be a
clear reference to the situation in which German Imperialism found
itself during the Great War. Caligari was meant to symbolize the
Kaiser, manipulating the submissive nation. Other circumstances
allow us to conclude that The Cabinet of Dr. Caligari was indeed
intended to replicate the bankrupt authoritorian state, but the planned
ending of the film, in which the hunted Caligari takes refuge in a
mental asylum of which he turns out to be the director, was substantially modified in the finished work and the whole story was

presented as the fantasies of a madman.

The significance of this reversal of point of view is very often exaggerated. Even if it was of fundamental importance in the context of the political situation of 1919, a much more important thing in the wider perspective seems to be the inspired, generalized rendering of the atmosphere during the first year of the Weimar Republic--the spiritual mood which brought about the development of Expressionism as a philosophical doctrine and an artistic trend.

The film undoubtedly owes more to the spirit of the paintings of Grosz and Kokoschka than to the terrifying stories of the Grimm brothers and E. T. A. Hoffmann. This was achieved in the first place by the painted, two-dimensional sets that establish the mood of the film and, while rejecting all accepted precedents, break with realism and replace it by an openly cubist, Gothic and theatrical visual style; a world of slanting walls, crooked chimneys, windy convulsively twisted passages and doors which open into the darkness.

The dense, nearly palpable atmosphere, achieved almost exclusively through the design and acting (the film technique is not worth mention), strives to reflect the complexity of mental states. The visual convention of the film serves not only as a commentary on the inner state of a sick mind, but more importantly, as a mirror image of the mood of a whole society overcome by insecurity, depression and near-rebellion. The considerable success scored by Warm, Reimann and Röhrig (designers of the film and members of the group, "Der Sturm"), automatically brought about a far-reaching revision of the traditional attitudes to design. As a result, German cinema would come to lock itself in studios for many years.

Thus, the first Expressionist film, although of considerable importance, in fact played a hindering role in the development of the cinematic means of expression, although in the very same work Willi Hameister achieved a substantial step forward in the principal speciality of German camerawork--the masterly maniuplation of light. This theatrical device turned out to be very appropriate for the needs of the cinema.

SIR ARNE'S TREASURE (Herr Arnes Pengar) Mauritz Stiller

Script: Gustaf Molander and Stiller, from the novel by Selma Lagerlöf. Photography: Julius Jaenzon (Interiors) and Gustaf Boge (Exteriors). Art Direction: Harry Dahlström. Cast: Hjalmar Selander (Sir Arne), Concordia Selander (His wife), Richard Lund (Sir Archie), Mary Johnson (Elsalill), Wanda Rothgardt (Sir Arne's daughter), Axel Nilsson (Torarin), Stina Berg (Hostess), Erik Stocklassa (Sir Regi-

nald), Bror Berger (Sir Philip), Gustaf Aronson (Captain), Dagmar
Ebbesen (Torarin's mother), Gösta Gustafsson (Clergyman).

Svenska Bio, Sweden.   5 reels, 7280 ft.

The two key directors in the silent period of Swedish cinema were
Mauritz Stiller and Victor Sjöström. The Finnish-born Stiller came
to Sweden and joined Svenska Bio in 1912, a few months before
Sjöström. His development was slow, and while Sjöström was making his best films, Stiller was still a beginner directing skillful but
slight comedies; he would soar higher after falling under the influence of the fatalistic Scandinavian literature. In 1919 Sjöström persuaded his colleague to make a screen version of a legend written
by Selma Lagerlöf. The result, Sir Arne's Treasure, is Stiller's
best film of all and, together with The Outlaw and His Wife, the
most outstanding achievement of the silent cinema in Sweden.

Like the other film, Sir Arne's Treasure is a story of
blighted love, and it is set in the late 16th century. Sir Archie
and two other Scottish mercenaries escape from a Swedish prison
and head towards the port of Marstrand, hoping to find a ship for
Scotland. On the way they ransack Sir Arne's rich farm, kill the
occupants and steal a treasure; the only survivor is the owner's
daughter, Elsalill. She goes to Marstrand, meets Sir Archie and
unaware of his crime falls in love with him.

For most of the film snow is the leitmotif of the story,
stressing the purity of feelings and creating a somewhat unreal atmosphere. In the final scenes however the lead is taken by the
sea: hoping to escape punishment for murder and robbery, Sir
Archie and his companions wait for the thaw to liberate the ice-
bound ship. They are attacked by the local people, Elsalill is
killed and Sir Archie captured. It is only then that the sea relents
and frees the ship. The sea is here a symbol of nature's domination over human affairs, a tempering force and a symbol of superior
justice. The film changes the chronology of the story in order to
simplify the dramatic line and clarify the characters' motivations.

Stiller was inclined to use primarily visual effects, such as
sharp contrasts of light and shadow and dynamic editing, while
Sjöström was a more contemplative director, relying on the facial
expressions of the actors and using long and rather static takes.
Sir Arne's Treasure impresses with its perfect screen recreation
of the Renaissance and with excellent acting. The editing is very
advanced, especially in the scene of the burning of Sir Arne's house,
full of tension and movement: the arrival of help from the nearby
farm is shown in parallel editing. The Expressionistic composition
of the long procession of women following Elsalill's body carried by
six men dressed in white became a "signature tune" of the silent
cinema; the essence of the atmosphere of the picture, it would be
quoted by Eisenstein in Ivan the Terrible.

BROKEN BLOSSOMS   David Wark Griffith

Script: Griffith, based on "The Chink and the Child, " a short story
in a collection, "Limehouse Nights, " by Thomas Burke. Photography: G. W. Bitzer and Hendrick Sartov. Cast: Lillian Gish (Lucy
Burrows), Donald Crisp (Battling Burrows), Richard Barthelmess
(Chang Huan), Arthur Howard (Burrows' manager), Edward Peil
(Evil Eye), George Beranger (The Spying One), Norman Selby (Prizefighter Kid McCoyh).

United Artists, U.S.A. 6013 ft.

Broken Blossoms is the first noble and great melodrama in the
cinema. After several lean years Griffith started work in United
Artists (which he co-founded) with his favorite Victorian theme of
oppressed innocence, making a film that was received enthusiastically by everyone. The scene is the 19th century Limehouse, the
slums of East London. A young Chinese, who came to England to
spread the teaching of love and peace, befriends a beautiful and
delicate girl terrorized by her boxer father. The innocent feeling
has a tragic ending: the brute discovers his daughter's association
with the non-white man and, having just lost a bout, batters her to
death. The Chinese does not bear the cruel trial to which his philosophy of life is submitted: he kills Battling Burrows and then
commits suicide.

The realist description of the scene of action does not matter
in Broken Blossoms, which clearly leans towards an allegory of Innocence destroyed by Civilization--hence Griffith's London, photographed in diffused lights and enveloped in a veil of phosphorescent
fog, more resembles a town from an Andersen fairy tale than a
real city. This atmosphere gives an unusual poetic character to the
intimate drama, narrated with Dickensian crusading passion and
obeying the rules of the unity of place, time and action. It is indeed surprising that after the exuberant Intolerance Griffith was
capable of making such an unspectacular and simple, but equally
moving film. The drama develops with a good sense of rhythm,
making use of the contrast of the quiet and lyrical scenes with dynamic and brutal ones.

Griffith was however sparing with the cinematic effects he
had pioneered earlier: the editing of Broken Blossoms is very restrained, close shots very few. The picture has an incomparable
intimacy and charm; as someone said, "Griffith showed himself to
be a master not only of shout but also of whisper." But even here
the director was not talking of people but incarnations of ideas; the
meek submissiveness of Lucy and the Chinese youth (symbolizing
Innocence) to the excesses of Evil is irritating.

Still, this time taste did not fail Griffith as it did in the
pacifist Hearts of the World (1918). Maybe only the solemn and
naive captions are a discordant note, but one easily forgets this in
the face of such an acting team as in Broken Blossoms. Lillian
Gish, the subtlest heroine of the silent cinema, gave here one of
her unforgettable, pastel performances; she was well partnered by
Richard Barthelmess, almost spiritually united with the brittle personality of his Chinaman.

POLIKUSHKA   Alexandr Sanin

Script: Valentin Turkin, Fyodor Otsep and Nikolai Efros, from the
story by Leo Tolstoy. Photography: Yuri Zhelyabuzhsky. Cast:
Ivan Moskvin (Polikushka), Vera Pashennaya (Akulina, his wife),
Yevgeniya Rayevskaya (Lady of the manor), V. Bulgakova (Her
niece), Varvara Massalitinova (Joiner's wife), S. Aydarov (Bailiff),
D. Gundurov (Gardener).

Russ, Russia.   6 reels, 4980 ft.   Released in 1922.

The first film show in Russia took place, before the Tsar, as early
as May 1896. For twenty years afterwards Russian films adopted
the same role of curiosity, crude entertainment and vehicle for
primitive literary adaptations (Pushkin and Tolstoy were the favorites)
as did films elsewhere. The key names in the early Russian cinema are those of Protazanov and Gardin; the films, although fascinating for a historian, resemble the American movies before The Birth
of a Nation. The real beginning of artistic activity in the Russian
cinema came as an aftermath of the Revolution.

Polikushka, a film made on a profit-sharing basis by what
can be best described as a film commune, is the most outstanding
work of the pre-Eisenstein era of the Soviet cinema. Firstly, this
is the first serious attempt at psychological portrayal of a protagonist. Secondly, it is an interesting and meticulously correct record
of rural life in Tsarist Russia. Thirdly, the performance given in
it by Ivan Moskvin, a distinguished theatrical actor, must be considered as remarkable.

A serf called Polikushka, a reformed delinquent, is sent by
his owner, who wants to show her trust in him, to a district town
to fetch a sum of money. Polikushka goes to sleep on the cart on
the way back; the money slips out from under his hat and is lost.
The man commits suicide in despair; his baby son, left without
supervision, drowns. In the last scene of the film the happy people
who found the money meet the funeral of the father and son.

Moskvin's portrayal of a simple drunken peasant is even now quite convincing; the film itself does not seem in the least naive, despite its melodramatic story. The film technique, naturally, was still relatively primitive with its immobile camera and no dramatic use of editing. Some faults can be offset against the extreme economies during the production: the cameraman exposed only around 6000 feet of negative film (reportedly almost the entire stock available in Russia at the time), while the present length of a screen print of Polikushka is 4980 feet. This implies a very low ratio of negative to positive footage, which could well be an all-time record.

1920

THE PHANTOM CARRIAGE (Körkarlen) (Thy Soul Shall Bear Witness) Victor Sjöström

---

Script: Sjöström, from the novel by Selma Lagerlöf. Photography: Julius Jaenzon. Art Direction: Alexander Bakó and Axel Esbensen. Cast: Victor Sjöström (David Holm), Hilda Borgström (His wife), Tore Svennberg (Georg), Astrid Holm (Sister Edith), Concordia Selander (Her mother), Lisa Lundholm (Sister Maria), Tor Weijden (Gustafsson), Olof Aas (Coachman), Nils Aréhn (Prison chaplain).

Svenska Bio, Sweden. 5 reels, 6122 ft.

The writing of Selma Lagerlöf is a recapitulation of centuries of Scandinavian folklore. Although the unique, brooding and romantic mood of her tales is very difficult to render on the screen, this has repeatedly been attempted: sometimes brilliantly as in Stiller's Sir Arne's Treasure, more often with only partial success as was in the case of his The Saga of Gösta Berling (1924). "The Phantom Carriage" is possibly the most difficult to handle in view of its highly complex narrative. Yet Sjöström's film version is a considerable success.

The story develops on New Year's Eve. According to a legend, the man who dies at midnight on that day will be compelled to carry the souls of the dead in his phantom carriage the following year. David Holm, a drunkard who terrorizes his family, is knocked unconscious during a fight at the cemetery and his villainous companion who died exactly a year earlier comes to fetch him in a phantom carriage. In a dream David re-lives his past and traces his downfall; just before the stroke of midnight he is saved thanks to the death of a charitable Salvation Army nurse and returns to his despairing family.

1920   -59-   L'Homme du large

The Phantom Carriage is not typical of the Swedish cinema
in its total lack of reference to the landscape and its reliance on a
limited number of interiors--indeed it seems closer to the German
Expressionist school.   The complicated story, involving even retro-
spections-within-retrospections was told with unhesitating clarity by
Sjöström who also gave here one of his best performances as an
actor.   The character of the film justified the use of a wide range
of technical tricks, of which the most often used was multiple exposure (at one stage four separate images are superimposed).

The Phantom Carriage is more than just a well-told story:
it is a drama of moral attitudes in which the mood and ideas are
conveyed through the purposeful choice of pictorial composition and
lighting.   It was given more impact by careful balance of the dream
sequences and the brutal realism of David's life story.   Because of
the reliance on cinematic technique this picture was bound to date
more than other Sjöström works, apart from the fact that the director felt more at home in outdoor dramas of simpler construction,
such as The Outlaw and His Wife.   Yet, despite its moralizing attitude, sentimentality and the naïve description of the life of the poor,
The Phantom Carriage is an evocative work with many beautiful
scenes--and the first genuine film of atmosphere.

L'HOMME DU LARGE   Marcel L'Herbier

Script: L'Herbier, from the story, "Un Drame au Bord de la Mer,"
by Honoré Balzac.   Photography: Lucas.   Cast: Roger Karl (Nolff),
Claire Prélia (His wife), Marcelle Pradot (Djenna), Jaque Catelain
(Michel), Charles Boyer (Guenn-la-Taupe), Lili Samuel (Lea), Marcel L'Herbier (Sailor).

Film Gaumont, France. 5512 ft.

While both Germany and Sweden developed their own national styles
in cinema, there was also an increase in creative activity in France.
The leader and principal theoretician of what became known as
French cinematic Impressionism was Louis Delluc.   The artistic
program of the Impressionists was the visual representation of
mental processes and their narrative style resembles that of the
novels of Marcel Proust.   The films were almost always rather
short and this includes Delluc's best works, Fièvre and La Femme
de nulle part (both made in 1921).   The main weakness of Impressionist cinema is its excessive formalism.   All these characteristics
are present in the work of L'Herbier, a former symbolic poet.

The story of L'Homme du large, a free adaptation of Balzac,
is rather rudimentary: a proud sailor loves the sea, hates the land-

lubbers and expects his son to follow his example. But Michel
prefers drinking in a tavern with his friends. The climax of the
family conflict is when he steals money and commits perjury. His
father decides to "put him into God's hands" and abandons him tied
up in a small boat which he pushes out to sea. Tragic and broken,
he swears to himself to keep the secret, but in the trivial happy
end Michel is saved by fishermen, takes a liking to the sea and returns to his father. His sister, who at first wanted to go into a
convent, marries a sailor.

The main stress in the film is visual, the individual shots
were treated as signs in a symbolic ideographic writing and were
combined along these lines. Although L'Homme du large is over-
acted it does offer a true and convincing description of life on the
Brittany coast with its white cliffs and wrathful sea. The details
of local custom, costume and landscape were here used even more
prominently than in the Swedish films of that time and one feels that
this was not always done with full dramatic justification.

THE GOLEM (Der Golem, wie er in die Welt kam) Paul Wegener
    and Carl Boese

Script: Wegener, based on a 17th-century legend. Photography:
Karl Freund. Art Direction: Hans Pölzig. Cast: Paul Wegener
(The Golem), Albert Steinrück (Rabbi Loew), Lída Salmonová (Miri-
am), Ernst Deutsch (Famulus, Rabbi's assistant), Otto Gebühr (Em-
peror Luhois), Lothar Müthel (Florian), Hannes Sturm (Rabbi Jehuda),
Greta Schröder (Girl with the rose), Max Kroner (Temple servant).

Projektions-AG Union, Germany. 5 reels, 6306 ft.

The old legend about the clay figure called the Golem has fascinated
the imagination of German film-makers for years with its mystical
quality and obvious cinematic potential. It was first made into a
film in 1914 by Henrik Galeen and Paul Wegener. The latter, a
famous actor, was for many years associated with the theatre of
the great Max Reinhardt; he first appeared in the cinema in Stellan
Rye's The Student of Prague, creating the first great acting performance in the German cinema.

Wegener had always been interested in the mystical and imaginary and in 1920 made another film version of the Golem legend.
The story is set in the ghetto of medieval Prague which, on the
Emperor's orders, is to be cleared of Jews. Rabbi Loew, endowed
with special powers, summons Biblical characters to the rescue and
puts life into a clay creature by placing a cryptic sign upon its
heart. The sacred Golem will save the Jews. The Imperial palace

is soon threatened with destruction and the frightened Emperor
promises to revoke the antisemitic decree if only the Rabbi checks
the liberated elements. But the Golem, prompted by a stellar con-
figuration, is overcome by destructive passion and mutinies against
its creator. Its deadly progress is checked only by the flower
borne by a little girl.

The Golem is closely related to the theatre of Reinhardt,
both through Wegener and through Pölzig, the art director. These
links materialized in the manner of staging of crowd scenes and in
the curiously lighted sets of winding passages, steep streets and
crooked houses with pointed roofs. The obsessive interest in as-
trology and the supernatural, the motif of metamorphosis (as in
The Student of Prague), the visual imagery, which at one point includes a projection of past events onto the wall, are all very characteristic of the contemporary preoccupations of the German cinema,
although the film cannot otherwise be considered typically Expressionist.

The atmosphere pervading The Golem severs its links with
reality and transfers it into the world of fairytale. The picture
could have become a great classic of the genre if it were not for
the disastrously naive subplot of the romantic love of a courtier
and a Jewish girl, and a somewhat incoherent narrative. Yet it
remains a considerable achievement and a very characteristic example of the fantastic style of the time. The full title of the picture
is The Golem, How He Came into the World and the idea of a figure brought to life seems to have inspired the handling of Dr.
Frankenstein's creation, the classic movie monster.

THE PARSON'S WIDOW (Prästänkan) (The Fourth Marriage of Dame
    Margaret) Carl Theodor Dreyer

Script: Dreyer, from a story by Kristofer Janson. Photography:
George Schnéevoigt. Cast: Hildur Carlberg (Margarete Peders-
dotter, the parson's widow), Einar Røds (Søfren), Greta Almroth
(His fiancée, Mari), Olav Aukrust and Kurt Welin (Seminarians),
Emil Helsengreen (Gardener), Mathilde Nielsen (Gunvar), Lorentz
Thyholt (Beadle).

Svensk Filmindustri, Stockholm, Sweden. 4921 ft.

In the years 1908-1915, prosperous Denmark had a very powerful
film industry which exported its products all over the world. Although the scripts were of low quality and, in their fatalistic mood,
exploited the bourgeois sensitivities of the audience, the cinema had
a great asset in the flourishing Danish theatre, which supplied very

good performers. One of them, Asta Nielsen, became the first great film actress. The most notable picture of that period was August Blom's Atlantis (1913). All this came to a close with the outbreak of the war, before Dreyer, the greatest director Denmark produced, had found his way into film direction.

Dreyer started as a journalist but later became a script-writer. His directorial debut, the complex melodrama The President (1919), foreshadowed his future visual style and was also the first study of the suffering of women--the central theme of Dreyer's work. Leaves from Satan's Book (1920) was a not very successful imitation of Intolerance, but the third film, The Parson's Widow, made like all his films from a literary original, was Dreyer's first outstanding work.

A young curate applies for a parson's job, preaches a rousing sermon and wins the post unaware of his obligation to marry the widow of his predecessor--or to be exact, of his three predecessors. He has to agree, but later installs his girl friend as a maid in the vicarage. The young couple join forces in vain attempts to get rid of the old woman. Finally they realize they have done an injustice to Dame Margaret; having made sure of the depth of their feelings the old lady then departs this life with grace and dignity.

Religion always fascinated Dreyer as can be seen in any of his pictures; his lifelong ambition was to make a film about the life of Christ. In The Parson's Widow the religious motif is rather ex-ternal than spiritual. Dreyer concentrated all his efforts on making an absolutely realistic stylistic exercise and shot the film in Nor-way in a genuine 17th-century museum village. The film-making betrays the influence of the Swedish cinema in its use of the lu-minous Scandinavian landscapes, but still, this charming picture quite obviously came to Dreyer with great ease.

The tone is unique in Dreyer's work, a mixture of sincere realism and comical touches. Søfren wins the preaching contest by surreptitiously sticking a feather in a competitor's hat; the beadle wakes the sleeping faithful with a long stick; the young man's futile attempts to be alone with his girl give rise to a series of comic scenes, the final one being the couple's trying to scare Lady Mar-garet to death.

WAY DOWN EAST   David Wark Griffith

Script: Anthony Paul Kelly, from the play by Lottie Blair Parker. Photography: G. W. Bitzer and Hendrick Sartov. Cast: Lillian Gish (Anna Moore), Richard Barthelmess (David Bartlett), Lowell Sherman (Lennox Sanderson), Kate Bruce (Mrs. Bartlett), Josephine

Bernard (Diana Tremont), Vivia Ogden (Martha Perkins), Mary Hay
(Kate Brewster), Porter Strong (Seth Holcomb), Florence Short (Eccentric aunt), Burr McIntosh (Squire Bartlett).

United Artists, U.S.A.   Originally approx. 9000 ft.; cut version,
7200 ft. 1931 music re-issue--110 mins.

Way Down East is, after Broken Blossoms, the second classical
screen melodrama, but it does not match the earlier works of
Griffith either in the narrative skill, or in the amount of inspiration
in developing the language of the cinema, or even in the quality of
the theme, which was here the naive story of a poor seduced girl.
Having been taken through a mock marriage ceremony and then abandoned by the seducer, Anne gives birth to a child which dies.   She
then takes a job as a servant at an austere puritan farming family.
When her past is revealed she is told to leave and tries to commit
suicide, but the son of her master saves and marries her.

Although the slow development of the story is animated by a
number of motifs characteristic of the American generic comedy--
quoted without much refinement but in exchange making the theme
closer to reality--the editing, Griffith's basic instrument of expression, plays no significant role at all until the finale.   It is only
here, in the scenes of the heroine's escape on the ice-floes of the
thawing river, that the master gave his Way Down East full brightness: the final scenes of this film are in fact the most decisive
ones for its stature.

Of course, Griffith's last successful picture has more positive
sides.   Among them is the photography, faithful to the period; success was achieved by the film's being made in the natural East
Coast scenery.   But above all is the greatest screen performance
of Lillian Gish, particularly moving in the scene of the baptism of
the dying child.   Her interpretation of the role reached the extremes
of naturalist acting in the spirit of the "living through" method professed by the famous Russian Konstantin Stanislavsky, but was invested with such irresistible charm that the content of the film is
not compromised but ennobled.

EROTIKON   Mauritz Stiller

Script: Stiller and Arthur Nordén, from the play, "A Kék Róka"
(The Silver Fox), by Ferenc Herczeg. Photography: Henrik Jaenzon. Art Direction: Axel Esbensen. Cast: Anders de Wahl (Professor Leo Charpentier), Tora Teje (Irene, his wife), Karin Molander (Marthe, his niece), Lars Hanson (Preben Wells, a sculptor),
Vilhelm Bryde (Baron Felix), Carina Ari (Schaname), Torsten Ham-

marén (Professor Sedonius), Elin Lagergren (Irene's mother), Martin Oscar (The Shah), Carl Wallin (Fur dealer).

Svensk Filmindustri, Sweden.   5998 ft.

The expansion of American films into European market after the end of the Great War dealt the death blow to the Swedish cinema. The Swedes tried to fight the competitors using their own weapon of light comedy, and pictures such as Erotikon, a lavish screen adaptation of a Hungarian vaudeville routine along the lines of Cecil B. DeMille, were expected to win back the lost audiences. While a marital triangle is usually a more suitable subject for a drama, the marital square cannot be treated otherwise than in a light vein.

The wife of an absent-minded professor of entomology loves a young sculptor while being in turn courted by a certain Baron Felix. The jealous sculptor suspects her of having an affair with Felix and tries to make the husband challenge the alleged lover to a duel. Finally, Irene marries the sculptor after a divorce from the professor who is in turn consoled by his attractive niece.

This intrigue proved to be sufficient for a zany and sophisticated comedy of manners, thriving on constant misunderstandings between characters and sexual innuendoes and as firmly set in the convention of the silent cinema as Clair's classic The Italian Straw Hat would come to be. Apart from his famous doom-laden sagas Stiller did direct several earlier comedies, and now showed himself able to make good use of the actors and innumerable humorous situations. For instance his employment of the "play within a play" principle during the scenes in the opera is interesting, with the stage action being an oblique comment on the actions of the real-life characters. On the other hand, the film suffers from rather long-winded dialogues, insufficient characterization and confused narrative.

In the final effect, Erotikon is a slight if amusing film. It is interesting that while it was inspired by the Hollywood productions (note the ironic treatment of the characters, but without even a trace of social criticism) it in turn exerted influence, on the feedback principle, on many American films, especially those of Lubitsch.

1921

DESTINY (Der Müde Tod) [also: The Three Lights; Between Worlds]
    Fritz Lang

Script: Lang and Thea von Harbou.

Framing Story; Photography: Erich Nitzschmann and Hermann Saal-
frank. Art Direction: Walter Röhrig. Cast: Lil Dagover and
Walter Janssen (The Lovers), Bernhard Goetzke (Death), Hans
Sternberg (Mayor), Carl Rückert (Minister), Max Adalbert (Notary),
Wilhelm Diegelmann (Doctor), Erich Pabst (Teacher), Karl Platen
(Chemist), Hermann Picha (Tailor), Paul Rehkopk (Gravedigger),
Max Pfeiffer (Watchman), Georg John (Beggar), Lydia Potechina
(Landlady), Grete Berger (Mother).

The Story of the First Light; Photography: Fritz Arno Wagner.
Art Direction: Hermann Warm. Cast: Eduard von Winterstein
(Caliph), Lil Dagover (Zobeide, his sister), Erika Unruh (Aisha, her
friend), Walter Janssen (The Frank), Rudolf Klein-Rogge (Dervish),
Bernahard Goetzke (El Mot, the gardener).

The Story of the Second Light; Photography: Fritz Arno Wagner.
Art Direction: Hermann Warm. Cast: Rudolf Klein-Rogge (Giro-
lamo), Lil Dagover (Fiametta), Walter Janssen (Giovanfrancesco),
Lothar Müthel (Messenger), Edgar Pauly (Friend), Lina Paulsen
(Nurse), Levis Brody (Moor).

The Story of the Third Light; Photography: Fritz Arno Wagner.
Art Direction: Robert Herlth. Cast: Karl Huszar (The Emperor
of China), Paul Biensfeld (A Hi, the magician), Lil Dagover (Liang),
Walter Janssen (Tiao Tsien), Bernhard Goetzke (Emperor's archer),
Max Adalbert (Chancellor of the Exchequer), Paul Neumann (Execu-
tioner).

Erich Pommer, Decla Film for Decla-Bioscop AG, Germany.   6
reels, 7582 ft.

"One cannot escape death, but he who loses his life gains it": this
beautiful Biblical thought, so close to the Teutonic philosophy of
life, is expressed in Destiny with matching visual power. The man
who did it was Fritz Lang, then still regarded as a highly rated beginner (he started as a scriptwriter and after taking to direction in
1919 had already made six films), but who in a couple of years
would become the driving force of the German cinema.

     Destiny is composed of three stories telling of the inevita-
bility of fate. The framing story is, according to a caption, set
"anywhere and at any time." A girl bargains with Death for the
life of her lover; Death agrees to spare him if she can keep alight
at least one candle out of three representing human lives. The
stories which follow take us to 9th-century Baghdad, 17th-century
Venice and semi-fantastic China and show the love of three couples
broken by death. All the candles are extinguished but Death offers
the heroine one last chance: any life in exchange for the life of the
boy. She offers her own and the lovers are reunited in death.

     Although the characters, the countries and the historical
periods change, Lang used the same actors in all episodes in order
to give Destiny the generalizing character of a moral dispute: the
message is each time drawn from a different environment but remains unchanged. The final conclusion of the film, that even fear
of inevitable death can be vanquished by the noble actions of man,
is one of the most distinctly stressed humanist manifestoes in the
cinema. Human dignity depends not on final victory but on action
itself, and although we cannot escape death, we must still fight
against it. To do is to be: this is the sense of existence according to Fritz Lang.

     The greatest value of Destiny, however, is not its Christian
message, but the gloomy poetry derived from the full cooperation
of all the stylistic elements: acting, sets, photography and lighting.
Lang creates unforgettable images on the screen--for instance, the
enormous Wall of Destiny or the great hall filled with thousands of
burning candles. In fact the entire picture is given an exceptionally
attractive visual appearance, further augmented by a number of technical tricks (a flying carpet, a wondrous steed, an army of Lilli-
putians). Destiny already contained the majority of the elements of
screen mythology and style of direction that would characterize the
whole of Lang's work and would enable him to reach his high position.

     On the other hand there are many things here which he did
not repeat later; the slow narrative pace of the story, the restraint
in the use of film editing, and the humorous tone in the Chinese
episode and in the presentation of the local dignitaries in the framing
story. In addition Lang threw in a captivating vision of a little Ger-

man town, one which can measure up to The Blue Angel.

Perhaps the most unforgettable thing about Destiny is the great performance of Bernhard Goetzke as the Angel of Death, to which Bengt Ekerot, in Bergman's allegorical The Seventh Seal (made 36 years later), surely owes a debt. Destiny is a modern and fascinating film; it talks of things which are always important in a way which has withstood the test of time.

THE KID   Charles Chaplin

Script: Chaplin. Photography: Rollie Totheroh. Cast: Charles Chaplin (Charlie the Tramp), Edna Purviance (Mother), Jackie Coogan (The Kid), Carl Miller (Artist), Tom Wilson (Policeman), Henry Bergman (Doss-house warden), Charles F. Riesner (Tough), Lita Grey (Flirtatious angel), Phyllis Allen (Woman with pram), Nelly Bly Baker (Slum nurse), Albert Austin (Dosser).

Charles Chaplin for First National, U.S.A.   6 reels, 5300 ft.

In January 1919 Chaplin formed United Artists together with Mary Pickford, Douglas Fairbanks and D. W. Griffith. The distribution of The Kid, Chaplin's first feature-length picture, was the first enterprise of the new film company. During the two preceding years the director's art had gone through a significant evolution: as soon as he started making films longer than two reels, his tone became more reflective, his frolics less frantic. This was when "out of the eyes of the Tramp looked a soul." From then on Chaplin soared higher than other comics who, with the sole exception of Buster Keaton, never graduated from buffooning grotesques.

The setting of The Kid is Victorian London, Chaplin's home town; Griffith's Broken Blossoms was set a few streets away. Charlie, a poor itinerant glazier, takes care of a waif. The two are shown working together some years later: the Kid breaks windows--Charlie glazes them. In the happy end the boy's mother, now a rich opera singer, takes care of them both.

The Kid marks the maturity of Chaplin's style; more of a melodrama than a comedy, it is the first complete example of the characteristic "bitter-sweet" blend of comic and tragic elements arranged in a carefully thought-out and dramatically logical structure. Tragic scenes, like the boy's being taken away to the orphanage, are alternated with veritable gems of screen humor, such as the scene in which the two are frying pancakes which Charlie subsequently counts like money. The humor is however somewhat toned-down and gentle: in Charlie's dream the suburban street is adorned

with garlands and the inhabitants fly using angel's wings--but don't
stop quarreling. The humanist message of The Kid--its concern for
the weak and helpless--started the series of films that would culminate in The Gold Rush. The main trump of the picture is of
course Jackie Coogan. This amazingly precocious five-year-old
gave, at Chaplin's side, a real dramatic performance with a proper
gradation of emotion--a role he would never match again.

After The Kid, Buster Keaton and Harold Lloyd, Chaplin's
main competitors, not wanting to be left behind without a fight, also
switched to making almost exclusively full-length features.

FOOLISH WIVES   Erich von Stroheim

Script: Stroheim. Photography: Ben Reynolds and William
Daniels. Art Direction and Costumes: Stroheim and Richard Day.
Cast: Erich von Stroheim (Count Vladislav Sergei Karamzin),
Maude George (Princess Olga, his cousin), Mae Busch (Princess
Vera, his cousin), George Christians (Howard Hughes, the American
Ambassador), Miss Dupont (His wife), Cesare Gravina (Gaston, the
counterfeiter), Malvine Polo (His daughter), Dale Fuller (Karamzin's
maid).

Universal, U.S.A. 18-20 reels (approx. 20,700 ft.), reduced to
12-14 reels (approx. 13,800 ft.) in the released version.

While millions were being killed on the fronts of the First World
War, the parasitic elite crowded the casinos of the Riviera. Stroheim refers to this contrast in his first outstanding film: a lady
sitting in an elegant restaurant drops her handbag; her officer neighbor does not pick it up because he has no arms. The grandeur of
the Monte Carlo scenery is background for an uncompromising attack on the ethics of the upper classes.

A supposed émigré Tsarist officer, staying in Monaco in the
company of his "Russian princesses" cousins, wanders between the
gaming rooms and the bedrooms of society ladies, not missing a
single opportunity. Karamzin lives off his "cousins'" chambermaid,
tries to seduce the wife of the American Ambassador when shelter-
ing from a storm and later "borrows" from her a sizeable sum under false pretences. When the jealous maid sets the villa alight,
Karamzin jumps out of the window and leaves the ambassador's wife
behind. Finally he is murdered by a counterfeiter whose feeble-
minded daughter he had seduced; his body is dumped into a stinking
sewer.

Stroheim, born in 1885, was an émigré from Vienna who rep-

resented himself in the U.S., where he came during the first years
of the century, as a member of Austrian society while being in fact
the son of a Jewish merchant. He was able to paint with insight
the vision of a milieu that he found both repulsive and fascinating.
He created a work remarkable for its nonconformist theme, penetrating psychological scrutiny, boldness of scope and formal brilliance. The dramatic potential of the interiors of a specially built
set--a full-scale replica of a Monagasque palace--was used to the
full. Stroheim was a follower of Griffith's doctrine (he was his assistant for a few years and achieved his first notice in the role of
a pharisee in Intolerance) that naturalness of surroundings is a pri-
mary condition for the credible behavior of actors. Softening lenses,
slow-motion shots, superimposed images, and low-key photography
are all dramatic components; the play of stripes of light and shadow
in all seduction scenes becomes a counterpoint to human littleness.

Foolish Wives is a film of violence and suggestive visual
symbolism which often recalls the contemporary German cinema.
The scene when the camera rapidly closes in on the maid's tormented eyes can be quoted as an American analogue of a similar shot in
Lang's Dr. Mabuse, the Gambler. Foolish Wives can be considered
the last part of an unofficial trilogy composed of Stroheim's first
three films: earlier parts were Blind Husbands (1918) and The
Devil's Passkey (1919). The latter was destroyed by the producer
shortly after release, but is considered to have been of only secondary importance. The common denominator of the trilogy is the
motif of a marital triangle, in which the woman is seduced by an
unscrupulous officer, played by Stroheim himself. Such thematic interests, expounded in a vehemently realistic style and with strong
sexual overtones, were understood as an attack on the principal
shrine of American morality--the institution of marriage. Accordingly, Foolish Wives was cut before release by almost a half.

When, a year later, the Motion Picture Producers and Dis-
tributors of America was formed under the aegis of Will Hays, the
Defender of Decency and Moral Standards, Stroheim's hands were
tied, Hollywood defeated him; the ostracized director would have all
his subsequent films--apart from the commerical Merry Widow
(1925)--either mutilated, or given to someone else to finish.

SOULS ON THE ROAD (Rojō no Reikon) Minoru Murata

Script: Kiyohiko Ushihara, based on the novel, "Children on the
Street," by Wilhelm Schmidtbonn and the play, "Lower Depths," by
Maxim Gorky. Photography: Bunjiro Mizutani and Hamataro Oda.
Cast: Kaoru Osanai (Yasushi Sugino), Haruko Sawamura (Youko,
his wife), Koreya Togo (Koichiro, their son), Mikiko Hisamatsu
(Fumiko, their daughter), Ryuko Date (Mitsuko, Koichiro's fiancée),

Yuriko Hanabusa (Peer's daughter), Sotaro Okada (Caretaker of
Villa), Kumahiko Mohara (Steward of Villa), Minoru Murata (Taro),
Komei Minami (Tsurikichi, a released convict), Shigeru Tsutamura
(Kamezo, a released convict).

Shochiku Kinema, Japan.   Approx. 8202 ft.

The first Japanese feature film was made as early as 1899, and
regular film production started around 1912.   Soon after, Japan had
thousands of movie theatres and Nikkatsu, the first film company,
produced over a hundred films a year.   Up to the present day Japanese pictures have followed one of two conventions: jidai-geki,
historical costume drama (set before 1868), and gendai-geki, which
deals with contemporary subjects.   The proportion which both these
conventions enjoy in Japanese film production varies; before 1915
historical subjects dominated.   This date however marks the beginning of the rapid transformation of Japan from an agricultural to an
industrial country and meanwhile Japanese film-makers were forming their art under foreign (mainly American) influence.

        Around 1918 several film-makers returned home after train-
ing in Hollywood.   The results were soon visible on the screen:
the use of modern narrative techniques, close-ups and dissolves
showed that the example of The Birth of a Nation did not go unheeded.   Among the intellectuals who wanted to spread modern western cultural achievements was the film-maker Karou Osanai.   In
1920 he was hired by the Shochiku Kinema Company and later founded another organization called Shochiku Kinema Research Studio.
Minoru Murata's Souls on the Road, its first production, is the first
outstanding Japanese film and also the earliest to contain distinct
social criticism.   The film was based on an interesting dramatic
principle derived from Griffith's Intolerance--the parallel development of separate plots which complement and counterpoint each
other.

        The setting of Souls on the Road is the mountainous country-
side of central Japan.   In the first of the two concurrent stories a
prodigal son who left the paternal home to study the violin in Tokyo,
returns with a wife and sick child to a hostile reception from his
father.   In the second story two ex-convicts wander hungrily around
the countryside in search of a livelihood and meet with understanding and help from the old caretaker of a peer's country villa.   Both
sub-plots finally come together: the two wanderers who set off full
of hope and courage for the future, find the rejected son dead in
the snow.

        The main dramatic device in the film is contrast: the con-
trast of the pessimism of one story with the optimism of the other,
the contrast of sunshine and overcast skies.   Murata gave further
evidence of his familiarity with foreign film production is his use of
landscape as a mood-creating element, his purposeful use of camera
set-ups, modern narrative editing and even the use of wipe and iris

(which again came from Griffith). Even the heroine is of the Hollywood type. On the other hand the use of trick photography (superimpositions) recalls, although with a lesser degree of skill, Sjöström's The Phantom Carriage.

Souls on the Road is indeed a very Western picture; this was predetermined by the choice of the scenario. The film's aura of sadness interestingly coexisted with the trends of mood in European art. This atmosphere is stressed by the photography of grey country roads, snowy fields and dark forests in winter, bare and superficially unattractive. Souls on the Road has something of the spirit of the desperate odyssey through the provincial roads of Italy in Federico Fellini's very much later La Strada.

WITCHCRAFT THROUGH THE AGES (Häxan) Benjamin Christensen

Script: Christensen. Photography: Johan Ankerstjerne. Art Direction: Richard Louw. Cast: Maren Pedersen (The Witch), Clara Pontoppidan (Nun), Tora Teje (Modern hysteric), Elith Pio (Young monk), Benjamin Christensen (Devil/Fashionable doctor), Oscar Stribolt (Fat monk), Johs Andersen (Chief Inquisitor), Karen Winther (Dame Anna), Emmy Schønfield (Marie, a seamstress), Alice O'Fredericks (Woman possessed by the Devil).

Svensk Filmindustri, Sweden, 6840 ft. Re-released in 1967 with sound and an English commentary (read by William Burroughs). Length of the sound version: 6840 ft., 76 mins.

This para-documentary treatise examined the origins and manifestations of witchcraft throughout the space of history. (1) The prologue describes early concepts of devils and witches using old documents and drawings. (2) The Middle Ages, the heyday of witchcraft and counter-witchcraft, are then surveyed, with possession, persecutive witch hunts, black magic, flagellation, perverted sexuality, general hysteria, and the somber business of the Inquisition given attention. (3) The film finds in 1920 that people once considered possessed by the Wicked One and treated as such are now inhabiting hospitals and mental institutions.

Witchcraft Through the Ages was made in Sweden by a Danish director whose later reputation rested mainly on his (note the title) Seven Footprints to Satan (1929), an American-made satire on Hollywood musicals. Here he splendidly created a dense atmosphere of gloomy superstition; the film's imagery was derived equally from medieval German and Dutch paintings and the lively imagination of the director, who used sophisticated chiaroscuro illumination of objects at unusual angles. Yet showing horrors was not an aim in it-

self. On the contrary, the enlightened Christensen, incredulous and
sceptical, identified witchcraft with hysteria and other forms of mental debility.

The absurd subject matter of the film is made more incisive
by startlingly realistic acting involving documentary-like sequences
in a modern mental asylum. The tone of the picture is a mixture
of ribald humor and the macabre shown with a cold, almost scientific objectivity. In all, Witchcraft Through the Ages is a technically precocious and very evocative (if uneven) vision of medieval times,
containing many grisly scenes of outrage, torture and pseudo-con-
fessions, and imaginative pictorial compositions, which often impart
a vicious and slightly anarchistic quality, delighting the surrealists
and possibly influencing the cinema of Luis Buñuel, the greatest of
them all.

SHATTERED (Scherben)   Lupu Pick

Script: Carl Mayer and Pick. Photography: Friedrich Weinmann.
Cast: Werner Krauss (Father), Edith Posca (Daughter), Paul Otto
(Inspector), Hermine Strassmann-Witt (Mother), Lupu Pick (Travel-
er).

Rex-Film GmbH, Germany. 5 reels, 4449 ft.

The Cabinet of Dr. Caligari triggered off animated artistic activity
in the German cinema, and gave rise to two very closely related
(although externally different) trends. One of them, known as "Expressionism," rejected reality in favor of stylized visual compositions and indulged in fantastic and terrifying stories of tyrants and
monsters. The second, the Expressionist chamber drama known as
"Kammerspiel" (from the type of stage play popular at the time),
was more closely related to real life. The two trends were joined
by the personality of Carl Mayer, one of the most influential scriptwriters the cinema ever had, and by the type of visual imagery preferred (the use of light).

Their treatments of reality are different: the Kammerspiel
exposes the basic failings of human nature rather than the destructive
influence of external forces, and has more in common with naturalist literature than with the theatre. The Kammerspiel rehabilitated
psychological drama, previously ridiculed by Expressionism, which
saw man as the plaything of mighty forces beyond his control. The
protagonists of the Kammerspiel are the bourgeois, the ordinary little people driven by the same feelings and passions as in the novels
of Zola, Dreiser and Norris--jealousy, hatred, frustration--emotions
which post-war Europe knew only too well. The Kammerspiel films

liked to obey the strict classical unities of action, time and place in the development of the plot, avoided captions (in Shattered there is only one, the essential "I am a murderer") and used their protagonists as symbols: the Mother, the Father, the Woman.

Lupu Pick's Shattered is the first outstanding Kammerspiel picture. There are only four participants in the drama: a daughter of a railway man is seduced by an engineer from the city; the girl's mother loses her mental balance when she learns of the affair and freezes to death while praying in front of the figure of a saint; the girl, rejected by her lover, tells all to her father who kills him and then stops an express train by waving a lantern (red in the original print) and then confesses the crime to the driver; the girl goes mad.

Shattered carries a distinct air of finality. The tragedy is stylized and in fact far removed from reality, but it is still related to the social scene: at the end of the film the director shows the rich guests in the restaurant car of the express looking impassively at the stricken, tragic Father. In his later New Year's Eve, Pick allowed this contrast to become a dominant dramatic thread.

SEVEN YEARS' BAD LUCK   Max Linder

Script: Linder.   Photography: J. Van Enger.   Cast: Max Linder (Max), Thelma Percy (Station agent's daughter), Alta Allen (Max's fiancée), Betty Peterson (Maid), Lola Gonzales (Hawaiian maid), Harry Mann (Chef), Chance Ward (Railroad conductor), Ralph McCullough (Max's valet), Hugh Saxon (Station agent), Cap Anderson (Jail bird), F. B. Crayne (False friend), Pudgy (the little dog), Joe Martin (Monk).

United Artists, U.S.A.   5 reels, approx. 5000 ft.

Max Linder was one of the greatest comedians of the silent cinema. Born in 1883 in France, in 1903 he became a theatrical actor and from 1905 appeared in the Pathé films. In the next few years he starred in scores of one- and two-reelers made from his own scripts, soon establishing the distinctive screen personality of a young man immaculately dressed in a smart morning coat, top hat, lacquered shoes and carrying a walking stick. Linder's restrained, modern acting was very far from theatrical, his use of mime and gesticulation, sparing and simple, and he displayed an amazing feel for the essence of the cinema. For these reasons he is often considered the first real film actor.

When starting the Keystone film company in 1912, Mack Sen-

nett, the creator of the American slapstick comedy, set himself as
a goal the promotion of an actor who would follow Linder's style of
acting. It was not easy in these early days when film comedians
were frantically bombarding each other with cream cakes, Charlie
Chaplin was still just funny and Buster Keaton was yet nothing. One
must also remember that Linder's style was very different from the
American type of humor, and hard to imitate.

Yet America did have a chance to have a Linder-type actor
in an American film: Linder himself came over and in the years
1921-23 made three feature films, so French in character as to be
almost considered imported productions. Seven Years' Bad Luck,
the first of them, is principally based on only one gag: a valet
breaks the mirror in front of which Linder shaves each morning
and persuades the cook to stand on the other side of the empty
frame and imitate their master's movements. When Max finds out,
he wants to give the cook a good beating, but instead breaks the already replaced mirror. The seven years of bad luck which follow
are the occasion for a display of a series of smaller, but brilliant,
gags, most of which concern the train journey. The most famous
sequence shows how Max, with amazing imagination and ingenuity,
avoids the ticket collector. In the end all his disasters give way
to seven years' happiness with his bride.

Seven Years' Bad Luck, with its complete dramatic logic,
charm and lightness, is one of the classical screen comedies. He
Linder's dandy is never heartless, and never really unhappy. He
exerted a great influence on cinema acting: Chaplin borrowed his
cane, Adolphe Menjou and Pierre Etaix, his screen personality--all
comedians in fact owe him something. Yet if one intends to search
for Linder's equivalent as a film director, one has to go to France
and to the early comedies of René Clair.

ELDORADO   Marcel L'Herbier

Script: L'Herbier. Photography: Lucas. Sets: Le Bertre and
Garnier. Cast: Eve Francis (Sybilla, the dancer), Jaque Catelain
(Hedwick, the painter), Marcelle Pradot (His fiancée), Philippe
Hériat (Hunchback), Claire Prélia.

Gaumont, France. 5577 ft.

The visual side of L'Herbier's early films by far overshadowed their
weepy and schematic plots: this is equally true of L'Homme du
large and Eldorado, a sentimental story about the life and tragic end
of a girl who works as a dancer at the "Eldorado" cabaret in Anda-
lusia in order to support her child. The heroine starts a relation-

ship with a young painter and finally commits suicide after being raped by a hoodlum.

L'Herbier employed most technical devices then in use in the cinema--sometimes he applied them with such boldness and imagination as to amount to a cultivated pictorial vision. Eldorado was styled after the works of the great Spanish masters (Ribera, Velasquez, Goya), the juxtaposition of the sun-drenched landscapes and dazzlingly white architecture with the smoky, velvety dusk of the interiors gives the film an authentic Spanish feel; frequent use was made of soft-focus photography and, as in the German Warning Shadows, shadows dancing on gauze backcloths--a device that was to become standard in the poetic cinema.

Some of the film (the scenes of the Holy Week procession) is almost documentary in character, but unfortunately L'Herbier expended more effort portraying the precious dilemmas of his heroes than trying to define his attitude to reality with more precision. All the same, Eldorado is one of the first attempts at subjective narrative in cinema, whereby the screen world is seen through the eyes of the characters: the fragile imaginings of a drunkard, the twisted visions of the despairing heroine, the Alhambra palace distorted to represent the creative ideas of a painter.

Eldorado is the last notable picture of a director who while obviously very talented, was obsessed by formalism and bookishness. For the next few years he was quick to follow the dominant trends and directions and made films as esoteric as they were pretentious; later, finally betrayed by his aesthetic longings, he resigned himself to commercial productions.

BACKSTAIRS (Hintertreppe) Leopold Jessner and Paul Leni

Script: Carl Mayer. Photography: Karl Hasselmann and Willy Hameister. Art Direction: Paul Leni. Cast: Henny Porten (Maid), Wilhelm Dieterle (Man), Fritz Kortner (Postman).

Henny Porten-Filmgesellschaft, Germany. 4 reels, 4521 ft.

Backstairs, one of the classical Kammerspiel dramas, is a work of the leading director of the Expressionist theatre, who gained wide recognition for his original treatment of stage space in which the central element was the steep stairs used as a device for establishing the relations between the characters. This was transferred to the cinema in Backstairs, and the title of the picture is, in the context, rather significant; the plot contains the essence of the Kammerspiel simplicity and totally dispenses with captions. A crippled and

jealous postman intercepts the letters written to a servant girl by
her absent lover.   Feeling abandoned and partly driven by pity the
girl visits the cripple in his flat.   The lover returns, struggles with
the rival who, using his last ounce of strength, kills him with an
axe.   In a state of shock, the girl throws herself down onto the
pavement.

While there is plenty of misery in Backstairs (and some understanding of it) there was not enough effort made (even on the
relative scale of this particular genre) to give the tragedy a definite
social edge, in the absence of which the picture draws close to horror melodrama.   This seems to be rather the fault of the directors
than of Carl Mayer, the distinguished scriptwriter, who had more
luck with his other filmed scripts and who himself never treated the
characters mechanically.   All the same, the picture is decidedly
more than a curiosity or a relic of its genre.   This is so because
of its classical simplicity, which in the final account always turns
out to be a permanent asset in the cinema.

1922

THE PILGRIM   Charles Chaplin

Script: Chaplin. Photography: Rollie Totheroh. Cast: Charles
Chaplin (Bogus clergyman), Edna Purviance (Girl), Kitty Bradbury
(Her mother), Mack Swain (Lay worker), Loyal Underwood (Dean),
Charles F. Riesner (Thief), Dinky Dean (Naughty boy), Sydney Chap-
lin (His father), May Wells (His mother), Henry Bergman (Sheriff
on the train), Tom Murray (Sheriff at Devil's Gulch), Monta Bell
(Policeman), Raymond Lee (Real clergyman), Florence Latimer,
Phyllis Allen and Edith Bostwick (Ladies of the parish).

Charles Chaplin for First National, U.S.A. 4 reels, 4300 ft.

The Kid was followed by two shorts, The Idle Class (1921) and Pay
Day (1922), and then by The Pilgrim, with which Chaplin concluded
his obligations to First National. A prisoner escapes from Sing-
Sing, steals the clothes of a clergyman who is enjoying a bath,
chooses at random on the map a town (called Devil's Gulch) to escape to. He is frightened by a policeman on the train, but nevertheless reaches his destination. There he is welcomed by a crowd
of parishioners awaiting their new pastor. The ex-prisoner gives
a splendid sermon, moves into the parish house and embarks upon
his pastoral duties. He would like to extricate himself from the
awkward situation, but is attracted by a beautiful girl (at whom he
makes eyes during services). Alas, another escaped convict appears
in town and the minister is soon unmasked.

   The Pilgrim does not contain even a mite of the sentimental
lyricism of The Kid. Chaplin replaced it with a satire so venomous
and a criticism so aggressive as to make the picture almost a political statement. The objects of attack are the provincial attitudes,
narrowmindedness, hypocrisy and bigotry. The use of the church in

the criticism (the film was originally to be called "The Minister")
encountered strong opposition and resulted in its being banned in
many states.   The very equation criminal = clergyman was considered objectionable, not to mention the notion that the ex-prisoner
feels so at home in the rural cosiness of neighborly visits, family
photographs and homemade cakes.   Most insufferable was the clear
implication that if it were not for the accidental encounter with a
fellow crook, Charlie would have been an exemplary minister.

The Pilgrim is one of Chaplin's funniest films although the
humor is of the satirical variety.   The best parts of it are the
famous mimed sermon on the story of David and Goliath, the splendid scene when a dreadful child is brought on a visit, whose tricks
Charlie bears until they are alone, Charlie's expert assessment (by
weight) of the content of the collection boxes and of course the final
scene in which, at the girl's request, the sheriff releases Charlie
on the Mexican border.   Bandits lie in wait on one side and the
Law on the other.   The end of the film comes as Charlie runs
astride the frontier.

DR. MABUSE, THE GAMBLER (Dr. Mabuse, der Spieler)   Fritz Lang

---

Script: Thea von Harbou, from the novel by Norbert Jacques.
Photography: Carl Hoffman.   Art Direction: Otto Hunte and Stahl-
Urach.   Cast: Rudolf Klein-Rogge (Dr. Mabuse), Aud Egede Nissen
(Cara Carozza), Gertrude Welcker (Countess Told), Alfred Abel
(Count Told), Bernhard Goetzke (von Wenk), Paul Richter (Edgar
Hull), Forster Larrinaga (Spoerri), Hans Adalbert von Schlettow
(Georg, Mabuse's chauffeur), Goerg John (Pesch), Karl Huszar
(Hawasch), Grete Berger (Fine), Fulius Falkenstein (Karsten, Wenk's
friend), Lydia Potechina (Losing lady), Julius Hermann (Schramm).

Erich Pommer, Ullstein-UCO Film, Germany.   Part I: "Der
Grosse Spieler," 6 reels, 11,470 ft.; Part II: "Inferno," 6 reels,
8399 ft.

Because of earlier commitments Lang could not undertake the direction of The Cabinet of Dr. Caligari, although it was in fact he
who suggested the vital idea of making that picture in the form of
a madman's tale.   He compensated himself for the loss of this attractive theme by making Dr. Mabuse, the Gambler, "the document
of the modern world" as he himself described the film.   Although
sensational cinema is almost as old as the movies themselves, it
was long devoid of artistic value and originality.   It is, however,
ennobled by the works of Lang.

The motif of the struggle between the Law and a criminal organization was Lang's obsession and first appeared in his The Spiders (1919). The early days of the post-war Weimar Republic provided an ideal setting for further explorations of this motif: anarchy, uncertainty, inflation, the spiritual rebellion of some and the apathy of others become a plague. Dr. Mabuse, the Gambler, a two-part thriller-melodrama adapted from a roman policier is meant to be a distorted reflection of those times, an allegory on the struggle between order and chaos.

Dr. Mabuse, a Genius of Crime, is the head of a powerful gang of killers, counterfeiters and gamblers. Using no fewer than ten different disguises Mabuse steals a secret trade contract, starts a panic on the stock exchange and makes huge sums as the result. By dint of his powers as a hypnotist he wins 150,000 marks at cards from a millionaire whom he arranges to be seduced by his accomplice. Dr. Wenk, a public prosecutor, and a certain Countess Told fight against Mabuse. Finally, surrounded by the police, Mabuse takes refuge in the workshop of his counterfeiters, goes raving mad, throws forged money in the air and ends up in an asylum.

Dr. Mabuse, the Gambler is a classic of anarchist cinema. It is not only that both the police and criminals are represented as similar competing gangs: Lang decided that chaos is the best tool for representing chaos and gave the picture a nearly absurd complexity. The impression of confusion was achieved through the colossal length of the picture, its long-winded, rambling, repetitive style, and the use of interesting symbols (circular forms represent chaos) and rather complicated visual compositions, which give the feeling of lack of direction. The impression of decadence is created by the distorted Expressionist décor of the gambling den. There are also repeated references to inflation, which at that time assumed astronomical proportions, and to the collapse of law and order. On the other hand, whatever Lang's intentions, the pace of the picture is far too slow despite rapid turns in the plot, and the editing is often inadequate and confusing. Some of this can be excused by the massive shortening process to which the film was subjected before release.

Dr. Mabuse, the Gambler is the most vertiginous flight of fancy in Lang's work. Its hero became a self-perpetuating myth and the director later had to resurrect him twice.

NOSFERATU (Nosferatu--Eine Symphonie des Grauens) Friedrich Wilhelm Murnau

---

Script: Henrik Galeen, from the novel, "Dracula," by Bram Stoker. Photography: Fritz Arno Wagner. Art Direction: Albin Grau.

Cast: Max Schreck (Graf Orlok, Nosferatu), Alexander Granach (Knock, an estate agent), Gustav von Wangenheim (Hutter, his employee), Greta Schroeder (Ellen, his wife), G. H. Schnell (Harding, shipowner), Ruth Landshoff (Annie, his wife), John Gottowt (Professor Bulwer), Gustav Botz (Professor Sievers), Max Nemetz (Captain of the "Demeter"), Wolfgang Heinz, Albert Venohr (Seamen), Guido Herzfeld (Innkeeper), Hardy von Francois (Doctor).

Prana Film Berlin GmbH, Germany. 5 reels, 6453 ft.

Friedrich Wilhelm Murnau was the inventor of horror cinema. But really, he did not invent it single-handed: Nosferatu is only the last link in the chain which led from the natural German gusto for the uncanny, evident even in fairy tales, through the atmosphere of anxiety and restlessness of post-war Germany and the fantastic but harmless tales of the Expressionists. But now this is the real thing. Murnau discovered the laws of horror cinema and made use of its principal elements--the constant feeling of anticipation and the use of details of décor as ominous symbols. Nosferatu, apart from being firmly based in German folk legends, was also inspired by the supposedly real cases of contemporary vampirism.

A solicitor's clerk is summoned to a Carpathian forest castle belonging to a Count Nosferatu. The vampire lord of the castle sleeps during the day in an earth-filled coffin and terrorizes the neighborhood at night. Later he sails down the Rhine in a rat-infested ship to a Hanseatic city where he spreads terror and disease, until he is vanquished by the powers of good, personified by the clerk's wife, Ellen. Nosferatu is taken by surprise by the light of day and dissolves into thin air.

Nosferatu is a curious sort of a psychological film: instead of studying the psychology of the characters, it manipulates that of the spectator. But the most remarkable thing about Nosferatu is not the gothic imagination of its creators, nor the acting (though Max Schreck is great), but the original and fruitful idea of shooting the film outside. The picture has none of the pseudo-theatrical sets of The Cabinet of Dr. Caligari and is all the better for it. It appears that optical realism is a much better vehicle for horror than weird designs: the vampire strolling down a sunny street is more terrifying.

The film uses many elements of uncanny poetic imagination: huge shadows on the walls, a ship gliding over phosphorescent waters, an eerie drive through the woods (which is partly shown in negative). The photography in Nosferatu is compositionally remarkable, but sometimes its technical execution does not match that of other Expressionist films.

CRAINQUEBILLE   Jacques Feyder

Script: Feyder, from the story of Anatole France. Photography:
Léonce-Henry Burel and Maurice Forster. Cast: Maurice de
Féraudy (Crainquebille), Jean Forest ("La Souris"), Félix Oudart
(Agent 64), Jeanne Cheiral (Madame Bayard), Marguerite Carre
(Madame Laure), Françoise Rosay (Customer), Marc Frederix (Her
son), Charles Mosnier (Dr. Mathieu, a witness), Numès (President
Bourriche), René Worms (Lemerle/Advocate), Roques (Agent 121).

Les Films Trarieux et Legrand, France. 5906 ft.

An excellent psychological portrayal, exceptional in the context of
contemporary cinema both from the point of view of the distribution
of dramatic accents and the choice of cinematic approach, Crainquebille was the first big, though underestimated, achievement of Feyder, the director who thereby introduced himself as a master of expressive simplicity in probing the interior of man. At a time when
cinema strove to become an art by developing original means of expression which maximally transform reality, Feyder abided by a
verbatim literary adaptation, rejected the obligatory movement, neglected the editing and took no interest in stressing the mood.

     The story of a poor vegetable seller's persecution by the law
is told realistically, with a leisurely, analytical precision. Unjustly
accused of having shouted "death to cops" at a policeman, Crainquebille is tried and because of his inarticulateness and pigheadedness
sentenced to 15 days in prison. He is ruined: customers turn away
from him, he loses the respect of neighbors and ends up as a tramp.
It is only through the friendship of a little boy that he can face life
again.

     Feyder gave the story charm and wry humor, avoiding both
pomposity and excessive realism--he added a happy ending to the
novel with that in mind. The portrayal of Les Halles, the former
Parisian early-morning vegetable market, adds a touch of personal
documentary to the picture and balances the highly subjective court
scenes. In these the feelings of the accused and his instinctive
fear of authority are conveyed by means of visual exaggeration; the
policeman, seen from below, towers over the judges and the accused who shrinks in the dock; his only defense witness is enveloped
in an unfriendly flood of light; the out-of-focus court room appears
to Crainquebille as a sea of eyeballs.

     These attempts at subjective narrative linked the picture with
the Impressionist avant-garde which then indisputably dominated the
French cinema, yet Feyder never registered his accession to any
trend. Because of this, he was, although acknowledged, never to

be popular with the public, for nobody could know that Feyder's style foreshadowed the cinema of the 50's.

L'AUBERGE ROUGE   Jean Epstein

Script: Epstein, from the tale, "Une Ténébreuse affaire," by Honoré de Balzac. Photography: Raoul Abourdier, assisted by Roger Hubert and Robert Fefebvre. Cast: Léon Mathot (Prosper Mangan), Pierre Hot (Innkeeper), Gina Manès (His daughter), David Evremond (Frederic Taillefer), Jacques Christiani (André Taillefer).

Pathé, France.   5085 ft.

During the three years that elapsed since the 25-year-old Jean Epstein first took interest in the cinema, he became acquainted with all its achievements, worked as Louis Delluc's assistant (1921), and had already in his debut (Pasteur, 1922) exhibited an impressive maturity of vision and an original, experimental use of variable camera angles. Epstein's following film, made only a few months later, caused a sensation in the world of French cinema, already agitated by the avant-garde. The young director instantly gained the reputation of an outstanding artist.

L'Auberge rouge, a highly complex sensational melodrama set in the period of the French Directoriat (1795-99), is both a recapitulation of the stylistic achievements of the silent cinema on reaching its maturity and an experiment in the use of the novel narrative method which involves complex time structure. Like the directors of the Nouvelle Vague who would forty years later spend whole weeks in film archives, Epstein gathered the fruits of his familiarity with cinema and with mathematical precision (he was, as a matter of fact, once seriously interested in mathematics) polished the form of his film.

The multitude of originally composed shots, frequent changes of narrative rhythm, slowed-down sequences, dissolves, multiple exposures, unusual camera movements--all these elements of the film director's craft were blended to form a coherent whole. The famous tracking shot around the circular table in the inn, or the very convincing attempts at subjective narrative, are Epstein's own successful contribution. The mood of L'Auberge rouge creates a very personal vision of reality and allows the spectator to look at events almost through the eyes of the protagonists.

The most interesting example of assimilating cinematic tools already developed by other directors is the culminating scene of the film, based on the precedent from Griffith's Intolerance: the preparations for an execution were edited in parallel with the desperate run of the girl carrying the proof of the convict's innocence. But in L'Auberge rouge there is no last minute rescue: help will come too late.

WARNING SHADOWS (Schatten, eine nächtliche Halluzination)   Arthur Robison

---

Script: Rudolph Schneider and Robison, after an idea by Albin Grau. Photography: Fritz Arno Wagner. Art Direction: Albin Grau. Cast: Fritz Kortner (Husband), Ruth Weyher (Wife), Gustav von Wangenheim (Lover), Alexander Granach (Showman), Fritz Rasp (Manservant), Eugen Rex, Ferdinand von Alten, Max Gülstorff (Cavaliers), Lilli Herder (Chambermaid), Karl Platen.

Pan-Film for Dafu-Film-Verleih GmbH, Berlin, Germany.   4 reels, 6568 ft.

Warning Shadows is one of the most evocative silent films and remains to this day one of the best portrayals of the imaginary in the cinema.   It is of further interest because of its ingenious story-within-a-story construction, which was here applied even better than Sjöström did in The Phantom Carriage.   Warning Shadows obeys the three classical unities: of action (the court intrigue set in the past and developing among six characters), of place (a palace), and of time (the party lasts as long as the picture).

A count becomes jealous on seeing the courtship between four cavaliers and his wife; one of them, "The Lover," nearly seduces her.   An itinerant conjurer appears at this point and, anxious to forestall the inevitable tragedy, suggests a performance of his shadow plays.   The room is converted into a theatre and the conjurer begins, with the help of cutouts, an oriental story of a cuckolded husband which (on the principle similar to the play in "Hamlet") illustrates the dilemma of the Count.   This story gives way to a hypnotic session (the picture is subtitled "a nocturnal hallucination") during which the subconscious and the inner instincts of the real-life characters are allowed to roam free.

This episode is a suggestion of a possible climax of the intrigue: the Count imagines his wife seduced by The Lover and witnesses a kiss in the mirror.   Mad with jealousy, he makes the cavaliers truss his wife with ropes and stab her with swords, and is later thrown out of the window himself.   However, the body mysteriously disappears.   We return at this point to the Oriental story which ends happily and then to the story proper which also comes to a quick conclusion: the show is over, the Count and the

wife are reconciled, The Lover leaves. Finally the conjurer rides
off.

The theme of the free play of overpowering passions is typical of the interests of the Expressionist cinema; the fact that
Robison, an American brought up in Germany, was a doctor of
medicine throws some light on the handling of this theme. (For instance, the suggestion of the split personalities of the characters is
significant.) In any case, the happy ending is certainly an unusual
touch in the Expressionist cinema which normally professed the
helplessness of man in the face of external forces.

While the Freudian overtones of Warning Shadows seem naive
today, the picture is notable because of its brilliant visual form.
The Cabinet of Dr. Caligari, the first Expressionist film, made a
great impression with its eccentric designs, but remained uninventive
from the point of view of lighting, the use of which was left for ensuing films (Vanina, e.g.) to explore. But it was Robison who for
the first time succeeded in giving light a more important role than
that of ornament. In Warning Shadows it became a genuine means of
expression and even the main source of the drama. The complex
use of shadows on diaphanous screens, reflections in mirrors, the
clever use of optical illusions (the Count sees two shadows touching
hands, yet his wife and The Lover are in fact away from each other
and only their projections overlap) give the picture a romantic air
of moody fantasy.

The variety of camera positions, the sensitive editing, the
great fluency with which the complex story is told gave Warning
Shadows the character of an assured and genuinely cinematic work
of art. The shadows in the title are the subject matter of the film,
not mere props.

THE THREE MUST-GET-THERES   Max Linder

Script: Linder. Photography: Harry Vallejo and Max Dupont.
Cast: Max Linder (Dart-in-Again), Bull Montana (Duke of Rich-
Lou), Frank Cooke (King Louis XIII), Catherine Rankin (The Queen),
Jobyna Ralston (Connie), Jack Richardson (Walrus), Charles Met-
zetti (Octopus), Clarence Werpz (Porpoise), Fred Cavens (Berna-
joux), Harry Mann (Bunkumin).

United Artists, U.S.A. 4 reels, 4900 ft.

After Seven Years' Bad Luck Max Linder made the less successful
Be My Wife (1922) and then another excellent comedy, The Three
Must-Get-Theres. The title is, of course, a verbal pun on "The

Three Musketeers," the classical cloak-and-dagger novel by Alexandre Dumas. Linder did not miss the chance of making a double parody--of the novel and of the film just made of it by Fred Niblo, starring Douglas Fairbanks.

The picture is a costume comedy and the familiar well-groomed personality of Linder is for once missing. Max appears in d'Artagnan's role as Dart-in-Again. On his way to Paris Max challenges each of the three "must-get-theres" and then joins them in fighting against the Duke of Rich-Lou's soldiers. The Queen's chambermaid, Connie, asks him to regain, before the King finds out, a brooch, a present from the King, which the Queen inadvertently gave to her lover. Max succeeds and as a reward is given permission to marry Connie and is made the fourth "must-get-there." The vehicles for humor are in this film anachronisms--fully intended and applied with intelligence and taste. The hero dons a Louis XIII costume and a straw hat with it, the "must-get-theres" use motorcycles, typewriters and telephones with complete imperturbability, one can spot Napoleon's bust on the Duke's desk. Yet the whole is never forced, but always subtle and hilariously funny. No wonder the film was again considered imported from Europe.

The Three Must-Get-Theres was the last outstanding Linder comedy, although he made two more, one in France and one in Austria. The private life of the great screen joker was very different from the carefree mood of his films: Linder died young, suicidally, in 1925.

VANINA (Vanina oder die Galgenhochzeit) Arthur von Gerlach

Script: Carl Mayer, from the short story, "Vanina Vanini," by Stendhal. Photography: Frederik Fuglsang. Art Direction: Walter Reimann. Cast: Asta Nielsen (Vanina), Paul Wegener (Octavio), Paul Hartmann (Governor), Bernhard Goetzke, Raoul Lange.

Projektions-AG "Union," Berlin, Germany. 5 reels, 5085 ft.

The tyrant character was an essential element of the German Expressionist films. A product of the national obsessions and idiosyncrasies, it had in a way already materialized as the director of a mental asylum who murderously manipulated the somnambulic Cesare in The Cabinet of Dr. Caligari. Vanina, which is based on a ballad by a French writer (and very faithful to its spirit), is a very typical Expressionist study of tyranny and oppression.

The story is set in a fictitious state ruled by a cruel crippled Governor who ruthlessly opposes any manifestations of popular

discontent. His daughter Vanina loves the leader of the rebels,
Octavio. The Governor throws Octavio into prison, then after the
entreaties of his daughter releases him and apparently agrees to
their marriage. However, during the wedding Octavio is again imprisoned and sentenced to death. Vanina challenges her father,
frees Octavio from his cell and attempts to escape with him from
the palace. In vain: when only one door separates them from freedom they are caught and the Governor (to fulfill the gruesome promise of the film's subsidiary title, "Wedding Under the Gallows")
reads out, in laughter, the death sentence. Vanina, unable to survive her lover, drops down dead.

Vanina has a very powerful visual style, based in great part
on the contrast between the rapid movement of the scenes of the
rebellion with the slow scenes in the palace. The acting, which
stresses the essential mood of despair and lack of hope, is convincing and astonishingly modern. The great Danish actress, Asta
Nielsen, gives a good performance in the title role and is fittingly
accompanied by Paul Wegener, known already from The Student of
Prague and The Golem.

The sequence of the lovers' escape is based on an original
concept, which runs counter to the ideas of Griffith and later to the
Soviet directors, that advocates the building of dramatic tension
through the increased rhythm of editing. In Vanina the slowed down
pace of the flight through the unending labyrinthine corridors achieves
the impression of overwhelming terror.

1923

COEUR FIDÈLE   Jean Epstein

Script: Epstein.   Photography: Paul Guichard, assisted by Stuckert
and Léon Donnot.   Cast: Léon Mathot (Jean), Gina Manès (Marie),
Edmond van Daele (Little Paul), Benedict (Father Hochon), Mme.
Maufroy (Mother Hochon), Melle Marice (Invalid), Madeline Erickson (Woman of the port).

Pathé, France.   5512 ft.

The dominant mood of the French Impressionist avant-garde of the
early 20's was that of escape from reality into the world of dreams.
This mood was coupled with an awareness of the futility of such a
solution.   The creative interests of the film-makers of the trend
(Marcel L'Herbier, Jean Epstein and Louis Delluc) were naturally
attracted by the people living on the social margin, by the world of
waterfront cafés, provincial fairgrounds and the themes of faraway
journeys, nostalgia and hopeless love.

These sentiments first appeared fully in Delluc's short Fièvre
(1921), the ephemeral drama of frustration and passion set entirely
in a Marseilles waterfront bar, but in Coeur fidèle become part of
the first true and poetic vision of the great port.   Epstein, the best
of the Impressionist directors, was able satisfactorily to combine the
story content of his films with formal experiments and at the same
time to evade the traps of excessive formalism which others found
too treacherous.   He knew how to make use of the achievements of
others: L'Herbier's subjective narrative, returns to the past, soft-
focus shots and superimpositions; the advanced editing of Griffith
and Gance; the poetic touch of Delluc.

Coeur fidèle, made from a script written in one night, tells

a story of the rivalry of two men, an honest worker and a petty
villain, for a waitress in a Marseilles waterfront café. After much
hesitation the girl chooses the villain; the worker wounds his rival
and is thrown into jail. After release he struggles with him again
and is about to lose when the crook is killed in the last moment by
a crippled girl. One is tempted to say that even the film's title is
naive, but its formal aspect more than makes up for it, transform-
ing what could easily be trivial into subtle and profound drama.

Impressionism, by its definition, gave priority to the study
of movement over immobility and saw reality as a sequence of brief
spells of motion, aiming to recreate on the screen the ever-fluid
world of the painting of Renoir, Cézanne and Monet. Epstein was
fascinated by movement; in the key scene of the film which is set
in an amusement park, each frame was used to create the sensation
of frantic whirling. Epstein placed the camera for a moment inside
the revolving merry-go-round, thereby making the spectator not
merely an observer but a participant in the screen events.

Although Coeur fidèle was shot on location and its photography is clinically precise, the overall impression of the film is
dreamlike. It was not the external realism of the décor which mat-
tered for the director--who achieves here a rare psychological precision, using each frame of the film as a key to a state of mind;
from his moody drama of overcast skies and pools glistening in the
light of dawn a fatalism emanated which in the next decade was to
impress deep marks upon the French cinema.

OUR HOSPITALITY   Buster Keaton and Jack G. Blystone

Script: Clyde Bruckman, Jean Havez and Joseph Mitchell. Photography: Elgin Lessley and Gordon Jennings. Cast: Buster Keaton (Willie McKay), Joe Roberts (Joseph Canfield), Natalie Talmadge
(His daughter), Leonard Chapman (James Canfield), Craig Ward
(Lee Canfield), Ralph Bushman (Clayton Canfield), Joe Keaton (Engineer), Edward Coxon (John McKay), Jean Dumas (Mrs. McKay),
Kitty Bradbury (Aunt Mary), Monty Collins (The Rev. Benjamin Dor-
sey), James Duffy (Train Guard), Joseph Keaton Talmadge (Willie
as a baby).

Buster Keaton/Joseph M. Schenck Productions, U.S.A.   7 reels,
6220 ft.

The beginnings of Buster Keaton's career were similar to those of
Chaplin: born in 1885, he performed from early childhood in a
family comedy act called "The Three Keatons," but it was not until
1917 (when Chaplin was at the height of popularity) that the comedian

Roscoe (Fatty) Arbuckle brought Keaton into films. Our Hospitality
is Keaton's first real feature; the film he made earlier the same
year, The Three Ages (1923), a parody of Intolerance, was in fact
still only a compilation of three one-reelers.

        1831: Willie McKay, a New York dandy, is summoned to
take possession of the family inheritance in the South.   During the
train journey he meets a girl who turns out to be his neighbor.
She invites Willie to join her, her father and brothers for dinner.
When the hero arrives at the house, he discovers with horror the
existence of a long-outstanding feud between the respective families.
One cannot assault a guest under one's own roof--and outside the
door Willie loses immunity--so at first he tries to extend his visit
using hilarious schemes and then tries to leave the house unnoticed.
A series of breakneck chases follow, the last of which, the most ingeniously staged, hovers on the brink of a waterfall. Willie mi-
raculously survives all and hurriedly marries the girl, just in time
to forestall a new assault. Now he is safe for good.

        In this picture Keaton provided a consistent dramatic line,
vastly superior to similar efforts by other comedians, including
Chaplin. Our Hospitality is a self-contained, tightly constructed
and impeccably logical drama, each episode of which serves as a
natural source of unexpected comical situations. Keaton's hero is
clumsy and always taken by surprise but never gives up and always
remains unperturbed--and always wins.

        Some of the gags (though not as many as in later films) re-
sult from the hero's encounters with inanimate objects, particularly
with technical inventions. "Onward sped the iron monster": the
side-splitting beginning shows Willie's journey by an archaic train
(the action of the film takes place a few years after steam engines
were first imported from England). Keaton had just discovered the
possibilities of the railway as a vehicle for humor; later he would
exploit them to the hilt in The General. Much humor is also derived from jocular references to the period and reconstructions of
detail.

        The prologue of Our Hospitality (which explains the reasons
for the family feud) contains an embryo of the future deep-focus
technique that allows several simultaneous actions to be conducted
within the same frame, but at different distances from the camera.
Our Hospitality marked the creative maturity of Keaton: not the
least of his skills was expert editing, clearly influenced by Griffith.

THE COVERED WAGON   James Cruze

Script: Jack Cunningham, from the novel by Emerson Hough. Pho-

tography: Karl Brown. Cast: Lois Wilson (Molly Wingate), J.
Warren Kerrigan (Will Banion), Ernest Torrence (Jackson), Charles
Ogle (Jesse Wingate), Ether Wales (Mrs. Wingate), Alan Hale (Sam
Woodhull), Tully Marshal (Bridger), Guy Olive (Joe Dunstan), John
Fox (Jed Wingate).

Famous Players-Lasky, U.S.A. 10 reels, 9407 ft.

In 1848 a wagon train leaves Kansas City for the 2000 miles trek to
Oregon. On the background of these pioneers' struggle with hunger,
the severity of elements, and the treachery of the Indians, Cruze
projected the struggle of two men for the favors of the fair Molly
Wingate. Will Banion, whom Molly loves, finally vanquishes the
villainous Sam Woodhull. When the news arrives of the discovery
of gold in California, the pioneers divide: some continue to Oregon,
others, including Will Banion go to seek their fortunes in the dig-
gings. Banion does find gold and joins Molly who is waiting for
him in Oregon.

The Covered Wagon is a celebrated epic of pioneering America, made in natural scenery with simplicity and admirable touches
of authenticity. It has warmth and wit without patriotic declarations
and flag-waving, excellent sequences of a river crossing, a buffalo
hunt and even a night sequence, something really remarkable in
1923 when no panchromatic stock was yet being used. The picture
excellently employed the achievements in film technique brought about
by D. W. Griffith: the shots are well photographed, well timed and
imaginatively edited.

The weakness of the film is the feeble and inconsistent story
and the conventional treatment of characters and their motives (thus
the Indians are wicked but the Whites, with rare exceptions, noble).
All this is not too serious a shortcoming if one considers the picture as an adventure story, an enthusiastic chronicle of conquest
which does not attempt any critical portrayal or social analysis of
those times.

The Covered Wagon, one of the most financially successful
films ever and one of the classic Westerns, was later mercilessly
copied.

A WOMAN OF PARIS Charles Chaplin

Script: Chaplin. Photography: Rollie Totheroh and Jack Wilson.
Cast: Edna Purviance (Marie St. Clair), Adolphe Menjou (Pierre
Revel), Carl Miller (Jean Millet, Marie's fiancé), Lydia Knott (His
mother), Charles French (His father), Clarence Geldert (Marie's

father), Betty Morissey (Fifi), Malvine Polo (Paulette), Henry Bergman (Maître d'hotel), Harry Northrup (Valet), Nelly Bly Baker
(Masseuse), Charles Chaplin (Station porter).

United Artists, U.S.A.   8 reels, 8395 ft.

The pictures of the great comic are so completely dominated by the
character of the Tramp that the spectator tends to forget that Chaplin also directed them all.   This situation is for once reversed in
the film in which Chaplin appears only in a tiny episode as a railway porter.   His first contribution to the United Artists (which he
co-founded) was intended to promote Edna Purviance, Chaplin's
partner in many films, as a dramatic actress in her own right.
Simultaneously, Chaplin wanted to fulfill his long-standing ambition
of making a "serious" drama which would prove to the world (and
to himself) that he is more than just a performer.

The intrigue of A Woman of Paris is shamelessly melodramatic and refers to the traditions of French sentimental literature.
A provincial girl is forced to part with her beloved, a painter, and
becomes the mistress of a Parisian man-about-town.   The painter
comes to Paris, discovers what has happened, but offers to take her
back all the same.   Marie rejects the offer of happiness thus driving
him to suicide.

Not only the theme of the film, but also the style of film-
making is untypical of Chaplin who proved himself to be a director
with sensitivity, imagination and technical skill.   The camera was
no longer static but often used close-ups and significant details; the
editing was vigorous; the use of dissolves improved the narrative
pace, although it seems to harm its fluency.   Wishing to make a
true and simple film, Chaplin tried to avoid excessive emotional
accents and chose a toned-down, precise psychological analysis of
the characters.   Only the naively optimistic ending (Marie joins her
dead lover's mother in work at a country orphanage) is a discordant
note.

Still, in those early days the relative immaturity of cinematic
art usually showed up more readily in conjunction with serious
themes than with comedies, and the picture is really more notable
because of its numerous good directorial effects rather than as a
whole.   Instead of a passing train we are shown the reflection of its
lights; the intimate relationship between the heroine and her rich
protector is instantly revealed by the shot of a man's collar falling
out of a drawer in her flat.   Some pictorial effects are substitutes
for the actual sound: thus the people in a restaurant turn their
heads because they heard the suicidal shot.

Chaplin displayed an obsessive, almost Stroheimian care
for the verity of every detail and shot restaurant scenes in real
restaurants with real waiters serving real champagne; the sets
all had four walls and the cameraman was working through a

hole in one of them! Among several good acting performances
the most interesting today is the one of Adolphe Menjou who would
soon become identified with the character of a suave and cynical
dandy. A Woman of Paris was not a commercial success and remains an isolated experiment in the career of Chaplin, who in his
following The Gold Rush returned to the ever-popular Tramp.

LA BELLE NIVERNAISE   Jean Epstein

Script: Epstein, from a story by Alphonse Daudet. Photography:
Paul Guichard, assisted by Léon Donnot. Cast: Blanche Montel
(Clara), Maurice Touzé (Victor), David Evremont (Maugendre), Max
Bonnet (Page), Pierre Hot (Father Louveau), Mme. Lacroix (Mother
Louveau).

Pathé, France.   5900 ft.

In comparison with Coeur fidèle, animated and pulsating with movement, La Belle Nivernaise embodies Epstein's relative change of
tone. The rapidly edited high drama had now given way to a quiet
and nostalgic reflection. La Belle Nivernaise is a story of paradise
lost and regained. The heroine is a girl adopted by a family of
bargees and living with them on a boat, "The Beauty of Nevers,"
floating endlessly across the inland waterways of France. Found and
taken away by her rich relatives, Clara is unhappy with town life
and finally decides to return to the barge.

As fine as it is simple, La Belle Nivernaise is one of the
best achievements of the Impressionist school and a classic of poetic cinema. The leading pictorial motif and the emotional key to
the work is water. The laziness of rivers and canals generates a
romantic mood and unhasty rhythm; the misty vistas of bridges and
slowly passing river banks have been compared to the paintings of
Corot and Renoir. In many ways, including of course the theme of
escape and return to a barge, the film foreshadowed Jean Vigo's
famous L'Atalante.

LA ROUE   Abel Gance

Script: Gance, with the collaboration of Blaise Cendrars. Photography: Léonce-Henry Burel and Bujard. Cast: Ivy Close (Norma), Séverin Mars (Sisif, the steam-engine driver), Gabriel de Gra-

vone (Elie, his son), Pierre Magnier (Engineer Hersain), Gil Clary,
Terof, Maxudian.

Abel Gance/Pathé, France.   34,450 ft., later cut to 13,780 ft.
Released in 1924.

A gigantic screen drama, La Roue remains in a way a balance sheet
of the first example the artistically ambitious feature film set for
itself to follow--the formula of the 19th-century novel.   Perhaps
even not only the novel, but that narrative arts in general; it is not
difficult to find in La Roue an intentional combination of elements
from all provinces of art: a romantic tragedy and a musical symphony with a grandiose finale.   Lack of moderation however is always treacherous and in this case amounts to a particularly serious
fault: it seems impossible to find another famous film which would
need trimming as badly as this one.   This applies to the already
shortened version, containing a mere 40 per cent of the original
footage.

        Such cinematic monuments were indeed a speciality of Abel
Gance, the man who deserves to be called the Victor Hugo of the
French cinema.   A former actor and playwright and later one of
the leaders of the Impressionist avant-garde, Gance began his best
creative period with the anti-war superproduction J'accuse (1919)
and ended it with the massive Napoléon (1927), which is shown on
three screens simultaneously.   La Roue, a film which took three
years to make and was almost entirely shot on location in the French
Alps and the railway station in Nice, is probably his most colossal
undertaking, not only in terms of length, but also in emotional intensity.   Gance unfolded here the drama of a steam-engine driver
(Sisif) and his son (Elie), both engrossed in hopeless love for an
adopted girl who is to them respectively daughter and sister.

        Norma, who had been orphaned in a disaster, was accepted
as a member of the family in early childhood and brought up together with Elie, both of them unaware of her past.   When she
grows up, Sisif comes to realize his true feelings for her, but after
an inner struggle agrees to Norma's planned marriage and her departure to the big city.   Elie also bids Norma goodbye with a heavy
heart: he does not know that she is not his real sister.   When
some time later he discovers the truth, his peace is lost forever.

        In a little railway station in the Alps where the father, his
sight failing after an accident at work, works a funicular, the son
can think only about his love.   The tragedy is fulfilled when after a
chance meeting between Norma and Elie the girl's jealous and mis-
informed husband tries to take revenge on the boy: the two fall into
a precipice clasped in a deadly embrace.   From now on Sisif and
Norma will be together again: the adopted daughter returns to her
now blind father to look after him for the rest of his days.

        La Roue did not succeed, both from the point of view of the

content and of the coherence of the work, which in Gance's intention
was to be a synthesis of motifs from Greek tragedy--those of Antigone, Sisyphus and Oedipus (note the blindness)--and romantic no-
tions of 19th-century French literature, as well as references to
contemporary art, particularly the work of Fernand Léger, a painter
who praised the beauty of modern technology. Not only did Gance
display a lack of a sense of aesthetic harmony and a really exceptional talent for dragging out the narrative, but to boot lowered the
value of the film by the naiveté of certain situations, infantile symbolism, and a multitude of pretentious literary allusions ranging
from Aeschylus to D'Annunzio.

And yet this melodramatic epic has found a place in cinema
history: its formal aspect, which contains almost all the syntactic
components of the language of film, is a splendid display of the possibilities of the new art. This applies especially to the editing, in
the development of which as a means of expression La Roue was one
of the turning points. It was Gance who first transplanted the experiments of Griffith onto European soil, who developed the use of
accelerating rhythm to increase the emotional temperature on the
screen (a device which would be brought to full mastery of Eisenstein), who convincingly rendered the complex emotional states of
his heroes by means of editing. Burel's photography in La Roue is
beautiful and precise, but also excessively self-conscious. All the
same, the editing accords it a truly great force of impact.

Particular fame for the film was won by the sequences of
the run of the steam engine: terse, genuinely interesting and at
that time most impressive studies of a world of rails, semaphors
and masses of steel carried into the distance. Individual shots here
follow each other so quickly as to create a simultaneous pictorial
consonance, something equivalent to the sounds of a multitude of instruments in an orchestra; thus they have created a cinematic symphony. In these parts of the film the director's intention to give a
powerful vision of the world of modern technology met with complete
success. Even though Gance exaggerated his portrayal of an almost
human emotional link between the man and the steam engine (which
is in fact one of the heroes of the film), still, this all-embracing,
pantheistic treatment of the world of great passions and enormous
mechanisms is something that modernist art could only envy the
maker of La Roue.

It is unfortunate that too many chords in this cinematic symphony sound false; ruthless time assaults even that which does remain noble: the editing, the convincingly real microcosm of a railway station, snowy Alpine landscapes, the occasional lyricism and
the poetry. If La Roue must still be called a masterpiece, it is
only the greatest of the failed masterpieces.

NEW YEAR'S EVE (Sylvester--Tragödie einer Nacht)   Lupu Pick

Script: Carl Mayer, from the outline by Klaus Richter.   Photography: Karl Hasselmann (Interiors) and Guido Seeber (Street scenes).   Cast: Eugen Klöpfer (Café owner), Edith Posca (His wife), Frieda Richard (His mother), Karl Harbacher, Julius E. Herrmann, Rudolf Blümner.

Rex-Film AG, Germany.   4 reels, 5016 ft.

For the scriptwriter Carl Mayer, New Year's Eve was the middle part of the trilogy of Kammerspiel dramas of which the first part was Shattered, and the third and greatest was to be The Last Laugh; for Lupu Pick it was his second important film.   New Year's Eve is in fact similar to Shattered in more ways than one: again, members of a petty bourgeois family are entangled in passions stronger than themselves; once more the director preserves the unity of place (limited to a small café and the adjoining streets), of time (the drama lasts exactly as long as the film itself), and of action.   The action is simple: a café owner cannot stand the hostility between his mother and his wife and kills himself on the stroke of midnight on New Year's Eve.

This piercing chamber drama, one of the so-called "instinct films," is built on the principle of contrast between the immobility and despair of the three people in the stifling enclosure, and the animation and all round rejoicing of the multitude celebrating the coming of the New Year--a contrast between darkness and glittering lights.   The intercut images of passers-by and beggars and the symbolic shots of the moon over the sea create a sort of visual allegory of the fate of the protagonists, giving the picture a steadily mounting dramatic rhythm which reaches a climax in the final scene.

New Year's Eve carries perhaps the heaviest stigma of finality and determinism of all the Kammerspiel dramas.   When the burden of suffering becomes too heavy to bear, one can either destroy the apparent source of it or commit suicide--such is the philosophy they profess.   The indifference of the world to the affairs of an individual can only be resolved in death.   So, while New Year's Eve is actually one of the best pictures of the trend and must be considered a fine psychological study, it cannot really count as a social document; in fact spiritually it belongs to the romantic cinema.   The Kammerspiel used objects as metaphors and symbols (for instance broken glass represents the fragility of human life) and their aura of authenticity was derived from the realism of locality and characters rather than from objective observations of the condition of man.   Everything is in New Year's Eve a stylized subjective vision rather than a description of life.

The proper and final conclusion of the social scene in the 20's was thus not to be drawn by the Kammerspiel directors but by Erich von Stroheim in Greed--uncompromising, corrosive and powerful.

1924

GREED   Erich von Stroheim

Script: Stroheim, based on the novel, "McTeague," by Frank Norris. Photography: Ben Reynolds and William Daniels. Art Direction: Richard Day and Stroheim. Editing: Stroheim and Rex Ingram. Cast: Gibson Gowland (McTeague), Zasu Pitts (Trina Sieppe), Jean Hersholt (Marcus Schouler, her cousin), Tempe Piggott (McTeague's mother), Erich von Ritzau (Traveling dentist), Sylvia Ashton ("Mommer" Sieppe), Chester Conklin ("Popper" Sieppe), Austin Jewell (August Sieppe), Joan Standing (Selina), Dale Fuller (Maria Macapa, a charwoman).

Goldwyn Co./MGM, U.S.A. Originally 42 reels, approx. 30,000 ft., reduced to 10 reels, approx. 7900 ft. in released version.

A brilliant study of the degeneration of man through poverty and unfulfilled aspirations, Greed is set amid German immigrants being assimilated into American society. A former miner and self-taught dentist marries a girl who wins $5000 in a lottery on their engagement day. The windfall becomes a disaster; Mac's lack of official qualifications as a dentist is denounced by Trina's former suitor, Marcus, and he has to stop his practice; the financial trouble grows more and more acute; fear of spending builds an insurmountable barrier of hatred between the sexually mismatched husband and wife. The result is murder: humanity slain by gold. Mac takes Trina's money and flees from town and Marcus joins the posse hoping for a reward for apprehending Mac. The two rivals finally fight a mortal struggle in Death Valley, where they perish from thirst and exhaustion.

    Stroheim contained in this work incomparably more than an illustration of the basic psychological truth that money does not

-97-

bring happiness. The theme of the frustrations of an ordinary man
was particularly close to Stroheim and probably reflected his long
experience as a Hollywood dogsbody. The adaptation of one of the
most important novels of American naturalist literature was meant
to be a mirror of life, a précis of knowledge about human nature.
The filming was done in 1923 in the natural scenery of San Francisco and Death Valley with a maniacal meticulousness for the realism of every detail.

Alas, the uncompromising Stroheim's inability to limit himself resulted in one of the greatest artistic tragedies in cinema history: the nine-hour running time of the film was not acceptable to
the producer. After three reductions in footage, of which Stroheim
conducted and sanctioned only the first, the multi-layered tale of the
land of the dollar populated by people overcome by an obsession for
social advancement was deprived of most of its background and reduced to one theme--that of the main characters. But even this
plot was not left in its entirety. Most of the courtship of Mac and
Trina is omitted as well as their first quarrel. Other abandoned
subplots are those of Mac's father, and of the mentally ill Maria
Macapa and Zerkow, the junkman.

Greed is great even in its abbreviated form. Its predatory
passion for truth, its dramatic temperature and tremendous power
of imagery are striking. The latter is specially in evidence in the
scenes of the wedding, the murder and the final mortal struggle in
the desert. Original metaphors were carefully chosen, so that the
objects which acquire a symbolic meaning can really exist in the
circumstances presented in the film: a bird--the symbol of life; an
aggressive cat--an omen of threat; the yellow tinting of certain details of the original print, a symbol of obsession with gold; the
funeral cortège seen through the window during the wedding reception.

Only two American films can match this apogee of Stroheim's art: Chaplin's The Gold Rush, which was made a year later,
and the giant work of the cinema of the 40's, Citizen Kane.

THE LAST LAUGH (Der letzte Mann) Friedrich Wilhelm Murnau

Script: Carl Mayer. Photography: Karl Freund, assisted by
Robert Baberske. Art Direction: Robert Herlth and Walter Röhrig.
Cast: Emil Jannings (Porter), Mady Delschaft (His daughter), Max
Hiller (Her fiancé), Emilie Kurz (His aunt), Hans Unterkirchen
(Hotel manager), Olaf Storm (Young guest), Hermann Valentin (Rich
client), Emma Wyda (Thin neighbor), Georg John (Night watchman).

Erich Pommer, UFA, Germany. 6 reels, 7595 ft., later reduced to 6680 ft.

The Last Laugh, one of the greatest and most influential of silent
films, was scripted by Carl Mayer, who had been responsible for
all the best Kammerspiel pictures.   The petty bourgeois story and
the way in which it is told recalls those chamber dramas but the
picture itself breaks free from any trends and movements in the
cinema.   The theme appears to have been suggested by Gogol's
novel, The Cloak, but comes also quite naturally in the context of
the traditional German obsession with the uniform as a symbol of
power and importance.

The hero of The Last Laugh is a porter in a Berlin hotel.
The splendid uniform makes him an object of admiration and respect
for the whole neighborhood.   Alas, because of his age he loses his
position and is demoted to lavatory attendant.   He tries to hide his
defeat and wears the old uniform when going home, but the truth is
revealed on the day of his daughter's wedding.   Now the neighbors
treat the old man with derision and contempt.   Broken, he with-
draws to the lavatory, where he will probably die....   But the
makers of the film, ostensibly in an impulse of pity (but really to
make the human tragedy more penetrating), added a tacked-on satirical ending whereby a millionaire dies in the arms of the hero,
leaving to him a fortune.   The old man turns now into a discerning
guest of the hotel which once saw his humiliation.

Perfection manifests itself in The Last Laugh as the organic
blending of all cinematic elements.   Mayer's script was faultlessly
translated into visual terms by Murnau, the erstwhile maker of
Nosferatu, and by Karl Freund at the camera; the great performance
of Emil Jannings gives a general human meaning to this story of an
insignificant man.   Above all The Last Laugh is a remarkable
achievement of film technique thanks to which it acquired a fullness
of expression that epitomizes the maturity and narrative fluency
characteristic of the highly developed silent cinema at the threshold
of sound.

The mobile camera hovers around the hero, precedes him
when he majestically descends the stairs in his glory, follows him
from above after his demise, and stops fascinated by the recurrent,
glittering, hypnotic, sparkling, symbolic revolving doors of the Atlantic Hotel.   The camera almost becomes the main actor in the
film and, by its very ubiquity, makes the captions superfluous (apart
from one explaining the reasons for the happy end).

Together with Dupont's Vaudeville, The Last Laugh is the
most mature offspring of Expressionism.   Visually it is a continuation of the best traditions of the graphic design of Grosz and Kokoschka, and gently evokes, especially in the dream sequence, the
dormant memories of The Cabinet of Dr. Caligari.

STRIKE (Stachka) Sergei Eisenstein

Script: The Proletkult Collective (Eisenstein, Grigori Alexandrov, Valeri Pletnyov and I. Kravtchunovsky). Photography: Eduard Tissé. Cast: Maxim Straukh (The Spy), Grigori Alexandrov (Fireman), Mikhail Gomorov (Workman), I. Ivanov (Chief of Security Police), I. Klyukvin (Militant worker), Alexandr Antonov (Organizer), Boris Yurtsev ("King" of the thieves).

Goskino and Proletkult, U.S.S.R. 6460 ft.

The 26-year-old Sergei Eisenstein, a director at the Proletkult theatre in Moscow, found it impossible to constrain his visual imagination within the limits of the theatrical spectacle. Then he discovered in cinema the powerful and versatile means of expression he had sought. Armed with solid stage experience and the teaching of Vsevolod Meyerhold, an immensely influential theatre director and creator of a theory of acting called "biomechanics," Eisenstein made Strike.

New developments in art always destroy old structures, but re-use the building materials. Eisenstein, a fanatical follower of the doctrine of revolutionizing existing forms of artistic expression, built completely novel achievements on the ruins of the arch-theatrical 16th-century Italian "commedia dell'arte," which used only seven archetypal characters and a set number of dramatic situations.

Strike is thus divided into six "acts" of similar length; the characters are purposely sketchy and instantly recognizable as types (Informer, Worker, Mother, Capitalist, etc.)--but they provide only a background. This is all that Eisenstein owed to the theatre: the rest was his own contribution. It is interesting that he used commedia dell'arte as a starting point in a film which in fact does not deal with individual characters. For years to come Eisenstein would make films whose heroes were human masses. One has to admit that such an interpretation of cinema agrees with the spirit of the Communist revolution. Eisenstein is thus rightly considered a leading revolutionary film director and his position in Soviet art corresponds to that of Meyerhold in the theatre and Vladimir Mayakovsky in the field of poetry.

The theme of Strike is the conflict between capital and labor. The film relates events in a Tsarist factory. A worker is falsely accused of stealing a micrometer and commits suicide in despair. His fellow workers, long discontented, come out on strike. Sporadic skirmishes with the police culminate in open confrontation and a terrible slaughter.

Eisenstein's film cuts across two trends in Soviet cinema: the newsreel-style "Kino Pravda" of Dziga Vertov and Kuleshov's story film. The principal artistic tool of the director is editing: for Eisenstein it constituted the essence of the cinema and he proved his theoretical concepts in practice. Strike is a classical example of the "montage of attractions" whereby every shot involves a visually suggestive or "attractive" object which helps to arrest the spectators' attention. Thus the conspirators meet in unusual places: under the factory roof, in an empty pool. Other stylistic devices include the purposeful use of repetitions which form a sort of recurring refrain. It seems that Eisenstein, eager to achieve maximum emotional impact and the most dynamism from a rather flimsy plot, overdid this means of expression.

Still another cinematic device is the "intellectual montage," based on the principle of justaposition of shots designed to generate, by their sheer additive effect, abstract ideas in the mind of the spectator (a massacre scene intercut with a shot of a bull being slaughtered should bring to mind the concept of Injustice). Mass scenes are intercut with others almost intimate in character, poverty is opposed to affluence, the hunger of the workers is set against the lavish dinners of the shareholders. (Perhaps intentionally, Eisenstein did not completely merge the scenes. He would always be a master of brilliant episodes rather than coherent films; this became increasingly evident in his later works.) Among the most memorable scenes are the workers' meeting at the factory with the camera performing a series of overhead pans above the participants, and that apocalyptic, almost Surrealist episode, worthy of Goya, when the mounted police pursue the strikers on the many floors of a tenement.

The style of Strike, reflecting as it does the complex origin of Eisenstein's aesthetic beliefs, is far from uniform: the director continuously employed the principle of contrast and served the spectator with rapid transitions of style, mood and idiom. As a whole, with the tragic finale, the film has the strong flavor of satirical political cartoon and while showing the work of spies and informers amounts to a real anthology of police methods.

Although Eisenstein disowned Strike, describing it as a case of "the infantile malady of leftism," the film is far more than a piece of history. It has a strange modern fascination. Formerly considered only the director's training etude, it now appears better and better in the eyes of the spectators. Strike is without a doubt one of the greatest directorial debuts in the cinema.

SHERLOCK JUNIOR   Buster Keaton

Script: Clyde Bruckman, Jean Havez and Joseph Mitchell. Photography: Elgin Lessley and Byron Houck. Cast: Buster Keaton (Sherlock Junior), Kathryn McGuire (Girl), Joe Keaton (Her father), Ward Crane (Rival), Jane Connelly, Erwin Connelly, Ford West, George Davis, Horace Morgan, John Patrick, Ruth Holley.

Buster Keaton/Joseph M. Schenck Productions, U.S.A.   5 reels, 4065 ft.

It is not often that film-makers give evidence of an awareness of one aspect of the basic nature of their medium: the amazing ability of the cinema to defy time.   Chaplin did not realize this; his camera just looks at the events but never appears to intervene in them. Likewise, there is no reference in Chaplin's work to the actual making of films. Keaton was different: in Sherlock Junior he used a pretext to make the screen action the hero's dream and took off for a flight of fantasy.   The hero is a cinema projectionist cum amateur detective. He courts a girl but his rival spitefully plants the girl's father's watch in his pocket, causing an accusation of theft and then disgrace.

Returning to his projection room work, Sherlock Junior falls asleep and imagines himself joining the action of the film he is showing: he wins the girl back by dint of his detective skills.   The idea of a real person entering the life of screen characters is fruit-ful as a comic vehicle: as the films are edited, the situations on the screen change faster than the hero's efforts to intervene. Kea-ton thus shows that he realized (Chaplin did not) what film editing is all about. René Clair's perceptive comment on this was that Sherlock Junior is the cinematic equivalent of Pirandello's famous stage play, Six Characters in Search of an Author, in which the theatre examines its sources. Keaton's experiment is unusual, in-telligent and with comic potential.

Because of its highly complex, nested action, Sherlock Junior is perhaps not the most successful Keaton picture, but certainly the one made with the most technical bravura (how on earth was it all done?) and ingenuity. One need say no more than mention the final fabulous, hair-raising motorcycle chase.

THE NAVIGATOR   Buster Keaton and Donald Crisp

Script: Clyde Bruckman, Jean Havez and Joseph Mitchell. Photog-raphy: Elgin Lessley and Byron Houck. Cast: Buster Keaton (Rollo Treadway), Kathryn McGuire (Girl), Frederick Vroom (Her father, owner of "The Navigator"), Noble Johnson (Cannibal chief), Clarence Burton, H. M. Clugston.

Buster Keaton Productions Inc., U.S.A.   6 reels, 5702 ft.

Rollo Treadway is an idle young millionaire. His marriage proposals are spurned by a girl whose father owns a ship, "The Navigator." By sheer coincidence (and quite independently) both Rollo
and the girl are aboard just as the ship is set adrift by a gang of
conspirators. The trouble is that there is not another living soul
with them.... Struggles with enormous and complicated machinery
is Buster Keaton's most recurrent theme, and it was never exploited better and with more ingenuity and consequence than in The
Navigator. Rollo of course can not only handle the ship's outsize
equipment (although his first attempts are rather clumsy), but also
conquer the girl's heart, avoid the cannibals through the rather eccentric use of a submarine, and reach the happy end.

The Navigator can be divided into a series of 12 distinct (but
smoothly and naturally joined) basic comic situations. The central
idea is that of the individual grappling with equipment designed for
a multitude; everything on "The Navigator" is too big, the hero has
to cook breakfast in a ship's galley equipped to feed five hundred.
This problem may be one of the reasons for the modern revival of
Keaton's popularity; in our times of loss of identity and concern with
the environment, Rollo's adventures easily find sympathy with the
audience.

Among other famous gags one can mention the inexplicably
swinging doors or the ominous face of the captain in the porthole
which turns out to be no more than a photograph thrown overboard.
When it comes to staging, Keaton's is inventive and extravagant.
In one scene the hero (immediately recognizable even in a diver's
suit) repairs the propeller on the sea bottom. In a stroke of Surrealist inspiration Keaton comes up with a great gag: the sign MEN
AT WORK under water!

This most picturesque tale of a modern Robinson Crusoe
rightly belongs among its makers' favorites (and it was Keaton's
most financially successful work). The richness of dramatic content of the film would be surpassed in Keaton's work only by The
General, made two years later.

NIBELUNGEN (Die Nibelungen)   Fritz Lang

Script: Thea von Harbou, from "Nibelungenlied," a German heroic
13th-century epic. Photography: Carl Hoffmann and Günther Rittau.
Animation: Walther Ruttmann. Art Direction: Otto Hunte, Erich
Kettelhut and Karl Vollbrecht. Costumes: Paul Gerd Guderian.
Cast: Gertrud Arnold (Queen Ute), Margarete Schön (Kriemhild),

Hanna Ralph (Brunhild), Paul Richter (Siegfried), Theodor Loos
(King Gunther), Hans Carl Müller (Gerenot), Erwin Biswanger
(Giselher), Bernhard Goetzke (Volker von Alzey, the minstrel),
Hans Adalbert von Schlettow (Hagen Tronje), Hardy von Francois
(Dankwart), Georg John (Mime, the smith/Alberich/Blaodel), Georg
Jurowski (Priest), Iris Roberts (Page), Rudolf Rittner (Rüdiger),
Rudolf Klein-Rogge (King Etzel), Hubert Heinrich (Werbel), Fritz
Alberti (Dietrich von Bern), Georg August Koch (Hildebrand), Grete
Berger (A Hun), Frieda Richard (Reader of the runes).

Erich Pommer for UFA, Germany. Part I: "Siegfrieds Tod," 7
reels, 10,551 ft.; Part II: "Kriemhilds Rache," 7 reels, 11,732 ft.

Destiny and Dr. Mabuse, the Gambler were so very Teutonic in
character and so successful at the box office that the management
of UFA decided to assign the husband-wife team Lang-von Harbou to
the boldest project the company had yet attempted. The idea was
to translate into visual terms the 13th-century heroic epic, "The
Lay of the Nibelungs" (used already by Richard Wagner as material
for his operatic cycle), and create a sort of cinematic national
monument, an apotheosis of the German Genius. Lang expended
great efforts on the project and after a year of intensive work produced a grand bipartite feature, which is one of the most pictorially
cultivated silent films.

Siegfried is the story of an innocent destroyed by the evil of
the world. The hero vanquishes the monsters, becomes invulnerable
to assault by bathing in the blood of the dragon he killed, arrives at
the court of Burgundy and asks for the hand of princess Kriemhild.
This is granted provided Siegfried conquers the bellicose Icelandic
Queen Brunhild for King Gunther. Brunhild and the traitor Hagen
unite against Siegfried and Hagen kills him during a hunt by hitting
the place on his back where a linden leaf fell during his blood bath
making it the only vulnerable spot on his body.

Kriemhild's Revenge is a somber study of a woman's vengeance for the death of her lover. Kriemhild marries Etzel (Atilla),
the King of the Huns and invites Gunther and Hagen to the palace.
Etzel refuses to kill Hagen while he is his guest, but agrees to a
personal combat. There is a massacre in which Kriemhild's brothers die, followed by the burning of the palace; finally she kills Hagen and is herself assassinated by one of her subjects.

The screen result certainly fulfills the hopes of the producers,
to invoke the gloomy atmosphere of a medieval legend with larger-
than-life heroes pursuing their aims--a mood typically grandiose,
pervaded by determinism and inevitability, and devoid of a touch of
lightness or humor. Nibelungen does not really try to explain the
motivation of the characters; it uses people only as part of the set
and is thus not a psychological film. While Nibelungen lacks the
human element, its visual aspect--the sets, lighting, editing, animation, trick photography--is most impressive. The film was made en-

tirely in the studio where Lang built hundreds of colossal sets: a
fire-breathing dragon, primeval forests, ships and cathedrals, all
perfectly credible, realistic and capable of matching any modern
production.

The visually most fascinating fragment of the film is the sequence of Kriemhild's nightmare in which two black hawks attack a
dove; it superbly recapitulates the mood of the work. The extremes
of emotional scale represented by the characters are reflected in
their dress (which together with the style of lighting is not realistic):
the immaculate Siegfried is dressed in white, Hagen in black. This
principle was later used, in reverse, by Eisenstein in Alexander
Nevsky. Nibelungen also inspired Ivan the Terrible, another Eisenstein work, and very interestingly compares with it, part for part,
from the point of view of the origin, the variation of tone, and the
pictorial conception.

Siegfried and Kriemhild's Revenge coexist on the counterpoint
principle: the first is slow but light in mood, the sets objective
and symmetrical, the camera fairly mobile; the second is somber
and dark, swollen with vengeance and desolation, the sets more eccentric, the camera work favoring close-ups of faces rather than
movement.

VISAGES D'ENFANTS   Jacques Feyder

Script: Feyder. Photography: Léonce-Henry Burel and Paul Par-
guel. Cast: Jean Forest (Jean), Victor Vina (His father), Rachel
Devirys (His stepmother), Arlette Peyran (Jean's stepsister),
Jeanne-Marie Laurent, Pierre Houyez.

Zoubaloff and Porchet, Lausanne, Switzerland. 7382 ft.

As Feyder's earlier Crainquebille foreshadowed Italian Neorealism
and the cinema of the 1950's through its style, Visages d'enfants
draws close to the films of that period on account of its psychological preoccupations, in particular its interest in the anxieties of
childhood. Thus the film is related in many ways to Les Jeux interdits, the 1951 work of René Clément. In Visages, the father of
an orphaned boy marries a young widow. Jean displays his resent-
ment of his new stepmother and her daughter by hiding his stepsister's doll in the snow. When the girl narrowly avoids death in
an avalanche, Jean throws himself into a torrent. He is saved by
his new mother and reconciled with her.

Feyder shot the film on location in Switzerland, achieving a
high visual standard through dramatic employment of the Valais lo-

cality; its folk costumes and snowbound mountain valleys provide a
clever visual equivalent of a child's inner life, a metaphor for the
innocence of childhood. At the same time the director took one
more step in the development of his simple, almost austere style:
while Crainquebille still contained close-ups (motivated by psychological intentions in a manner similar to Dreyer's The Passion of
Joan of Arc), here all this was over. What has remained is simplicity, beautiful photography, the subtle rendering of the psychology
of a child. Although Feyder often found sentimentality hard to
avoid, he still has made a refined and simple film in which the little Jean Forest, who appeared in Crainquebille, gives a convincing
and charming performance.

THE IRON HORSE   John Ford

Script: Charles Kenyon, from the story by Kenyon and John Rus-
sell. Photography: George Schneidermann and Burnett Guffey.
Cast: George O'Brien (Davy Brandon), Madge Bellamy (Miriam
Marsh), Charles Edward Bull (Abraham Lincoln), William Walling
(Thomas Marsh), Fred Kohler (Deroux), Cyril Chadwick (Peter Jes-
son), Gladys Hulette (Ruby), James Marcus (Judge Haller), Francis
Powers (Sgt. Slattery), J. Farrell McDonald (Cpl. Casey), James
Welch (Pvt. Schultz), Colin Chase (Tony), George Waggner (Col.
"Buffalo Bill" Cody).

Fox, U.S.A. 11,335 ft.

John Ford, the leading personality in the American cinema from the
silents to the early 70's, came to Hollywood in 1913, and in the
next eight years made over 35 feature films. In 1924 he directed
his first really outstanding picture and the biggest project Fox had
yet attempted. The Iron Horse is an epic about the construction of
a transcontinental railroad. The basic situation itself is full of
suspense: the race between the Union Pacific and Central Pacific
to be first to complete their railroads. Against this background a
man searches for his father's murderer and courts the daughter of
one of the chief engineers. Finally Davy Brandon becomes a rail
worker himself.

    Ford built miles of railroad track and a full-scale shanty
town on location in Nevada. There was a cast of 5000, but the
real hero and the spiritus movens of the story is the railway. The
director launched here his later classical theme of a team of people
facing a difficult task and dexterously blended suspense with sentimentality and campfire scenes with shots of silhouettes of riders
against the sky. This mixture became his hallmark, although years

were to pass before Ford again made a film of comparable class.

WAXWORKS (Das Wachsfigurenkabinett)   Paul Leni

Script: Henrik Galeen. Photography: Hjalmar Junge. Art Direc-
tion: Leni, Fritz Maurischat and Alfred Junge. Cast: Wilhelm
Dieterle (Young poet/Rinaldo Rinaldini), John Gottowt (Showman),
Olga Belejeff (His daughter), Emil Jannings (Haroun-al-Raschid),
Conrad Veidt (Ivan the Terrible), Werner Krauss (Jack the Ripper).

Neptun-Film AG, Berlin, Germany.   4 reels, 7028 ft.

Together with Nosferatu, Vanina and Dr. Mabuse, the Gambler,
Waxworks is the most typical film of the "demonic Expressionism"
with its recurrent tyrant character.   It is also, appropriately for the
last fully Expressionist picture, a review of past motifs, a sort of
anthology of tyrants--tyranny appears in Waxworks in triplicate.
Films composed of several separate stories were in vogue in Germany, and indeed none of the episodes in Waxworks carries enough
substance to justify a separate picture. The film begins at a fun
fair where wax figures are on display. A young poet (played by
Wilhelm Dieterle who was to become the leading director of American film biographies) is asked by the showman to compose essays
about the fiercest of them. The framing story serves only as an
excuse for entering the world of fancy.

        The first episode, featuring Emil Jannings in a rare comedy
part of Haroun-al-Rashid involved in a series of humorous encounters with a pastry cook and his wife, is the least successful of the
three, and demonstrates with its sick humor that the burlesque approach is very difficult to use in the context of a basically sober
theme. The remaining stories, while having no real intellectual
message, can certainly terrify the spectator. The one telling of
the pursuits of Ivan the Terrible stresses the elements of sadism
and cruelty (e.g., the hourglass before the eyes of the dying torture victims) and leaves the mad Tsar furiously turning the hourglass over and over (this ending interestingly coincides with that
of Dr. Mabuse, the Gambler).

        The last episode develops into a classical cinematic nightmare.
The poet has fallen asleep in the process of writing his stories and now
fancies himself fleeing, in the company of the showman's daughter,
from the pursuit of Jack the Ripper. This part of Waxworks, visually
based on double exposure, creates an interesting vision of the so-
familiar fun fair eeriness and very strongly invokes the feeling of
alarm and fear. The fact that it merges with the framing story

gives it a feel of a bad dream which continues into waking hours.

Pictorially Waxworks is impressive with its twisted, typically
Expressionist sets, high-contrast lighting, and chiaroscuro vistas of
a nightmarish Kremlin.   The makers of the picture were a veritable
gathering of celebrities and their names alone explain a lot about it.
The director was Paul Leni, who had collaborated with Reinhardt
and Jessner on many theatrical projects; the script was written by
Galeen, production supervised by Robert Wiene, the director of The
Cabinet of Dr. Caligari; and the cast brought together the very best
German actors.

HE WHO GETS SLAPPED   Victor Sjöström

Script: Carey Wilson and Sjöström, from the play, "Tot, Kto
Poluchayet Poshchelechiny," by Leonid N. Andreyev. Photography:
Milton Moore. Cast: Lon Chaney ("Ho Who Gets Slapped"), Nor-
ma Shearer (Consuelo), John Gilbert (Bezano), Tully Marshall
(Count Mancini), Marc MacDermott (Baron Regnard), Ford Sterling
(Tricaud), Harvey Clarke (Briquet), Paulette Duval (Zinida), Ruth
King ("He's" wife), Clyde Cook, Brandon Hurst and George Davis
(Clowns).

Louis B. Mayer, U.S.A. 7 reels, 6953 ft.

The fate of the Swedish silent film school was sealed when both its
great directors left the country for Hollywood; Sjöström went in
1923 and Stiller, accompanied by Greta Garbo, in 1925. He Who
Gets Slapped, the second picture Sjöström made during his seven-
year American adventure, is an adaptation of a successful play by
the writer who depicted the decadent life in Russia just before the
First World War.

Sjöström transferred the literary original to the screen with
all its fatalistic ballast: a scientist who at one stroke loses both
his wife and his brilliant discovery to a dishonest man tries to
drown his misery in laughter by becoming a circus clown. His
speciality is being slapped on the face. He falls in love with a
bareback rider, but fate--alias evil Baron Regnard--strikes again.
To prevent the girl from marrying his rival the clown releases a
lion from the cage, and in the final scene, mortally stabbed, stag-
gers around the arena to the delight of the audience.

While the scripts of Sjöström's American pictures were not
always suitable for him, the fatalism of He Who Gets Slapped recalls the mood of his great Swedish films. The main strength of
the picture (one has to throw out the melodramatic intrigue at once)

are the camera work and the lighting. As a clear visual key for expressing the humiliation and anguish of the hero, Sjöström uses high contrasts of light and shade, a most unusual practice in the brightly and evenly lit Hollywood studios--a clown drenched with a spotlight in the middle of a dark arena, the key face-slapping scene.

In the choice of theme and situations, Sjöström's film foreshadowed The Blue Angel of Sternberg. But while Sternberg's picture is firmly rooted in reality, the far-fetched script of He Who Gets Slapped makes too much use of fate as a source of dramatic conflicts, thus taking the sting out of the human tragedy.

1925

BATTLESHIP POTEMKIN (Bronenosets "Potyomkin") Sergei Eisenstein

---

Script: Nune Agadzhanova-Shutko. Photography: Eduard Tissé.
Cast: Alexandr Antonov (The Sailor Vakulinchuk), Vladimir Barsky
(Captain Golikov), Grigori Alexandrov (Lieutenant Giliarovsky), Mikhail Gomorov (Sailor), N. Poltavtseva (Teacher), B. Vitoldi (Woman
with the pram), Repnikova (Woman on the steps), Marusov (Officer),
I. Bobrov (Recruit), Andrei Fait (Officer), Alexandr Levshin (Short
officer).

Goskino, U.S.S.R. 5709 ft.

"There is no art without conflict": this statement by Eisenstein
never had a fuller demonstration on the screen than in this film,
which reconstructs the events on the battleship "Prince Potemkin"
and in Odessa harbor during the unsuccessful 1905 revolution, and
which was to become an artistic summary and recapitulation of its
time. Battleship Potemkin was made in homage to that first Russian
revolution and designed to have a scope and scale comparable with
Fritz Lang's Nibelungen. The story was at first going to be one of
the seven parts of a cinematic fresco to be called Towards Dictatorship. Partly by accident and partly by intuition, Eisenstein decided
to devote the whole film to the sailors' mutiny on the "Prince Potemkin," one of the ships of the Black Sea fleet.

The dramatic construction of the whole is based on the rules
of classical tragedy and comprises five parts, of which each is a
separate whole with an exposition, culmination and solution. Part
I: the sailors refuse to eat verminous meat, which the doctor falsely declares clean. II: the captain orders the execution of those
who complain, but the sailors refuse to shoot their brothers; officers

are cast overboard; one sailor is killed. III: citizens of Odessa
gather round the body on the wharf; anger mounts. IV: the people
of Odessa send supplies to the battleship; the army massacres the
crowds watching the operation from the Odessa steps; when the ship
starts shelling the barracks, the massacre stops. V: a naval
squadron approaches the "Potemkin," whose men signal "brothers";
the ship is allowed to sail away freely.

An almost mathematically rigorous composition, whose perfection is unmatched in the cinema, provides a framework for a
film not only completely homogeneous, but also spontaneous and dynamic. The generalizing uniformity of Battleship Potemkin was
achieved not only by Eisenstein's employment of the traditional
means of expression offered by the cinema, fine arts, literature and
even musical harmony (which has a visual parallel in this silent
movie), but also by blending these with completely innovative elements.

The most important among these elements are the editing of
the crowd scenes, especially brilliant in the all-too-famous Odessa
Steps sequence (which was incidentally not in the script and was introduced after Eisenstein visited the city); the free treatment of
time which allowed the director through editing, to expand cinematic
time in relation to real time (in that sequence in the ratio of 3:1);
the preservation of the classical dramatic construction even in the
absence of an individual hero; and the masterly build-up of pathos
and tension achieved by increasing the pace and the dramatic use
of the lettering of the titles, although it must be admitted that the
actual text is often naively propagandist. It is interesting that the
suppression of individual heroes did not stop Eisenstein from commanding complete emotional involvement, though there is no one with
whom the spectator can identify.

Battleship Potemkin is the greatest cinematic realization of
Militant Art, an unsurpassed illustration of the aesthetic beliefs of
Soviet art--but above all an Internationale of the cinema, a striking-
ly beautiful banner of Revolution.

THE GOLD RUSH   Charles Chaplin

Script: Chaplin. Photography: Rollie Totheroh and Jack Wilson.
Cast: Charles Chaplin (The Lone Prospector), Mack Swain (Big Jim
McKay), Tom Murray (Black Larsen), Georgia Hale (Georgia),
Betty Morissey (Her friend), Henry Bergman (Hank Curtis), Mal-
colm Waite (Jack Cameron, the local Don Juan).

United Artists, U.S.A. Originally 9760 ft., cut for release to 9
reels, 8555 ft.

In The Gold Rush Chaplin created the film through which he wanted
to be remembered: a story of a weak and insignificant gold prospector, set in Alaska during the Great Gold Rush of 1898.   Charlie,
one of the thousands who came to the Klondike, is rescued from the
thug Larsen by Big Jim.   Charlie meets Georgia in a bar and falls
in love with her.   He is disappointed when the girl fails to come to
his New Year's party.   Big Jim asks Charlie to help him in his
prospecting and the two after a dramatic night in a gale do strike
it rich.   During a triumphant return journey to the States, Charlie
meets Georgia on the ship and introduces her as his fiancée to the
reporters.

This masterpiece has outgrown even the intentions of its
maker and became one of the most popular films of all time.   The
reasons for this are not difficult to find: Chaplin's tragicomedy is
told not only with universally comprehensible simplicity, blending
incomparably the elemental joy of laughter with the most intimate
emotion, touching on the simplest and deepest feelings, it is also a
materialization of the optimistic faith in life, a beautiful love story,
a film very personal to every ordinary man.   Finally, The Gold
Rush is a magic materialization of dreams of adventure: at the end
Chaplin offers his hero not only his beloved but also the gold, on
whose destructive influence he has previously reflected many a time
in the film.   But could he refuse the fulfillment of dreams to the
one who humbly lived by hope, though tossed on waves?

It is not the finale which is the most delightful and most
memorable part of The Gold Rush.   The scenes forever contributed
to the history of cinema are, in the first place, the dream of the
dance of the buns conducted by the hero on Christmas Eve, the feast
of the starving gold-diggers during which they gracefully eat their
boots, the fight against the bear, the first dance with the beloved,
the struggle against the gale and the dramatic moments in the hut
suspended over a precipice.   The richness of invention presented
here would be enough to serve several excellent films, but The
Gold Rush is only one and unrepeatable.

VAUDEVILLE (Varieté) [Variety]   Ewald André Dupont

Script: Leo Birinski, from the novel, "Der Eid des Stephan Huller, "
by Felix Holländer. Photography: Karl Freund. Art Direction:
Oscar Werndorff. Cast: Emil Jannings (Boss Huller), Lya de Putti
(Bertha-Marie), Warwick Ward (Artinelli), Mady Delschaft (Boss's
wife), Georg John (Sailor), Kurt Gerron (Docker), Charles Lincoln
(Actor).

Erich Pommer, UFA, Germany. 7 reels, 9331 ft.

The great German cinema of the early 20's was coming to an end:
Waxworks was the last outstanding work of the "demonic Expressionism," Vaudeville marked the close of the Kammerspiel and the arrival of a realistic-minded period. On the other hand, this work by
an ex-critic cannot be wholly claimed by the Kammerspiel, but
seems to be rather an intelligent summing up of the earlier formal
achievements of the Expressionists--a continuation of The Last Laugh,
that great film which towered above any classification.

    The story of Vaudeville came from police chronicles and is
shown in a realistic, matter-of-fact manner, free of the symbolism
of the films of Pick or Jessner. A prisoner, about to be released,
tells the prison governor his life story. He had been nicknamed
"Boss" Huller and ran a paltry show in an amusement ground.
When somebody brought to him a beautiful provincial girl who wanted
to work as a dancer, Huller, a married man, lost his head over
the girl and ran away with her. The couple worked as circus acro-
bats and joined the acrobat Artinelli to form a very successful trio.
One day Boss learned that his girl was unfaithful to him, killed his
rival and paid for his crime in prison.

    As always happens when a potentially melodramatic story is
told by a sensitive director, a simple and noble picture is made instead of a trivial and superficial one. Jannings' brilliant acting
watched by a constantly mobile camera allowed Dupont to convey a
non-banal psychological reflection, which never tries to indulge in
pretentious generalizations. But it is the fine modesty of execution
which permitted him to achieve greatness.

    Vaudeville is one of the best pictures in the cinema about the
shoddiness and agony of circus performers' life, a very fruitful
theme which produced Chaplin's The Circus, Sjöström's He Who
Gets Slapped and Bergman's brilliant Sawdust and Tinsel.

THE BIG PARADE   King Vidor

Script: Harry Behn, from the play, "What Price Glory," by Lau-
rence Stallings. Photography: John Arnold. Cast: John Gilbert
(James Apperson), Renée Adorée (Mélisande), Hobart Bosworth (Mr.
Apperson), Claire Adams (Justyn Reed), Robert Ober (Harry), Tom
O'Brien (Bull), Karl Dane (Slim), Rosita Marstini (French mother).

MGM, U.S.A. 13 reels, 12,550 ft., released version 12 reels,
11,519 ft. Originally some sequences in two-color Technicolor.

For the first time the true war, devoid of the romantic halo of an
adventure, appeared on the screen. What is more, there are no

emphatic accusations: the war is seen through the eyes of an ordinary private in the U.S. Army, who goes to the French front as
a boy unaware of the cruel facts of life, and returns as a bitterly
experienced invalid. The story is told by King Vidor, one of the
most careful observers and most honest directors in the American
cinema. He tried to be objective, even indifferent; he wanted to
give his account of the story of an ordinary man whose fate is not
in his own hands, but who is nonetheless emotionally involved in his
situation, although both the script itself and the theme of the atrocities of the First World War make such indifference impossible from
the very start.

    The message of Vidor's film is clear, even when taken with-
out its evocative title: to condemn, it is sufficient to show a glimpse
of a soldier's girl disappearing in the distance as he leaves for the
front, a nightmarish and near-abstract pattern of shell-holes on the
battlefield; a silent minuet of attacking soldiers mowed down by enemy fire. In spite of so many films on the horrors of war, there
are many acute observations in The Big Parade which have not been
superseded, even by the more uncompromising ones.

MASTER OF THE HOUSE (Du Skal Aere Din Hustru) [Thou Shalt
   Honor Thy Wife] Carl Theodor Dreyer

Script: Dreyer and Svend Rindom, from the play, "Tyrannens
Fald" (The Fall of a Tyrant), by the latter. Photography: George
Schnéevoigt. Art Direction: Dreyer. Cast: Johannes Mayer (Victor
Frandsen), Astrid Holm (Ida, his wife), Karin Nellemose (Karen,
their daughter), Mathilde Nielsen (Mads, the nanny), Clara Schøn-
feld (Ida's mother), Johannes Nielsen (Doctor), Petrine Sonne
(Washerwoman), Aage Hoffman and Byril Harvig (The boys).

Palladium Film, Denmark. 7730 ft.

After returning home from Germany where he directed the drama
Mikaël (1924) sustained in the spirit of the then prevailing Kammerspiel, Dreyer transformed onto the screen a stage play about
the conversion of a domestic tyrant. A tetchy middle-class husband
terrorizes his wife, children--even the canary. Finally, persuaded
by the old nanny, the maltreated wife leaves the marital household.
The husband is deprived of the comforts to which he is used and it
is only then that he realizes the wickedness of his behavior; con-
trite, he asks his wife's forgiveness.

    As Vaudeville in Germany took advantage of the experiences
of the Expressionist chamber drama, so does Dreyer in Denmark.
But he freed his morality play from the stylization and symbolism

characteristic of the Kammerspiel and created the archetype of a
psychological film.   The story develops almost entirely between
three people in the claustrophobic enclosure of a tiny flat, between
kitchen and dining room, canary cage and a cuckoo clock.   The
household is faithfully recreated in the studio, with even working
gas, water and electrical installations.

    The pedantic registration of the characters' behavior with a
mobile camera far removed the film from its stage prototype and
foreshadowed the masterly The Passion of Joan of Arc.   Master of
the House is characterized by a severe realism and restraint in the
acting, a touch of humor and the precision of the rather obtrusively
concluded dramatic structure.   This picture is one of the fullest
examples of Dreyer's attitude as a Protestant moralist.

SEVEN CHANCES   Buster Keaton

Script: Clyde Bruckman, Jean Havez and Joseph Mitchell, based
on the comedy by Roi Cooper Mergue. Photography: Elgin Lessley
and Byron Houck. Cast: Buster Keaton (Jimmie Shannon), Ray
Barnes (Billy Meekin), Snitz Edwards (Lawyer), Ruth Dwyer (Mary
Jones), Frankie Raymond (Her mother), Jean Havez (Man on the
landing).

Buster Keaton Productions Inc. U.S.A. 6 reels, 5113 ft.

Years are passing but Jimmie Shannon is too shy to tell Mary
Brown of his love for her.   Then he learns that he has inherited a
fortune, but on condition that he gets married the very same day.
Keaton's hero--as always--takes the shortest route, but the girl rejects him, annoyed at the abrupt and mawkish proposal.   The film
tells of Jimmie's fight against the clock in the name of love and the
prospective legacy.   The result, of course, can be guessed.   So
can the happy ending; but before the film comes to that Keaton goes
through astonishing variations on his usual theme of the struggle
with unfriendly fate.

    When a friend, trying to help, publishes the story of the
search for a wife by the millionaire-to-be in the newspapers, a battalion of prospective brides (as it happens, terrifying old spinsters)
besiege and obstinately pursue the poor fellow.   This gives rise to
the picture's best scene, shortly before the end, when the hero escapes an avalanche of thousands of boulders.   The weakness of
Seven Chances lies in its too eccentric story which gives the described events a somewhat mechanical inevitability.   Also the pace
of the film seems too frantic.   The result, although enjoyable, is
a little less charming than Keaton's usual standard.

THE JOYLESS STREET (Die freudlose Gasse)   Georg Wilhelm Pabst

---

Script: Willy Haas, from a novel by Hugo Bettauer. Photography:
Guido Seeber, Kurt Oertel and Robert Lach. Art Direction: Hans
Sohnle and Otto Erdmann. Cast: Greta Garbo (Greta Rumfort),
Asta Nielsen (Marie Leschner), Valeska Gert (Frau Greifer, ma-
dame of a brothel), Einar Hanson (Lieutenant Davy), Jaro Fürth
(Counselor Rumfort), Werner Krauss (Butcher), Robert Garrison
(Canez), Agnès Esterhàzy (His daughter).

Hirschel-Sofar, Germany. 11,155 ft.

Vienna in the period of post-war inflation: interminable lines in
front of shops, depressing interiors of tenement houses, a crisis in
the beliefs of the declining middle classes, the brutality of upstart
speculators and the humiliation of decent people. The Joyless
Street has two intertwined plots. The first is the story of Greta
Rumfort, daughter of an impoverished official, who is saved from
poverty and prostitution by the love of a young American lieutenant.
The second is the story of Marie Leschner, a prostitute who kills
her unfaithful lover and reports his suicide, but later confesses to
the police.

The third film in the career of one of the most outstanding
directors of the twilight of the silent films and the dawn of the talkies, contained documentation unencountered until then of the facts of
life in the Twenties. As did Dupont in Vaudeville, Pabst completely
ignored the symbolism so recently omnipresent on German screens.
Neither did he follow up the social implications of the plot, which
would anyway probably have been unacceptable in the cinema at the
time. Instead, he attempted to show abjectively the "true life,"
using the contrasts of poverty and luxury as a dramatic device and
consciously avoiding the artificial aesthetic stylization which was
then almost obligatory. The result is a partial success: the shattering screen vision of poverty and desperation (note the famous
scene outside the butcher's shop) can irritate the viewer with the
obtrusiveness of its cinematic effects and, even more, with its melodramatic plot; the latter has always been the weakest point in
Pabst's work.

But Pabst has a trump card to play in The Joyless Street--
Greta Garbo, who creates here her first truly great performance.
A few years later the unknown Swedish actress would become Holly-
wood's greatest star.

GO WEST   Buster Keaton

Script: Keaton, Raymond Cannon and Lex Neal. Photography:
Elgin Lessley and Bert Haines. Cast: Buster Keaton (Friendless),
Howard Truesdale (Owner of Diamond Bar Ranch), Kathleen Myers
(His daughter), Ray Thompson (Foreman), Brown Eyes (Herself).

Buster Keaton Productions Inc., U.S.A.   7 reels, 6293 ft.

"Go West, young man": Friendless, the penniless hero decides to
follow that slogan in search of his fortune. He crosses America by
jumping freight trains and finally finds work on a ranch. He manages quite well in spite of his ignorance of animal husbandry, but
when he fails to find a sympathetic soul among his fellow cowboys,
he develops a friendship with a cow. Brown Eyes is going to be
sold and Friendless accompanies her on the cattle train to town.
When the train is ambushed, it turns out that the hero has, by himself, to escort the enormous herd to its destination; but he can
handle even that!

        Buster Keaton, however, here unusually sentimental and
rather far from his best achievements, could not quite handle the
picture as a whole: most of Go West amounts in fact to an undy-
namic enumeration of often very forced gags, and it is only in the
last sequence that a feeble comedy turns into a champagne cow opera
which makes the spectator forgive Keaton his previous lethargy.
These scenes of the cattle roaming through the streets of Los An-
geles give rise to some likeable gags and the final chase of Friendless and the police evoke Keaton's earlier Cops (1921)--perhaps the
most brilliant short slapstick comedy ever made.

1926

MOTHER (Mat) Vsevolod Pudovkin

Script: Nathan Zarkhi, from the novel by Maxim Gorky. Photography: Anatoli Golovnya. Cast: Vera Baranovskaya (Pelageya Vlasova), Nikolai Batalov (Pavel, her son), A. P. Chistiakov (Mikhail, her husband, a locksmith), Ivan Koval-Samborsky (Pavel's friend), Anna Zemtzova (Girl student), N. Vidonov (Misha), V. Savitzky (Secret policeman), Vsevolod Pudovkin (Police officer), F. Ivanov (Prison Governor), I. Bobrov (Young prisoner), V. Uralsky (Student), A. Gromov (Revolutionary).

Mezhrabpom-Russ, U.S.S.R. 5906 ft.

Mother was the feature film debut of the greatest master of the silent Soviet cinema besides Eisenstein. Having made Chess Fever (1925), a likeable two-reeler which gives a humorous account of a Moscow chess tournament, and an educational documentary about Pavlov's experiments on the functioning of the brain, the 30-year-old Pudovkin was commissioned by the Education Minister to direct a completely different (and much more weighty) project. His job was to transfer to the screen one of the most outstanding novels of revolutionary literature, tracing the rise of class awareness among the proletarians of Tsarist Russia, using a weary middle-aged woman as an example.

1905: Pavel Vlasov's father, a drunkard and police informer, is killed while trying to break a strike. Pavel himself is a revolutionary. When the police come looking for hidden weapons his mother reveals where they are hidden, hoping thereby to save her son. But Pavel is given a long jail sentence. The mother realizes her grave mistake and begins to cooperate with the revolutionaries. When Pavel escapes from prison mother and son take part in a demonstration and are both killed by the police.

The principal rule observed strictly and often dogmatically on nearly all prestige Soviet film adaptations has been fidelity to the literary original. Even though in these early days the rule was not so rigorously applied, the main objective of the makers of Mother was to render the message of the book on the screen. This did not mean, however, photographing it page by page: Zarkhi introduced quite substantial changes to the story in order to bring out the main plot with more clarity.

For his part Pudovkin solicitously constructed the psychological motivation of the drama, which is subsequently faultlessly conveyed by Vera Baranovskaya and Nikolai Batalov--the outstanding actors from the famous Moscow Art Theatre. Their roles were developed in the spirit of the method of Stanislavsky, which urges a total identification of the actor with the portrayed character and a great economy of gesture. This is how Mother achieved the feel of moving and intimate truth when describing the experiences of a person fighting for happiness--her own, her son's and those of the likes of her who live a life without hope.

Yet the position of Pudovkin's film among the great achievements of the cinema owes not so much to the actual content, but to the form through which it is conveyed. Mother is a testimonial to the might of the language of the cinema, a model of narrative structure and one of the best examples of the artistic use of film editing. While Eisenstein promoted "intellectual montage" consisting of the dramatic collision of consecutive frames, Pudovkin employs the so-called "constructive montage," which above all concerns the fluent bridging of the narrative phrases in order to be more direct and communicative.

Mother constitutes almost a review of the functional use of poetic allegories for commenting on the action (the best known example of this is the visual association of the workers' demonstration with the images of ice breaking on the river), for revealing the latent motives of human actions (the reaction of the prisoners to the arrival of spring), and for conveying mental states (as in the scene where the mother gives her son the news of the planned prison break). The first of Pudovkin's great pictures proved that pictorial finesse need not weaken the dynamism of a film but, on the contrary, can enhance its emotional impact.

THE GENERAL   Buster Keaton and Clyde Bruckman

Script: Keaton and Bruckman.   Photography: J. Devereux Jennings and Bert Haines.   Cast: Buster Keaton (Johnnie Gray), Marian

Mack (Annabelle Lee), Glen Cavender (Capt. Anderson), Jim Farley
(General Thatcher), Frederick Vroom (Southern general), Charles
Smith (Annabelle's father), Frank Barnes (Annabelle's brother), Joe
Keaton, Mike Denlin and Tom Nawm (Union generals).

Buster Keaton Productions Inc., U.S.A.   8 reels, 7500 ft.

Buster Keaton reached the level at which the content of his picture turns into something much weightier than an excellent com-
edy--it becomes a near-philosophical generalization.   The story
of the ordinary little man who performed heroic feats for his beloved, based on an authentic episode of the American Civil War, is
told in a manner completely unlike that of Chaplin's films but, in
its spirit, is very close indeed to the classic Chaplinesque theme
of the modest man who fights for his happiness.

While, however, Chaplin always tried to make the spectator
identify himself with his Tramp, Keaton remained proud and aloof.
How paltry seem the enterprises of the run-of-the-mill, middle-
class hero as played by Harold Lloyd (the third famous American
comic of the silent burlesque), when compared with the feats of
Keaton's hero, who bravely resists the might of enormous machines
and foils crowds of enemies!   Even if he is a bit frightened, this
does not affect his ways: he is too involved in overcoming obstacles
in the pursuit of the two loves of his life--a girl and ... a steam
engine.   Even if he makes mistakes and suffers setbacks, they do
not affect his resolve.   To despair means to add one evil to another, and the practical Johnnie Gray cannot afford any delay.

In The General he is in a particular hurry: he is fighting
the whole of the enemy army, and there is no joking with the military, even if they are as incompetent as this satirical peep at one
of the heroic pages of U.S. history would seem to suggest.   A little
steam-engine driver, turned down for military service by the Con-
federates as being more useful as an engineer, is mistakenly rejected as a coward by his beloved Annabelle Lee.   He pursues his
engine, "The General," which was stolen with his beloved aboard by
Northern spies.   He unknowingly crosses the enemy lines, over-
hears the Unionists' secret plans, rescues the girl, regains the
engine, successfully fights a whole battalion of pursuers and returns
to a hero's welcome and a commission.

The plot is built symmetrically around the central motif of
the rail chase which of course became for Keaton an inexhaustible
source of comic situations.   Precision of dramatic construction, always strong in Keaton's pictures, is here at its peak in spite of the
fact that both Battling Butler, made earlier in the same year, and
the subsequent College (1927) are far from perfect in this respect.
Keaton caught the essence of the historical period impeccably (it
has since become a cliché that the hero of The General is a figure
taken straight from a daguerrotype).   The best gags are built on
the principle of surprise to the hero or to the audience and often

on situations in which only the audience knows what has happened
(for instance when the sword with which Johnnie struggled flies out
of the scabbard to impale the enemy sniper). Yet one does not feel
for one moment that the story is so built as to serve only as an excuse for gags.

Anyway, it is not the gags and not the dramatic construction
that matter most in The General: the greatness of the film is
achieved with the seemingly motionless face and the expressive sil-
houette by which the great Buster Keaton conveys the experiences of
his lonely hero.

THE LODGER (A Story of the London Fog) Alfred Hitchcock

Script: Hitchcock and Eliot Stannard, from a novel by Mrs. Belloc
Lowndes. Photography: Baron Ventimiglia (Hal Young). Cast:
Ivor Novello (Lodger), June (Daisy Bunting), Marie Ault (Mrs.
Bunting, her mother), Arthur Chesney (Mr. Bunting), Malcolm Keen
(Detective Joe Betts, Daisy's fiancé).

Gainsborough, G.B. 7685 ft.

London at the turn of the century. Jack the Ripper, who strikes
regularly once a week and always slays a blonde woman, terrorizes
the whole town. The description of the murderer is known: he is
dressed in a long black cape and carries a black valise. When a
man answering this description rents a room in a London house,
first the landlady, then her daughter and the daughter's detective
fiancé, and later the whole town, harbor suspicions that the lodger
is Jack the Ripper. It nearly comes to a lynching. But the man
is nothing of the sort.

The Lodger is the first of many (and the most successful of
all) adaptations of Mrs. Lowndes' popular novel. The motif of a
wrongful accusation seems to be one of Hitchcock's favorites; it was
to be employed later on the occasions of I Confess (1952) and The
Wrong Man (1957). Only one year after Hitchcock's debut as a director (in The Pleasure Garden, 1925), all the clearly crystallized
features of his style of directing appeared; and for the first time
Hitchcock appears personally in an episode. The Lodger contains
obvious parallels to the contemporary trends in world cinema, especially German, and it is interesting to compare it with Lang's
Metropolis with its motifs of the propagation of rumor and crowd
hysteria.

With its skillful replacement of acoustic effects by visual effects (when the lodger paces up and down his room above, we see

his feet through a specially constructed transparent ceiling), the
film is an example of a mature silent film, ready for the introduction of sound. The greatest assets of The Lodger are the excellently balanced, brisk rhythm of the narrative and the very well rendered atmosphere of foggy London.

METROPOLIS Fritz Lang

Script: Thea von Harbou, from her own novel. Photography:
Karl Freund and Günther Rittau. Art Direction: Otto Hunte, Erich
Kettelhut and Karl Vollbrecht. Cast: Alfred Abel (Joh Fredersen),
Gustav Fröhlich (Freder), Brigitte Helm (Maria/robot), Rudolf
Klein-Rogge (Rotwang), Fritz Rasp (Slim), Theodor Loos (Josaphat),
Erwin Biswanger (No. 11811), Heinrich George (Foreman), Olaf
Storm (Jan), Hanns Leo Reich (Marinus), Heinrich George (Grot).

UFA, Germany. 13,743 ft.

The Germans set out to create a film which would overshadow the
Hollywood superproductions with its scale, scope and technical
standards. The direction was, of course, entrusted to Lang, the
maker of Nibelungen. Metropolis is a 21st-century city built on
slavery and ruled by Joh Fredersen. When his son, Freder, falls
in love with Maria, a girl who preaches the gospel of love and
peace, the ruler of Metropolis commissions Rotwang, an inventor,
to create Maria's double to spread mutiny among the workers. When
their children are the mutiny's first victims, the workers kill the
false Maria; Freder saves the real one and achieves reconciliation
between capital and labor.

    The expectations of the commissioners of Metropolis were
fulfilled--the picture is a giant as far as execution is concerned.
But it certainly is not an artistic giant: all that is worst in Lang--
his tendency toward arid formalism, pomposity, and a cruel mechanistic
view of the world--was here brought to the forefront and overwhelms
the content of the film. These contents, however, leave even more
to be desired. The abortive vision of the society of the future,
divided into a class of masters and a class of slaves which unite
spiritually in the finale in the name of Love, is repellent with its
ahumanism and terrifying by the display, in the darkest colors, of
the Teutonic national spirit.

    Metropolis is one of the extremely rare examples of a film
which remains in the annals of cinema achievement despite its reactionary social attitudes and formal faults, thanks to the fascinating
dynamism of direction in the crowd scenes (Lang relies here on
Reinhardt's theatrical examples and uses the crowds of extras as

an elastic material for creating mobile geometrical structures), the masterly photographic compositions, the lighting and the really magnificent design.

THE SCARLET LETTER   Victor Sjöström

Script: Frances Marion, from the novel by Nathaniel Hawthorne. Photography: Hendrick Sartov. Cast: Lillian Gish (Hester Prynne), Lars Hanson (The Rev. Arthur Dimmesdale), Henry B. Walthall (Roger Prynne), Karl Dane (Giles), William H. Tooker (Governor), Marcelle Corday (Mistress Hibbins), Fred Herzog (Jailer), Jules Cowles (Beadle), Mary Hawes (Patience), Joyce Coad (Pearl), James A. Marcus (French sea captain), Chief Yowlachie (Indian), Polly Moran (Townswoman).

MGM, U.S.A.   9 reels, 8229 ft.

In Puritan New England the 17th century was a time of austerity, witch hunts, intolerance and persecution. A woman is branded with an A (for Adultress) after giving birth to a child. Years later, her husband returns from Indian captivity; her pastor lover, realizing that their plan to escape together is hopeless, reveals publicly the A he has branded on his flesh, confesses his guilt and dies in her arms. The Scarlet Letter is not in the class of the masterly The Wind, that would be made two years later--but was already its harbinger. The story telling is still a little conventional and stiff and lacks the passionate, instinctive involvement of the later film. Yet Sjöström was clearly on the way to regaining his former greatness.

His first encounter with Lillian Gish produced an excellent performance from the former star of Griffith's films, and the picture's success is to a great extent due to her. But perhaps it also stems from the Scandinavian character of the drama, so close to Sjöström, in which the love of two young people is destroyed by the puritan severity of social conventions.

BATTLING BUTLER   Buster Keaton

Script: Paul Gerard Smith, Albert Boasberg, Charles Smith and Lex Neal, from the play by Stanley Brightman and Austin Melford. Photography: J. Devereux Jennings and Bert Haines. Cast: Buster Keaton (Alfred Butler), Snitz Edwards (His valet), Sally O'Neil (The mountain girl), Walter James (Her father), Bud Fine (Her brother),

Francis McDonald (Alfred Battling Butler), Mary O'Brien (His wife), Tom Wilson (His trainer), Eddie Borden (His manager).

Buster Keaton Productions Inc., U.S.A.   7 reels, 6969 ft.

Father, disturbed by his son's inability to cope with life, sends him on a camping holiday in the mountains in the hope of making a man of him.   The trip indeed becomes a crucial test for the ninny: although Alfred's sporting activities are rather hopeless, he meets a beautiful girl and is forced to impersonate a famous boxer in order to impress her derisive father and brothers.   The trouble begins when Alfred has to face the real Battling Butler; but love gives him wings.

This time Keaton was not generous with gags, but he nonetheless included two excellent episodes in Battling Butler: one of them is the delightful quadrille of the duck hunt in the beginning of the film, and the other, of course, the culminating fight of David and Goliath.   Also remarkable is the prologue, in which the spectator may discover, even more pronouncedly than in Our Hospitality, the deep-focus technique which would be later ascribed to Welles. What is more, it is used in the scene of the parents' talk about the future of their son, strikingly similar to the celebrated episode in Citizen Kane.

WINGS OF A SERF (Krylya Kholopa) [Ivan the Terrible]   Yuri
   Tarich

Script: Konstantin Schildkredt, Victor Shklovsky and Tarich. Photography: Mikhail Vladimirsky.   Cast: Leonid Leonidov (Ivan IV), I. Klyukvin, Nikolai Prozorovsky (Nikishka), Vladimir Korsh-Sablin (Prince Ivan), S. Askarova (Tsarina), S. Garrel, I. Kachalov.

Sovkino, U.S.S.R.   7008 ft.

A young serf with a passion for science finds his way to the court of Tsar Ivan the Terrible and demonstrates the flying machine he has invented.   The boyars (rich landowners), enemies of progress, oppose its use; prejudice and politics lead to the inventor's death.

Wings of a Serf, a naturalistic historical drama, is one of the most interesting achievements of this stream in the silent Soviet cinema, which ran parallel to the avant-garde led by Eisenstein, Pudovkin and Kuleshov.   Despite a somewhat stereotyped plot and the black-and-white view of the psychology of the characters, the picture contains a wealth of social detail of the time and is impres-

sive also for its monumental scale of set design, which was in all
probability inspired by the monolithic German cinema of the 20's
(Lang's Nibelungen and Metropolis). There is also a truly regal,
though theatrical, performance by Leonid Leonidov. What is particularly interesting is that Wings of a Serf is to a certain degree
an archetype for Eisenstein's Ivan the Terrible, made 18 years later.

DEATH BAY (Bukhta Smerti) Abram Room

Script: Boris Leonidov, from the story, "V Bukhte 'Otrada'," by
Alexei Novikov-Priboy. Photography: Yevgeni Slavinsky. Cast:
Nikolai Saltikov (Surkov, machinist), Alexei Kharlamov (Captain of
the ship), Nikolai Okhlopkov (Seaman), Andrei Fait (Alibekov, security service chief), L. Yurenev (Masloboev, a stoker), V. Yaro-
slavtsev (Ivan Razdolny).

Goskino, U.S.S.R. 7493 ft.

Soviet screen epics about the Revolution were not yet in 1926
tainted by "Social Realism," that Communist doctrine by which artists were exhorted to depict the new social system in symbolic,
dignified works achieving great visual and ideological impact through
their poster-like feel--a doctrine that resulted more often than not
in lifeless, conventional and stilted works. In his debut Room gave
one episode in the ruthless struggles of the Russian Civil War in a
semi-documentary, un-ponderous style. He used the narrative
methods of American gangster drama and enriched these with a
painstaking psychological and moral analysis of people faced with
life-and-death situations. The main character of Death Bay is a
mechanic on a Red Guard ship, who strives in vain to preserve his
neutrality even in the face of mortal conflict. But revolution does
not grant asylum even to those who stand aside. "There is no
shortcut through fire"--this would be a description of those times
in the title of another Soviet film, made forty years later.

1927

THE PASSION OF JOAN OF ARC (La Passion de Jeanne d'Arc)
  Carl Theodor Dreyer

Script: Dreyer and Joseph Delteil, based on the original record of
the trial and supposedly on the novels, "Vie de Jeanne d'Arc" and
"La Passion de Jeanne d'Arc," by the latter. Photography: Rudolf
Maté, assisted by Barth Kottula. Art Direction: Hermann Warm
and Jean Hugo. Costumes: Valentin Hugo. Historical Adviser:
Pierre Champion. Cast: Louise Renée Falconetti (Joan of Arc),
Eugène Silvain (Pierre Cauchon, Bishop of Beauvais), Maurice
Schutz (Nicolas Loyseleur, Canon of the Rouen Cathedral), Michel
Simon (Jean Lemaître), Antonin Artaud (Jean Massieu), Ravet (Jean
Beaupère, Canon of Paris and Besançon), André Berley (Jean
d'Estivet, Canon of Bayeux and Beauvais, the prosecutor), Jean
d'Yd (Guillaume Evrard), André Lurville, Jacques Arna, Alexandre
Mihalesco, R. Narlay, Henri Maillard, Léon Larive, Jean Hemme,
Henri Gaultier, Paul Jorge and Jean Aymé (Judges).

Société Générale de Films, France. Originally 7251 ft., cut to 6680 ft.

Joan of Arc: a theme which gave the cinema at least two great
films (Dreyer's in 1927 and Bresson's in 1961), and, indirectly,
Panfilov's outstanding picture in 1970. Or perhaps it was not the
theme itself but the form it took in the hands of the great Danish
director Dreyer that stimulated the imagination of his successors
in exploring the motif of a woman fighting for her beliefs. The
perfection of The Passion of Joan of Arc is the result of the director's discovery of the best arena for demonstrating his ideas--
the human soul.

    Dreyer wanted his actors to identify psychically with the
screen characters and built an atmosphere of great concentration,

-126-

dispensing with make-up. He wanted to place his protagonists above
the actual time and place and did this by selectively eliminating details of the period from the frame and by limiting the background to
a bare minimum. Thus the overwhelming proportion of the film was
shot in three ascetic interiors only and the camera goes into the
open only in the last scene.

     The Passion of Joan of Arc, the record of the last day in
Joan's life, concentrates not so much on observation of the Rouen
trial, as on scrutiny of the faces of the accused and her judges,
reflecting each person's inner self magnified in close-ups, related
to each other and evaluated through the angles from which they are
seen. This extraordinary use of the language of the cinema, which
brings to one's mind irresistible comparisons with the modern television technique, is coupled with dynamism and power drawn by the
director from the Soviet film school.

     The effect is not in the least weakened by the absence of the
spoken word. While giving the captivating battle of words in the
form of titles, Dreyer did not neglect the narrative rhythm which
gives more weight to the actors' lines; the huge close-ups of faces
are a counterpoint of the written word and, conversely, the titles
turn into a fascinating commentary on the facial expressions of the
characters. This is how one of the greatest portrayals of a tormented human being was created on the screen, profound and true.
Renée Falconetti's great performance as Joan remains one of the
highlights of all cinema, and reaches its climax in the final scene
of the death at stake, a powerful symbol of the fight for freedom.

THE END OF ST. PETERSBURG (Konyets Sankt-Peterburga)
   Vsevolod Pudovkin

Script: Nathan Zarkhi. Photography: Anatoli Golovnya. Cast:
A. P. Chistyakov (Worker), Vera Baranovskaya (His wife), Ivan
Chuvelov (Ivan, a peasant), V. Chuvelov (Friend from his village),
V. Obolensky (Lebedev, steel magnate), A. Gromov (Revolutionary),
Vladimir Tzoppi (Patriot), Nikolai Khmelyov, M. Tzibulsky (Stock-
brokers), Vsevolod Pudovkin, Vladimir Fogel (German soldiers),
Sergei Komarov (Police officer).

Mezhrabpom-Russ, U.S.S.R.   8202 ft.

The End of St. Petersburg is the middle part of Pudovkin's screen
trilogy illustrating the paths by which the protagonists came to join
the Revolution. The first part of the cycle was Mother, the third
would be Storm Over Asia. Now the hero is a country boy whom
poverty drives to the city. He begins his political education as a

strike-breaker, later passes through a Tsarist prison and the misery of First World War trenches, and finally becomes a soldier of the Revolution and a participant in the storming of the Winter Palace.

This time acting was not as important to Pudovkin as in Mother, and although the director stuck to the individual rather than to collective heroes, it was only as a statistical representative of millions. The most important thing was to give a broad generalizing treatment of the causes and the development of the October Revolution: thus the drama of an individual is replaced by the drama of history.

Despite its unevenness, The End of St. Petersburg is Pudovkin's greatest film and the most involving one. It is also on the point of closest approach between the styles Pudovkin and Eisenstein. Apart from a psychologically rather sketchy treatment of the characters (which one may interpret as a step towards Eisenstein's collective hero), the narrative often employs symbolic shortcuts and lets itself be broken up by quasi-journalistic inserts. The overall impression is that of an emphatic epic--more so perhaps in this case than in Mother. The editing deviates from the Pudovkinian "constructive montage" to the advantage of the sharp collision of frames (e.g., the grim trenches of the First World War opposed to the agitation on the stock exchange). Pudovkin, following the precedent of Eisenstein, who from necessity employed fluent editing, created in The End of St. Petersburg one of the best achievements of the Soviet silent cinema.

SUNRISE   Friedrich Wilhelm Murnau

Script: Carl Mayer, from the story, "Der Reise nach Tilsitt," by Hermann Sudermann. Photography: Charles Rosher and Karl Struss. Cast: George O'Brien (The Man), Janet Gaynor (The Wife), Margaret Livingston (The Woman from the City), Bodil Rosing (The Maid), J. Farrell MacDonald (The Photographer), Ralph Sipperly (The Barber), Jane Winton (The Manicurist), Arthur Housman (The Obtrusive Gentleman), Eddie Boland (The Obliging Gentleman).

Fox Film Corporation, U.S.A.   10-11 reels, reduced to 9 reels, 8729 ft.

"The progress of German screen Expressionism is horizontal, there is no ascending path to follow here," complained a critic. This certainly is not true about the works of F. W. Murnau, who remained an Expressionist even after his move to America: the roots of Sunrise are firmly planted in the German screen tradition. As many

other distinguished European directors did, Murnau came to Hollywood; Carl Mayer, the great scriptwriter, was also in America.
Sunrise is a simple film, with a simple country couple as its main
characters. A fisherman is seduced by a woman from the city and
plans to drown his wife in the lake. The wife guesses his intentions, but after a storm during which she almost really drowns,
they are reconciled.

Sunrise is a film about Love Victorious, a homage to the
simple feelings of simple people--with the overtones of a fable about
the struggle of Good and Evil. The woman from the city personifies Evil; the wife, like Ellen in Nosferatu, is Goodness itself.
The metaphor itself as well as the polarization and sublimation of
characters is typical of the German cinema. But to register the
minutest twists of the psyche, Murnau followed the practices of the
modern novel from Proust to Joyce: the description, harmonious
and full, of a man's inner workings comes first. A film director
has only the camera at his disposal; so, the camera takes over as
narrator and achieves perfect fluency: the reflection of mental processes by means of images is here excellent.

The mood, imagery and style are subordinate to the characters' feelings. There is the unreal, dreamy atmosphere of the
country when the husband is being seduced, with glittering lights
and a halo around objects, while the town sequences are sharp and
realistic. There is one great scene in the film, simple to describe
but most complex psychologically: the joyous journey home, by
tram, of the newly reconciled couple, while the view through the
window becomes, as in a dream or a symbolic novel, a recapitulation of their life.

OCTOBER (Oktyabr) [Ten Days That Shook the World] Sergei
Eisenstein

Co-director: Grigori Alexandrov. Script: Eisenstein and Alexan-
drov. Photography: Eduard Tissé. Cast: Vasili Nikandrov (Lenin),
N. Popov (Kerensky), Eduard Tissé (A German), Nikolai Podvoisky
(Podvoisky), Boris Livanov (Tereshchenko, minister).

Sovkino, U.S.S.R. 9272 ft.

The intellectual quality of narration puts October forty years ahead
of its time, yet the film, in spite of errors and imperfections, is
more than a brilliant avant-garde experiment; it is a mature and
full achievement. October is in a way different from Eisenstein's
earlier Battleship Potemkin, which was an artistic treatment of
actual events. This time the director made a reconstructed docu-

ment of the ten days in October 1917 that shook the world (thus the alternative title of the film) and the preceding events of that February and July. This is indeed a very specific document, often turning into an epic poem, a political propaganda poster--and is far from the compositional perfection of the previous film.

October was in the first place to be a practical demonstration of Eisenstein's aesthetic beliefs. He modified his "montage of attractions" into the concept of "intellectual montage" whereby each frame is treated as a sign, and the collision (not blending) of two frames/signs produces, just as in Japanese ideographs, a third composite sign. An example is the juxtaposition of shots showing a Menshevik making a speech at a Congress with scenes of balalaika-playing. Apart from this rather obvious simile, there are many others in the film, far less intelligible.

Besides the next, failed work, The Old and the New (1929), October carries the heaviest cargo of metaphors, emphasis, Futurist influences and satirical commentary, although the last is often cryptic. It is also a demonstration of the dangers which await an artist who applies theoretical concepts in practice too rigorously. For example, the procedure of "typage" (casting actors who only externally resemble the characters they are playing) which was satisfactory before, now fails--consider the film's portrayal of Lenin.

The striking dynamism of Eisenstein's vision, however, compensated for all shortcomings, created its own aesthetic laws and, more than that, has beaten actual history out of shape with its compelling suggestiveness. The storming of the Winter Palace was in reality quite different, but after October sanctioned this fictional portrayal it came to be quoted in documentaries as the actual authentic event. It became Eisenstein's second screen myth--the first was the Odessa Steps massacre in Battleship Potemkin, which was the fruit of directorial imagination, but which is often treated as historical fact. The famous scene of the opening of the bridges, a symbol as powerful as it is hypnotic, is a great example of the magic of the cinema.

THE WEDDING MARCH   Erich von Stroheim

Script: Stroheim and Harry Carr. Photography: Ben Reynolds and Hal Mohr. Sets: Stroheim and Richard Day. Cast: Erich von Stroheim (Prince "Nicki" von Wildliebe-Rauffenburg), Fay Wray (Mitzi), George Fawcett (Prince Ottokar, Nicki's father), Maude George (Princess Maria Immaculata, Nicki's mother), Cesare Gravina (Mitzi's father, a violinist), Dale Fuller (Catherine, his wife), Hughie Mack (Keeper of the vineyard), Mathew Betz (His son · Schani, the butcher), George Nichols (Schweisser, a magnate), Zasu Pitts (Cecelia, his daughter), Anton Wawerka (Emperor Franz-Joseph I).

Famous Players-Lasky, U.S.A. Originally 14 reels, cut to 11 reels, 10,170 ft. One sequence in color.

"Marriage without love is only sacrilege and mockery. This film is dedicated to true lovers." Stroheim showed with this motto of The Wedding March that the accusations of anarchism and perverted cynicism leveled at him after Foolish Wives were quite unjust. It now seems from perspective that part of the trouble was that audiences tended to identify the director with the despicable characters he played. Moreover, many fell into a familiar trap and considered that to show is to endorse. By grace (or, more correctly disgrace) of this argument, many artists, not necessarily film-makers, have found themselves in difficulties. The Wedding March is not a pessimistic display of base instincts at work, but the defense of pure, noble feeling assaulted by money and social mores.

After Greed, a single excursion into the lower social regions, Stroheim set out for the land of his youth, Vienna at the beginning of the century. The Wedding March tells of the love between a young prince and Mitzi, the daughter of a café violinist; a love defeated by money. Nicki is the last descendant of a faded aristocratic family, who for the sake of patching up their finances is forced to marry Cecelia, the crippled daughter of a licentious corn plaster magnate. Mitzi herself has to marry her butcher fiancé, Schani. The banal theme of marriage of convenience, attains the rank of an authentic, moving tragedy in the hands of a director obsessed with a passion for unmasking evil.

Brutal and repulsive eroticism, tendencies to naturalistic exaggeration, ostentatious display of baseness and perversion are used here to indict moral evil. In short, Stroheim's imagery is not far from what was later considered the hallmark and invention of Luis Buñuel: characteristic symbols (birds in cages, as in Greed), and the combination of softly-lit flower compositions and religious motifs (in love scenes) with a calculated display of physical deficiency (Cecelia) and sadism (Schani). The two fathers, a prince and a bourgeois, lie drunk under a table in a brothel and discuss the marriage of their children.

It is interesting that Stroheim's films, with their obsessive interest in the aristocracy do not really evince class consciousness. In The Wedding March the dividing line does not run, as it might seem, between social classes. Rather, the decisive factor is the length of time which has passed since the individual characters were corrupted by money; it is only money which puts people into two antagonistic camps.

THÉRÈSE RAQUIN (Du sollst nicht ehebrechen)   Jacques Feyder

Script: Feyder, Fanny Carlsen and Willy Haas, from the novel by
Émile Zola. Photography: Friedrich Fuglsang and Hans Scheib.
Art Direction: Andrei Andrejev and Eric Zander. Cast: Gina
Manès (Thérèse Raquin), Wolfgang Zilzer (Camil, her husband),
Hans Adalbert von Schlettow (Laurent, her lover), Jeanne-Marie
Laurent (Madame Raquin), Paul Henckels (Office manager).

Zelnick (D.E.F.U.), Berlin, Germany. 10 reels, 10,614 ft.

In the same year Stroheim made his somber Viennese The Wedding
March in America, Feyder transferred to the screen in Germany one
of the most interesting novels of French naturalist literature and
made thereby a film in many aspects similar to Stroheim's. The
external appearances, the place of action and execution of both films
are different, but the intention is the same: arraignment of the
false morality which brings about human tragedies and leads to
crime. Even the creative method is similar: the director of
Thérèse Raquin follows Zola, the author of the book, in naturalistic
stressing of details of the décor and in outlining the stifling, oppressive atmosphere and the dominating role of instincts.

   Thérèse, a niece of Madame Raquin, a Paris shopkeeper,
marries, without love, the old woman's feeble son, Camil. Then
Camil's friend becomes Thérèse's lover; they together drown the
husband and represent the crime as an accident. The lovers now
get married, to the mother's delight, but tormented by remorse
finally confess to the crime. When Madame Raquin writes the letter informing the police, Thérèse and Laurent commit suicide. The
style of the film seems to have been influenced by the spiritual
mood in the country where it was made: it bears distinct traces of
the Kammerspiel with its gloomy penumbra, its tendency to symbolism (a goldfish circling inside the aquarium symbolizes the anxiety and boredom of the heroine's married life), its pessimistic
vision of the self-destruction of man by ungovernable inner compul-
sions. But Thérèse Raquin is far from any psychological clichés
and does not set out to prove forcibly a point assumed a priori.

   The main components of Feyder's drama are atmosphere and
penetrating psychological observation; the director avoided cheap effects, and using simple fine accessories created one of the most
perfect chamber dramas of the silent cinema.

THE ITALIAN STRAW HAT (Un Chapeau de Paille d'Italie) René
   Clair

Script: Clair, from the play by Eugène Labiche and Marc Michel.
Photography: Maurice Desfassiaux and Nicolas Roudakoff. Art Direction: Lazare Meerson. Cast: Albert Préjean (Fadinard, the
bridegroom), Olga Tschechowa (Anaïs de Beauperthuis), Marise
Maïa (Bride), Yvonneck (Nonancourt, her father), Alice Tissot
(Cousin), Alex Bondi (Her husband), Pré Fils (Bobin), Vital Gey-
mond (Lieutenant Tavernier), Paul Olivier (Deaf Uncle Vésinet),
Alex Allin (Félix, a servant), Volbert (Mayor), Jim Gérald (Beauperthuis), Alexandrov (Valet), Valentine Tessier (Customer).

Films Albatros, France. 6800 ft.

"At its present stage of development the cinema cannot remain a
visual art and at the same time express thought": in accordance
with his words, Clair opposed stilted literary conventions of film-
making and already appeared, in Paris qui dort (1923), his first
work, as an enthusiast of dynamic movement on the screen. How
perfidious fate turned out to be! The directors of the Nouvelle
Vague who in the late 50's revolutionized the principles of cinematic
narration, blended exactly these conventional literary means of expression with new formal propositions and it was Clair himself, the
master of the "old" French cinema, whom they censured most for
the triviality of his plots and for the scrupulous contriving of his
scripts at the desk.

       But it was only 1927; Clair in his sixth film transported to
the screen a somewhat stale mid-19th-century boulevard vaudeville,
and did it with admirable lightness and originality. He transposed
the plot to turn-of-the-century Paris, thereby making the costumes
and the whole milieu ridiculous (25-year-old clothes always seem
comical, not being old enough to become fashionable again; look at
the clothes in the films of the late 50's!); parodied the theatrical
idiom of the plot, and solved the problem of dialogues, always
present in silent films, by replacing them with mimed, balletic conventions.

       Clair distinctly improved upon Labiche's ideas, made the
plot clearer, and piled the screen adventures around the search for
a duplicate of a Florentine straw hat eaten by a horse. When Fadinard, about to be married, drives through a forest in a coach,
his horse eats a hat fixed to a tree. Madame Beauperthuis, to
whom the hat belonged and who was there at a tryst with her hussar
captain lover, dares not to come back without it for fear of her
jealous husband. The lovers stay at the bridegroom's home and exhort him to find a replacement for the hat. Unknowingly Fadinard

tells the story to the cuckolded husband himself. But before it
comes to a duel, it turns out that a deaf uncle has bought an identical hat as a wedding present, and so everything ends well. The
two basic comical situations in the film are the opening scene in
the forest and the adventures of the uncle who is deaf as a post.

As a result of Clair's efforts, a shallow comedy is transformed on the screen into a parody of a vaudeville, delightful in its
rhythm and lightness of touch (note the famous quadrille of the lan-
ciers), but also full of biting anti-bourgeois satire. There are visible influences of Surrealism, of which Clair's famous short Entr'acte
(1924) was the fullest expression. The success of the film was enormous and not only in France but abroad; Clair acquired the leading
position in the film world that was to be his for thirty years. Hardly any film director has enjoyed as much.

UNDERWORLD   Josef von Sternberg

Script: Robert N. Lee and Charles Furthman, based on a project
by Ben Hecht. Photography: Bert Glennon. Cast: George Bancroft ("Bull" Weed), Evelyn Brent ("Feathers" McCoy), Clive Brook
("Rolls Royce"), Larry Semon ("Slippy" Lewis), Fred Kohler (Buck
Mulligan), Helen Lynch (His girl), Jerry Mandy (Paloma).

Famous Players-Lasky/Paramount, U.S.A. 8 reels, 7643 ft.

Underworld was an impressive start to a series of American gangster films, and a turning point in the career of Josef von Sternberg.
Viennese by origin, and having for eleven years patiently climbed the
steps of a film career in Hollywood, Sternberg made his debut with
Salvation Hunters (1925)--in his own opinion the only sincere work of
art in his entire career, and the only one which bears his directional
credo. Experimental, semi-amateur and produced for next to nothing, this symbolic drama was influenced by the German Kammerspiel and attracted critical attention by its interesting formal aspect.
Sternberg seemed to be on the way to success and was given the direction of further films. But his interests were not understood;
Sternberg took on inappropriate scripts and as a result his following
two films (one was taken over by another director) were failures.

It was only Hecht's scenario for Underworld which allowed
Sternberg to display the fullness of his talent. Bull Weed, a tough
but generous and sentimental gangster, kills a rival and is imprisoned. Feathers, his girlfriend and Rolls Royce, his drunken lawyer
protégé, try to organize his escape, but the plan misfires. Thinking he was betrayed, Bull escapes all the same. When his friends
join him the police mount a siege. Seeing that they are in love and

that they are still loyal to him, Bull understands and tells them to
go away before he dies from police bullets. Underworld is at once
a sensational picture, faultlessly composed and finely told and an intelligent psychological sketch, containing convincing portraits of the
underworld protagonists. The motif of a criminal besieged by the
police was to appear again and again in the cinema (Marcel Carné).

Sternberg was not interested in action as such, as were the
directors of crime films before him; neither did he follow the sociological causes of crime as would be done by the "gangster series"
proper that started with Little Caesar. He was primarily a psychologist. The cinema of passions, the cinema of problems and
moral dilemmas is in Underworld also the cinema of formal brilliance and great visual power. The formal aspect was, as a matter of fact, the most important to the director: Sternberg created
"moving paintings," excellently handled the composition of the photography and its Expressionist chiaroscuro, used significant details
which increase suggestiveness and build up the atmosphere of the
film's interiors, and expertly distributed the elements of stability
and motion in the frame. Many shots are striking: the fluorescent
fogs, the sun's rays which steal into the dusty flat where Bull barricades himself from the police; the white feathers in shabby, dusty
rooms give the story a touch of desperate poetry.

Sternberg was an able student of Griffith in narrative style,
and added a talent for brief, incisive storytelling to the list of
achievements of the American school of film editing (note the succinct description of the raid on the jeweler's shop). But he could
not free his films of pollution from melodrama: in Underworld this
fault disappeared in the rapid flow of the story, but in a few years
it would reappear and cause Sternberg's downfall.

BED AND SOFA (Tretya Meshchanskaya) [Three Sharing]   Abram
    Room

Script: Victor Shklovsky and Room. Photography: Grigori Gibyer.
Cast: Nikolai Batalov (Kolya, the husband), Ludmila Semyonova
(Ludmila, the wife), Vladimir Fogel (Volodya, the friend), L.
Yureniev, E. Sokolova.

Sovkino, U.S.S.R.   6644 ft.

A marital triangle: a theme which nearly always leads to the banal
in cinema. But not in this case. Room's film is very strongly set
in the reality of the Moscow of the 20's and is original from the
point of view of the plot and the psychology. In addition it is a
faithful mirror of the customs and thought of the times. A husband

goes on a trip and leaves his wife in the charge of a friend.   The
friend takes her to the movies, for an aeroplane trip and finally becomes her lover.   The husband returns, learns what has happened
and resigns himself to sleeping on the sofa while the lover shares
the marital bed with his wife.   The two men team up in bullying the
girl.   She becomes pregnant but they both deny responsibility.   So,
having declined an abortion, she leaves them both.

Bed and Sofa touches problems which coincide with Women's
Liberation, discussions on abortion and woman's role in society.
The film was scripted by Shklovsky, the distinguished Russian
literary critic, and its plot is said to have been based on details
of the private life of the great revolutionary poet Vladimir Mayakovsky.   Great merit lies in the method of execution: the small room
in which the story develops copies an average big-city living room
during the housing shortage, and the street scenes are authentic.
Bed and Sofa is a reminder that the hidden camera method was not
introduced by the Nouvelle Vague in the 50's, but by the Soviet documentary and later feature film, and in the silent period.   In the real
scenery the people are also real, and the observation of reactions
and attitudes is intimate, penetrating and excellent.

Room, who had made himself known the previous year with
Death Bay (1926), related the surprising adventures of his protagonists in a tone half-serious, half-satirical; already the original title
of the film (meaning "Third Bourgeois Street") was a joke.   This
ambivalence of the mood of the film corresponded very well with the
peculiar conglomerate of customs and behavior in a society then in
the process of creation, a society whose social relationships had so
recently been overturned.

THE LOVE OF JEANNE NEY (Die Liebe der Jeanne Ney)   Georg
    Wilhelm Pabst

Script: Ladislaus Vajda and Rudolf Leonhardt, based on the novel
by Ilya Ehrenburg. Photography: Fritz Arno Wagner and Walter
Robert Lach. Cast: Edith Jeanne (Jeanne Ney), Brigitte Helm
(Young blind girl), Hertha von Walther (Coach), Uno Henning (Andreas), Fritz Rasp (Kalibiev), Wladimir Sokoloff (Bolshevik friend).

UFA, Germany. 6 reels, 8671 ft.

After the brutally realistic The Joyless Street, Pabst made an excursion into the realm of psychoanalytical drama.   Secrets of a
Soul (1926) was a feature-film lecture on the theories of Freud, in
which the director had a lively interest.   Yet it is not a remarkable
achievement; the film is formally original (visually it is based on

multiple exposure), but as a whole was a naive attempt at translating the language of science into the language of cinema.

Pabst's next serious essay was the screen version of a novel
whose action takes place during the Soviet Civil War, a story of the
love of a French girl and a young Russian Communist, set in the
Crimea and in Paris. This extraordinary screen adaptation, which
seriously changed the sense and the ending of the novel, aroused
Ehrenburg's protests. But even though, as the result of the adaptation process, the script was loaded with psychological nonsense additionally aggravated by Pabstian melodramatics, the director shot
this script respecting completely his principle of fidelity to the
milieu. This meant realism in the description of the Soviet Rus-
sians--to Westerners of 1927 a real novelty--and, more importantly,
care for the authenticity of the scenery. The major part of the outdoor scenes was shot using a mobile hand-held camera, and the realistic touch so obtained was enhanced by the imaginative editing.
Even the shortest scene consists of a multiplicity of shots taken
from different angles, joined in a perfectly fluid way and creating
the impression of a completely three-dimensional observation.

Pabst employed in this film the fruits of Pudovkin's formal
experiments. He also used, though with lesser success, the narrative American editing technique. In both cases however, he enriched the experiences of others by his own impressive ideas: his
future films would all be masterly pieces of film-making, although
Pabst was to achieve maturity of content only with the arrival of the
sound era.

THE CIRCUS   Charles Chaplin

Script: Chaplin. Photography: Rollie Totheroh. Cast: Charles
Chaplin (Charlie the Tramp), Allan Garcia (Circus proprietor),
Merna Kennedy (His stepdaughter, an equestrienne), Harry Crocker
(Rex, king of the high wire), Betty Morissey (Vanishing lady),
George Davis (Conjurer), Henry Bergman (Old clown), Steve Murphy
(Pickpocket), Stanley Sanford (Ringmaster), John Rand (His assistant),
Doc Stone (Prizefighter).

United Artists, U.S.A. 7 reels, 7032 ft.

The period after making The Gold Rush was one of the most difficult
in Chaplin's life. Entangled in the vicissitudes of his private life,
which for many months was known to the public, he was from all
directions attacked for his beliefs and supposed immorality. The
director passed through a mental low and, not surprisingly, could
not be an optimistic joker. The Circus is the story of a tramp who

is unjustly suspected of theft and takes refuge in a circus. He accidentally runs onto the arena, delights the public and is hired as a
clown. But he soon ceases to be funny and has to do menial jobs.
He falls in love with a beautiful equestrienne, but she prefers the
handsome high-wire artist. The circus leaves and Charlie is alone
in an empty arena. Litter is the only trace of dashed dreams.
Charlie looks at a paper star on the floor, kicks it aside with
resignation and walks away.

The Circus is the weakest (and saddest) picture in Chaplin's
mature period. But it is not a failure; among its best parts are
the particularly touching, bitter finale and the starting sequence of
the chase of Charlie, a policeman and a thief--the richest in gags.
One of the comic situations is brilliant: Charlie and a thief hide
from pursuit as moving figures on a circus Aunt Sally stall. There
is a scene in this sequence too which was undoubtedly an inspiration
for the culminating scene of Welles' The Lady from Shanghai--the
game of hide-and-seek in the hall of mirrors.

The strongest asset of The Circus is Chaplin's role--in all
probability his greatest achievement as an actor.

THE FORTY-FIRST (Sorok Pervyi)   Yakov Protazanov

Script: Boris Lavrenyov and Boris Leonidov, from the story by the
former. Photography: Pyotr Yermolov. Cast: Ada Voytsik
(Mariutka), Ivan Koval-Samborsky (Govorukha-Otrok), Ivan Strauch
(Comissar Yevsukov).

Mezhrabpom-Russ, U.S.S.R. 6184 ft.

The first of two famous screen adaptations of the short story about
the Red Guard girl who fell in love with the wounded counter-revolu-
tionary officer entrusted to her care. Nowadays Protazanov's film
finds itself in an astonishing situation with respect to Chukhrai's
adaptation, made 29 years later. Namely, it turns out to be externally much more faithful to what it describes than the later film,
in spite of being directed by the most eclectic (although still one of
the best) of the first generation of Russian film-makers, who in the
20's found themselves under fire for their "traditionalism" and
"bourgeois mentality."

On the other hand, Chukhrai's The Forty-First (made in
1956) was the first harbinger of the rejuvenated post-Stalinist Soviet
cinema which tried to break out of the shackles of schematic and
propagandist morbidity. Why does the first, silent version seem to

be more true?   Certainly because its substance is rawer and closer
to being documentary cinema; perhaps also because it was made
closer in time to the events it describes.   It has none of the future
mythology of the revolutionary heroes which developed during the
30's with the films about Chapayev and Maxim.

It is equally true to say that the director's role in the 1927
Forty-First was only that of a skillful craftsman.   Yet the film is
something more than an illustration of the story with pictures: it
compensates for the lack of psychological characterization of the
protagonists (which are nevertheless drawn quite convincingly) by
rich and precise observation of their background.   This is especially
evident in such sequences as the crossing of the Kara-Kum desert
or the bivouac in the Turkmenian village.

The director intelligently used some of the achievements of
the Soviet avant-garde cinema and built the natural climate of the
film on the foundation of technical skill fortified by the use of attractive scenery.

EN RADE   Alberto Cavalcanti

Script: Cavalcanti and Claude Heymann.   Photography: James
Rogers.   Art Direction: Erik Aess.   Cast: Catherine Hessling
(Kitchen maid), Nathalie Lissenko (Laundress), Georges Charlia
(Her son), Tommy Bourdel (Dock hand), Philippe Hériat (The Idiot,
once a sailor).

Editions Pierre Braunberger, France.   6420 ft.

A poetic Impressionist film, summing up the formal achievements
of the silent French avant-garde, En Rade is one of the classical
expressions in the cinema of the motif of waterfront cafés and hopeless desires to escape.   It provided the link connecting both the
short Fièvre (1921) by Delluc, the avant-garde's theoretician, and
Epstein's Coeur fidèle with the later Quai des Brumes, in which the
motif would return with new strength in the new style of Poetic Realism.

En Rade, the film by Cavalcanti, a roving Brazilian director,
is devoted entirely to those quay-side yearnings.   It starts with the
motto "The call of the sea--nostalgia" and tells of the romantic
plans of a boy from Marseilles and a little waitress.   These plans
of escape towards the Happy Islands are blighted, of course; brutal
reality fills the heroine with distrust and makes her draw back with
fear before the fulfillment of the vision of happiness.

The softening lens was used here to provide a visual key for
expressing the world of dreams and was of basic importance in creating the mood of the film. En Rade was to find an interesting
parallel, both in the theme and style, in Sternberg's American The
Docks of New York (1928).

SEVENTH HEAVEN   Frank Borzage

Script: Benjamin Glazer, based on the play by John Golden. Pho-
tography: Ernest G. Palmer. Cast: Janet Gaynor (Diane),
Charles Farrell (Chico), Ben Bard (Brissac), David Butler (Gobin),
Albert Gran (Boul), Gladys Brockwell (Nana), Emile Chautard (Père
Chevillon), George Stone (Sewer Rat), Jessie Harlett (Aunt Valentine
Vulmir), Lillian West (Arlette), Marie Mosquini (Madame Gobin).

Fox Films Corporation, U.S.A.   9 reels, 8500 ft.

Seventh Heaven is an archetypal Hollywood romance. Although the
setting is Paris during the First World War, the French capital is
shown in the soft colors of Victor Hugo's mid-19th-century novels.
A poor but honest girl, tormented by her horrible sister, is in love
with a street cleaner. Their idyll is broken when he is called up
for the army. The war ends but during the armistice celebrations
she learns that he has been killed. The girl refuses to believe this
and her instinct is right: although blinded, he does come back.
The story is shown with plenty of sentimentality but the director obviously kept some distance from the story and did not treat it with
deadpan seriousness. A certain disarmingly naive charm, in fact,
saves the film from ridicule.

Seventh Heaven was made entirely in the studio, which often
resulted in bad continuity (compare the ascent and descent of the
stairs--different each time!), and the supporting cast tended to
overact. The main protagonists however, did quite well: they later
became a very popular "ideal couple" and were starring as a love
team for over seven years. They appear, separately, in two of
Murnau's American films--Janet Gaynor is the heroine of the great
Sunrise. A curious aspect of the film are the dialogues: the cast
of this silent American production is obviously speaking French!

1928

STORM OVER ASIA (Potomok Chingiskhana) [The Heir to Genghis-Khan] Vsevolod Pudovkin

---

Script: Osip Brik, from the story by Ivan Novokshonov. Photography: Anatoli Golovnya. Cast: Valeri Inkizhinov (Bair, a Mongol hunter), A. Dedintsev (Commander of the occupation forces), Paulina Belinskaya (His wife), Anna Sudakevich (His daughter), F. Ivanov (Lama), V. Tzoppi (Smith, agent for fur company), A. P. Chistyakov (Commander of a partisan detachment), Vladimir Pro (Missionary scholar), K. Gurnyak (English soldier with leggings), Boris Barnet (English soldier with cat), I. Inkizhinov (Bair's father).

Mezhrabpomfilm, U.S.S.R. 10,144 ft.

The inner transformation of the individual, the main motif of Pudovkin's work in his golden period, is this time illustrated by a young Mongolian boy, Bair, who from a primitive nomadic hunter metamorphoses into a national leader in the fight against the British colonialists. Father sends Bair to the market in town to sell a fine fox skin. Bair wounds a dishonest English fur dealer and takes refuge with a guerrilla detachment. During a skirmish with the British he is taken prisoner and sentenced to death. Before the execution a document is found inside Bair's amulet according to which the boy is the heir of Genghis Khan; the British make him the "ruler of Mongolia." During the celebration banquet Bair notices one of the ladies wearing his fox skin. He will not be the pawn of the occupying forces and as the symbolic storm starts, escapes through the window to lead the fight against them.

The plot of Storm Over Asia was developed with much more clarity than The End of St. Petersburg (or even Mother); Pudovkin directed the film with much lightness and ease--perhaps because of

the lower specific gravity of the content. The dynamic story, which
is in principle a sensational drama, was an excellent opportunity for
the employment of Pudovkinian editing and its rhythmical properties
are much more prominently apparent than in the previous films.
The construction of many episodes was based entirely on the pulsating movement of the frames (the launching of the chase after the
incident in the market, the preparation for the celebrations in the
monastery, the dance of the monks, the epilogue). The photography
was no less perfect. Golovnya faultlessly exploited the possibilities
afforded by the attractive locale.

   In the final analysis, Storm Over Asia with its clarity and
fine content, is one of the most perfect examples of the formal
beauty of a silent film. It was, unfortunately, the last great work
of its maker: Pudovkin was not to achieve such scale of expression
again. The appearance of Storm Over Asia in England provoked
questions in Parliament and a general uproar--the uniforms of what
was assumed to be the "White" army "were discovered to be British!"

THE WIND   Victor Sjöström

Script: Frances Marion and John Colton, from the novel by Dorothy
Scarborough. Photography: John Arnold. Cast: Lillian Gish (Let-
ty), Lars Hanson (Lige), Montagu Love (Roddy), Dorothy Cumming
(Cora), Edward Earle (Beverly), William Orlamond (Sourdough), Laon
Ramon, Carmencita Johnson and Billy Kent Schaefer (Cora's children).

MGM, U.S.A. 8 reels, 6824 ft.

Mojave, the sandy wilderness of Arizona: unfriendly landscape,
crude people. In such surroundings lives a frail girl who cannot
communicate with the relatives who look after her. She escapes
from them and marries a farmhand whom she does not love. She
has a home. But she has no peace. Aggressive nature exerts a
destructive influence over the people, pushes them to brutality and
violence and predetermines their fate. The girl has to kill in self-
defense and buries the corpse. In vain: the sand is ceaselessly
blown by the wind--the wind which appears in this scenery as the
only master, and which becomes for the director the key motif, an
almost inestimably valuable dramatic element.

   Lillian Gish never played a better role; Sjöström, who opened
his great career with the open spaces of A Man There Was, now
closed it with this excellent drama set in the deserts of America.
After The Wind he would direct three unimportant films, and would
still later divide his time between working as artistic advisor to a
Swedish film company and occasional acting assignments. (The best

of them was when Sjöström was 78: his famous role as Professor
Isak Borg in Bergman's <u>Wild Strawberries</u> brought his name back
from obscurity shortly before his death.)

THE CROWD   King Vidor

Script: Vidor, John V. A. Weaver and Harry Behn. Photography:
Henry Sharp. Cast: Eleanor Boardman (Mary Sims), James Mur-
ray (John Sims), Bert Roach (Bert), Estelle Clark (Jane), Daniel G.
Tomlinson (Jim), Lucy Beaumont (Mother), Dell Henderson (Dick),
Freddie Burke Frederick (Junior), Alice Mildred Puter (Daughter).

MGM, U.S.A.   9 reels, 8957 ft.

Everyday urban America: a story of an average man, one of the
cogs in the machine of Industrial Civilization. John is a petty clerk
in a huge New York company. He meets a girl, marries her, they
have two children. The daughter is run over by a car; John, overwhelmed with grief, loses his concentration at work and is sacked.
It is difficult to find another job; his wife decides to leave him after
a quarrel. Then John wins a couple of dollars in a competition for
an advertising slogan, and the whole family enjoys an evening together.

     <u>The Crowd</u> is a faithful description of the milieu it focuses
upon; as a film it has a distinct affinity with the future Neorealist
style--and at the same time is the first great epic of 20th-century
alienation.   The scene in which the desperate father pleads with the
crowd to keep quiet after the death of his child acquires the rank of
a powerful symbol. With <u>The Crowd</u> Vidor went counter to the then
current intoxication with the joys of the Jazz Era, zealously cultivated by almost all his Hollywood colleagues. He was sober and
bitter, yet did not touch on the strings of fatalism and, as in <u>The
Big Parade</u>, avoided taking an openly critical stance.

     The inner strength of <u>The Crowd</u> results not only from the
story itself, but also from the perfection of its conveyance. Vidor's
picture is one of the best examples of precise, mature language in
the silent cinema. In it, American and European experience in
film-making were harmoniously blended. The passage from direct
realist observation to the generalizing metaphor about a modern society was based on the achievements of German Expressionism, both
spiritually (the Kammerspiel) and technically (as in the famous tracking shot from street level to an upper floor in an office block, which
resembles the sweeping pans of <u>The Last Laugh</u>). But these foreign
models were only the starting point for a picture which cannot easily
be classified, other than as a fine and independent work.

THE FALL OF THE HOUSE OF USHER (La Chute de la maison
    Usher) Jean Epstein

Script: Epstein, from two stories by Edgar Allan Poe--"The Fall
of the House of Usher" and "The Oval Portrait." Assistant Director:
Luis Buñuel. Photography: Georges Lucas, assisted by Jean Lucas.
Art Direction: Pierre Kefer. Cast: Jean Debucourt (Roderick
Usher), Marguerite Abel-Gance (Madeline Usher), Charles Lamy
(Guest).

Jean Epstein Films, France. 4921 ft.

A poetic horror film--the most outstanding achievement of this genre
in cinema history. Epstein, after several years of experiments interspersed with commercial pictures, summed up his investigations
of the means of expression of avant-garde Impressionism--which
makes The Fall of the House of Usher a sort of anthology of the
language of the pre-sound French school. The scenario of the film,
based on the plot by the master of the fantastic short story, tells
of a curious drama in an aristocratic English family: the young
Lord, painting his wife's portrait, finds to his horror that, as the
work progresses, life correspondingly drains from his Lady. But
the painting must be finished, the family tradition demands it....

    The mood of the scenery in which the story takes place is
achieved by an exemplary employment of both natural means and
technical expertise. Epstein shot the location sequences of the film
in the gloomy autumn landscape of the marshy Sologne country. He
consistently stressed such elements of design as the candles in the
huge, empty rooms of the castle. The camera work employed
mostly lazy tracking and panning shots, and introduced a magnificent
scale of variable lighting. The key role rests with multiple exposure, and trick and slow-motion photography: the whirling leaves,
the pendulum of a clock, books falling out of shelves by themselves,
phantom candles accompanying the funeral cortège. These elements
have combined to produce an unrepeatable, elegiac film.

PANDORA'S BOX (Die Büchse der Pandora) Georg Wilhelm Pabst

Script: Ladislaus Vajda and Joseph R. Fliesler, after two plays--
"Erdgeist" (1893) and "Die Büchse der Pandora" (1904), by Frank
Wedekind. Photography: Günther Krampf. Cast: Louise Brooks
(Lulu), Fritz Kortner (Dr. Peter Schön), Franz Lederer (Alva Schön,

his son), Carl Goetz (Papa Brommer), Krafft Raschig (Rodrigo
Quast), Alice Roberts (Countess Anna Geschwitz), Daisy d'Ora
(Peter Schön's fiancée), Michael von Newlinsky (Marquis Casti-
Piani), Siegfried Arno (Stage manager), Gustav Diessl (Jack the
Ripper).

Nero-Film AG, Germany.   8 reels, 10,676 ft.

Pandora's Box is the film in which Pabst came closest to his ideal
of deriving mood from the external layer of the portrayed reality,
not forcing it on the spectator by stylization and deformation.   That
this is so is perhaps because the story of Pandora's Box is so unimportant compared with the atmosphere of the film--and certainly
because the main role was played by Louise Brooks.   The 22-year-
old American dancer, who shone only in Pabst's films, was exactly
like the girl Wedekind described: a messenger of fascinating sensuality, leading all around her to disaster.

        Lulu, a cabaret dancer, makes her lover break his engage-
ment to the daughter of the Minister of the Interior, and marry her
instead.   During the night after the wedding, her husband asks her
to shoot him.   Lulu is accused of murder but escapes from court.
She casts her spell upon the dead man's son and travels abroad with
him.   She narrowly avoids being sold to a harem and later becomes
a prostitute in London where she ends up as a victim of Jack the
Ripper.

        Actress Brooks dominates the whole of the picture, leveling
out the imperfections of the plot which push the film towards abstract, primitive symbolism.   But it was above all the film-making
which decided the atmosphere and the rank of Pandora's Box: that
is, the excellent composition of the photography, strongly Expressionist through its contrasting use of light and the three-dimension-
ality of the cinematic space, created--as in the theatre of Max Rein-
hardt--by lighting the deep background.

LONESOME   Pál Fejös

Script: Edward T. Lowe Jr. and Tom Reed, from a story by
Mann Page.   Photography: Gilbert Warrenton.   Cast: Barbara
Kent (Mary),   Glenn Tryon (John),   Fay Holderness (Overdressed
woman), Gustav Partos (Romantic gentleman), Eddie Phillips (The
Sport).

Universal, U.S.A.   6785 ft.   Talking sequence and sound effects.

A protest against the dehumanizing force of modern life, a defense
of the identity of an individual lost in the crowd. What King Vidor's
The Crowd showed in the sphere of a social drama, Lonesome does
within the convention of the lyrical cinema. The protagonists are a
telephone operator and a mechanic, lonely in the anthill of New York.
They meet by accident at Coney Island amusement park and are
separated before they have time to exchange names or addresses.
Fate rectifies the mishap after they have lost hope of finding each
other: they live in the same tenement. From this moment perhaps, their lives will take on more color. A simple story, related
with subtlety, humor, and above all, truth. Lonesome is both a
love sonnet and a sociological document, uncommon in the American
cinema at the time.

LES DEUX TIMIDES   René Clair

Script: Clair, based on a one-act comedy by Eugène Labiche and
Marc Michel. Photography: Robert Batton and Nicolas Roudakoff.
Art Direction: Lazare Meerson. Cast: Maurice de Féraudy (Thi-
baudier), Pierre Batcheff (Frémissin), Vera Flory (Cécile Thi-
baudier), Jim Gérald (Garadoux), Françoise Rosay (Frémissin's
aunt).

Films Albatros/Sequana, France.   5668 ft.

Les Deux timides is Clair's second screen adaptation of a stage
vaudeville (written by the same authors, Labiche and Michel) and
his second success. Even though the picture may be less spectacular
than The Italian Straw Hat, it is bolder and qualitatively even better.
Les Deux timides is a comedy of manners and tells of the efforts of
a young lawyer to secure the hand of a girl of good family in competition with another suitor, his brash and repugnant sometime client.
The girl's father is sympathetically inclined to the lawyer but, alas,
cannot make his position clear to the other suitor.

The style of the film refers to the Max Linder tradition and
also to the spirit which pervades The Gold Rush. The balletic
quality of The Italian Straw Hat is here partly replaced by the Chaplinesque human warmth. There is also an abundance of the technical
tricks Clair was always very fond of. As the young lawyer delivers
his defending speech, the camera does not show the speaker but illustrates the content of the argument. When he gets confused and
eventually mistakes the beginning for the end, the camera follows
suit: the pictures stumble, stop, only to rush forward as the thread
of argument is picked up; at one stage the action is shown back to
front.

Clair split the frame in two several times, for instance to show what the rivals plan to do to each other.   Among the gags unstintingly supplied by the director one must distinguish those which can be described as acoustic without the sound: the explosions of children's firecrackers, the servant putting her fingers in her ears, the backfiring of a car engine.   While some film-makers, such as Keaton and Chaplin, felt very well in the silent world, the universal and agile Clair was visibly limited by it.

CROSSWAYS (Jūji-ro)   Teinosuke Kinugasa

Script: Kinugasa. Photography: Kohei Sugiyama. Art Direction: Bonji Taira. Cast: Junosuke Bando (Rikiya), Akiko Chihaya (Okiku, his sister), Yukiko Ogawa (O-ume), J. Soma (False policeman).

Kinugasa Productions/Shochiku, Japan.   5841 ft.

Kinugasa began his career in films as a female impersonator. When women were no longer forbidden to appear in films, he took to direction and established, with little money, his own company, Kinugasa Motion Picture League.   His first production, the avantgarde A Page of Madness (1926), was a commercial failure and, in order to pay his debts, Kinugasa was forced to make commercial films for a while before he could return to his ambitious search for the essence of the cinema.   Crossways, a film made with exceptional care and refinement, well reflects the director's own depressed mood at that period.

The story of this--as Kinugasa called it--"samurai film without duels" is set in the 18th century in the Yoshiwara entertainment quarter of Tokyo.   Rikiya, a young man infatuated with a geisha called O-ume, believes he has killed his rival at an archery ground. He flees, wounded, to his sister Okiku who tries to help him. Okiku attempts to enlist the help of a false policeman but has to kill him in self-defense when he tries to rape her.   It is now she who needs help and protection from the law.   Tempted to see O-ume again, the weak and delirious Rikiya dies from shock on seeing his supposed victim, and his sister in vain waits for him at the crossroads.

Although the film is ostensibly part of the traditional samurai historical genre, called jindai-geki, it is in fact quite unusual for the Japanese cinema of the 20's: the protagonists are presented as earthy creatures and the young samurai is not a haughty and immaculate hero, but a man suffering and haunted by mental breakdown.   The formal aspect of Crossways is even more distant from the national Japanese convention.   It was mostly shot from the point

of view of the hero and has a free time structure that dispenses
with the chronology of events in order to create the feel of the confused memories and hallucinations of a wounded man.

Kinugasa worked only at night and had the sets painted a
deep grey, creating a genuine "symphony in grey." The mood of
drabness and depression is stressed by the low-key photography.
The overall effect was compared by the director himself to a drawing in Chinese ink. The editing, which operates with short simple
shots and often uses suggestive detail (like the take of a cat being
attracted by the blood in Rikiya's wounds), shows clearly the influence of the Soviet cinema and its "analytical montage." There is
also some Expressionist montage (in the scenes of hallucinations)
which reminds one of similar effects in Pabst's Secrets of a Soul
(1926).

Kinugasa's excellent feel for the essence of the cinema allowed him to create the most outstanding Japanese film of the silent
era. Contrary to common belief it was not the much later Rashomon, but Crossways which marked the European discovery of the
Japanese cinema--a discovery that was unfortunately later forgotten.
Still, Crossways is the only early Japanese film widely known in the
West. This is in all probability due to the fact that the only print
of the film in existence was the one Kinugasa left in Britain, in the
National Film Archive, in 1930 while on "sales tour" of Europe.
By the late 60's the director had made over 100 films. He became
famous again in the 50's for his brilliant use of color, particularly
in two films--Gate of Hell (1953) and The White Heron.

THE DOCKS OF NEW YORK   Josef von Sternberg

Script: Jules Furthman, suggested by "The Dockwalloper," by John
Monk Saunders. Photography: Harold Rosson. Cast: George Ban-
croft (Bill Roberts), Betty Compson (Sadie), Olga Baclanova (Lou),
Clyde Cook ("Sugar" Steve), Mitchell Lewis (Third Engineer), Gustav
von Seyffertitz ("Hymn Book" Harry), Lillian Worth (Steve's girl),
Guy Oliver (The Crimp), May Foster (Mrs. Crimp).

Famous Players-Lasky/Paramount, U.S.A. 8 reels, 7202 ft.

The Docks of New York is the last part of Sternberg's trilogy of
the underworld of which the first part was Underworld and the middle part (and the weakest)--The Drag Net (1928). It is a story of
two failed people. A coal stoker rescues a girl from drowning and
marries her as a joke. He is about to leave her the next morning
when his conscience awakens and he returns to save the girl from a
false charge of murder. When she is later accused of possessing

stolen clothing he confesses to the crime and serves 60 days in prison for her sake. The girl promises to wait for him.

The pictorial richness of the interiors in the earlier Underworld was in this film achieved, with equal success, out of doors. The painterly, soft-focus treatment of the urban scenery, the use of atmospheric phenomena for visual ends (foggy quays, glistening wet streets) and the fine Expressionist manipulation of the lighting gave the picture the most perfect visual form in all of Sternberg's work and created a suggestive atmosphere of tension, of a scuffle with fate. The dramatic intensity of this story from the lower depths of New York is even higher than in Underworld. Sternberg draws the colorful characters with sympathy and skill and well contrasts the fragility of Betty Compson with the brutal strength of George Bancroft.

The close-knitting of the photography and the psychology of the characters made The Docks of New York one of the most narratively precise films of the dusk of the silent period and foreshadowed the brilliant The Blue Angel. The film, although rather underestimated at the time (partly because it was released in the same week as the Al Jolson talkie), exerted nonetheless a considerable influence on the cinema, particularly on the French Poetic Realist films, similar in theme (quay-side was their chief motif), mood and pictorial form.

STEAMBOAT BILL JR.   Charles F. Reisner

Script: Carl Harbaugh. Photography: J. Devereux Jennings and Bert Haines. Cast: Buster Keaton (Willie), Ernest Torrence (Steamboat Bill), Tom Lewis (His mate), Tom McGuire (King), Marion Byron (His daughter), Joe Keaton (Barber).

Buster Keaton Productions Inc., U.S.A. 7 reels, 6400 ft.

While lesser screen comics put most stress on the cinematic technique, the great ones, Chaplin and Keaton, rely mainly (perhaps conventionally) on the plot. The stories of the unperturbed victim of inanimate objects are often complex almost to absurdity. "Romeo and Juliet" à la Buster Keaton: Romeo-Willie is the son of the owner of a well-worn steam packet; Juliet--the daughter of a banker who also has a boat, but smarter and more modern.

The parents are (of course) rivals, and the feeling between their children does not make the situation easier. Willie's father, a simple and intolerant man, has in fact a grudge against his son, not only because of his beloved, but also because of the eccentric clothes in which he arrives home after studying in Boston: a beret, a moustache and a ukulele to boot!

Steamboat Bill, as a man who respects work, decides to make an expert sailor out of his son. And he could even have been successful, and his son's romance wrecked, if life had not given Willie a chance to display bravado and industriousness. In the culminating scene of the cyclone, photographed with a mobile camera and based, as a matter of fact, on an episode from Keaton's childhood, the brave sailor not only saves the lives of his kin (including his future father-in-law), but is even able, in the surrealist finale, to find under water the pastor needed for solemnizing his marriage!

QUEEN KELLY   Erich von Stroheim

Script: Stroheim. Photography: Ben Reynolds, Gordon Pollock and Paul Ivano. Art Direction: Robert Day and Stroheim. Cast: Gloria Swanson (Patricia Kelly, an orphan), Walter Byron (Prince "Wild" Wolfram von Hohenberg Falsenstein), Seena Owen (Queen Regina V, his cousin and fiancée), Sidney Bracey (Prince Wolfram's valet), William von Brincken (Adjutant to Prince Wolfram).

Joseph P. Kennedy, United Artists, U.S.A. 8 reels, 9843 ft. in the released version.

All Stroheim's films have something of a fairy tale about them, and Queen Kelly is a classical story of a little girl and a prince, set in the Kingdom of Kronberg--an imaginary country, but somehow recalling Hapsburg Austria. The heroes are a typical product of Stroheimian imagination; the plot, an obvious travesty of "The Merry Widow": Prince Wolfram, engaged to marry the Queen, meets a convent girl called Kelly while out riding. The Queen discovers the romance, whips Kelly out of the palace and arrests Wolfram. The girl unsuccessfully tries to drown herself.

Back in the convent there is a summoning telegram from her aunt, the proprietress of a brothel in German East Africa. Kelly marries a rich old degenerate (who quickly dies) and takes over her aunt's trade; her ways earn her the nickname of "Queen Kelly." Finally Wolfram goes to Dar-es-Salaam, marries Kelly and takes her back to Kronberg where she becomes his consort after the assassination of the Queen. Thus Kelly becomes queen after all.

The main dramatic device in the film is that of contrast. The opening scenes of Prince's riding excursion are pastoral and serene while the Palace scenes are full of suggestive sensuality and soft lights among which the near-naked Queen, wrapped in white fur

and carrying a kitten, lounges in her lavish bed decorated with a
row of cupids. In turn, the African sequence (incomplete in the released version, but some footage was recently found) has an aura of
vulgarity, corruption and dark passions.

Queen Kelly was Stroheim's swan song. After about a third
of the shooting production was stopped because of the director's disregard for budgetary limits and the arrival of the "sound revolution."
One of the greatest, but also one of the most undisciplined film-
makers with respect to his producers, Stroheim would after this be
only a great actor, gradually becoming synonymous with the part of
a Prussian officer. He played this standard role in 1936 in Renoir's
great La Grande illusion.

In 1950 Stroheim appeared beside his Queen Kelly heroine,
Gloria Swanson, in Billy Wilder's Sunset Boulevard. There he
played himself: a fallen angel, a film director who has become his
star's butler. This analogy is an absolutely fascinating commentary
on Stroheim's career, especially since Sunset Boulevard contains a
direct quote from Queen Kelly, the hypnotic scene of Kelly's prayer
in the candle-lit chapel. After Queen Kelly Stroheim directed, it
is true, one more film--Walking Down Broadway (1933), but it is
second rate.

After the break in production, Queen Kelly was finally assembled, thanks to the efforts of Gloria Swanson, by Josef von
Sternberg, who added titles and music as well as the ending in
which Kelly drowns, and Wolfram commits suicide beside her coffin.
Despite these intrusions, Queen Kelly remains the fullest manifestation of the cinema of Erich von Stroheim not constrained by either
the producers or, since the film was not released in the U.S.A.,
the censors. The film provides additional fuel for a discussion of
Stroheim's undoubted influence on Luis Buñuel. The parallel between Kelly and the American-Viennese heroines in Ophüls films is
also interesting.

Never in Stroheim's work had suggestive sexual symbolism
been used more extensively; the near-saturated atmosphere of sadistic sensuality is manifested even in the set designs and is, indeed, in places excessive. The whip-wielding Queen, sharply contrasted to the somewhat effeminate Prince, is the most drastically
portrayed sadistic heroine in the whole of the director's work. Yet
against this background Stroheim's intentions--the defense of genuine,
spontaneous feeling between two people in defiance of a degenerate
world of lust and hypocrisy--came out with even more prominence.

FINIS TERRAE   Jean Epstein

Script: Epstein. Photography: Joseph Barth and Joseph Kottula,
assisted by Louis Née and Raymond Tulle. Acted by the seaweed
collectors and fishermen of the islets in the Ouessantin archipelago.

Société Générale de Films, France. 6972 ft.

The same year in which Epstein made The Fall of the House of
Usher, his fullest work in the style of the "poetic avant-garde,"
witnessed a surprising (and final) turn in his development. Finis
Terrae is a para-documentary film shot in the islands off the Brittany coast. With it, he began his second creative period, completely different from the first. From then on Epstein would be making
simple films, but full of emotion, about the sea and the people living
from it.

Fascinated by the life of the inhabitants of the island of
Ouessant, some of whom he met during a trip to the Atlantic coast,
Epstein arrived there in the autumn of 1927. With a severity worthy
of Hemingway he filmed a story he heard in a fishing village: a
boy is hurt during the seaweed harvest and develops an infection;
attempts to transport the unconscious patient to the mainland fail
when the waves push the boat out to the high seas. A doctor leaves
Ouessant, performs an operation during the storm and, together
with the resuscitated patient, arrives back to the welcome of the
locals who have waited on the shore the whole night.

Epstein, always reluctant to work with professional actors,
engaged as performers the people the film is about--and though he
was not always able to make them act naturally, he did not waste
the potential force of expression offered by the authenticity of nature.
He did not add to this picture anything which might have disturbed
its stylistic balance and, with his simple narrative, achieved a lasting result.

LES NOUVEAUX MESSIEURS   Jacques Feyder

Script: Charles Spaak and Feyder, from the play by Robert de
Flers and Francis de Croisset. Photography: Georges Périnal
and Maurice Desfassiaux. Art Direction: Lazare Meerson. Cast:
Gaby Morlay (Suzanne Verrier), Henri Roussel (Comte de Montoire-
Grandpré), Albert Préjean (Jacques Gaillac), Henri Valbel (An ex-

treme leftist deputy).

Films Albatros/Sequana, France.   8280 ft.

A satire on the parliamentarians of the French Third Republic,
made in a mellow, but vitriolic tone. Although the film was made
by Feyder, the boulevard comedy style in which it is sustained was
the property of the director's friend, René Clair. Feyder also took
from Clair his gusto for deriding people who are ridiculous but want
to appear serious and respectable. The story of an upstart ex-
electrician who becomes in turn a tycoon, a member of parliament
and a minister and who competes with his political rival, an old
marquis, for the favors of a beautiful dancer, is a satire directed
against the whole parliament, without differentiating shades of political opinion. Those statesmen who, though radical in opposition,
quickly become institutionalized after gaining power, are especially
under fire.

Les Nouveaux messieurs must have been an accurate hit at
the ways of political leaders and the political situation at the time,
as it was subjected to the censor's scissors and, before release,
was presented by him (free of charge) with an additional absurd
title: The parliament presented here is not the French Parliament,
but only the fruit of the imagination of the film's authors. In the
psychological cinema of Feyder this is quite an exceptional picture,
and proof of the versatility of his directorial craft. After all, his
previous work was the grim Thérèse Raquin, and his next, the
American melodrama The Kiss (1929), with Greta Garbo.

THE SPIES (Spione)   Fritz Lang

Script: Thea von Harbou, from her own novel. Photography:
Fritz Arno Wagner. Art Direction: Otto Hunte and Karl Vollbrecht.
Cast: Gerda Maurus (Sonia), Willy Fritsch (Donald Tremaine, "No.
326"), Rudolf Klein-Rogge (Haghi), Lupu Pick (Dr. Matsumoto),
Lien Deyers (Kitty), Craighall Sherry (Miles Jason), Fritz Rasp
(Colonel Jellusic), Louis Ralph (Morrier), Hertha von Walther (Lady
Leslane), Paul Hörbiger (Franz, the chauffeur).

Fritz-Lang-Film for UFA, Germany.   10 reels, 14,318 ft.

Discouraged by the financial failure of Metropolis, Lang returned
to the sensational genre in which he felt more confident, and made
a picture in many ways similar to the earlier Dr. Mabuse, the
Gambler. It is only that in The Spies spying is substituted for
gambling, the change most probably brought about by the spy fever

which swept many European countries in the late 20's.   So now
Lang scared the audience--in the Teutonic spirit of the brothers
Grimm--with the struggle between spies and counter-intelligence in
a fictitious state of Novomia, and created a classical sensational
picture.

The supposedly crippled Haghi, pushed around in an invalid
chair by a doting nurse and constantly surrounded by a cloud of
cigarette smoke, poses as the manager of a major bank while really
directing an extensive network of international spies.   When a foreign government assigns an agent, Tremaine, to investigate thefts
of diplomatic documents, Haghi replies by sending Sonia, his own
agent.   The love affair between the two leads to Haghi's undoing:
in the slightly surrealist finale the master-criminal, disguised as
a clown, fires at his own head and then asks for the curtain to
descend.

The Spies is no less a display of Lang's technical virtuosity
than his earlier (or later, for that matter) works.   The rambling
and confused style of Dr. Mabuse, the Gambler is replaced by an
examplary economy of narrative which often condenses complex
events to a short series of brilliant shots.   Particularly fine in
this context is the scene of the railway crash by which Haghi unsuccessfully tries to eliminate Tremaine.   Visually the film is
equally restrained; the compositions are refined and simple and
there is frequent use of large open planes and studied contrasts of
light and shade.

The Spies is another study of an obsession in Lang's work:
although it is clearly implied that the activities of the chief villain
(note the equation, banker = criminal) are the by-product of the
war, spying is for him something more than vice, it is an aim in
itself, an all-consuming, irresistible passion.   It is also significant
that Lang used the actor, Rudolf Klein-Rogge, who also played Mabuse.   Interestingly, Lupu Pick, the director of Shattered is cast
as one of the agents.

THE CAMERAMAN   Edward Sedgwick

Script: Clyde Bruckman and Lew Lipton.   Photography: Elgin
Lessley and Reggie Lanning.   Cast: Buster Keaton (Luke Shannon),
Marceline Day (Sally), Harry Gribbon (Cop), Harold Goodwin (Stagg),
Sidney Bracy (Editor).

MGM, U.S.A.   8 reels, 6995 ft.

The era of the silent cinema was coming to a close--and together with it waned the fortunes of Buster Keaton. In 1928 Keaton gave up his own production company and signed a contract with MGM. The Cameraman, the first film shot after this disastrous decision was taken, was the beginning of the end. Keaton, it is true, would still contribute a good performance to a silent Spite Marriage, but there he was not the scriptwriter, nor the director, nor (as he still was in The Cameraman) the producer. He would be demoted to the role of actor, and the gags of his invention would be "improved" beyond recognition by others.

The Cameraman was as a premonition of things to come, a farewell to the good old days. This dramatic comedy is a sort of summing up of the great comic's career and it contains many reminders from his former pictures. It is a film about a film, and as such a kind of paraphrase of Sherlock Junior. The Cameraman is a story of a street tintype photographer who, encouraged by his sweetheart, buys a movie camera instead. The trouble is that he does not really know how to use it.

He gets launched with a ship, makes a mess of a freelance documentary about a regatta (in which Sally is taking part) and a clever monkey steals from the camera a film about a Chinatown tong war. Finally however the film is found and it is revealed what a brave chap Buster was. In the final scene he walks along Broadway acknowledging a hero's welcome, unaware that it is addressed to a certain Mr. Lindbergh whose car is just behind.

The initial situation is the source of many gags concerning the technical problems of making films. Buster, of course, manages to make every error possible. Yet the film lacks lightness: Edward Sedgwick, formerly a director of horse operas starring Tom Mix, and later of trivial Flip and Flap comedies, clearly favored humor of a more primitive type than Keaton's. Alas, the maker of The General was too high-brow for MGM and thus not profitable enough....

ELISO   Nikolai Shengelaya

Script: Sergei Tretyakov, Oleg Leonidov and Shengelaya, from the short story by Alexandre Kazbegi. Photography: Vladimir Kereselidze. Cast: Alexandre Imedashvili (Astamir, a foreman), Kokta Karalashvili (Vazhiya), Kira Andronikashvili (Eliso), Alexandre Zhorzholyani (General), Cecilia Tsutsunava (Zazubika), I. Mamporiya (Seydula).

Goskinprom-Gruzya, U.S.S.R.   7546 ft.

A Georgian historical epic, evoking the tragic fate of a nation paci-
fied in 1864 by the Tsarist Russian Empire. The authorities start
a big drive to appropriate the best arable lands and force the peasants away. The conditions in which the villagers are evacuated are
terrible. When one of the women dies the party is in near panic.
Then one of the elders orders a folk song to be played. Eliso, his
daughter, starts to dance.... The doom-laden atmosphere disappears.

        The style of the film is based on the Eisensteinian models
of ponderous para-documentary reconstruction, but at the same time
is decidedly different from the style of Battleship Potemkin or October in its use of editing and the pace of its narration. Long, deep-
focus shots dominate, only occasionally punctuated with close-
ups. The majestic rhythm of Shengelaya's cinematic poem appears
to be organically ingrown to the land of which it speaks. The raw,
but ravishingly beautiful mountain landscapes, in a way a co-director of the picture, determine the atmosphere of the work and explain human actions and characters.

THE HONEYMOON   Erich von Stroheim

Script: Stroheim and Harry Carr. Photography: Ben Reynolds and
Hal Mohr. Cast: Erich von Stroheim (Prince "Nicki" von Wildliebe-
Rauffenburg), Zasu Pitts (Cecelia, his wife), Fay Wray (Mitzi),
Mathew Betz (Schani, her husband).

Famous Players-Lasky, U.S.A. Originally over 13,000 ft.; 9938
ft. in version released in Europe.

Pressure from the producers forced Stroheim to divide the film
which he planned to call The Wedding March into two parts, of
which the second was released as The Honeymoon. Cecelia and
Nicki spend their honeymoon in a Tyrolean mountain château. Although they were not married of their own choice, a genuine affection develops between them. In the meantime in Vienna, Mitzi
marries her butcher fiancé Schani, who, still jealous of the love of
Nicki and Mitzi, decides to shoot Nicki during a hunt. Cecelia
tries to protect her husband and is herself fatally wounded. Her
father is overcome with grief, while Nicki's mother expresses her
pleasure at the financially successful match.

        Stroheim, who never took cognizance of the dramatic poten-
tial of film editing, again failed to contain his intentions in a compact form. After three years of production and continued defiance
of the allotted budget, he entered into another conflict with the producer who demanded substantial cuts. Stroheim could not cope with

the editing of the footage, which had dragged on since 1923. As a result The Honeymoon was taken from him and placed in Josef von Sternberg's hands, who, despite Stroheim's protests, added a prologue summing up the first part and cut around 30 per cent of the material, distorting the dramatic skeleton of the picture. The most important omissions are those of the wedding night scenes and of the final fight between the two rivals--Schani and Nicki. In effect the villain survives the title "The End," a unique precedent in the moralist cinema of Erich von Stroheim.

WHITE SHADOWS IN THE SOUTH SEAS   Woodbridge S. Van Dyke

Script: Jack Cunningham, from the novel by Frederick O'Brien.
Photography: Clyde De Vinna, George Nagle and Bob Roberts.
Song, "Flower of Love," by William Axt and David Mendoza. Cast:
Monte Blue (Dr. Matthew Lloyd), Raquel Torres (Fayaway), Robert Anderson (Sebastian, a merchant).

Cosmopolitan Productions, U.S.A.   7968 ft., 88 mins.

Chronologically, this is the first qualitatively successful sound film: a curious mixture of exotic melodrama and sincere registration of the destructive effects of white civilization in the Polynesian Islands. While colonists introduce the natives to liquor, drugs and prostitution, Sebastian, a greedy merchant, tries to liquidate Lloyd, the doctor who opposes these practices, by locking him up in a sinking ship. But Lloyd survives and reaches an island unknown to white civilization, where he marries the chief's daughter and lives happily until, driven by greed, he contacts the colonists trying to sell some of his pearls. The merchants arrive to colonize the island and Lloyd is killed while trying to drive them back.

The film was begun in Tahiti by Robert Flaherty, director of the most famous documentaries of the 20's--Nanook of the North (1921) and Moana (1925), a poetic impression from Samoa. But Flaherty soon gave up the direction of the film, which, contrary to his artistic credo, went beyond a faithful registration of reality, and in which the roles of aborigines were to be played by professional actors. Woodbridge S. van Dyke, his successor, and future initiator of the Tarzan screen series, was only a skilled craftsman, but he succeeded in containing in White Shadows in the South Seas enough authenticity to save the film from being solely a maudlin love story.

THE HOUSE IN TRUBNAYA STREET (Dom na Trubnoy) Boris
Barnet

Script: B. Zorich, Anatoli Marienhof, V. Shershenevich, Victor
Shklovsky and Nikolai Erdman. Photography: Yevgeni Alexeyev.
Cast: Vera Maretskaya (Paranya Pitunova, country girl), Vladimir
Fogel (Hairdresser Golikov), Sergei Komarov (Lyadov), Anna Sudake-
vich (Marisha), Yelena Tyapkina (Golikov's wife), Ada Voytsik
(Fyenya), V. Batalov (Semyon Byvalov), Boris Barnet (Director).

Mezhrabpom-Russ, U.S.S.R. 5764 ft.

A Moscow tenement house during the period of the New Economic
Policy which started in Russia in 1921: like Room's Bed and Sofa,
The House in Trubnaya Street is an interesting record of the way
of life of the era--but this time distinctly in the spirit of anti-
bourgeois satirical comedy. While relating the adventures of a
country girl who becomes a servant in the rich family of a hairdresser (rich, that is, according to the principle that the shrewd
lower-middle classes are the first to benefit from upheavals, and
the war and revolution are just over). Barnet made use of Chaplin's recipies: he knew how to exploit the vexatious attributes of
inanimate objects, splendidly observed the characters and mixed a
touch of sadness into the gaiety. All this was conducted with great
vigor but also with moderation, resulting in the most interesting
Soviet comedy of the pre-sound period.

Noteworthy are not only the extended comic episodes (especially the scenes of the amateur theatrical performance, the pursuit of
a goose among the street traffic, and the hairdresser's party), but
also the skill with which cinematic matter has been related to the
realities of life. Thus the camera often leaves the enclosure of a
studio set of a tenement block and goes out into the street--and
here, as in Bed and Sofa, hides in the crowd and registers life in
the raw.

OUR DAILY BREAD [Title in released version: CITY GIRL]
Friedrich Wilhelm Murnau

Script: Berthold Viertel and Marion Orth, from the play, "The
Mud Turtle," by Elliott Lester. Photography: Ernest Palmer.
Cast: Charles Farrell (Lem Tustine), Mary Duncan (Kate), David
Torrence (Lem's father), Edith Yorke (Lem's mother), Dawn O'Day

(Marie), Dick Alexander (Mac), Tom Maguire (Matey), Guinn Williams, Edward Brady and Jack Pennick (Reapers).

Fox Film Corporation, U.S.A.   Originally 8465 ft.

Our Daily Bread is one of the four films Murnau made in America. It came after Sunrise and Four Devils (1928) but before Tabu. This was of course the period during which sound was being introduced into cinema and this was the reason for the unhappy history of the picture. It was shot as a silent and could have been a box-office success if it had not been for the disastrous hesitation of the producers over the release. Vital months were lost and the picture, retitled City Girl turned into an unwanted product of a past era.

The dramatic principle of Our Daily Bread is the contrast between city and country life which Murnau so splendidly used in Sunrise. An inexperienced country boy is sent to the city to sell a crop of wheat and returns home with a bride. The despotic, puritanical father rejects the girl as a gold-digger and it is only after a very dramatic showdown during a stormy night on the farm that she can finally be accepted.

Although Our Daily Bread does not match Sunrise and its drama lacks such passionate romantic power, the film does have great scenes. One of them is the arrival of Lem and Kate at the farm shown with a camera relentlessly gliding over cornfields blown by the wind and perfectly conveying youthful intoxication with happiness. Another scene is the horse-cart drive of the reapers through the fields which has something of the hypnotic quality of Nosferatu.

1929

HALLELUJAH!   King Vidor

Script: Wanda Tuchock and Richard Shayer. Dialogues: Ransom
Rideout. Photography: Gordon Avil. Music: Irving Berlin and
Negro Spirituals. Cast: Daniel L. Haynes (Zeke), Nina Mae McKin-
ney (Chick), William Fountaine (Hot Shot), Harry Gray (Parson
Johnson), Fannie Belle De Knight (Mammy), Everett McGarrity
(Spunk), Victoria Spivey (Missy Rose), Milton Dickerson, Walter
Couch, Walter Tait (Johnson Kids), Dixie Jubilee Singers.

MGM, U.S.A.   9711 ft., 108 mins.

Hallelujah! is the first masterpiece of the sound cinema.   The newly discovered means of expression was used here in an astonishingly
creative manner.   What is more, the film explored the use of silence in the sound film.   Not the mandatory muteness of before,
which ruled the entire picture, but dramatic silence, which turns
out to be one of the most evocative instruments in creating the magic
of the cinema.

    The story of Hallelujah! develops entirely among Alabama
blacks.   A farmhand, Zeke, falls for the seductive Chick and loses
the family money to her lover Hot Shot.   In the fight which follows
Zeke accidentally kills his brother.   Having vowed to repent he becomes a famous evangelist, but again falls under Chick's spell.
When she turns out to be an unfaithful wife, Zeke pursues the lovers
and kills Hot Shot; Chick dies in an overturned coach.   Prematurely
released from jail Zeke is forgiven by his family and consoled by a
childhood friend.

    The most admirable example of the discriminating use of the
soundtrack is in the scene of the night pursuit through wooded

marshes in which the dramatic tension is stepped up by the abrupt
cry of a vigilant bird, the splash of disturbed water and the panting
of the antagonists. The close of the scene is accompanied by the
ominous absence of any sound; the fugitive perishes strangled by his
rival.

It is significant that nobody in the early sound cinema followed Vidor's example, perhaps with the exception of Sternberg in
The Blue Angel, and the soundtrack continued generally to be used
as a vehicle solely for screen loquacity, the recording of the vocal
prowess of the actors, and the tacking on of a musical illustration
to the plot. Of course, Hallelujah! also has a musical score, and
an outstanding one. This drama of human passions is accompanied
by magnificent blues songs, Negro spirituals, work songs and classical jazz themes.

The contemporary objections (mostly by American critics) to
the protagonists as being "hardly typical" seem ridiculous today (was
Hamlet "typical"?) and it is not even clear whether Vidor intended
to make primarily a "socially conscious" film. Hallelujah! is a
revelation not only because of its use of sound. It is also the first
film with an all-black cast that treats the black community without
paternalism and condescension, and as such remained unrivaled for
the next 25 years. It is also one of the earliest registrations of
American folklore in feature cinema--a multilayer work, of which
examples are extremely rare.

DIARY OF A LOST GIRL (Das Tagebuch einer Verlorenen) Georg
Wilhelm Pabst

Script: Rudolf Leonhardt, from the novel by Margarethe Boehme.
Photography: Sepp Allgeier. Cast: Louise Brooks (Thymiane Hen-
ning), Edith Meinhardt (Erika), Vera Pawlowa (Aunt Frida), Josef
Rovenský (Henning, the pharmacist), Fritz Rasp (Meiner, the shop
assistant), André Roanne (Count Osdorff), Arnold Korff (The Old
Count Osdorff, his uncle), Andrews Englemann (Director of the
House of Correction), Valeska Gert (His wife), Francisca Kinz
(Meta), Sybille Schmitz (Elisabeth, the first governess).

G. W. Pabst Film GmbH, Berlin, Germany. 8 reels, 9393 ft.

In Diary of a Lost Girl Pabst repeated the intentions of Pandora's
Box, his previous film, in that he wanted to demonstrate the strength
of instinct in man and to mount an attack on the hypocrisy and double standards of the bourgeoisie. The accusations are here leveled
by a girl with a heart of gold whom an ignoble seducer has pushed
into prostitution, but who has not stripped her of her dignity. Such

an idea, from third-rate literature, hardly surviving print, is ennobled by Pabst and by the fascinating Louise Brooks, the leading
actress in Pandora's Box.

The heroine's melodramatic innocence opposed to the degeneration of a whole array of bourgeois types suggests inevitable (and
probably not coincidental) associations with the cinema of Erich von
Stroheim. However while Pabst refers to the Hollywood master
through the type of intrigue, the formal aspect is rather unrelated--
one need mention only Pabst's employment of rapid, descriptive
editing, or the Pudovkinian camera positions which were used to relate characters to each other (as in the shot of supervisor and leader in the approved school). Stroheim could never do any of these
things.

Diary of a Lost Girl is less of a film of atmosphere than
Pandora's Box; also, it cannot really be considered (as the director
would have liked) a realistic description of a real situation, since
the style of direction clearly diverges from that. Pabst's last silent
picture is above all a display of the wonderful, subjective expressiveness of the language of the cinema of the 20's.

SUCH IS LIFE (Takový Je Život)   Karl Junghans

Script: Junghans. Photography: László Schäffer. Cast: Vera
Baranovskaya (Washerwoman), Theodor Pištěk (Her husband, a coal-
man), Máňa Ženíšková (Their daughter), Wolfgang Zilzer (Her fiancé),
Jindřich Plachta (Tailor), Manja Kellerová (His wife), Eman Fiala
(Pianist), Valeska Gert (Girl in a pub), Uli Tridenska (Washerwom-
an's friend), Max Körner (Coal shop owner).

Bukáč-Pištěk, Czechoslovakia. 6201 ft.

For several years Karl Junghans, a Sudeten German, collected with
help from his friends, the wherewithal to make a film about the unhappy life and tragic death of a poor washerwoman. Money was
scarce during the shooting, but the film did see the light of day in
the end. As sometimes happens with films made in similar circumstances, the result turned out to be very good, deeply lived through
--and also technically competent, which is much more rare. The
somber tale set among the proletariat of Prague penetrates with its
mood of melancholic resignation. Its warmth and understanding of
people condemned to life without hope is impressive. The sequence
of the Sunday excursion to the country is particularly memorable.

The style of Such Is Life brings the film close to the post-
Expressionist works of German "critical realism," which however

never themselves reached a comparable standard. Junghans used a much wider range of means of cinematic expression and intelligently compiled the creative methods of virtually the entire silent cinema from Sjöström to Eisenstein. Vera Baranovskaya gives a deeply moving performance as the washerwoman who dies after pouring boiling suds over herself.

THE GHOST THAT WILL NOT RETURN (Privideniye, Kotoroye Ne Vozvrashchayetsya) Abram Room

---

Script: Valentin Turkin, from a story by Henri Barbusse. Photography: Dmitri Feldman. Cast: B. Ferdinandov (José Real), Olga Zhizneva (Clemance), Maxim Strauch (Police agent), D. Kara-Dimitriev (Intelligence boss), L. Yureniev, K. Gurnyak.

Sovkino, U.S.S.R. 7644 ft.

A parable, ravishing in its external form, of a man in the cogs of the mechanism of terror, set in a fictitious Latin American state. After ten years of captivity an imprisoned revolutionary is given one day of holiday. He uses the spell of "freedom" for a journey to his home settlement where he helps organize a strike. Mortal danger hangs over him all the time: he is going to be shot dead in a faked escape attempt. An atmosphere of tension and anxiety was injected into the film by the placement of the hero in a hostile and arid world of empty, light planes and solids, where one cannot possibly hide, and which deprive man of his privacy and paralyze his will. Even the prisons are here spacious, full of light--and all the more cruel.

The refined geometric style of the photography, obtained through the use of Constructivist* set designs and a multiplicity of camera angles, played here a key role in building the internal system of meaning of the film, acting as a sort of psychological commentary and giving The Ghost That Will Not Return the quality of a generalizing essay on the meaning of freedom. As inspired camera work, influenced by the trends of modern art, it would still be of great value and interest even without all these connotations. Thanks to its visual form and the editing, Room's film counts among the most interesting achievements of the Soviet cinema of the 20's.

---

*Trend in art, mainly in Russia 1914-30, giving expression to the search for new forms which would reflect the present. In stage design Constructivists used abstract geometrical structures.

FRAGMENT OF AN EMPIRE (Oblomok Imperii)   Friedrich Ermler

Script: Katerina Vinogradskaya and Ermler. Photography: Yevgeni Schneider. Cast: Fyodor Nikitin (Filimonov), Ludmila Semyonova (His wife), Yakov Gudkin (Wounded Red Guard), Valeri Solovtsov (Culture and education officer), Vyacheslav Viskovsky (Factory owner), Sergei Gerasimov (Menshevik).

Sovkino, U.S.S.R.   7228 ft.

Fragment of an Empire is more than a psychological drama based on a capital idea. It is a film where, apart from the presence of mature examples of the Soviet style of editing and the influences of German Expressionist films (especially in the war flashback), the spectator will quite unexpectedly find elements characteristic of much later trends in the cinema (like the dramatically open ending or the Resnais-ian quality of the recurring images of the past).   The capital idea was to show the enormous changes in post-revolutionary Russia through the eyes of a worker, former soldier of the Revolution, who after 10 years of isolation from society caused by amnesia, returns to his native St. Petersburg from a village in the back of beyond.   But there is no more St. Petersburg--it has become Leningrad; and everything around provokes a confrontation between the pre-revolution reality known to the hero and the present.

Yet the motif of the discovery of a new life only provides the dramatic skeleton of the film, which is very far from the brashness of a propaganda picture. Fragment of an Empire is, apart from its value as a mine of sociological observation, above all a chamber psychological study--very accurate, full of subtlety and warmth.   The actor was with this film restored to grace in the Soviet cinema, which for nearly a decade relied principally on editing as the means of expression.   The talent of Ermler appeared here for the first time in full, and Fragment of an Empire established him as the leading director of a psychological trend in the Soviet cinema.

THE BLUE EXPRESS (Goluboi Ekspress)   Ilya Trauberg

Script: Leonid Ierikhonov and Trauberg. Photography: B. Khrennikov and Jurgis Stilianudis. Cast: Sergei Minin (Englishman), Yakov Gudkin and Ivan Savelyev (Overseers), I. Sernyak (Secretary),

I. Arbenin (Missionary), A. Vardul (Coolie), Sun Bo-yang, Chou Hsi-fan, Chang Kai.

Sovkino, U.S.S.R. 5577 ft.

The growth of revolutionary conflict in the Far East: what Pudovkin in Storm Over Asia unrolled on the wide steppes of Mongolia, the 24-year-old Trauberg, the young assistant of Eisenstein on October, enclosed in the limited space of railway carriages. The passengers on the train, in which the tense action of the film takes place, are a symbolic cross-section of China society, from coolies to obese merchants. The European merchants and officials travel first class guarded by armed soldiers while the third class is filled by the ordinary people. The film brings the two worlds to a direct confrontation and the poor take over the train.

As a matter of fact there are many symbols here (the director was clearly under Eisenstein's influence), the principal one being the uncheckable run of the express train controlled by pariahs, a sign of the forthcoming changes beyond the Great Wall. Trauberg also took from his master the great dynamism of expression, the pathos, certain elements of editing, and employed them skillfully in the genre of sensational drama: there is none of the artificiality of imitation here, though the director of The Blue Express did not later prove his talent by any other work.

MOTHER KRAUSE'S JOURNEY TO HAPPINESS (Mutter Krausens Fahrt ins Glück) Phil Jutzi

---

Script: Jan Fethke and Willy Döll, based on stories told by Heinrich Zille to his friend Otto Nagel and photographed in the scenes immortalized by Zille's drawings. Photography: Phil Jutzi. Cast: Alexandra Schmitt (Mutter Krause), Ilse Trauschold (Her daughter Hanna), Holmes Zimmermann (Her son Paul), Friedrich Gnass (Max, a workman), Gerhard Bienert (Lodger), Vera Sacharova (His sweetheart), Fee Wachsmuth (Her child).

Prometheus-Film, Germany. 7 reels, 10,817 ft.

"One can destroy a man with a house just as well as with an axe"-- such is the motto of the film probably most representative of the post-Kammerspiel "new objectivity," the naturalistic trend in the German cinema initiated by Pabst's The Joyless Street. The works of the trend revolved around the person of Heinrich Zille, a Berlin graphic artist and journalist; Mother Krause's Journey to Happiness was made after he died, but was also a result of his inspiration.

The film relates the tragedy of a woman earning her living by selling newspapers who by taking a scoundrel for a lodger brings disaster upon her family. The children go off the rails and the mother finally turns on the gas tap in despair, thus departing for her "journey to happiness." The background of the events is the authentic working-class quarters of North Berlin, registered in a series of documentary sequences. The train of thought of the picture is quite interesting: on the one side there is the fatalistic turning of the other cheek to fate, but on the other, the discovery of new, positive attitudes in society personified here in the worker friend of the seduced girl who believes in struggle and not surrender.

The film was made in the time of the strongest influence of the German left, the period from the victorious 1928 elections until the Great Depression of 1929. The makers did not overtly promote either of the two attitudes to reality: they took the position of observation and wait-and-see.

BLACKMAIL Alfred Hitchcock

Script: Hitchcock, Benn W. Levy and Charles Bennett, from a play by the latter. Photography: John Cox. Music: Hubert Bath and Henry Stafford. Cast: Anny Ondra (Alice White), John Longden (Frank Webber, the detective), Sara Allgood (Mrs. White), Charles Paton (Mr. White), Donald Calthrop (Tracy), Cyril Ritchard (Artist), Hannah Jones (Landlady), Harvey Braban (Chief Inspector), Phyllis Monkman (Charlady).

British International Pictures, GB. 7667 ft., 85 mins.

In self-defense a girl kills a painter who attempted to rape her in his studio. The murder hunt is led by her policeman fiancé who quickly guesses what had happened. The situation is further complicated when a shady character begins to blackmail the hero. Yet blackmail does not pay and justice--though not quite in accordance with the law--is done; the detective directs suspicion towards the blackmailer who, in the famous chase sequence on the roofs of the British Museum, falls to his death. Hitchcock first made the picture as a silent and immediately afterwards re-shot the dialogue sequences (as post-synchronization was not yet available).

Curiously, it is the inventiveness and versatility in the em-

ployment of the sound that is the greatest asset of <u>Blackmail</u>:
Hitchcock used the new means of expression not only as a way of
avoiding captions but as a dramatic device, a counterpoint and commentary to the plot. The skill with which the director stepped up
suspense and created the atmosphere of threat foreshadowed his
best films. No wonder then that <u>Blackmail</u>, the first British talkie,
was also one of the most financially successful.

Another interesting aspect of the film is the moral ambiguity
of the story, a feature for which Hitchcock later became famous
(another example is <u>The Secret Agent</u>). The point is that the police
never find out who killed. It is true that the heroine was not really
guilty, but still.... Hitchcock did at first plan to end the film with
the girl's arrest--but commercial pressures made him change his
mind.

SPITE MARRIAGE Edward Sedgwick

Script: Ernest S. Pagano, from a story by Lew Lipton. Photography: Reggie Lanning. Cast: Buster Keaton (Elmer Edge-
mont), Dorothy Sebastian (Trilby Dew), Edward Earle (Lionel
Benmore), Leila Hyams (Ethel Norcrosse), Will Bechtel (Frederick
Nussbaum).

MGM, U.S.A. 9 reels, 7047 ft.

Spite Marriage, a film released when the talkies were well under
way, marked Keaton's last appearance in the silent cinema. It is
the story of the conquest of a beautiful actress's heart by an awkward and ordinary trousers-presser in a tailor shop. One day he
succeeds in getting a job on the stage play in which his beloved is
the star. The hero is lucky: as sometimes happens, disappointment with a fiancé spawns a whim for marrying just anybody--and
the delighted hero just happens to be around. He succeeds in
thwarting the rejected lover's attempts to get rid of him and does
marry the girl, to be united with her in love and happiness after a
series of incredible adventures.

The comic situation is made prime use of and Spite Marriage,
although less dynamic, is no worse than many earlier Keaton comedies. He himself seems somewhat subdued, more tragi-comical
than comical. This was the end of the great comic; the most modern
ace of the silent slapstick comedy (both as an actor and as a commentator on life) was never able to find himself in the new conditions of the talkies. He did not have a suitable voice and he was
also too preoccupied with his miming style of acting, formed in the
vaudeville before he came to Hollywood.

Keaton was still to give several vignette performances, most famous of which is one of a bridge player who says just one highly significant word, "pass," in Wilder's <u>Sunset Boulevard</u>, but was not to regain his due recognition until shortly before his death, after 35 years of obscurity.

SUN (Sole)   Alessandro Blasetti

<u>Script</u>: Aldo Vergano and Blasetti.   <u>Photography</u>: Giuseppe Caracciolo and Giorgio Orsini.   <u>Cast</u>: Dria Paola, Lia Bosco, Anna Vinci, Marcello Spada, Rolando Constantino, Vasco Creti, Vittorio Vasar, Rinaldo Rinaldi, Igino Nunzio, Vittorio Gonzi, Arnaldo Baldaccini, Sante Bonaldo, Arcangelo Aversa.

Augustus Films, Italy.

Blasetti, a young journalist campaigning against the rustiness of Italian drawing-room film production, started a film company with a few friends with the intention of putting into practice his beliefs in the need for realism in the cinema.   In accordance with this the company's first production tells about the life of the peasants working on the reclamation of marshes and waste land in the Po valley.

The dramatic axis of the film is the conflict between the young people and the old who accept changes with reluctance and distrust.   In effect, Blasetti's original contribution seems to reside rather in the formal aspect of the film than in its content.   It is true that the script carries a clear social message, but while making the film Blasetti let his temperament carry him away and made primarily an impressive if somewhat too exalted poetic etude, which contemplates the beauty of the countryside and the dignity of man at work.   The refined photographic compositions, expert editing, emphatic mood, and use of non-professional actors, all indicate clear influences from the works of Sergei Eisenstein.

The story of the film, however, stopping short of social conclusions while referring to the government sponsorship of the land reclamation, caused <u>Sun</u> to be fully endorsed by the Mussolini régime.   Thus, unexpectedly, Blasetti made an official film.   But he was not enthusiastic about being acclaimed the champion of the Italian fascist cinema: in his other pre-war films he would generally try to preserve an independent stand.

ALIBI   Roland West

Script: West and C. Gardner Sullivan, from the play, "Nightstick,"
by John Wray, J. C. Nugent and Elaine Sterne Carrington. Photography: Ray June. Cast: Chester Morris (Chick Williams, "No.
1065"), Harry Stubbs (Buck Bachman), Mae Busch (Daisy Thomas),
Eleanor Griffith (Joan Manning), Irma Harrison (Toots), Regis
Toomey (Danny McGann).

United Artists, U.S.A. 8167 ft., 91 mins.

The underworld before the advent of the "gangster series": Little
Caesar would be made a year later, but the sound cinema was already starting to take increased interest in gangsters. Alibi is a
brutal picture of a ruthless scuffle between the police and the underworld, seen from the more traditional point of view, that of the
guardians of public order, and not through the eyes of the criminals,
as in the films of Sternberg and the majority of the later pictures
in which the detection of crime is no longer the point. A man,
newly released from prison, murders a policeman during a robbery
and escapes. When he becomes a suspect, his trusting young wife,
the daughter of another cop, tries to arrange an alibi for him but
is shattered to learn the truth. He is trapped by a detective whom
he shoots down in cold blood.

The most important things in Alibi seem to be the para-
documentary character of the staging and the tone of an honest re-
port--but at the time of its release the film was valued mainly for
its skill in handling the sound. This was indeed used with ingenuity:
after the killing of the policeman the other cops communicate by hitting metal objects with rubber batons; the monotony of prison life is
stressed by the rhythmical sound of steps. Alibi is thus one of the
first technically competent sound films.

RAILS (Rotaie)   Mario Camerini

Script: Camerini, from Corrado D'Errico. Photography: Ubaldo
Arata. Cast: Maurizio D'Ancora, Käthe von Nagy, Daniele Crespi,
Giacomo Moschini.

Saci, Mailand, Italy.

The Italian Neorealism, which dates from Rossellini's Rome, Open
City, was to take its shape as an artistic program only with the end
of the Second World War. Yet, already by 1929 two of its harbin-
gers had appeared. One of these was Blasetti's Sole, the other,
Rails. Rails is Camerini's seventh film, thus it has a maturity and
balance which compensate for a certain predictability of the script.
But the essence of its artistic success was the break with studio
work, both in the literal and figurative sense.

The film is a story of a young couple who travel by train in
search of work, of their little worries and joys and their eventual
success. Camerini focused his attention on the ordinary people,
the passengers in the third-class carriages to whom he unobtrusively
opposes the rich people traveling first class. This element makes
Rails an unexpected parallel of Trauberg's The Blue Express in
Russia. But the presentation of the everyday Italy of small railway
stations was here not in itself the aim, and was used only for the
stronger exposition of the background, on which Camerini, who was
to become a master of the subtle comedy of manners, projected his
warm psychological observations of the protagonists.

1930

EARTH (Zemla) Olexandr Dovzhenko

Script: Dovzhenko. Photography: Danilo Demutski. Cast: Semen
Svashenko (Vasil), Stepon Shkurat (Opanas, his father), Ioulya Solnt-
seva (Vasil's sister), Mikola Nademsky (Father Semen), Yelena
Maximova (Vasil's fiancée), Pyotr Masokha (Foma), Nikolai Mikhailov (Priest), I. Franko (Koulak), O. Umanets (Chief of Council), P.
Petrin (Speaker), E. Bondina (Young peasant), L. Lashchenko (Young
koulak).

VUFKU, Kiev, U.S.S.R. 5591 ft.

The last masterpiece of silent cinema, a work full of such beauty
and technical brilliance that it has assumed the rank of a near-
philosophical generalization. Dovzhenko, a Ukrainian scriptwriter
and director and a glorifier of his native land, was, besides Eisenstein and Pudovkin, the third master of the Soviet silent cinema.
Earth is his greatest film. Vasil, a country boy, organizes a
Kolkhoz (farm cooperative), with a group of friends despite his
father's indignant opposition. When the cooperative starts work the
rich peasants set out to assassinate Vasil. He is murdered at
night, at full moon, as he comes back from his beloved along a
country road.

Never perhaps were such close links with nature portrayed
on the screen, not even in the Swedish cinema of which these links
were the spiritual core. The frames of the film, swollen with the
breath of nature, are a counterpoint to human actions and states of
mind--and man is an inherent part of the living organism of the
earth. Dovzhenko showed this symbiosis with touching purity, in
the tonality of an incomparable, poetic day-dream. The three
"movements" which express the author's credo fullest are the mag-

ically fluid prologue, in which a dying old man in a country orchard
serenely says farewell to the world; the central climax of youthful
intoxication with life (the dance); and the phenomenally composed
final sequence of the funeral of the murdered hero.

A pregnant woman, who was part of the funeral cortège,
turns back when she feels the first signs of the approaching childbirth. In this scene Dovzhenko perfectly expresses the noble pathos
and the invincible optimism which vanquishes the drama of death: a
child is born, new life begins. The emotions expressed here are
close to those in many poems by Dylan Thomas, particularly in the
volume, "Deaths and Entrances."

Earth is Dovzhenko's reply to The Old and the New (1929),
in which Eisenstein glorified the conquest of nature by peasants
united in collective farming. Dovzhenko, whose story is also centered around the process of Stalinist collectivization, expressed a
diametrically different attitude. During the funeral the sunflowers
bow before the head hero: the director understands nature not as
an element to be conquered, but as a realm friendly to man. He
makes us admire and respect nature, a message that seems now
even more topical than back in 1930.

CITY LIGHTS   Charles Chaplin

Script: Chaplin. Photography: Rollie Totheroh, Gordon Pollock
and Mark Marklatt. Music: Chaplin. Cast: Charles Chaplin
(Charlie the Tramp), Virginia Cherrill (Blind girl), Florence Lee
(Her grandmother), Harry Myers (Eccentric millionaire), Allan
Garcia (His butler), Hank Mann (Prizefighter), Henry Bergman
(Mayor/janitor), Albert Austin (Street-sweeper/shady character),
Stanhope Wheatcroft (Head waiter), John Rand (Tramp), James
Donnelly (Foreman dustman), Eddie Baker (Referee), Robert Parrish
(Newsboy).

United Artists, U.S.A. 7815 ft., 87 mins.

There are few films made more meticulously than City Lights.
Chaplin, who had not yet regained his mental poise after personal
difficulties, continually changed the crew and actors and shot certain fragments of the film an incredible number of times, for example the prologue, which is decisive for the understanding of the plot.
He wanted to achieve perfection through the extreme technical simplicity of the narrative. The aim of these efforts was most important to him at a time when screens were already dominated by
the sound films whose loquacity Chaplin hated.

The talkies, filmed mainly in medium close-ups and medium long-shots, prostituted his beloved miming art; his intention in City Lights was thus to stress the role of the mime, in which an actor acts with his whole body. Although, at least for commercial reasons, the film had to have a soundtrack it dispensed with dialogue: Chaplin gave it only his own musical score. He did not miss an opportunity to make a jest at the expense of sound films, whose technique of voice recording was then far from perfect: the soundtrack in the scene of the unveiling of the monument, instead of the voice of the speaker, conveys the abrupt murmur of a wind instrument.

The basic situation of City Lights, an ordinary man's struggle for his dignity, is a typically Chaplinian one that remained practically unchanged in the 15-year period from The Gold Rush to The Great Dictator. The reason for this is undoubtedly the presence of a common denominator in all these films--the character of Charlie the Tramp. This time he is in search of a living in a big city. Escaping from a policeman, he ends up in front of the stall of a poor blind florist girl in such a way that she takes him for somebody very rich. That night the hero saves a drunken millionaire from a suicidal death; the near-victim offers him his friendship-- only as it turns out, until he sobers up.

But in the meanwhile Charlie, having a car and money at his disposal, strengthens his myth with the girl. As a result of further events, he gets hold of a considerable sum of money for her in order that she may regain her sight; but Charlie finds himself behind bars for alleged theft. When he leaves jail they meet again. The florist, of course, does not recognize him by sight, but she recognizes him by touch: this final scene is one of the most beautiful and heartrendingly tender in all cinema history. There are, besides, more scenes in the film in which emotion comes to the forefront; but, as usual with Chaplin, they are interspersed with hilarious situational gags: this blend has always guaranteed the high stature of Chaplin's pictures.

THE BLUE ANGEL (Der blaue Engel) Josef von Sternberg

Script: Carl Zuckmayer, Karl Vollmöller and Robert Liebmann, from the novel, "Professor Unrat," by Heinrich Mann. Photography: Günther Rittau and Hans Schneeberger. Art Direction: Otto Hunte. Music: Friedrich Holländer. Cast: Emil Jannings (Professor Immanuel Rath), Marlene Dietrich (Lola Frölich), Kurt Gerron (Kiepert, a magician), Rosa Valetti (Guste, his wife), Hans Albers (Mazeppa), Eduard von Winterstein (Headmaster), Reinhold Bernt (Clown), Hans Roth (Beadle), Rolf Müller (Angst, a student), Rolant Varno (Lohman, a student), Karl Balhaus (Ertzum, a student),

Robert Klein-Lörk (Goldstaub, a student).

UFA/Paramount, Germany/U.S.A.   9728 ft., 108 mins.

"End of a Tyrant"--such is the subtitle of the novel that was the starting material for the script of The Blue Angel, and such is the meaning of Sternberg's film. Basking in fame, the father of the gangster cinema traveled in the opposite direction to that of the majority of the outstanding European directors of the period: Murnau, Stiller and Sjöström were attracted by Hollywood, but Sternberg, Viennese in origin but brought to the United States as a child, returned to Europe. The German film company UFA wanted to deprive the Americans of their leading role in the cinema at all costs.

The imported master did not fall short of expectations and made a film which is not only brilliant, but very attractive. Such an outcome was made possible, among other things, by the freedom with which he was able to show on the screen the touchy problems of aggressive sexuality--a freedom not easy to come by in Hollywood. The Blue Angel is full of allusions and symbols with erotic overtones. The climate they create is very reminiscent of the films of another ex-Austrian--Erich von Stroheim.

But Sternberg's intentions were different from those of the maker of Foolish Wives: the purpose of his film was to give a penetrating study of the spiritual interior of Germany, a country where the general obsession with discipline leads to the uninhibited discharge of destructive instincts as soon as an opportunity arises. The restrictive bourgeois mentality brings calamity and downfall upon those who betray the unassailable rules of society: this is how lack of freedom leads to degeneration.

The Blue Angel provides a capital summary of the sentiments which lay at the roots of Expressionism and does it not in the sphere of screen mythology but in a behavioristic study of the mechanism of human actions. As such, the film is an analysis of the psychological situation which the whole world would soon come to know under the name of Fascism.

The plot of The Blue Angel is rather simple: a high-school master, whom his students hate, calls on the star of a traveling cabaret to complain about her corruption of his pupils. The consequences of the visit are disastrous: the teacher loses his head over the seductive artiste, marries her, leaves the school and descends to the lowest levels of degradation. When, some years later, the cabaret visits the town again, he has to appear in front of his former students and town officials crowing "cock-a-doodle-doo" in a lamentable stage sketch. This piercing cock-a-doodle-doo is the most magnificent scene in the careers of both Jannings and Sternberg.

To the striking visual aspect of the film, which at least

matches that of his former works, the director of The Blue Angel
added dramatic power, and, a new element, a dense cobweb of suggestive innuendoes. He felt quite at home in the new sound cinema,
and was able to exploit the new medium at his first attempt not only
with technical correctness, but also to create the mood: in the
tense pauses in the dialogue, in the classical crowing sequence, in
the symbolic motif of the old song about fidelity rung by the chimes
of the town-hall clock and in the frivolous cabaret songs sung by
Marlene Dietrich.

Marlene was to be for Sternberg the same femme fatale as
is her screen Lola-Lola for the hero of the film: the director discovered his star and, fascinated by her, implacably rolled down
from the highest peak of his creative career--without a doubt, The
Blue Angel. While making run-of-the-mill spy films for Marlene,
he allowed her to achieve full brightness, but he himself frittered
his talent away.

SOUS LES TOITS DE PARIS   René Clair

Script: Clair. Photography: George Périnal and Georges Raulet.
Art Direction: Lazare Meerson. Music: Armand Bernard. Cast:
Albert Préjean (Albert), Pola Illery (Pola), Gaston Modot (Fred),
Edmond Gréville (Louis), Bill Bocket (Bill).

Films Sonores Tobis, France. 8302 ft., 92 mins.

In contrast to Chaplin, Clair was an enthusiast of sound in the
cinema from the very beginning, although he joined his great colleague in opposing the loquacity which soon came to dominate the
screens. To Clair, the spoken word was an auxiliary means of expression which obviated over-long visual explanations--and he proceeded to express his message through images, sound and music.
Music (or, to be exact, song) plays a special role in Clair's first
sound film, because his intention was to render the spirit of life in
a Parisian suburb, which is best expressed by what is being sung
there. Accordingly, the whole film is sustained in the convention
of a popular song.

Sous les toits de Paris is the story of an undecided girl
whose favors are sought by three men: Fred the gangster, Albert
the street singer and his friend Louis. The most promising feeling
seems to be that between Pola and the prepossessing Albert. Alas,
he is innocently imprisoned for supposed theft; when he comes out
his place in Pola's heart is already taken by Louis. Even a game
of dice for the girl does not help.

Sous les toits de Paris was a step forward in the development of the individual style of Clair, independent of the influences of the lyrical tragicomedy à la Chaplin which are here even stronger than in Les Deux timides. This film was the beginning of the populist school in the French cinema which would develop parallel to the other trends and would, in a modified form, appear again in pictures as seemingly remote as Truffaut's of the late 60's (Baisers volés). The characteristic features of this school are the warm lyricism, the straightforward attitude to the protagonists, the apparent realism of events and the completely light-hearted tone. The climate of the whole allows the spectator to forgive Clair many flaws, as much in the content as in the dramatic structure of the film.

In Sous les toits de Paris, some of the flaws resulted from the avowed avoidance of dialogue which did not always bring good results since the natural flow of the story is occasionally disturbed and certain passages give the impression of a silent production with tacked-on sound. Also, some flaws resulted from the insufficient characterization of the protagonists and for others, the leading actress is to blame.

But there are many things in Clair's film which are successful and innovatory: take the use of sound without the image (a quarrel in darkness) and image without the sound (a scene in a café as viewed from the outside), or the splendid mobility of the camera (the celebrated opening tracking shot which introduces the inhabitants of the suburb and reveals their response to the waltz sung by Albert). The most important achievement is the rhythmic quality of the narrative, based on the blending of the picture and the sound, which would appear with even more strength in Clair's next film, Le Million.

WESTFRONT 1918   Georg Wilhelm Pabst

Script: Ladislaus Vajda and Peter Martin Lampel, from the novel, "Vier von der Infanterie," by Ernst Johannsen. Photography: Fritz Arno Wagner and Charles Métain. Cast: Gustav Diessl (Karl), Fritz Kampers (The Bavarian), Claus Clausen (Lieutenant), Hans Joachim Moebis (Student), Gustav Püttjer (The Hamburger), Jackie Monnier (Yvette), Hanna Hoessrich (Karl's wife), Else Heller (Karl's mother).

Nero-Film AG, Germany. 8766 ft., 97 mins.

Apathetic waiting for death: this is how the best of the early pacifist pictures sees the situation on the front in the fourth year of the

Great War. Pabst's fidelity to reality gave the story about four German soldiers killed one by one at the front an extraordinary expressiveness, and already in his first sound film introduced himself as the most outstanding individual stylist of the technical breakthrough in the cinema.

Westfront 1918 does not for one moment depart from the raw registration of facts, either towards emphatic symbolism or obtrusive naturalism. The monotony, mud, cold and boredom of the wartime landscape dominate the picture; armed confrontation does not appear here as atrocity, but above all as nonsense. It is true that Pabst did not raise the question of the causes of the war and did not analyze the evolution of the awareness of his protagonists, yet through the manner in which he treated his heroes he still took a clear political stand. Germany in 1931 found itself on the crossroads and the screens were full of praise for the homegrown armed forces, but Pabst clearly declared himself in the pacifist camp.

From the formal point of view, Westfront 1918 is a demonstration of the director's adaptability to the new conditions of filmmaking. The former fast and snappy editing was replaced by long takes with a mobile camera; the sound, although technically far from perfect, was used with great sense of economy and exclusively as immanent sound: music, alien to the line of thought of the film, was excluded.

ALL QUIET ON THE WESTERN FRONT   Lewis Milestone

Script: Maxwell Anderson, Del Andrews, George Abbott and Milestone, from the novel, "Im Westen nichts Neues," by Erich Maria Remarque. Photography: Arthur Edeson. Music: David Broekman. Cast: Lew Ayres (Paul Baumer), Louis Wolheim (Katchinsky), John Wray (Himmelstoss), Raymond Griffith (Gerard Duval), Slim Summerville (Tjaden), Russell Gleason (Müller), William Bakewell (Albert), Arnold Lucy (Kantorek), Ben Alexander (Kemmerich), Scott Kolk (Leer), Owen Davis Jr. (Peter), Beryl Mercer or Zasu Pitts in the European version (Mrs. Baumer), Edwin Maxwell (Mr. Baumer), Yola D'Avril (Suzanne).

Universal Pictures Corporation, U.S.A.   12,411 ft., 138 mins.

An adaptation of the most famous pacifist novel, written when World War I was over and World War II had not yet begun. This is literature on the screen rather than a cinematic transformation of the book--but literature excellently understood and well illustrated with images. Even in the first of his outstanding films Milestone showed his ability to bring the literary material to life: a series of narrative episodes, generic scenes and anecdotally treated situations ar-

ranges itself on the screen in an expressive war almanac, whose
main strength is the lack of gloomy prophecies and demoniacal
visions.

1915.   In a German town a group of senior schoolboys volun-
teer for the army under the influence of their fanatical teacher.
They experience the sordid reality of the trenches soon enough.
The central character is Paul Baumer, a subtle and sensitive boy.
All his school friends are killed one by one, but Paul survives
until 1918.   As the enemy fire dies away, he is killed while reaching for a butterfly among the barbed wire, just as the radio com-
munique announces: "All quiet on the Western Front."

The film contains no analysis of the causes of the war.
Milestone had no first hand experience of the Western Front and
in recreating it on the screen he had to rely on the book and on
miles and miles of documentary footage.   He got it right: the war
appears as common, which makes it even more cruel--and all the
more nonsensical.   The fact that the protagonists of the film are
German is quite unimportant; if they were French it would not make
much difference.   Milestone emphasized this in one of the three sequences of the film: when two soldiers, a German and a Frenchman, lie in a shell-hole while the successive attacks and counter-
attacks of the exhausted armies roll over them.

All Quiet on the Western Front spells out the absurdity of
war and attacks the concept of "hostility of nations," both by its
general tone and through the dialogues.   This was the message of
the novel, a classic written by a German of French descent whose
real name was Kramer, but who made it into a pseudonym by spelling it back to front in French.

This is obviously an early sound movie: the actors, not
used to the advantage of the sound still put too much stress on
gesticulation, and overact as a result.   The sound recording is not
too good; this is apart from the occasional low literary quality of
the dialogue.   And, to put all the faults together, there is some sentimentality (prayers in hospital).

The battle scenes in All Quiet on the Western Front are
merely a documentary registration of an unending slaughter, and
Milestone abandoned here all embellishments characteristic of the
rest of the film (like the meeting with the French girls), and drew
close to the severity of the German counterpart of his film--Pabst's
Westfront 1918.   Just as spectacle was avoided, so was commentary.
Even if commentary occasionally appears, it is an artistically justified exception--like the story, shown in a series of dissolves, of
the pair of boots which death transfers from one owner to another.

LITTLE CAESAR Mervyn Le Roy

Script: Francis Edwards Faragoh and Robert N. Lew, from the novel by W. R. Burnett. Photography: Tony Gaudio. Cast: Edward G. Robinson ("Rico" Bandello), Sidney Blackmer (Big Boss), Glenda Farrell (Olga Strassoff), Ralph Ince (Pete Montana), Douglas Fairbanks Jr. (Joe Massara), William Collier Jr. (Tony Passa), Thomas Jackson (Flaherty).

Darryl F. Zanuck, Hal Wallis for Warner Bros., U.S.A. 80 mins.

When Darryl F. Zanuck, the new production head of Warner Bros., set out to encourage films dealing with topical problems, no subject deserved attention more than urban gangsterism, the plague of the Prohibition years. The making of films on gangster themes had in fact already been initiated in the silent cinema by Joseph von Sternberg's Underworld, but the so-called "gangster series" started in earnest only in 1930.

While Sternberg was primarily interested in the psychological motivation of his protagonists, the gangster series assumed a sociological attitude, trying to trace the mechanism and social causes of urban crime in America. The heroes of the three principal gangster films (Caesar Enrico Bandello in Little Caesar, Tom Powers in Wellman's Public Enemy, Tony Camonte in Scarface) are in fact variations on the same personality: all come from a Catholic immigrant background, suffer from sexual inadequacy and climb the ladder of vice and treachery to reach the inevitable violent end.

Little Caesar is the portrait of a criminal who, after defeating rival gangs, becomes the king of the underworld in control of the entertainment industry in the city, until, betrayed by a woman, he dies from police bullets. Awareness of the power of his crime organization raises incredible conceit and indomitable haughtiness in Little Rico and surpresses all human reactions, including even the self-preservation instinct. He does not commit his crimes out of greed. Not at all: as a self-avowed superman he is interested only in power itself.

Le Roy took up the heritage of Sternberg's films and presented the gangster world with authenticity and ruthlessness, in a cold, almost predatory manner. Little Caesar is dominated by the excellent performance from Edward G. Robinson: the title role ensured for the unknown actor a leading position in Hollywood. The hero's dying words have become part of cinema lore, "Mother of mercy, is this the end of Rico?," and the picture itself was the first in a series of screen portrayals of underworld heroes.

THE BIG HOUSE   George Hill

Script: Frances Marion. Photography: Harold Wenstrom. Cast:
Chester Morris (Morgan), Wallace Beery (Butch), Lewis Stone
(Warden), Robert Montgomery (Kent), Leila Hyams (Anne), George
F. Marion (Pop), J. C. Nugent (Mr. Marlowe), Karl Dane (Olsen),
De Witt Jennings (Wallace), Mathew Betz (Gopher), Claire McDowell
(Mrs. Marlowe), Robert Emmett O'Connor (Donlin), Tom Kennedy
(Uncle Jed), Tom Wilson (Sandy), Eddie Foyer (Dopey), Roscoe
Ates (Putnam), Fletcher Norton (Oliver).

Cosmopolitan Productions, U.S.A.   7901 ft., 88 mins.

The inside of a prison--microcosm of the outside world with all its
conflicts and passions isolated and magnified. Although gangster
dramas had been in vogue for some years, the cinema somehow did
not follow gangsters in their inevitable progress and was slow at
taking cognizance of prison life as a potentially fruitful dramatic
theme. In The Big House this omission was rectified.

      A modern prison is seen by a new pair of eyes, a prisoner
in on a comparatively light charge. Apart from modern conveniences
and gadgets the prison contains really hellish places. The prison
population is dominated by one of the convicts, a brutish and con-
ceited thug. The agony is made more acute by the introduction of
scenes from the outside world, when one of the prisoners escapes
and falls in love with his cellmate's sister. The interpersonal conflicts culminate in a riot.

      The best thing about The Big House is the lack of any "hu-
manist" touches. Hill was impersonal (note the huge nightmarish
dining hall), ruthless and clinical; the expert script dispensed even
with the usual motif of friendship between cellmates. At the same
time this is one of the pictures which belong to the "cinema with a
social conscience" in America. It set out to attract public attention
to the basic wrong of the penitentiary system, i.e. that prisons
create, not reform criminals. This is shown very convincingly in
one of the plots in which a tough prisoner turns step by step into
a villain under the pressure of events.

      Prison themes were to stay in the cinema for ever after.
Problems similar to those explored here would appear in the 50's
in France (André Cayatte and others) and were to yield some really
interesting films.

MURDER [German title: MARY] Alfred Hitchcock

Script: Alma Reville, from the play, "Enter Sir John," by Cle-
mence Dane and Hellen Simpson. Photography: Jack Cox. Cast:
Herbert Marshall (Sir John Menier), Nora Baring (Diana Baring),
Phyllis Konstam (Dulcie Markham), Edward Chapman (Ted Mark-
ham), Miles Mander (Gordon Druce), Esmé Percy (Handel Fane),
Donald Calthrop (Ion Stewart).

British International Pictures, GB. 10,499 ft., 117 mins. The
film was made in two language versions: English and German.
Above credits are for the English version.

Murder is a rare Hitchcock whodunit. The type of film usually cultivated by the director can be described as a "suspense story" or,
if one prefers, a "thriller." It is usually a picture in which dramatic tension is sustained and increased throughout and where the
discovery of the villain (if he is not known from the very beginning)
often seems almost superfluous. Hitchcock confesses that he does
not like making films where all the interest is concentrated in the
ending.

The plot of Murder is set in the circus milieu. A young
artiste is accused of murdering a friend, tried and sentenced to
death on circumstantial evidence. But a member of the jury, not
convinced of her guilt, undertakes his own investigation and finds
that the real murderer was the fiancé of the accused. It is interesting to see how a cinematic and not in the least theatrical film can
be made from a stage play, and especially interesting that Hitchcock
even goes so far as to use the arch-theatrical "play within play"
technique for the purpose of generating suspense.

The most remarkable thing in Murder is its technical virtuosity. The visual form of the film reminds one of the works of
German Expressionism and seems very suitable in the context of
crime and guilt. Imaginative use was also made of the sound:
speech was used not realistically but to convey the subjective feelings of the characters. Thus the loud pronouncements of the guilt
of the accused are heard over a shot of the face of the only person
who believes in her innocence; internal monologue (i.e. monologue
from behind the frame and with no lip movement) was also used.

Hitchcock shot Murder in two simultaneous versions, English
and German, using different actors in each. This procedure was
rather unsuccessful, apparently because of the language difficulties.
Murder employs, probably for the first time, the principle of the
incredulous jury member, which later became a classical starting
point for crime films.

1931

KAMERADSCHAFT   Georg Wilhelm Pabst

Script: Ladislaus Vajda, Karl Otten and Peter Martin Lampel, from an idea by Otten. Photography: Fritz Arno Wagner and Robert Baberske. Sets: Ernö Metzner and Karl Vollbrecht. Cast: Fritz Kampers (Big miner), Alexander Granach (Kaspers), Ernst Busch (François), Gustav Püttjer (Thin man), Daniel Mandaille (Emile), Georges Charlia (Jean), Pierre Louis (Georges).

Nero-Film AG Berlin-Paris/Gaumont-Franco-Film Aubert, Germany/France.   8373 ft., 93 mins.

One of the greatest disasters in the history of mining occurred in 1906 in a coal mine near Courrières on the French-German border. The Germans took part in the rescue operation, helping their French comrades.   These real events became the starting point of Pabst's greatest film: the action was moved forward to 1921, and the main underlying theme became praise for human cooperation forged in the fight against a common adversary.

The script contains many allusions to the First World War, it also openly refers to the antagonisms which arose between the French and the Germans in the course of the rescue, but only in order to stress more strongly the conclusion that international cooperation is necessary.   Pabst mentioned only in passing what six years later became the theme of Renoir's La Grande illusion, that social divisions are deeper and more permanent than national divisions.   This noble message was supported by Pabst with brilliant film-making: the episodes which take place in the mine were shot not on location, but in the studio.   Paradoxically, this did not weaken the realism, but reinforced it, probably because, in the interest of verisimilitude, Pabst forced the actors to work in conditions which amounted to a safety hazard.

The style of <u>Kameradschaft</u> is very remote from that of <u>Pandora's Box</u>: the director's aim was neither to obtain atmosphere nor to achieve fine visual compositions. He strove towards psychological realism, faithful description of the milieu, and a clear message—and this is all contained in this concrete and tangible film, as concrete and tangible as the work of the miners all over the world to whom <u>Kameradschaft</u> was dedicated.

But this is not all: Pabst allowed himself a sarcastic reflection and introduced an ending in which the French and German border guards ceremonially replace the underground border grill which had been symbolically broken down earlier. This silent scene, banned by the censor and recently rediscovered, is about one minute long. It turns out to be the best in the film although the quality of the print is lower than in the rest of the film and the image unclear; the glowing lights, higher contrast and lack of sound give the episode a touch of a sinister symbolic vision.

M   Fritz Lang

<u>Script</u>: Thea von Harbou, based on a newspaper report by Egon Jacobson. <u>Photography</u>: Fritz Arno Wagner. <u>Music</u>: Edvard Grieg, the motif of part I of the "Peer Gynt" suite No. 1, Op. 46. <u>Cast</u>: Peter Lorre (Franz Becker, the murderer), Otto Wernicke (Inspector Lohmann), Ellen Widmann (Mrs. Beckmann), Inge Landgut (Elsie), Gustav Gründgens (Schränker), Theodore Loos (Groeber), Fritz Gnass (Burglar), Fritz Odemar (Card Sharper), Paul Kemp (Pickpocket), Theo Lingen (Confidence trickster), Ernest Stahl-Nachbaur (Chief of police), Franz Stein (Minister), Georg John (Blind beggar).

Nero-Film AG, Germany.   10,525 ft., 117 mins.

<u>M</u> is a classic of crime cinema, one of the best works of the genre and one of the best pictures of Lang, who broke once and for all with gigantomania and the Teutonic ornamentation of his productions of the late 20's (<u>Metropolis</u>): his ambition was this time to create a sort of reportage with documentary values, based on real events and judicial records (particularly the Kürten, Hartmann and Grossmann cases), and even using documentary film materials on the work of the police.

The central character is a psychopathic child murderer—a public enemy who will be apprehended by the public. Everybody in the city takes part in tracking the maniac down and his final apprehension is not so much the result of the work of the police as of the underworld, for which the psychopath is a real threat, as he keeps the cops on constant alert. "We have had enough of the police and the mess they make of everything," declare the bosses of the underworld and organize a hunt of their own, which Lang wittily counterpoints by showing the activities of the official guardians of public order.

In the excellently conducted narrative an important role is played by the sound. Despite the fact that the director is making his first sound film, he shows inventiveness and originality. Such acoustic effects as the mother calling the missing child, the recurring musical passage from Grieg's "Peer Gynt" whistled by the murderer, or the frightened panting which betrays him when he hides in the attic of an empty office building, amount even after so many years to some of the best examples of the creative use of sound.

<u>M</u> is an attractive and fascinating thriller, but it also has less obvious values underneath the appealing exterior. (This is apart from the question whether some of the factors for which we value the film were in fact intended by its creators.) The climactic scene of the underworld holding a kangaroo trial for the murderer is especially disturbing. Peter Lorre brilliantly portrayed him as an unhappy and deeply disturbed man. Admittedly, society has to eliminate such people, but how? Lang touched here on the basic dilemma of any judicial system. The great question of the finale is left unanswered; <u>M</u> ends full of doubt and compassion for human failings.

THE THREEPENNY OPERA (Die Dreigroschenoper)   Georg Wilhelm
   Pabst

<u>Script</u>: Leo Lania, Belá Balázs and Ladislaus Vajda, from the play by Bertold Brecht, inspired by the "Beggar's Opera" (1728), by John Gay. <u>Photography</u>: Fritz Arno Wagner. <u>Sets</u>: Andrei Andreiev. <u>Music</u>: Kurt Weill and Theo Mackeben. <u>Cast</u> (German version): Rudolf Forster (Mackie Messer), Carola Neher (Polly Peachum), Valeska Gert (Mrs. Peachum), Fritz Rasp (Peachum), Reinhold Schünzel (Tiger Brown), Lotte Lenja (Jenny), Hermann Thimig (Priester), Ernst Busch (Street singer), Vladimir Sokoloff (Prison warder).

Nero-Film AG/Tobis-Klangfilm/Warner Bros., Germany/U.S.A.
10,161 ft., 113 mins.

<u>The Threepenny Opera</u>, a screen version of the famous stage spectacular which three years earlier had had a great triumph at the

Berlin Theater am Schiffbauerdamm, was actually made earlier in
the same year as Kameradschaft and although it belongs to the
greatest films of Pabst, is rather exceptional from the point of
view of his aesthetic (although not his social) interests. It was an
extremely difficult screen adaptation--yet an unqualified success.
In order to achieve it, Pabst had of course to abandon his realist
views and his concept of "non-ornamentation" of life--and he did
this with complete consistency.

The play, anarchistic not only in content but also in form,
is transformed on the screen into a dramatically compact construction and the unavoidable loss of the elemental quality of the theatre
is compensated for by the precise fluidity of the screen narrative.
The unity of the whole was achieved by the creation of a unique atmosphere which permeates the picture and which in a sense resembles the dreamlike quality of the later films of the Nouvelle Vague.
Thus the action takes place among Andreiev's sets exaggerating real
dimensions and stylized after the Victorian fin-de-siècle; Wagner's
stunning photography de-concretizes the image by the constant movement of the camera and surrounds objects with a halo of glamor and
light.

Yet despite these concessions to a poetic convention, Pabst
did not abandon the Brechtian view of society. On the contrary--
some anti-bourgeois accents were actually strengthened (note for instance the added subplot of Polly Peachum's bank) and the culminating scene of thousands of beggars emerging from dark side streets
and alleys onto the brightly lit route of the Royal procession, counts
among not only the most excellent visually, but also the most radical
in the German cinema of the early 30's.

The fluency with which the Brechtian songs were incorporated
into the screen action is quite remarkable: The Threepenny Opera,
the film which was not intended to be a musical, is ahead of America cinema in the naturalness and ease with which the songs and the
dialogue scenes are combined, by twenty years. A great deal of
credit for the perfection of the final result is also owed to the excellent cast.

All the same, Brecht was not satisfied with what his play became on the screen. What is more--he brought a legal suit against
the company which produced the film. And he won it. Yet this
does not prove him right....

TABU   Friedrich Wilhelm Murnau and Robert J. Flaherty

Script: Muranu and Flaherty. Assistant Director: David Flaherty.
Photography: Floyd Crosby and Flaherty. Music: Hugo Riesenfeld.

Cast: Anna Chevalier (Reri, the young girl), Matahi (boy), Hitu
(old chief), Kong Ah (Chinese merchant), Jean, Jules and other
non-professionals from Bora-Bora and Tahiti.

Murnau-Flaherty Production, U.S.A.   90 mins.

Flaherty's documentary from the South Seas, Moana (1925), was a
considerable commercial success. Encouraged by this and hoping
to capitalize on the increased popular interest in exotic themes
which provided a momentary escape from the hard reality of the
day, Paramount arranged the cooperation of Flaherty and Friedrich
Wilhelm Murnau, the great German director of subtle psychological
films who had arrived in America in 1926. As a result the two
left for the Society Islands where Flaherty provided the story (that
he do so was insisted upon by the producers) and the ethnological
advice, since he was familiar with the locale and acted as one of
the cameramen; the direction was in the hands of Murnau.

     The simple intrigue, quite in the spirit of Flaherty's re-
maining pictures, tells of the love of a pearl-diver and a girl who
is destined to be a priestess of her tribe. The escape of the lovers
to a paradise-like island is in vain: the girl is taken away and the
boy drowns having failed in his pursuit.

     Love destroyed by social conventions: the motif so essen-
tially European and present in the cinema from the very beginning
appears as no less penetrating discovered in the lives of the natives
of Bora-Bora. Tabu is an interesting blend of the elements of vitality and destruction, obtained through the cooperation of two artists
of brilliance but of fundamentally different interests.

     Flaherty's foremost preoccupation had always been to praise
the symbiosis of man and nature, while Murnau questioned the meaning of existence and the workings of fate. Thus the story of doomed
love turned into a universal philosophical discourse about the problems
common to different cultures and a nostalgic vision of paradise lost
by urban civilization. This is independent of the fact that these two
so different concepts of the function of the cinema were difficult to
reconcile and the cooperation between Murnau and Flaherty broke up
prematurely.

     Tabu still preserves distinct hallmarks of both its creators
and remains a fascinating mixture of Murnau's somber sentimentality
and Flaherty's documentary matter-of-factness, an oddly touching
fairy tale full of impressive visual beauty.

LE MILLION   René Clair

Script: Clair, based on the musical comedy by Georges Berr and M. Guillemaud. Photography: Georges Périnal and Georges Raulet. Sets: Lazare Meerson. Music: Georges Van Parys, Armand Bernard and Philippe Parès. Cast: René Lefèvre (Michel), Annabella (Béatrice), Louis Allibert (Prosper), Vanda Gréville (Vanda), Paul Olivier ("Father Tulipe," a gangster), Odette Talazac (Prima donna), Constantin Stroësco (Sopranelli, the tenor), Raymond Cordy (Taxi driver).

Films Sonores Tobis, France.   8029 ft., 89 mins.

As the silent The Italian Straw Hat was a parody in mime of the conventions of vaudeville, Le Million, a sound film, became a parody of the operetta. Prosper and Michel, two artists troubled by financial difficulties, buy a lottery ticket which wins a million. But the jacket with the ticket in the pocket is stolen by a thief nicknamed "Father Tulipe." The friends recover it after a breakneck chase through police stations and an opera stage, where the jacket is used as a prop.

By this time Clair had achieved mastery in his craft: this stylized Parisian comedy was built with a watchmaker's precision in both the compositional and stylistic aspects. The content is slight and unimportant--it constituted only a pretext for creating a mathematically precise framework of a film operetta, and also served as an excuse for satirizing the stuffy conventions of theatre, opera and loquacious cinema, which the director found so unbearable. The confrontation with theatrical artificiality is carried out quite openly: Clair unashamedly reveals that the sets are made of paper and cardboard and that, to put it mildly, there are flagrant contradictions between the spirit and the matter.

The skill displayed is worthy of high praise, but all the same, it was impossible to discard all conventions. The stylized operetta still remains an operetta; after all, even a masterful parody of shoddiness is not enough to create new lasting values. The main strength of Le Million is its formal virtuosity.

GIRLS IN UNIFORMS (Mädchen in Uniform)   Leontine Sagan

Co-director: Carl Froelich. Script: Christa Winsloe and F. D.

Andam, from the play, "Gestern und Heute," by the former. Photography: Reimar Kuntze and Franz Weihmayr. Music: Hansom Milde-Meissner. Cast: Dorothea Wieck (Fraülein von Bernburg), Hertha Thiele (Manuela von Meinhardis), Emilie Unda (Headmistress), Ellen Schwanneke (Ilse von Westhagen), Hedwig Schlichter (Fraülein von Kosten), Gertrud de Lalsky (Manuela's aunt).

Deutsche Filmgemeinschaft GmbH, Germany. 8799 ft., 98 mins.

A woman's voice in the political discussion on the future of Germany, a country which was still at the crossroads, but soon to sink into the gloom of Hitlerism. Although the film is set in the period before the First World War, the message is relevant enough. Girls in Uniforms is a story of a sensitive girl lost in the Prussian atmosphere of a Potsdam boarding school for the daughters of the poorer officers of Emperor Wilhelm II.

        The school, run along military lines, seeks to instill in the girls the ideals of absolute obedience to authority ("you are the future mothers of soldiers," says the headmistress) and personal self-denial. The heroine finds sympathy only with one woman teacher and transfers all her feelings onto her. This affection is taken for lesbianism and leads to a dangerous spiritual conflict; deprived of the possibility of seeing her ideal, Manuela attempts suicide.

        Lack of freedom as a source of emotional anomalies is a thesis similar to that in Sternberg's The Blue Angel, but is here presented with subtlety and gentleness of description--not in the form of a protest or an indictment of Prussian methods of education, but in the spirit of placid persuasion. This is a doubtful solution from the point of view of the picture's crusading potential, but certainly valuable from the artistic angle, especially since the delicate style is well suited to the touchy but never superficially treated theme of the anxieties of an emerging woman. A very important aspect of Girls in Uniforms is the excellent acting.

THE CONGRESS DANCES (Der Kongress tantzt) Erik Charell

Script: Norbert Falk and Robert Liebmann. Photography: Carl Hoffmann. Sets: Walter Rohrig and Robert Herlth. Costumes: Ernst Stern. Music: Werner R. Heymann. Cast: Lilian Harvey (Christel Weinzinger), Willy Fritsch (Tsar Alexander I/The Tsar's double), Conrad Veidt (Prince Metternich), Lil Dagover (The Countess), Adele Sandrock (The Princess), Otto Wallburg (Bibikov), Carl Heinz Schroth (Pepi, Metternich's Secretary), Julius Falkenstein (Minister of Finance).

Erich Pommer/UFA, Germany.   9098 ft., 101 mins.

The Congress Dances is the greatest achievement of the German
film operetta, a picture full of genuine charm, waltzing rhythm and
lightness.   It was led by the skilled hand of the former director of
the spectacular Berlin stage revues.   The crowds of extras and an
abundance of sets recreating the period of the Vienna Congress of
1815, do not overbalance the film in the slightest: Charell felt like
a fish in water in the realm of the cinema and fulfilled all the expectations of his producers, who wished to crown a series of film
roles by the prepossessing duo Lilian Harvey/Willy Fritsch with a
gigantic historical parade.

        Of course, there is just as much history here as is needed:
the adventures center around behind-the-scenes intrigues, in which
the main role--the appropriate manipulation of the political intentions
of Tsar Alexander I--is entrusted to a beautiful Viennese girl. Christel is to be punished when a bunch of flowers she threw during a parade accidentally lands on the Tsar's head but Pepi, who is in love
with her, intervenes. Pepi is the secretary of Metternich, the Austrian foreign minister; when it turns out that the Tsar is crazy about
Christel (there was the address of her shop in the bunch of flowers),
Metternich hopes this will take the Tsar's attention away from politics.   But the Tsar's double is introduced into the play and these
hopes are thwarted.   During a gala ball a telegram arrives: Napoleon has escaped from Elba and landed in France.   Everybody
leaves and Christel's hopes of going to St. Petersburg are dashed.
But there is always the loving Pepi....

        Excellent photography gave the film wings: Hoffmann's cam-
era was in constant movement; the several-hundred-yard tracking
shot of the heroine's coach ride with the Tsar throughout Vienna has
its own niche in cinema history.

A PASS TO LIFE (Putyovka v Zhizn) [Road to Life]   Nikolai Ekk

---

Script: Ekk, Alexandr Stolper and Regina Yanushkevich. Photog-
raphy: Vasili Pronin. Music: Yakov Stollyar. Cast: Nikolai
Batalov (Sergeyev), Ivan Kyrla (Mustafa), Mikhail Dzhagofarov (Kol-
ka), V. Vesnovsky (His father), Regina Yanushkevich (His mother),
Mikhail Zharov (Fomka Zhigan), M. Gonta (Lolka), Alexandr Novikov
(Vaska), A. Antropova (Inspector Skryabina).

Mezhrabpomfilm, U.S.S.R. 10,827 ft., 120 mins.

The Russian Revolution left thousands of homeless orphans behind.

The fate of these children and the efforts of the social workers who tried to restore the young dropouts to the community are the themes of the first Soviet sound feature film in the strict sense of the word. A teacher organizes a cooperative factory in an old monastery which is to be run by the children themselves. Lack of materials temporarily stops work; an adolescent gang from Moscow provokes a violent conflict with the residents which ends in tragedy—but the work will continue.

A Pass to Life is certainly an uneven film: journalistic ambitions are entwined with melodrama and the portrayal of the criminal underworld is rather overdone. But what also counts is the film's sincerity, interesting semi-documentary sequences (scenes of the round-up of the deliquents from the cellars of abandoned houses), and the strength with which it carries its message, a strength reinforced by characteristic Russian warmth and affection. Considerable credit for this is due to the actors, chosen according to the "typage" procedure, and of whom a considerable percentage were recruited from the labor colony near Moscow.

The sound was not yet consistently employed; there are silent passages and an abundance of captions (which were to persist in the Soviet cinema until the war). All the same, in several scenes Ekk managed to make acoustical effects into very essential, even crucial dramatic components, particularly in the final scene in which the buzz of the preparations for the celebration is brought into collision with the silent homage to the murdered friend.

HOTEL PARADIS   George Schnéevoigt

Script: Flemming Lynge, from the novel by Einar Rousthøjs.
Music: Kai Normann Andersen. Cast: Eyvind Johan-Svendsen (Heinrich Schultze), Karen Caspersen (Emilie Schultze), Kirsten Møller (Rosa, their daughter, as a child), Inger Stender (Rosa as an adult), Holger Reenberg (Kleinsorg), Jon Iversen (Pastor Seeligmann), Svend Melsing (Max von Krakow), Elith Pio (Fridolin), Karen Poulsen (Tosse-Grethe), Robert Schmidt (Hangman).

Nordisk Film, Denmark. 9629 ft., 107 mins.

Hotel Paradis is one of the first Danish sound films; it was directed by the man who was earlier a cameraman on several of Dreyer's films. It is a melancholy story of a couple who lease a hotel on the coast and, unable to pay rent, murder their only guest for money—only to spend the rest of their lives in an agony of remorse. Perhaps not a very cinematic plot, indeed a theatrical one: but Schnéevoigt's handling of it makes Hotel Paradis a veritable film of atmosphere, heavy with an almost tangible air of existential sadness. That, and the two excellent leading roles, more than outweigh a certain sentimentality (for which the film was criticized at the time, but which is not so apparent to modern eyes), and an imperfect incorporation of the dialogue into the picture, which was a common flaw during the first years of sound.

PUBLIC ENEMY   William A. Wellman

Script: Harvey Thew, from the story by Kubec Glasmon and John Bright. Photography: Dev Jennings. Cast: James Cagney (Tom Powers), Jean Harlow (Gwen), Edward Woods (Matt Doyle), Joan Blondell (Mamie), Beryl Mercer (Mrs. Powers), Donald Cook (Mike Powers), Mae Clarke (Kitty), Mia Marvin (Jane), Leslie Fenton ("Nails" Nathan), Robert Emmett O'Connor (Paddy Ryan).

Warner, U.S.A.   85 mins.

The gangster's progress: Tom Powers' path from an indulgent middle-class background to big time crime leads through petty thefts, robbery of fur warehouses and first murders in inter-gang warfare, to the final coming of age--the liquor racket. His end is easy to predict and as violent as his life: Tom's trussed corpse is dumped on his mother's doorstep.

Public Enemy is the most typical classic of the gangster series, in the sense that its principal value is its registrative, factual, "journalistic" quality--and also because the scriptwriters did not base the plot on facts from police chronicles or on lives of known gangsters, but tried to give a synthetic, sociological vision of the road to crime of an ordinary member of the underworld, from childhood to tragic end.

Wellman treated the protagonist of his film as more than an insect under an entomologist's magnifying glass; he studied the man with commitment, more--with sympathy. The director justified this attitude by his intention to place responsibility for the events he showed onto the social conditions after the Great Crisis. However, sympathy for a gangster seemed too dangerous when the difficulties of everyday life left many obligatory moral rules suspended in the air.

The short period of the flowering of the gangster film was soon to come to an end after the fierce offensive of the Daughters of the American Revolution and the American Legion. Their argument, still very much alive now, was that description of crime incites to crime; even the fact that gangster cinema condemned gang-

sterism was left unheeded. The disease of gangsterism was too
dangerous to be discussed with full frankness.

THE FRONT PAGE Lewis Milestone

Script: Ben Hecht, Bartlett Cormack, Charles Lederer and Charles
MacArthur, from the play by Hecht and MacArthur. Photography:
Glen MacWilliams and Bert Camm. Cast: Adolphe Menjou (Walter
Burns), Pat O'Brien (Hildy Johnson), Mary Brian (Peggy Grant),
Edward Everett Horton (Bensinger), Walter Cartlett (Murphy),
George E. Stone (Earl Williams), Mae Clarke (Molly Malloy), Slim
Summerville (Mr. Pincus).

United Artists, U.S.A. 101 mins.

A situation comedy set in the milieu of the Chicago court journalists:
ruthless newshounds exploit an approaching execution while a crafty
editor tries to keep his star reporter on the job by hook or by
crook.   The situation is further complicated when the condemned
man escapes and hides in the newspaper office. The Front Page is
an exemplary screen adaptation of the very famous Hecht-MacArthur
stage play, a satire stigmatizing the professional anesthesia of tabloid journalism.   So successful was it in fact that not only were
there three film versions, it was revived on Broadway in 1969 and in
1972 in London.

      The difficulty Milestone faced making the picture was to
transplant the basically stable play into the medium of the cinema
while losing nothing of its wit. He solved the problem by putting
the camera in constant motion: although the action moves little in
the physical sense of the word, the camera in a series of pans
achieves the feel of breadth and space.   To break entirely with the
stage Milestone added a number of realistic touches; one of them
was the use of sets with four walls, instead of the usual three.
From then on the flow of sparkling, intelligent dialogue and the
piling up of quid pro quo situations could proceed unimpeded.

      Adolphe Menjou, whose roles were always of worldly, so-
phisticated men, was here--very surprisingly--cast as a cynical
editor, and did very well in the part. (When he adapted the same
play to the screen a few years later, under the title His Girl Friday, Howard Hawks added an interesting twist to the story by casting a woman in the important role of the star reporter.)

MARIUS   Alexander Korda

Script: Marcel Pagnol, from his own play. Photography: Ted Pahle. Music: Francis Grammon. Cast: Raimu (César Ollivier), Pierre Fresnay (Marius, his son), Orane Demazis (Fanny), Alida Rouffe (Honorine), Fernand Charpin (Honoré Panisse), Robert Vattier (Monsieur Brun), Paul Dulac (Félix Escartefigue), Mihalesco (Piquoiseau), Edouard Delmont (Second Mate), Giovanni (Ferry boatman), Milly Mathis (Aunt Claudine Foulon), Maupi (Chauffeur), Oueret (Felicite), Vassy (An Arab).

Marcel Pagnol/Paramount, France. 11,235 ft., 125 mins. (originally 130 mins.).

This film is the first part of the "Marseilles Trilogy," based on Marcel Pagnol's stage plays; parts made later are Fanny and César. The film is definitely more the property of Pagnol than of Korda, who was in this case only the executor of the intentions of the author. Pagnol, who already in the early 30's was a known comedy dramatist, became in the cinema the disciple of the doctrine of "tinned theatre," which propounded the literal transformation of stage plays onto film. Of course, such an approach was quite wrong in principle, but the cinema of the early sound years, which did not have sufficiently crystallized narrative methods at its disposal, found it impossible to avoid. Pagnol encountered fierce opposition from the followers of "pure cinema," but this did not change his stand one bit.

Pagnol was not in fact as orthodox as he would have liked us to believe, although it is true that the films made from his plays (he became a film director himself in 1934) were characterized by the irritatingly immobile camera and the prevalence of inflexible medium long-shots. It must be said however that he did not avoid the use of exteriors and, after all, the careful preparation of dialogues was not equivalent to making the way actors say them theatrical. There are two reasons for the success of the dialogue: first, because both the Marseilles Trilogy and the later films (of which The Baker's Wife is the best) are very closely connected with the everyday life of the French Provence and thus with its dialect; and second, because the main roles were played by truly outstanding actors, who knew how to adapt to the required artistic convention.

The first part of the trilogy initiates the story of Marius, the boy who loves Fanny, a seller of crabs, as much as he loves the sea. The call of faraway journeys, a theme which persisted in the French cinema throughout the inter-war period, appears in the end to have the upper hand.... Marius is not a film of atmosphere, as could be expected from the plot, but a witty generic tale. The

strongest trump of the screen Pagnol is indeed the richness of folkloristic and psychological observation which partly obscures the
stage pedigree of his films.

VAMPYR, OU L'ÉTRANGE AVENTURE DE DAVID GRAY (American
  title: NOT AGAINST THE FLESH) - Carl Theodor Dreyer

Script: Dreyer with Christen Jul, from "Carmilla" and "Room
in the Dragon Volant" in In a Glass Darkly by Joseph Sheridan
Le Fanu. Photography: Rudolf Maté and Louis Née. Art Di-
rection: Hermann Warm, Hans Bittmann and Cesare Silvagni. Mu-
sic: Wolfgang Zeller. Cast: Julian West, alias Baron Nicolas de
Gunzburg (David Gray), Henriette Gérard (Marguerite Chopin, the
Vampire), Maurice Schutz (Owner of the castle), Rena Mandel (Gi-
sèle, his daughter), Sybille Schmitz (Léone, his daughter), Jan
Hieronimko (Doctor), Albert Bras, N. Babanini (Servants), Jane
Mora (Nurse).

C. T. Dreyer Filmproduktion/Tobis-Klangfilm, Germany. 8957 ft.,
99 mins, later cut to 6070 ft., 67 mins.

A screen adaptation of a 19th-century tale of horror: a young man
arrives in the village of Courtempierre, where a vampire aided by
a villainous doctor terrorizes the castle owner and his two daughters,
finally causing the death of the father and one of the girls. The
picture ends with a scene that has become a classic of subjective
narrative: David Gray, sitting on a cemetery bench, imagines his
own funeral which is shown through his own eyes as he is lying in
the coffin.

This film, totally unexpected coming from the creator of The
Passion of Joan of Arc, was in all probability undertaken for economic reasons, although in fact Dreyer did have a free choice of
theme. So, Vampyr was a temporary change which a Dutch aristo-
crat-cum-cinema-enthusiast, who quite successfully appears in the
title part, agreed to finance. Under Dreyer's hand the second-rate
literary material transformed into a perhaps weird, but certainly
fascinating (and of course formally brilliant) debate about the inner
anxieties of man.

It is significant that, like some other outstanding directors
in their first sound films (to mention only Chaplin's City Lights),
Dreyer almost eschewed spoken dialogue in favor of subtitles, which
in fact have an importance of their own in stressing narrative rhythm. The avoidance of dialogues was certainly dictated primarily
by the director's desire to create a film of atmosphere along the
lines of Epstein's The Fall of the House of Usher (although the tech-

nical difficulties inherent in shooting a sound film in three languages
at once must have also played a part).

The mood-creating elements here are, first, the silence interrupted by disturbing sounds, then the misty images filmed through
diffusion discs, and then of course the locations so indispensable to
the horror genre: a cemetery, a deserted mill, an old decrepit
château. In Vampyr Dreyer created something very rare for the
concrete art of the cinema--a world in which nothing seems real.

CITY STREETS   Rouben Mamoulian

Script: Max Marcin and Oliver Garrett, from a story by Dashiell
Hammett. Photography: Lee Garmes. Cast: Gary Cooper (The
Kid), Sylvia Sidney (Nan), Paul Lukas ("Big Fella" Maskal), William
Boyd (McCoy), Guy Kibbee (Pop Cooley), Stanley Fields (Blackie),
Wynne Gibson (Agnes), Betty Sinclair (Pansy).

Paramount, U.S.A. 6633 ft., 74 mins.

Rouben Mamoulian was one of the most versatile and most eclectic
Hollywood film-makers. Born in Russia, he at first worked as a
theatrical and operatic director in London and New York. His films
are very varied, ranging from the horror story, Dr. Jekyll and Mr.
Hyde (1931), to the weepy pseudo-psychological melodrama, Queen
Christina (1933), with Greta Garbo, and the first Technicolor movie
ever, Becky Sharp (1935). Mamoulian never hesitated to transplant
theatrical elements into the cinema, as well as effects observed
from other directors. He did not really have a personal style, but
was certainly a thorough craftsman or even--if one considers the
celerity with which he assimilated the discoveries of others--an innovator.

City Streets, his second film, is a conventional gangster
drama of Prohibition era bootlegging. A shooting gallery attendant
loves the daughter of a beer racketeer who wants him to join his
gang. The young man finally does in order to help the girl who is
in jail charged with a gang war killing; but when she is released
the two escape the world of crime and head towards a new life.

The film is notable for its sense of style: the soft lighting,
free and fluent camera movements and the visual and acoustic symbols (the ominous sound of a passing train during a chase, the recurrent shots of statuettes of cats and a bird in a cage used in a
context similar to that in Greed). There is also interesting use of
internal monologue whereby the thoughts of the heroine (i.e. the obsessive word "beer," just like Hitchcock's "knife" in Sabotage (1936)

--where even the same actress was used) are heard over a close-up of her face with no lip movement.

    Actually, City Streets is more of a love story than a drama of violence and in this sense it is related to Underworld and the later They Live by Night. The film never shows a killing and can afford intimations of tenderness as in the scene in the prison visiting room. This tone was in fact predetermined by the choice of leading actors. In City Streets, gangsters are not ape-like mobsters like the hero of Scarface but are shown to have human feelings and in the case of Gary Cooper can be even remarkably sympathetic. Thus Mamoulian stays clear of the imperatives of the "gangster series" and is more interested in the process by which a decent man is engulfed by crime, even if he allows him to escape in the end.

EMIL AND THE DETECTIVES (Emil und die Detektive) Gerhard
    Lamprecht

Script: Billy Wilder, from the novel by Erich Kästner. Photography: Werner Brandes. Music: Allan Gray. Cast: Kathe Haack (Frau Tischbein), Rolf Wonkhaus (Emil, her son), Olga Engl (Grandmother), Inge Landgut (Pony Hutchen), Fritz Rasp (Man-in-the-bowler-hat), Rudolf Biebrach (Superintendent Jeschke), Hans-Joachim Schaufuss (Gustav-with-the-motor-horn), Hans Richter (Flying Stag), Hubert Schmitz (Professor), Hans Albrecht Lohr (Young Tuesday).

UFA, Germany. 6670 ft., 74 mins.

Conflict with German teenagers is dangerous, as the crook who inconsiderately robs the young hero finds out to his cost. The 12-year-old Emil is sent by his mother to take 140 marks to his grandmother in Berlin. The Man-in-the-bowler-hat steals the money while the boy is asleep during the journey. Emil discovers the loss and, with a crowd of Berlin youngsters led by Gustav-with-the-motor-horn, follows the thief everywhere. Emil's rational actions, backed up by the organizational talents of his loyal friends, achieve results of which even the police would not be ashamed to boast.

    In the impressive, elemental final sequence the villain is caught beyond appeal and bright, cheerful justice and order overcome the darkness of the world of crime. The Man-in-the-bowler-hat turns out to be a bank robber long wanted by the police, Emil receives the reward for his arrest and returns to a civic reception in his home town.

    Emil and the Detectives is a very successful screen adapta-

tion of the famous boys' story. It is done with humor, lightness of
touch and an extraordinary naturalness in its treatment of the young
heroes, so much so that it gives the impression that it was not directed by an adult but by one of the children. The story was re-
filmed a number of times and in various countries, but with much
inferior results.

The script was written by Billy Wilder, at that time an Austrian scriptwriter who had started his career by scripting the well-
known documentary People on Sunday (1930), directed by Robert
Siodmak (at that time also an Austrian). In 1934 Wilder went to
America and, while still scripting his films, became one of the
major Hollywood directors.

AN AMERICAN TRAGEDY   Josef von Sternberg

Script: Samuel Hoffenstein, based on the novel by Theodore Dreiser.
Photography: Lee Garmes. Cast: Phillips Holmes (Clyde Griffiths), Sylvia Sidney (Roberta Alden), Frances Dee (Sondra Finch-
ley), Irving Pichel (Orville Mason), Frederick Burton (Samuel Griffiths), Claire McDowell (Mrs. Samuel Griffiths), Wallace Middleton
(Gilbert Griffiths), Vivian Winston (Myra Griffiths), Arnold Korff
(Judge), Richard Kramer (Deputy Sheriff Kraut).

Paramount, U.S.A. Approx. 90 mins.

After the triumph of The Blue Angel Sternberg made two more films
with Marlene Dietrich, both spy melodramas and both popular successes. Surprisingly, his next undertaking was an adaptation of
Dreiser's grim realist novel about a young man, the son of mis-
sionaries, who, driven by a passion for social advancement, intends
to murder his pregnant working-class girl friend to be free for a
financially successful match. He is brought to trial and convicted
when the girl accidentally drowns.

The novel is in its intention an arraignment of the society
which has destroyed the hero's sense of values, a demonstration of
the damage done to him by a Puritan upbringing. It was in this
spirit that Sergei Eisenstein wanted to film the novel during his stay
in America (telling the story as a stream-of-consciousness monologue), but his script was rejected by Paramount as a piece of Communist propaganda. Sternberg, who never even saw Eisenstein's
script, approached the problem outlined in the novel quite differently. He argued that Clyde Griffiths' tragedy is not necessarily
brought about by the faults of American society but by the character
of the man and is equally conceivable elsewhere.

In other words, Sternberg's view was that this is not primarily an "American" tragedy. Consequently the director disre-
garded the social implications of the book (causing the author's fury
and a court case which Dreiser lost) and while actually using the
original literary dialogue exclusively, centered on psychological realism, which he enforced by his inimitable visual poetry and contrasts of light and shade. Sternberg's An American Tragedy (a box-
office flop in America but a success in Europe) is a study of frustration and dashed aspirations, counterpointed by recurring shots of
water.

L'OR DES MERS   Jean Epstein

Script: Epstein. Photography: Christian Matras, assisted by Albert Bres and Joseph Braun. Acted by the inhabitant-fishermen of
the island of Hoedick.

Synchro-Cine, France. Approx. 6562 ft. Originally a silent film,
released in 1933 with sound and music (by Devaux and Kross-Hert-
man), which was not approved by the director.

A poor old fisherman finds a chest on the sea shore and is convinced it contains a treasure. His neighbors hold similar beliefs.
To get hold of the supposed gold, one of the young men of the village
tries to win the favors of the lucky man's daughter. When in the
end it turns out that the chest contains only glass, the boy already
loves the girl for real....

The third of Epstein's Brittany films, after Finis Terrae and
the medium-length Mor-Vran (1930), is, like the first, a reconstruction of an authentic happening, made with the participation of the inhabitants of the isle of Hoedick. Simplicity, slowness of rhythm,
and poetry: a complete contrast to the path that most of the cinema
of the first years of sound had taken. It is not surprising then that
Epstein lived to receive the highest praise after the premiere of
L'Or des mers--but he did not live to gain popularity. The artist
striving for ascetic beauty became lost in the noise of the sound
cinema.

TELL ENGLAND   Anthony Asquith and Geoffrey Barkas

Script: Asquith, from the novel by Ernest Raymond. Photography:
Jack Parker, Stanley Rodwell and James Rogers. Cast: Carl Har-

bord (Edgar Doe), Tony Bruce (Rupert Ray), Fay Compton (Mrs. Doe), Dennis Hoey (Padre), C. M. Hallard (Colonel), Frederick Lloyd (Captain Harding), Gerald Rawlinson (Doon), Lionel Hedges (Sims), Sam Wilkinson (Booth), Wally Patch (Sgt. Instructor), Hubert Harben (Mr. Ray).

British Instructional, G.B.   8530 ft., 95 mins.

Anthony Asquith, son of the first Earl of Oxford and Asquith, began taking interest in films in the 20's and attracted critical attention with his fourth picture, A Cottage On Dartmoor (1929), a melo-dramatic thriller which was said to have "out-Hitchcocked Hitch-cock" and which proved Asquith's independent style.   Tell England, an early sound film, is a war picture based on a dramatic principle similar to that in Richardson's The Charge of the Light Brigade: that of contrast between the quietness and peaceful comfort of rural England and the brutality of the battlefield.

        The subject matter is the Gallipoli Campaign--a bloody oper-ation conducted by the Allied forces in Turkey in 1915-1916; the story concerns a young upper-class Englishman who is torn out of his idyllic home life to take part in the war.   The battle scenes, especially the sequences of the landing on the peninsula, are es-pecially powerful.   In general the picture displays quite a high standard of cinematic craftsmanship with its skillful cutting and imaginative use of incidental sound and music, and remains--in case it means anything--the best British war film made before the Second World War.

1932

¡QUE VIVA MEXICO!   Sergei Eisenstein

Co-director: Grigori Alexandrov. Script: Eisenstein. Photography: Eduard Tissé.

Produced by Upton Sinclair, U.S.A.

A masterpiece which does not exist: the nearly complete material was never assembled in the intended form, either by its director or by the producer, who--annoyed by the escalating budget and protracted time of execution--took the film away from Eisenstein. Such was the end of the Soviet master's trip to the West, which began in 1929.

        To begin with Eisenstein worked in Western Europe, where he carried out studies that were to broaden his theory of "intellectual montage." In 1930 he crossed the Atlantic. Paramount offered him the direction of a film, but none of the projected adaptations of eminent literary works (among others, Dreiser's "An American Tragedy" and Joyce's "Ulysses") ever materialized. Then the writer Upton Sinclair decided to finance a film about Mexico, leaving the director a very wide margin of creative freedom. But Eisenstein could not be contained within it. A conflict resulted, one of the reasons for which was the fact that the director wanted to make a silent film, with only the folk songs as musical illustration. It would have been extremely difficult to distribute such a film at the time when the movie public were totally conquered by the talkies.

        In April 1932 Eisenstein returned to the U.S.S.R., and his ¡Que Viva Mexico! is preserved only in fragmentary form in several other films intended as partial recreations of the originally envisaged form; one of them, Time in the Sun, was assembled by Mary Seton, the director's assistant; another (Eisenstein's Mexican Project), by Jay Leyda. The finished work was to consist of six parts, and would convey the essence of that complex country of great contrasts, violent passions and magnificent history--the whole richness of the land fascinated Eisenstein and he wanted to create its image in a manner commensurate with its great latent potential.

The prologue was to be a documentary report from Chichén Itzá, the ancient sacred city of the Mayas. The first of the four stories following the prologue, "Sandunga," is the story of the love of a young Indian couple from Tehuantepec. The second, "Fiesta," takes place during a feast and deals with the traces of Spanish influence in Mexican culture: the principal elements here are the corrida, the religious procession, and the impious passion of a woman for her husband's friend.

"Maguey," the third story, tells of a ruthlessly suppressed mutiny of peons, provoked by the rape of an Indian girl by a stranger invited to the property of the landowner. The last story, "La Soldadera," is the only part of the work which was never filmed. It was to be the life of a woman accompanying the revolutionary detachments of Villa and Zapata. Her husband is killed in battle at the moment when his child is born: the culmination of the motif of life and death intertwined, which for Eisenstein was the key to the essence of Mexico.

The film was to have been closed by an epilogue symbolizing the past and the future of the country: in the carnival procession of the Day of the Dead, people of all social classes are marching hidden behind masks of Death. When the masks are taken off--it turns out that they concealed not only the living, but also the dead. The living are the Mexican people; the dead, the ruling classes.

Eisenstein's intentions were excellently understood by the photographer, Eduard Tissé; the pictorial appearance of the work--compositionally ravishingly pure, using deep contrasts of white and black--not only deserves acclaim as the most beautiful in cinema history, but is at the same time extraordinarily appropriate for the spirit of the planned emotional survey of the country.

If only Eisenstein could have completed his work and personally edited the material, one would have to expect some authentic artistic sensation--quite apart from the fact that he is credited with more artistic inventiveness in ¡Que Viva Mexico! than was really the case. Eisenstein and Tissé provided a stylistic example which was used later equally by Mexican, Brazilian and Cuban directors.

All the same, the Latin American cinema, which only developed during the 60's, discovered for itself that the style of the exotic expression of the essence of this part of the world, and not only the vision of one artist, however brilliant. Eisenstein could simply sense the pulse of that land and express it in the most excellent visual form.

I WAS BORN, BUT....   (Umarete-wā Mita Keredo) Yasujiro Ozu

Script: Akira Fushimi and Ozu. Photography: Hideo Mohara.
Cast: Hideo Sugawara (Elder son), Tokkan-Kozo (Younger son),
Tatsuo Saito (Father), Mitsuko Yoshikawa (Mother), Takeshi Saka-
moto (Boss).

Shochiku, Japan. Approx. 5340 ft.

The first Japanese sound film was Heinosuke Gosho's The Neighbor's
Wife and Mine (1931), but as in Western countries the established
silent directors resolutely opposed conversion to the new medium.
The two most important reasons for it were the Japanese traditionalism, and the prospective unemployment of the popular benshi who
interpreted films to the audience.

     Yasujiro Ozu, one of the greatest film directors of his coun-
try, who started his career in 1923 and had already by 1931 attracted attention with several of his films, exploited the capabilities
of the silent cinema for a further three years. After Chorus of
Tokyo (1931) he made another comedy film called I Was Born,
but....

     The humiliation of adults is more acute and unjust when seen
through the eyes of children. (This motif appears repeatedly in the
cinema and would later become particularly penetrating in the ending
of Bicycle Thieves.) Two boys of eight and ten are shown in their
first encounter with social inequality: their father subserviently
fawns upon his boss, the father of their playmate, and acts the
buffoon in his home movies. The brothers, indignant and humiliated,
go on a hunger strike. But two little boys cannot change the established order in which some people are bosses and others only petty
clerks. Such is life....

     Charlie Chaplin was first to discover the piercing power of
sad comedy. Here Ozu made a similar discovery in Japan: he obtained humor from the clash between the disarming naiveté of the
children and the ridiculous values and conventions of the grown-ups.
Ozu told the story with humor and lightness, well aware that a more
serious tone would not only have been less effective, but also falsely
dramatic. All this was done without separate comic devices, without gags in the traditional sense of the word, but simply by the use
of natural comic situations. The scene for instance in which the
home movies are shown is hilarious: this is all so true!

     This unobtrusive style gave the film an aura of benevolent
gentleness, a near-philosophic composure of attitude, which earned
I Was Born, but.... the status of one of the last great silent films.

Ozu's style was in principle established; already here the technique was simple, dissolves were rejected and editing was done by simple cuts.

Ozu occupies an exceptional position in the cinema of his country--that of minstrel of the family life of the middle classes. The plots of his films are often very similar; some, like this one, might seem unimportant, but Ozu profoundly understood his protagonists and knew how to obtain great tragedies from small events. The way in which the director filmed his heroes is significant: since the Japanese do not use chairs but floor mats, the natural step to take in search of realism was to look at them from their own eye level. Thus the camera rested on the floor: this was said to have given the cameraman, who had to crawl a lot, a serious abdominal ailment.

POIL DE CAROTTE Julien Duvivier

Script: Duvivier, from the novels, "Poil de Carotte" and "La Bigote," by Jules Renard. Photography: Armand Thirard. Music: Alexandre Tansman. Cast: Robert Lynen (François, "Poil de Carotte"), Harry Baur (Monsieur Lepic), Catherine Fonteney (Madame Lepic), Christiane Dor (Annette), Colette Ségal (Mathilde), Maxime Fromiot (Félix Lepic), Louis Gauthier (Godfather), Simone Aubry (Ernestine), Marthe Marty (Honorine).

Film d'Art (Vandal et Delac), France. 8450 ft., 94 mins.

Subtlety and poetry, characteristics which were always the most valuable in the films of Julien Duvivier, in the 30's one of the leading French directors, appear in Poil de Carotte at their simplest and purest. Duvivier's first famous film remains also his best: it is perhaps more modest than his later works, but is also free from their pretentiousness and melodramatics. It is in fact surprising that it is this picture which turned out to be so good.

Starting in 1919 Duvivier had made nearly 20 films to date, among them an earlier silent version of Renard's novel, but he had never before achieved even a shade of the perfection of his second Poil de Carotte. (Neither would it be approached by the author of the novel in his own screen version of the book, made in the 40's.) The story of an unloved sensitive eight-year-old, set in rural France, certainly makes an interesting theme if a risky one: it is all too easy to fall into weepy emotionality with a story of this sort.

Duvivier did not avoid emotion, but offered it with originality. The most touching of the scenes in which poetic emotion comes to

the forefront is the brilliantly staged ceremony of "marriage" of
the boy and his playmate. The brutal reality and the rustiness of
backwater France are contrasted with the bucolic world of the little
hero's imagination--a very suitable motif for giving vent to directorial critical passion, as French cinema was to find out repeatedly
in the future. Yet it was Duvivier who was here one of the first
and best.

The value of Poil de Carotte was substantially increased by
the manner of execution: a fast narrative pace and vigorous editing
assured the proper tempo of the story and neutralized sentimentality.
In his later work Duvivier would not always find it so easy.

I AM A FUGITIVE FROM A CHAIN GANG   Mervyn Le Roy

Script: Howard J. Green, Brown Holmes and Sheridan Gibney,
from the novel by Robert E. Burns. Photography: Sol Polito.
Cast: Paul Muni (James Allen), Glenda Farrell (Marie, his wife),
Helen Vinson (Helen), Preston Foster (Pete), Edward J. McNamara
(Warden), Sheila Terry (Allen's secretary), Allen Jenkins (Barney),
Berton Churchill (Judge).

Warner Bros., U.S.A. 91 mins.

Mervyn Le Roy, one of the initiators of the realistic "gangster
series" and one of the most socially committed American directors
in the 30's, was particularly interested in the anomalies inherent
in the enforcement of law and order. Thus Little Caesar was a
warning of the disease of gangsterism and They Won't Forget was
to be a passionate denunciation of lynch law. His I Am a Fugitive
from a Chain Gang, a scorching attack on the American penal system, is based on a famous novel published as the memoirs of a
convict (who was said to have been still on the run when the film
was released).

A demobilized soldier is accused of a crime he did not commit and sentenced to ten years' hard labor. Somehow he escapes,
covers his tracks, studies for an engineer's diploma and finally becomes an executive in a sizeable company. His landlady, who has
blackmailed him into marriage, denounces him when he wants to
divorce her for another girl. Following legal advice Allen sur-
renders to the police, confident of being granted immediate parole.
But this is rejected and he escapes again....

Le Roy shows how a man is changed under the pressure of
an unjust accusation and the terrible conditions of prison life, which
he depicts in scenes close to apocalyptic. This is how a criminal

is made and one cannot state this with more poignance than in the
famous last exchange in the film, during a surreptitious meeting between the fugitive and his girl: "But how do you live?"--"I steal."
He then disappears into the night not wanting to endanger her.

Although the director simplified his task a little by making
the hero innocent (the treatment of prisoners by sadistic guards
would have been inhuman anyway), this was one of the first films
(the pioneer was Crainquebille) to take up the theme of the antagonism between the individual and the machinery of justice.   The anguish and insecurity of a man on the run and the oppressive and
unrelieved mood of cold despair of the prisoners is conveyed by the
almost documentary style of the narrative and the photography.

Much, too, is owed to Paul Muni, who earlier the same
year appeared in Scarface. This extraordinarily adaptable actor
would come to be seen in a variety of roles, including those of
famous men--Pasteur and Zola--but would never be better and more
winning.   The big box-office success of I Am a Fugitive from a
Chain Gang added much impetus to the social trend in American
cinema and the picture produced actual changes in the chain gang
practice.

LIEBELEI   Max Ophüls

Script: Hans Wilhelm and Curt Alexander, from the play by
Arthur Schnitzler. Photography: Franz Planer. Art Direction:
Gabriel Pellon. Music: Theo Mackeben. Cast: Wolfgang Lie-
beneiner (Fritz Lobheimer), Magda Schneider (Christine Weiring),
Luise Ullrich (Mitzi Schlager), Willy Eichberger (Theo Kaiser),
Paul Hörbiger (Hans Weiring, Christine's father), Gustaf Gründgens
(Baron Eggerdorff), Olga Tschechowa (Baroness Eggerdorff).

Elite Tonfilm Production, GmbH, Germany. 7920 ft., 88 mins.

Romantic Vienna at the turn of the century. Cafés, boulevards,
military balls--such are the death throes of Imperial Austria. The
mixed sentiments of exhilaration and foreboding are at the roots of
the writings of Arthur Schnitzler, on whose play Ophüls based his
first great film.   The director's work centered around two themes:
women in love and Vienna. Curiously, that great herald of Vienna
had spent only 10 months there, when at the unusually early age of
24 he was engaged to direct at the State Theatre.

Liebelei is a story of the beautiful and innocent love of an
army officer and the daughter of an opera musician, a love on a
collision course with codes d'honneur, bourgeois attitudes and the re-

.mains of the Hapsburg empire. Fritz is killed in a duel by the belatedly jealous husband of his former mistress; Christine commits
suicide when she hears of his death. The tragic end, a rule in
Ophüls' films, suits his pessimistic philosophy; the idea of purifica-
tion through love would later be adopted by the French Poetic Re-
alists.

Liebelei is a film of lingering sadness and a curious determinism. This atmosphere is typical of Ophüls, perhaps vital to
him, although the plot itself, the story of love and death, is essentially timeless. Already by the first scene of his first important
film (an opera performance of Mozart's "Entführung aus dem Se-
rail"), Ophüls has declared his allegiances: like Mozart he was a
master of innuendoes. His principal stylistic tool was the elaborate
but never self-conscious camera movement. He made his camera
climb stairs, follow coaches in long tracking shots (for instance in
the fine scene of the sleigh ride through the snowbound forest), or
whirl around dancing couples. He was always inventive: in the
dance scene the dancers whirl in opposite direction to the camera
circling around them.

Liebelei ended his German era, to be followed by many years
of exile. During that time the director would leave a trail of excellent pictures on both sides of the Atlantic.

À NOUS LA LIBERTÉ   René Clair

Script: Clair. Photography: Georges Périnal. Art Direction:
Lazare Meerson. Music: Georges Auric. Cast: Raymond Cordy
(Louis), Henri Marchand (Émile), Rolla France (Jeanne), Germaine
Aussey (Maud, Louis's mistress), Paul Olivier (Uncle), Jacques
Shelly (Paul, Jeanne's suitor), André Michaut (Foreman), Alexandre
d'Arcy (Gigolo), Léon Lorin (Old man), Vincent Hyspa (Orator).

Films Sonores Tobis, France. 8720 ft., 97 mins.

In 1932 the world seemed to be moving relentlessly toward the total
subjugation of man by machines--a danger to the quality of life and
a threat to liberty. Such a mood prevailed everywhere, but was
probably strongest in France. The beginnings of technological
breakthrough and the accompanying social conflicts increased by the
unhappy economic situation of the country after the Great Crisis,
justified this black view of the future.

René Clair was the first to try to present this train of
thought on the screen. Fortunately, he did not, in À nous la liberté,
strike the tone of a serious philosophical dissertation, an approach

which always dates quickly. This protest against the blind rush
toward automated life was disguised as a grotesque and concealed
its leftist tendencies with the allegorical character of the story.
The whole is certainly successful, if a bit undecided.

The protagonists are Louis and Émile, two former prisoners.
Louis managed to escape and become the owner of an ultramodern
phonograph factory, Émile served his term in full and now delights
in the joys of freedom. He becomes a worker in the factory; an
accidental meeting of the two friends proves to the rich one that the
swap of a prison cell for an executive's office was only jumping out
of the frying pan into the fire. In the final scene the tycoon, although also spurred by circumstances (his jailbird friends begin to
blackmail him), leaves his business to the workers and walks with
his friend towards the horizon: Long Live Freedom!

The final success certainly did not come easily to Clair; the
best proof of this is the fact that his next excursion into social satire, Le Dernier milliardaire (1934), turned out to be his worst
film. In A nous la liberté it is clearly seen that the director did
not feel at home in the solid concreteness of cubist designs; he was
also undecided in his choice and balance of serious and comic scenes.
Luckily for the whole however, the comic elements prevailed and excellently cement and strengthen the structure of the story, giving
the picture the good-humored, easy-going, straightforward atmosphere, which is always the greatest trump of Clair's works.

The personality of Émile, a dropout hero who rejects social
conventions, makes a considerable contribution to the creation of
this atmosphere--until Porte des Lilas there would be no comparably
vivid and prepossessing character in Clair's films. The tramp
character, the reminiscences (from City Lights) of the drunken friendship between a rich man and a poor and even the final shot with the
two friends walking down the country road into the distance, introduced into the film distinct Chaplinesque accents, which were indeed
not new in Clair's work.

Chaplin reclaimed the debt with interest: four years later
he made Modern Times, a film clearly inspired by À nous la
liberté. This gave rise to a law suit by the copyright holders of
the French film. The inglorious case was finally cut short by
Clair's statement: "If my film inspired him, this is to me a great
honor."

SCARFACE (Shame of a Nation) Howard Hawks

Script: Ben Hecht and Seton I. Miller, from the novel, "Shame of
a Nation," by Armitage Trail. Photography: Lee Garmes and L.

William O'Connell. Music: Adolph Tandler and Gus Arnheim.
Cast: Paul Muni (Tony Camonte = Al Capone), Ann Dvorak (Cesca,
his sister), Karen Morley (Poppy), Osgood Perkins (Johnny Lovo =
Johnny Torrio), Boris Karloff (Gaffney = Bugs Moran), C. Henry
Gordon (Guarino), George Raft (Gino Rinaldo), Purnell Pratt (Gar-
ston, a publisher), Vince Barnett (Angelo), Ines Palange (Mrs.
Camonte), Harry J. Vejar (Big Louis Costillo = Big Jim Colosimo),
Edwin Maxwell (Police chief), Tully Marshall (Editor), Henry Armetta
(Pietro).

Howard Hughes and Hawks, The Cabeo Company, U.S.A. 8264 ft.,
92 mins.

Together with Little Caesar and Public Enemy, Scarface is one of
the grand classics of the "gangster series" and the best picture
Howard Hawks made in the 30's.   Tony Camonte, the (anti)hero is
a thinly disguised Al Capone and the film traces the main episodes
of his career including the St. Valentine's Day Massacre and the
murder of Legs Diamond and ends--as always--with the protagonist
himself riddled with bullets. Hawks is a master of cinematic craft
and knows how to pervade each film he makes with an aura of expertise and surety.

Here craft was supported by genuine inspiration. Scarface
is sustained in a naturalist convention and unrelentingly charts the
ruthless world which excludes normal people. The audience witness
28 murders (and hear several referred to); to complete the picture
even the police are seen to be repulsive. It is characteristic that
although Scarface never approves of Tony's felonies, the spectator's
sympathy is unmistakably on his side despite that the director intended the film (as he stresses in the moralizing introduction) to
attract the attention of the establishment to the reign of gangsterism.

Paul Muni in his first important film role admirably builds
the complex title character: unsubtle, brutal, vain, arrogant, stupid, delighting in gaudiness and vulgarity and incestuously attracted
to his sister. Other gangsters are also fascinating: the coin-flipping
"Little Boy" (whom Tony later murders out of jealousy); Boris Karloff as the mobster Gaffney; Tony's simple secretary who pulls a
gun on a telephone when annoyed by the caller. Le Garmes' photography is remarkable with its deep contrasts and suits perfectly
the grim scenery of classic and ferocious gun battles in the twilit
streets of Chicago.

Scarface has an interesting use of visual symbols: the coin
flipped in the air recalls transience of human life; the sign of the
cross, which obsessively (and often with great ingenuity) accompanies
every murder, represents death. Hawks built the gang warfare into
an ironic and morbidly humorous high drama of perverted diplomacy,
which has sometimes been compared to the court intrigues in 15th-
century Venice.

COUNTERPLAN (Vstrechnyi)   Friedrich Ermler and Sergei Yutkevich

Script: Leo Arnshtam, D. Del, Ermler and Yutkevich. Photography: Joseph Martov, Alexandr Gintsburg and Vladimir Rapoport. Music: Dmitri Shostakovich. Cast: Vladimir Gardin (Babchenko), Maria Blumenthal-Tamarina (His wife), Tatyana Guretskaya (Katya), Andrei Abrikosov (Pavel), Boris Tenin (Vasya), Boris Poslavsky (Skvortsov, an engineer), M. Pototskaya (His mother), A. Alekseyev (Factory director), Nikolai Kozlovsky (Lazarev, an engineer), V. Sladkopevtsev (Morgun), J. Gudkin (Chutochkin).

Rosfilm, U.S.S.R.   10,400 ft., 116 mins.

A prototype of the "production" film--a genre of the Communist cinema which was meant to praise workers who achieved impressive production targets, but which soon turned into a stuffy bore. The most primitive variety of production films came to dominate Soviet screens and would be responsible for the 20-year period of eclipse of their cinema. However, all the later faults--schematic representation of people and situations, brash propaganda, forcibly embellished reality--were not yet present in Counterplan.

This classic story of a production undertaking at a Leningrad factory (to exceed the required production targets by building a much bigger turbine--thus the alternative title of the film is Turbine 50,000) and of the difficult assimilation of an old-fashioned worker into a socialist crew, still preserves sincerity in its tissue. More: it is a valuable document of the time when the power of Soviet industry was being created. On the other hand however, it is a very uneven film. Its positive sides, apart from undoubted authenticity, are the psychological differentiation of the characters, the Constructivist use of sound and the excellent performance by Gardin; the negative, the forcible bringing to life of the screen characters by giving them generic characteristics (a rather common trouble with Soviet films), imprecise dramatic construction, theatrical tendencies, and the lack of the intimate touch and warmth in presenting characters that were still apparent in Ermler's Fragment of an Empire.

For the latter fault Yutkevich cannot be blamed; he had been making good films for several years and would later prove to be as penetrating a psychologist as Ermler, his co-director. The faults of construction, austerity and a certain illustrative role of the film with respect to the script, can be blamed on the conditions under which it was made. For the premiere to take place, as planned, on the 15th anniversary of the outbreak of the Revolution, the shooting was done in incredible haste and the material assembled even without the usual control screening. Admittedly, the race with time was won both by the makers of the film and by its heroes--but the re-

sults of this race are different in each case; the film suffered, but
the turbine is probably still going strong.

ARROWSMITH   John Ford

Script: Sidney Howard, from the novel by Sinclair Lewis. Photog-
raphy: Ray June. Music: Alfred Newman. Cast: Ronald Colman
(Dr. Martin Arrowsmith), Helen Hayes (Leora), A. E. Anson (Pro-
fessor Gottlieb), Richard Bennett (Sondelius), Claude King (Dr.
Tubbs), Beulah Bondi (Mrs. Tozer), Myrna Loy (Joyce Lanyon),
Russell Hopton (Terry Wickett), De Witt Jennings (Mr. Tozer).

Goldwyn/United Artists, U.S.A.   108 mins.

The eternal choice between personal happiness and sacrifice in the
name of progress: the hero of Ford's film is a young doctor, a
specialist in tropical diseases, who comes to a famous Institute
from a rural background and discovers a serum to counteract cattle
plague only to find that his discovery has been anticipated. Most of
the action of the film is set in the unromantic West Indian jungle
where the doctor continues his work and where his wife falls victim
to the plague.

Ford was carried on the anti-bourgeois wave in American
literature and cinema and adopted an anti-Babbitt stand in his criticism of the rivalry and hypocrisy in the medical profession. The
film, made from the well-known novel, closes on the familiar Ford
note of optimism and faith in man and his dignity. With its honesty
of observation of the characters--but in the absence of striking dis-
coveries--it becomes an interesting essay on sacrifice and perseverance. This opinion is shared by Ford who counts the film among
his favorites.

BEFORE MATRICULATION (Přēd Maturitou)   Vladislav Vančura and
    Svatopluk Innemann

Script: Vančura, Julius Schmitt and Josef Neuberg. Photography:
Otto Heller and Václav Vích. Music: E. F. Burian. Cast: Jind-
řich Plachta (Kleč, a teacher), František Smolík (Donát, a teacher),
Antonín Novotný (Simon), Miroslav Svoboda (Kafka), Gustav Hilmar
(His father), Věra Gabrielová (Marta), Zora Myslivečková (Eva),
Bohdan Lachman (Headmaster).

A-B Film, Czechoslovakia.   8858 ft., 98 mins.

Before Matriculation is a very psychologically convincing drama of
the emotions and anxieties of adolescence.   Kafka and Simon, two
high school students, are in love with a girl from another school.
As a result of conflict with the headmaster both are expelled after
a master is injured trying to prevent Kafka from committing suicide.   With the help of another teacher the two finally graduate
from another school and all ends well.   The central problem of Before Matriculation is the attitude of the teacher to the students and
its message is that schoolmarmish authoritarianism should be abandoned in favor of friendship with the students.   This was how Vančura debuted as a director: the leading pre-war Czech writer had
always taken a lively interest in the cinema and even in the 20's had
written several (unused) scripts.   Before Matriculation is notable for
its very good acting team; the parts of the young people are played
by high school pupils from Prague.

MARIE, A HUNGARIAN LEGEND (Tavaszi Zápor; Marie Legende
     Hongroise) Pál Fejös

Script: Ilona Fülöp and Fejös.   Photography: Peverell Marley and
István Eiben.   Music: László Angyal and Vincent Scotto.   Cast:
Annabella (Maria Szabo), István Gyergyai (Steward), Ilona Dajbukát
(Manageress), Karola Zala (Boss of "Fortuna").

Hunnia Film/Les Films Osso, Hungary/France.   6092 ft., 68 mins.
The film was made in four language versions.

A screen adaptation of an old Hungarian folk legend about seduced
maidens who, after reaching Heaven, protect their illicit daughters
from a similar fate.   The heroine of the film is a servant girl seduced by a rich man.   Dismissed from service for immorality, she
gives birth to a daughter, who is taken away from her.   Marie
goes mad, becomes a vagrant and finally dies under the statue of
a saint.   After death she works in the heavenly kitchen and, seeing
her daughter with a young man, sprinkles the couple with water
from a golden cup thus interrupting their amours.

     Fejös returned to Hungary after nine years abroad during
which he had made six films in Hollywood (including of course the
celebrated Lonesome) and two films in France.   Here he emotionally
praised the beauty of his homeland in the first (and only pre-war)
worthwhile Hungarian picture.   The very sparing use of dialogue,
the noble composition of the frame, and the use of editing as the
principal means of expression, link Marie, a Hungarian Legend with

the style of the silent cinema.   Annabella, the French actress who would soon after play the main role in Clair's Quatorze Juillet, unexpectedly seems quite at ease cast as a Hungarian peasant girl.

WHAT RASCALS MEN ARE! (Gli Uomini, Che Mascalzoni!)   Mario
   Camerini

Script: Mario Soldati, Aldo De Benedetti and Camerini.   Photography: Massimo Terzano and Domenico Scala.   Music: Cesare A. Bixio and Armando Fragna.   Cast: Vittorio De Sica, Lia Franca, Cesare Zoppetti, Pia Locchi, Anna D'Adria, Giacomo Moschini, Tino Erler, Maria Montesano, Didaco Chellini, Carola Lotti, Gemma Schirato.

Cines, Italy.   5975 ft., 66 mins.

A little story of misunderstanding, quarrels and truces between a Milan chauffeur and his beloved, a drugstore clerk.   The story develops in the grounds of the Milan fair.   What Rascals Men Are! is the first of a series of films which brought Camerini the nickname of "The Italian René Clair."   The theme is perhaps similar to those of Clair (for instance Sous les toits de Paris and Quatorze Juillet) but without his poetry.   This is compensated for by the Italian temperament.   A small-time, good-hearted piece of bourgeois realism, skillfully and copiously spiced with humor, containing interesting observations and taking full advantage of the individual actors.

FANNY   Marc Allégret

Script: Marcel Pagnol, from his own play.   Photography: Nicolas Toporkoff.   Music: Vincent Scotto.   Cast: Raimu (César Ollivier), Pierre Fresnay (Marius, his son), Orane Demazis (Fanny), Alida Rouffe (Honorine), Fernand Charpin (Honoré Panisse), Robert Vattier (Monsieur Brun), Milly Mathis (Aunt Claudine Foulon), Paul Dulac (Félix Escartefigue), Maupi (Chauffeur).

Les Films Marcel Pagnol--Les Établissements Richebé, France. 11,309 ft., 126 mins. (originally 142 mins.).

The middle part of Pagnol's "Marseilles Trilogy," of which the individual parts were filmed by different directors: Marius, the first

part, by Alexander Korda; Fanny, by Marc Allégret; and César, by
Pagnol himself.   Marius has gone off to sea and left Fanny pregnant; her parents advise her to marry Panisse, an elderly rich widower, to give the baby a name and a home, rather than wait five
years for Marius to come back.   Fanny agrees.   On his death bed
Panisse, who understood everything, makes Fanny promise to marry
Marius when he returns, for the sake of her child.

Allégret paid almost no attention to the visual aspect of the
film and placed the main stress on the dialogue--the result is the
stiffest and the most theatrical of the three parts.   However, it
splendidly captures the unrepeatable spirit of the life in Provence--
and this, apart from the high standard of acting, is its main value.
"Fanny" turned out to be the most frequently filmed of all Pagnol's
plays.   A year later Almirante transferred it to the screen in Italy
and a 1961 American version was to be directed by Joshua Logan.
All the same, the first screen adaptation remains the best.

1933

QUATORZE JUILLET René Clair

Script: Clair. Photography: Georges Périnal. Art Direction: Lazare Meerson. Music: Maurice Jaubert. Cast: Annabella (Anna), Georges Rigaud (Jean), Pola Illery (Pola), Raymond Cordy (Taxi driver), Paul Olivier (Monsieur Imaque, the drunken eccentric), Raymond Aimos (Charles), Thomy Bourdelle (Fernand).

Films Sonores Tobis, France. 8856 ft., 98 mins.

Paris, René Clair's native city, has always been a key motif in his films: from a silent documentary, La Tour (1928), about the Eiffel Tower, through the charming Sous les toits de Paris, which established Clair as the minstrel of the Parisian suburbs, to his most recent pictures. After a passing change of theme in À nous la liberté the director returned here to his beloved city. The title refers to France's annual national holiday and the intrigue, so reminiscent of Sous les toits de Paris, revolves around this one day.

A taxi driver and a beautiful girl, neighbors across the street, meet on the evening of the 13th of July and take to each other. The situation is complicated by the return of Jean's coquettish former mistress; their paths diverge further when Anna's mother dies and the girl has to move out. Jean begins to keep the company of petty criminals; while acting as a lookout he realizes that Anna works in a bar that is to be robbed; he thwarts the plans of his cohorts, breaks with them and with his unfaithful mistress and returns to Anna.

The treatment of the theme is more episodic here than in Clair's earlier films, and Quatorze Juillet is more of a series of picturesque scenes cemented by a simple plot and, to quote the di-

rector's own words, "does not attempt to offer any general conclusions about reality." This is only a good-humored, slightly ironic
trifle, and the protagonists (among them the drunken M. Imaque, a
splendid figure) are treated with jovial indulgence. It is a comedy
with a touch of sadness, slower in pace, more lyrical and reflective
and less stylized than before. Quatorze Juillet has often been described as a masterpiece of populist cinema. This does not seem
entirely justified: this tale about ordinary Parisians is faithful not
so much to realism as to the motifs of proletarian mythology; it is
a masterpiece of cinema for ordinary people rather than about ordinary people.

It is remarkable that all this was based on decidedly second-
rate ingredients, on a story which, if treated differently or simply
by someone else, would undoubtedly have resulted in a piece of
screen confectionery. Instead, it was turned into a warm, entirely
unselfconscious, natural tale about the simplest human problems.
While offering no stylistic surprises or technical innovations, it remains in the memory as a pleasant, bitter-sweet vision of a Parisian
street. The superb lightness of touch is, above all, the most impressive feature of Quatorze Juillet.

LE GRAND JEU   Jacques Feyder

Script: Feyder and Charles Spaak. Photography: Harry Stradling
and Forester. Music: Hans Eisler. Cast: Françoise Rosay
(Blanche), Pierre-Richard Wilm (Pierre Martel), Marie Bell (Flor-
ence/Irma), Charles Vanel (Clément), Georges Pitoëff (Nicholas
Ivanoff), Pierre Larquey (Gustin), Pierre Labry (Canteen attendant),
Camille Bert (Colonel), Pierre de Guingand (Captain), André Dubosc
(Bernard Martel), Lyne Clevers (Dauville).

Films de France, France. 10,676 ft., 118 mins.

A rejected lover joins the Foreign Legion to seek forgetfulness in a
new life in North Africa. He soon gains a reputation for cynicism,
drink and reckless bravery. In Morocco he meets a woman decep-
tively like Florence (who had left him in France). He falls in love
with her, but he cannot forget the other. When he inherits some
money he decides to marry, but before he does he accidentally
meets Florence who rejects him again. His life collapses and having
had his death forecast by a fortune-teller he rejoins his battalion and
goes to seek death.

It is extremely rare that such a melodramatic-exotic intrigue
results in a picture so fine and convincing as Le Grand jeu. Feyder's first film after his return from the United States (where he was

in fact not an artist, but only a craftsman making French and German versions of American productions) places him at once among the leading French directors of the mid-30's. The picture is also of historical importance as a harbinger of the new trend of Poetic Realism soon to be regnant in the cinema. Feyder later explained the reasons which led him to make a film from such a dubious script by saying that escapism and exoticism were at the time of his return to France almost an imperative in the cinema and any attempts at treading on the ground of truth, especially social truth, met with so much resistance that they had to be abandoned.

Luckily the director was interested in the Pirandellian motif of the duality of human nature (which Hitchcock would also tackle in Vertigo, using an astonishingly similar story) and was able to use it in a context which on the one hand satisfied the audience and on the other allowed him to experiment at will with the psychological subtleties and details of the plot. The banal and the melodramatic were forced into the far background in the picture. Feyder capitalized above all on the atmosphere of drowsiness brought about by the heat and shoddiness, torpor and flies; made serious and open references to lust; delineated with precision and fidelity the colonial milieu, and with his characteristic psychological mastery created a vision of human fate that is true, moving and universal.

It is not only the hero who cannot cope with the internal crisis: Feyder presents a whole constellation of shipwrecked lives, both in the ranks of the Foreign Legion and in the two women with whom the hero is involved. One of them is a singer in a sleazy cabaret and reminds the hero of his lost Florence (in both roles Feyder cast Marie Bell, but in the case of the singer the voice was dubbed by Claude Marcy), the other, a fortune-teller hotel proprietress who looks after Pierre and is secretly in love with him. In this part Françoise Rosay creates an unforgettable character of a jaded, heavy-lidded and enigmatic old woman.

It is just such characters, lost, trying in vain to escape from the vicious circle of fate, which were to people the French screens in the period of Poetic Realism.

PASSING FANCY (Dekigokoro) [A Caprice]   Yasujiro Ozu

Script: Tadao Ikeda, from a story by James Maki. Photography: Shozaburo Matsumoto. Cast: Takeshi Sakamoto (Kihachi), Tomio Aoki (Tomio), Den Ohinata (Jiro), Nobuko Fushimi (Harue), Chôko Iida (Otome).

Shochiku, Japan. 9052 ft.

The second outstanding silent film Ozu made after the introduction
of sound, Passing Fancy came a year later than the brilliant comedy
I Was Born, but.... As in some of Ozu's earlier films, the plot
is situated in Shitamachi, a poor area of Tokyo. The protagonists
are two brewery workers and a young girl. The director treats
them with a warmth and humor which somehow recalls Steinbeck's
novel "Cannery Row."

Ozu's main concern was always with daily life: Kihachi's
son is ill, Harue thinks of becoming a geisha to raise some money
for his treatment, Tomio manages to secure a loan; to repay it he
will have to go far away to work, but Kihachi insists on going instead.

With the beginning of the sound era, Ozu's style became
visibly simpler and even less ornate than before; he abandoned the
use of optical effects, but otherwise preserved all his characteristic
touches: the low camera positions (so that the sets had to have ceilings), long static shots and editing by simple cuts. Passing Fancy
is a film which radiates intimacy and simple charm and contains a
number of masterly comic scenes (the little son waking his father
in the morning, the introductory sequence in the theatre when a number of people pick up the same empty purse). The joyous finale of
Kihachi's swim from the ship is one of the film's few outdoor scenes.
Takeshi Sakamoto created in Passing Fancy maybe the most prepossessing male character in the early Japanese cinema.

1860   Alessandro Blasetti

Script: Blasetti, Emilio Cecchi and Gino Mazzucchi, from a story,
"La Processione Incontro Garibaldi," by the latter. Photography:
Anchise Brizzi and Giulio De Luca. Music: Nino Medin. Cast:
Aida Bellia (Gesuzza), Giuseppe Gulino (Carmine), Gianfranco Gia-
chetti (Father Costanzo), Otello Toso, Maria Denis, Mario Ferrari,
Laura Nucci, Totò Majorana, Cesare Zopetti, Vasco Creti and Si-
cilian peasants.

Cines Pittaluga, Italy. 6926 ft., 77 mins.

In the years 1848-1870, a sacred period for Italy known as the
"Risorgimento," the partitioned country was liberated and united
under the leadership of Giuseppe Garibaldi. In 1860 Sicily and
Naples were liberated and power vested in an Italian king. 1860,
the most outstanding Italian film made before the Second World War,
is a patriotic tale about a Sicilian highlander and his wife. The
population of a little village are persecuted by the Bourbon soldiers;
the resistance is led by the local priest. Everybody is anxiously

awaiting the landing of Garibaldi. The hero, one of the insurgents, is sent to Genoa to tell the liberation forces that the time is ripe for attack and joins the famous "thousand" which is shown embarking. The climax of the picture is the visually splendid battle of Catalafimi.

Although the structural axis of 1860 is the story of two people, the real hero is the whole Italian nation. A host of sensitively and individually portrayed characters file through the screen, among them Garibaldi himself--shown not as a star statesman, but as only one of many freedom fighters. The theme of the film agreed with the political doctrines of the Mussolini regime which considered itself heir to the noble traditions of the heroic past; as a result, as happened before with Sun, Blasetti found himself in concord with the official point of view. All the same, in his stressing of the role of the whole nation, he represents a progressive approach to history, refraining from unnecessary rhetoric.

The narrative of 1860 is conducted with simplicity and directness; the shooting was done on real Sicilian locations and most of the actors--including those in leading parts--were amateurs. Thus the creative method displayed in the picture is basically close to the future Neorealist practice--indeed, 1860 is justly considered a forerunner of Neorealism, not only because of the manner of execution, but also because of the great strength with which the patriotic message is conveyed.

The differences between Blasetti and the post-war Italian directors (apart from Visconti) rest mainly in the pictorial aspect. In 1860 the visual appearance is of vital importance; as in Sun, Blasetti knew how to convey the whole beauty of the sun-drenched landscape, but this time he stopped short of the previous aesthetic over-emphasis.

THE TESTAMENT OF DR. MABUSE (Das Testament des Dr. Mabuse) Fritz Lang

---

Script: Thea von Harbou. Photography: Fritz Arno Wagner and Karl Vash. Cast: Rudolf Klein-Rogge (Dr. Mabuse), Otto Wernicke (Inspector Lohmann), Oscar Beregi (Dr. Baum), Gustav Diessl (Kent), Vera Liessem (Lily), Karl Meixner (Hofmeister), Theodor Loos (Dr. Kramm), Georg John (Winkler, Baum's assistant), Theo Lingen (Jeweler), Paul Henckels (Counterfeiter), Gerhard Bienert (Detective).

Nero-Film AG, Germany. 122 mins.

Eleven years after Dr. Mabuse, the Gambler, Mabuse came to life
again on the screen. As before he is the main protagonist of a
thriller, but one which now also contains distinct political overtones.
It starts where the earlier film left off: Mabuse is locked up in a
mental asylum. His spiritual influences are unimpaired and he hyp-
notizes Dr. Baum, the director of the asylum, into allowing him to
organize and direct a criminal gang which commit robberies, attack
factories and railways, and counterfeit currency. After many adventures a detective uncovers these activities. Dr. Mabuse dies,
but the director continues with the felonies, is unmasked and finally
goes mad himself.

The activities of a Genius of Crime's gang bring to one's
mind certain associations with the activities of the Brown Shirts.
The avowed intention of Lang was to compromise Hitler's doctrines
by putting them into the mouths of criminals. The result was that
Goebbels banned the film as soon as it was made. The Nazis however did not manage to annihilate The Testament of Dr. Mabuse.
Leaving Germany after turning down an offer to become the official
film director of the Third Reich, Lang smuggled one print of the
picture abroad and Europe was given a chance to take note of his
allegoric forecast of the times to come.

It is not in fact a very striking allegory, even if an intentional one: the film is a rather excessively played out study of the
fear felt by the unexpectedly attacked society and by a police inspector fighting a mysterious enemy. It was a nice touch on the
director's part to preserve Inspector Lohmann (played by the same
actor) from the previous M. Yet Lang did not repeat the success
of that film; the dramatic line was not given enough amplitude, the
constant sustaining of tension weakened--as always in such cases--
the power of expression. For this reason The Testament of Dr.
Mabuse finds itself above the standard of skilled craftsmanship in
only a few scenes.

THE PRIVATE LIFE OF HENRY VIII   Alexander Korda

Script: Lajos Biró and Arthur Wimperis. Photography: Georges
Périnal. Music: Kurt Schroeder. Songs and lyrics: King Henry
VIII. Costumes: John Armstrong. Cast: Charles Laughton (Henry
VIII), Robert Donat (Culpeper), Binnie Barnes (Katheryne Howard),
Merle Oberon (Anne Boleyn), Franklyn Dyall (Cromwell), Wendy
Barrie (Jane Seymour), John Loder (Thomas Peynell), Everley
Gregg (Catherine Parr), Frederick Cully (Duke of Norfolk), William
Austin (Duke of Cleves).

London Film Productions, G.B. 8664 ft., 96 mins.

British cinema had been in a state of limbo for many years before
the advent of sound, but then there was a surge of activity: Hitchcock began to seem interesting, there was a promising documentary
school and, in 1931, Alexander Korda, a Hungarian, arrived in
Great Britain via Hollywood to inject new life into historical cinema.
His formula is an anecdotal approach to the heroes: in his "private
lives" series, the characters are shown informally, in slippers in
the cosiness of the bedroom instead of in the din of battle.   It is
the characterization which matters, the plot is subordinated and--to
the despair of historians--the facts are distorted.   Charles Laughton
gives a great, and for British cinema classical, performance in the
title role, endowing the King with sneering cruelty, monstrous glut-
tony, roguishness, viciousness and sentimentality.   The camera of
Georges Périnal took good care of the veracity of the period.   A
new development in historical drama perhaps, but one wonders
whether it is any more true to life.

DON QUIXOTE (Don Quichotte)   Georg Wilhelm Pabst

Script: Alexandre Arnoux and Paul Morand, from the novel, "El
ingenioso hidalgo Don Quijote de la Mancha," by Miguel de Cervantes Saavedra.   Photography: Nicolas Farkas and Paul Portier.
Music: Jacques Ibert.   Cast: Fyodor Shalyapin (Don Quijote), Dor-
ville (Sancho Pança), Mady Berry (Sancho's wife), René Donnio
(Carrasco), Mireille Balin (Duchess), Vladimir Sokoloff (Captain of
police), Charles Martinelli (Duke), Renée Valliers (Dulcinea).

Vandor Film S.A.R.L./Nelson Films Ltd., France/G.B.   7072 ft.,
78 mins.

The excellent Kameradschaft failed in its confrontation with the German public, but enjoyed great popularity in France.   Perhaps this
was one of the reasons why Pabst left Germany and abandoned the
serious themes of his previous works.   One way or the other, the
move to Paris closed the period of Pabst's greatness and Don
Quixote is his last achievement of any calibre.   His adaptation of
the Cervantes classic saga about the wanderings of an eccentric
gentleman (played by the great opera singer Shalyapin) and his faithful servant is primarily notable for its visual aspect.

Pabst returned to the style of silent cinema, choosing elaborate camera angles and displaying beautiful photography served in
short, vigorously cut shots.   The scene of the joust with the windmills is in perspective an example of the masterly editing increasingly forgotten in the noise of the sound cinema.   But this is not quite
enough to fend off a certain academic coolness which sets in.   Unlike
the hero of his film, Pabst is not prepared to fight the windmills;

with the outbreak of the Second World War he would return home, and although he would not lower himself to the official line of Nazi cinema, he would remain in the shade, from which he momentarily emerged in the mid-50's with The Last Act (1955).

THE RIVER (Řeka) Josef Rovenský

Script: Jan Reiter, Rovenský and Jindřich Snížek. Photography: Jan Stallich Music: Josef Dobeš. Cast: Jarmila Beránková (Pepička), Váša Jalovec (Pavel), Jaroslav Vojta (His father), Hermína Vojtová (His mother), Jan Sviták (Poacher), Rudolf Deyl (Teacher), Antonín Marlé (Merchant).

Jan Reiter, Czechoslovakia. 77 mins.

A story of the calf love of two 14-year-olds, sustained partly in the tonality of a naive folk story and partly in that of a poetic fairytale. The River is the outstanding directorial debut of a well-known actor who died in 1937. The film is characterized by noble photography, which discovers the beauty of the Czech countryside, and slow narrative rhythm, delicately tuned to the pulse of nature. It is a film typical of that trend in the Czechoslovak cinema which brought it its greatest successes in the period between the two world wars.

The River was as a matter of fact one of the group of Czech films which received a prize at the Venice Biennale in 1934; the other two were, The Earth Sings (1933), the fine documentary about Slovakia directed by Karel Plicka, and Ecstasy (1932), the famous psychological drama in which Gustav Machatý boldly (but unfortunately with unnecessary avant-garde pretentions) attempted to refer to controversial erotic themes.

1934

L'ATALANTE   Jean Vigo

Script: Vigo and Blaise Cendrars, from the original scenario by
Jean Guinée. Photography: Boris Kaufman. Music: Maurice
Jaubert. Cast: Jean Dasté (Jean), Dita Parlo (Juliette), Michel
Simon (Père Jules), Gilles Margaritis (Peddler), Louis Lefèvre
(Boy), Raya Diligent (Bargeman), Maurice Gilles (Barge owner).

J. L. Nounez, France. 7343 ft., 82 mins (cut from 89 mins).
The film was released, shortened and re-edited as Le Chaland qui
passe; it was restored to its original form in 1945.

Jean Vigo, an artist of extraordinary promise, made only three
films before this one: the medium-length À propos de Nice (1929),
Zéro de conduite (1933), and a short documentary about a French
champion swimmer. Their "poetic" feel was doubtless reinforced
by the unruly, violent imagination of the director and his anarchistic
tendencies, obviously related to Surrealist art. L'Atalante, finished
days before the director's death, is a film about the life of the
bargemen of the Seine. It invites analogies with Epstein's La Belle
Nivernaise, which also used a boat's name as the title.

The plot of the film is rather ordinary and involves basically
only four people living on the barge: three adults and a young boy.
The captain of a barge is deserted by his wife who, bored by the
uneventful life, follows her lover to Paris. Some time later, disenchanted and repentant, she is brought back. The personalities of
these water people are drawn with conviction and understanding.
They do not quite move in a dream world--their link with reality
is ensured by the colorful eccentric with a heart of gold: the ta-
tooed Père Jules, who lives in a cabin full of curiosities and who
brings the errant wife back to her husband.

-222-

What might seem another soft-focus, soft-hearted picture is in fact a realistic one. The poetic stylization never covers feebleness of purpose and not only does not weaken the realism, but reinforces it. Vigo speaks through slow camera movements, and the delicate texture of photography often done at twilight (for example, the memorable scene of the bride on the quay at dawn). There are also a few underwater shots. Life, love and forgiveness--such are the themes of L'Atalante and although some scenes do seem now overly sentimental, the film has great passionate romantic power.

CHAPAYEV   Sergei and Georgy Vasiliev

<u>Script</u>: Sergei and Georgy Vasiliev, from the novel by Dmitri Furmanov. <u>Photography</u>: Alexandr Sigayev and A. Xenofontov. <u>Music</u>: Gavriil Popov. <u>Cast</u>: Boris Babochkin (Chapayev), Boris Blinov (Furmanov), Leonid Kmit (Petka), Varvara Myasnikova (Anna), Illarion Pevtsov (Col. Borozdin), Stepon Shkurat (Potapov, a Cossac), Boris Chirkov (Peasant), V. Volkov (Yelan), Nikolai Simonov (Zhikhariev), G. Vasiliev (Lieutenant).

Lenfilm, U.S.S.R.   8760 ft., 97 mins.

A leading classic of revolutionary cinematic battlepieces: a story, based on a genuine biographical account, of the unit led by a self-styled Cossack Ataman, who declared himself on the Communist side.   In order to make of the hero--a somewhat anarchistic popular leader--a real Red Army officer, a political commissar is delegated to his unit.   The film relates the process of change in Chapayev's personality, who after incipient resistance gradually begins to accept the discipline of the regular armed forces and, blending this with the fantasy of a man of the steppes, becomes one of the heroes of the struggle against counter-revolution.

The construction of the plot is exceedingly clear, the dramatic line a model: one can say that Chapayev was already a classic at the moment of its creation.   It is interesting that the film was made by directors who never distinguished themselves later, and who had had their debut only four years previously: proof that a careful and meticulous analytical approach to a theme alone can sometimes give results of quite a high standard.

The values of the film lie neither in the skillful staging nor in the visual part--the tonality of photography is rather rugged, bringing the film closer to a documentary than to a cinematic poem. The quality of the final effect lies above all in the authentic character of the script, the care in transferring it to the screen and in the creation of full-blooded characters.   This would have been diffi-

cult without full cooperation from the actors; they were faultlessly
cast and created characters which really remain in one's memory.
This applies particularly to the hero.

MAN OF ARAN   Robert Flaherty

Script: Robert, Frances and David Flaherty. Photography: Robert
Flaherty. Music: John Greenwood. Cast: Colman "Tiger" King
(Man of Aran), Maggie Dirrane (His wife), Michael Dillane (Their
son), Pat Mullin, Patch Ruadh, Patcheen Flaherty, Tommy O'Rourke
(Shark hunting crew).

Gainsborough Films, G.B. 6900 ft., 77 mins.

After spending some time in England making a short, Industrial
Britain (1931), Flaherty went to his native Ireland and became fascinated by the Aran Islands, a group of three main and many smaller
islands lying some 15 miles west of the Galway coast, of which
Inishmore is the largest. It might be that Flaherty was under the
influence of Epstein's recent Finis Terrae, which he rated very highly. This way or another, having been given a free hand and financial support by Michael Balcon (producer of the entertainment films
of Stevenson and Hitchcock), Flaherty intended to return to contem-
plating the basic beauties of human existence and make a strict
documentary to be called "Man Against the Sea."

These intentions evolved considerably during the director's
two-year residence in the islands and Man of Aran is neither a
rigorous documentary, nor--despite its title--a film about people.
It tells about the sea storming the rocky cliffs with all its might,
about the variability of the ocean and its austere beauty. In Tabu
Flaherty was forced by the producer to introduce fictional elements;
in this film he did it under the pressure of day-to-day monotony.

To give the film life, he put the action back a hundred years,
when the locals were still hunting the sunfish or the great basking
shark, and used the hunt as the climactic scene. Thus fiction
again triumphs over reality. Although credible, this scene remains
at odds with facts. It is only the film-making, with its passionate
and meticulous observation, that is documentary in character.

In Flaherty's cinema the traditional division between documentary and feature seems no longer in force; although human actions do provide the dramatic axis of this film, the observation of
them is in fact limited only to outdoor existence: there is nothing
about the emotions, love or family life which Flaherty was always
before so eager to portray. He shows people mending their boats,

fishing, cultivating potatoes--the only possible crop, which has to
be grown in soil collected from rock crevices and supplemented with
seaweed brought from the shore.

Yet it does not seem right to criticize Man of Aran for its
insufficient attention to the human element; the film reflects a seg-
ment of reality, but not the one which would traditionally be given
here. Flaherty's camera apparently captured the essence of Aran
and achieved an intimate integration with the condition of life of its
people, who were delighted with the film, even though there is little
about life itself in it. A real flaw of the picture, as with many
documentaries, is the failure to achieve sustained dramatic tension--
the uneven exposure and poor quality of the sound are excusable in
view of the difficult conditions of the shooting.

IT HAPPENED ONE NIGHT   Frank Capra

Script: Robert Riskin, from the story, "Night Bus," by Samuel
Hopkins Adams. Photography: Joseph Walker. Music: Louis
Silvers. Cast: Clark Gable (Peter Warne), Claudette Colbert
(Ellen Andrews), Walter Connolly (Alexander Andrews, her father),
Roscoe Karns (Shapley), Jameson Thomas (King Westley), Alan Hale
(Danker), Ward Bond (Bus driver), Arthur Hoyt (Zeke), Blanche
Frederici (His wife), Harry Bradley (Henderson).

Columbia, U.S.A. 104 mins.

It Happened One Night was a hit of the screens of 1934, and the
winner of five principal Oscars (best film, director, script, actor,
and actress). While such honors have not always been an indication
of the quality of the film, this time the public and the jury of the
Academy of Motion Picture Arts and Sciences were quite right. It
Happened One Night is one of the best comedies made in the United
States--and not only the best, but also one of the most sympathetic.

The slight (in fact exceptionally trivial) story of the adventures of a tenacious and prepossessing reporter and the rebel
daughter of a millionaire during a coach journey from Miami to
New York (concluded, how else, by marriage) achieved that level of
sophisticated fun on which the relationship between reality and the
actual plot becomes unimportant. This was above all, due to the
merit of the director.

Capra, sometime gagman for Mack Sennett, became in one
move a director generally admired for his warm treatment of nearly
all characters, his ability for humorous description of the milieu,
and the conflict-free quality of the film, which allows one to forget

the hard reality of the day. Separate laurels are due to the actors, who were little known before, but who after this film advanced to the position of Hollywood's leading stars.

General satisfaction with the success of It Happened One Night was not shared only by undershirt makers. Clark Gable ruined them. When the spectators saw in one of the scenes that the hero bares his splendid torso when he takes his shirt off, the above mentioned article stopped finding customers. Thus is the power of the movies!

THE YOUTH OF MAXIM (Yunost Maksima) Grigori Kozintsev and
    Leonid Trauberg

Script: Kozintsev and Trauberg. Photography: Andrei Moskvin. Music: Dmitri Shostakovich. Cast: Boris Chirkov (Maxim), Stepan Kayukov (Dyoma), Valentina Kibardina (Natasha), A. Kulakov (Andrei), Mikhail Tarkhanov (Polivanov), M. Shchelkovsky (Foreman), S. Leontyev (Engineer), P. Volkov (Worker).

Lenfilm, U.S.S.R. 8786 ft., 98 mins.

Maxim was the second revolutionary hero (Chapayev was the first) to appear on Soviet screens. He is a fictional personality, and yet is perhaps even more vivid in the memory of the cinema-goer of his country. The intention of the film's creators was to illustrate the history of the Communist movement in Russia in a tripartite series of pictures, through the adventures of the hero. The "Maxim Trilogy" starts in 1910, when Maxim, a young St. Petersburg factory worker, first comes across the Bolshevik movement and ends in 1918 when he is appointed by the new government to head the national bank.

The first part of the series follows the hero through underground activity consisting of agitation and distribution of leaflets in the factory, confrontations with the police and imprisonment from which he finally manages to escape. The screen Maxim became such a popular character that he was later introduced into an episode in quite another film, A Great Citizen; the actor could never escape the memory of his famous role--proof of how real the details of Kozintsev and Trauberg's story must have been.

These two had been collaborating since the early 20's; even in the silent period they were counted among the leaders of the Soviet avant-garde. In 1922 they founded the "Factory of the Eccentric Actor" (abbreviated as FEX) and propagated a style which was a conglomeration of pop culture, acrobatics and crazy burlesque. The

manifesto of the company stated among other things that an actor
in no case should be allowed to think about the psychological aspect
of his part.   They dared to make not only entertainment films (Adventures of Oktyabrina, 1924), but even adaptations of respected
literary classics (The Cloak, 1926) in a similar spirit!

In the early 30's the youthful frenzies (Kozintsev was 17
when FEX was started) give way to a more serious view of life:
the directors made themselves heard through the interesting drama,
Alone (1931), about a woman teacher fighting backwardness in the
Altai mountains.   But some fantasy still remained--and it is thanks
to it that Maxim is such a full-blooded screen character, a man
shown not from the angle of official propaganda, but from a private
perspective, as a youth who not only works and thinks, but also
falls in love and enjoys life with a vigor that would serve two people.

The personality of Maxim fits well into a background full of
carefully preserved details and peopled by equally convincing characters, photographed with modest accuracy by Moskvin.   The tonality
of photography in fact never goes beyond different shades of grey,
and yet it can sometimes be intimate, sometimes use Expressionist
chiaroscuro, and sometimes be brutally somber--but it is always
suited to the action.

While Chapayev became the archetypal Soviet battle film, The
Youth of Maxim and its sequels, The Return of Maxim and The
Vyborg Side, are the classical revolutionary psychological dramas.
Later efforts in both genres never managed to repeat the success
of the originals, but instead resorted to ponderous and stilted con-
ventions and irritating one-dimensional standardized plots.

TONI   Jean Renoir

Script: Renoir and Carl Einstein, based on the material gathered
by J. Levert for his novel, "Toni."   Photography: Claude Renoir
and R. Leduc.   Music: Bozzi.   Cast: Charles Blavette ("Toni"--
Antonio Canova), Jenny Hélia (Marie), Celia Montalvan (Josepha),
E. Delmont (Fernand), Andrex (Gaby), Max Dalban (Albert, the
foreman), Kobachevitch (Sebastian).

Films d'Aujourd'hui, France.   7743 ft., 86 mins.

This film is considered in France, together with Feyder's Le Grand
jeu, to be a turning point in the interests of the national cinema in
the 30's.   Toni was the second significant work by Renoir, one of
cinema's greatest individualists (the first was La Chienne (1931), a

naturalistic and cruel drama of passion; interesting, but more important as a social phenomenon than an artistic one). Renoir's early films had been made in the mid-20's in the Impressionist idiom with which the director was naturally associated as the son of Auguste Renoir, one of the greatest Impressionist painters. In the later period, Renoir, whose interest in the cinema was awakened by the great impact Stroheim's Foolish Wives made on him, turned, as Stroheim did, toward somber psychological studies which mercilessly explore the interior of man.

Toni, a fatalistic drama of the passions raking the Italian-Spanish immigrant community in Provence, is such a film. An Italian quarryman nicknamed Toni falls in love with Josepha, the daughter of a Spanish immigrant. Having surprised Josepha making love to Albert, his friend, Toni marries another girl. Josepha soon regrets her marriage to Albert and plans to escape with a lover; she kills Albert who surprises her stealing his money for the journey. While trying to help her by disposing of the body, Toni is shot dead by a xenophobic French peasant. A train arrives at the station bringing a new batch of Italian immigrants.

On first sight this seems to be a primitive melodrama; it is not, however, a melodrama but life itself. Not simply because the film is based on a real crime passionel from police records, but primarily because Renoir knew how to recreate this authentic report on the screen, subtly and simply. His careful observation of the milieu and his avowed avoidance of studio work later led to the director's films being named as precursors of Neorealism. But this is only part of the justice which should be done to Renoir. In fact Toni goes a step further than the Italian Neorealists: here the sound was not added by post-synchronization, but was directly recorded.

PENSION MIMOSAS Jacques Feyder

Script: Charles Spaak. Photography: Roger Hubert. Art Direction: Lazare Meerson. Music: Armand Bernard. Cast: Françoise Rosay (Louise Noblet), Paul Bernard (Pierre Brabant), Alerme (Gaston Noblet), Lise Delamare (Nelly), Jean Max (Romain), Arletty (Parachutist), Paul Azaïs, Nane Germon, Raymond Cordy.

Films Sonores Tobis, France. Approx. 110 mins.

Feyder continued with his examination of human emotions: this time he painted a portrait of the cynical and perverse woman owner of a small pension in the South of France, who unexpectedly experiences a great and tragic feeling for a young boy. But the intrigue

was left aside and the film concentrates on the observation of the
psychology and behavior of a group of people embittered and deprived of hope, people whom a passion for roulette has pushed onto
a social margin.

Feyder not so much develops the theme as probes into its
depth, disregarding care for an expressive narrative for the sake of
a meticulous verification of situations. The director found an excellent collaborator in Françoise Rosay, whose extremely complex part
counts among the greatest achievements of French cinema acting.
Spiritually, Pension Mimosas is very close to the Poetic Realism
which was soon to come into existence.

While however the silent Crainquebille was ahead of its time
and foreshadowed the style of film-making of the 40's and 50's,
Pension Mimosas seems on its part related to the future psychologi-
cal-literary trend known as Nouvelle Vague, quite apart from whether
Malle, Franju or Truffaut admit their debt to Feyder or are even
conscious of it. Literature, often even of doubtful quality, was used
by the director of Pension Mimosas as a foundation on which he
built a precise script; but when it came to the shooting, psychological
improvisation done with close cooperation from the actors tended to
take over the main roles and the final result is quite substantially
different from the starting material.

All this had little in common with the standard method of
film-making at that time, which--especially in American cinema--
consisted of photographing a script. Yet it reminds one quite distinctly of the films of the Nouvelle Vague, though without their spontaneity and innuendoes. What is more, both Le Grand jeu and Pension Mimosas may be seen from an angle close to such films as Le
Feu follet or La Tête contre les murs: through the eyes of people
who realize the limitations of their environment.

The difference between Feyder and the later French directors
rests in the method of communicating with the audience; the director
of Pension Mimosas, a master of psychological cinema, relied on
actors rather than on images supported by music. Yet his next
film, Carnival in Flanders, would be for a change a brilliant display
of pictorial sensitivity.

THE MAN WHO KNEW TOO MUCH Alfred Hitchcock

Script: A. R. Rawlinson and Edwin Greenwood, from an original
theme by Charles Bennett and D. B. Wyndham-Lewis. Photography:
Curt Courant. Music: Arthur Benjamin. Cast: Leslie Banks
(Bob Lawrence), Edna Best (Jill Lawrence), Peter Lorre (Abbott),
Frank Vosper (Ramon Levine), Hugh Wakefield (Clive), Nova Pil-

Revolt of the Fishermen   -230-   1934

beam (Betty Lawrence), Pierre Fresnay (Louis Bernard).

Gaumont British, G.B.   74 mins.

Hitchcock followed the successful Murder with four very bad films.
It was only when he associated himself with Gaumont British that he
regained his former touch and directed several pictures that are
among his best.   Hitchcock seldom makes straight thrillers and the
plots of his films are stories of which crime constitutes only an
element, if a very important one.   This is why, as in this case, he
often departs from the literary material.

The favorite recipe throws innocent passers-by into the midst
of sensational events with rapidly changing scenery--in this case
Swiss mountains, then suburban London, then an Albert Hall symphony concert.   An English couple in Switzerland learn a secret
from a dying man; their child is kidnapped by a spy ring wanting to
prevent them from revealing the secret.   The couple find the gang
in London and, after a masterly and suspenseful scene of a thwarted
political assassination followed by a siege, regain the child.   The
gang is liquidated by the police.

The tempo of the film changes as fast as its scenery: the
slow and awesome pace of certain sequences gives way to fast and
rapidly edited ones (the concert).   A good, somewhat nostalgic,
portrayal of the London of the past is of further interest.   The Man
Who Knew Too Much is a kind of allegory on the classic theme of
the conflict between Good and Evil--both treated in almost abstract
terms and in a way reminiscent of Fritz Lang.   In 1956 Hitchcock
remade this picture.   This is also of interest, but for different
reasons.

REVOLT OF THE FISHERMEN (Vosstaniye Rybakov)   Erwin Piscator

Script: Georgy Grebner, from the novelette, "Der Aufstand der
Fischer von Santa Barbara," by Anna Seghers.   Photography:
Pyotr Yermolov and Mikhail Kirillov.   Music: Ferenc Sabó, V.
Ferré and N. Chemberdzhi.   Cast: Alexei Diky (Kedennek), Y.
Glizer (His wife), F. Ivanov (Nehr), Emma Tsesarskaya (Katarina
Nehr), Vera Yanukova (Maria), N. Gladkov (Hull), D. Konsovsky
(Andreas), N. Izvodsky (Desak), A. Safroshin (Bruyk), S. Martinson
(Bredel, garden keeper).

Mezhrabpomfilm, U.S.S.R.   8891 ft., 99 mins.

Revolt of the Fishermen, an unusual combination of theatrical and cinematic styles and also of the styles of silent and sound cinema, is the work of a German avant-garde theatre director whose leftist political beliefs and lack of success with Berlin audiences had forced him to leave Germany. On the invitation of a Soviet film company he transferred to the screen a German novel about a fishermen's strike ruthlessly put down by the army.

A young sailor Andreas pretends to be a strikebreaker but blows up one of the fishing ships with dynamite. At the funeral of a murdered striker, the mourners, incited by a funeral oration, attack the soldiers; massacre follows. The film ends with an appeal to the fishermen to unite. Piscator had already made a similar statement on the stage: his epic film presentation and interpretation of the facts, done from the point of view of a political journalist, will in emotional effect leave no one indifferent.

Both the director's attitude and the content of the novel are close to Eisenstein's cinema. It is thus not surprising to find that Piscator distinctly relied on Eisenstein's style, especially in the dynamic second part of the film. On the other hand, the early parts have more in common with the films of Lupu Pick and the early works of Pabst, and even--in so far as the mood is concerned --with the French Impressionist school.

Against the background of this stylistic mixture, the individual sequences of the film seem structurally incoherent and there is evident an indecision in the handling of the soundtrack, which nonetheless includes some interesting formal ideas from the border areas of cinema and theater (the internal monologue of the hero is heard from behind the screen and somewhat resembles the ancient Greek dramatic chorus which comments upon events). Yet the shortcomings of Revolt of the Fishermen are compensated for by the interesting visual aspect of the film, especially its second part.

JOLLY FELLOWS (Vesyolye Rebyata) [Jazz Comedy] Grigori Alexandrov

---

Script: Alexandrov, V. Mass and Nikolai Erdman. Photography: Vladimir Nilsen. Music: Isaac Dunayevsky. Cast: Leonid Utyosov (Kostya Potekhin), Lubov Orlova (Anyuta), Maria Strelkova (Yelena), Yelena Tyapkina (Stepmother), Fyodor Kurikhin (Man with a torch), G. Arnold (Frascini, conductor from Paraguay), R. Erdman (Music teacher).

Mosfilm, U.S.S.R. 8455 ft., 94 mins.

"Twelve musical attractions roughly glued together by the plot"--this

is how Eisenstein's long-standing collaborator described his debut
in a full-length feature. Alexandrov had indeed been Eisenstein's
assistant on Strike (that is, during the period of the "montage of
attractions"). Jolly Fellows is something quite new to Russia:
Alexandrov, who had just returned from a stay of several years in
the West, blended the patterns of the American musical vaudeville
with the Russian indigenous folk comedy and a whimsy reminiscent
of the Factory of the Eccentric Actor.

A crazy spree results, one which could--if thought about--
leave a lot to be desired, but which is too straightforward to be
judged with severity. A Crimean shepherd is mistaken for a distinguished conductor by a lady opera singer. Invited to her home
he arrives with his animals and causes complete havoc. Later, he
is again mistaken for the conductor in Moscow and has to conduct
in his place. In the end he does choose a musical profession, but
as leader of a jazz band.

The Russian elementality, joie de vivre and the skillful connection of the picture with the soundtrack (which is, as it happens,
not quite technically perfect) assured great success for the film both
in Russia and abroad. A separate success emerged for Lubov Orlova, who in spite of trying to be funny at all costs and in all places,
has too much charm not to succeed. The best movement in the
film is the scene of the fight among the members of the Soviet
Dixieland group, capitally illustrated with jazz music.

OUR DAILY BREAD   King Vidor

Script: Vidor and Elizabeth Hill, from an idea found in "Reader's
Digest." Dialogues: Joseph L. Mankiewicz. Photography: Robert
Planck. Music: Alfred Newman. Cast: Tom Keene (John), Karen
Morley (Mary, his wife), John T. Qualen (Chris, a farmer), Bar-
bara Pepper (Sally), Addison Richards, Harry Holman.

United Artists, U.S.A. 80 mins.

With his previous films, The Crowd and The Big Parade, King Vidor
proved his social interests. Now in his only independent and personal film--made possible through great sacrifice--he shows an attempt to solve the unemployment caused by the Great Crisis. The
Depression was at its deepest and Vidor incorporated the leftist intellectuals' hopes when F.D.R. came to power.

The film is about an agrarian commune: John, unemployed,
and Mary, his wife, move to a deserted farm which they have inherited from a relative. They are joined by others in a similar

situation. Vidor quite unnecessarily tried to animate the story with
a subplot, in which the hero is seduced by a blonde vamp. During
their escape together John finds a stream in the mountains and returns to the cooperative to help build the irrigation canal which will
save the crops that have been hit by drought.

This final enthusiastic scene is made with considerable technical prowess, using the mobile camera in a near-documentary manner, and with quick cross-cutting, clearly inspired by a Soviet film
The Earth Thirsts (1930), directed by Yuli Rayzman. In all, the
film is a sincere but utopian proposition. Our Daily Bread lacks
the acuteness and passion of The Grapes of Wrath, but should we
really expect film-makers to propose successful social reforms?

BOULE DE SUIF (Pyshka) Mikhail Romm

Script: Romm, from the short story by Guy de Maupassant. Pho-
tography: Boris Volchok. Cast: Galina Sergeyeva (Elisabeth
Rousset--"Boule de Suif"), Andrei Fait (Lt. d'Eyrick), Faina
Ranevskaya (Mme. Loiseau), Anatoly Goryunov (M. Cornudet), M.
Mukhin (Count), Y. Mezentseva (Countess), T. Okunevskaya and
P. Repnin (M. and Mme. Carré-Lamadon).

Mosfilm, U.S.S.R. 6211 ft.

A rather unusual debut for the leading Soviet director: a silent
film made well after the close of the silent era. The 33-year-old
Romm stood before an uneasy choice: he could either embark upon
an independent directorial career in the sound cinema, but with a
rather undefined future, or he could transfer to the screen one of
de Maupassant's most famous short stories with modest means and
using the already outdated silent conventions. Romm chose the
lesser evil and surprised everybody with his excellent transference
to the screen of a text whose adaptation without dialogue seemed a
somewhat hopeless undertaking.

The Franco-Prussian war of 1871: a prostitute nicknamed
"Boule de Suif" travels by stagecoach from Rouen to Le Havre.
The girl shares her food with a group of bourgeois who travel with
her and earns their sympathy. When the coach is stopped by a
Prussian officer, everybody persuades "Boule de Suif" to submit
herself to him. Freed thanks to her, the traveling companions
nonetheless turn their backs on her and a German soldier is the
only one to share his bread with her.

The method of adaptation chosen by Romm is based, of all
things, on that of Dreyer's in The Passion of Joan of Arc: the di-

rector used close-ups which stress the reactions of characters and
sustained the dramatic tempo of the story with the quick dissolves
of talking faces.   Even the emotional pattern of the film--a lonely
girl versus a bunch of unappetizing townspeople--finds an analogy in
Joan of Arc's situation.   Romm's film could perhaps have been an
even more resonant closing chord from the cinema without words,
were it not for a tendency to force easy conclusions on the spectators, additionally reinforced by the over-acting of some of the cast.

All the same, Boule de Suif is a significant example of how
a really talented artist can overcome serious limitations.   The same
short story will be used as the basis of Christian-Jaque's remake
of the film; and--more indirectly--of Ford's Stagecoach.

MASKERADE   Willy Forst

Script: Walter Reisch.   Photography: Franz Planer.   Music:
Willy Schmidt-Gentner.   Cast: Paula Wessely (Leopoldine Dur),
Adolf Wohlbrück (Heideneck, the artist), Olga Tschechowa (Anita
Keller), Hilde von Stolz (Gerda), Peter Peterson (Prof. Carl Har-
randt), Walter Janssen (Paul Harrandt, opera musical director),
Julia Serda (Countess M.), Hans Moser (Zacharias).

Tobis-Sascha Filmindustrie AG, Austria.   9270 ft., 103 mins.

In the early 30's, soon after sound was introduced into films, the
Austrian cinema attracted the world's attention for a brief period.
This was primarily through Max Ophüls and his film Liebelei which,
while being technically German (if one is to go by production company), remains the classic screen manifestation of the proverbial
Viennese lightness.   The other leading personality in Austrian films
was Willi Forst, a well-known theatrical actor who debuted as a
film director in Unfinished Symphony (1933), the story of the life of
Schubert.

Maskerade, his second picture, brings to life, as Liebelei
did, turn-of-the-century Vienna--the Imperial capital, city of romantic waltzes, forgotten memoirs, melancholy love affairs and
fashionable salons.   The story of the film revolves around the identity of a nude lady in a newspaper drawing.   There are rumors and
guesses, and in the end the fashionable painter Heideneck, the
favorite of the ladies, trying to extricate himself from his awkward
position, gives a name at random.   The name turns out to be that
of an honest (but poor) dame de compagne of an old aristocratic
lady.   The two fall in love, and this triggers off a typical high-life
drama of jealousy involving the painter's former mistress and the
well-known surgeon whose wife had been the real model.

All this would have been quite unimportant (or even worse than that) if it were not for Forst's superb lightness of touch and his unerring balancing of the tragic and comic accents in the story which makes Maskerade a charming carnival comedy, blending sentimentality, music, dance and a nostalgic atmosphere of Good Old Vienna. The distinguished cast is overshadowed by Paula Wessely, a famous theatrical actress, who gives a remarkable performance as a shy and unimpressive girl in love with a social lion.

CRIME AND PUNISHMENT (Crime et châtiment)   Pierre Chenal

Script: Christian Stengel, Vladimir Strichevsky and Chenal, from the novel by Dostoyevsky. Photography: Joseph-Louis Mundviller. Music: Arthur Honegger. Cast: Pierre Blanchar (Rodion Raskolnikov), Harry Baur (Porfiri, the magistrate), Madelaine Ozeray (Sonia), Alexandre Rignault (Razoumikhin), Madeleine Beruber (The Moneylender), Catherine Hessling (Yelizaveta), Marcelle Géniat (Mrs. Raskolnikov), Lucienne Demarchand (Dunia), Marcel Delaitre (Marmeladov), Daniel Gilbert (Zamiatov).

Compagnie Générale des Productions Cinématographiques, France. 8820 ft., 98 mins.

For nearly forty years Chenal's film remained the best screen adaptation of Dostoyevsky's great novel about the poor philosophy student Raskolnikov who, to test his theory that a man of genius is not bound by the law, murders a woman usurer and her servant. He lives a life of remorse and fear until, under the influence of the saintly harlot Sonia, he confesses to the crime.

This adaptation can be considered outstanding only in the relative sense, since the scriptwriter and director sensibly gave up from the very outset the impossible task of transmitting the entire complexity and ambiguity of the literary original. They had to limit themselves to telling the story of one man and his demons and to bypass for one thing the magnificently full personality of Sonia (which is one of the most endearing female characters in all literature, but in the film little more than a symbol of conscience).

Still, what does remain in Chenal's Crime and Punishment-- the criminal intrigue upon a psychological background--is elaborated with inventiveness and care. The fascinating duel of words and wits between Raskolnikov and the examining magistrate, which received particular attention from the makers of the film, must be counted among the outstanding achievements of acting (Harry Baur's performance is very nearly definitive) and directing in the early French sound cinema. Equally remarkable was the camera work especially

in its use of lighting and composition of the frame in creating the
nightmarish atmosphere of the drama.

THE WAVE (Pescados) [Redes]   Fred Zinnemann

Co-direction: Emilio Gómez Muries. Script: Agustín Velázquez,
Henwar Rodakiewicz, Vásques Chavez and Paul Strand. Photography:
Paul Strand. Music: Silvestre Revueltas. Cast: Silvio Hernández
(Miró), Gloria Morel (His wife), Juan José Martínez Casado (His
friend), Antonio Lara, Gabriel Figueroa.

Paul Strand for Secretaría para la Educación, Mexico. 65 mins.

The Wave is a visually excellent cinematic poem about Mexican
fishermen, given social overtones from the fight against the exploiting owners. Spiritually this film is almost a continuation of Eisenstein's ¡Que Viva Mexico! and Strand's photography brings to mind
irresistible associations with the deep contrasts of Eduard Tissé's
compositions. But the debuting Zinnemann and Strand (who was
commissioned to produce the film by Mexican Minister of Education
Chavez) were perhaps even more inspired by the real life of this
land than were the Soviet artists two years before. The earlier
contacts of the young director with Robert Flaherty were probably
not without influence on the final semi-documentary appearance of
The Wave. Yet the film contains more than an impressive description of landscape and people: the visual impact is used to emphasize
its ardent commitment, a feature always characteristic of Zinnemann.

ANGÈLE   Marcel Pagnol

Script: Pagnol, based on the novel, "Un de Beaumugnes," by Jean
Giono. Photography: Willy. Music: Vincent Scotto. Cast: Orane
Demazis (Angèle), Henri Poupon (Clarius, Angèle's father), Toinon
(Mother), Jean Servais (Albin), Fernandel (Saturnin), Edouard Del-
mont (Amédée), Andrex (Louis).

Les Films Marcel Pagnol, France. 150 mins.

Pagnol, who with his doctrine of "canned theatre" introduced so
much fracas into French cinema, here stood behind the camera for

the first time. Rather unexpectedly, he did not transfer to the
screen one of his own plays (César, the third part of the Marseilles
Trilogy would see the light of day only after another two years).
Instead, he adapted for the screen a story by Jean Giono, another
well-known French writer, whose style of writing was in fact akin
to his own (even if his attitude to life was not).

Pagnol made his film in a manner completely in disagree-
ment with his avowed theories: although Angèle abounds in dialogues,
they are always dialogues which spring naturally from situations.
The action develops invariably in rural settings and rural interiors.
In short, Angèle has no trace of theatricality at all. Deserted by
her lover, Angèle returns home with an illegitimate child. She is
contemptuously rejected by her father even though Albin, another
man, wants to marry her. Albin gradually overcomes the father's
objections to the marriage and achieves a reconciliation between
him and his daughter.

The juicy full-bloodedness of the characters of the film and
their good-hearted humor assured a colossal popularity for Angèle,
but only among the French public. Foreign audiences were simply
not familiar enough with the idiom and local specificity of the picture. This would soon change and postwar Western audiences would
come to accept even the Japanese samurai films without much opposition. But at the time Angèle was made, the regional character
of a film did not facilitate its export.

THE LOST PATROL   John Ford

Script: Dudley Nichols and Garrett Fort, from the story, "Patrol,"
by Philip MacDonald. Photography: Harold Wenstrom. Music:
Max Steiner. Cast: Victor McLaglen (Sergeant), Boris Karloff
(Sanders), Wallace Ford (Morelli), Reginald Denny (George Brown),
J. M. Kerrigan (Quincannon), Billy Bevan (Herbert Hale), Alan
Hale (Cook), Brandon Hurst (Bell), Douglas Walton (Pearson), Sam-
my Stein (Abelson), Howard Wilson (Flyer), Neville Clark (Lt. Haw-
kins), Paul Hanson (Jock Mackay).

RKO Radio Pictures, U.S.A.   74 mins.

A classic Ford movie in which the director used his favorite dramatic device: a group of people, driven by a common purpose,
are isolated and clinically analyzed. In 1917 a British army patrol
is lost in the Mesopotamian desert. Their officer is killed and an
NCO takes command. The men are being shot one by one by invisible enemy snipers. As in his other films with a similar motif,
The Grapes of Wrath and Stagecoach, Ford aims at giving character

studies of his protagonists, even if he does not arrive at startling psychological discoveries.

This must be to a great degree blamed on the acting which is old-fashioned and often very wooden indeed. Boris Karloff, later of Frankenstein fame, who plays here a religious fanatic, behaves as if he was Frankenstein's monster already. Only Victor McLaglen, an old Ford regular (who plays the sergeant, the last survivor of the group) passes with flying colors. But Ford did what he could: despite having a distinct theatrical touch the film does create the atmosphere of harsh and oppressive desert conditions with a threat from an unknown enemy.

THE YOUNG TREES   (Młody Las)   Józef Lejtes

Script: Anatol Stern, Jan Adolf Hertz and Lejtes, from the play by Jan Adolf Hertz. Photography: Albert Wywerka. Music: Roman Palester and Marian Neuteich. Cast: Adam Brodzisz (Stefan Kiernicki), Stefan Jaracz (Kiernicki, school inspector), Maria Bogda (Wanda), Mieczysław Cybulski (Janek Walczak), Bogusław Samborski (Starogrienadsky, headmaster), Kazimierz Junosza-Stępowski (Pakotin), Antoni Bednarczyk (Sirotkin), Michał Znicz (French master), Władysław Walter (Terteńko, janitor), Tekla Trapszo (Mrs. Walczak).

Libkow-Film, Poland.   6726 ft., 75 mins.

1905: a pupils' strike at one of the Warsaw High Schools. They were demanding Polish education and protesting against the police methods of the Tsarist administration (Poland was at that time under Russian rule). Political and social objectivity and lack of crass nationalism equipped the picture with the truly moving atmosphere of youthful patriotism. The director gave The Young Trees a poignant narrative and displays skill in leading the excellent theatrical actors. This is one of the very few prewar Polish films which achieved international recognition.

1935

THE INFORMER   John Ford

Script: Dudley Nichols, from the novel by Liam O'Flaherty. Photography: Joseph H. August. Music: Max Steiner. Cast: Victor McLaglen (Gypo Nolan), Heather Angel (Mary McPhillip), Preston Foster (Dan Gallagher), Margot Grahame (Kattie Madden), Wallace Ford (Frankie McPhillip), Una O'Connor (Mrs. McPhillip), Joseph M. Kerrigan (Terry), Joseph Sawyer (Bartley Muiholland), Neil Fitzgerald (Tommy Conner), Donald Meek (Pat Mulligan), D'Arcy Corrigan (Blindman).

RKO Radio Pictures, U.S.A.   91 mins.

The Informer, a screen version of the novel written by the director's cousin, is the fulfillment of Ford's lifelong intention of making a film about "The Troubles" in Ireland, the country of his parents. The story is laid in Dublin during the Sinn Fein uprising, in 1922. Gypo Nolan, a simple and brutal man, is excluded from the underground organization.   Hunted by the British, rejected by the Irish, he leads a paltry life and plans to emigrate to America with his girl.   To obtain the money for the tickets he denounces his friend to the Black and Tans for the £20 bounty.   Eaten by remorse and fear, he betrays himself, is sentenced to death by his former comrades and dies early in the morning in a deserted church.

Ford did not betray even a trace of political involvement and instead focused all his attention on the protagonist and his motivation, trying to examine the psychology of betrayal, moral fall and fear.   The director masterfully created an atmosphere of impending doom, very appropriate for the theme of crime and punishment, and augmented it by choosing a strict claustrophobic unity of time and place--the action of The Informer takes one night and is limited to a small section of Dublin.

The mood was achieved primarily by dint of the soft atmospheric photography, the use of sharp contrasts of light and shadow, studied pictorial compositions (which are not always justified), recurrent visual motifs ("wanted" poster, shipping line advertisement) and rather emphatic symbols (blindman knocking at the pavement with his cane symbolizes Destiny, just as in the later Poetic Realist films of Marcel Carné). The principal asset of the film is the brilliant performance of Victor McLaglen, subtly conveying the roughness and naiveté of one of the classical screen antiheroes.

The Informer was made in a fantastically short time (reportedly: script, six days, shooting, 17 days), which is undoubtedly the reason for its greatest failure, the technical shoddiness that is only too evident. In spite of this the picture collected four Oscars (leading role, direction, script, music), riding on the crest of the wave of increased interest by Americans in European themes, after the homegrown gangster films had died a sudden death.

JÁNOŠÍK   Martin Frič

Script: Frič, Karel Hašler and Karel Plicka, from the play by Jiří Mahen, based on an 18th-century Slovak legend. Photography: Ferdinand Pečenka. Music: Miloš Smatek. Cast: Pal'o Bielik (Jánošík), Zlata Hajdúková (Anka), Andrej Bagár (Sándor), Theodor Pištěk (Count Markušovský), Elena Hálková (Zuzka), Filip Dávidík (Janíčko), Roza Schlesingerová (Fortune teller), Jánko Borodáč (Judge).

Lloydfilm, Czechoslovakia.   7546 ft., 84 mins.

Jánošík is a visually striking ballad about the legendary 18th-century Slovak brigand who wallopped the tyrannical Hungarian nobles and helped the poor. He was caught and put to death in 1713 after refusing to plead for the Emperor's mercy. Outstanding pictorial qualities, a compelling elementality of content and a noble theme combine in this best (and most internationally successful) prewar Czechoslovak picture.

The earlier activities of its director were exclusively in the field of popular comedy where he had indeed some success (Heaveho!, 1934). However, comedy has always been a more difficult field than drama, and thus Frič, undoubtedly an able director, also struck the right chord in Jánošík, and while adopting the style of a folk tale, created a film as classically fine as it is simple and moving. The director was very much assisted by his co-script-

writer Karel Plicka, an enthusiastic admirer of Slovakia, and by
Ferdinand Pečenka, whose refined photography seems sometimes
almost excessively contemplative, yet never ceases to be vivid and
dynamic.

Sustained in the convention of romantic legend, Jánošík would
perhaps not command such power of expression if it were not for
the final change of tone: the last sequence transforms into the cruel
drama of the wronged highlanders whom the hero wants to strength-
en in their fight against injustice by his voluntary death.

CARNIVAL IN FLANDERS (La Kermesse héroïque) [In German:
Die klugen Frauen] Jacques Feyder

Script: Charles Spaak and Bernard Zimmer. Photography: Harry
Stradling. Sets: Lazare Meerson. Music: Louis Beydts. Cast
(French version): Françoise Rosay (Burgomaster's wife), Jean
Murat (Duc d'Olivares), André Alerme (Burgomaster), Micheline
Cheirel (Siska), Lyne Clevers (Fishmonger's wife), Maryse Wend-
ling (Baker's wife), Ginette Gaubert (Innkeeper's wife), Marguerite
Ducouret (Brewer's wife), Louis Jouvet (Chaplain), Bernard Lancret
(Jan Bruegel), Alfred Adam (Butcher), Arthur Devère (Fishmonger),
Marcel Carpentier (Baker), Pierre Labry (Innkeeper), Alexandre
Darcy (Captain), Claude St. Val (Lieutenant), Delphin (Dwarf).

Films Sonores Tobis, France. 10,800 ft., 120 mins. Film made
in French and German language versions.

The Flemish school of painting come to life on the screen: until
the 60's Feyder's picture remained the best vision in the cinema of
a distant historical epoch. Seventeenth-century Flanders is recreated here not only with exceptional attention to detail, but also
with humor and lightness. 1616: Spanish occupation forces arrive
at the little town of Boom. The mayor and elders, followed by the
rest of the town's male population, are overcome by terror--no
doubt things will not be good, there will be sacking of houses,
probably also bloodshed. Thus they all proceed to vanish from the
face of the earth.

The women, annoyed at such cowardice, resolve to welcome
the soldiers and defend themselves with their natural weapons.
The Spaniards are astonished by the hearty reception and become
as meek as lambs; they not only do not pillage Boom, but even
benefit its inhabitants. It is thanks to them that the marriage of
the Mayor's daughter (which he is against) to a certain young painter, Jan Bruegel, can be arranged. Next day there is nobody in the
town who is not satisfied.

The Belgian audience however were far from satisfied at
such view of history: the country was on the brink of political
riots! Feyder had a lot of explaining to do to convince people that
he was not a traitor in the pay of foreign governments. Thus a
director who only twice in his career ventured into the realm of
film comedy twice landed himself in trouble because of it. He
never touched a similar theme again and it is only unfortunate that
he was not to achieve success in the field of drama either.

Although the only film of any standing he came to make before the advent of the war, La Piste du Nord (1939)--a coarse dynamic tale set in the snows of Canada--is a new development in
Feyder's style, it is, despite its values, inferior to his earlier
works. After the fall of France, Feyder moved to Switzerland,
where he died in 1948.

LE CRIME DE M. LANGE   Jean Renoir

Script: Jacques Prévert, from an idea by Renoir and Jean Cas-
tanier. Photography: Jean Bachelet. Music: Jean Wiener. Cast:
René Lefèvre (Amédée Lange), Jules Berry (Batala), Odette Florelle
(Valentine), Nadia Sibirskaïa (Estelle), Sylvia Bataille (Edith), Henri
Guisol (Meunier), Maurice Baquet (Charles), Marcel Levesque (Con-
cierge Bessard), Odette Talazac (His wife).

Obéron, France. 90 mins.

"The only personal thing which I can contribute to this absurd and
cruel world is my love": such was Renoir's credo, and its traces
could already be discerned in the bitter sympathy for the hero of
Toni. It was expressed, however, with the greatest strength of conviction in Le Crime de M. Lange. Lange is an author of crime
stories, an employee of a small, failing publishing house. When
the bankrupt owner vanishes, escaping his creditors, Lange starts
a cooperative which soon boasts considerable achievements. The
profits are shared between the members, but there is also a fund
for helping others. The reappearance of the boss, who unscrupu-
lously plans to appropriate the fruits of their efforts, results in
tragedy: Lange kills the rascal and flees abroad with his girl.
They are caught by border guards--and set free when the girl tells
the story of the crime.

Le Crime de M. Lange was made in completely different
conditions, and with different starting material than Toni. Renoir
abandoned location shooting, amateur actors and documentary fidelity for the sake of the symbolic and stylized script written by
Prévert, the future spiritual father of the French Poetic Realism.

He used this script, however, not in the romantic "Prévertian Spirit," but as a vehicle for his own cold observation of life. The result is a film which complements precise detail with a disturbing, even a little uncanny, atmosphere of blended grotesque and black humor. He was to continue with this imagery in his future kaleidoscopic La Règle du jeu, but here it appeared in a much more coherent form.

The film was made during the rapid turn of France towards the Left; after the abortive Fascist takeover bid, the Popular Front was formed. Renoir declared his full support for it, and traces of this are visible in Le Crime de M. Lange, both in the social overtones of the story of the publishing cooperative opposed to the cynical owner and in the warm characterization of the Parisian suburban milieu. Renoir's next film was La Vie est à nous (1936), a propaganda montage made for the French Communist Party.

THE GHOST GOES WEST   René Clair

Script: Robert Sherwood, Geoffrey Kerr and Clair, based on Eric Keown's "Punch" story, "Sir Tristam Goes West." Photography: Harold Rosson. Music: Misha Spoliansky. Cast: Robert Donat (Murdoch Glourie/Donald Glourie), Jean Parker (Peggy Martin), Eugene Pallette (Joe Martin), Elsa Lanchester (Lady Shepperton), Everly Gregg (Mrs. Martin), Hay Petrie (The MacLaggan), Morton Selten (Old Glourie), Elliot Mason (Mrs. Macniff), Patricia Hilliard (Shepherdess), Jack Lambert, Colin Leslie, Richard Mackie, J. Neil More and Neil Lester (Sons of MacLaggan).

London Films, G.B.   8200 ft., 91 mins.

After the failure of the second of his social pamphlets, Le Dernier milliardaire (1934), Clair left France, to return only after the war. The first leg of his emigration odyssey was London, where he brought to the screen the exquisitely ingenuous story of a Scottish ghost, burdened with the duty of inflicting family vengeance and his descendant-double, who tries to get out of financial trouble by selling the ancestral castle. It is bought by an American millionaire who has it dismantled and reassembled across the Atlantic, complete with ghost.

Deprived of home ground under his feet, the director did not repeat the brilliance of his first sound films; the final American sequences especially of The Ghost Goes West come apart at the seams, the style draws close to theatrical-Hollywoodian, and the picture is overloaded with the dialogue against which Clair formerly so sharply protested. All the same, the wit and inventiveness of the French master achieved here a reasonable success. This applies particularly to the "Scottish" part of the film, which contains a veritable gem of screen humor: the historical flashback, explaining how Murdoch's ghost came about.

PETER IBBETSON   Henry Hathaway

Script: Vincent Lawrence, Waldemar Young, Constance Collier, John Meehan and Edwin Justus Mayer, from the novel by George du Maurier and the play by Nathaniel Raphael. Photography: Charles Lang and Gordon Jennings. Music: Ernst Toch. Cast: Gary Cooper (Peter Ibbetson), Ann Harding (Mary, Duchess of Towers), John Halliday (The Duke of Towers), Ida Lupino (Agnes), Douglas Dumbrille (Col. Forsythe), Virginia Weidler (Mimsey), Dickie Moore (Gogo), Doris Lloyd (Mrs. Dorian), Gilbert Emery (Jenkins), Donald Meek (Mr. Slade), Christian Rub (Major Duquesnois), Elsa Buchanan (Madame Pasquier).

Paramount, U.S.A. 7433 ft., 83 mins.

A curious period tale of love stronger than death: two children live in a house in Paris in the mid-19th century. When the boy's mother dies, he is taken to England where he changes his name to Peter Ibbetson and later becomes a promising architect. Commissioned to rebuilt the Duke of Towers' stables, he recognizes the Duchess as his childhood playmate. The Duke, sensing the affinity of the two, becomes insanely jealous and is accidentally killed by Peter who is thrown into prison. Through visions the two maintain an almost tangible spiritual link which even death cannot sever.

The story of Peter Ibbetson scarcely survives print. It is the camera which appears to be responsible for much of the picture's character. When Peter Ibbetson was made, it was scorned by most critics for its sentimentality and also (which is a calculated risk anyone making a film from a well-known literary work takes) for not agreeing with the prevailing vision of the popular novel. Yet the film was warmly welcomed by those connected with Surrealist art and with the passing years turned into a legend: in the so-called Brussels anti-plebiscite of 1958 Peter Ibbetson was voted, by outstanding critics, to be one of the ten best films ever made!

To anyone familiar with the work of Buñuel, Breton or Kyrou it is not difficult to see why these Surrealists received the film as a revelation: in Peter Ibbetson dreams are not treated as moody intrusions, but as independent autonomous entities--and this notion is dear to Surrealist art. To a degree unmatched, perhaps, until Letter from an Unknown Woman, sentimentality in this picture transcends the limits of a mere convention and succeeds in conveying a thing very difficult to communicate in the cinema: the feel of spiritual contact.

CAPTAIN BLOOD   Michael Curtiz

Script: Casey Robinson, from the book by Rafael Sabatini. Photography: Hal Mohr. Music: Erich Wolfgang Korngold. Cast: Errol Flynn (Peter Blood), Olivia de Havilland (Aranella Bishop), Lionel Atwill (Col. Bishop), Basil Rathbone (Levasseur), Ross Alexander (Jeremy Pitt), Guy Kibbee (Hagthorpe), Henry Stephenson (Lord Willoughby), Leonard Mudie (Baron Jeffreys), Robert Barrat (Wolverstone), Hobart Cavanaugh (Dr. Bronson), Donald Meek (Dr. Whacher).

Warner Bros., U.S.A.   10,829 ft., 120 mins.

Captain Blood, the spirited adaptation of one of the most popular adventure novels, was never surpassed in the serious variety of cloak-and-dagger films. With no regard for logic and probability (but without a tongue-in-cheek attitude to the protagonists), and with plenty of fancy and an excellent flow and pace in the story, Michael Curtiz led his hero from one adventure to another.

In the subplots of Captain Blood the spectator can find all the component motifs of the genre: noble love and elegant duels, the felonies of the wicked and the subterfuges of the wily, exotic landscapes and boldly staged sea battles, noble pirates and not-quite-so-noble representatives of the Law. Errol Flynn towers over all this: Captain Blood was the first film of this elemental screen hero, who is no worse than even Douglas Fairbanks, his legendary predecessor of the silent period.

WIFE, BE LIKE A ROSE (Tsuma Yō Bara no Yoni) [U.S. title: Kimiko]   Mikio Naruse

Script: Naruse, from the stage play by Minoru Nakano. Photography: Hiroshi Suzuki. Music: Noboru Ito. Cast: Sadao Maruyama (Shunsaku Yamamoto), Tomoko Ito (Etsuko, his wife), Sachiko Chiba (Kimiko, his daughter), Yuriko Hanabusa (Oyuki, his mistress in the country), Setsuko Horikoshi (Shizuko, her daughter), Kaoru Ito (Ken'ichi, her son), Kamatari Fujiwara (Shingo, Etsuko's elder brother), Chikako Hosokawa (Shingo's wife).

PCL, Japan. 6644 ft., 74 mins.

Shomin-geki: a specifically Japanese genre of cinema that subtlety merges melodramatic and tragicomic motifs in which the atmosphere of the story is permeated with a cheerful attitude to life tinged with both understanding humor in exposing the failings of human nature and melancholic reflection on the randomness of fate.

The beginnings of this genre, which tells about the life of the lower-middle classes, date from the middle 20's. It was a short period in Japanese history when progressive forces exerted a strong influence and as a result the cinema was allowed more freedom in the choice of themes. The directors could go beyond the conventions and make films with marked social interests, like Paper Doll's Whisper of Spring (1926), directed by the then leftist Kenji Mizoguchi.

Naruse was, together with Gosho and Ozu, the leading shomin-geki film maker; his best works appeared in the 50's, but even before the war he became known with a beautiful tale about the mature acceptance of the sovereignty of others. Wife, Be like a Rose tells of the discovery of the wisdom of life by a young girl living alone with her poet mother. The father has abandoned the family and tied himself to another woman; after many years the daughter decides to persuade him to return.

When they meet the girl realizes that she has in front of her not an unequivocal sinner, but a man who could not communicate with his intellectual wife and established a new family with someone closer to him. The prepared words of condemnation are not uttered; reality can never be enclosed within moral clichés. Naruse presents this simple truth with a finesse and psychological penetration rarely achieved--and equally rarely appreciated--outside Japan.

MARYŠA   Josef Rovenský

Script: Otakar Vávra, Rovenský and Vladimír Wokoun, from the play by Alois Mrštík and Vilém Mrštík. Photography: Karel Degl. Music: Josef Dobeš and Jiří Fiala. Cast: Jiřina Štěpničková (Maryša Lízalová), František Kovařík (Her father), Hermína Vojtová (Her mother), Jaroslav Vojta (Vávra, miller), Vladimir Borský (Francek), Ella Nollová (His mother), Marie Glázrová (Rozárka).

Monopol, Czechoslovakia. 9514 ft., 106 mins.

In Slovakia at the end of the 19th century, a beautiful girl is forcibly married off to a rich miller. The outcome of the mismatch is tragic: Maryša poisons her husband. Rovenský transferred to the screen a naturalistic play which, at the time of its creation (1893) had full social motivation but which became more and more stale with the passing years, giving it credibility and fullness of expression while preserving the social and psychological context of the story. He made the film a painterly replica of the colorful world of elementality and passion.

The carefully preserved folklore is here not a mere ingredient but is organically linked with the story and the dialogues have none of the pretentiousness so common in rural dramas on the screen. It is indeed a pity that Maryša could not have been made in color; as a matter of fact one of the scenes (the wedding) was shot on color film, but could not be included in the final print in view of its insufficient technical quality. Similar imperfections frustrated all the early attempts in the field of color cinema in Europe as well as in Hollywood, which was at that time more technically advanced.

The first feature-length color movie, The Black Pirate (1926) starring Douglas Fairbanks, had been made ages before but did not cause a landslide. One of the reasons for this was the simultaneous mastering of the sound--the more attractive of the new means of expression. But the main reason was the high cost of research on the improvement of Technicolor, the first color system, and the strict secrecy which shrouded the processing of the exposed stock.

The first film whose colors roughly resemble reality is Mamoulian's much later Becky Sharp (1935). It was the first picture shot in the improved three-color system and also the first to contain a scene in which color is used as a genuine dramatic element. The most impressive picture of the 30's from the point of view of the color quality was Hathaway's western The Trail of the Lonesome Pine (1936), but a long time was to pass before color became a real artistic factor in the cinema.

PEASANTS (Krestyaniye)   Friedrich Ermler

Script: Manuel Bolshintsov, V. Portnov and Ermler. Photography: Alexandr Gintsburg. Music: Venedikt Pushkov. Cast: Yelena Yunger (Varvara Nechayeva), Boris Poslavsky (Yegor Nechayev), A. Petrov (Gerasim Platonovich), Yekaterina Korchagina-Alexandrovskaya (His mother), Nikolai Bogolyubov (Nikolai Mironovich, Head of Political Affairs), Ivan Chuvelyov (Kostya), V. Lukin (Matveyev).

Lenfilm, U.S.S.R.   10,171 ft., 113 mins.

A characteristic portent of the atmosphere of threat and the fear of the hidden internal enemy which mounted in the U.S.S.R. Economic difficulties created suspicions of sabotage, government pressure met with real resistance, resistance resulted in repressions. A period came during which the political psychosis would claim millions of victims.

The cinema, which was treated in Russia with great seriousness in accordance with Lenin's teaching, was given a propaganda task: it was to show the destructive methods adopted by the individual enemies of Communism. In particular the rural areas were concerned, where a "collectivization" met with the peasants' resistance. The film, which illustrates the struggle of the authorities against the rich peasants, was given to Ermler, the director who enjoyed official confidence. He was thus in a lucky position, as he had considerable creative freedom. Ermler had already, in the period of Fragment of an Empire, proved himself to be a seasoned psychologist.

He started out from the agreed basic situation in quite an unexpected direction: his somber, naturalistic tale of a bloody social conflict in a Siberian collective farm is perhaps not entirely convincing as far as the actual facts are concerned; yet it reveals the mentality of people of those times with striking precision, and supports it, within the same convention, by the solid motivation of the attitudes of each of the parties to the conflict. Even that forced practice of making the characters "credibly human" at all costs, which on other occasions had jarred so much in Soviet cinema, can be excused here, because it is the hostile and wicked rich peasant who was given human dimensions, while the commisar who fights him, visibly less intelligent, was forced to maneuver intricately in a rather unfriendly community. In the final result, the film, although certainly far from perfect, is still one of the more interesting Soviet productions of the last years before the war.

I'LL GIVE A MILLION (Darò un Milione)   Mario Camerini

Script: Cesare Zavattini, Ivo Perilli, Camerini and Ercole Patti, from "Buoni per un Giorno, " by Cesare Zavattini and Giaci Mondaini. Photography: Otello Martelli and Carlo Montuori. Music: Gian Luigi Tocchi. Cast: Vittorio De Sica, Assia Noris, Luigi Almirante, Mario Gallina, Fausto Guerzoni, Romolo Costa, Franco Coop, Vinicio Sofia, Claudio Ermelli, Cesare Zoppetti, Umberto Sacripante.

Novella Film, Italy.

What can be the outcome of a millionaire's caprice of offering a
fortune to the first person who will prove to be really magnanimous?
One of the outcomes can surely be a decent comedy, especially when
the part of the millionaire disillusioned with life and masquerading
as a poor man is played by Vittorio De Sica, and the script is written by Zavattini. This was the debut of this dynamo, who were later to generate half of the great films of Neorealism.

I'll Give a Million is the most fanciful of Camerini's lyrical
pictures, full of psychological nuances and good-hearted irony in
describing his fellow Italians. The earlier reminiscences of Clair
(in What Rascals Men Are!) are also in evidence here and are joined
by the echoes of Capra (the plot) and Chaplin (the motif of a millionaire who wants to commit suicide and is saved by a pauper--a
clear reference to City Lights). The makers of I'll Give a Million
undoubtedly used the ideas of others, but presented them in a different spirit in the Italian context, and steered clear of any social
accents--quite understandable in the times of Mussolini.

THE THIRTY-NINE STEPS   Alfred Hitchcock

Script: Charles Bennett and Alma Reville, from the novel by John
Buchan. Photography: Bernard Knowles. Music: Louis Levy.
Cast: Madeleine Carroll (Pamela), Robert Donat (Richard Hannay),
Lucie Mannheim (Miss Smith-Annabella), Godfrey Tearle (Professor
Jordan), Peggy Ashcroft (Crofter's wife), John Laurie (Scottish
crofter), Helen Hayes (Mrs. Jordan), Frank Cellier (Sheriff), Wylie
Watson (Mr. Memory).

Gaumont British, G.B.   87 mins.

The totally absurd plot of John Buchan's novel gave rise to a film full
of imagination, extravagance, genuine tongue-in-cheek humor and--
right from the lettering of the titles--the flavor of the 30's, now not
without appeal. Even if The Thirty-Nine Steps lacks logic, it does not
lack speed: the rapid diametrical changes of the situation of the hero
are the motor of the plot. The dramatic principle is one of a double
chase: an unknown girl is stabbed to death in the flat of a young Canadian who pursues the murderers, a sinister spy ring, to Scotland, and is
himself wanted by the police for the very same crime.

Although the picture does not match the excellence of Hitchcock's
best films, it has a certain nostalgic interest as a review of his favorite
motifs: the conflict of forces of good and evil; the hero saved by the
love of a woman; ordinary people being suddenly involved in momentous events. The train journey, almost inevitable in a Hitchcock film, here gives rise to exciting scenes on the Forth Bridge.

1936

MODERN TIMES   Charles Chaplin

Script: Chaplin. Photography: Rollie Totheroh and Ira Morgan.
Music: Chaplin. Cast: Charles Chaplin (Charlie the Tramp),
Paulette Goddard (Working-class girl), Henry Bergman (Café owner),
Chester Conklin (Mechanic), Allen Garcia (Manager of a steel works),
Lloyd Ingraham (Prison governor), Louis Netheaux (Drug addict),
John Rand (Jailbird), Stanley Sanford (Man working next to Charlie
on the conveyor belt), Hank Mann (Charlie's cellmate), Mira McKin-
ney (Wife of the prison chaplain).

United Artists, U.S.A.   7634 ft., 85 mins.

It was only in 1936, eight years after the introduction of sound
cinema, that Chaplin finally decided to break his screen silence.
Yet even then he did it half-heartedly. Although equipped with
musical score and background sounds, Modern Times lacks the direct spoken word (apart from the hilarious and brief episode when
Charlie, working as a waiter, sings a nonsense song) and thus really at heart remains a silent picture. On the other hand, this seems
strangely consistent with the message of the film, which is the protest of an ordinary man against the dehumanization and mechaniza-
tion of life brought about by technological progress.

      Charlie is a mere cog in the assembly line of an ultramodern
factory; his duty is to tighten just one nut. In order to save time
the management experiments with a machine for feeding workers
while they work and the innovation is tried out on Charlie. All this
drives him crazy and, accordingly, he is sent to a mental asylum.
After his release, Charlie searches for work in vain and ends up
arrested as the leader of a Communist demonstration (while in fact
he only picked up a red flag which had fallen off the end of a long

truck). He does all right in a comfortable jail but is, alas, soon
released. He befriends a waif girl who is threatened with arrest
and the two go together through the joys and miseries of life.

The theme and many of the details of Modern Times were
based on René Clair's À nous la liberté; this fact brought about a
widely publicized court case whereby the German owners of Clair's
film unsuccessfully sued Chaplin for copyright infringement. The
key to Modern Times is the clash between the basically old-fashioned
Tramp character with the ultramodern world of today. A simple
man is unhappy in a world dominated by machines and it is significant that it is only in jail that he seems satisfied. But the Chaplinesque panacea for all problems is still effective--the departure
into the distance along a dusty country road.

Modern Times is a sort of anthology of Chaplin's cinema, a
recapitulation of motifs from his earlier works. The film is literally bursting with ideas and the brilliant gags are not all possible to
enumerate, although among the most memorable are the scene with
the feeding machine and Charlie's odyssey through a variety of jobs,
factory worker, night watchman in a department store, and singing
waiter. The multitude of separate comic episodes tend to become
autonomous and in places seriously threaten the homogeneity of the
whole picture. On the other hand, this generates a valuable new
quality--an episodic, caricatural, cartoon-strip style.

Of course, the theme of Modern Times is today even more
relevant (and the film seems better understood) than when it was
made and the great success of its re-release in the early 70's
comes as no great surprise. Chaplin is still torn between satirizing
the dreaded technological inventions and deriding the sound cinema
(when he can sing he does not care to use proper words). But
Modern Times is the last picture in which he does not speak; curiously in his next, The Great Dictator, Chaplin would be guilty of
garrulity!

PARTIE DE CAMPAGNE   Jean Renoir

Script: Renoir, from the short story by Guy de Maupassant. Pho-
tography: Claude Renoir and Jean Bourgoin. Editing: Marguerite
Renoir. Music: Joseph Kosma. Cast: Sylvia Bataille (Henriette),
Georges Darnoux (Henri), Jane Marken (Madame Dufour), Gabriello
(M. Dufour), Jacques Borel (Rudolph), Paul Temps (Anatole), Ga-
brielle Fontan (Grandmother), Jean Renoir (Papa Poulin), Marguerite
Renoir (Servant).

Panthéon Productions, France. 3700 ft., 41 mins. Production of
the film was interrupted; the existing material was edited and re-

leased in 1946.

Taking the external characteristics of Partie de campagne, one
should describe it as an example of a literary adaptation which
achieved complete unison with the intentions of the original author.
Yet to say only so much is to say nothing at all. For Renoir,
while preserving the whole outline of the plot of Maupassant's short
story (which is one of his typical subtle etudes of moods and feelings), used it only as the starting point for a poetic essay which
praises the beauty of nature and acknowledges its mighty influence
on the human psyche. While Dovzhenko in Earth gave the fullest
expression to the natural symbiosis of peasant and soil, in Partie
de campagne Renoir perfectly expressed the dazzling experience of
townspeople's encounter with nature.

The story is set in 1860 and describes the visit of the family
of a Parisian shopkeeper to the country. Although afraid of the
"man-eating pike," the shopkeeper and his son-in-law-to-be Anatole
try fishing but finally settle for a nap. Meanwhile the mother and
daughter are courted by two men, one of whom is an enjoy-it-while-
it-lasts hedonist, while the other has a more serious attitude to
pleasure. The ladies are allocated in accordance with these beliefs.
The irony is that it is the serious one who finally seduces the
daughter, thereby ruining her future life with a down-to-earth husband.

The reflections of light in the leaves and grasses, the singing
of birds, the provocative glittering of the surface of the river all
paralyze the routine of city life while letting evolve new feelings
and longings. These very images and this atmosphere can easily
be found in the paintings of Auguste Renoir the great father of the
brothers Jean and Claude. But while Auguste and his fellow Impressionists could only speak with short phrases, as it were, Jean
and Claude composed an entire song, of extraordinary fluidity and
fascinating lightness. Still, their film is a song rather than a symphony.

Admittedly, Partie de campagne does not even characterize
its protagonist fully, but it was not its aim to do so. It set out to
describe one basic experience, that of revelation. The manner in
which this was done is an example of understatement in the cinema,
a demonstration that new and complex feelings can be expressed
with hardly any touches of the camera. A miniature can sometimes
be more revealing and more complete than a large canvas.

All this is independent from the fact that Renoir never fully
completed his study of the collision of the pure world of nature with
the triviality of urban life. First the illness of one of the main
actors interrupted the shooting. Renoir, who in this period enthusiastically explored different regions of cinema, did not find the
time later to finish the work and also rejected Prévert's proposals
for adding to the existing material. It was only after many years

that the film saw the light of day, assembled as a medium-length
feature. It is impossible to judge what Partie de campagne would
have been like if the original idea of the film had been realized.
But apart from that it is excellent even in its existing abbreviate
form.

WE FROM KRONSTADT (My iz Kronshtadta)   Yefim Dzigan

Script: Vsevolod Vishnevsky. Photography: Naum Naumov-Strazh.
Music: Nikolai Kryukov. Cast: Vasili Zaichikov (Comissar Mar-
tinov), Grigori Bushuyev (Artiom Balashov), N. Ivakin (Burmistrov),
Oleg Zhakov (Jan Draudin), Raisa Yesipova (Yekaterina Tyman),
Pyotr Kirillov (Valentin Bezprozvany), E. Guni (Anton Karabash),
Mikhail Turinenko (Junker).

Mosfilm, U.S.S.R. 8711 ft., 97 mins.

Like Chapayev, We from Kronstadt could also be considered a
classic on the day of its premiere--perhaps even more so: all the
component elements of the film are so impeccably balanced and the
whole composed with such inner conviction that it does not deviate
at all towards formalist academism or towards political propaganda.
On the other hand, while in Chapayev a leading revolutionary was
the center of attention, We from Kronstadt is, at least in part, a
continuation of the collective character of Eisenstein's silent cinema:
the protagonists are the Kronstadt sailors who defended St. Petersburg from the advancing White forces in October 1919. From the
battalion the film is about, only one man will survive the ruthless
encounters with Yudenich's army. He will witness and participate
in the final victory.

Authorship of We from Kronstadt certainly cannot be credited
only to its director. Dzigan, a good craftsman who had never before (or since) made films of comparable standard, was here rather
a coordinator of the work of the whole creative team and the executor of the intentions of the script, written by a playwright who
thus proved his intimate understanding of the specific qualities of
cinema as a medium. Vishnevsky spent two years preparing the
projected film and the shooting took more than a year. How different the ways of achieving perfection can be!

It was the scriptwriter who was mainly responsible for the
slow progress of the production; with great patience he tried to
achieve full authenticity and three-dimensional verisimilitude. These
intentions were fully respected by the cameraman and the actors.
To make the sea convincing in its role as a wrathful witness of the
dramatic events, for instance, the shooting was done in stormy

weather. The desired three-dimensional aspect of the film was achieved by Naumov-Strazh with an impressive display of pictorial effects.

The photography, with its crude autumnal texture, was no more a vital component of the dramatic line than was the sound-track, whose originality and emotional impact ensured for it an exceptional position in the whole Soviet cinema of the 30's. Even Eisenstein and Prokofiev in Alexander Nevsky had not achieved such an entrancing effect as did Kryukov with his method of blending natural sounds with music. The memorable scenes of the film in which the sound itself plays a decisive role are the desperate attack of the singing battalion and the extermination of the sailors' band. In the first of these scenes the song now and again comes through the din of the battle, and now and again is overshadowed by it; in the second, the musicians dying one after another desperately give strength to their fighting comrades by playing louder and louder on the decreasing number of musical instruments. When death terminates the efforts of the orchestra's last member, a powerful salvo from the ships of the Baltic Fleets bursts into the dying sound of the tuba. It is a forceful symbol of the ruthless struggle, shown here with a poetry which the Soviet cinema found extremely difficult to match later.

MR. DEEDS GOES TO TOWN   Frank Capra

Script: Robert Riskin, from the short story, "Opera Hat," by Clarence Budington Kelland. Photography: Joseph Walker. Music: Howard Jackson. Cast: Gary Cooper (Longfellow Deeds), Jean Arthur (Babe Bennett), George Bancroft (MacWade), Lionel Stander (Cornelius Cobb), Douglas Dumbrille (John Cedar), Raymond Walburn (Walter), Margaret Matzenauer (Madame Pompani), H. B. Warner (Judge Walker), Warren Hymer (Bodyguard).

Columbia, U.S.A.   10,391 ft., 115 mins.

America under the New Deal: the slogans of the day are social solidarity and respect for the rights of the ordinary man. Capra, as usual, praises the virtues of the middle classes and laughs at the faults of the rich--and steeps his film in good-natured, optimistic faith in justice on the one hand and thorough cinematic skill on the other. It is thus hardly surprising that the director became even more popular with the public than he did after It Happened One Night.

Mr. Longfellow Deeds, a small-town, tuba-playing, postcard-poet, totally unexpectedly inherits twenty million dollars. Provincial and naive when he arrives in New York, he is surrounded by

parasites. A woman journalist writes stories in newspapers about
him while pretending to be his friend. But the two finally fall in
love and love in Capra's films is always victorious. The girl
comes to Deeds' rescue when his relatives, in an attempt to get at
his money, try to declare him insane; the hero's brilliant court
oration deals a final blow to the evil forces.

Despite its very naive (though very funny) plot, the film is
a faithful mirror of its time. This is probably because it is a
comedy: it is significant that, for instance, Chaplin's City Lights
tells us more about the Depression than many a solemn drama.
Indeed, Capra reached regions close to Chaplin, when through sentimental naiveté he achieved deep emotion. He was not to repeat
this success in Mr. Smith Goes to Washington (1939), where certain
critical accents proved to be misguided, and instead of sympathy,
evoked pity in the audience.

The greatest asset of Mr. Deeds Goes to Town is, without a
doubt, Gary Cooper: simple, charming and irresistibly sympathetic.

OSAKA ELEGY (Niniwa Erejī/Niniwa Hika)   Kenji Mizoguchi

Script: Mizoguchi and Yoshikata Yoda. Photography: Minoru Miki.
Cast: Isuzu Yamada (Ayako), Kasuke Koizumi (Junzo, her father),
Chiyoko Okura (Sachiko, her younger sister), Shinpachiro Asaka
(Hiroshi, her elder brother), Benkei Shiganoya (Sonosuke Asai, her
patron), Yoko Umemura (Sumiko, his wife), Eitaro Shindo (Fujino),
Kunio Tamura (Doctor).

Daiichi Eiga, Japan. 8009 ft., 89 mins.

The most penetrating female portraits in the whole of the Japanese
cinema were drawn in the films of Kenji Mizoguchi, the director
who from his early silent film Paper Doll's Whisper of Spring
(1926) until Street of Shame, his last completed picture, remained
faithful to the theme of the analysis of the female character, whatever the tonality of the individual film or its social and historical
setting. In the 20's and 30's Mizoguchi moved with ease between
styles and genres--from satirical comedies to imitations of Expressionism, from realist social dramas to poetic ballads about artists--
but the woman was nearly always in the center. In his youthful
films she was treated with admiration for her beauty and merits; in
the later ones, with penetration and irony but always with seriousness.

Mizoguchi created the portrayal of the heroine of Osaka
Elegy with exceptional care; a main reason being the personal links

tying him to the scenery of the poor quarters of that large industrial city. Yoshikata Yoda was asked by the director to polish the visual aspect of the film ad infinitum; but when the work was finished it became obvious that Mizoguchi had achieved something entirely over-shadowing his 56 previous films.

Osaka Elegy, like most of his works, is centered around the motifs of blind fate and women's sacrifice for the sake of men. The theme is of a girl, a telephone operator, who ruins her life when she becomes her aging boss's mistress for the sake of several hundred yen which she needs for her unemployed father. The di-rector set it in a carefully reconstructed street by the canals in Osaka. Seemingly, the film does not lack melodrama. It also con-tains naturalistic elements. Yet this is a film that does not have to be ashamed of component parts of doubtful provenance.

Mizoguchi really could transfer life to the screen. The rea-sons for it are easy to find: the ardor, candor and social passions so characteristic of him, especially in his youth. The formal as-pect of Osaka Elegy is in principle only of subsidiary importance. Mizoguchi, who had always displayed great pictorial sensitivity, this time attached more weight to the realism of images than to their aesthetic refinement. As far as the narrative method is concerned, it was in fact Osaka Elegy in which the director first began to es-tablish his later characteristic long-lasting shots, with the camera far from the object and the actors entrusted with achieving the dy-namic accents. The decisive elements of the film are the realistic climate and the very convincing role of Isuzu Yamada.

FURY   Fritz Lang

Script: Bartlett Cormack and Fritz Lang, from a story by Norman Krasna. Photography: Joseph Ruttenberg. Music: Franz Wax-man. Cast: Spencer Tracy (Joe Wilson), Sylvia Sidney (Katherine Grant), Walter Abel (District Attorney), Bruce Cabot (Kirby Daw-son), Edward Ellis (Sheriff), Walter Brennan ("Bugs" Meyers), George Walcott (Tom), Frank Albertson (Charlie), George Chandler (Milton Jackson), Arthur Stone (Durkin), Morgan Wallace (Fred Gar-rett), Roger Gray (Stranger), Edwin Maxwell (Vickery), Howard Hickman (Governor), Jonathan Hale (Defense Attorney), Leila Ben-nett (Edna Hooper), Esther Dale (Mrs. Whipple), Helen Flint (Franchette).

MGM, U.S.A.   8530 ft., 95 mins.

After leaving Germany in 1933, Lang went first to France, where he made a mediocre comedy, Liliom (1934), and later the same

year arrived in America.   For almost two years he had trouble
finding work; finally he co-scripted and directed Fury, a picture in-
dicting lynch law.   Fury is based on a real incident.   On his way
to a meeting with his fiancée after a long separation, Joe Wilson is
arrested as a suspected kidnapper.   The rumors exaggerate the evidence and twist facts and soon nobody in town doubts Joe's guilt.

The bloodthirsty citizens besiege the jail and blow it up, but
the prisoner manages to escape in the turmoil.   He swears vengeance on the mob and with the help of his brothers plants evidence
proving his death.   As a result 22 people are tried for murder.
Joe is persuaded by his girl to come to the court as the verdicts of
guilty are being handed down and admit the truth, thus saving the
lives of people who are morally murderers.

The duality of human nature, the potential for evil in ordinary
decent people always fascinated Lang.   Here he indulged himself
doubly: he shows evil instincts to be present both in the townspeople, who suddenly turn into wild beasts, and in their would-be
victim, in whom injustice liberates the craving for revenge.
Lang comments: "Lynch is only the result of a certain situation....
Often it all starts with the best of intentions."   Still, there were
6010 people lynched in America in the fifty years before Fury was
made.

Lang makes his point with remarkable restraint.   The hero
is not an unequivocal goodie and--which is worth noting--the sheriff
does have a reason to suspect him (a five-dollar bill, part of the
ransom money, was found in his possession).   It is only violence
which Lang condemns.

Fury is an expert film and certainly Lang's best work outside Germany.   His understanding of smalltown America, precise
observation of different types of people, and skill in building up tension are impressive.   Especially interesting are the short, powerful snaps of the increasing hysteria in the town.   The use of a documentary film of the attack on the prison gives the picture a nice,
matter-of-fact touch.   To all this Lang adds his original, and sad-
dening, psychological reflection and a touch of wry humor.   Thus
the director finally discarded the gloomy demonism and larger-than-
life ornamentation characteristic of his films in the 20's.   Fury
opened up to Lang all doors in the American film industry.   It also
contained Spencer Tracy's first big role.

SISTERS OF THE GION (Gion no Shimai)   Kenji Mizoguchi

Script: Mizoguchi and Yoshikata Yoda.   Photography: Minoru Miki.
Cast: Isuzu Yamada (Umekichi, the Elder Sister), Yoko Umemura

(O-Mocha, the Younger Sister), Eitaro Shindo, Benkei Shiganoya, Namiko Kawashima, Fumio Okura, Taizo Fukami, Reiko Aoi.

Daiichi Eiga, Japan. 70 mins.

Sisters of the Gion constitutes a distinct continuation of Osaka Elegy, Mizoguchi's previous picture--in its method of describing the world, in the choice of theme and in the dramatic construction. As in that film, there is here no properly developing dramatic line, but only a certain situation, precisely depicted by a succession of small but characteristic events. This time also Mizoguchi talks about women. One of the two sisters of the title, to whom more attention was given, bears considerable similarity to the heroine of Osaka Elegy (and is portrayed by the same actress).

       She is a beginner geisha in the entertainment district of Kyoto; her dreams are of work in Tokyo or getting married. She wants to push through life regardless, treating her position as the result of an unfriendly world dominated by egoistic men. She wants to give tit for tat and is prepared for anything that may improve her social status. The elder sister is different: she has no illusions and finds consolation for the future in an inner discipline and the ability to accept her fate. In the light of the ironically bitter con-clusion of the film she was undoubtedly right. The more the younger sister wrestles with fate, the more futile are her efforts, and her further life will probably not be very different from that of the hero-ine of Imamura's The Insect Woman of nearly 30 years later: in pre-war Japan the "modern" attitude to life had, as yet, practically no chance of achieving its aim.

BALTIC DEPUTY (Deputat Baltiki)   Alexandr Zarkhi and Yosif
     Kheifits

Script: D. Del, Zarkhi, Leonid Rakhmanov and Kheifits.   Photog-raphy: M. Kaplan. Music: Nikolai Timofeyev. Cast: Nikolai Cherkasov (Prof. Polezhaev), M. Domasheva (His wife), Boris Livanov (Bocharov), Oleg Zhakov (Dr. Vorobyov), A. Melnikov (Kupryanov), M. Dubrava (Printing apprentice), N. Kakharinov (Yard-keeper), A. Mazurin (Menshevik).

Lenfilm, U.S.S.R. 8622 ft., 96 mins.

Just after the Revolution, the Russian intelligentsia, quite under-standably, took a decidedly distrustful (or openly hostile) attitude toward the new regime. Only very few among the outstanding men of learning could conceive of a wider perspective beyond the current

situation when the ruthlessness of the conflict between the old and
the new made it seem dangerous to espouse active (and compromis-
ing) stances. To such individuals belonged a famous Moscow botanist, Kliment Timiriazev, and it is on his life that Zarkhi and Kheifits base themselves in their attempt to present the model of an intellectual who declared himself on the Bolshevik side.

The film was to turn out to be invaluable for both internal
and foreign propaganda. The shooting was preceded--as for We
from Kronstadt--by a prolonged period of collecting, documenting
and researching customs and psychology and polishing the dramatic
structure of the script. Zarkhi and Kheifits did this with all the
more ardor as they had had no chance of shining thus far in their
work on rather unspectacular and down-to-earth themes. Baltic
Deputy was an important opportunity and was exploited to the full.
Yet another remarkable portrait of a revolutionary hero was made--
this time a very specific hero, though no less vivid than Chapayev
or Maxim.

Much credit for this achievement goes to Nikolai Cherkasov,
later the grandiose protagonist of Eisenstein's last films. It is
nearly incredible, the way in which this 32-year-old music-hall
comedian managed on the screen to become a somewhat eccentric
scholar with one foot in the grave. He would not have got the part
if the directors had not come to know him when he appeared in
their earlier film (they were repeatedly to show their good judgment in appreciating the psychological predispositions of actors).
The details of the personality of the professor molded on Timiriazev
are portrayed in the film with an exceptional care, at moments excessive, but through its character as an intimate diary the film
avoids ideological obtrusiveness, which was rampant in the Soviet
cinema of the period.

And this was not meticulousness suspended in a vacuum: the
background is equally rich. Although the style of Baltic Deputy is
somewhat episodic (independently of the fact that the individual
scenes are quite skillfully joined together), it is just this episodic
character which helps the film to convey a number of interesting
observations about the people and the times during the creation of
the Soviet government.

REMBRANDT   Alexander Korda

Script: Carl Zuckmayer. Photography: Georges Périnal. Art
Direction: Vincent Korda. Costumes: John Armstrong. Music:
Geoffrey Toye. Cast: Charles Laughton (Rembrandt van Rijn),
Gertrude Lawrence (Geertke Dirx), Elsa Lanchester (Hendrickje
Stoffels), John Bryning (Titus van Rijn), Richard Gofe (Titus as

child), Meinhart Maur (Ornia), Walter Hudd (Banning Cocq), John
Clements (Govaert Flink), Henry Hewitt (Jan Six), Abraham Sofaer
(Dr. Menassen), William Fagan (Mayor), George Merritt (Church
warden), John Turnbull (Minister), Sam Livesey (Auctioneer).

London Film Productions, G.B.   7913 ft., 88 mins.

The huge box-office success of The Private Life of Henry VIII triggered off a veritable avalanche of imitations.   Korda was of course
not idle himself, but he entrusted to others several scripts to direct which continue his ironical-anecdotal approach to history, while
he acted only as executive producer.   Rembrandt, the best picture
based on this historical approach, was however directed by Korda
himself.   It is perhaps open to discussion whether The Private Life
of Henry VIII exerted any influence on the frivolous Carnival in
Flanders, but there is no doubt at all that, conversely, Feyder's
film inspired Korda's painterly treatment of Rembrandt's epoch.

        This screen biography describes the later period in the life
of the Dutch master.   Compared to similar efforts of this type, it
sounded a much more serious tone, at moments nearly Chaplinesque
in its pathos.   For this the director as much as Charles Laughton
was responsible.   The part of Rembrandt is not only rich and ribald, but also intimate and moving; his interpretation certainly
counts as one of the best achievements of this outstanding actor.
Yet even Charles Laughton appearing in a picture whose beautiful
visual aspect imitates the old Dutch chiaroscuro paintings did not
bring the anticipated response.

        Fate is sometimes vicious: Rembrandt, a film clearly su-
perior to The Private Life of Henry VIII both in the care of staging
and in artistic taste, was received with indifference by the public
and the producing company suffered a considerable loss.   As a result Korda was discouraged from further attempts along similar
lines, and returned to film direction (without results meriting mention) only after four years.

THE SECRET AGENT   Alfred Hitchcock

Script: Charles Bennett, from the play by Campbell Dixon, based
on the novel, "Ashenden," by W. Somerset Maugham. Photography:
Bernard Knowles. Music: Louis Levy. Cast: Madeleine Carroll
(Elsa Carrington), Peter Lorre (The General), John Gielgud (Richard
Ashenden), Robert Young (Robert Marvin), Percy Marmont (Caypor),
Florence Kahn (Mrs. Caypor), Charles Carson (R), Lilli Palmer
(Lilli).

Gaumont British, G.B.   7816 ft., 87 mins.

As in the previous The Man Who Knew Too Much, Hitchcock used
a foreign locale and national characteristics with dramatic purpose.
Ashenden, an intelligence agent, travels to Switzerland to liquidate
a spy and kills somebody else by mistake.   The plot itself does not
seem to be a particularly good dramatic vehicle: in the director's
own opinion the fact that the axis of the plot is a basically· negative
purpose (the killing), considerably slows down the action.   The audience is simply not wholeheartedly on the side of the hero.   Yet
Hitchcock added his unmistakable touch, which took the film away
from shallow waters and transformed it into a suspenseful and original thriller: the spy headquarters are situated in a chocolate factory; the dead organist-spy's body slumped on the organ manual
sounds a constant and ominous note.

The outcome of the controversy over the final railway crash
scene shows how vulnerable films are to censorship and how easily
the moral implications of a picture may not only be changed, but
reversed.   The train, bound for Constantinople and carrying Ashenden, his wife, their accomplice, nicknamed "Mexican," and the spy,
is bombed by British aircraft.   The spy is trapped in the wreckage;
Mexican offers him a flask of brandy.   When the spy drinks, Mexican shoots him and then picks up the flask and drinks himself.   The
censor objected to this ending.   In the released version therefore
the situation is reversed.   Mexican slips the injured spy a gun and
is shot for his pains.   In other words, it was the timing of the
drink which was considered immoral!

CÉSAR   Marcel Pagnol

Script: Pagnol, from his own play.   Photography: Willy.   Music:
Vincent Scotto.   Cast: Raimu (César Ollivier), Pierre Fresnay
(Marius, his son), Orane Demazis (Fanny), André Fouché (Cesariot
Panisse), Fernand Charpin (Honoré Panisse), Edouard Delmont (Dr.
Félicien Venelle), Milly Mathis (Aunt Claudine Foulon), Robert Vat-
tier (M. Brun), Alida Rouffe (Honorine), Doumel (Fernand), Paul
Dulac (Félix Escartefigue), Maupi (Chauffeur).

Les Films Marcel Pagnol, France.   10,852 ft., 121 mins.

In the early 30's, when the first screen adaptations of Marcel Pagnol's stage plays were being made, the outcome was not much different from the general style of French cinema.   French movies
were clearly short of breath and the profuse dialogues of "canned
theatre" burdened not only Marius and Fanny, but most of their con-

temporary films. In the late 30's all was different: French cinema distinctly gravitated towards minor scales of mood and in spite of the fact that César and other late Pagnol films shook off their theatrical heritage and became truly cinematic, they were now, with their coarse folk temperament, even more alien to the rest of French production than before.

César is the last part of the Marseilles Trilogy. César is the big and jovial owner of the waterfront bar. Panisse, his friend and Fanny's husband, dies. Fanny's son Césariot thinks he is Panisse's child, but Fanny tells him that his father is really Marius who went off to sea. Marius is now back and runs a garage; somebody tells Césariot that Marius is involved with a gang of criminals. Césariot follows it up and finds the story to be a joke. Marius, Fanny and Césariot are finally reconciled.

The plot is here perhaps less interesting than in the earlier parts but the film-making is definitely better. The film has a powerful, authentic mood, organically united with the Provençal milieu, and dominated by the extraordinary personality of Raimu. The great actor created here the first of his three best roles; the others were to be the main parts in The Baker's Wife and Strangers in the House.

PÉPÉ LE MOKO   Julien Duvivier

Script: Henri Jeanson, Duvivier and Roger d'Ashelbé, from the novel by the latter. Photography: Jules Kruger and Marc Fossard. Music: Vincent Scotto and Mohamed Yguerbuchen. Cast: Jean Gabin (Pépé le Moko), Mireille Ballin (Gaby), Line Noro (Inès), Charpin (Régis), Saturnin Fabre ("Grand Père"), Gabriel Gabrio (Carlos), Lucas Gridoux (Slimane), Dalio (L'Arbi), Fréhel (Tania), Gilbert Gil (Pierrot), Roger Legris (Max).

Paris Film Productions, France. 8855 ft., 98 mins.

A Parisian ex-gangster on the run hides in the Casbah, the Arab quarter of Algiers; he has broken with the past, but his former crimes do not allow him to emerge. As long as he can shelter among narrow alleyways he is safe, but nostalgia appears--and a beautiful woman, straight from the cabarets of Paris. Pépé le Moko leaves his sanctuary and heads toward the sea to meet his girl; there he is claimed by a police bullet.

From an aesthetic point of view this is a most outstanding picture, not only because of the brilliance of the narrative technique but also through the directorial inventiveness in many epi-

sodes, which are often quoted as examples of masterful staging (a
collision between the actual voice of an ex-singer with her record
of many years ago; the falling corpse which sets the juke-box in
action; the excellent editing rhythm of the hero's final descent from
the Casbah to the sea).

Visually, the film is closely related to Le Grand jeu and,
like that film, it foreshadowed Poetic Realism. This can be seen
in its pessimistic mood and the classic motif of the hero's being
too weak to overcome his longings. If it was not for Duvivier's
fatal lack of a sense of proportion, Pépé le Moko would doubtless
have been one of the best French pictures of the 30's.

The melodrama which Feyder so carefully played down in his
films was stressed with relish by the director of Pépé le Moko; the
psychological depth so vital to Renoir did not concern Duvivier at
all, although he included more than enough of local color and stressing of mood. (The screen Casbah, however, is of studio origin).
Thus Duvivier wasted the opportunity to reach a lasting position in
French cinema, yet he did exert a very considerable influence on
its development--a fact which tends not to be generally appreciated.
His work is underestimated as eclectic and ideologically thoughtless.

THE THIRTEEN (Trinadtsat)   Mikhail Romm

Script: Yosif Prut and Romm. Photography: Boris Volchek.
Music: Anatoli Alexandrov. Cast: Ivan Novoseltsev (Commander),
Yelena Kuzmina (His wife), A. Chistyakov (Geologist), Andrei Fait
(Lt. Col. Skuratov), Pyotr Masokha (Sviridenko), I. Kuznetsov
(Akchurin), A. Dolinin (Timoshkin), I. Yudin (Petrov), V. Kulakov
(Balandin), D. Zolts (Levkoev), S. Krylov (Zhurba), S. Kozminsky
(Gusev), A. Kepikov (Muradov), A. Kuliev (Kuliev).

Mosfilm, U.S.S.R. 7726 ft., 86 mins.

The beginnings of Romm's career as a director are without a doubt
among the most unconventional in the cinema: after his debut with
the silent Boule de Suif (the last Soviet film to lack a soundtrack),
he was given the task of transplanting the plot of John Ford's The
Lost Patrol to the setting of the Soviet border territory in the Kara-
Kum desert. There would be nothing very remarkable in this if it
were not for the fact that Romm had not seen the American film.

This time, fortunately, although the funds allotted him were
again meager, the film was at least shot on location. The crew
was almost decimated by monstrous heat (and the actors did not escape either--there are only 12 protagonists and not 13 as the title

would suggest), but Romm made an interesting picture. It can be
called an exterior chamber drama, because the stress is placed
not on the spectacular, but on the study of human actions in a
critical situation. This choice, forced in fact by the circumstances,
turned out to be quite right. Not surprisingly so: the director had
already in his first film shown his great talent as a psychologist.

LA BELLE ÉQUIPE   Julien Duvivier

Script: Duvivier and Charles Spaak. Photography: Jules Kruger
and Marc Fossard. Music: Maurice Yvain. Cast: Jean Gabin
(Jeannot), Charles Vanel (Charlot), Raymond Aimos (Tintin),
Viviane Romance (Gina), Marcelle Géniat (Grandmother), Raymond
Cordy (Drunkard), Jacques Baumer (M. Jubette), Charpin (Gen-
darme), Raphaël Medina (Marie), Micheline Cheirel (Huguette),
Robert Lynen (René), Charles Granval (Proprietor), Charles Dorat
(Jacques).

Ciné-Ayrs, France. 8500 ft., 94 mins.

In La Belle équipe the populist tendencies à la René Clair were
married to the leftist moods of the French Popular Front. The
picture was made during Duvivier's best creative period, which
would end with La Fin du jour. The story is of the "ten little nig-
ger boys" type: five unemployed men invest 100,000 francs that
they won in the state lottery in a small cooperative inn which they
build themselves on the banks of the river Marne to cater for Sunday trippers and anglers. There are two girls with them, one good,
one bad. For one reason or another the friends fall out of the
scheme one by one.

The film has humor, joie de vivre, good characterization,
interesting details of custom--and unfortunate melodramatics, which
Duvivier found impossible to fend off. The best proof of the feebleness of the director's backbone in giving in to commercial pressures are the two endings of La Belle équipe to cater for different
audiences--one optimistic and sustained in the carefree, Capra-
esque mood of the rest of the film, and the other tragic. The
tragic version, in which one of the two remaining friends shoots
the other over the unfaithful wife who toys with both of them, seems
more in tune with the pessimistic spirit pervading the French cinema
at the time and was thus probably more appropriate.

THE ONLY SON (Hitori Musuko) Yasujiro Ozu

Script: Tadao Ikeda and Masao Arata, from a story by James
Maki. Photography: Shojiro Sugimoto. Music: Senji Ito. Cast:
Chôko Iida (Otsuné Nonomiya), Shinichi Himori (Ryosuke, her son),
Masao Hayama (Ryosuke as a boy), Yoshiko Tsubouchi (Sugiko, his
wife), Chishu Ryu (Ookubo, the teacher), Tomoko Naniwa (His wife),
Mitsuko Yoshikawa (Otaka).

Shochiku, Japan. 7831 ft., 87 mins.

The Only Son was Ozu's first sound film. Like other grandmasters
of silent cinema, including Chaplin, he had long been reluctant to
use sound. Despite this, for the past three years his films, made
in the outdated silent convention, had won the highest Japanese film
award. All the same, the final introduction of dialogues was inevitable, both because of commercial pressures and the director's
wish to take note in his films of the more complex human situation
in Japan following the onset of the period of economic depression in
1935.

Ozu's cinema employs a limited number of basic themes and
the plots of some of his films are so similar that they almost seem
to be copies of each other. Yet great tragedies can be pent up in
austere simplicity, and there are static scenes in The Only Son in
which dramatic tension is brought almost to breaking point. A
mother slaves at a little wool factory in the mountains and sacrifices all for the sake of her son, a university student in remote
Tokyo. He hopes to find a good job with good prospects when he
graduates, but finds nothing better than teaching an evening course
at a school. The mother sees the defeat of his dreams and her
hopes of a happy old age with her only son are destroyed. She is
left alone.

Ozu's use of sound in this picture, as happened often with
last-ditch opponents of it, sets a creative example. His style had
finally matured: more restrained and reserved (although the dramatic content actually became more profound), it was to survive the
advent of color and remain unchanged until the 60's.

THE STORY OF LOUIS PASTEUR William Dieterle

Script: Sheridan Gibney and Pierre Collins. Photography: Tony

Gaudio. Cast: Paul Muni (Louis Pasteur), Josephine Hutchinson
(Marie Pasteur), Anita Louise (Annette Pasteur), Donald Woods (Dr.
Jean Martel), Fritz Leiber (Dr. Charbonnet), Henry O'Neill (Dr.
Émile Roux), Porter Hall (Dr. Rossignol), Raymond Brown (Dr.
Radisse), Akim Tamiroff (Dr. Zaranoff), Walter Kingsford (Napoléon
III), Iphigenie Castiglioni (Empress Eugènie).

Warner Bros., U.S.A.   7856 ft., 85 mins.

The cinema was for a time overcome by a vogue for screen biographies: apart from the trend professing to "view history through a
key-hole," led by Alexander Korda, a second convention began to
appear. Its aim was to instruct and to popularize knowledge about
great human achievements by portraying the life of their creators.
Nobody yet dreamed about the third approach, which would seriously
analyze the motives and psychology of outstanding personalities.

The worthwhile achievements within the "popularizing" convention were principally the work of William (Wilhelm) Dieterle, a
German actor and director, former student of Max Reinhardt, whose
best known acting performance was in Leni's Waxworks, and who
came to America in 1932. The first of his "bio-pics" was a film
about Louis Pasteur, founder of bacteriology and inventor of the
method of inoculation for hydrophobia (rabies).

Pasteur can be best described as an honest film, an excellent
character study, avoiding sentimentality and sustained in the best
spirit of American democratic traditions. The pace of the story is
occasionally slow; the clarity and care with which the hero's beliefs
are presented on the screen draws close to infantilism but never
ceases to be serious. Of the greatest importance for the picture
was Paul Muni, who would subsequently appear in a series of biographical films, and who built here a complete portrayal of the
great scientist, with his modesty, patience, perseverance and sense
of humor. All these things would perhaps not have been sufficient
for the picture to be more than correct--but Dieterle wielded one
more trump, which usually shifts the balance of success in the cinema: that is his passion for personal expression.

THEATRE OF LIFE (Jinsei Gekijō)   Tomu Uchida

Script: Toku Kameyabara, adapted by Yasutaro Yagi, based on the
novel by Shiro Ozaki. Photography: Tatsuyuki Yokota. Cast:
Kaichi Yamamoto (Hyotaro), Isamu Kosugi (Hyokichi, his son),
Kimio Tobita (Hyokichi in his boyhood), Kazuko Yoshida (Omine,
Hyotaro's wife), Reizaburo Yamamoto (Kiratsune, a gangster),
Chieko Murata (Osode), Kiyo Kuroda (Orin).

Nikkatsu, Tokyo, Japan.   10, 636 ft., 118 mins.

A screen adaptation of an autobiographical novel about a young man
"entering life" during his studies at the famous Waseda University
in Tokyo.   The youthful integrity of the hero, his noble gallant traditions absorbed from literature, his first love illusions--all this
rapidly disintegrates in confrontation with the ruthless rules of the
world of power and money.

Memories of one's youth are always romantic--all the more
so since the Japanese daily reality in the period of the rapid growth
of militarism was definitely even more grim than that of the early
1920's, the period portrayed in the film.   It is therefore not surprising that Theatre of Life enjoyed (and enjoys) a colossal popularity in Japan, and brought Tomu Uchida a considerable reputation.
He deserved it: a year later he would make a rather uneven, but
very ambitious social drama, The Naked Town (1937).   Soon after,
but before the outbreak of the war, came one of the most outstanding Japanese films of the period--his Earth.

TUDOR ROSE (U.S. title: Nine Days a Queen)   Robert Stevenson

---

Script: Miles Malleson, from a story by Robert Stevenson.   Pho-
tography: Mutz Greenbaum.   Cast: Cedric Hardwicke (Earl of
Warwick), John Mills (Lord Guildford Dudley), Felix Aylmer (Ed-
ward Seymour), Leslie Perrins (Thomas Seymour), Frank Collier
(Henry VIII), Desmond Tester (Edward VI), Gwen Ffrangcon-Davies
(Mary Tudor), Martita Hunt and Miles Malleson (Jane's parents),
Sybil Thorndyke (Ellen), Nova Pilbeam (Lady Jane Grey).

Gainsborough Pictures, G.B.   7077 ft., 78 mins.

The traditional approach to historical subjects in the cinema inevitably involves an all-out costume display with as many extras
as possible and a battle from time to time to enliven the action.
This convention, although not without impressive achievements, in
the majority of cases led to run-of-the-mill productions.   A new,
informal approach to historical figures was started by Korda's The
Private Life of Henry VIII, and the title of that film itself gives
some idea of where the change lay: it was simply that cinema began to treat kings and queens as private individuals and not inscrutable statues.   Although the events they describe remained
basically the same, the emphasis was placed elsewhere.

One of the most interesting examples of this new genre of
chamber dramas is Tudor Rose, the story of a 16-year-old girl

lost in the hubbub of policy-making.   The film is set in the period
following the death of Henry VIII (1547), which triggered off a ruthless struggle for power in England.   The Earl of Warwick appears
to come out as the victor when he deals successfully with the rivalry between Edward and Thomas Seymour by executing Thomas.
When Edward VI, the young and sickly new king, dies, Warwick
marries off his son, Lord Guilford Dudley, to Lady Jane Grey, thus
making her Queen.   The director of the film was right in not de-
pending on the suspense of actual events as the source of drama--it
would be bad policy in historical pictures, where the outcome of
events is generally known by the audience.

Stevenson turned this into an advantage: knowledge of the
events to come adds to the picture the mood of inevitability and
actually gives the actors' performances more depth.   In the title
role of the tragic nine-day (or 14-day, according to some) Queen of
England (Mary Tudor was, of course, to rally her supporters and
depose Jane) was young Nova Pilbeam, who two years earlier appeared as a child in Hitchcock's thriller The Man Who Knew Too
Much.

1937

LA GRANDE ILLUSION   Jean Renoir

Script: Charles Spaak and Renoir. Photography: Christian Matras. Music: Joseph Kosma. Cast: Jean Gabin (Maréchal), Pierre Fresnay (de Boeldieu), Erich von Stroheim (von Rauffenstein), Marcel Dalio (Rosenthal), Julien Carette (Actor), Gaston Modot (Engineer), Jean Dasté (Teacher), Georges Peclet (Soldier), Dita Parlo (Else), Jacques Becker (English officer), Sylvain Itkine (Demolder).

Les Réalisations d'Art Cinématographique, France. 10,530 ft., 117 mins.

It seems ironic, perhaps ominous, that this pacifist film was made barely two years before the outbreak of a war. Or should one say that it was the war which, tragically, proved Renoir right? La Grande illusion is set during the First World War and is based on the memoirs of a certain French officer who escaped seven times from German captivity. Two Frenchmen, Captain de Boeldieu, an aristocrat and professional soldier, and Lieutenant Maréchal, in civilian life an ordinary mechanic, are shot down over enemy lines. After being transferred from camp to camp they finally arrive in a fortified castle commanded by the war invalid Major von Rauffenstein who originally took them captive.

De Boeldieu and the commandant, both educated members of the international aristocracy obeying the same code d'honneur, find a natural affinity; sometimes they speak English which others, of less privileged origin, do not understand. Despite all differences, de Boeldieu, Maréchal and the Jew Rosenthal, who was in civilian life a rich banker and who shares his food parcels with everybody, develop a genuine comradeship. De Boeldieu sacrifices his life to

distract the guards' attention from the escape of the other two who
finally succeed in crossing the frontier to neutral Switzerland.

The "great illusion" of the title is the belief that the causes
of wars are national animosities. Class divisions are stronger and
Renoir derides the idea that people who speak the same language
are natural friends. The aristocrats from two enemy countries
still have more in common than two Frenchmen of unequal social
status. The fact that von Rauffenstein is compelled to shoot de
Boeldieu changes nothing, being just part of the artificial code of
war and not the expression of real emotions. These are best demonstrated when the German commandant cuts a geranium flower to
honor his dead French colleague.

Here are two career officers who <u>need</u> the war to be able to
exist and consider it an extension of their peacetime code of behavior, and who are blindly followed by ordinary soldiers to whom
war is only a tiresome duty. On the other hand Maréchal later received assistance and affection from a Bavarian peasant woman.
As long as the present social divisions are in force, Renoir declares the "desperate adventure" of war inevitable.

He deliberately immersed <u>La Grande illusion</u> in the deceptive
inactivity of a POW camp. The artificial conditions of isolation and
extratemporality allowed him a better perspective in looking at war
and absolved him of the traditional easy melodramatics of antiwar
tirades that depend on heroism in battle. For this reason the director's characteristic coolness became an asset, making his approach to the theme more intellectual than emotional. Renoir produced his demonstration with a wonderful Pascalian lucidity and
achieved a result of great subtlety and ardent calm.

The tone of the picture is brilliantly varied--from the hilarity
of the scenes involving the funny actor-prisoner, to the muted emotion of the great scene at de Boeldieu's bedside, to the eruption of
patriotism when the POW's dressed as women during an amateur
cabaret burst into the French national anthem on hearing of their
country's forces taking an important fortress (which with intentional
irony Renoir shows changing hands several times in the film). The
photography in <u>La Grande illusion</u> is reminiscent of <u>Toni</u>, conveying
the essence of the period through its crude bleakness, emanating a
mood of idealism combined with faith to reality. The three leading
roles (with von Stroheim giving a wonderful performance as a German) are classics of cinema acting.

So is the whole film, and not only among pacifist productions.
<u>La Grande illusion</u> dwarfs them all, including the earlier <u>All Quiet
on the Western Front</u>, and carries a universal message valid not
only in wartime. "To be killed in the war is a tragedy for a com-
moner, but for you and me it is a good way out," says de Boeldieu
to von Rauffenstein. "I have missed my chance," confesses the
German. De Boeldieu did not miss his own; his exit was an honor-
able death. But the real victory is shown to rest with the two

ordinary men who escape towards a new life.

THE RETURN OF MAXIM (Vozvrashcheniye Maksima)   Grigori
    Kozintsev and Leonid Trauberg

Script: Kozintsev, Lev Slavin and Trauberg. Photography: Andrei
Moskvin. Music: Dmitri Shostakovich. Cast: Boris Chirkov
(Maxim), Valentina Kibardina (Natasha), Alexandr Zrazhevsky
(Yerofeyev), A. Kuznetsov (Turayev), Mikhail Zharov (Dymba),
Vasily Vanin (Nikolai), A. Chistyakov (Mishchenko), Yuri Tolubeyev
(Bugay), A. Bondi (Menshevik), Vasily Merkurev (Student), N.
Kriuchkov (Soldier).

Lenfilm, U.S.S.R.   10,112 ft.,   112 mins.

The second part of the "Maxim Trilogy" (the first was The Youth of
Maxim). Summer 1914: the hero, just released from internal exile,
takes up revolutionary activity once again with all his old energy,
additionally fortified by the experience gained behind the bars of
Tsarist prisons. The party sends him to a factory where the Mensheviks try to disrupt the unity of the workers. Maxim craftily obtains information about the factory management's moves against the
workers and organizes a strike. All this does not prevent him, of
course, from living as before and loving his faithful Natasha. An
armed confrontation with the police is interrupted by the outbreak of
the First World War; the film ends with Maxim leaving for the front
in a soldier's uniform.

Of the three parts of the trilogy, The Return of Maxim displays the richest palette, ranging from the intimate lyricism of certain scenes to the style in others of a heroic epic (though a style
very different from that of Eisenstein and Pudovkin); from comedy
mood to notes of genuine tragedy; from a social report to quasi-
journalistic crusading. The freedom with which the point of view is
varied, the fluency in blending such different component elements,
and the domination of scenes of rather intimate character (in which
the vivid folk touch of Kozintsev and Trauberg is impressive) combine to make the middle part of the trilogy the best of the cycle.

BEZHIN MEADOW (Bezhin Lug)   Sergei Eisenstein

Script: Alexandr Rzheshevsky, after an authentic story by Pavel

Morozov. <u>Photography</u>: Eduard Tissé. <u>Music</u>: Gavriil Popov.
<u>Cast</u>: Viktor Kartashov (Stepok), Boris Zakhava (Father), Yelizaveta
Telesheva (Praskovia Osipovna, collective farm manager), Erast
Garin (Her husband), Vasily Orlov (Uncle Vasya, a political agitator),
Igor Pavlenko (Policeman), Nikolai Okhlopkov (Joker), L. Yudov
(Communist youth), Gorelov (One-legged koulak), F. Filipov (Doctor),
Savitsky (Bearded peasant), Berezovskaya (Girl in the forest), N.
Maslov, Y. Zaytsev, P. Zhuravlev (Subversives).

Mosfilm, U.S.S.R. Production of the film interrupted; 1967 reconstruction supervised by Sergei Yutkevich. Length of reconstructed
version: 31 mins.

It is an irony of fate that after ¡Que Viva Mexico! Eisenstein's next
film would also never be finished. The events leading to this are
among the most unusual in cinema history and contain as many mys-
teries as they have unexpected circumstances. Eisenstein decided
to transfer to the screen a script based on the story of a Urals boy
scout, Pavel Morozov, who died in 1932 by the hand of his own father while defending a cooperative farm from sabotage by rich peasants.

The script itself is full of abortive emphasis, stilted and
artifical dialogues and psychological absurdities, at variance not
only with logic but also with the Russian character. Eisenstein did
not mind; he was fascinated by the theme of sharp conflicts in col-
lectivized rural Russia and wanted to treat the literary material only
as a starting point for his own vision. And create it he did: a
heroic child is photographed in the halo of a saint on an icon, the
bloody fight for the practical application of Communist agricultural
methods acquires an outright Biblical dimension, the "ideological
thread" is dominated by poetic allegory and brilliant form.

But in vain are the revelatory pre-Welles attempts at deep-
focus staging; in vain, the stunning photography by Eduard Tissé, the
tonality of which would be compared to beaten silver by an outstanding Soviet critic. The picture did not conform to the usual patterns
and the rulers of the Soviet film industry ordered it changed. Eisenstein agreed, aware that he has allowed himself--as before in The
Old and the New (1929)--to be carried away by his imagination, and
that the crude propaganda is only one of the many faults of the material. For instance, the scenes of the joyful devastation of an
Orthodox church which is being converted into an educational center
are clearly dissonant; the director handled them in a manner worthy
of a naive enthusiast of the Chinese Cultural Revolution.

The changes subsequently introduced are substantial. With
Isaak Babel's help, Eisenstein completely rewrote the script, replaced the overly ostentatious actor portraying the father, and toned
down the poetic vehemence.

Unfortunately, he was still not understood. The raw, un-

1937

-273-

Drôle de drame

edited material was shown by the overzealous bosses of film industry to Stalin, who ordered work on Bezhin Meadow to stop. The official reason for which was the formalism and obscurity of the film. Apart from the absurdity of making the decision before seeing the final print, the question remains whether the alleged excess of formalism genuinely existed. This question will probably never be answered. Those times were too exotic for one to assess the film on the basis of an incomplete reconstruction made 30 years later. In fact this reconstruction reveals an unexpected amount about Eisenstein's intentions, if one takes into account that it is based exclusively on discarded footage found mainly in the director's home (the negative and all prints were destroyed during the war). The individual shots included in it came mainly from the first version of the film and only a few episodes from the second are included.

DRÔLE DE DRAME   Marcel Carné

Script: Jacques Prévert, from the novel, "His First Offence," by J. Storer-Clouston. Photography: Eugen Schüfftan. Art Direction: Alexandre Trauner. Music: Maurice Jaubert. Cast: Louis Jouvet (Soper, Bishop of Beckford), Michel Simon (Irwin Molyneux), Françoise Rosay (Margaret Molyneux), Jean-Louis Barrault (William Kramps), Jean-Pierre Aumont (Billy), Nadine Vogel (Eva), Alcover (Inspector Gray), Henri Guisol (Buffington), Madeleine Suffel (Companion), Jenny Burnay (Mrs. Pencil), Sinoël (James), Annie Cariel (Elizabeth Soper).

Edouard Corniglion-Molinier, France. 8800 ft., 97 mins.

The French, who have traditionally distrusted the British, have managed several digs at them in films, all of which were child's play in comparison with Drôle de drame (although ridiculing the British was not the prime objective of the picture, only the legacy of the novel on which it is based). Marcel Carné's second feature is a surrealist, grotesque comedy, an all-out joke at the expense of the principal British institutions--the Anglican Church, Scotland Yard and even the English Sunday.

The story, set in a Victorian London, is as absurd as it is complicated: an Anglican bishop calls at the home of his unruly cousin, a respectable botanist who also secretly writes crime novels under an assumed name. When the botanist's wife apparently disappears (she has really gone to fetch some breakfast because the servants have all left), the bishop suspects the husband of murdering her. Then the botanist also vanishes, reappearing as his Sherlock Holmes alter ego and jumping into action. The supposed crime is thus investigated by the supposed criminal himself, and it is of course the bishop who now becomes the suspect.

Carné shot the film in a handful of not particularly realistic studio sets with some of the very best French actors, who created a whole gallery of absurd characters (Jean-Louis Barrault plays the fierce murderer, Kramps, who kills butchers because of his love for animals). Drôle de drame is just what the title says it is: a funny drama, the sort of farce which only the French can do well. It is all smooth, intelligent, sophisticated, equipped with brilliant dialogues, typically complex--and incredibly modern.

On the other hand, some subplots (like the romance between the milkman and the secretary) are really superfluous. Drôle de drame is an anarchistically distorted mixture of sharp observation and wild fantasy, and it is curious that the visionary London presented in the film has a ring of truth about it. Although this picture remains Carné's only venture into the realm of comedy, in 1937 it gave an oblique promise of the director's later interest in drama, not least because it was the beginning of his cooperation with the scriptwriter Jacques Prévert.

THEY WON'T FORGET   Mervyn Le Roy

Script: Robert Rossen and Aben Kandel, from the novel, "Death in the Deep South, " by Ward Greene. Photography: Arthur Edeson. Music: Adolph Deutsch. Cast: Claude Rains (Andy Griffin), Gloria Dickson (Sybil Hale), Edward Norris (Robert Hale), Otto Krüger (Michael Gleason), Allyn Joslyn (Bill Brock), Lana Turner (Mary Clay), Elisha Cook, Jr. (Joe Turner), Linda Perry (Imogene Mayfield), Cy Kendall (Detective Laneart).

First National, U.S.A. 8657 ft., 96 mins.

Lynch-law: the theme used by Lang in Fury was taken by Le Roy to its logical extreme. On a public holiday in a city in a Southern state a girl is found murdered in a near-empty secretarial school. There are three suspects: the headmaster, the Negro janitor and a young Northerner who was the girl's teacher. An ambitious, vote-thirsty district attorney, seeing an opportunity for making political capital, choses the Northerner as the most suitable defendant, stirs up prejudice with the help of a mudracking local paper, twists the evidence, and despite the protests of the national press and a strenuous defense has the man sentenced to death.

When the governor commutes the sentence the convict is lynched by the townspeople and judicial murder is substituted for by

mob rule. They Won't Forget, one of the principal "socially committed" pictures of the 30's, offers no way out, and at the end
(which solves no problems and which explains nothing) the director
does not even bother to tell us whether the lynched man was in fact
guilty. Unlike Fury there are no mitigating circumstances offered
and no implication that "lynch can start from the best of intentions."

Le Roy steeped the film in a sustained somber tone and
added a number of skillful touches, the best known of which is the
use of a mailbag snatched by a passing train as a sinister metaphor
for hanging. Nevertheless They Won't Forget, the once-bold film,
now seems a little academic, with bad dialogues, an irritating use
of back projection even in the simplest interior sequences, and some
scenes which have since been worn thin and were too predictable
anyway.

The star role in the picture was taken not by the main character, but by Claude Rains, who gives an exquisite portrayal of the
district attorney--devious, clever and ruthless. Still, the principal
values of They Won't Forget, a merciless study of the workings of
prejudice and the excellent characterization, remain. In its cheer-
less mood the picture foreshadowed a long trail of films noirs.

SNOW WHITE AND THE SEVEN DWARFS   Walt Disney

Story Adaptation: Dorothy Ann Blank, Richard Creedon, Merrill De
Maris, Otto Englander, Ted Sears, Earl Hurd, Webb Smith and
Dick Richard, from the fairy tale, "Sneewittchen," in a collection,
"Kinder- und Hausmärchen," by Jacob and Wilhelm Grimm. Anima-
tion Supervision: David Hand. Character Designing: Albert Hurt-
ler and Jose Grant. Music: Larry Morey and Frank Churchill
(Songs), Leigh Harline and Paul J. Smith (Background score).
Voices: Adriana Caselotti (Snow White), Lucille La Verne (Queen),
Roy Atwell (Doc), Billy Gilbert (Sneezy), Scotty Mattraw (Bashful),
Otis Harlan (Happy), Pinto Colvig (Grumpy and Sleepy), Harvey
Stockwell (Prince). Margery Belcher, (later Marge Champion) mod-
elled for Snow White.

RKO Radio Pictures, U.S.A. 7490 ft., 83 mins. Technicolor.

The name of Walt Disney had already been linked with animated
cinema from the beginning of the 20's--and became famous with the
appearance of Mickey Mouse in Steamboat Willie (1928), his first
sound animated film. Well contrived, Mickey Mouse rapidly became a favorite of the audience; more--a film star of the first mag-
nitude and this all over the world. After this first (and probably
the best) humanized animal, others marched onto the screen, among

them Pluto and Donald Duck. Disney rapidly expanded his film company, and in 1929 started making "Silly Symphonies"--animated nur-
sery rhymes in which the principal element was the musical rhythm,
synchronized with the movement inside the frame. In 1932 Disney
introduced color into his work.

The next logical step was of course an animated full-length
feature. For the theme, Disney chose a fairy tale; but he transferred it on to the screen in a spirit different both from that of the
original (by the Grimm brothers) and from his own earlier shorts,
which can all be summarized in principle as crazy chases and scuf-
fles in the catch-as-catch-can convention. Thus the characteristic
American dynamism was now replaced by the equally American
sweet lyricism.

One must say that the quality did not gain from this change.
The slowing down of the narrative brought out all the verbatim realism of the drawings, especially evident in the design of the Princess and her Prince; saccharine melodrama stole into the story.
A sober look at the whole might make one ask whether a simple
description of the film as kitsch would not settle the problem. Yet
Disney was a splendid juggler of the emotions of the audience and
although his domain is a good few flights of stairs below Chaplin's,
it is still the same house: it is impossible not to like Snow White
and the Seven Dwarfs.

It could in fact be that Disney's intentions were of the best
and the primitivism of the imagery was caused by the desire to get
across to the kids. It is also doubtful whether, at the time when
the film was made, anybody was seriously concerned with more ambitious designs for children's films, especially since the adults themselves were most attracted by just this style. These reservations
apply rather to the world of humans than to those of animals or
plants, where very penetrating observations abound, conveyed with
inventiveness and wit. The best effects are those connected with the
music--not only excellently composed but really splendidly employed
to illustrate the images.

UN CARNET DE BAL   Julien Duvivier

Script: Jean Sarment, Henri Jeanson and Bernard Zimmer. Pho-
tography: Michel Kelber, Philippe Agostini and Pierre Levent.
Music: Maurice Jaubert. Cast: Marie Bell (Christine Surgère),
Françoise Rosay (M. Audié), Harry Baur (Père Dominique Regnault),
Louis Jouvet (Joe), Pierre Blanchar (Thierry), Raimu (François
Patusset), Fernandel (Fabien), Pierre-Richard Wilm (Eric Irvin),
Robert Lynen (Jacques Dambreval).

Productions Sigma/Société de Production et Exploitation du Film
"Un Carnet de bal," France.   9830 ft., 109 mins.

A young widow finds an old dance program and decides to trace the
suitors from her first ball.   One has committed suicide because of
his hopeless love for her.   The others are failures, products of
compromise between mediocrity and unfulfilled ambitions.   They are
an ex-lawyer turned criminal, a common smalltown mayor, a monk,
an epileptic doctor abortionist in the dock district of Marseilles, a
stupid village barber, an aloof mountain guide.   The ballroom she
remembered turns out to be a commonplace town hall, but there is
a beaming girl there experiencing her first ball.... On her disillusioned return home the heroine learns that the eighth man, the
one she loved, was for many years her neighbor across the lake
but had died a week before.

Striving for happiness is useless, time shatters the illustions
of youth.   Melancholy pervaded the French cinema in the pre-war
years.   It seems significant that the best episodes of this composite
film are the most pessimistic ones--the chilling encounter of the
heroine with the crazed mother who does not believe in her son's
death many years ago, and the scene in the dockside consulting
room where evil and despair are condensed (Duvivier found an interesting visual key to the mood of the latter episode: he shot it
with a tilted camera.)

One can criticize Un Carnet de bal on many counts: although
dramatically well-balanced, the episodes are too "typical" and too
purposely diversified with respect to place of action and types of
people involved.   Through a fault common to episodic films, it became more of a collection of shorts joined together by the personality of the heroine and the motif of a journey.   The dialogues spell
out things well left to the spectator to infer.   Even the basic situation is hardly credible (all those broken people, so much misery,
and all because of her!) and Marie Bell, cold and aloof, does not
help in elucidating this mystery.

Un Carnet de bal contains, however, many outstanding acting
performances (it was designed in the first place to bring together
the best French actors) and some genuine visual inventiveness (the
whirling couples from the past appear realistically on the background of the contemporary action, usually on white draperies).
These factors make the film an interesting period piece, especially
for the amateurs of pre-war French cinema.   Although to be honest
its claims to being a classic of poetic cinema do not now seem
particularly strong, yet Jaubert's beautiful "Valse grise" does linger
on in one's memory.

DEAD END   William Wyler

Script: Lillian Hellman, from a play by Sidney Kingsley. Photography: Gregg Toland. Art Direction: Richard Day. Music: Alfred Newman. Cast: Sylvia Sidney (Drina), Joel McCrea (Dave), Humphrey Bogart ("Baby Face" Martin), Wendy Barrie (Kay), Claire Trevor (Francey), Allen Jenkins (Hunk), Marjorie Main (Mrs. Martin), Billy Halop (Tommy), James Burke (Mulligan).

Samuel Goldwyn, U.S.A.   8473 ft., 94 mins.

Dead End, a dramatic vision of New York slums, is a fruit of the social tendencies which developed in American cinema under the New Deal.   Near the East River, fashionable apartments meet waterfront tenements.   Wyler presents a gallery of people from the social margin who live there: an unemployed architect, a woman kept by a rich businessman, and hooligan youths who paddle in dirty water, commit petty thievery, idolize gangsters and whose whole future can be read in their faces.

The central character is a dapper and sinister gangster, who spent years in jail and is currently wanted for killing eight people in inter-gang warfare.   He has come here to see his mother and his one-time girlfriend, but already has new plans--kidnapping the boy who lives in the elegant residence nearby.   For Humphrey Bogart this was the second famous role; a year earlier he became famous as Dillinger--another gangster--in a very poor screen version of Robert Sherwood's play "The Petrified Forest."

This new generation of American movie gangsters is of theatrical origin.   They descend from the pages of the plays of Sherwood, Lillian Hellman and Maxwell Anderson.   They are not strong and ruthless proletarians treated with a touch of sympathy (as in the erstwhile "gangster series") but rather neurotic middleclass dropouts, products of the frustrating influences of modern civilization.   Bogart would be cast as an outlaw many times in the years to follow and would always give his characters profoundly human features.

In Dead End also there is a lost and unhappy man concealed under a thick layer of brutality and cynicism, a man who never forged his fate but let himself be driven by it.   He will be killed by the dropout architect whom the bounty will perhaps allow to fulfill his desperate dream of leaving Dead End.   Bogart's performance was made even more credible by Wyler's precise psychological delineation of other characters and his care in giving the "mirror of life" quality to the scenery--a gigantic set which extended for a whole urban block.

1937   -279-   Humanity Like a Paper Balloon

The director was assisted by Gregg Toland who in his first
really important work was at the threshold of a great period of collaboration with Welles and Ford; the dusky quality of the photog-
raphy--its deep shades--underline the grim mood of the story.   The
occasional melodramatic accents have very little bearing on the expression of Dead End as a whole--doubtless one of the most uncompromising prewar American films.

HUMANITY LIKE A PAPER BALLOON (Ninjō Kami Fusen)   Sadao
   Yamanaka

Script: Shintaro Mimura. Photography: Akira Mimura. Music:
Chu Ota. Cast: Kan'emon Nakamura (Shinza, a barber), Chojuro
Kawarazaki (Matajuro Unno, a masterless samurai), Shizue Yama-
gishi (Otaki, his wife), Sukezo Suketakaya (Chobei, a landlord),
Tsuruzo Nakamura (Genko, a dealer in goldfish), Hisako Hara
(Otetsu, his wife), Choemon Bando (Yabuichi, a blind masseur),
Noboru Kiritachi (Okoma, the daughter of the big shop Shirakoya).

Toho, Japan. 7717 ft., 86 mins.

A critical look at past centuries and a polemic on the legend of
samurai chivalry were not in the least a monopoly of Japanese directors of the 50's and 60's.   Even before the Second World War
two distinguished directors, Mansaku Itami and Sadao Yamanaka, assumed a basically negative attitude to the national past and debunked
the myths of former heroes.   Yamanaka made his first film at 23
in 1932, and three years later was already an acknowledged director
who knew how to employ exceptionally fluent editing and how to give
his films a beautiful visual form, sometimes compared to that of
old national paintings.

   Humanity Like a Paper Balloon, Yamanaka's greatest achievement, gives an idea of what the director could have achieved in the
cinema.   The story develops in the Tokugawa era of the 18th century, in a poor quarter of Tokyo, where impoverished samurai live
a paltry life among people of lower social classes to whom they are
now equal in status.   The essence of degradation is not only the
economic situation, but also the symbolic inability to fulfill the
basic requirements of the code of knighthood: a fall from a pedestal
allows one to learn the truth about the human condition and this
causes the starving samurai to neglect his strict principles and give
help to a needy man.   When circumstances force him as a man of
honor to commit suicide, he will not be able to do this by the obligatory harakiri: hunger had made him sell his sword for rice.

   The young director does not intend to limit himself to a faith-

ful conveyance of the period: he concentrates not so much on historical details as on the sociological aspect of the story. The effect of this is the supertemporal quality of the screen expression--
and thus the film contains a clear analogy to the present, which is
additionally stressed by the style of the acting. This was considered too bold for 1937: Yamanaka was called to the army as a
non-commissioned officer (an exception among filmmakers of that
time in Japan) and died a year later on the Chinese front.

YOUNG AND INNOCENT [U.S. title: The Girl Was Young] Alfred
    Hitchcock

Script: Charles Bennett and Alma Reville, from a novel by Jose-
phine Tey. Photography: Bernard Knowles. Music: Louis Levy.
Cast: Derrick de Marney (Robert Tisdall), Nova Pilbeam (Erica),
Percy Marmont (Colonel Burgoyne), Edward Rigby (Old Bill), Mary
Clare (Erica's aunt), John Longden (Kent), George Curzon (Guy),
Basil Radford (Uncle Basil).

Gainsborough Pictures/Gaumont British, G.B.   7560 ft., 84 mins.

The story of Young and Innocent, set in the English countryside, is
based on the dramatic principle of the double chase, familiar from
another Hitchcock classic, The Thirty-Nine Steps. As a matter of
fact, another motif, that of a man being saved by a woman, is also
the same.

    A woman is found strangled on the beach and police suspi-
cions are centered on the victim's former lover, the belt of whose
raincoat was found near the body. A policeman's teenage daughter
believes in the lover's innocence and helps him to escape arrest
and to find the real murderer. They discover the raincoat of the
back of a tramp who tells them that the murderer had a twitch in
his eye. This leads to the star scene of the film, the tea-dance
at a seaside hotel, where the mystery is resolved in an amazing
tracking shot. The camera starts from a general view of the ballroom and tracks down 145 feet to come to rest four inches in front
of the drummer's eye: there is a twitch in it! Hitchcock likes
technical displays, but never uses them as an aim in itself: he
later used a similar shot for creating suspense in Notorious. And,
of course, he made Rope--the only feature film ever done in a single shot.

LENIN IN OCTOBER (Lenin v Oktyabre) Mikhail Romm

Co-direction: Dimitri Vasiliev. Script: Alexei Kapler. Photography: Boris Volchek. Music: Anatoli Alexandrov. Cast: Boris Shchukin (Lenin), Nikolai Okhlopkov (Vasili), V. Pokrovsky (Dzerzhinsky), Vasili Vanin (Matveyev), K. Korolov (Vasili's wife), A. Kovalevsky (Kerensky), N. Sokolov (Rodzianko), Nikolai Svobodin (Rutkovsky), J. Shatrova (Anna Mikhailovna), Nikolai Arsky (Blinov), Ivan Lagutin (Filer), I. Golshtab (Stalin), N. Chaplygin (Kirilin), V. Ganshin (Zhukov), B. Vladislavsky (Karnaukhov).

Mosfilm, U.S.S.R. 9954 ft., 111 mins.

Twenty years after the Soviet Revolution and 13 years after his death, Lenin was already a myth. Romm had to have this fact in mind when making the film, which was to rise atop many more or less successful productions based on the lives of heroes made by other Soviet directors. Lenin in October gives the account of the most crucial period of the Revolution, from Lenin's arrival from Finland in October 1917 until the taking of the Winter Palace. Yet, in spite of being cast on this momentous historical background, this is a personal portrait, almost an intimate one: it tries to consider its hero as a person rather than a charismatic figure surrounded by a halo of grandeur.

This was an extremely difficult task--how many outstanding portrayals of famous personalities are there in the cinema? Another difficulty with this type of film is that it stretches the historical knowledge of a spectator, especially a foreign one, to the utmost. It is therefore all the more praiseworthy that the film did not become a propaganda fanfare or a cryptic and obscure chronicle. Another thing is that the political facts of life at the time produced some quite ludicrous historical inaccuracies in the film, such as an exaggeration of the role of Stalin in the events and the presentation of Trotsky as a sinister villain (although in 1917 he and Lenin were in fact good friends).

Absolutely crucial in a biography is the correct casting: the main part is taken by Boris Shchukin, whose portrayal of Lenin, natural and entirely un-monumental, deserves the most credit in the whole enterprise. Lenin in October is the first of a spate of films dealing with the Leader at different historical periods and adopting different approaches, and which are of rapidly decreasing degrees of interest: such, for instance is its immediate sequel-- Lenin in 1918 (1939).

THE LIFE OF ÉMILE ZOLA   William Dieterle

Script: Norman Reilly Raine, Heinz Herald and Geza Herczeg.
Photography: Tony Gaudio. Music: Max Steiner. Cast: Paul
Muni (Émile Zola), Gale Sondergaard (Lucie Dreyfus), Joseph
Schildkraut (Capt. Alfred Dreyfus), Gloria Holden (Alexandrine Zola),
Donald Crisp (Maître Labori), Erin O'Brien-Moore (Nana), John
Litel (Charpentier), Henry O'Neill (Col. Piquart), Norris Carnovsky
(Anatole France), Robert Barrat (Major Walsin-Esterhàzy).

Warner Bros., U.S.A. 10,482 ft., 116 mins.

Among William Dieterle's screen biographies the most famous is
the one based on the life of Zola, the realist French novelist.   The
main reason for this was the film's topical associations with the in-
famous trial that followed the burning of the German Reichstag in
1933.   The Nazis caused the fire and then accused the Communists
and Jews, thus justifying Hitler's assumption of dictatorial powers.
At the root of these associations was the major episode in Zola's
life: the dramatic public campaign he led in the defense of Alfred
Dreyfus, the French General Staff Captain.

     In 1894 Dreyfus, a Jew, was jailed for espionage on ridicu-
lously dubious "evidence." It took 12 years to overcome the inertia
and hypocrisy of the establishment and get Dreyfus released.   The
film takes certain liberties with historical facts (in order to increase dramatic tension and make the point more clearly) and centers mainly on this particular chapter of the great writer's activity.
Zola's early life, his friendship with the painter Cézanne, and the
beginnings of his literary fame are all charted briefly.   When Mme.
Dreyfus appeals to Zola for help he sacrifices all, writes the manifesto "J'Accuse," loses a libel suit, escapes to England, and returns to France when the Dreyfus case is reopened.

     The Zola here is perhaps not very true to the actual per-
sonality, but is made convincing by Paul Muni's acting, undoubtedly
the greatest asset of the film.   The screen characterization of the
French society, which the director presents to clarify his reason-
ing, also does not quite correspond to reality.   There are more
Hollywood tricks here than in the previous film about Pasteur, both
of melodramatic and comic variety.   Thus The Life of Émile Zola
cannot be considered a historical document.   But it survives independently from the facts it depicts--as a story of a man's devotion
to an idea.

IL SIGNOR MAX   Mario Camerini

Script: Camerini and Mario Soldati, from the material by Amleto
Palermi. Photography: Anchise Brizzi. Music: Renzo Rossellini.
Cast: Vittorio De Sica, Assia Noris, Rubi D'Alma, Lilia Dale,
Giovanni Barrella, Umberto Melnati, Mario Casaleggio, Caterina
Collo, Virgilio Riento, Romolo Costa, Luciano Dorcaratto, De-
siderio Nobile, Michele Contessa, Otello Polini, Walter Grant,
Gianfranco Zanchi.

Astra, Italy. 7300 ft., 81 mins.

A comedy of errors: a street newspaper seller becomes involved
with high society and, as might be expected, lives through a number
of adventures. Among Camerini's pre-war films, Il Signor Max
was the last successful one. It adopted a rather different attitude
to reality than did its predecessors. This time the director ironically derided the high life and declared his sympathies on the side
of the ordinary people, while actually stopping short of clear social
conclusions. These circumstances (and of course the plot itself)
make the similarities of Il Signor Max to the cinema of Frank Capra
particularly striking, especially Mr. Deeds Goes to Town. Gary
Cooper also is not without a parallel: as always in Camerini's
films of that period, the main part was played by Vittorio De Sica
who, before becoming an outstanding film director, was the favorite
Italian actor.

1938

ALEXANDER NEVSKY (Alexandr Nevsky)   Sergei Eisenstein

Assistant Direction: Dmitri Vasiliev. Script: Pyotr Pavlenko and
Eisenstein. Photography: Eduard Tissé. Music: Sergei Proko-
fiev. Art Direction: Iosif Shpinel. Cast: Nikolai Cherkasov
(Alexandr Nevsky), Nikolai Okhlopkov (Vasili Buslai), Alexandr
Abrikosov (Gavrilo Oleksich), Dmitri Orlov (Ignat, Master Ar-
mourer), Vasili Novikov (Pavsha, Governor of Pskov Province),
Nikolai Arski (Domash Tverdislavovich, a Novgorod boyar), Vera
Ivasheva (Olga, the Maiden of Novgorod), Anna Danilova (Vasilisa,
the Maiden of Pskov), Varvara Massalitinova (Amelfa Timofeievna,
Buslai's mother), Vladimir Yerschov (Von Balk, Master of the Teu-
tonic Order), Sergei Blinnikov (Tverdilo, Commander of the Pskov
Army and a traitor), Ivan Lagutin (Ananiash, a Black Monk), Lev
Fenin (The Bishop), Naum Rogozhin (A Black Monk).

Mosfilm, U.S.S.R. 9987 ft., 111 mins.

A year after the abortive Bezhin Meadow Eisenstein was given yet
another official assignment. In view of an uncertain political situation, especially in the field of relations with Germany, it was considered necessary to make a propaganda film which would recall a
remote historical incident involving a fight against the Germans
while praising Russian national qualities and the internal strength
of the Russian people. Alexander Nevsky is set in the 13th century,
when the aggressive priest-knights of the Teutonic Order invaded
Russian lands and took Pskov. The inhabitants of the threatened
Novgorod turn for help and leadership to the heroic Prince Alexander
Nevsky, who rouses the masses of peasants and townspeople and
defeats the enemy.

Eisenstein perfectly fulfilled the task. In spite of having

been under the supervision of Dmitri Vasiliev, the watch-dog appointed to stop the unruly master from excessive formalism, he
made a picture full of power, visual beauty and great sophistication. Since there is little historical information available about the
hero, realism would be only reinforced fiction and would be inappropriate in a film meant to rouse enthusiasm and edify rather than
portray the period or analyze psychological motivation. The convention adopted by Eisenstein can be described as a historical legend,
an epic opera of which the heroes are not real people but symbols,
stylized incarnations of ideas. The battles are here not between
armies but between ideologies.

Accordingly Alexander Nevsky has very little characterization and almost no dialogues; it is very demanding on the spectator
because of its almost completely symbolic and figurative treatment
of the plot, slowness of pace and unusually pronounced reliance on
the refined pictorial compositions. The prevailing mood is that of
heroic elation, the stylistic principle is that of contrast. Contrary
to the usual moral terminology for Good and Evil, Black symbolizes
Russia and White, the German invaders. The helmets of the Russians are sharp and pointed, those of the Germans round and sinister (both types nevertheless being historically correct).

The film is an example of a rare unison between image and
sound. The soundtrack is used with a genuine dramatic purpose;
every scene bears the stamp of close cooperation between Eisenstein and Prokofiev, the famous composer. The leading musical
motif is a slow chorale or oratorio and is used as a background.
In the forefront are a multitude of sounds, all significant and all
sharply contrasted. The sounds sustained in gay major keys symbolize the pipe-blowing Russians; the melancholy minor keys are
identified with the Germans and their horns and trumpets.

The editing tended to play a much lesser role than in Eisenstein's earlier work--the battle scenes for instance left many opportunities unused. It seems that the external pressures on the director were responsible. The composition of the frame depends on the
mood: in the tense battle scenes it is asymmetric, with unevenly
distributed lights and shadows and variable camera angles; in leisurely peace-time sequences, for instance in the beginning which
shows Alexander Nevsky as a fisherman, the compositions are balanced and symmetrical, the shots longer and more stable.

From among many scenes of great visual beauty one might
mention the enthusiastic symbolic sequence of torches flaming in the
Novgorod streets and the final battle on the ice which is unfortunately incomplete in most prints shown in the West. Eisenstein went so
far in his pursuit of pictorial refinement that he sometimes disre-
garded technical execution, and the film has obvious accelerated
projection in the horse-riding scenes, and makeshift stage design.
A more serious fault is the rather unacceptable verbose propaganda
in the finale.

THE CHILDHOOD OF MAXIM GORKY (Detstvo Gorkovo)   Mark
Donskoy

Script: Ilya Gruzdev and Donskoy, from Maxim Gorky's autobio-
graphical novel, "Childhood." Photography: Pyotr Yermolov.
Music: Lev Schwartz. Cast: Alexei Lyarsky (Alyosha Peshkov),
Varvara Massalitinova (Akulina Ivanovna), Mikhail Troyanovsky
(Kashirin), Daniil Sagal (Tsyganok), J. Alexeieva (Varvara), Vasili
Novikov (Yakov), A. Zhukov (Mikhail), K. Ziubko (Grigori, the fore-
man), Igor Smirnov (Lonka), A. Tikhonravov (Neighbor).

Soyuzdetfilm, U.S.S.R.   9032 ft., 100 mins.

The second half of the 19th century, a fascinating period in the history of Russia: in a world full of sharp contrasts and antagonistic
forces which can make a man climb to the top and fall back down
into the mud, the childhood of one boy passes. He is called Alyosha
Peshkov, and as Maxim Gorky he would become one of the greatest
realist writers of his country and his works would be classics of
modern literature. The images of his youth, contained in a cycle
of three autobiographical novels, were transferred onto the screen
with all the power of suggestion of the literary original, and with
such fidelity to it that one feels as if the author himself was standing behind the camera. Yet all this was done by a director who in
his previous 10-year career had not shown any such wide abilities.

Still, the reasons for the congenial quality of the film are obvious: the maker of the "Trilogy of the Young Gorky" has the same
inimitably Russian soul in his breast as the hero of his tale. Donskoy's cinema is above all emotional cinema, and not aesthetic or
intellectual. Furthermore, the director was distinctly inspired by
the literature although he had a great visual imagination of his own:
he created a picturesque screen world, in which the elements of
brutality and lyricism, cordiality and hatred are intertwined--the
world of the provincial merchant-artisan-beggarly Russia, peopled
by individuals depicted with all their national directness and characteristic ostentation.

Alyosha stays at his grandfather's house in Nizhny Novgorod.
The family quarrels constantly about money; Grandmother Akulina
is the uniting influence. Alyosha strikes a contact with his grandfather who sensitizes him to injustice and to the problems of others.
The estate is partitioned and soon financial problems become acute.
Alyosha sets off to earn his living among people. Nature is in symbiosis with this biological world of a village on the Volga--nature,
in accordance with the deepest tradition of Russian art, friendly to
man, even if full of stormy internal forces. The landscape is very
strongly linked to the plot of the film, although not to the point of

becoming a participant in the drama--it is rather a commentator, a rhythmic counterpoint, an instrument for stressing moods and emotions.

In The Childhood of Maxim Gorky, the first part of the trilogy, this emotional quality of style is most convincing and candid; the characters are seemingly drawn with too much contrast, yet each of them is invested with some crumb of tenderness, even if hidden deeply under a barbarian casualness. It is not the people who bear the guilt for their sins: they are degraded by the world of money and violence, a world which can be and will be changed. It can be changed because Nature allows man to become great even when he originates in poverty and pain.

QUAI DES BRUMES   Marcel Carné

Script: Jacques Prévert, from the novel by Pierre Mac Orlan. Photography: Eugen Schüfftan and Louis Page. Sets: Alexandre Trauner. Music: Maurice Jaubert. Cast: Jean Gabin (Jean), Michèle Morgan (Nelly), Michel Simon (Zabel), Pierre Brasseur (Lucien Legardier), Robert Le Vigan (Michel Krauss, painter), Aimos (Quart-Vittel), Edouard Delmont (Panama), Marcel Pérès (Driver), René Génin (Doctor).

Grégor Rabinovitch, France. 8064 ft., 90 mins.

The mood of dejection and impending doom which overwhelmed prewar France was reflected in all provinces of art, and in the cinema appeared in the form of a trend known as "Poetic Realism." "Realism"--because of its genuine interest in authentic description of the social scene; "poetic"--because of the manner in which this description is put forward, involving a romantic mythology of Love, Destiny and the all-pervading desire to escape from dire reality.

The most important personalities among the leaders of the Poetic Realist School were Jacques Prévert and Marcel Carné. Prévert--the author of melancholic poems and stories and a brilliant scriptwriter, whose great influence on the cinema can only be compared to that of Carl Mayer, the key figure in the German Expressionism--supplied spiritual fuel for the trend. Carné, a former assistant of Feyder (and also on Le Grand jeu and Pension Mimosas), directed the best films of the School. His own first two works were Jenny (1936) and the semi-surrealist comedy Drôle de drame.

Quai des Brumes is the first true classic of the Poetic Realist School. Prévert rediscovered the novel (written in 1927) and changed its setting from Paris to Le Havre, to be able to capitalize

on the "great port" motif which always fascinated the French.
Jean, an army deserter, arrives in the fog-bound port town and
falls in love with Nelly, a girl whom he meets at a quay-side inn.
The girl is being terrorized by her wicked guardian Zabel, who has
murdered her fiancé. To avoid the police Jean uses the passport
of a painter who committed suicide, and joins the crew of a ship
bound for Venezuela. He is forced to kill Zabel who tries to rape
Nelly and just as the ship is about to leave is himself shot dead by
a cowardly crook.

This is how dreams of refuge and happiness are shattered:
there is no pity in the world in which Fate is man's only master.
With its moon-like port town enveloped in fog and inhabited by symbolic people with exotic-sounding names, Quai des Brumes creates
a fantastic, stylized world in which reality and imagination merge
into one, but which is still essentially real and true. The most
tangible quality is the sense of anxiety and finality.

The film is remarkable from the formal point of view and
all the elements of style are perfectly blended and balanced. The
script does not contain one word too many; the soft photography and
the less-than-real sets of Trauner seem markedly influenced by
Sternberg's thematically similar The Docks of New York and are the
main factors in generating the poetic atmosphere; the editing is
rhythmical and purposeful.

The part of Nelly puts Michèle Morgan onto a path leading to
the position of the greatest French film star, and brings her together with Jean Gabin, another favorite of the public. It is characteristic that it is only the lonely heroine and the abandoned dog
which remain alive at the end of Quai des Brumes, a picture whose
frame of mind is perhaps best rendered by the desperate sound of
the siren of the "Louisiana" as Jean, her would-be passenger, lies
dead on the quay.

PYGMALION Anthony Asquith and Leslie Howard

Script: W. P. Lipscomb, Cecil Lewis and Asquith, from the play
by George Bernard Shaw. Photography: Harry Stradling. Music:
Arthur Honegger. Cast: Wendy Hiller (Eliza Doolittle), Leslie
Howard (Professor Higgins), Wilfrid Lawson (Alfred Doolittle),
Marie Lohr (Mrs. Higgins), Scott Sunderland (Colonel Pickering),
David Tree (Freddy), Jean Cadell (Mrs. Pearce), Everley Gregg
(Mrs. Eynsford Hill).

Gabriel Pascal Productions, G.B.   8609 ft., 96 mins.

The first screen versions of George Bernard Shaw's plays had already been made in the early 30's. "Pygmalion" itself was filmed in 1935 in Germany and in 1937 in Holland. The reason for the failure of these attempts is not difficult to find: Shaw's theatre relies greatly on fine dialogue, basically incompatible, one would think, with the primarily visual art of the cinema. This is why so many film adaptations of stage plays are slow and verbose. With "Pygmalion" the difficulty is doubled, since the language itself lies at the very root of the intrigue.

A famous professor of phonetics encounters a Cockney flower girl in the Covent Garden market and to win a bet makes a true lady out of her through intensive training in elocution and savoir faire. Finally, he falls in love with his creation. The success of the film is due to Asquith's genuine cinematic sense which allowed him to translate the basically theatrical plot into visual terms. The dialogue is here not obtrusive at all; yet in fact Pygmalion not only preserves the essence of Shaw's theatre, complete with its mocking tone, but even holds its own in terms of cinema: the sequence of Eliza's linguistic progress which compresses long effort into a series of brief shots, is a classical example of skillful narrative editing.

Asquith treated the text with great respect and retained the original chronology and the details of the story. The crucial scene of the Ambassador's ball, during which Eliza's skills are tried out, was written--at Asquith's suggestion--by George Bernard Shaw himself. Among the galaxy of English stage actors who created an array of well-characterized types here is the co-director, Leslie Howard, as Professor Higgins and the splendid Wendy Hiller in the difficult part of Eliza. Little wonder Pygmalion is a light and charming comedy.

JEZEBEL   William Wyler

Script: Clements Ripley, Abem Finkel and John Huston, from the play by Owen Davis, Sr. Photography: Ernest Haller. Music: Max Steiner. Cast: Bette Davis (Julie), Henry Fonda (Preston Dillard), George Brent (Buck Cantrell), Mary Lindsay (Amy), Donald Crisp (Dr. Livingstone), Fay Bainter (Auntie Belle), Richard Cromwell (Ted), Henry O'Neill (General Bogardus), Spring Byington (Mrs. Kendrick), John Litel (Jean La Cour), Gordon Oliver (Dick Allen), Janet Shaw (Molly Allen).

Warner Bros., U.S.A. 9495 ft., 106 mins.

Wyler's cinema--precise, full of shades of meaning, subtle over-

tones and at times rare fascination--reveals itself in Jezebel with
all its brightness. In fact not only the style, but also the theme
is extremely characteristic of the director. Jezebel is the Biblical
nickname for an independent and egoistic woman. Such is Julie,
the spoiled and arrogant New Orleans belle, who for the sake of a
specifically understood emancipation defies every social convention
of the 1852 Louisiana, but who in time of real trial can show true
greatness.

Julie's appearance at a ball in a red dress (instead of the
customary white) leads to the breaking of her engagement to a handsome and ambitious young banker and leaves her with an aristocratic
roué to sweeten her frustration. When he, Pres, returns and falls
ill with yellow fever Julie does not hesitate to follow him to possible
death on the quarantine island.

The melodramatic, most complex character of the title is
brilliantly portrayed by Bette Davis. The heroines of several of
Wyler's pictures made in the 40's were to be similar to her: at
times noble, at times repellent, but always full of style and independence. The scripts used by Wyler, one of the most versatile of
Hollywood directors, would similarly be slick and shoddy although
he mixed the conservatism of the traditional American cinema with
the latest innovations and with splendid psychological intuition.
Wyler would in fact always handle scripts typical of the Hollywood
factory of dreams, but would never be bothered by this.

Instead of concealing the shortcomings of the starting material, as Feyder did in Le Grand jeu, he gave it credibility and
conviction, both through the precision of his analysis of man and
the obsessive attention to detail, almost worthy of Griffith and Stroheim. Even if the world reflected in his melodramas is not the
real one, it is still certainly powerful. If it is not externally
credible, it appears to have credibility of a higher order: it tells
the truth about the human character.

LES DISPARUS DE SAINT-AGIL   Christian-Jaque

Script: Jacques Prévert (under the pseudonym Jean-Henri Blanchon),
from a novel by Pierre Véry. Photography: Marcel Lucien.
Music: Henri Verdun. Cast: Erich von Stroheim (M. Walter, the
English master), Michel Simon (M. Lemel, the drawing master),
Aimé Clariond (M. Boisse, the headmaster), Serge Grave (M.
Planet), Armand Bernard (Fermier), Robert Le Vigan (César),
Jean Claudio (Sorgues), Marcel Mouloudji (Macroy), Claude Roy
(Little Claude), Jean Bouquet (Fernier).

Dimeco, France. 9279 ft., 102 mins.

Christian-Jaque, a film-maker who could never be classified as a member of any trend or creative school but was above all else a thorough craftsman, was an interesting--and very French--director. While having no great achievements to his name, he contributed to the cinema a likeable less-than-real mood in his pictures, particularly the two early ones: Les Disparus de Saint-Agil and The Murder of Father Christmas. In a dream-like provincial boarding school three boys form a secret society and become the astonished witnesses of the mysterious gradual disappearance of other pupils. The events are to take a more serious turn and finally the boys round up a gang of counterfeiters working in the school.

The makers of Les Disparus de Saint-Agil openly declared their abandonment of any pretense to reflecting actual reality and treated the film as an exercise in generating a powerful atmosphere of semi-reality. Untroubled by the question of the credibility of events, they indulged in an excursion into the realm of cinematic fantasy disguised as a romantic thriller. Poetry emerges here with mystification and with recurrent, faintly anarchistic satirical tones (best seen in the scenes of the rehearsal of the school orchestra and the amateur theatre performance). Some of this special atmosphere can be traced back to Christian-Jaque's earlier assistantship to Duvivier, but most of it originates from Prévert, the scriptwriter who was one of the generators of Poetic Realism.

The gallery of eccentric types in the school is amusing (why film directors take such delight in caricaturing schoolteachers is a subject for a separate study), the main attraction among them being Erich von Stroheim as the enigmatic language teacher. A year earlier Stroheim gave a famous performance in Renoir's La Grande illusion; this is another of the idiosyncratic roles with which he graced the cinema after he ceased to direct his own films.

VOLGA-VOLGA   Grigori Alexandrov

Script: Mikhail Volpin, Nikolai Erdman and Alexandrov. Photography: Boris Petrov. Music: Isaak Dunayevsky. Cast: Lyubov Orlova (Strielka), Igor Ilinsky (Byvalov), Vladimir Volodin (Pilot), Pavel Olenev (Uncle Kuzya), A. Tutyshkin (Alyosha Trubyshkin), S. Antimonov (Yard keeper), M. Mironova (Byvalov's secretary).

Mosfilm, U.S.S.R.   9406 ft., 105 mins.

After Jolly Fellows, subtitled "A Jazz Comedy," Alexandrov tried to transplant a revue melodrama onto home soil; but Circus (1936) was not particularly successful. So, the director returned to some of the motifs already used in Jolly Fellows, and created a kind of

satirical multi-character comedy, of course richly adorned with
music.

A bureaucratic manager of a balalaika factory (a hilarious
character, a real descendant of Gogol's revisors) receives an invitation to send a team to the Moscow Musical Olympiad. There are
two musical societies in the factory willing to go: light (led by
Strielka, a musically talented girl, at present employed as a post-
woman) and operatic. Both groups sail down the Volga, in separate
paddle-boats, causing a lot of fracas even before the competition
proper starts. The bureaucrat also causes a lot of trouble, but
these efforts are doomed since youth always wins.

This time the script was not, as in previous films of Alexandrov, "a collection of attractions," but was solidly based on the
classical dramatic axis of a journey. Former eccentricity was likewise replaced by a certain discipline in the madness presented,
subordinated to the dancing rhythm at which events develop, swaying
like the waters of the Volga which carry the protagonists. The result is the best of all Soviet comedies, very populist in character,
very typical of its country--and very funny.

THE LADY VANISHES   Alfred Hitchcock

Script: Sidney Gilliat and Frank Launder, from a novel by Ethel
Lina White. Photography: Jack Cox. Music: Louis Levy. Cast:
Margaret Lockwood (Iris Henderson), Michael Redgrave (Gilbert),
Paul Lukas (Dr. Hartz), Dame May Whitty (Miss Froy), Googie
Withers (Blanche), Cecil Parker (Mr. Todhunter), Linden Travers
(Mrs. Todhunter), Mary Clare (Baroness), Naunton Wayne (Caldi-
cott), Basil Radford (Charters).

Gainsborough Pictures, G.B. 8650 ft., 96 mins.

The Lady Vanishes is doubtless the most amusing of all Hitchcock's
films, a delightful fantasy untroubled by the laws of logic or probability. On a transcontinental train home from the Balkans a young
English girl meets a charming old lady who shortly after mysteriously disappears. Although other passengers deny ever having seen
her, Iris and her young musician friend persist in their search,
find the lady (who is a British intelligence agent), unmask an evil
spy ring and escape unhurt to London where all three meet again
in a charming scene at the Foreign Office.

The Lady Vanishes takes place almost entirely aboard the
train and impresses with the precision and purposefulness of the
movements of the camera enclosed within the space of a few rail-

way carriages on a set barely thirty yards long. Even the studio
sets and the frequent use of back projection do not detract from the
film.   The detail was used with mastery (the name of the lady written on a misty window as a proof of her existence, the heavy panting of a locomotive brought to a standstill on a side line).   The
cast put together an arch-Hitchcockian assortment of excellently
characterized amusing types: Basil Radford and Naunton Wayne are
a slightly caricatural couple of cricket-crazy English gentlemen
abroad.

The Lady Vanishes, the last significant film Hitchcock made
before moving to America, was released barely three months before
the war.   The preoccupation of his last British films with espionage
and political assassination was an ominous portent of the times to
come.

THE GUILD OF THE KUTNÁ HORA MAIDENS (Cech Panen Kutno-
    horských)   Otakar Vávra

Script: Vávra and Zdeněk Štěpánek, from the comedy plays,
"Zvíkovský rarášek" and "Paní mincmistrová," by Ladislav
Stroupežnický. Photography: Jan Roth. Music: Jaroslav Křička
and Miloš Smatek. Cast: Zdeněk Štěpánek (Mikuláš Dačický from
Heslov), Ladislav Pesěk (Očko), Václav Vydra (Master of the mint),
Helena Friedlová (His wife), František Smolík (Toll collector and
town councilor), Jiřina Šejbalová (His wife), Theodor Pištěk (Head
of village), Antonie Nedošinská (His wife), Elena Hálková (Their
daughter), Gustav Hilmar (Mládek), Hana Vítová (His daughter),
Adina Mandlová (Rozina), Bedřich Karen (David Wolfram), František
Kreuzmann (Steward), Ladislav Boháč (Zdeněk), Jaroslav Vojta
(Father Bonifác), Karel Dostal (Emperor Rudolf II).

Lucerna, Czechoslovakia.   8530 ft., 95 mins.

A large-scale historical spectacle set in Kutná Hora, a Czech
town, famous for its silver ore, which blossomed during the Renaissance.   The hero is a certain Mikuláš Dačický, a slyboots, a Don
Juan, a patriot and an enemy of injustice.   When Mikuláš arrives
in Kutná Hora, husbands and fathers are sleepless.   Also in town
is a German alchemist, David Wolfram, who has fascinated the Emperor Rudolf II with the prospect of making silver out of nothing,
while he is in fact lining his pockets by exploiting the local mines
with the connivance of corrupt local dignitaries.   Poor people who
protest at the injustice and poverty are thrown into prison.

Mikuláš manages, after much trying, to unmask the charla-
tan who, as it turns out, also wants to abduct the pretty wife of a

local dignitary. The hero also succeeds in conquering his beloved, the only woman in town who has resisted him so far. The Guild of the Kutná Hora Maidens is, apart from Jánošík, the most interesting Czechoslovakian picture about the past--and not only for its vigorous and carefully correct reconstruction of the late 16th century, but also because of its topical references to the period of the Treaty of Munich; in 1938 the film was considered in Czechoslovakia to be more of a patriotic manifesto (with its motif of resistance to German influence), than a lighthearted costumer. The visual aspect of the picture is distinctly reminiscent of Feyder's Carnival in Flanders, and maybe not without design.

THE VYBORG SIDE (Vyborgskaya Storona)   Grigori Kozintsev and Leonid Trauberg

---

Script: Kozintsev and Trauberg. Photography: Andrei Moskvin and G. Filatov. Music: Dimitri Shostakovich. Cast: Boris Chirkov (Maxim), Valentina Kibardina (Natasha), Natalia Uzhvi (Yevdokia), Mikhail Zharov (Dymba, anarchist), A. Chistyakov (Mishchenko), Yuri Tolubeyev (Bugay), Maxim Strauch (Lenin), Mikhail Gelovani (Stalin), A. Kuznetsov (Turayev), Leonid Lubashevsky (Sverdlov), B. Zhukovsky (Lawyer), D. Dudnikov (Ropshin), I. Nazarov (Lapshin).

Lenfilm, U.S.S.R.   10,748 ft., 119 mins.

The last part of the "Maxim Trilogy" (Part I was The Youth of Maxim and Part II, The Return of Maxim). The victory of the Soviet Revolution promotes the hero from an ordinary factory job to a responsible executive post in the national economy. Of course Maxim has no idea about the financial operations of the bank of which he has become commissar, and his administrative staff has no intention of helping him at all. But what about the craftiness and common sense of a former St. Petersburg worker?

Maxim sets up a team of trusted people who will assist him to introduce order and start proper work in the most difficult period of national reorganization when everything is no longer as simple and clear-cut as during the fight against Tsarist rule. Maxim succeeds in thwarting the destructive plots of internal enemies and, as the film ends, once again puts on uniform, this time to fight the German interventionists. It is, as a matter of fact, not only the hero who has a difficult time: Kozintsev and Trauberg also had to put most effort into the plot of the last part of their epic, and the result is not always satisfactory.

The Vyborg Side lacks breadth in places, it has lengthy

patches and exaggerations and even some traces of propagandist
simplifications in the best Stalinist vein. Even the photography is
less subtle, somewhat documentary in character--it has clarity, it
is true, but it lacks atmosphere. However, the impetus built up
during the previous parts proves sufficient to give even the final
installment the best characteristics of the "Maxim Trilogy" and
worthily closes the saga of the contribution of a private citizen to
the Revolution.

YOU CAN'T TAKE IT WITH YOU   Frank Capra

Script: Robert Riskin, from the stage play by George S. Kaufman
and Moss Hart. Photography: Joseph Walker. Music: Dmitri
Tiomkin. Cast: Jean Arthur (Alice Sycamore), Lionel Barrymore
(Martin Vanderhof), James Stewart (Tony Kirby), Edward Arnold
(Anthony P. Kirby), Misha Auer (Kolenkov), Ann Miller (Essie Car-
michael), Spring Byington (Penny Sycamore), Samuel S. Hinds (Paul
Sycamore), Donald Meek (Mr. Poppins).

Columbia, U.S.A. 11,366 ft., 126 mins.

Ordinary people are happier than millionaires--they do not have to
bother with keeping up appearances, they form eccentric families,
where mother writes thrillers, father makes fireworks which alert
the whole district, daughter loves ballet dancing.... And money?
Money, the "it" of the title, is not all!

     If only the lugubriousness of the rich does not get in the way,
everything will go well: this is more or less the philosophy of the
last of Capra's fully successful prewar films, each of which became
in its time a veritable fountain of joy for everyone. As in Mr.
Deeds Goes to Town, the notes of social criticism ring quite loud,
and as in that picture, the film never goes outside the jocular convention. Maybe it was easier so--and also more sensible.

AMONG PEOPLE (V Lyudyakh) [Out in the World]   Mark Donskoy

Script: Ilya Gruzdev, from the autobiographical novel by Maxim
Gorky. Photography: Pyotr Yermolov. Music: Lev Schwartz.
Cast: Alexei Lyarsky (Alyosha Peshkov), Varvara Massalitinova
(Akulina Ivanovna), Mikhail Troyanovsky (Kashirin), I. Kudriavtsev
(Sergeyev), N. Berezovskaya (His wife), J. Lilina (Matryona Ivanov-

na), I. Zarubina (Natalya), D. Zerkalova ("Queen Margot"), A.
Timontayev (Smuryi), Nikolai Plotnikov (Zhikharev, ikon painter).

Soyuzdetfilm, U.S.S.R.   8957 ft., 99 mins.

Among People is the name of the middle part of the "Trilogy of the
Young Gorky." The rudiments of style are here very much the
same as in the first part (The Childhood of Maxim Gorky), and
Among People does not lean towards the exaggerated symbolism and
the primitive imagery which would destroy the quality of the last
part, My Universities (1939). All the same, the film is much more
static and less cohesive than its predecessor, and has become more
of a series of observations of different social environments in provincial Russia; some of them are faithful and vivid, others overdone
and irritating.

The 13-year-old Alyosha works as a dogsbody for his drafts-
man uncle. He reads passionately--at night because of the family's
hostile attitude to reading. He leaves to become, first, a washer-
up on a ship where he develops a friendship with the cook who
strengthens his will to study, then a painter of ikons. Later he returns to his grandmother's for a while only to leave home again.

Among People does not have the harmony or the narrative
fluency which characterized the beginning of the trilogy. The individual episodes are rather monotonously joined together by fade-
outs and fade-ins, the action is forcibly pushed forward by captions.
The life, which in The Childhood of Maxim Gorky literally emanated
from the screen, begins to acquire the taste of a somewhat theatrical mise en scène; spontaneity is turned into stiff academicism.
All this was to hang heavily over Donskoy's future work, but here
these faults were not yet too pronounced.

Among People counts in the first place as a further part of
an impressive epic fresco showing the decomposition of the old Russia as seen through the eyes of a sensitive boy who is seeking good
fortune for himself and others. Sweepingly drawn characters which
file through the screenplay are portrayed with variable success by
the actors--certainly with less consistency than in the earlier part.
Yet one part undoubtedly overshadows all others--that of Varvara
Massalitinova. Her Grandmother Akulina is one of the best female
roles in the Soviet cinema.

LA BÊTE HUMAINE   Jean Renoir

Script: Renoir, from the novel by Émile Zola. Photography:
Curt Courant. Music: Joseph Kosma. Cast: Jean Gabin (Jacques

Lantier), Simone Simon (Séverine), Fernand Ledoux (Roubaud),
Julien Carette (Pecqueux), Blanchette Brunoy (Flore), Jenny
Hélia (Philomène), Colette Régis (Mme. Victoire), Jean Renoir
(Cabuche).

Paris Film Productions, France.   8910 ft., 99 mins.

La Marseillaise (1937), that massive and ambitious project, "a film
for the people created by the people," was an almost complete failure. In it Renoir intended to praise the unity of a nation in the
face of injustice and exploitation in the style of an epic fresco
blended with the personal drama of the ordinary fighters in the
French Revolution; it is not so much a failed masterpiece as simply
mediocrity; it is heavy, theatrical and primitively done.

    Le Bête humaine was, for a change, not a film planned by
Renoir himself, but suggested to him, yet he made it with full
strength of conviction. The theme of Zola's novel was of course
close to Renoir's interests; he had started his ruthless probing of
the nature of man in La Chienne (1931) and expressed it best in
Toni. The somber mood of the book closely coincided with the atmosphere in France at the time, where the Popular Front lay in
ruins and war was in the air. In effect the picture is very much
like its literary source: pessimistic, brutal and ruthless.

    Lantier, a locomotive engineer from an alcoholic family,
loves Séverine, the wife of a deputy station master who had in the past
killed her elderly lover. Goaded by his mistress, Lantier is about
to murder the husband but kills her instead in one of his brain-
storms. Finally, unable to bear the guilt, he throws himself from
his train.

    Renoir prepared with great care for the shooting and included
in La Bête humaine many scenes of striking visual power and an unmistakably true touch (e.g., the opening train ride to Le Havre,
which brings back the memories of Gance's railway symphony, La
Roue; the meeting on the railway tracks in the rain; the discovery
of the murdered Séverine). As usual, the director exercised remarkable persuasiveness and psychological insight, which were in
addition expressed with exceptional fullness by the outstanding actors. The precision in observing human behavior is here close to
that achieved by the hidden camera method and "open" dramatic
thread of 25 years later.

    In spite of that however the film turns out to be far from
perfect: it is a bit over-contrasted even in view of its naturalistic
convention and an unbalanced dramatic line, in places giving the impression more of a notebook than of a finished work. The cause of
these failings was here the same as in the case of La Marseillaise
(1937), and would from now on appear in many of Renoir's
pictures: it can best be described as the incompatibility of idea
and form, the failure to translate the intentions of an artist into images.

THE CITADEL   King Vidor

Script: Ian Dalrymple, Frank Wead and Elizabeth Hill, from the novel by A. J. Cronin. Photography: Harry Stradling. Art Direction: Lazare Meerson and Alfred Junge. Music: Louis Levy. Cast: Robert Donat (Andrew), Rosalind Russell (Christine), Ralph Richardson (Denny), Rex Harrison (Dr. Lawford), Emlyn Williams (Owen), Basil Gill (Dr. Page), Dilys Davis (Mrs. Page).

MGM, G.B. 10,042 ft., 112 mins.

In 1938 Metro-Goldwyn-Mayer decided to expand into the British film industry. Of the three films made in all, The Citadel, directed by the great King Vidor, is the only worthwhile effort. An idealistic young doctor works hard in a Welsh mining village. He does some original research into silicosis among miners, but the ignorance and prejudice of the inhabitants cause him to interrupt work and move to London. At first he starves, but later accidentally meets a university colleague and joins him in the ranks of fashionable doctors who for astronomical fees treat the imaginary diseases of rich snobs. It is only when the hero's best friend dies through the professional ignorance of a colleague during an easy operation, that Andrew reflects and decides to pursue not money, but duty to society.

The Citadel, a successful screen version of Cronin's elevating novel about two facets of medicine, splits into two distinct parts according to locality. The episodes in the mining village are shown with realism and honesty, the London scenes with scoffing satirical wit. If the film's naive philosophy, which preaches man's elevation through hardship, is objected to, the criticism should be addressed to the author of the book (which is rendered on film with great fidelity of spirit) rather than to Vidor.

The Citadel was made with an almost entirely British cast. The main fault of the film is the emphatic and not very credible Robert Donat who shows himself to be a better leading man for Hitchcock than for Vidor. The best performance in the picture is that of Ralph Richardson as the hero's permanently drunk but nonetheless idealistic friend.

BANK HOLIDAY [U.S. title: Three on a Weekend]   Carol Reed

Script: Rodney Ackland and Roger Burford, from an original story by
Hans Wilhelm and Ackland.   Photography: Arthur Crabtree.   Cast:
John Lodge (Stephen Howard),   Margaret Lockwood (Catherine),   Hugh
Williams (Geoffrey), Rene Ray (Doreen), Merle Tottenham (Milly),
Linden Travers (Ann Howard), Wally Patch (Arthur), Kathleen Har-
rison (May), Garry Marsh ('Follies' manager), Jeanne Stuart (Miss
Mayfair), Wilfrid Lawson (Police Sergeant), Felix Aylmer (Surgeon).

Gainsborough Pictures, G.B.   7744 ft., 86 mins.

If one discounts the Hungarian-born Korda, and Hitchcock, who was
just about to emigrate to America, Carol Reed was the only outstanding director in the fog-bound British cinema of the late 30's.
The success (critical and box-office) of Bank Holiday, his fifth picture, was made possible by the abandonment of historical spectacles
of the sort of The Private Life of Henry VIII and other such like
fairy tales for the benefit of the reality of the day.   This evolution
is doubtless encouraged by the splendid achievements of the British
documentary cinema, and runs parallel to the emergence of the
"populist cinema" in France.

The last Monday of August is an annual holiday in England.
Just before leaving for a long-planned weekend at the seaside with
her bank clerk boyfriend, a young London nurse sees the death of
a maternity patient and has to break the news to the dead woman's
husband.   Although she and the young man travel first class and
plan to stay at the Grand Hotel, she cannot forget that experience
and slowly comes to realize her love for the widower.   Driven by
a premonition she returns to London just in time to save him from
suicide.

In Bank Holiday the dramatic plot was skillfully blended with
the comedy element provided by a Cockney family on their communal excursion, the would-be beauty queen and her ugly girlfriend
and the splendid sketch of Wilfrid Lawson as the Sussex policeman.
The feel of the popular holiday was here very well rendered, the
English setting painted with a richness of detail and the characters
drawn so well that the spectator almost forgives Reed the far-
fetched story and the fact (often obvious) that the film was made almost entirely in the studio.

PETER THE FIRST (Pyotr Pervyi)   Vladimir Petrov

Script: Alexei Tolstoy, Petrov and N. Leshchenko. Photography:
Vladimir Yakovlev and Vyacheslav Gordanov. Music: Vladimir
Shcherbachev. Cast: Nikolai Simonov (Tsar Peter I), Alla Tarasova
(Ekaterina), Nikolai Cherkasov (Prince Alexei), Mikhail Zharov
(Menshikov), Mikhail Tarkhanov (Field Marshal Sheremetev), Viktor
Dobrovolsky (Fedka/Yaguzhinsky), N. Roshefor (Demidov), F. Bog-
danov (Brovkin), Irina Zarubina (Yefrosinya), K. Gibshman (Buino-
sov), Vladimir Gardin (Count Tolstoy), N. Litvinov (Shafirov), G.
Orlov (Zhemon).

Lenfilm, U.S.S.R.   Part I: 9236 ft., 103 mins., Part II: 11,230
ft., 125 mins.

Tsar Peter I "opened the window onto Europe" and created the
foundations of a modern Russian state. This theme was taken up
by the Soviet cinema in the period when even the thus-far neglected
historical cinema was expected to convey a propaganda message.
This epic picture is made with breadth and, trying to excuse situational simplifications and the overdone "generic" character of the
protagonists by its avowed populist character, it seeks to address
itself to a wide audience.

       The first part of Peter the First is brisk and dynamic. The
editing and the staging of mass scenes reaches to the heights of the
silent Soviet classics, but the second part is lengthy and static and
unsuccessfully tries to represent the complexity of the social and
political situation at the threshold of the historic breakthrough in
the development of Russia.

THE ADVENTURES OF ROBIN HOOD   Michael Curtiz and William
    Keighley

Script: Norman Reilly Raine and Seton I. Miller, based on a 14th-
century legend. Photography: Sol Polito and Tony Gaudio. Music:
Erich Wolfgang Korngold. Cast: Errol Flynn (Sir Robin of Locks-
ley, "Robin Hood"), Olivia de Havilland (Maid Marian), Basil Rathbone (Sir Guy of Gisbourne), Claude Rains (Prince John), Patric
Knowles (Will Scarlet), Eugene Pallette (Friar Tuck), Alan Hale
(Little John), Melville Cooper (High Sheriff of Nottingham), Ian
Hunter (King Richard), Una O'Connor (Bess), Montagu Love (Bishop
of Black Canons), Leonard Willey (Sir Essex).

Warner Bros., U.S.A.   9292 ft., 103 mins.   Technicolor.

What should be the crowning theme for the Curtiz-Flynn team after
the success of their Captain Blood?   Of course, the extraordinary
deeds of Robin Hood!   This time the adventures of the hero are
over-accomplished from the point of view of the script and the direction; there are too many effects which are designed to enliven
the situations (but which are, taking things indulgently, addressed
to children).   Still, the carefree elemental cinema does have its
own aesthetic laws, in terms of which The Adventures of Robin
Hood must doubtless be a considerable achievement.   Special attractions are the decent color photography and the very spectacular, although conventional, final fight.

1939

LE JOUR SE LÈVE   Marcel Carné

Script: Jacques Viot and Jacques Prévert. Photography: Curt
Courant and Philippe Agostini. Art Direction: Alexandre Trauner.
Music: Maurice Jaubert. Cast: Jean Gabin (François), Jacqueline
Laurent (Françoise), Arletty (Clara), Jules Berry (Monsieur Valen-
tin), René Genin and Mady Berry (Caretakers), Bernard Blier (Gaston),
Marcel Pérès (Paulo), Jacques Baumer (Police inspector), René
Bergeron (Café owner), Gabrielle Fontan (Lady on the staircase),
Arthur Devere (M. Gerbois), Georges Douking (Blindman), Germaine
Lix (A singer).

Sigma-Frogerais, France.   7995 ft., 87 mins.

The dramatic content of Le Jour se lève, the purest and stylistically
most dignified Poetic Realist film, is much simpler and more static
than that of Carné's earlier Quai des Brumes.   A foundry worker
kills an evil man and barricades himself in the attic room of a suburban tenement house; the events which led to the tragedy are shown
in three flashbacks as François waits for the police assault.   He
had fallen in love with a girl under the strange spell of a certain
Monsieur Valentin, a cabaret dog trainer.   François is at first mis-
led by Valentin's false claim to be the girl's father but finally kills
him when he realizes that the destruction of others is Valentin's
only mission in life.   As the day breaks and the police launch their
attack, François commits suicide in his lonely room.

Le Jour se lève is an example of a rigorous and purposeful
narrative structure in which no detail is unimportant.   The strict
limitations imposed on the plot, set virtually in one room and extend-
ing over a few hours, are reminiscent of the conventions of Greek
drama.   Also the mood of overwhelming fatalism, the use of sym-

-302-

bols (with a blindman representing Destiny), the motif of self-administered justice (compare Antigone), and even the use of the "chorus" of neighbors, were intentionally classical. In these respects Carné emulated the dramatic conventions of the German Kammerspiel, in particular Pick's New Year's Eve.

It is also an example of a film for which set design was an absolutely vital element. Trauner built a studio replica of the sad metropolitan outskirts suffused in a dull early morning light; it is remarkable how perfectly ordinary elements which are not in the least beautiful can add up to produce a semi-real mood of melancholic elevation. Every object in François' room is significant, some are almost actors in the drama and become starting points for flashbacks which, as is usual in screen references to the workings of the human memory, start from the principle of visual association.

Typically for Poetic Realism, sentimentality (take the motif of the love of two orphans with near-identical names, François and Françoise) merges with a matter-of-fact objectivity in describing the details of everyday life and the work in the foundry; this in turn gives way to the poetic license of lyrical love scenes among flowers. André Bazin described Le Jour se lève as "a masterpiece of proletarian tragedy." Jean Gabin, the hero of Quai des Brumes, is present in virtually every frame of the picture and gives another classic portrayal of a screen Outsider, comparable with the archetypal characters of the American Western. Jules Berry's part as the sinister Monsieur Valentin is also a classic; in Carné's next film, Les Visiteurs du soir, Berry would portray Satan himself.

Quai des Brumes and Le Jour se lève excellently render the mood of spiritual defeat regnant in prewar France, so well in fact that the subsequent military defeat would actually be blamed, by the collaborationist Vichy government, on Carné's destructive influence! As previously, the final chord is an acoustic one and the final desperate sound of the alarm clock summoning the dead hero to work at 6:20 a.m. would ring resoundingly in many future French films. The sentiments which pervade Le Jour se lève are in fact to continue well into the postwar years, giving rise to the French variety of film noir and also acquiring intellectual respectability under the name of Existentialism.

STAGECOACH John Ford

Script: Dudley Nichols, from the story, "Stage to Lordsburg," by Ernest Haycox. Photography: Bert Glennon and Ray Binger. Music: Richard Hageman, W. Franke Harling, Louis Gruenberg, Leo Shuken and John Leipold, adapted from 17 American folk tunes of the early 1880's; arranged and conducted by Boris Morros. Cast:

John Wayne (The Ringo Kid), Claire Trevor (Dallas), Thomas
Mitchell (Dr. Josiah Boone), George Bancroft (Curley Wilcox),
Andy Devine (Buck), John Carradine (Hatfield), Louise Platt (Lucy
Mallory), Donald Meek (Mr. Peacock), Berton Churchill (Gatewood),
Tim Holt (Lieutenant Blanchard).

United Artists, U.S.A. 8730 ft., 97 mins.

Unanimously considered to be the most outstanding example of the
classical Western, Stagecoach is in fact a film for which this traditional classification is too narrow. Admittedly, this is construc-
tionally the clearest and technically the most dynamic example of
the archetypes of the genre involving all the traditional characters
of a Commedia dell'Arte of the Wild West, complete with the dramatic axis of a journey which sometimes becomes an escape, sometimes a search, sometimes a chase. There is a matchless sequence
of an attack by Indians and there are the motifs of a chivalrous villain and just vengeance.

But the conventional mold of the protagonists did not stop the
director from a precise analysis of their psychology--Ford's picture
foreshadowed the later fashion for supplementing the old stereotype
with a moral and psychological motivation, and thus seems to be an
obvious prototype of the future Superwestern. It is significant that
Stagecoach appears to be not so much a spectacle as an almost intimate drama involving people in exceptional (or outright ultimate)
situations. The film is of model construction and carefully preserves the principle of the "three unities": it thus consciously ennobles the genre and must be considered the turning point between
the conventions of the traditional Western and the realistic Western.
The latter type, which strove to discard clichés and to tell the truth
about human behavior but still resort to euphemisms, would dominate
throughout the 40's.

The appearance of High Noon would start the 15-year period
of the domination of the "psychological Superwestern," which was to
consider mainly moral arguments. In the late 60's, under distinct
Italian influence, the "biological Western" would appear, bringing
into focus above all drastic "flesh and blood" naturalistic description.
From the point of view of the dramatic situation, Stagecoach is in
a way a remake of The Lost Patrol (a varied group of people facing
outside threat)--and if Ford were not an expert in making Westerns,
one might almost wonder whether simply a certain dramatic situation was not just mechanically transplanted onto the Wild West.

It was not so, and the proof is not only in Ford's later work,
but also the fact that the dramatis personae of Stagecoach obviously
feel at home in the New Mexico locality: a cowboy, honest but
hunted as a criminal; a sheriff of integrity but not of absolute de-
pendability; a permanently drunk doctor; the pregnant wife of a captain whose detachment is busy chasing Indians; a banker who committed a fraud; a cardsharp of good family; a liquor salesman; a

prostitute with a heart of gold.   They are all traveling by stagecoach from Tonto to Lordsburg, some from duty, some under
duress, some to fulfill family revenge.

The journey will be dangerous: desperate Apache Indians
attack the stagecoach near the end of the journey.   The breakneck
chase ends with a last-minute rescue.   The dramatic encounter
with the Indians serves as a catalyst for uncovering the real features of character, so far hidden under the mask of pretense and
social position.   The people who arrive at Lordsburg are different
from those who boarded at Tonto, at least different with respect to
their traveling companions.   Ford filled the space between these construction frames with a mastery he would not later reach.   The psychology here is not only precisely observed and credible, but revealed with great sense of humor.

From the point of view of the narrative rhythm Stagecoach is
really faultless.   This is seen with special clarity in the sequence
of the Indian attack, in which the long shots of the pursuers and the
frantic escape are edited in between the close-ups of the passengers.   In the moments when the waving curve of tension falls, Ford
could be lyrical and truly poetic (the childbirth scene; Dallas and
Ringo Kid at dinner).   The mood was often created through the art-
ful use of the montage of associations, reminiscent of the silent
Soviet films.

This careful and serious approach to the Western theme gave
the thus far disdained brand of popular cinema a much higher rank:
what was a mere convention became transformed into truth.

LA RÈGLE DU JEU   Jean Renoir

Script: Renoir.   Photography: Jean Bachelet.   Music: Roger
Désormière (from Wolfgang Amadeus Mozart, Pierre Alexandre
Monsigny, Camille Saint-Saëns and Johann Strauss).   Cast: Marcel
Dalio (Robert de la Cheyniest), Nora Gregor (Christine),   Jean Renoir
(Octave), Roland Toutain (André Jurieux), Mila Parély (Geneviève de
Marras), Paulette Dubost (Lisette), Julien Carette (Marceau), Gaston
Modot (Schumacher), Pierre Magnier (General), Eddy Debray (Cor-
neille), Pierre Nay (Saint-Aubin), Odette Talazac (Mme. de la Plante),
Richard Francoeur (la Bruyère), Claire Gérard (Mme. la Bru-
yère), Léon Larive (Cook).

Société de Production et de Distribution des Films de Jean Renoir/
Nouvelle Edition Française, France.   112 mins.

Whether or nor La Règle du jeu, one of the most enigmatic, ambivalent and disturbing pictures in cinema history, is Renoir's greatest film, it would be difficult to find in his work another so personal and at the same time so strongly related to the cinema of Erich von Stroheim. Of course, La Règle du jeu is Stroheim translated into French, a combination of venomous satire and a curious narrative convention, a little like the plays of Alfred de Musset and a little like vaudeville, but still strangely appropriate for telling a classical society melodrama whereby a man of uncomplicated soul is introduced into a world obsessed by social status and moral conventions.

André Jurieux, a famous aviator, loves Christine, the neglected wife of the owner of a country château. Through the good offices of Octave, a friend of the family (a music critic who once wanted to be a virtuoso but was too lazy, splendidly played by Renoir himself), André is invited to a hunt during which the amorous pursuits of the society people are intertwined with those of the servants. Everybody is betrayed by everybody else and knows it perfectly well. But nobody cares--this is the rule of the game. (Another rule, a caricature of this one, is in force among the servants).

Unless the rules collide or a stranger, unadapted to the convention, appears, the game proceeds smoothly. But a disruption of the rules must end in tragedy. Christine decides to leave her husband, who is himself preoccupied with another woman, and elope with André. She waits for him in the garden wearing an overcoat borrowed from her maid Lisette. The jealous gamekeeper, Lisette's husband, who throughout the film has tried to forestall her flirtation with a new servant, mistakes Christine for his wife and kills the approaching André with a shotgun. The death is represented as an accident.

Renoir said that his intention was to make a light comedy which would only very occasionally strike a more serious note and thus incline the spectator to reflection. If so, he missed his target by an astronomical margin: La Règle du jeu is a cruel drama in which comedy elements (such as the theatre performance during the social gathering) play only the role of blood-curdling intermezzos and make Renoir's ruthless jibe at the imperfection of human nature all the more penetrating.

One of the causes of this situation is the director's characteristic coldness, his inability to treat the protagonists with any degree of intimacy, his failure to give the picture the polish and smoothness which, when applied to excess in pre-war Hollywood productions, could make even bandits prepossessing. Here people are turned into insects and impassively examined under a magnifying glass. In spite of this, La Règle du jeu is a brilliant film, although one cannot resist the conclusion that it is a good deal more ambitious than the director's wildest expectations--and certainly more biting, as was demonstrated by the violent reaction of a certain part of the audience.

From the formal point of view La Règle du jeu oscillates
from the near-documentary quality of Toni, through a slapstick
chase to being a grotesque spiced with black humor; Renoir appears
to be the first to have attempted such a mixture on the screen. He
was also one of the first to use the deep-focus narrative, which so
far had been experimented with, rather timidly, only by Wyler,
Ermler (in A Great Citizen) and Buster Keaton. As a matter of
fact Renoir himself had already tried the deep-focus technique--in
Boudu Saved from Drowning (1932).

Yet the greatest innovation was the very concept of the picture, which in the context of the political and social situation in
France at that time (1939) acquired an additional layer of meaning
and importance: La Règle du jeu became a modern tale about
corpses in a dead man's house. Although when released it could
offend some people, it was not (and could not have been) understood,
coming as it did at a time when Citizen Kane, that review of cinematic styles and conventions, was yet to be made. Reassessment
was made only after the war and since then La Règle du jeu has
been considered one of the classics of the world cinema.

THE STORY OF THE LAST CHRYSANTHEMUM (Zangiku Monogatari)
    Kenji Mizoguchi

Script: Yoshikata Yoda and Matsutaro Kawaguchi, from the novel by
Shofu Muramatsu. Photography: Shigeto Miki and Yozo Fuji.
Music: Shiro Fukai. Cast: Shotaro Hanayagi (Kikunosuke Onoe),
Kakuko Mori (O-toku), Gonjuro Kawarazaki (Kikugoro Onoe V), Yoko
Umemura (O-sato, his wife), Tokusaburo Arashi (Shikan Nakamura),
Kokichi Takata (Fukusuke Nakamura), Ryotaro Kawanami (Esudayu),
Nobuko Fushimi (Eiryu, a geisha), Kinnosuke Takamatsu (Matsusuke
Onoe), Junnosuke Hayama (Kanya Morita), Tamitaro Onoe (Tamizo
Onoe), Hideo Nakagawa (O-toku's uncle), Hisayo Nishi (His wife),
Benkei Shiganoya (Genshun, a masseur).

Shochiku, Japan. 143 mins.

Towards the end of the 1930s the Japanese cinema achieved not only
artistic maturity but also, mainly through the works of Ozu and
Mizoguchi, international recognition. Mizoguchi's reputation was
established largely by his Osaka Elegy and Sisters of the Gion, both
made in 1936. The next few years however witnessed the rise of
Japanese militarism, which culminated in the Manchurian Campaign
and Pearl Harbor, and Mizoguchi found it impossible to continue the
social-commitment interest of these films in the new "heroic period."

Under direct official pressure the cinema usually resorts (compare the films of the occupied countries of Europe) to neutral historical themes. National characteristics became even more in evidence than before in the style of Japanese films: slow, languorous camera movements, longer and closer shots, the typical harmony and visual balance of the frame, the dramatic role of lighting and subtle pictorial symbolism. It is interesting that the artistic quality was not in the least impaired.

Kenji Mizoguchi found his refuge in the Meiji Era, a crucial period in Japanese history--a happy choice, as the director always felt best in costume films. The plot of The Story of the Last Chrysanthemum starts in 1885. The synopsis sounds like third-rate sentimental literature, but the film is great. It tells the story of Kikunosuke Onoe, a celebrated Kabuki theatre actor, but the real theme is the self-sacrificing love of O-toku, a servant girl through whom he is able to achieve greatness. She first points out the shortcomings in his art, and when he leaves the home of his father, a famous actor, she follows him through the years of poverty and humiliation, of work in third-rate traveling companies, during which he develops into a true artist. She dies when Kikunosuke, now in triumph, leads a ceremonial festive boat procession amidst exploding fireworks.

It is very difficult to describe from where in fact the brilliance of the film is derived. Most probably it comes from the subtlety of Mizoguchi's treatment of the theme, his excellent creation of a complicated network of human relationships and his radiant, pulsating style. The theatre scenes are nearly hypnotic, shown in a hieratic, ritualistic manner. Nobody ever showed so well the difficult process of the improvement of an actor's art: here this is almost tangible.

The Story of the Last Chrysanthemum is basically a film of interiors: the theatre, the home--even the narrow streets of the metropolitan suburbs acquire a chamber character. The story develops at a leisurely pace with the camera slowly hovering in the background; as always with Mizoguchi, objects appear to emanate a light of their own. The use of sound is interesting with natural noises incorporated into the plot and serving a dramatic purpose.

EARTH (Tsuchi)   Tomu Uchida

Script: Ryuichiro Yagi and Tsutomu Kitamura, from the novel by Takashi Nagatsuka. Photography: Michio Midorikawa. Music: Akihiro Norimatsu. Cast: Isamu Kosugi (Kanji), Akiko Kazami (O-tsugi, his daughter), Donguri-boya (Yokichi, his son), Kaichi Yamamoto (Ukichi), Bontaro Miake (Heizo), Reisaburo Yamamoto

(Kane, a horse dealer), San-emon Suzuki (Gen-san), Masako Fuji-
mura (Tami), Chieko Murata (Landowner's wife), Mieshi Bando
(Katsu), Mari Koh (O-kume), Kyosuke Sawa (Hikozo), Chie Mitsui
(Yoshie, his wife), Miyoko Sakura (Aki, his daughter), Isamu Yone-
kura (Kumakichi), Toshinosuke Nagao (Village policeman).

Nikkatsu, Japan.   92 mins.

What Dovzhenko's films, and partly the Jacques Rouquier documentary Farrébique (1946) are to European cinema, Tomu Uchida's
Earth is to Japan.   Yet how different were the conditions in which
these films were created!   Dovzhenko's poetic Earth was in principle designed to be a propaganda film supporting rural collectivization; Uchida started from opposite, anti-official, positions, and made
the film in secret--unknown even to the management of his own stu-
dio--since it was obvious that on the verge of the Second World War
a realistic picture of the destitution of rural Japan, made even more
acute by the whole series of disasters which befall the protagonists,
absolutely could not suit the ideological line of the régime.

     The director could not look for help among producers who
thought that everybody had his own trouble and did not need others',
especially peasants'.   Yet when the film finally managed to squeeze
through onto the screens, it had a striking success--the result of
the power of expression achieved by the director.   Uchida rented a
small piece of land in a poor village and transformed his actors into authentic peasants using primitive methods to cultivate their rice-
fields.   The shooting lasted the whole year and the film was made
in cyclic form, in accordance with the rhythm of nature: no wonder
the outcome is a picture full of power and truth.

     The director did not idealize the peasants: they are pre-
sented as downtrodden, simple and limited, branded by the struggle
for their livelihood.   The dramatic events shown are not exceptional,
but are identified with everyday existence.   At the same time Earth
turns out to be more than just a naturalistic registration of peasants'
lives.   Uchida took the contemplative stand, an attitude of hope
which originates partly from Buddhist philosophy, partly from faith
in man, in whom the sense of the commonness of his condition will
in the end liberate the feeling of solidarity, and partly from the
1939 attitude of tightening the belt and turning towards the always
vivid forces of nature.

     Uchida's work is also a poetic film, characteristic of the
Japanese forms of expression and revealing the deep links between
the Japanese man and nature.   Moods change here with the natural
tonality of the seasons, the bamboo grove is both witness and con-
fessor to human affairs, the flora is here not an ornament, but a
brotherhood of biological individuals neighboring man through the
wall of the house.   Thus Earth has one more aspect, unintentional
on the part of the director: it is a veritable key to the mentality
of his country.

HIS GIRL FRIDAY   Howard Hawks

Script: Charles Lederer, from the play, "The Front Page," by
Ben Hecht and Charles MacArthur. Photography: Joseph Walker.
Music: Morris W. Stoloff. Cast: Cary Grant (Walter Burns),
Rosalind Russell (Hildy Johnson), Ralph Bellamy (Bruce Baldwin),
Gene Lockhart (Sheriff Hartwell), Helen Mack (Mollie Malloy),
Porter Hall (Murphy), Ernest Truex (Bensinger), Cliff Edwards
(Endicott), Clarence Kolb (Mayor), Roscoe Karns (McCue), Frank
Jenks (Wilson), Regis Toomey (Sanders), Abner Biberman (Diamond
Louis), Frank Orth (Duffy), John Qualen (Earl Williams).

Columbia, U.S.A. 8242 ft., 92 mins.

His Girl Friday is one of the handful of successful remakes of good
films. Yet it is a remake with a difference: the part of Hildy
Johnson, the star newspaper reporter, played by Pat O'Brien in
Milestone's The Front Page is played in Hawks's film by a woman--
Rosalind Russell. Interestingly, the idea of changing the sex of one
of the principal characters was a splendid one and, apart from creating many new dramatic situations, added an entirely new level to
the film in comparison with its predecessor. The story is now not
only a battle of wits, but also a battle of the sexes.

        Walter Burns, the editor of the Morning Post, is visited by
Hildy Johnson, a fellow journalist and his former wife, who is about
to get married again. Preparations for the execution of Earl Williams, a disturbed and pathetic accidental killer are under way and
the corrupt sheriff expects the hanging to bring him votes in the
approaching elections. When Williams escapes at the last minute,
Burns senses a scoop and, displaying incredible ingenuity, persuades
Hildy to cover the story for the Post. His tricks include having
Hildy's groom-to-be arrested for alleged theft. After some breakneck events, the story is written, corrupt electioneering exposed,
Williams saved from the gallows; Hildy remains on the job and--
what else?--remarries Burns.

        The main trump of Hecht and MacArthur's original stage play
is its brilliant dialogue. While in Milestone's film the dialogue was
toned down a bit for the screen, here, thanks to the scenarist
Lederer, it regains full brightness. The camera, incessantly on
the move, scrutinizes the limited and mainly interior field of action,
only briefly to dwell on people's faces or on the rolltop desk in
which the murderer is hidden.

        This is a no-holds-barred vision of tabloid journalism whose
"gentlemen of the press" are cynical and motivated by the pursuit
of news to the exclusion of normal human feelings. When a girl,

intimidated by the reporters, jumps out of the window in despair, they look down and one of them shouts "she's moved!" Perhaps unwisely, Hawks's main preoccupation, unlike Milestone's, is with the question of whether Walter will succeed in keeping Hildy on the job; the problem of whether the execution will be avoided is really only secondary.

But a compensating advantage is the fact that His Girl Friday has had much more success than The Front Page in explaining to audiences just why Hildy's journalistic skills are so indispensable to her editor. This is due mainly to the very good acting of Rosalind Russell and Cary Grant.

THE STARS LOOK DOWN   Carol Reed

Script: J. B. Williams, from the novel by A. J. Cronin. Photography: Mutz Greenbaum. Art Direction: James Carter. Music: H. May. Cast: Michael Redgrave (David Fenwick), Margaret Lockwood (Jenny Sunley), Emlyn Williams (Joe Gowlan), Nancy Price (Martha Fenwick), Edward Rigby (Robert Fenwick), Allan Jeayes (Richard Barras), Cecil Parker (Stanley Millington), Linda Travers (Laura Millington), Milton Rosmer (Harry Nugent, MP), George Carney ("Slogger" Gowlan).

Grafton, G.B. 9270 ft., 103 mins.

After Bank Holiday, The Stars Look Down is Reed's second outstanding picture. It is also in a way a continuation of the interests of that film but given in a more coherent and less episodic form. The miners in a village in the Northeast of England refuse to work because of the unsafe conditions in the mine. The management retaliates with repressions. The son of the miners' leader struggles to get a university scholarship to obtain the education necessary to fight more effectively against poverty and exploitation. These hopes are dashed when he marries disastrously to an unfaithful girl and becomes the local schoolmaster. The film culminates in a pit disaster caused by the greed and callousness of the management.

The greatest value of The Stars Look Down is the passionate and realistic vision of a mining village and the pits, which can stand comparison with Kameradschaft. Yet the film as a whole cannot: while Pabst gave his picture only a rather rudimentary story and concentrated on the dramatic events in the pit, Reed tried to combine the socially-oriented theme and several really powerful scenes with a fictional and often melodramatic story, a combination which is less successful on the screen than in Cronin's novel.

Michael Redgrave in the main role gave one of his best early performances: he did not try to symbolize the struggle of Capital versus Labor, he is just a credible, ambitious working-class boy. On the other hand Reed had serious problems with handling the other end of emotional scale: the character of the mine owner, just as in most Soviet films, lacks motivation, depth and credibility and this remains the main deficiency of The Stars Look Down. Although several of Reed's later films are better than this one, they are somewhat remote and less direct.

LA FIN DU JOUR   Julien Duvivier

Script: Duvivier and Charles Spaak. Photography: Christian Matras. Music: Maurice Jaubert. Cast: Victor Francen (Marny), Louis Jouvet (Saint-Clair), Michel Simon (Cabrissade), Madeleine Ozeray (Jeanette), Gabrielle Dorziat (Mme. Chaubert), Arthur De-vère (Manager), Arquillière (M. Lucien), Sylvie (Mme. Tusini), Joffre (M. Philemon), Mme. Lherbay (Mme. Philemon), Jean Coquelin (Delormel), Pierre Magnier (M. Laroche), Granval (Deau-bonne), Jean Aymé (Victor), Tony Jacquot (Pierre), Gaby Andreu (Danielle), Gaston Modot (Innkeeper).

Regina, France. 8400 ft., 93 mins.

Charles Spaak, after Prévert the most outstanding prewar French scriptwriter, and thus necessarily one of the promulgators of Poetic Realism, found a theme perfectly consonant with the moods of the future trend: a shelter for old actors, a world without tomorrow, a world of illusions, of bitter memories, of the insufferable squab-bles of people branded by a professional stigma and the expectation of death. The once successful live by their memories, the failures still hope to be given a chance to shine.

The central character is Saint-Clair, once a great casanova who now sends to himself letters supposed to come from "admirers." Also at the shelter is his former mistress and a man whose life was shattered after Saint-Clair seduced his wife. Back from the Riviera where he frittered away an unexpected legacy, Saint-Clair wants to prove his power over women by persuading a young girl to commit suicide. This is prevented and the film ends with a tribute to the acting profession over the grave of an actor who always wanted to appear in a great role but when given the chance died without uttering a word.

The dramatic potential of the theme is exploited to the full, the excellent actors are doubly true since they play themselves, melodrama is not so much played down as justified by the specific character of this small and isolated milieu. The atmosphere of the film is a mirror of the mood of the whole of France at that time: La Fin du jour tells about the twilight of the whole interwar period.

A GREAT CITIZEN (Veliky Grazhdanin)   Friedrich Ermler

Script: Mikhail Bleyman, Mikhail Bolshintsov and Ermler. Photography: Arkadi Koltsaty. Music: Dmitri Shostakovich. Cast: Nikolai Bogolyubov (Pyotr Shakhov), Ivan Bersenev (Kartashov), Oleg Zhakov (Borovsky), Aleksandr Zrazhevsky (Dubok), Zoya Fyodorova (Nadia), G. Semyonov (Kolesnikov), J. Altus (Kats), Boris Poslavsky (Sizov), A. Kuznetsov (Vershinin), Pyotr Kirillov (Briantsev), Boris Chirkov (Maxim), Ivan Kuznetsov (Ibragimov), I. Rayskaya-Dore (Shakhov's mother), L. Yemelyantseva (Loseva).

Lenfilm, U.S.S.R.   Part I: 10,535 ft., 117 mins.   Part II: 15,222 ft., 169 mins.

Ermler was commissioned in A Great Citizen to show the class struggle with respect to industry as he had done in Peasants with rural U.S.S.R. The ideological line he was given to follow involved the exposure of the "internal enemy," who tries to stop the rapid industrialization through sabotage or even assassination of prominent individuals. The model personality was Kirov, one of the Soviet leaders, murdered in unexplained circumstances in Leningrad in 1934. A specific feature of the situation was that it was in fact Kirov's death that was used by Stalin as a pretext for unleashing a wave of political persecutions, which in the general perspective-- the personal tragedies of many, many people apart--actually very much weakened the Soviet economic and military apparatus.

Ermler based himself on some details of Kirov's biography-- but, as in Peasants, he did not conjure up a flat political poster; A Great Citizen is above all a formally interesting, complex journalistic essay about a man who builds a new world. Of course, it was impossible not to include the rudiments of the official party line in such a solemn prestige work; hence the rough treatment accorded to Mensheviks and Trotskyites, whom the film unequivocally brands as the blackest enemies of the people.

Shakhov, a party secretary in the "Red Metalworker" factory, strives to improve on tractor production in 1925. He wins a temporary victory over the reactionaries after his article exposing their machinations appears in Pravda. The plot of Part II develops in 1934. Enemies of the people have not given up and now try to kill Shakhov during a hunt. This is thwarted when a bribed gamekeeper confesses. A foreign spy who is camouflaged as a party secretary

causes a serious production accident. Just before the subversives
are arrested they assassinate Shakhov during an award ceremony.

The film gives prominence not to the destructive internal
struggle but to the problem of creation, the awakening of enthusiasm
in new people, people converted by the exemplary stand of the hero.
It is understandable that Ermler could not convey this message
through a mere association of images: he had to saturate the film
with dialogues, and he did it with consistency; but this did not make
the narrative static. In the long shots, which dominate, the camera
is rarely immobile, and when it does stop, the characters are in
motion: interframe editing is often in evidence even to the extent
of drastically changing the distance of the camera from the object
within a single shot.

An important role is played by lighting, which is one of the
main architects of the emotional impact; but even more important
is the Ermlerian psychological intimacy and care for detail. A
Great Citizen is a lame film--but, in view of its values, it must
still be considered as one of the most interesting prewar Soviet
pictures.

OF MICE AND MEN   Lewis Milestone

Script: Eugene Solow, from the novel by John Steinbeck. Photog-
raphy: Norbert Brodine. Music: Aaron Copland. Editing: Bert
Jordan. Cast: Burgess Meredith (George), Betty Field (Mae), Lon
Chaney Jr. (Lennie), Charles Bickford (Slim), Roman Bohnen
(Candy), Bob Steele (Curley), Oscar O'Shea (Jackson), Granville
Bates (Carlson), Leigh Whipper (Crooks), Noah Berry Jr. (Whit).

United Artists, U.S.A. 9569 ft., 106 mins.

The year 1940 saw two films made from the writings of John Steinbeck. One of them was of course Ford's celebrated version of The
Grapes of Wrath; the other was Of Mice and Men, a somber story
of aggression, friendship and compassion set in a community of
itinerant farmhands. George, a brisk and energetic man and his
simple-minded friend Lennie flee from a posse and wander around
the country looking for work. They arrive at a farm and in vain
try to live peacefully. The owner is cruel, his son cheeky and the
son's wife frivolous and bored. The girl's fascination with Lennie's
animal strength ends in her accidental death and George shoots Lennie dead rather than allow him to be caught and punished.

The theme seems even less handsome, and more difficult to
handle on the screen, than the dustbowl drama of the Oakies in The

Grapes of Wrath. Yet Milestone gave a penetrating and sensitive
insight into life among the sun-scorched fields of the South. He
discovered the insecurity and desperation of the life of farm workers, and created a romantic, stylized vision of rural life which often
strikes evangelical tones of mercy and compassion. It must be said
that Steinbeck's philosophy is basically very naive but the film defends itself from the threat of sentimentality by its tone of a simple
morality tale and the sincere nobility of its intentions.

For another thing, Milestone perfectly solved the considerable
difficulties of casting which are brought to attention by almost every
stage revival of the play. Lon Chaney gives a particularly fine performance, probably the best in his career. Aaron Copland's clear
and resonant score well underlines the mood and the issues of the
film.

THE BAKER'S WIFE (La Femme du boulanger) Marcel Pagnol

Script: Pagnol and Jean Giono from an episode in the novel, "Jean
le Bleu," by Giono. Photography: G. Benoit and R. Ledru. Music:
Vincent Scotto. Cast: Raimu (Baker), Ginette Leclerc (His wife),
Charles Moulin (Shepherd), Fernand Charpin (Marquis), Robert Vat-
tier (Curé), Robert Bassac (Schoolmaster), Charles Blavette (Tonin),
Dullac (Casimir), Julien Maffre (Pétugue), Jean Castan (Esprit),
Alida Rouffe (Céleste), Maximilienne (Angèle), Odette Roger (Miette),
Charblay (Butcher), Michel (Barthélemy), Maupi (Barnabé), Edouard
Delmont (Rustic).

Les Films Marcel Pagnol, France. 10,450 ft., 116 mins.

The Baker's Wife is a satirical comedy of characters set, like the
earlier "Marseilles Trilogy," in Pagnol's beloved sunny Provence.
When the wife of a baker in a little village runs off with the shepherd
in the service of the local Marquis the baker refuses to bake any
more bread. This causes consternation and unease in the community
and results in the organization of a field search under the leadership
of the three local celebrities: the Marquis, the Curé and the Schoolmaster. The missing wife is soon found and life proceeds as before.

This is however not the point in this uncomplicated story.
What Pagnol really wanted to do is survey a little universe, uncover
the hidden cruelty and passions lying beneath a seemingly idyllic
rural life, and disclose the narrowness, selfishness and pettiness of
the local establishment. No one is spared: the dogmatic and syco-
phantic priest who fawns upon the hypocritical Marquis despite the
latter's numerous love affairs; the ridiculous schoolmaster.

Only the cuckolded husband is treated with sympathy: the
pathetic and tragic baker in the incomparable classical performance
of Raimu personifies the great dramas of little people.   The weakness of the film--as usual with Pagnol's cinema--is its excessive
stability resulting from an over-reliance on dialogue.   The Baker's
Wife is for the French cinema a study for La Règle du jeu, that
vitriolic and brilliant social statement.

YOUNG MR. LINCOLN   John Ford

Script: Lamar Trotti. Photography: Bert Glennon. Music: Alfred
Newman. Cast: Henry Fonda (Abraham Lincoln), Alice Brady (Abi-
gail Clay), Marjorie Weaver (Mary Todd), Arleen Whelan (Hannah
Clay), Eddie Collins (Eph Turner), Pauline Moore (Anne Rutledge),
Richard Cromwell (Matt Clay), Donald Meek (John Felder), Judith
Dickens (Carrie Sue), Eddie Quillan (Adam Clay), Spencer Charters
(Judge Bell), Ward Bond (John Palmer Cass), Milburn Stone (Doug-
las), Cliff Clark (Sheriff).

20th Century-Fox, U.S.A.   9054 ft., 101 mins.

The portrayal of the early life of a famous man is an attractive
subject for a feature film.   It can deal with things usually not widely known, while avoiding the difficulties of the approach to an established celebrity which the numerous directors working on the lives
of people from Napoleon to Lenin were to find out for themselves.
John Ford attempted the biographical drama of the early life of the
great President, showing his progress from a humble provincial
storekeeper to a successful lawyer.   The tall pensive young man
finally decides to follow a legal career after the death of the girl he
loves.

Most of the story takes place in the town of Springfield
where Lincoln practices as a lawyer and where he conducts his
first spectacular case--the defense of the two Clay brothers accused of murder during an Independence Day ball.   The mother of
the accused herself thinks one of them is the killer and is in agony
when the prosecution exhorts her to reveal which one.   Lincoln
cleverly cross-examines one of the witnesses and shows that he is
the real murderer.

John Ford's approach to the theme was mainly anecdotal and
only broadly based on facts.   Whether or not Lincoln said these
things was unimportant, the important thing was Lincoln as a moral
standard.   To Ford, who always stressed a patriotic note in his
films, Lincoln appeared as a legend, a synonym for uprightness and
probity, an almost Christ-like figure.   The film, although a little

over-sentimental and lacking pace in places (though not in the court
scenes), does convey the spirit of American enthusiasm which Walt
Whitman wrote about. This is to a great extent due to Henry Fonda
in one of his best early roles.

CONFESSIONS OF A NAZI SPY   Anatole Litvak

Script: Milton Krims and John Wexley, based on materials gathered
by Leon G. Turrou, former FBI agent. Photography: Sol Polito.
Cast: Edward G. Robinson (Edward Renard), Francis Lederer
(Schneider), George Sanders (Schlager), Paul Lukas (Dr. Kassell),
Henry O'Neill (Attorney Kellogg), Dorothy Tree (Hilda Keinhauer),
Lya Lys (Erika Wolff), Grace Stafford (Mrs. Schneider), Ely Malyon
(Mrs. McLaughlin), James Stephenson (British Intelligence agent),
Celia Sibelus (Mrs. Kassell), Joe Sawyer (Werner Renz), Sig Ru-
mann (Krogman), Hans von Twardovsky (Wildebrandt).

Warner Bros., U.S.A.   9152 ft., 102 mins.

Only in the late 30's had the world come to realize the tangibility
of the Nazi threat. The cinema took note of the situation first by
making more or less oblique references to Nazi Germany, mainly
in thrillers (Hitchcock), but later became more explicit in such pictures as Chaplin's The Great Dictator and Litvak's Confessions of
a Nazi Spy. The latter film was based on the materials from the
trial of a German spy ring accused of stealing secret plans and
made use of the services of a former FBI Nazi intelligence expert.

The aim was to draw attention to the strength and influence
of Nazi intelligence all over the world, but especially in the U.S.A.
A middle-aged Scotswoman acts as a link between the U.S. network
and Berlin. Nazi agents are everywhere: on transatlantic liners
and in thousands of branches of the German-American Bund. Litvak
dispensed with a fictional plot and chose the style of the semi-
documentary "March of Time" newsreel, which Orson Welles later
found so useful in Citizen Kane and which became a standard device
of the thrillers in the late 40's. A spoken commentary and a number of maps and diagrams were also included.

Confessions of a Nazi Spy was made in an atmosphere close
to that which it creates in the audience (and which also accompanied
the making of The Great Dictator): official and semi-official demands and protests from the Nazi government, threats to U.S. ex-
ports and to the relatives of the participants in the film living in
Germany. This may be one of the reasons why the picture shows
the Nazis in an aura of domination and threat, although the psychological (and psychopathic) motivation of the agents seems quite

responsibly investigated.

Confessions of a Nazi Spy was not only a suspenseful and
gripping thriller, surrounded by a ring of truth and urgency, but a
warning of a threat which still seemed remote but was soon to develop into a nightmare.

WUTHERING HEIGHTS William Wyler

Script: Ben Hecht and Charles MacArthur, from the novel by Emily
Brontë. Photography: Gregg Toland. Sets: James Basevi.
Music: Alfred Newman. Cast: Merle Oberon (Cathy), Laurence
Olivier (Heathcliff), David Niven (Edgar), Flora Robson (Ellen Dean),
Donald Crisp (Dr. Kenneth), Hugh Williams (Hindley), Geraldine
Fitzgerald (Isabella), Leo G. Carroll (Joseph).

Samuel Goldwyn, U.S.A. 9361 ft., 104 mins.

Wuthering Heights is of course an adaptation of the famous English
romantic novel. Heathcliff, an orphan, is brought up together with
Catherine and Hindley Earnshaw in a house on the Yorkshire moors
called "Wuthering Heights." When Hindley becomes master of the
house, he treats Heathcliff as a servant; Catherine, whom Heathcliff loves, marries Edgar Linton for financial reasons. Unaware
of this, Heathcliff swears revenge; makes a fortune elsewhere, returns, marries Isabella Linton whom he treats badly in order to
humiliate her brother (whom he also ruins at cards). He continues
the affair with Catherine, but his beloved dies in childbirth. Finally, when following a vision of the dead girl, Heathcliff is killed by
Edgar Linton.

The story, which actually comprises only the first part of
the book is told in a series of flashbacks by a faithful servant.
To capitalize on the more colorful costumes the period of the film
was changed from Regency to Georgian and the whole made in Hollywood using a hothouse imitation of the Yorkshire moors (which is
in fact much like the real thing). One cannot really criticize the
film for simplifying the psychological problems of the complex
novel. Wyler, quite rightly, decided to exploit in the first place
the Gothic potential of the story and concentrate on its awesome
hero.

Accordingly, Wuthering Heights creates a very powerful atmosphere of a mixture of depression and determination (most pronounced in the very evocative beginning full of horror and doom)--
although this is not necessarily the atmosphere equivalent to that
of the novel. At the same time it is the over-emphasis on mood

which in the absence of adequate psychological analysis and with the
story line pushed into the background, is the main flaw of Wuthering
Heights.

For brief spells the picture becomes falsely romantic, and
this is reinforced by the soft and fuzzy photography, so different to
that in Wyler and Toland's earlier Dead End. There is also a
truly disastrous ending with the two dead protagonists soaring heaven-
ward to the accompaniment of an angel choir. The film used some
of the leading British actors, but most credit must go to Laurence
Olivier.

GULLIVER'S TRAVELS   Dave Fleischer

Script: Dan Gordon, Cal Howard, Ted Pierce, I. Sparber and Ed-
mond Seward, from the novel by Jonathan Swift. Photography:
Charles Schettler. Music and Lyrics: Ralph Rainger and Leo Robin.
Singing Voices: Jessica Dragonette (Princess Glory), Lanny Ross
(Prince David).

Max Fleischer Productions, U.S.A. 6871 ft., 76 mins. Technicolor.

After the success of Snow White and the Seven Dwarfs, Disney made
further full-length animated films and quickly gained a monopoly in
the genre. The challenge was timidly taken up by the Fleischer
brothers, the elder of whom, Max, had been working in animation
for more than twenty years and was the author of the popular characters Coco the Clown and Betty Boop.

Gulliver's Travels, an adaptation of a famous literary classic, does not bring anything new to the genre; the drawings are
close to the early style of Disney, naturalistic and one-dimensional,
and the animation is technically imperfect. It is however impossible to deny the authors of this adaptation of Swift for children a
good dose of inventiveness and wit, especially in taking pictorial
advantage of the wonders in which the novel abounds. The Fleischer
brothers would never repeat the success of their first full-length
animation; for the next twenty years in children's animation one
would talk only about Disney's productions.

NINOTCHKA   Ernst Lubitsch

Script: Charles Brackett, Billy Wilder and Walter Reisch, based
on a story by Melchior Lengyel. Photography: William Daniels.
Music: Werner R. Heymann. Cast: Greta Garbo (Ninotchka),
Melvyn Douglas (Leon), Ina Claire (Swana), Bela Lugosi (Razinin),
Sig Rumann (Iranoff), Felix Bressart (Buljanoff), Alexander Granach
(Kopalski), Gregory Gaye (Rakonin), Rolfe Sedan (Hotel manager),
Edwin Maxwell (Mercier), Richard Carle (Gaston).

MGM, U.S.A. 9925 ft., 110 mins.

Ninotchka is the first picture in which the American cinema took
cognizance of the existence of a Communist Russia. The Soviet
government sends three emissaries to Paris on a mission to sell
jewels confiscated from a countess during the Civil War. When the
envoys seem to be over-indulging in the newly-found Western lux-
uries, a drab ex-soldier girl (incredibly, Greta Garbo) is dis-
patched to save the project. Ninotchka however falls in love with
a French aristocrat and after a spell back home, defects.

The task of making this mild anti-Soviet (or rather anti-
Stalinist) satire was given to Lubitsch, the expert on elegant salon
comedies. The director succeeded because he overcame the standard trouble with this sort of film: getting the details right. Lubitsch talks only about things which he knows (which is more than,
for instance, Hitchcock managed in Torn Curtain, 1966), and the
use of Communist jargon, references to five-year-plans and collective farming do not sound a wild fantasy only because of the mocking bravura with which he leads the story.

The film is based on the principle of contrast: the fast pace
of the Paris episodes are opposed to the grim Russian sequences,
the incipient dogmatic orthodoxy of the heroine is transformed into
glowing womanhood under the "decadent" influence of Parisian life.
It is however Greta Garbo in her first comedy part who is the main
source of light here and to whom most credit for the picture's success is due. She subtly conveyed the metamorphosis of her heroine, and did not everdo her slogan-chanting indoctrination in the beginning.

From the middle 20's Garbo gave a series of brilliant performances in Hollywood and became a super-star which outshone all.
Yet it is only fair to say that none of her American films ever approached the standard of the European ones, particularly Pabst's
The Joyless Street, to which she owed her early fame. It is tragic
that the cinema wasted one of its greatest actresses by making her
portray a gallery of sentimental heroines.

1940

THE GRAPES OF WRATH   John Ford

Script: Nunnally Johnson, from the novel by John Steinbeck. Photography: Gregg Toland. Music: Alfred Newman. Cast: Henry Fonda (Tom Joad), Jane Darwell (Ma Joad), John Carradine (Casey), Charley Grapewin (Grampa Joad), Dorris Bowdon (Rosasharn), Russell Simpson (Pa Joad), O. Z. Whitehead (Al), John Qualen (Muley), Eddie Quillan (Connie), Zeffie Tilbury (Grandma Joad), Frank Sully (Noah), Frank Darien (Uncle John), Darryl Hickman (Winfield), Shirley Mills (Ruth Joad).

20th Century-Fox, U.S.A.   11,660 ft., 130 mins.

The celebrated odyssey of the Joads, a family of Oklahoma tenant farmers forced off their land by dustbowl conditions and ruthless landlords. The ten of them set off in a jalopy truck to California in search of work. The journey is a nightmare: the grandparents die one after another, the husband of the pregnant Rosasharn vanishes without a trace. The mirage of Californian well-being soon fades in the eyes of the Joads. During a strike in protest against exploitation by greedy farmers, Casey, one of the party, is murdered. Tom Joad kills a policeman in revenge and has to flee promising to fight for a change of social order. The remainder of the party set off again.

It is ironic that Ford does not like his most famous picture: the distinguished crusading novel set in the years of crisis and deprivation left him little freedom in the script. All the director could do was to change the order of some scenes and redistribute certain dialogues. All the same, the principal motif of a "miniature society" is classically Fordian.

Ford secured the cooperation of Gregg Toland, the greatest American cameraman, who found a perfect visual key to the spirit of the work. The camera towers over the film, discovering hidden facets of ordinary, ugly objects, grimly enumerating endless highways and transit camps surrounded by barbed wire. Some images are symbolic, like the opening shots of Tom Joad who has just been released from prison: a tiny figure walking along the road. Everything in The Grapes of Wrath is as drab and cold as the barrel of a gun, and yet the film commands a great epic power and turns the report on the wanderings of a family into a universal drama enacted beneath overcast skies.

Without being unkind to the director it must be said that few films rely on photography more than The Grapes of Wrath. Surprisingly, the dustbowl of the 30's lent itself readily to artistic pictorial description and the images of the film very interestingly compare with the works of the great photographers (such as Dorothea Lange, Arthur Rothstein and Ben Shahn, the then employees of the U.S. Farm Security Administration), which were used, for example, in the New York Museum of Modern Art "The Bitter Years" exhibition in 1962. Most great but tragic works of art (for instance the novels of Dostoyevsky) are basically heartening, and The Grapes of Wrath also ends on a note of optimism: the scene of Tom's farewell to his mother contains the essence of the picture, professes the spirit of persistence and affirmation of life and stresses the palpable links of the heroes with the soil--while there is life there is hope.

Ford well alternated the tones of intimacy and pathos, but in the later part, driven by the desire to be faithful to the book, included too many dialogue scenes which are unnecessarily static and discursive. The Grapes of Wrath had excellent acting from the entire cast. The most memorable roles are those of Henry Fonda as the ex-criminal Tom and Jane Darwell as Ma Joad, the Mother-Earth, the symbol of determination and the uniting influence in the family. This performance brought her an Oscar; another was received by the director.

THE GREAT DICTATOR   Charles Chaplin

Script: Chaplin. Photography: Karl Struss and Rollie Totheroh. Music: Meredith Wilson. Cast: Charles Chaplin (Adenoid Hynkel, Dictator of Tomania/Jewish barber), Paulette Goddard (Hannah, the Jewish girl), Jack Oakie (Benzino Napaloni, Dictator of Bacteria), Reginald Gardiner (Schultz), Billy Gilbert (Herring), Henry Daniell (Garbitsch), Grace Hayle (Madame Napaloni), Carter de Haven (Bacterian ambassador), Lucien Prival (Officer), Eddie Gribbon and Hank Mann (Storm troopers), Maurice Muscovitch (Mr. Jaeckel), Emma Dunn (Mrs. Jaeckel), Bernhard Gorcey (Mr. Mann), Paul

Weigel (Mr. Agar), Chester Conklin (Man being shaved), Leo White
(Barber).

United Artists, U.S.A.   11,319 ft., 126 mins.

The virtually silent Modern Times finally convinced Chaplin that he
could survive in the cinema only if he started making sound films.
The thought of parodying Hitler first occurred to him in 1938, and
the idea of playing two roles at once was suggested by Alexander
Korda and accepted eagerly when Chaplin realized that this gave him
an opportunity to use a double dose of satire--and a double dose of
mimic art. The Great Dictator was finally released in 1940, after
two years of production (which was interfered with from all quarters), when Germany commanded half of Europe and the United
States was still neutral.

Chaplin however was never neutral and indulged in a devastating piece of political satire whose main cutting edge lies in splendidly ridiculing Hitler's absurd showmanship and thereby compro-
mising his ideas. It was said that the immediate reason for Chaplin's attack was that Hitler stole his moustache. This opinion is a
clever key if not to actual motifs, at least to the sentiments of the
film.

The Great Dictator is based on the classical comedy principle
of a striking likeness between two completely different people, and
the title in the beginning, "All likeness between the Jewish barber
and the dictator Hynkel is purely coincidental," strikes one as a
superbly absurd joke if one considers that Chaplin appears in both
roles. In addition, by using a standard Hollywood expression he is
also taking a dig at the film industry with which he had long been
at odds.

The Great Dictator starts during the First World War in the
State of Tomania. An awkward private soldier, in civilian life a
barber, loses his memory in an airplane crash and finds himself in
a mental asylum. He is released after power in the country has
been assumed by a certain Jew-hating Hynkel. Tomania is plagued
by poverty and unemployment and the dictator's opponents are kept
in concentration camps. Hynkel's storm troops harass Charlie and
destroy his barber shop in the ghetto; Charlie is sent to a camp.
Hynkel signs a treaty with another dictator. Charlie escapes from
the camp in disguise just as Tomania invades a neighboring state.
He is accidentally taken for Hynkel and uses this likeness to make
a pacifist address.

The Great Dictator is an astonishing but very uneven film.
The whole is based on the combination of two narrative conventions:
Chaplin talks as dictator, but uses mime as the barber. The point
is that his activities as the barber are markedly less funny, and
the humor seems strained. On the other hand, the scenes with
Chaplin as Hynkel are great. Particularly powerful and devastating

is the meeting between Hynkel and Napaloni, dictator of Bacteria (a spoof of Mussolini) and these scenes belong to the very best in all Chaplin's work.

A special guardsman sticks out his tongue to lick stamps; the encounter between the two dictators, overtly courteous but riotous in private, culminates in a battle with dishes full of spaghetti during a state banquet. The star scene is doubtless the alegorical, absurd, lyrical and sensuous dance of Hynkel with a world-balloon: when it explodes, the mighty dictator fearfully climbs a curtain. In another great scene Charlie shaves a client in strict time to Brahms' Hungarian Dance.

The weakness of The Great Dictator resides in the diametrical changes of mood: the lyrical scenes in the ghetto coexist rather unhappily with the all-out satire in the dictator's palace. Chaplin was determined to apply his bittersweet mixture rather than concentrate on parody alone as in Shoulder Arms or The Pilgrim. It has also been said that Chaplin sometimes went too far and that the concentration camp is not a suitable location for humor. But would he have made the picture as it is had he been aware of the full extent of the Nazi atrocities? Another flaw is the excess of side episodes unnecessarily diverting the audience's attention from the main theme and harming the dynamism of the whole.

Chaplin still was not conversant with the technique of sound cinema: the final six minutes of the film are taken up entirely by the passionately humanist speech about freedom and equality of all people by the barber mistaken for the dictator. Although Chaplin's intentions are here obviously commendable (and of topical propaganda value) the use of "straight" declamation seems naive and uncinematic. All this does not detract too much from The Great Dictator, a comedy which tells us more about dictatorship than many other "serious" films and which remains one of the most penetrating accusations against Fascism in the cinema.

FANTASIA   Walt Disney

Story Direction: Joe Grant and Dick Huemer. Direction of individual numbers: Samuel Armstrong, James Algar, Bill Roberts, Paul Satterfield, Hamilton Luske, Jim Handley, Ford Beebe, T. Hee, Norm Ferguson and Wilfred Jackson. Music Direction: Edward H. Plumb. Music played by the Philadelphia Symphony Orchestra conducted by Leopold Stokowski playing the following items: (1) Toccata and Fugue in D Minor--Johann Sebastian Bach; (2) "The Dance of Elves," from the suite Op. 71a of the ballet, "The Nutcracker"--Pyotr Tchaikovsky; (3) The Sorcerer's Apprentice--Paul Ducas; (4) Part I of the suite of the ballet, "The Rite of Spring"--Igor Stravin-

sky; (5) Sixth Symphony ("Pastoral") in F Major, Op. 68--Ludwig
van Beethoven (fragments); (6) "Dance of the Hours," from the third
act of the opera, "Gioconda"--Amilcare Ponchielli; (7) A Night on Bald
Mountain--Modest Moussorgsky; (8) Ave Maria, song Op. 52 no. 6--
Franz Schubert.

Walt Disney Productions, U.S.A.   11,361 ft., 126 mins.   Technicolor.

Fantasia is without a doubt the most original Disney film.   Attempts
at illustrating music with images had been made before in short
films by, among others, Fischinger (Musical Studies, 1930-1933)
and Alexeieff (Une Nuit sur le Mont Chauve, 1933). Fantasia is composed of seven short episodes of animated feature cinema, combined
with documentary elements (in the introduction and the intermezzos between individual parts), and even educational cinema (not always
competent).

        The transposition of sound into images is often trivial and
the designs sometimes close to kitsch.   The method adopted more
often gives an excellent musical background to Disney's cartoons
than a genuine visual illustration of the themes of the composers.
Yet the whole is a success because of Disney's pictorial and musical
inventiveness and his ability to blend humor and emotion.   At times
a fascinating unity of picture and sound is achieved and in its overall effect the film is a not unimportant instrument for popularizing
music, made-to-order for the capacities of the American public.

THE RETURN OF FRANK JAMES   Fritz Lang

Script: Sam Hellman.   Photography: George Barnes and William
V. Skall.   Music: David Buttolph.   Cast: Henry Fonda (Frank
James), Gene Tierney (Eleanor Stone), Jackie Cooper (Clem), Hen-
ry Hull (Major Rufus Todd), J. Edward Bromberg (George Rynyan),
Donald Meek (McCoy), Eddie Collins (Station agent), John Carradine
(Bob Ford), George Barbier (Judge), Ernest Whitman (Pinky),
Charles Tannen (Charlie Ford), Lloyd Corrigan (Randolph Stone).

20th Century-Fox, U.S.A.   8280 ft., 92 mins.   Technicolor.

A screen hit often becomes a stimulus for the making of sequels of
various kinds.   Such a continuation was made of Henry King's Jesse
James (1939), a rather mediocre variety of the tale of a bandit belonging to the pantheon of Western heroes.   Yet The Return of Frank
James is by no means a pale imitation of the original, as is common in such cases.

For his debut in the Western genre Lang made a totally autonomous and original picture, whose relationship to the preceding film consists merely of the same outline of the plot in which the murdered Jesse James' brother single-handedly avenges his death. While King was simply interested in giving a popular version of the life story of a bandit (somewhat whitewashed in accordance with the prevailing fashion), Frank James was with Lang given a completely different dimension: he was designed to fit the classical Lang personality of a Proscribed Man, internally noble, but pushed on to the path of crime by an unfriendly environment.

The film is narrated with great skill and it seems that it differs even more from the classical traditions of the genre than did Stagecoach of the previous year, in that not only the psychological, but also the moral pattern is revised. This pioneering character of The Return of Frank James was as a matter of fact unnoticed; the Lang morality tale seemed in 1940 to be a pollution of the rules of the Wild West and a mechanical transplant of alien European traditions. It is not impossible that this interpretation is correct so far as the actual origins of Lang's intentions are concerned.

But the result obtained deserves high praise: Lang did not feel a stranger in the new scenery and knew how to use exteriors with great skill; the rhythmical quality of the narrative is impressive as is his direction of the actors. The Return of Frank James is, apart from The Ox-Bow Incident, the most interesting achievement of the Western genre in the early 40's.

FOREIGN CORRESPONDENT   Alfred Hitchcock

Script: Charles Bennett and Joan Harrison. Photography: Rudolf Maté. Music: Alfred Newman. Cast: Joel McCrea (Jonnie Jones, reporter), Laraine Day (Carol Fisher), Herbert Marshall (Stephen Fisher, her father), George Sanders (Herbert Folliott, reporter), Albert Bassermann (Van Meer), Robert Benchley (Stebbins), Eduardo Cianelli (Krug), Edmund Gwenn (Rowley), Harry Davenport (Mr. Powers).

United Artists, U.S.A.   10,798 ft., 120 mins.

Foreign Correspondent, like all Hitchcock's pictures, contains something which unmistakably identifies the director. A young American journalist (following the principle of small people involved in great affairs) finds himself in the middle of a diplomatic incident whereby a Dutch diplomat carrying an important secret treaty is kidnapped in London by the Nazis. The hero, aided by an English girl, fol-

lows him to Holland. The plot is further complicated by the fact
that the girl's father is a disguised Nazi agent. All ends well, of
course, with the agent killed and the young couple back in London.

The last sequence, in which the young man broadcasts to
America about the war, is Hitchcock's first contribution to the war
effort. The director, typically, does not forget to employ the best
of what the Dutch locality has to offer him (a great scene of windmills with sails rotating in the wrong direction, an escape among
the forest of umbrellas on a rainy day). He also uses an interesting (but to his dismay, generally unnoticed) technical device in the
final plane crash scene: it is all done in one shot, without a cut,
from the moment the plane is diving down until water runs into the
cockpit through the broken glass!

DR. EHRLICH'S MAGIC BULLET William Dieterle

Script: John Huston, Heinz Herald and Norman Burnside, from an
idea by the latter. Photography: James Wong Howe. Music:
Max Steiner. Cast: Edward G. Robinson (Dr. Paul Ehrlich), Ruth
Gordon (Mrs. Ehrlich), Albert Bassermann (Dr. Koch), Otto Krüger
(Dr. Emil von Behring), Donald Crisp (Minister Althoff), Maria
Ouspenskaya (Franziska Speyer), Montagu Love (Professor Hartmann),
Sig Rumann (Dr. Hans Wolfert), Donald Meek (Mittelmeyer), Henry
O'Neill (Dr. Lentz).

Warner Bros., U.S.A. 9253 ft., 103 mins.

It sometimes happens that the best film of a director becomes the
least known and the least appreciated. On the other hand, it is difficult to talk of special injustice in the response to Dr. Ehrlich's
Magic Bullet. Although Dieterle did not abandon the essence of his
previous approach to biographic cinema, nor did he contain in it
more considerable formal achievements, this story of the discoverer
of Salvarsan (an anti-syphilis drug which revolutionized therapy) is
still more ambitious than his previous work: not as a portrayal of
the protagonist against the background of the period, but as a study
of a scientist obsessed by a passion for discovery.

Perhaps because Dr. Ehrlich is the least known of the personalities whom Dieterle presented on the screen, and maybe because of the lack of distraction from subplots, the picture has a
particularly high degree of credibility, and its hero becomes a
figure especially close to the spectator and worthy of his admiration.
In the final sequences of Dr. Ehrlich's Magic Bullet the director
achieved to the highest degree that which was his aim in all his
undertakings of a similar kind: the atmosphere of fascination with

the involvement in work for the benefit of humanity.

NORTHWEST PASSAGE   King Vidor

Script: Laurence Stallings and Talbot Jennings, from the novel by
Kenneth Roberts. Photography: Sidney Wagner and William V.
Skall. Music: Herbert Stothard. Cast: Spencer Tracy (Major
Rogers), Robert Young (Langdon Towne), Walter Brennan (Hunk
Marriner), Ruth Hussey (Elizabeth Browne), Nat Pendleton ('Cap'
Huff), Louis Hector (the Rev. Browne), Robert Barrat (Humphrey
Towne), Lumsden Hare (Lord Amherst), Donald McBride (Sgt.
McNott), Isabel Jewell (Jennie Coit).

MGM, U.S.A. 11,378 ft., 126 mins. Technicolor.

Northwest Passage chronicles a dramatic episode which occurred in
1759 in the American colonies. When the Indians brutally exter-
minate white settlers, a penal detachment of Roger's Rangers is
sent to avenge their deaths. A harsh and strenuous trek through
marshland and forests, in the face of danger from both the Indians
and the French, ends with the massacre of the Indians at St. Francis. A weary and famished remnant of the expedition force returns
home.

      The concept of Vidor's picture, according to the classic re-
cipe of The Iron Horse, was to show the inner transformation of an
individual in the face of exceptional, dramatic events. The director
chronicled the expedition with vividness and veracity, but also with
an excessively bare realism, which sometimes seems to have become an end in itself. On the other hand, in describing the world
where the wounded are left behind and the survivors drink hard,
this is a lesser fault than sentimentality would have been. Although
the dialogue of Northwest Passage is flat in places, this does not
detract from the character of the film which, in addition, is one of
the outstanding examples of early color photography.

MAJOR BARBARA   Gabriel Pascal

Script: George Bernard Shaw, from his own play. Photography: Ronald
Neame. Costumes: Cecil Beaton. Music: William Walton. Cast:
Wendy Hiller (Major Barbara), Rex Harrison (Adolphus Cusins),
Robert Morley (Undershaft), Robert Newton (Bill Walker), Sybil

Thorndyke (The General), David Tree (Charles Lomax), Penelope
Dudley-Ward (Sarah Undershaft), Marie Lohr (Lady Britomart Undershaft), Emlyn Williams (Snobby Price), Deborah Kerr (Jenny Hill).

Pascal Film Productions, G.B.   10, 886 ft., 121 mins.

It is hardly surprising that the second successful screen adaptation
of a George Bernard Shaw play was undertaken by the Hungarian-
born Gabriel Pascal, the man who earlier had produced with great
success the first--Pygmalion.   Admittedly, "Major Barbara" is
easier to transfer to the screen: this story of an armaments tycoon's daughter--who is a major in the Salvation Army and falls in
love with a young professor of Greek--is a good deal more dynamic
and less dependent on dialogue than "Pygmalion."   Before the film
was made the play had a fantastic success on the English stage (six
revivals in London alone) and Pascal should have considered himself lucky to be able to reuse the outstanding theatrical actors.
Apart from being safe sailing such a practice usually makes a film
more popular with the public.

    The director's approach to the text was scrupulous and full
of respect, yet cuts in the dialogue were made where required.   As
a result Major Barbara is a competent film of a charming utopian
play.   Of additional interest is the well-photographed near-documentary portrayal of prewar London, particularly the East End where
most of the story is set.

THE PHILADELPHIA STORY   George Cukor

Script: Donald Ogden Stewart, from the play by Philip Barry.
Photography: Joseph Ruttenberg. Music: Franz Waxman. Cast:
Cary Grant (Dexter Haven), Katharine Hepburn (Tracy Lord), James
Stewart (Mike Connor), Ruth Hussey (Liz Imbrie), John Howard
(George Kittredge), Roland Young (Uncle Willie), John Halliday
(Seth Lord), Virginia Weidler (Dinah Lord), Mary Nash (Margaret
Lord), Henry Daniell (Sidney Kidd), Lionel Pape (Edward), Rex
Evans (Thomas), Russ Clark (John).

MGM, U.S.A.   10, 087 ft., 112 mins.

A sparkling stage play which became a successful screen comedy,
more--a Hollywood classic.   This is an achievement in itself and
is due primarily to Donald Ogden Stewart's most skillful script,
which gives the witty--if empty--intrigue high polish and good pace.
The Philadelphia Story chronicles the hours preceding the second
marriage of a rich society woman.   Tracy Lord is going to marry

a dull wealthy man. The preparations for the wedding are rather
complicated by the arrival of her first husband (Cary Grant) and a
social gossip reporter (James Stewart) who, with a woman photographer, is assigned to the event. Through Stewart's machinations
the wedding is finally cancelled.

The main strength of the picture is the competent acting:
Katharine Hepburn repeated her Broadway performance and James
Stewart won an Oscar for his part. It is curious that only a year
earlier Hepburn had been named as a fatal box-office risk by theatre owners. Although much of its one-time appeal has evaporated
from The Philadelphia Story, the film survives as, among other
things, a memory of a bygone glamorous world.

GASLIGHT   Thorold Dickinson

Script: A. R. Rawlinson and Briget Boland, from the play, "Angel
Street," by Patrick Hamilton. Photography: Bernard Knowles.
Music: Richard Addinsell. Cast: Anton Walbrook (Paul Mallen),
Diana Wynyard (Bella Mallen), Cathleen Cordell (Nancy), Robert
Newton (Ullswater), Frank Pettingell (Rough), Jimmy Hanley (Cobb),
Minnie Raynor (Elizabeth), Mary Hinton (Lady Winterbourne), Marie
Wright (Alice Barlow), Jack Barty (Chairman of Music Hall),
Aubrey Dexter (House agent), Angus Morrison (Pianist).

British National, G.B.   7983 ft., 88 mins.

The British prototype of film noir: a psychological thriller set in
Queen Victoria's reign. A notorious murder is committed in a
house in a fashionable part of London, but neither the killer, who
ransacked the house, nor the police can find the famous rubies belonging to the victim. Fifteen years later a happy couple move into
the house. Happy, that is, until the husband slowly but systematical-
ly makes his wife believe she is going mad....

The London of 1880, shown through the prism of sentiment
for the good old days, appears on the screen as a city of top-hatted
police, music halls with comic songs and can-can dancing and servants praying with their masters before a meal; on this correctly
and charmingly shown background, Dickinson built a suggestive atmosphere. But most of his attention went toward ensuring the psychological credibility of the complex relationship of the couple, and
the graduation of tension; for this reason the film was shot--on a
genuine multi-room set--in chronological order of scenes.

But the director, despite his narrative skill, did not achieve
a perfect result; the tradition of film noir was not yet developed and

in its absence Dickinson did not equip Gaslight with the harrowing, haunting quality of a nightmare.   Partial responsibility may always be vested in the actors and perhaps not without reason: Diana Wynward is too pliable and disoriented and Anton Walbrook not intense enough.   The result is only an interesting period melodrama.   The aura of glamor which surrounds Gaslight is not only a reflection of its true quality; it also comes from such things as the subsequent box-office success and dramatic circumstances that surrounded the film a few years later.

When the American producers decided in 1944 to make another screen adaptation of the play by Hamilton, reissues of Dickinson's original were stopped and attempts made to destroy the negative and all existing prints.   A similar fate was earlier designed for Pépé le Moko, fortunately in both cases without success.

1941

CITIZEN KANE   Orson Welles

Script: Herman J. Mankiewicz. Photography: Gregg Toland.
Music: Bernard Herrmann. Art Direction: Van Nest Polglase and
Perry Ferguson. Editing: Robert Wise and Mark Robson. Cast:
Orson Welles (Charles Foster Kane), Dorothy Comingore (Susan
Alexander Kane), Joseph Cotten (Jedediah Leland), Everett Sloane
(Mr. Bernstein), George Coulouris (Walter Parks Thatcher), Ray
Collins (James W. Gettys), Ruth Warrick (Emily Norton Kane),
Erskine Sanford (Carter), William Alland (Thompson, the butler/
Newsreel narrator), Agnes Moorehead (Kane's mother), Richard
Baer (Hillman), Paul Stewart (Raymond, Kane's butler), Fortunio
Bonanova (Matiste, singing master), Joan Blair (Georgia), Buddy
Swann (Kane as a child), Harry Shannon (Kane's father), Sonny Bupp
(Kane III).

RKO Radio Pictures, U.S.A.   10,750 ft., 119 mins.   16 secs.

A vast, gargantuan fresco, an unequalled analysis of American
dreams, a seethingly dynamic work of the screen cutting across
styles and conventions. The film tells the life story of a newspaper
potentate, Charles Foster Kane. This fictitious character was given
features common to the leading American capitalists and was so
closely based on the life of William Randolph Hearst that it was
nearly barred from the screen. The controversy which preceded
the premiere lasted for several months, but in the end Welles was
victorious, both through his determined opposition to Hearst's
schemes and through his strong position in the world of cinema.

    Before making Citizen Kane, which brought him acclaim as
a genius, Welles was already a rising star: he had had much success as a theatrical actor and director, ran his own Mercury Thea-

tre Company and in 1938 was responsible for the most famous pro-
duction in the history of broadcasting--the adaptation of H. G. Wells'
"The War of the Worlds." This realistic unannounced report of a
Martian invasion of Earth caused a public panic in the Eastern
States. Welles' first venture into film was the semi-amateur Too
Much Johnson (1938), meant to be shown in conjunction with a stage
play, but never released.

He embarked on a professional career in the cinema in 1939,
his reputation allowing him to get an extremely advantageous contract from RKO, a company in grave financial difficulties.
Welles was given unlimited creative freedom. At first he wanted to
adapt Conrad's "The Heart of Darkness," telling it in the first person: the camera would be identified with the hero. Both this project, and another for making a film of a banal thriller, "Smiler with
a Knife," were shelved--fortunately, as they gave way to one of
cinema's most brilliant works.

Citizen Kane is based on the script by Mankiewicz originally
called "American" into which Welles introduced only very slight
changes. However, his characteristic flamboyance and desire to
make a personal, exclusive film led him to add his name as a
scriptwriter. Ironically, it would be in this capacity that he would
win the only Academy Award in his career.

Charles Foster Kane dies in the loneliness of his grandiose
residence, Xanadu; his dying word is "rosebud." What does "rosebud" mean? A reporter is assigned to investigate the mystery and
interviews the people closest to the deceased: the editor of one of
his newspapers; its former theatre critic, Kane's friend; Kane's
estranged second wife, and finally his butler. Their subjective
stories form the structural skeleton of the film and assemble themselves into a portrait of the dead publisher. Now the audience can
take an active part in the creative process, comparing different
statements and images. Significantly, the jigsaw is a symbol which
recurs throughout the film and clearly symbolizes the tortuous in-
quest undertaken by the reporter.

Welles thus completely broke with the established concepts
of psychological drama whereby action is just shown to the spectator.
Here there is no chronology of action: time becomes plastic. It
can be stopped, speeded up, reversed. Absolute time is dead: it
was killed in science by Einstein, in literature by Proust and Joyce,
and in the cinema by Citizen Kane. This is a drama of loneliness,
its central problem is the impossibility of interhuman communication, a constant motif of contemporary art. The reporter will never
learn what Kane's dying word meant. The interior of man is un-
fathomable, his real passions hidden. The mystery will only be un-
veiled in the finale by the objective witness of the drama, the film
camera, and those who want to penetrate the inner life of others
are shown--at the beginning and at the end of the film--the notice
on the gate of Xanadu: "NO TRESPASSING."

Citizen Kane, which was intended by its author to be a wonder of cinematic technique, consists in great part of elements which were thus far considered irreconcilable, logically contradictory and anticinematic. Welles did not care about aesthetic correctness, and overturned the sacred principles of the cinematic language with dilettantish abandon; from the arsenal of means of cinematic expression he picked only the elements he needed. He is a great codifier rather than an innovator of the type of Griffith or Eisenstein, but all the same he introduced a host of new ideas into cinema.

This applies in the first place to the deep-focus technique--the simultaneous staging of the action on several planes of the same frame. This technique enriches the dramatic content of the frame, stressing the ambivalence of human actions and the complexity of fate. The classic is the scene from Kane's childhood staged simultaneously on three planes: furthermost from the camera Kane is seen sledding; nearer, his father is immersed in uneasy thought; while closest to the camera is his mother talking to the visitors.

This manner of visual representation of situations required the use of special optics. In coping with technical problems Gregg Toland was a windfall for Welles: he used specially coated 24 mm lenses stopped down to f:8 and equipped with additional irises. The effect is a high-contrast, crystal-sharp photography with all objects in focus regardless of their distance from the camera. This in turn required tremendously intensive lighting and the use of ultra-fast super-XX film, and entailed such problems as the necessity to equip the sets with ceilings (in view of the wide angle of the camera vision). This was also exploited as a dramatic device; an appropriate choice of camera position gives in some scenes the feeling of the protagonists being overwhelmed, in others it monumentalizes them; the latter device is incidentally one of the principal stylistic effects in the film.

A great part in giving the movie its remarkable suggestiveness and force of expression was played by Toland's camera work: long tracking and panning shots and choice of angle suspend the film in a peculiar space-time precipice and give it an incomparable feeling of moving through a labyrinth. It is complemented by the deformation of the image and monumentalization of the soundtrack, both also novel effects. Many means of expression which Welles took in fact from the cinema past give the impression of being brand new--either because of their use in an unusual context, or because of their having fallen into disuse during the 30's. For instance, Welles resurrects dissolves and fade-outs, fast, nervous editing, symbolic detail.

Editing is in many instances trivial, cocquetish and tries à la Welles to impress at all costs--but is often wonderfully innovatory. Take the editing "on the soundtrack": 13 years pass between two parts of the same sentence in which Thatcher wishes Kane, "Merry Christmas ... and a Happy New Year." Another example

is the amusing portrayal of the growing estrangement of Kane and
his first wife: a series of breakfast scenes, the lapse of time between which is revealed by the different but always fashionable
clothes, is punctuated by dissolves, but joined together by the seemingly continuous conversation which becomes more and more sparing
and finally ceases....

Last but not least--the acting. The whole cast is excellent,
but Welles, with his brilliant portrayal of the title character from
youth until old age, once and for all established himself as one of
cinema's most distinguished actors. The grandiose and eclectic
style of Citizen Kane is also extremely varied: the elegiac, slow
opening sequence is followed by the noisy "News of the March"
newsreel (made with a hand-held camera and deliberately scratched
for "authenticity"), which is in turn followed by the lighthearted
scenes of Kane's welcome at the newspaper office after his return
from Europe.

The individual elements of Welles' work often come close to
obtrusive--though often intended--mediocrity, but taken as a whole
they are doubtless the work of a genius. "Rosebud," seemingly so
crucial to the film, was only a pretext. It clearly constitutes an
element from second-rate literature; Welles himself considers it a
cheap Freudian gimmick. Citizen Kane does not attempt to explain
the whole of a man's life with one word; on the contrary, it proves
how futile is such an attempt.

The word uttered by the dying man loses on the screen its
original material sense; re-echoed by the finale ROSEBUD becomes
a poetic symbol of the eternal anxiety of man, of the lost innocence
of childhood, the perished snows of yesteryear.

US KIDS (Nous les gosses)   Louis Daquin

Script: Marcel Hilero, Gaston Modot and Marcel Aymé. Photog-
raphy: Jean Bachelet. Music: Marius-François Gaillard. Cast:
Jean-Pierre Joffroy (Rozet), Georges Regnier (André), Jean Buquet
("Tom Mix"), Bernard Dayde (Doudou), Louise Carletti (Mariette),
Gilbert Gil (M. Morin), Pierre Larquey (Finot), André Brunot
(Police inspector), Émile Genevoix (Fat Charles), Raymond Bus-
sières (Gaston), Lucien Coëdel (Laurent's father).

Pathé-Cinéma, France. 8175 ft., 90 mins.; later cut to 7649 ft.,
84 mins.

The cinema of the 1940's, which generally found its fuel in the affairs of everyday life and was addressed to ordinary people, had its

roots further back than 1941. Yet Daquin's debut can doubtless be
considered the very first signal of the changes that would culminate
in Italian Neorealism. It is true, that signal originated in Paris,
not in Rome, but no wonder: in comparison with the film industries
in the other countries overwhelmed by war, the French directors
had more creative freedom.

Although working in a country officially collaborating with the
Nazis (as Vichy France was), they were not on the one hand subjected to the merciless pressures of the propaganda machine or on
the other to the reefs of censorship. All this is reflected in the
higher standard of wartime French cinema as compared with that of
other occupied countries. Louis Daquin, connected with the Resistance Movement, took advantage of the favorable circumstances: Us
Kids is not only an unassuming tale of the comradeship of schoolboys
in one of the suburbs of Paris, but also an allegory addressed to
the whole of French society; an allegory of unity in the face of ad-
versity, and one as skillfully smuggled in as it was widely understood.

When one boy breaks a huge shop window, his friends mo-
bilize their skills and ingenuity to raise the money to pay for it and
overcome all sorts of difficulties including regaining the cash after
it had been stolen. This modest film, based on a script written before the war, became a manifesto of the vitality of the French national spirit and a harbinger of the forthcoming renaissance in the
French cinema. The film owes its renown above all to its freshness, which is especially clear against the dull and confirmist background of wartime film production. Its quality transcends the level
of current topicality.

Daquin, using Renoir's prewar experience, brought genuine
scenery and simple acting to the screen, and threw in the additional
attractions of proletarian humor and ingenious execution. The excellent use of the cleverly devised plot, dynamic acting, brisk and
laconically conducted intrigue and the natural presentation of the
children's world make one disregard the occasional situational stereo-
types.

THE MALTESE FALCON   John Huston

Script: Huston, from the novel by Dashiell Hammett. Photography:
Arthur Edeson. Music: Adolph Deutsch. Cast: Humphrey Bogart
(Sam Spade), Mary Astor (Brigid O'Shaughnessy), Gladys George (Iva
Archer), Peter Lorre (Joel Cairo), Barton MacLane (Lt. Dundy),
Lee Patrick (Effie Perine), Sidney Greenstreet (Kasper Gutman),
Ward Bond (Det. Polhaus), Jerome Cowan (Archer), Elisha Cook Jr.
(Wilmer Cook), Murray Alper (Frank Richman).

Warner Bros., U.S.A.   9037 ft., 100 mins.

A significant date in American cinema history: an adaptation of
one of the most famous books of American literature noir opens the
era of the black thriller. The Maltese Falcon had actually been
made into a film twice before, in 1931 and 1936; but it was only
Huston, a beginner director and later a master of stories of adventure, who gave the story this characteristic disturbing climate of
the border between dream and reality. While doing so Huston did
not resort to cheap effects: he used simple narrative and succinct
and clever dialogue, and brought out the mood by excellent stressing
of the visual appeal of dusky interiors.

Most of the features that were to characterize the genre are
already present in Huston's film: ambivalence of attitudes and actions, exclusion of the police from participation in the mainstream
of events, not always referring to them in a complimentary way,
situational innuendoes, and the final futility of the ruthless pursuit
of a goal. It is only the psychoanalytical motivation, later so typical of American thrillers, which is missing. It would in fact be
an alien intrusion here, since the motor of the plot is almost exclusively primitive emotion in which greed, the frenzy to possess,
is dominant.

This destructive power overcomes not only the rivals for the
ownership of a legendary figure of a Maltese falcon, but also the
private eye (portrayed by Bogart) somewhat accidentally entangled
in the intrigue. In his final decision to bring the crime to light,
his sense of justice and solidarity with his murdered colleague is of
as much importance as the logic of efficient action and also the fact
that $1000 is too low a price for a conscience.

Spade is employed by a mysterious woman to elucidate a
man's disappearance. Soon enough he discovers her connections
with an international gang involved in the pursuit of a jewel-studded
falcon statuette. He gets involved in their internal rivalries, solves
two murders and finally gets hold of the falcon. In vain, for the
treasure is a fake and the woman whom Spade loves turns out to be
the villain.

The appearance on the screen of a story which so radically
does without the goodies-baddies characterization of the protagonists,
which presents brutal strength as the only valid argument, and
whose action takes place outside the domain of establishment law is
important in another context: The Maltese Falcon is practically the
first decisive attempt at breaking through the official Hollywood
"morality code" that had been in force for some years. The gangster cinema, whose heyday in the 30's had practically ended with
Scarface as the result of the offensive on the part of the guardians
of morals and loyalty, was here resurrected and given a new character and meaning.

Instead of a reflection of reality on the screen we now have
fictional elements, the mentality and motivation of characters become more complex and are not, as before, mere variations on a
certain pattern of psychologies; literal observation is replaced by an
atmosphere of restlessness which evades the senses. These new
elements are in many cases used only to impress the audience with
abstract mystery, but not always: the sublime kind of film noir
does offer its own vision of man, one which interestingly compares
with the moods lying at the roots of Existentialism.

SULLIVAN'S TRAVELS   Preston Sturges

Script: Sturges. Photography: John Seitz. Music: Leo Shuken
and Charles Bradshaw.   Cast: Joel McCrea (John L. Sullivan),
Veronica Lake (The Girl), Robert Warwick (Mr. LeBrand), William
Demarest (Mr. Jones), Franklin Pangborn (Mr. Casalsis), Porter
Hall (Mr. Hadrian), Byron Foulger (Mr. Valdelle), Margaret Hayes
(Secretary), Torben Meyer (Doctor), Robert Greig (Sullivan's but-
ler), Eric Blore (Sullivan's valet).

Paramount Pictures, U.S.A.   8202 ft., 91 mins.

An original and ambitious film by Sturges, one of the leading writer-
directors of American cinema; a blend of banal comedy and of an
unexpectedly serious look at the America of the underprivileged.
A successful director of screen musical comedies wants to make
films about poverty and, despite protests from the producers, leaves
for a journey through America to research the subject in disguise.
Twice, because of a girl and because of illness, he is forced to reveal his true identity. It is only the third time that he is lucky.
But not quite: while distributing money to the hobos on the railway
siding he is attacked, robbed and left unconscious in an empty carriage. His attacker is killed by a steam engine, and the police,
thinking the body is Sullivan's accuse the poor man of murdering
himself. He is sentenced, but gets off in the end--and loses interest in the poor.

The controversial, but bitterly sensible conclusion of the
film is that escapist entertainment is needed after all as a defense
against the dreariness of everyday life. Thus Sturges supplemented
in a way the cinema of Frank Capra, making his films into social
parables and moving among similar rags-to-riches situations. For
instance in the director's debut, The Great McGinty (1940), a tramp
rises to become a governor; also Sullivan in Sullivan's Travels is
suddenly transplanted into a completely new social environment.

Many of Sturges's ideas about poverty are worn-out clichés,

which gives the film a double edge since it discloses Hollywood's real ignorance of social conditions. But Sturges did not assume the patronizing attitude of an absolving padre; he was bitter, ironic and here opened the door, behind which lie rather unpleasant facts of life, a bit wider.

THE MURDER OF FATHER CHRISTMAS L'Assassinat du Père Noël)
   Christian-Jaque

Script: Charles Spaak, from a novel by Pierre Véry. Photography: Armand Thirard. Music: Henri Verdun. Cast: Harry Baur (Cornusse), Raymond Rouleau (The Baron), Renée Faure (Catherine), Marie-Hélène Dasté (Mother Michel), Robert Le Vignan (Villard), Jean Brochard (Ricomet), Jean Parédès (Kappel), Fernand Ledoux (Mayor), Héléna Manson (Marie Coquillot).

Continental-Films, France. 9439 ft., 105 mins.

A fairy-tale romantic thriller set in a mountain village covered with Christmas snow. An old map-maker, who has a beautiful daughter, tours the village every Christmas Eve dressed as Father Christmas. A Baron, who loves the daughter, makes the map-maker drunk and borrows his costume. And later an unknown body is found dressed as Father Christmas in a local church, and a famous diamond is missing. ....

Fantasy and witty observation of customs, a poetic look at the world of children and horror drama: Christian-Jaque uses a similar style to that of Les Disparus de Saint-Agil, although this time he did not start from reality filtered through the imagination of his protagonists, but consciously obliterated the borderline between the real and the imaginary worlds. Further, he considerably enlarged the palette of the means of expression with inventive direction, interesting reminiscences from the past achievements of French cinema (the notable scene in the inn), and remarkable photography, especially of the night winter landscapes.

THE LITTLE FOXES William Wyler

Script: Lillian Hellman, from her play. Photography: Gregg Toland. Music: Meredith Wilson. Cast: Bette Davis (Regina Giddens), Herbert Marshall (Horace Giddens), Teresa Wright (Alexandra

Giddens), Richard Carlson (David Hewitt), Patricia Collinge (Birdie Hubbard), Dan Duryea (Leo Hubbard), Charles Dingle (Ben Hubbard), Carl Benton Reid (Oscar Hubbard), Jessie Grayson (Addie).

RKO Radio Pictures/Samuel Goldwyn Productions, U.S.A.   10,408 ft., 116 mins.

"Take us the foxes, the little foxes that spoil the vines: for our vines have tender grapes." The little foxes from the Song of Solomon are the four members of a monstrously greedy Southern family: Regina and her brothers Ben and Oscar are determined to get money for the profitable purchase of a cotton mill by hook or by crook. They "borrow" Regina's husband's bank securities; when he discovers the theft Regina deliberately causes his death. The play, a great Broadway hit, while unhesitant in baring human foibles and weaknesses, tends to be somewhat mechanically macabre and on film was itself a setback for Wyler. The literary basis of the film quite simply lacks the touch of humanism, that tinge of understanding which separates dramatic proficiency from true art.

But to do the director justice, he made the most of it: the play with little plot was transformed into a psychological study of a woman's ravenous greed, of corruption and complicity. It is notable rather for smooth direction and technical expertise than depth. Toland's camera hovers above characters' heads, follows them in their somber mansion, uncovers furtive facial expressions and latent smiles. The main element of pictorial composition is the huge mahogany staircase, a pointless, wordless symbol of "broken American dreams." The film is a powerful evocation of the dense, claustrophobic atmosphere of avarice and vengeance.

Bette Davis gives a celebrated performance but rather more harrowingly frightening than profound. The inquisitive, truth-searching quality of Dead End is lost and The Little Foxes is merely an impressive O'Neill-ian drama plus an unnecessary romantic plot plus some scenes of real power. One of such moments is the finale: Regina's daughter, the only person she cares for, defiantly leaves her with the sudden realization of her wickedness.

SERGEANT YORK   Howard Hawks

Script: Abem Finkel, Harry Chandlee, Howard Koch and John Huston, from "War Diary of Sergeant York," edited by Sam K. Cowan, "Sergeant York and His People," by Cowan, and "Sergeant York--Last of the Long Hunters," by Tom Skeyhill. Photography: Sol Polito and Arthur Edeson (war sequences). Music: Max Steiner. Cast: Gary Cooper (Alvin C. York), Walter Brennan (Pastor Rosier

Pile), Joan Leslie (Gracie Williams), George Tobias ("Pusher" Rose), Stanley Ridges (Major Buxton), Margaret Wycherley (Mother York), Ward Bond (Ike Botkin), Noah Berry Jr. (Buck Lipscomb), June Lockhart (Rosie York), Dickie Moore (George York), Clem Bevans (Zeke).

Warner Bros., U.S.A.　12,055 ft., 134 mins.

One of the partial successes of Hawks' cinema: the story of the great career of a simple, ambitious Tennessee boy striving for the rural bliss of buying a piece of land and marrying his beloved. It is ostensibly based on the life of a real person, but we must not treat this genealogy too seriously. For York is a mixture of a true, commonsense American and a naive idealist and so is Sergeant York--a mixture of two different films, a clash of two conventions. The first part is a brilliantly photographed, endearing portrayal of rural life in the South and its simple joys (without a single Negro in sight) with well-drawn and psychologically finely developed characters. The affection between York and his mother is particularly touching.

Later when York goes to war and becomes a national hero, the film loses its balance and pace; its excessive patriotism now seems humorous, but it was doubtless justified as necessary propaganda in the days of Pearl Harbor. The photography deteriorates and comes to rely on back projection. It is only Gary Cooper who comes out of it victorious and cements the film. His convincing, warmly prepossessing portrayal of York brought him his first Academy Award.

HOW GREEN WAS MY VALLEY　John Ford

Script: Philip Dunne, from the novel by Richard Llewellyn. Photography: Arthur Miller. Music: Alfred Newman. Cast: Walter Pidgeon (Mr. Gruffydd), Maureen O'Hara (Angharad Morgan), Donald Crisp (Mr. Morgan), Anna Lee (Bronwen Morgan), Roddy McDowall (Huw Morgan), John Loder (Ianto Morgan), Sara Allgood (Mrs. Beth Morgan), Barry Fitzgerald (Cyfartha), Patrick Knowles (Ivor Morgan), Ann Todd (Ceiwen), Richard Fraser (Davy Morgan), James Monks (Owen Morgan).

20th Century-Fox, U.S.A.　10,654 ft., 118 mins.　Technicolor.

How Green Was My Valley is the story of a collapse of a way of life. The picture is narrated in flashback, as the boyhood memories of Huw Morgan, the youngest of six children of a family living in a

mining village in a South Wales valley. The story is set at the
turn of the century and begins when Huw is 12 and the valley is
beautiful and green. The happiness of the mining community is
slowly eroded by the greed of the mine owners and the resulting
disputes. Huw's father disagrees with his four sons about the
strike. They leave home and finally emigrate. The daughter, who
loves the local minister, ceases to be part of the community when
she is forced to marry a mine owner's son. The father is killed
in a mining accident. The once idyllic valley is now black with
slag heaps, the inhabitants impoverished and bitter. Finally Huw
also leaves his native village.

When making the film of the famous novel, the objective
foremost in Ford's mind was fidelity to the literary material. It
was a difficult task: the book is written in a highly individual style
and has a very intimate, local character based on the author's personal experience. To boot, Ford had no firsthand knowledge of the
subject. He tried to compensate for it by extreme care in staging
and meticulous attention to detail. The value of the film resides
just in that--the careful and warm description of local customs and
way of life: the wages which are dropped into Mrs. Morgan's
spread apron as her husband and sons come back from work, the
ritual bathing in the back kitchen, the meal times, the household
with pottery plates over the mantlepiece.

Yet this fidelity to the novel does not reach further and the
film, despite a basically similar theme, is a long way from the
passionate involvement of The Grapes of Wrath. How Green Was
My Valley is Ford vanquished by the conventionality of Hollywood:
the story is mightily sentimental despite its austerity, the houses
and rooms too big and too tidy, the life of the characters difficult
but somewhat mechanically predictable. So, despite taking all his
dialogues from the novel, Ford missed its gist, and made an impressive and elegant, but basically phony film.

How Green Was My Valley was one of the bigger Hollywood
productions at the time; it cost millions and was shot on a specially
built set of an entire Rhondda Valley mining village. Although
somewhat uninvolving it is certainly pleasant to watch because of
the excellent photography and beautiful music sung by a Welsh choir.

THE SEA WOLF   Michael Curtiz

Script: Robert Rossen, from the novel by Jack London. Photography: Sol Polito. Music: Erich Wolfgang Korngold. Cast: Edward G. Robinson ("Wolf" Larsen), Ida Lupino (Ruth Webster), John
Garfield (George Leach), Alexander Knox (Humphrey Van Weyden),
Gene Lockhart (Dr. Louie Prescott), Barry Fitzgerald (Cooky), Stan-

ley Ridges (Johnson), Francis McDonald (Svenson), David Bruce (Young sailor), Howard da Silva (Harrison).

Warner Bros., U.S.A.   8979 ft., 100 mins.

An expert and very faithful adaptation--despite the abandonment of some philosophical references--of Jack London's tale about a satanic captain who exercises the rights of a dictator on his ship, the "Ghost." The film is the story of the captain's persecution of a group of people aboard: the cabin boy who is a fugitive from justice, the dypsomaniac ship's doctor and a couple who were picked up by the "Ghost" after a sea collision--a writer and a girl escapee from a reformatory.

The Sea Wolf is brilliantly done from every point of view: excellent in-depth psychological studies, an almost tangible atmosphere of terror, a world in which the basic principles of humanity have ceased to exist. Curtiz gives an impressive example of his functional studio film-making: the film was shot in specially built tanks and is technically immaculate. All available means cooperate harmoniously in creating the powerful climate. In this, the soundtrack is specially noteworthy, with its menacing natural sounds of the creaking timbers of the ship, and excellent musical score. At the head of the splendid acting team is Edward G. Robinson, who thoroughly exploits the rich possibilities of his role as the sadistic Wolf Larsen.

HORSE (Uma)   Kajiro Yamamoto

Assistant Direction: Akira Kurosawa. Script: Yamamoto. Photography: Hiromitsu Karasawa (Spring), Akira Mimura (Summer and studio), Hiroshi Suzuki (Autumn) and Takeo Ito (Winter). Music: Shigeaki Kitamura. Cast: Hideko Takamine (Ine, girl who loves the horse), Keita Fujiwara (Jinjiro, her father), Chieko Takehisa (Saku, her mother), Kaoru Futaba (Ei, her grandmother), Takeshi Hirata (Toyoichi, her younger brother), Toshio Hosoi (Kinjiro, her youngest brother), Setsuko Ichikawa (Tsuru, her younger sister), Sadao Maruyama (Mr. Yamashita, a school teacher), Sadako Sawamura (Kikuko, his wife), Yoshio Kosugi (Zenzo Sakuma, Jinjiro's friend), Tsuruko Mano (Mrs. Sakuma), Soji Kiyokawa (Mr. Sakamoto, judge of the horse market).

Toho, Japan.   11,581 ft., 129 mins.

While the realist and populist tendencies in Italian and French cinema are not surprising in the context of the early 1940's, in Japan at the peak of nationalism and militarist propaganda, <u>Horse</u> is really something extraordinary. Here a year after Pearl Harbor a pastoral, lyrical tale is told about an adolescent girl and the colt she breeds, a story of quiet family life in a poor mountain village. The narrative consists of a cycle of episodes centered around the passing of the seasons. The character of the film resembles Uchida's <u>Earth</u> and was basically as typical of the Japanese national style as it was untypical of the time it was made (the shooting of <u>Horse</u> was being prepared from 1937). The film had a certain propaganda role in exhorting the people to breed horses for army use; Kurosawa was its co-director.

The greatest assets of this semi-documentary poetic story are its careful simplicity and subtlety coupled with the beautiful presentation of nature. Much credit for the final result goes to the 17-year-old Hideko Takamine--a Japanese equivalent of Judy Garland or Natalie Wood--who radiates much of the charm which the film reflects back to the audience.

SUSPICION   Alfred Hitchcock

<u>Script</u>: Samson Raphaelson, Joan Harrison and Alma Reville, from the novel, "Before the Fact," by Francis Iles. <u>Photography</u>: Harry Stradling. <u>Music</u>: Franz Waxman. <u>Cast</u>: Cary Grant (John Aysgarth), Joan Fontaine (Lina MacKinlaw), Nigel Bruce (Beaky), Sir Cedric Hardwicke (General MacKinlaw), Dame May Whitty (Mrs. MacKinlaw), Isabel Jeans (Mrs. Newsham).

RKO Radio Pictures, U.S.A.   8928 ft., 99 mins.

The heroine of <u>Suspicion</u>, approaching the dangerous prospect of becoming an old maid, leaps into marriage when the opportunity arises. She is soon to repent when she realizes that her newly married, impulsive husband is a liar and an extravagant dandy. But is he trying to murder her as well? It would appear so--but since the film is told through the eyes of a naive loving wife, the spectator--and the heroine herself--can never be sure. It is indeed as an exercise in understatement, a portrayal of the workings of the imagination, that the film can claim success.

The picture, good-humored to start with, soon becomes a classical study of the build-up of tension: Hitchcock plays the main trump of his art. Skillful and convincing psychological strata accompany a banal and rather uninteresting story shot in technically trivial (even by Hitchcock's standards) studio sets. And yet this glossy-fashion-magazine film does have glimmers of brilliance. For example, in the scene where the husband carries a drink up

the stairs to his wife's bedside, Hitchcock puts a lighted bulb <u>inside</u>
the glass of milk. This promotes an otherwise inconspicuous object
to a magnetic center of attraction and becomes a classic of purely
visual narration. <u>Suspicion</u> was Hitchcock's second American film,
and everything in it--actors, scenery, atmosphere--was still completely English.

49TH PARALLEL   Michael Powell

Script: Rodney Ackland and Emeric Pressburger, from a story by
the latter. Photography: Frederick Young. Music: Ralph Vaughan
Williams. Cast: Richard George (Kommandant Bernsdorff), Eric
Portman (Lt. Hirth), Raymond Lovell (Lt. Kuhnecke), Niall MacGin-
nis (Vogel), Peter Moore (Kranz), John Chandos (Lohrmann), Basil
Appleby (Jahner), Laurence Olivier (Johnnie Barras), Finlay Currie
(The Factor), Anton Walbrook (Peter), Glynis Johns (Anna), Leslie
Howard (Philip Armstrong Scott), Raymond Massey (Andy Brock).

Ortus Films, G.B. 11,070 ft., 123 mins.

The first British feature film commissioned by the Ministry of Information formed in Britain after the outbreak of the war: a sensational story of a group of six German submarine crewmen sent on
a sabotage mission to the shores of America, who push their way
through Canadian territory to the still neutral U.S.A. The propaganda aspect of the film is the showing of the changes in the attitudes of the Canadians, who so far have shunned politics and now
change their position on encountering the awe-inspiring Nazis. Its
value resides in the credibility of the skillful and nonstereotyped
narrative, whose strength clearly derives from its reference to the
British documentary school which in the 30's and early 40's claimed
great triumphs: this documentary trend, led by John Grierson,
Paul Rotha, Basil Wright and later Humphrey Jennings, was the
basis of the great revival of British cinema during the war.

WESTERN UNION   Fritz Lang

Script: Robert Carson, from a novel by Zane Grey. Photography:
Edward Cronjager and Allen M. Davey. Music: David Buttolph.
Cast: Randolph Scott (Vance Shaw), Robert Young (Richard Blake),
Dean Jagger (Edward Creighton), Virginia Gilmore (Sue Creighton),
John Carradine (Doc Murdoch), Slim Summerville (Herman), Chill

Wills (Homer), Barton MacLane (Jack Slade), Russell Hicks (Governor), Victor Kilian (Charlie), Minor Watson (Pat Grogan).

20th Century-Fox, U.S.A. 8491 ft., 94 mins. Technicolor.

A classic variation on the Western theme--an episode of the settling of the West in the individualistic interpretation of Lang who, as a European, was able to give the worn-out theme a new look, a sort of freshness, and at the same time abide fully by the traditions of the idealized West. The story concerns the laying of telegraph wires from Omaha to Salt Lake City in 1861; the skeleton of the plot is the rivalry of two members of the team for the sister of Edward Creighton, the engineer who leads the pioneers. The dramatic situations are not too inventive: white bandits want to get the wires down; there are their mysterious (and inevitable) links with one of the pioneers.

What assures the place of Western Union among the classics of the genre is the tight, brisk, unrepetitious narrative, excellent use of locations (as in The Return of Frank James), and the original handling of color (the forest fire, cloud effects), although this is at times blemished by excessive showiness (the synthetic, electric-blue moonlight). The film is a very typical representative of Lang's American period: skill, competence and originality of approach to old subjects merges with a remote, enigmatic abstract quality; the director was never to succeed in repeating the passionate involvement of his German films.

1942

LES VISITEURS DU SOIR   Marcel Carné

Script: Jacques Prévert and Pierre Laroche. Photography: Roger Hubert. Art Direction: George Wakhevitch and Alexandre Trauner. Music: Maurice Thiriet and Joseph Kosma. Cast: Arletty (Dominique), Alain Cuny (Gilles), Marie Déa (Anne), Fernand Ledoux (Baron Hugues), Jules Berry (The Devil), Marcel Herrand (Renaud), Gabriel Gabrio (Hangman), Roger Blin (Monster showman), Pierre Labry (A Lord), Jean D'Yd (Bear showman).

André Paulvé, France. 8807 ft., 98 mins.

A medieval ballad about the omnipotence of love and the struggle of Satan against Good. Prévert and Carné, the two leaders of Poetic Realism, remained almost completely faithful to the philosophy of their prewar films, even in a work set in the remote 15th century. This was not entirely their choice: the majority of the creative film-makers remaining in France preferred to move into the realm of extratemporal abstract themes, in exchange for relative creative freedom.

The creators of Les Visiteurs du soir had still more reason than anyone to seek refuge in themes not directly related to reality: they were violently attacked by the collaborationist Vichy government for allegedly demoralizing the French public with their decadent Quai des Brumes and Le Jour se lève. Paradoxically, it was the very same orthodox wartime critics who sanctioned the term "Poetic Realism" and saw this movement as predominantly leftist, while Carné's school deserved in fact the name of Black Poetic Realism, and in Les Visiteurs du soir functioned equally well in the conventional climate of legend.

The dusky port towns of the earlier films give way to the
sunny Provence of 1485.   The bored Devil sends two young envoys
to earth to spread discord and sin.   Gilles and Dominique arrive at
Baron Hugues' castle during the ceremony of the betrothal of the
Baron's daughter Anne.   They start their sinister trade soon enough,
but only until Gilles' romantic love for Anne resists the power of
evil.   Irritated, the Devil himself arrives at the castle....

Carné, a sworn aesthete, gave the legend a fascinating visual
form.   The film, with its tall white-walled proud castles, has been
described as a symphony in white.   The lazy camera movements
give the feel of majesty; the shots are stable, long and usually contain a group of people; the symbols are fresh and stem organically
from the plot; technical tricks (like the resurrection of the bear) are
well done and imaginative; the soundtrack impresses with the in-
cantatory quality of the dialogue and the sad medieval songs.   In
short, the slow-moving climate of the Middle Ages has been captured perfectly: a langorous world of sleeping beauties, black and
white magic and pure feelings.

The film is one of the most outstanding of its kind; even in
the prologue, showing minstrels riding through the mountainous landscape of Haute Provence, its visual beauty is striking.   The later
scenes of the ball and the feast, modelled on medieval art, are
visually excellent, dramatically expert, well acted and make one forgive the surfeit of literary dialogue as well as a certain loss of consistency in the latter part of the film (from the Devil's arrival at
the castle).   Even if Les Visiteurs du soir is not a faultless work,
even if the director sometimes happens to be excessively precious,
we are rewarded with the purity and clarity of the images and the
psychological analysis which never loses the ring of truth.

Surprisingly, the only Carné film completed during the war
is also the most optimistic of his outstanding works: Satan does in
the end turn the lovers into stone, but even this cannot stop their
hearts beating.   This edifying finale made such a strong impression
in 1942 that it came to be generally understood as a symbol of the
invincibility of the Resistance Movement.   This was not intended by
Prevert and Carné, but shows that the inner power of some symbols does in certain situations exert a spontaneous heartening influence.

THE MAGNIFICENT AMBERSONS   Orson Welles

Script: Welles, from the novel by Booth Tarkington.   Photography:
Stanley Cortez, Harry J. Wild and Russell Metty.   Music: Bernard
Herrmann and Roy Webb.   Editing: Robert Wise and Mark Robson.
Cast: Joseph Cotten (Eugene Morgan), Dolores Costello (Isabel Minafer),

Anne Baxter (Lucy), Tim Holt (George Minafer Amberson), Agnes
Moorehead (Fanny), Ray Collins (Jack), Richard Bennett (Major Am-
berson), Erskine Sanford (Benson), J. Louis Johnson (Sam), Don
Dillaway (Wilbur Minafer), Charles Phipps (Uncle John).

RKO Radio Pictures, U.S.A.   Originally 131 mins., cut to 7940 ft.,
88 mins.

A saga of the decline and fall of a patrician American family and
the birth of a new industrial civilization; the story of how the arrogant George Minafer Amberson got his comeuppance. The Magnificent Ambersons is one of the classical cases where second-rate
literature metamorphoses on the screen into an original and powerful film. After Citizen Kane, brilliant but not entirely understood
at the time, Welles gave way to the producers' pressure to make a
more popular picture. Yet again they were in for a disappointment:
the film was too intelligent. In consequence The Magnificent Ambersons was partly re-edited, cut by over 3000 feet and given a different ending, all without Welles' approval. But in spite of all this
the inimitable Welles touch is stamped upon the film as firmly as
ever.

The weakness of the film is the story itself; indeed Booth
Tarkington contributed very little to the excellence of the film adaptation. Welles seems to have been aware of this inherent weakness
and simply delivered the commentary with tongue-in-cheek reverence;
in this and other aspects (the neo-Greek chorus of the townsfolk) the
director overrode the limitations of the literary material by giving
the film a dramatic core. The commentary, in 1942 a complete
novelty, gives the film a much more serious climate and dimension,
on one hand close to the style of Faulkner, on the other reminiscent
of Thornton Wilder's play "Our Town."

As far as the story is concerned, the salvage operation is
only partly successful, and the ballast of melodramatic plots and
lack of coherence lie heavily on the film. But this is more than
redeemed by its formal richness. The foremost formal achievement is the further development of the deep-focus technique which
substantially augments the density and intellectual ambivalence of
the work. Welles avoided editing by cutting and not only conducted
several actions simultaneously within the same take, but sometimes even within the same frame, transferring the center of attention from one part of the frame to another, a process in which
lighting plays an even greater role than acting. He also used,
probably for the first time ever, TMTs--the ten-minute-long dialogue takes in which the camera angle changes very little (but is
as always chosen with great originality).

The formal aspect of Citizen Kane was ravenously innovatory,
in spite of being mainly a powerful blend of old but often forgotten
elements. The style of The Magnificent Ambersons is much more
composed. Yet cinematic novelties were still introduced--indeed,

perhaps even more than before. Among them, apart from those already mentioned, are the dialogue, partly improvised by the actors
themselves (who, as in Citizen Kane, came from the theatre), the
application of the radio broadcasting technique used to create a sort
of synthetic dialogue from scraps of different conversations, and the
new way of sound editing which uses the music functionally.

One is entitled to expect that a Welles unfettered by financial
considerations might far surpass the frontiers of contemporary cinema in his further works. Unfortunately, The Magnificent Ambersons, an ironic reflection on the senselessness of human pride, suffered a financial defeat. Its author lost the trust of producers; his
next genuinely personal film would be made--under quite different
conditions--only after another five years.

OSSESSIONE   Luchino Visconti

Script: Mario Alicata, Antonio Pietrangeli, Gianni Puccini, Giusep-
pe De Santis and Visconti, from the novel, "The Postman Always
Rings Twice," by James Cain. Photography: Aldo Tonti and Do-
menico Scala. Music: Giuseppe Rosati. Cast: Clara Calamai
(Giovanna), Massimo Girotti (Gino), Juan de Landa (The Husband),
Elia Marcuzzo (Lo Spagnuolo), Dhia Cristani (Anita), Vittorio Duse
(Lorry driver), Michele Riccardini, Michele Sakara.

ICI Roma, Italy. 135 mins.

Ossessione marked the distinguished debut of an uneasy member of
a Milanese princely family who picked up film-making experience
at Renoir's side and who would later become one of the most distinguished personalities in the Italian theatre and cinema. Ossessione is a story of passion, crime and punishment based in outline
on the American thriller but transplanted into a strictly Italian environment. Giovanna, an innkeeper's wife, falls in live with Gino,
a vagabond they employ as an assistant. The lovers murder the
husband in a fake car crash. Remorse and fear breed antagonism
and mutual suspicion between the couple; finally Gino leaves. Reconciliation comes when Giovanna tells him she is expecting a child.
Their happiness is not to last: she dies in a car crash and the
police arrest Gino for double murder.

The premiere of Ossessione was a landmark in Italian cinema. For the first time the real life of the country appeared on
the screen, the life of conflict-torn people from the provincial
towns and wide open spaces of northern Italy. As with the slightly
earlier, but much milder and more traditional Four Steps in the
Clouds, Visconti's film would later acquire the reputation of being

the first masterpiece of Neorealism. It deserves such a description without a doubt but this does not mean that all the merit of the film lies in its contribution to one of the most important stylistic trends in the cinema. The tangible reality of everyday life is here placed in the background and not in the center of the drama.

The climate of the story if very strongly related to naturalism and to the French Poetic Realism, which was as a matter of fact stressed with distaste by the official critics after the film's premiere. There are also strong links with Dostoyevsky, in whose circle of existential themes Visconti always moved. Ossessione is primarily interested in making psychological, rather than social discoveries. Of course, real characters can be created more easily than authentic scenery--and this is the reason for the creative method Visconti used in Ossessione: his intentions are simply different from those of the directors of other classics of Neorealism.

Visconti's principal aim was not to reflect reality populated by real people, but to convey a behavioristic observation of an individual immersed in the stream of life. So, Ossessione, a unique film from the crossroads of different styles and trends, has a status superior to that of other early Neorealist works. Its merit is the transplantation of the Renoirian anthropomorphic tendencies onto this movement and the enrichment of the Italian cinema by attracting its attention to the interior of the human being.

THE ROAD TO HEAVEN (Himlaspelet) Alf Sjöberg

Script: Sjöberg and Rune Lindström, from the play by the latter. Photography: Gösta Roosling. Music: Lillebror Söderlundh. Cast: Rune Lindström (Mats Ersson), Eivor Landström (Marit Knutsdotter), Gudrun Brost (Solomon's wench), Anders Henrikson (Good Father), Arnold Sjöstrand (Rood painter), Holger Löwenadler (Solomon), Emil Fjellström (Gammel-Jerk), Björn Berglund (Josef), Inga-Lilly Forsström (Maria), Anita Björk (Anna).

Wivefilm, Sweden. 9500 ft., 106 mins.

A stylized folk legend about the human condition. A country lad, Mats, despairing after the tragic loss of his beloved, wanders in search of Heaven. Instead of God he meets the Devil in his quest, who takes advantage of his weaknesses and pushes him towards perdition. After death the roaming hero is summoned by the Creator to a paradise meadow which appears to coexist in a fourth dimension with earthly reality. Mats spent his youth on the same meadow and his cottage stands nearby. Similarly, God and the Devil exist in the real as well as in the supernatural dimension:

God appears as a benign, well-dressed old gentleman in a top hat.

The visual form of this morality play is based directly on the naive popular beliefs of peasants, and its spiritual climate is entirely contained within traditional Scandinavian Protestant attitudes. It is one of the cinema's very few excursions into the realm of instinctive, naive faith. All by the grace of God: this is the message of the play, written by a young theology student, which Sjöberg transferred to the screen with its author in the main role. In parts the result draws too close to conventional melodrama, but the director's main achievement lies somewhere else: in giving the film an exceptional visual form which counts among the best in the cinema of the 40's, and which refers directly to folklore and to Sjöström's and Stiller's silent films.

With its volatile photography, finely chiseled contrasts, skill in taking advantage of the potentialities of the landscapes, The Road to Heaven signifies the spiritual rebirth of the Swedish cinema and its return to importance in European film.

IN WHICH WE SERVE   Noël Coward and David Lean

Script: Coward. Photography: Ronald Neame. Music: Coward. Cast: Noël Coward (Captain Edward Kinross), John Mills (O/S "Shorty" Blake), Bernard Miles (C. P. O. Walter Hardy), Celia Johnson (Mrs. Alix Kinross), Joyce Carey (Mrs. Hardy), Kay Walsh (Freda Lewis), Derek Elphinstone (Number One).

Two Cities Films (Noël Coward), G.B. 10,295 ft., 114 mins.

Great Britain at war: although the struggle would never move onto the island itself, its reality--as Coward and Lean's film relates--could be felt at every step. The story of the fight of the crew of the destroyer "Torrin" against the (almost unseen) Nazi air force and navy was based on the recollections of the captain and his men. "This is the story of a ship" declares the commentary and onto the odyssey of shipwrecked men clinging to a life raft, Coward interposed retrospections of their lives--service in the Navy, home leave, marriages, partings.

In Which We Serve, one of the earliest of the series of British war films which included The Way to the Stars, San Demetrio, London and The Way Ahead, is the best and probably the most characteristic of all with its tone of serious concentration, simplicity, lack of overt jingoistic sentiments, and, above all, authenticity in the paradocumentary narrative. This is all the more remarkable since Coward, the instigator and scenarist of the film, was in his prewar interests very remote not only from the cinema but also from real life. This comedy playwright and theatrical actor felt best among the so-called intellectual themes and smart, sparkling dialogue.

Traces of Coward's old style can still be felt here in the complicated, polished narrative structure and, unfortunately, in the heavy weight of his unavoidably patronizing attitude to the lower social orders. But the rest is really typical of the sentiments in wartime England and it does catch the spirit of marine warfare just as, for example, the American Action in the North Atlantic.

THE OX-BOW INCIDENT (Strange Incident) William A. Wellman

Script: Lamar Trotti, from the novel by Walter Van Tilburg Clark. Photography: Arthur Miller. Music: Cyril J. Mockridge. Cast: Henry Fonda (Gil Carter), Dana Andrews (Martin), Mary Beth Hughes (Rose Mapen), Anthony Quinn (Mexican), Marc Lawrence (Rev. Farnley), William Eythe (Gerald), Henry Morgan (Art Croft), Jane Darwell (Ma Grier), Matt Briggs (Judge Tyler), Harry Davenport (Arthur Davies), Frank Conroy (Major Tetley).

20th Century-Fox, U.S.A. 6772 ft., 75 mins.

A condemnation of lynch law in a western which thematically far exceeds the mores of the genre, at least as they were in the 40's. The Ox-Bow Incident is an account of how in 1885 in Nevada three innocent men were hanged as supposed rustlers and murderers by a group of 28 "decent citizens" led by a sadistic ex-major and a ruthless harridan. The essence of The Ox-Bow Incident would be found in a similar context only very much later in the films of Arthur Penn (for instance in The Chase): moral anxiety stemming from awareness of the existence in the submerged streams of American life of the very same dark forces which in their European mutation organized themselves in the form of Fascism.

Wellman, who had earlier bared his critical claws with Public Enemy, A Star Is Born (1937) and Nothing Sacred (1937), developed the theme with the consistency of a moral treatise-- nothing was simplified, nothing conceded for the sake of formal appeal. The style of the narrative was strictly regulated by the requirements of the argument. Static scenes and dialogue dominate, yet the style of directing is never too close to the theatrical: even the presence of painted backdrops does not invalidate the authentic, pensive concentration.

The precise analysis of the behavior, the credibility of wide-

ly varied psychological characterization, the suggestive mood and
natural style of acting combine to produce a convincing picture both
from the aesthetic and the moral point of view. The Ox-Box Incident is among the most intelligent and original achievements of the
American cinema of the period.

I MARRIED A WITCH René Clair

Script: Robert Pirosh and Marc Connelly, from the novel, "The
Passionate Witch," by Thorne Smith and Norman Matson. Photog-
raphy: Ted Tetzlaff. Music: Roy Webb. Cast: Veronica Lake
(Jennifer), Fredric March (Wallace Wooley), Susan Hayward (Estelle
Masterson), Cecil Kellaway (Daniel), Robert Benchley (Dudley White),
Elizabeth Patterson (Margaret), Robert Warrick (J. B. Masterson),
Eily Malyon (Tabitha), Viola Moore (Martha), Mary Field (Nancy),
Nora Cecil (Harriet).

Paramount, U.S.A. 6800 ft., 76 mins.

During the seven years which passed after making The Ghost Goes
West, Clair did not score a single success. Air pur--a shot-on-
location film about the summer holidays of boys from the poor dis-
tricts of Paris--could have become something novel in the director's
oeuvre but was not finished because of the outbreak of the war.
The Flame of New Orleans (1941), Clair's first Hollywood production
after moving to the U.S.A. badly misfired. It was only to be a return to the world of ghosts and fantastic comedy that would stimulate the maker of The Italian Straw Hat to regain his sometime brilliance.

      This time the ghost is rather appealing since it materializes
as Veronica Lake. The unfortunate witch, played by one of the
principal platinum blondes of the screen, was burned at the stake
in the 17th century and plays the role of the executor of the curse
cast on the descendants of her denouncer--and in her free time assumes the form of smoke and inhabits a bottle. Clair excellently
exploited the capabilities offered by the script.

      Dancing in the footsteps of Méliès's wonders of cinema, he
used a richness of tricks; interlaced the real and fantastic world into a closely-knit whole; employed sound splendidly; charmed with
the number and pace of the gags, and did not miss a chance to sa-
tirize the realities of provincial life in America. For the first
time in many years he also returned to a lyricism close to that of
Chaplin. The whole qualifies 100 per cent, of course, as "papa's
cinema," which was so knocked about later by the young generation
of French directors; but how appealing it is here!

GOUPI MAINS ROUGES   Jacques Becker

Script: Pierre Véry, from his novel. Photography: Pierre Monta-
zel. Music: Jean Alfaro. Cast: Fernand Ledoux (Goupi Mains
Rouges), Georges Rollin (Goupi Monsieur), Blanchette Brunoy
(Goupi Muguet), Line Noro (Marie des Goupi), Robert Le Vigan
(Goupi Tonkin), Maurice Schutz (Goupi l'Empereur), Germaine Ker-
jean (Goupi Tisane), Arthur Devère (Goupi Mes Sous), René Génin
(Goupi Dicton), Guy Favières (Goupi la Loi), Marcelle Haina (Goupi
Cancan), Albert Rémy (Jean, the domestic).

Films Minerva, France. 8550 ft., 95 mins.

The year 1943 was for the French cinema above all the year of the
success of new creative individuals. This was a mere coincidence,
as Clouzot, Autant-Lara, Bresson and Becker did not set out any
common program. On the contrary, each of them was a more or
less independent director. They were all of a similar generation,
and almost middle-aged--perhaps a significant fact in analyzing their
individual postures. Apart from age there was one more thing they
had in common--a strong conviction of the importance of psychological analysis in the cinema.

This is quite evident in Goupi Mains Rouges, a story involving a family of Massif Central peasants. There are 12 Goupis
in all, all different and at odds with each other, apart from when
they commonly face the law. When one of them is robbed and another murdered, they decide to solve the mystery and while doing
this discover a hidden treasure. As in his other films, Becker
was here not so much a painter of individual portraits as the painter of the milieu; sometimes an unusual milieu, as in his debut
Dernier atout (1942), where he jokingly parodied the gangster demi-
monde.

In Goupi Mains Rouges he was very close to the soil and has
given one of the most genuine studies of the French rural community. The important aspects of this picture are a wise technical restraint, excellent characterization and suggestive atmosphere. On
the surface it would seem that he gravitated towards a documentary
realism, but it is only apparent: in fact Becker is much nearer to
the poetic spirit of the prewar French cinema.

FOUR STEPS IN THE CLOUDS (Quattro Passi fra le Nuvole)
  Alessandro Blasetti

Script: Giuseppe Amato, from a story by Cesare Zavattini and Piero Tellini. Photography: Václav Vích. Music: Alessandro Cicognini. Cast: Gino Cervi (Paolo Bianchi), Adriana Benetti (Maria), Aldo Silvani (Her father), Giacinto Molteni (Her grand-father), Guido Celano (Her brother), Giuditta Rissone (Paolo's wife), Enrico Viarisio (Commercial traveller), Carlo Romano (Bus driver), Lauro Gazzolo (Ticket collector), Silvio Bagolini (Trombone player).

Cines-Amato, Italy. 7800 ft., 87 mins.

Among the already established leading Italian directors, Blasetti was the one from whom the signal to abandon the banal cosmopolitanism and calligraphy characteristic of the Italian cinema during the Fascist period could most be expected to come. It was given in Four Steps in the Clouds--the first film for nearly ten years in which the director returned to his old doctrine of cinema linked to the life of the nation. The modest story of a bewildered and common traveling salesman who is given the chance to show human feelings during one of his journeys when he acts the supposed husband in front of a pregnant girl's parents, would exert--together with Ossessione--a distinct influence on the Italian cinema of the first postwar years.

In spite of this the film has no features of a manifesto. It was simply enough that as in Visconti's films a true Italy appeared on the screen, the Italy of poor and troubled people, of everyday affairs, of common joys and worries. Especially the first part of Blasetti's comedy, which takes place in a crowded bus, comes across despite its unrefined observations as a striking novelty and a veritable photograph of life. The fact remains that the director seems to have been carried away by his revelations. Four Steps in the Clouds is certainly a film of only medium class: its second, lyrical-nostalgic part is a little weaker than the first. Neorealism, it was clear, could gain more by listening to the tune of Ossessione than by cultivating (which it would often do) the life-reflecting generic quality of Blasetti's film.

MRS. MINIVER William Wyler

Script: Arthur Wimperis, George Froeschel, James Hilton and Claudine West, from the novel by Jan Struther. Photography:

Joseph Ruttenberg. <u>Music</u>: Herbert Stothart. <u>Cast</u>: Greer Garson
(Mrs. Kay Miniver), Walter Pidgeon (Clem Miniver), Teresa Wright
(Carol Beldon), Dame May Whitty (Lady Beldon), Reginald Owen
(Foley), Henry Travers (Mr. Ballard), Richard Ney (Vin Miniver),
Henry Wilcoxon (Vicar), Christopher Severn (Toby Miniver), Clare
Saunders (Judy Miniver), Helmut Dantine (German flyer).

MGM, U.S.A.   12,010 ft., 134 mins.

After the precocious <u>The Great Dictator</u>, this was only the second
American film to show the war raging in remote Europe. When
<u>Mrs. Miniver</u> was being planned war was something less than real
to an average American, a remote spectre which grew closer and
was soon to become part of his ordinary life: by the time the film
was released Pearl Harbor was over and Churchill had just made
his famous speech: "We shall go to the end...". Wyler's intention was basically part of the military effort. He wanted to show
the impact of war on and through the eyes of ordinary people.

The starting material, a series of newspaper articles about
wartime England, was as respectable as it was limited in its outlook: at first war means goodbye to roses for the affluent upper-
middle-class heroine. Later, her eldest son joins the RAF, her
husband helps in the dramatic evacuation from Dunkirk with his
pleasure boat, while she herself overpowers a wounded German air-
man in the garden. Wyler displayed the maximum of realism acceptable within the framework of the existing convention of a salon
melodrama, and while moving along lines not too distant from his
previous <u>The Little Foxes</u>, made a perfectly decent film.

The England of <u>Mrs. Miniver</u> is credible, although somewhat
annoyingly God-fearing and class-ridden but certainly more probable
than might be expected from a Hollywood film. But in the film-
making as well as from the dramatic point of view the film doubtless
belongs to the essentially American tradition of the serene optimism
of ordinary people that Capra's films show. The greatest asset of
the picture is Greer Garson in the excellent title role, memorable
in the air-raid scene when she quietly reads "Alice in Wonderland"
to her children in the deceptive sanctuary of a shelter. For today's
taste <u>Mrs. Miniver</u> is too closely related to the glycerine tradition
of the 1930's family melodrama; but it shows its real value when
compared with the low quality of other similar pictures at that time.

NEXT OF KIN   Thorold Dickinson

<u>Script</u>: Dickinson, Basil Bartlett, Angus MacPhail and John Dighton.
<u>Photography</u>: Ernest Palmer. <u>Music</u>: William Walton. <u>Cast</u>:

David Hutcheson (Intelligence officer), Mervyn Johns (Mr. Davis,
"No. 23"), John Chandos ("No. 16"), Nova Pilbeam (Beppie Lee-
mans), Stephen Murray (Mr. Barratt), Phyllis Stanley (Miss Clare),
Richard Norris (Private Jimmy), Geoffrey Hibbert (Private John),
Mary Clare (Mrs. Webster), Frederick Leister (Colonel).

Ealing Studios for the Directorate of Army Kinematography, G.B.
9152 ft., 101 mins.

Soon after Gaslight, a melodramatic thriller, Dickinson was assigned
to a project of a completely different kind: the aim was to attract
the attention of the troops and Home Guard to the need for secrecy
("Be like Dad: keep Mum"). What was originally to be a short
film sponsored by the Ministry of Propaganda and meant strictly for
the Army grew into feature length and was eventually given a wide
release (after cuts which reduced the number of allied dead). It
was a big commercial success.

Next of Kin, whose story was written by a real security officer, shows what might result from careless talk in wartime. A
raid is planned on a harbor in occupied France. German intelligence notices movements of troups in Britain and sends agents who
listen to indiscreet remarks, resort to blackmail and intimidation
and, taking advantage of negligence, "borrow" the aerial map and
in the end locate the planned operation. The British suffer heavy
casualities. It is interesting how Dickinson was able to transgress
the limitations of a propaganda undertaking, exploit the thrilling
facets of real life and make a fascinating, dramatically tight and
convincingly played film--a review of intelligence methods sustained
in the tone of an entertaining reminder.

PONTCARRAL   Jean Delannoy

Script: Bernard Zimmer, from the novel by Alberic Cahuet. Photography: Christian Matras. Music: Louis Beydts. Cast: Pierre
Blanchar (Colonel Pontcarral), Annie Ducaux (Garlone), Suzy Carrier (Sybille), Jean Marchat (Rozans), Guillaume de Sax (Fournier
Sarlovèze), Marcel Delaitre (Austerlitz), Lucien Nat (Garon), Louvigny (Comte de Mareilhac), Charlotte Lyses (Mme. de Mareilhac),
Simone Valère (Blanche de Mareilhac), Charles Granval (Marquis
de Ransac).

Pathé Cinéma, France. 9200 ft., 102 mins.

A salon melodrama from the period of the Second Empire; a film
in which the wartime censorship saw something quite other than did

the French cinema public.   This was not the result of a zealous
attempt to find as many anti-official innuendoes as possible in films
seemingly remote from contemporary reality.   Pontcarral is a Napoleonic officer condemned to death for conspiracy against Louis
XVIII but subsequently pardoned by Charles X.   Living in retirement he is torn between the loves of two sisters.   After 1830 Pontcarral becomes colonel again under Louis Philippe and dies a glori-
ous death during the African campaign.

In the personality of its hero, uncompromisingly faithful to
the ideals of Bonapartism and haughtily questioning the imposed
rule of the Bourbons, Pontcarral manages to smuggle through moods
quite close to the Resistance Movement, supplementing them with a
handful of satirical analogies between the rule of Louis XVIII and
the rule of Marshal Pétain.   The importance of Delannoy's film
would still be merely historical if it were not for the subtlety of
execution, which is here displayed for the first time by the later
director of La Symphonie pastorale.   The nostalgic, delicate portrayal of the unusual hero--the man who was too strict, proud and
too immersed in ideals to realize his deep desire for love--amounted
to one of the more interesting episodes in the French psychological
cinema of the 40's.   Pierre Blanchar made a considerable contribution towards this end, totally immersing himself in this difficult
role.

THERE WAS A FATHER (Chichi Ariki) Yasujiro Ozu

Script: Ozu, Tadao Ikeda and Takao Yanai. Photography: Yushun
Atsuta. Music: Gyoichi Saiki. Cast: Chishu Ryu (Mr. Horikawa,
a middle-school teacher), Shuji Sano (Ryohei, his son), Haruhiko
Tsuda (Ryohei as a boy), Takeshi Sakamoto (Mr. Hirata, a teacher,
Horikawa's friend), Mitsuko Mito (Fumiko, Hirata's daughter and
Ryohei's fiancée).

Shochiku, Japan.   8491 ft., 94 mins.

This poem of paternal love tells of the feelings of a father who sets
the upbringing of his son as his aim in life--a fulfilled aim: he
dies at the moment when the boy is independent and setting up a
family of his own.   And then during the funeral journey the urn
with the father's ashes, instead of being carried with piety in the
son's hands, is put aside.   The son takes no interest in memories,
but talks to his young wife about everyday matters.

It is hard to decide, even in the light of the evasive explanations Ozu gave after being attacked for such an unedifying ending,
whether he was giving vent to nostalgic reflection about transience

in the film's finale or whether he wanted to comment on the moral
indifference of wartime. But the fact remains that the most outstanding Japanese film director before Kurosawa did not want to
obey the dictates of military propaganda either in the details or in
the very choice of theme.

Like Ozu's films of the 30's, There Was a Father is a tale
about parents and children containing delicate pastel studies of characters. The war is absent from the screen--as it was in The Toda
Brother and his Sisters (1941), the only other film the director
made in the period 1937-48. Because Ozu did not want to do what
was expected of him, he was again drafted, as he was in the late
1930's. But he would not be killed as was Yamanaka; in the 50's
he was further to prove his great talent by a whole range of new
and tranquil works about the Japanese acceptance of life.

STRANGERS IN THE HOUSE (Les Inconnus dans la maison) Henri
    Decoin

Script: Henri-Georges Clouzot, from the novel by Georges Simenon.
Photography: Jules Kruger. Music: Roland-Manuel. Cast: Raimu
(Hector Loursat), Juliette Faber (Nicole Loursat), Jacques Baumer
(Rogissart), André Reybaz (Emile Manu), Marcel Mouloudji (Luska),
Jean Tissier (Ducup), Héléna Manson (Mme. Manu), Lucien Coëdel
(Jo), Marc Dolnitz (Edmond Dossin), Jacques Denoël (Destrivaux
Junior), Pierre Ringel (Daillat Junior), Jacques Grétillat (Judge).

Continental-Films, France. 8590 ft., 94 mins.

A skillful adaptation of a novel, based on real events, and written
by the most popular French crime writer; a film which in a way became an ancestor of André Cayatte's Avant le déluge. The story
takes place in a little town where the adults are busy only with
their affairs and intrigues, and the bored teenagers of good families,
with the help of a delinquent acquaintance, form a criminal gang.
When a body is found at the house of an eccentric, alcoholic ex-
lawyer, and it turns out that his own 18-year-old daughter Nicole
is involved, the local bourgeoisie, anxious to put an end to the
scandal, welcome the news that a scapegoat has been found by the
police--a student in love with Nicole. But the girl's father, in
whom parental responsibility has been awakened, undertakes the
defense and forces a confession out of the real murderer.

In accordance with the spirit of the times, the film contains
the rattle of the theories of the fatal influence of non-Arians (one
of the characters is conspicuously Jewish). This fairly typical
wartime production from the Paris branch of UFA would not have

reached a high rank if it had not been for Raimu: the great actor created here his last outstanding role as the ex-lawyer who conducts the examination of the consciences of the culprits.

CASABLANCA   Michael Curtiz

Script: Julius J. Epstein, Philip G. Epstein and Howard Koch, from a play by Murray Burnett and Jean Alison. Photography: Arthur Edeson. Music: Max Steiner. Cast: Humphrey Bogart (Rick Blaine), Ingrid Bergman (Ilsa Lund), Paul Henreid (Victor Laszlo), Claude Rains (Capt. Louis Renault), Conrad Veidt (Major Heinrich Strasser), Sydney Greenstreet (Señor Ferrari), Peter Lorre (Ugarte), Madeleine LeBeau (Yvonne), Dooley Wilson (Sam).

Warner Bros., U.S.A.   9225 ft., 102 mins.

An exotic and melodramatic thriller which in a typically Hollywoodian style refers to anti-Nazi activities far from the fronts of the Second World War. For those who wanted to reach America from the occupied countries of Europe, the path led through Casablanca and Portugal. Casablanca, with its flourishing black market in currencies and documents, operations of Nazi and Allied Intelligence and atmosphere of decadence and threat. Bogart played Rick Blaine, a disenchanted café owner who meets Ingrid Bergman, his former mistress but now the wife of a fugitive Resistance leader. The memories of a broken love affair are projected onto the background of Bergman's efforts to get false passports for herself and her husband.

Casablanca was one of the most popular American films of the 1940's and is now something more--a cult movie. Its reputation is not undeserved, for this is an atmospheric film par excellence. Everyone contributed something to this end: Curtiz directed with faultless feel for the style, rallied a cast of famous expatriates (no wonder the cosmopolitan atmosphere of the film is done so well) and skillfully evaded the reefs of melodrama and illogic in the plot. The quality of the final effect was assured thanks to Arthur Edeson's sensitive low-key photography and Max Steiner's score.

1943

THE CROW (Le Corbeau) Henri-Georges Clouzot

Script: Clouzot and Louis Chavance. Photography: Nicolas Hayer.
Music: Tony Aubain. Cast: Pierre Fresnay (Dr. Germain),
Pierre Larquey (Dr. Vorzet), Micheline Francey (Laura), Ginette
Leclerc (Denise), Louis Seigner (Dr. Bertrand), Héléna Manson
(Marie), Noël Roquevert (Saillens), Antoine Balpétré (Dr. Delorme),
Roger Blin (Cancer sufferer), Sylvie (His mother).

Continental-Films, France. 8399 ft., 93 mins.

Slanderous poison pen letters swamp a little town. At first the
calumnies of "The Crow"--as the author signs himself--are treated
with reluctant distaste and incredulity but later they set people
against each other, uncover cherished secrets, release reserves of
hatred and intolerance and lead to crime. In his brilliantly made
thriller Clouzot carried out a deep study of group psychology and
went far beyond the usual confines of the genre, whose rules he
otherwise strictly obeyed. The power of the generalizations of The
Crow doubtless stems from the outward projection of the director's
state of mind: the pessimism, the bitter reflections about the common human littleness, and the motifs of the devaluation of handi-
capped people in the eyes of the public and the resulting compensa-
tion claimed by these people, were quite natural for a man who
struggled against tuberculosis all his life.

The illness had already thwarted the director's plans; his interesting debut, an adaptation of a thriller called L'Assassin habite
au 21 (1942), took place when the director was 35. The Crow,
made a year later, instantly placed Clouzot among the leading French
directors. Referring in an original manner to Expressionism, ade-
quately naturalistic, and pulsating with inner rhythm, the film re-

veals a fully formed and independent artistic personality. The Crow
is the most classical French film noir which admirably creates the
atmosphere of all-embracing suspicion and almost makes one believe
in the independent, material existence of evil. It is interesting to
note that the genre seems most poignant in the context of the realities of life in the 1940's, not only in Europe but also in America.

The photography uses deep contrasts of light and shadow and
almost dispenses with half-tones in many scenes, which often acquire symbolic meanings: during one of the conversations among
the two doctors the light from the electric bulb alternately leaves
the participants in light and in darkness, creating an interesting
visual comment on the problems of Good and Evil. The sinister
intensity which he can invest in his symbols even if they are ordinary objects (broken mirror) is characteristic of Clouzot.

Unfortunately, the theme of the picture coexisted rather unhappily with the mood of occupied France; the glaringly critical
presentation of the community in a provincial French town seemed
in 1943 to be a betrayal of the country's interests. The protests--
against wickedness hidden beyond the respectable front of trust-
worthiness and decency, against the intolerance exhibited in baiting
the man who does not conform, against thoughtless judgment from
appearances, against the psychology of the informer--thus in fact
against many attributes of Nazism--were not understood.

And so, history itself would prove Clouzot right: the accuser would become the accused; the director who with reputedly
excessive scepticism showed how the misunderstanding even of noble
ideals breeds evil and hatred would, because of The Crow, be
barred from work in films for several years after the war.

DAY OF WRATH (Vredens Dag) Carl Theodor Dreyer

Script: Dreyer, Mogens Skot-Hansen and Poul Knudsen, from the
play "Anne Pedersdotter" by Hans Wiers-Jenssen. Photography:
Karl Andersson. Music: Poul Schierbeck. Cast: Thorkild Roose
(Pastor Absalon Pederssøn), Lisbeth Movin (Anne Pedersdotter, his
second wife), Sigrid Neiiendam (Merete, his mother), Preben Ler-
dorff Rye (Martin, his son from first marriage), Anne Svierker
(Herlof's Marte), Albert Høeberg (The Bishop), Olaf Ussing (Lau-
rentius), Sigurd Berg (Chaplain), Herald Holst (Steward).

Palladium Copenhagen-Tage Nielsen, Denmark. 9432 ft., 105 mins.

The political situation in occupied Europe narrowed the thematic
range available to directors; very often they escaped into the world

of historical subjects. The result was a number of films of timeless internal concentration. While in France Bresson was making
Les Anges du péché, in Denmark the 55-year-old Dreyer was shooting his first film in almost 12 years, a somber morality play about
the cruel times of prejudice and institutionalized violence of the Inquisition.

1623: a slow-moving period of witch-hunts and all-embracing
suspicion. Anne, the second wife of an old pastor, gives refuge to
an alleged witch. She discovers that Anne's own mother was saved
from the stake by the pastor in exchange for her daughter's hand.
The conflict between Anne and her vicious-tongued mother-in-law only
increases when Anne falls in love with her stepson. Tormented by feelings of guilt she comes to believe in being a witch herself; this belief
is reinforced when the pastor, to whom she confesses her infidelity,
dies from the shock. Denounced as a witch during his funeral and
abandoned by her lover, Anne is burned at the stake.

Day of Wrath examines the workings of divine law and medi-
tates on the tortuosity of human fate, treating it as coming directly
from God. His laws themselves are never disputed, but only acknowledged. The main concern of the director was to confront and
examine the attitudes of the two witches, one of whom confesses
under torture, the other volunteers to die, convinced of her sins.
Stemming from this is an acknowledgment of the human desire for
contact if not with the divine, at least with the supernatural. Dreyer's film is a Protestant version of Les Anges du péché. Human
conflicts (as in Bresson's cinema) are never on the surface, but have
to be discovered; inscrutable faces conceal great passion; each character creates a spiritual world of his or her own.

The most striking feature of the film is its dignity. In keeping with the subject it moves exceedingly slowly; the plots are developed simultaneously. Pictorially, it offers beauty and a Protestant
discipline often called architectonic; it has a classical composition
stressing the essential and discarding accessories, and a reliance on
contrasts of light and shade resembling, in their serene dignity,
Dutch paintings. The result is a unique projection of the human interior onto physical objects; it is only in the few exterior scenes
that the characters are subordinated to the majestic beauty of nature
--as in Vampyr, ou l'étrange aventure de David Gray, wide river
vistas and dusty country roads.

The soundtrack is equally spartan and the sound effects rare:
there is only the profuse dialogue, which is simply the spoken
thoughts of the characters. The camerawork is dominated by long
and slow horizontal pans and inquisitive close-ups of faces. The
strict, parallel composition is reinforced by the similarity of the
scenes at the stake at the beginning and the end, while the voices
of a boys' choir sing the reminder "Dies Irae." There is none of
the scoffing skepticism of Christensen's Witchcraft Through the Ages;
all is objective and one cannot help feeling that for the director
witchcraft constitutes reality.

This supreme flight of fancy would be matched only by Dreyer's own Ordet and by Bergman's The Seventh Seal.

JUDO SAGA (Sugata Sanshiro) Akira Kurosawa

Script: Kurosawa, from the novel by Tsuneo Tomita. Photography: Akira Mimura. Music: Seichi Suzuki. Cast: Susumu Fujita (Sugata), Denjiro Okochi (Shogoro Yano, his teacher), Takashi Shimura (Hansuke Murai), Yukiko Todoroki (Sayo, his daughter), Yoshio Kosugi (Saburo Momma, ju-jitsu teacher), Ranko Hanai (Osumi, his daughter), Ryunosuke Tsukigata (Gennosuke Higaki), Akitake Kono (Yoshima Dan), Soshi Kiyokawa (Yujiro Toda), Kunio Mita (Kohei Tsuzaki), Akira Nakamura (Toranosuki Niiseki), Sugisaku Aoyama (Tsunetami Iimura), Kuninori Kodo (Priest), Ichiro Sugai (Police chief).

Toho, Japan. 7106 ft., 79 mins.

Very few first films are as mature as Kurosawa's debut. Judo Saga is mature both as a manifestation of technical expertise and as a personal point of view. His own individual style is here clearly visible, as it is in almost all his later films. Kurosawa had time enough to prepare his artistic program, even though war conditions were not particularly conducive to the creative debut of a director whose credo was the spreading of good in the world. Only after seven years of apprenticeship as a scriptwriter and assistant (which is by Japanese standards a considerable period) was Yamamoto's brilliant pupil given the green light by the producers for an independent start.

Kurosawa's own script achieved the golden mean between his personal interests and the propagandists' demands. In the tale of a young judo champion the latter see above all praise of samurai gallantry and inner strength; but the finished film has more of Kurosawa's spirit than of the spirit of Japanese national vigor. The plot is set in the 1880's, when the new, noble school of judo starts to drive out the ruthless ju-jitsu. The hero, who came to Tokyo to study the combat technique, soon proves to be the ablest judoka. But his spiritual values do not match his physical prowess, and those are the crucial values required by the master Yano from Sanshiro Sugata: judo is more than a school of battle, it is also a way of life.

The process by which a young person achieves maturity, begins to understand the nature of life and betters himself through self-discipline constitutes the axis of the film. Kurosawa praised the sort of moral strength which leads to internal nobility. He did

not do this in a reflective mood: Judo Saga is very expressive,
full of striking contrasts of violent movement and stillness, sound
and silence. It often disturbs the rhythm of nature only to immerse
itself again in its majestic peace. Although this narrative style excellently reflects the essence of judo, it was chosen for other reasons: Kurosawa revealed himself here as an opponent of arrogant
militaristic self-confidence and also the nationalistic trend in Japanese cinema, which was particularly encouraged during the war. No
wonder that his break with the static and sparing style was not ap-
plauded at home in 1943. It is outright ironic that Kurosawa was
later accused of eclectic non-Japanism by the very critics who discovered the great cinema of the Far East only after the success of
Rashomon.

AIR FORCE   Howard Hawks

Script: Dudley Nichols and William Faulkner (dialogue). Photography: James Wong Howe. Music: Franz Waxman. Cast: John
Garfield (Winocki), John Ridgely (Captain Quincannon), George Tobias (Corporal Weinberg), Harry Carey (Crew Chief), Edward S.
Brophy (Marine sergeant).

Warner Bros., U.S.A. 11,182 ft., 124 mins.

Air Force is the most impressive of the American war films made
during the war and that with most claim to being a classic. The
film tells of the odyssey of the crew of a flying fortress, surprised
in the air by the news (on the radio) of the Japanese attack on
Pearl Harbor and searching for a landing space somewhere still out
of enemy control. The story is comprised of a series of flights
and dangerous landings on various islands on the Pacific, culminating in the attack by the "Mary Ann" and other planes on the accidentally sighted Japanese fleet.

    The script of Air Force, although packed with exciting mo-
ments, was still burdened with the slicked-down smoothness characteristic of the films made during the 30's. It was Hawks'
contribution to the war effort and stressed the principles of complete loyalty and team unity and their role in victory. Sustained in
the style of a colorful--though frightening--adventure, it somewhat
easily fortifies the spectator with its optimistic faith in victory, as
if the United States still did not know what the armed confrontation
with Japan meant. (Hawks is guilty of triviality when he shows the
enemy as a savage mob.)

    But the true face of that war was captured through the virile
and austere style of direction, the spontaneous frankness of the pro-

tagonists' behavior, and the low-key emotionality of the famous scene of the commander's death in the field hospital, supposedly written by William Faulkner. The commander dies in a hospital bed believing that the plane is taking off with the crew aboard and that the hum of fans is the engine noise. Hawks, one of whose numerous specialties is aerial films, created here definitely one of the best pictures of its kind; the air battle scenes are particularly impressive.

LES ANGES DU PÉCHÉ   Robert Bresson

Script: Raymond-Leopold Bruckberger, Jean Giraudoux and Bresson. Photography: Philippe Agostini. Music: Jean-Jacques Grunenwald. Cast: Renée Faure (Anne-Marie), Jany Holt (Thérèse), Sylvie (Prioress), Mila Parély (Madeleine), Marie-Hélène Dasté (Mother Saint-Jean), Yolande Laffon (Anne-Marie's mother), Paula Dehelly (Mother Dominique), Sylvia Monfort (Agnès), Gilberte Terbois (Sister Marie-Josèphe), Louis Seigner (Prison Governor).

Productions Synops/Roland Tual, France. 73 mins.

Bresson, an erstwhile assistant of René Clair and a freshly-released P.O.W., made the scenario of a priest interested in the cinema into a refined and almost completely mature vision, containing all the features of his unique art--a first picture that instantly made him a director of major stature, the spiritualist-in-chief of modern cinema. Both his obsessive motives are present in the film: loneliness and martyrdom. Anne-Marie, a girl from an affluent bourgeois family enters a Dominican convent of the Sisters of Béthanie, devoted to the rehabilitation of women with criminal records. She dedicates herself to helping a young delinquent, Thérèse, whose response is hatred and defiance. But Anne-Marie will not give up; even when she is dismissed from the convent for pride she will sacrifice her life to earn Thérèse's redemption.

There is little visible action in the film; the theme is the slow process of moral (not psychological) transformation; a conflict rather of souls than of personalities; an elevated game in which the stake is salvation. These are things of the spirit and Bresson rejected a direct approach to the subject. He ordered his actors to limit their facial expression: a negation of modern acting methods. With the deepening of the spiritual content of Bresson's films the acting becomes progressively more restrained.

The dialogues in Les Anges du péché are projections of the soul on the screen. This is why the philosophical dialogues of Giraudoux are so suitable to that cinema which does not rely on psychology, but on an overriding Providence. Bresson's films are

remarkable for their rare unity of content and their external form,
ascetic in appearance yet internally stressed almost to breaking point.
The perfect visual key to the problems of sacrifice and inner elevation
is the muted, mat high-key photography which suggests spiritual
purity; destiny looms as gray shadows over the characters.

But Bresson has not avoided the dangers associated with the
theme: in many scenes (especially those portraying internal anxieties) melodramatics are not far from the surface.   There is also
some superficial smoothness in the rounded-off plot and a certain
glycerine quality in the photography; the music is obtrusive.   But
despite minor imperfections, Les Anges du péché is a work of invincible truth and scorching internal conviction, a fearless examination of the eternal anxieties of man.

LIFEBOAT   Alfred Hitchcock

Script: Jo Swerling, from a story by John Steinbeck.   Photography:
Glen MacWilliams. Music: Hugo Friedhofer.   Cast: Tallulah
Bankhead (Constance Porter), William Bendix (Gus Smith), Walter
Slezak (Willy, Captain of the submarine), Mary Anderson (Alice
Mackenzie), John Hodiak (John Kovac), Henry Hill (Charles D. Rit-
tenhouse), Heather Angel (Mrs. Higgins), Hume Cronyn (Stanley
Garett), Canada Lee (George Spencer, called "Joe").

20th Century-Fox, U.S.A.   8645 ft., 96 mins.

One of the experiments Hitchcock made so frequently in the 1940's,
this film takes place wholly in a lifeboat in the mid-Atlantic that is
carrying a group of survivors from a ship torpedoed by a Nazi submarine.   They later pick up the captain of the U-boat which was also sunk.   He proves to be the most resistant of them all and steers
the boat off course towards a German ship.   That is, until the others discover what is going on.   The camera never leaves the boat
and shows the action almost exclusively in close-ups; the spectator's
attention is guided by significant objects (the gold bracelet used as
fish bait, the typewriter); music is almost eliminated and the reliance
on dialogue is greater than usual.   The effect resembles present-
day television technique.

Lifeboat represents its author's contribution to the war effort.   It is not a thriller but a psychological drama, a conversation
piece aimed at expounding and summing up the attitudes of the allies
and the Nazis, an artificial microcosm of the troubled world.   There
are obvious dangers in doing this, as indeed in any political allegory.
The arrangement of the characters is obtrusively socially representative (one woman journalist plus one Communist sailor plus one mil-

lionaire, etc.) but does not exclude some interesting observations
and reflections on national mentalities. In conclusion, it is a
demonstration of the superiority of German discipline and a plea
for closing allied ranks (although the killing of the Nazi captain is
morally highly suspect).

Hitchcock, as always, appears personally in his film. In
Lifeboat his choice is, if not bizarre, certainly unusual--he is the
victim of a before-and-after newspaper advertisement for "banting"
(i.e., weight reducing)!

THE CHILDREN ARE WATCHING US (I Bambini Ci Guardano)
   Vittorio De Sica

Script: Gherardo Gherardi, Cesare Giulio Viola, Adolfo Franci,
Margherita Maglione and De Sica, based on the novel, "Prico," by
Cesare Giulio Viola. Photography: Giuseppe Caracciolo. Music:
Renzo Rossellini. Cast: Emilio Cigoli (Father), Isa Pola (Mother),
Adriano Rimoldi (Lover), Luciano De Ambrosis (The boy, Prico).

Scalera-Invicta, Italy. 85 mins.

Vittorio De Sica, having already appeared in a number of light
comedies both on stage and in films, was in the 1930's a popular
leading actor. In 1940 he decided to try his hand as a director.
His first four films are not particularly interesting examples of the
Camerini style--a familiar mixture of frivolity and sentimentality à
la Chaplin. But the fifth picture, The Children Are Watching Us,
surprised everybody. De Sica had turned into a vicious critic of
the society he had so far amused.

Here is the country of the triumphant bourgeoisie, which out-
wardly appears grandiose and dreams heroic dreams, but within
conceals mediocrity, hypocrisy and sordid dealings. The dark side
of the marital triangle is the theme which De Sica had so far exploited in the comedy vein. The mother of a four-year-old boy
leaves her husband to follow another man. Then she returns and
a brief reconciliation follows; but she continues to see her lover.
The husband, unable to stand the humiliation and worrying over his
son, commits suicide. The boy, lonely and unwanted, is sent to
an orphanage where we part with him on the huge grim staircase.

The script was written by six scenarists and although one of
them, Zavattini, was to emerge as a driving force in the Italian
cinema for many years to come, this is probably the reason why
the structure of the film is somewhat loose, rather like a series of
episodes. De Sica is cool, clinical and subdued; he leaves no room

for light relief or for sentimental emphasis. As in the later
Bicycle Thieves the social background of the story is, interestingly,
carefully delineated and starkly realistic and thus all the more
heartbreaking.

Most of De Sica's later films are about children, some of
them better than this, but he would never again manage to get such
a touching performance from a little actor, one which is among the
handful of really significant cinematic children's performances.

SAN DEMETRIO, LONDON   Charles Frend

Script: Robert Hamer and Frend, from the official account by F.
Tennyson Jesse. Photography: Ernest Palmer. Music: John
Greenwood. Cast: Walter Fitzgerald (Chief Engineer Charles Pol-
lard), Arthur Young (Capt. George Waite), Ralph Michael (2nd Of-
ficer Hawkins), Neville Mapp (3rd Engineer Willey), Barry Letts
(Apprentice John Jones), Michael Allen (Cadet Roy Housden),
Mervyn Johns (Greaser John Boyle), Robert Beatty ("Yank" Pres-
ton), Gordon Jackson (Messboy John Jamieson), Frederick Piper
(Boatswain W. E. Fletcher).

Ealing Studios,   G.B. 9480 ft., 105 mins.

Autumn 1940; the Second World War in the Atlantic. The British
tanker "San Demetrio" is sent to America to bring a cargo of petrol.
When the return journey is almost over, the convoy is attacked by
a German battleship. The captain orders the abandonment of the
blazing ship. Most of the crew are soon rescued, but one boat
drifts for two days. Then the men sight a burning ship--it is the
"San Demetrio." The skeleton crew reboard, extinguish the flames,
save the cargo and manage to reach Britain using a school atlas for
navigation.

This praise of the heroism of the merchant navy in wartime,
a semi-documentary studio production shot in primitive conditions
and using unsophisticated means, delights just by its simplicity,
frankness and directness. The optimism so badly needed for raising
morale in wartime is not at all an alien intrusion, but constitutes
an organic whole with the climate of the picture. The influence of
the British documentary school of the 30's is here even more in
evidence than in In Which We Serve. Like that film, San Demetrio,
London was based on real events.

DOUCE   Claude Autant-Lara

Script: Jean Aurenche and Pierre Bost, from the novel by Michel Davet.   Photography: Philippe Agostini.   Music: René Cloërec. Cast: Odette Joyeux (Douce), Roger Pigaut (Fabien Marani), Marguerite Moréno (Countess de Bonafé), Jean Debucourt (Count Engelbert, Douce's father), Madeleine Robinson (Irène, governess), Gabrielle Fontan (Estelle), Julienne Paroli (Thérèse), Paul Frankeur (Julien).

Société Parisienne de l'Industrie Cinématographique, France. 9982 ft., 111 mins.

Claude Autant-Lara, already 40 years old, launched at last into the part of his career that would after the war earn him the status of one of the leading masters of the French psychological cinema.   The man who would later make Le Diable au corps began his work in films in 1923 and soon after did the short Construire un feu (1927), the first film to be made in Henri Chrétien's Hypergonar System (forerunner of CinemaScope and an invention unfortunately to be forgotten for more than a quarter of a century).   The proper directorial start for Autant-Lara was Mariage de Chiffon (1941), an adaptation of a fin-de-siècle romance, impressive for its fine narrative rhythm and sensitive rendering of the Good Old Times, and Lettres d'amour (1942) which, while developing the concepts of its predecessor but this time in a Second Empire setting, as an antiaristocratic satirical comedy, was used to make social comments.

Douce is a somber drama of passion and intrigue in an aristocratic Parisian family at the close of the 19th century.   Virulent psychological description, an atmosphere suggestive of amoral egoism, and elegant scenery as a background for human littleness: indeed if it were not for a certain melodramatic superficiality Douce would deserve comparison with Stroheim and Renoir.   Seventeen-year-old Douce, living with her widowed crippled father at the luxurious residence of her relatives, secretly loves the young estate manager.   She learns of his planned escape to Canada with her governess, Irène, whom the father also craves to marry.   Douce starts a risky intrigue whereby she elopes with the young man. She intends to leave him, but is killed in a fire at the opera.

Even with this doubtful finale Autant-Lara's first fully mature film is a considerable achievement so far as social criticism in the French cinema is concerned, not least because the unconventional contents are supported by a very meticulous formal aspect.   The credit for this is due not only the director but also other members of the company--particularly the actresses and the inventive Philippe Agostini, who suggestively handled the chiaroscuro photography.

SHADOW OF A DOUBT   Alfred Hitchcock

Script: Thornton Wilder, Alma Reville and Salley Benson, from a
story by Gordon McDonnell. Photography: Joseph Valentine.
Music: Dmitri Tiomkin. Cast: Joseph Cotten (Charlie Oakley),
Teresa Wright (Charlie Newton), MacDonald Carey (Jack Graham),
Patricia Collinge (Emma Newton), Henry Travers (Joseph Newton),
Hume Cronyn (Herbie Hawkins), Wallace Ford (Fred Saunders).

Universal, U.S.A.   9715 ft., 108 mins.

To the question, "What do you fear most?," Hitchcock might well
have answered, "Logic." Thornton Wilder's script, however,
liberated the director from such troubles, providing the source
material for a film neatly buttoned up from the logical and the psychological points of view. Another of Wilder's contributions was
the faithful portrayal of the attitudes and way of life of a provincial
American town, to which the anxiety of the Big World arrives in the
person of the mysterious Uncle Charlie. He is respected by all and
considered a paragon of civic virtues; it is only his adoring niece
who, by piecing together scraps of conversations and odd events at
the house, comes to realize that Uncle Charlie is in fact a New
York variety of Landru, the murderer of women. So, Uncle Charlie
will in turn try to kill her as well....

      This time Hitchcock shoots the film on location (which is its
second trump) and gives music a major part to play in building up
the tension--a disturbing tune from the Viennese Waltz, "The Merry
Widow," emerging from behind the frame. (Is it accidental that
Hitchcock once made a film called Waltzes from Vienna, 1933?)
Shadow of a Doubt is a typical example of the "small town" kind of
picture so frequent in the 40's, and it is interesting that the director
observed provincial life so well although he had only arrived in
America the previous year. What is more, Shadow of a Doubt virtually launched the genre of the American film noir, which was to
flourish later in the decade. But the master of suspense did not
stop at that; this is the first time that he went beyond "straight"
intrigue and, by injecting the plot with the elements of moral dispute, made a basically moralist (and quietly anti-establishment) picture.

MARIA CANDELARIA (Xochimilco)   Emilio Fernández

Script: Fernández and Mauricio Magdaleno. Photography: Gabriel Figueroa. Music: Francisco Dominguez. Cast: Dolores Del Rio (Maria Candelaria), Pedro Armendariz (Lorenzo Rafael, her fiancé), Miguel Inclan (Don Damian), Alberto Galan, Rafael Icardo, Margarita Cortès, Julio Ahuet, Béatriz Ramos.

Clasa Film Mondiales, Mexico. 110 mins.

The credit for introducing Mexican cinema to an international audience must undoubtedly go to Emilio Fernández and Gabriel Figueroa. In reverse order however; the role of the director of photography in determining the final, impressive form of the film was greater than that of the director. Had therefore Fernández--selector of fictional themes and film director, and thus theoretically the main author of the film--consciously demoted himself to the role of the supplier of dramatic material, which was then visually realized by Figueroa? It seems so. The content of their pictures is hardly innovatory, but their visual aspect aroused general admiration and brought Figueroa a record number of international prizes.

Of course, one could have a substantial objection to his art: this is not so much camera work as artistic photography. But this attitude would take no account of the sources of Figueroa's inspiration; for the monumental dignity of his photography stems directly from the traditions of Mexican art, which so faithfully records the inner rhythm of life in that country. It is significant that Tissé also expressed himself through frames of similar majesty in Eisenstein's ¡Que Viva Mexico! Tissé was as a matter of fact a model for Figueroa, who openly admitted being inspired by the style of the Soviet cameraman, not only in the composition of the frame, but also in his characteristic use of chiaroscuro.

Maria Candelaria, the second of Figueroa and Fernández's significant films, differs somewhat in character from the others. Its tone is closer to realism than to symbolic emphasis; the narrative, mainly thanks to the editing, is more dynamic. The story, although contained within the convention of a folk melodrama, includes--apart from one more variation on the legend of the wronged poor--some interesting information about the way of life of Mexican peasants of the early 20th century. The negative features of rural mentality, superstition and outright medieval intolerance, are exploited by the perfidious landowner for the persecution of a proud couple.

The husband is thrown into prison for the theft of medicines for his sick wife; the wife sits as a model for a painter from near-

by Xochimilco in order to earn some money. The vindictive landowner spreads a rumor that she sits in the nude: this is enough.
The wife was already resented as the daughter of a woman of dubious morals and the village deals with the disgrace by organizing a
hunt for the unfortunate Maria Candelaria. This climactic sequence
is perhaps the best episode in all the work of Fernández and Figueroa: the expressive photography is here accompanied by dynamic
narration and a high emotional content in the acting. In their later
films, Pueblerina and Maclovia, such spontaneity would be lacking: the
studied frames, unsupported by a vivid inner rhythm and using
closer shots than Maria Candelaria, seem to carry a certain academic coolness.

ADÉMAÏ, BANDIT D'HONNEUR   Gilles Grangier

Script: Paul Colline, Noël-Noël and Grangier. Photography: Maurice Barry. Music: Gallois-Montbrun. Cast: Noël-Noël (Adémaï),
Georges Grey (Mandolino), Gaby Andreu (Fortunata Brazzia),
Guillaume de Sax (Police adjutant), Alexandre Rignault (Freddo, the
bandit), René Génin, Charles Lemontier, Jean Morel, Marthe Mel-
lot, Marcel Pérès, Renée Corciade, Maurice Schutz.

Les Prisonniers Associés, France. 87 mins.

A brisk generic farce of which the theme is the unfortunate obligations of Corsican family vengeance. In accordance with tradition,
Adémaï, a kind-hearted Parisian shop assistant who would not harm
a fly and who seems an outright blunderer, must do his duty as,
alas, he comes from the island where honor and vendetta are syn-
onimous. To boot, Adémaï is unfortunate enough to be his family's
last hope, as all his male relatives have been exterminated in earlier feuds. Nonetheless, everything ends happily, according to the
good old models of the silent burlesque (the methods of which the
makers of Adémaï prove to be conversant with).

This film is not a direct reference to the world of slapstick
comedy: its raw material is rather intelligent cabaret-type gags
married to plebeian humor. The most vital element of Adémaï is
the personality of Noël-Noël, one of the most popular comedians of
the French stage and later of the screen. It is he who was the
spiritus movens of the whole frolic. The director's task was only
to register it.

NINE MEN   Harry Watt

Script: Watt. Photography: Roy Kellino. Music: John Green-
wood. Cast: Jack Lambert (Sgt. Watson), Richard Wilkinson (Of-
ficer), Gordon Jackson (Young 'un), Frederick Piper ("Banger" Hill),
Grant Sutherland (Jock Scott), Bill Blewett (Bill Parker), Eric
Micklewood ("Booky" Lee), John Varley ("Dusty" Johnstone), Jack
Horsman (Joe Harvey).

Ealing Studios, G.B.   6040 ft., 67 mins.

Just as San Demetrio, London and In Which We Serve relate the
war adventures of British sailors, Nine Men tells of the desert battles in the Middle East. The picture dispenses with intricate plot
or fine turns in the narrative; the intention was to show objectively
and clearly what the soldier's task was like in this testing time.
Here is an infantry platoon attacked during a journey by an enemy
plane; their commanding officer is killed, their only means of transport burned out. A sergeant takes command of the survivors.
Having entrenched themselves in a desert mound, the men take up
the fight against the crew of a German transporter. It comes to
close combat; the gallant stand of the British carries them through
the critical moments before the tanks come to their assistance and
help in the final victory.

This story was to illustrate the thesis that the harder the
training the easier the battle: it is with that purpose that it is told
by the sergeant (a participant in the actual events) to newly drafted
troops under his supervision. The young men are heartily fed up
with the tiresome drills and are raring to go to the front; but the
sergeant's story will convince them that the skills with which their
older colleagues defeated the enemy were gained during the careful
preparations.

Thus Watt's film also contains elements of topical propaganda,
though quite objective and indeed useful in many other situations.
In the first place, however, it is an unassuming witness of the stand
of the British soldier in everyday war. Watt's work originated directly from the British documentary school; no wonder then that this
para-documentary feature was also made as an authentic narrative.
He knew, however, how to enrich the style of this rather ordinary
and unspectacular story by a superior element: the human verity of
the characters of his protagonists.

SAHARA   Zoltan Korda

Script: John Howard Lawson and Korda, from an incident in the
Soviet film, The Thirteen. Photography: Rudolf Maté. Music:
Miklos Rozsa. Cast: Humphrey Bogart (Sgt. Joe Gunn), Bruce
Bennett ("Waco" Hoyt), Lloyd Bridges (Fred Clarkson), Rex Ingram
(Tambul), J. Carroll Naish (Giuseppe), Dan Duryea (Jimmy Doyle),
Richard Nugent (Capt. Jason Halliday), Patrick O'Moore (Ozzie
Bates), Louis T. Mercier (Jean Leroux).

Columbia, U.S.A. 8775 ft., 97 mins.

Desert warfare as in Nine Men, but seen from Hollywood: while
that film showed authentic people in real situations, Sahara cared
more for attractive plot and bright execution. An American unit
stranded in the Sahara desert picks up a group of Allied stragglers
whose commander relinquishes his command to them. They chase
the Germans away from a well to which they have been directed and
which turns out to be a mere trickle: it bursts open just when the
Germans surrender. The war is in Korda's film not only a duty to
society which has to be fulfilled, but also a dramatic adventure.

     All the same, as in Air Force and some other American
films of the period, a certain new look at man in critical situations
can be perceived which breaks with old clichés and stresses the
catalytic influence of crisis in forming ties of comradeship and
bringing out noble features of character. It was still not the hymn
to citizens in uniform that Wellman's The Story of G. I. Joe was to
be, but it did contain the first notes of it, the first attempts to look
at war from trench level.

     The film owes a lot to the personality of Humphrey Bogart
whose performances always contributed a mighty charge of humanism
to a picture: the sergeant from Sahara is not so much a uniformed
civilian as one of the many in the same situation who had been
forced by circumstances to fight in a just cause.

LE CIEL EST À VOUS   Jean Grémillon

Script: Albert Valentin and Charles Spaak. Photography: Louis
Page. Music: Roland-Manuel. Cast: Madeleine Renaud (Thérèse
Gauthier), Charles Vanel (Pierre Gauthier), Jean Debucourt (Larcher),
Léonce Corné (Dr. Maulette), Albert Rémy (Marcel), Robert Le Fort

(Robert), Raoul Marco (M. Noblet), Raymonde Vernay (Mme. Bris-
sard), Michel François (Claudinet).

Les Films Raoul Ploquin, France.   9514 ft., 106 mins.

Everyone can reach for greatness, everyone has a chance to become
a hero. This is the philosophy of Grémillon's film, which was
based on the breaking of a world aviation record in 1937 by a
modest provincial woman whose husband, an aircraft mechanic, had
infected her with the bug of the wide open skies. Everything depends on perseverance, on the inner flame that makes one disregard probability, the consequences of failure and even the interests
of one's family: one can lose, but how worthwhile it is to try!

     Thérèse Gauthier's road to success is neither strewn with
roses, nor straight; to start with, she was perhaps not quite even
conscious she was on it. But because of this the story appears
more convincing and more moving: it constitutes a clear demonstration that it is strength of character which is the most important
human feature. The style of the film consciously befits a scenario
written without "effects"; it is rough, sparing, sometimes even appearing awkward, but this did not stem from lack of invention on
the part of the director.

     Grémillon, who distributed the dramatic accents very well,
did not rely on the direct visual appeal of the picture. His aim
was to convey the idea, the general reflection, that his heroes are
not unique. This was why he resorted to everyday life, to seemingly ordinary French provincial events. As with Daquin's Us Kids,
Le Ciel est à vous is part of the same current which will lead to
Neorealism after the war--and as with Us Kids, it voices faith in
the potential of the French people.

ACTION IN THE NORTH ATLANTIC Lloyd Bacon

Script: John Howard Lawson, from a story by Guy Gilpatric.
Photography: Ted McCord. Cast: Humphrey Bogart (Joe Rossi),
Raymond Massey (Capt. Steve Jarvis), Alan Hale ("Boats" O'Hara),
Julie Bishop (Pearl), Ruth Gordon (Mrs. Jarvis), Sam Levene
("Chips" Abrams), Dane Clark (Johnnie Pulaski), Peter Whitney
(Whitey Lara), J. M. Kerrigan (Caviar Jinks), Charles Trowbridge
(Rear Adm. Hartridge).

Jerry Wald, Warner Bros., U.S.A. 11,546 ft., 128 mins.

It is 1942; American Liberty ships are convoying munitions to the

Soviet Union by the Northern route. The film follows the adventures of one of them, the "Seawitch," on a trip from Halifax to
Murmansk. The ships are doggedly hunted by U-boats and the Luft-
waffe. After a brave fight and having accounted for two enemy
planes and two submarines, the ship reaches port safely.

Bacon's film, skillfully made and well acted, stands out in
comparison with the other productions of the time by its matter-of-
factness. There are none of the usual contraptions of a naval film
and none of the inevitable messroom intrigues. Bogart plays the
first officer who takes command in an emergency. What a completely different type of seaman he is here compared to his de-
ranged Captain Queeg in The Caine Mutiny of several years later!
Action in the North Atlantic is an American counterpart of San
Demetrio, London. Together with Lewis Seiler's Guadalcanal Diary
(1943) this is the film closest to the British wartime style of film-
making with its pursuit of authenticity and sincerity and its avoidance
of emphasis.

MADAME CURIE   Mervyn Le Roy

Script: Paul Osborn and Paul H. Rameau, from the book by Eve
Curie. Photography: Joseph Ruttenberg. Music: Herbert Stothart.
Cast: Greer Garson (Marie Curie), Walter Pidgeon (Pierre Curie),
Henry Travers (Eugène Curie), Albert Bassermann (Prof. Jean
Perot), Robert Walker (David LeGros), C. Aubrey Smith (Lord Kel-
vin), Dame May Whitty (Mme. Eugène Curie), Reginald Owen (Dr.
Becquerel), Victor Francen (President of university), Elsa Basser-
mann (Mme. Perot), Van Johnson (Reporter).

MGM, U.S.A. 11,184 ft., 124 mins.

The last interesting film of the Hollywood series of screen biographies of outstanding personalities in the world of science. The way
in which Le Roy handled the theme did not in principle differ in any
respect from that of William Dieterle, the most successful representative of the biographic genre. The same earnest avoidance of
forcing the heroes' lives to appear more colorful and romantic, the
same popularizing intentions, the same conviction of the modest
greatness of the subject, and the avoidance of an emphatic grandiose
style.

The result seems unimpressive, but remains--despite its
limitations--quite convincing, all the more because Greer Garson,
here at the height of her acting attainments, could contain in the
screen personality many touches of the warmth, subtlety, and
strength of will that were so characteristic of Marie Curie. The

performance of Walter Pidgeon as the sky, delicate Pierre Curie,
dedicated to science, is also very good. It is indeed through the
personalities of the main performers that the film often reaches
moments of noble emotion--for instance in the scenes of the decision on their future work, the discovery of radium and the silence
after Pierre's tragic death in a street accident.

THE MORE THE MERRIER   George Stevens

Script: Robert Russell, Frank Ross, Richard Flournoy and Lewis
R. Soter. Photography: Ted Tetzlaff. Music: Leigh Harline.
Cast: Jean Arthur (Connie Milligan), Joel McCrea (Joe Carter),
Charles Coburn (Benjamin Dingle), Richard Gaines (Charles J.
Pendergast), Bruce Bennett (Evans), Frank Sully (Pike), Clyde Fill-
more (Senator Noonan), Stanley Clements (Morton Rodakiewicz), Don
Douglas (Harding).

Columbia, U.S.A.   9365 ft., 104 mins.

War-time discomforts in 1943 Washington: bureaucracy, spy fever,
over-population and the resulting accommodation difficulties.   Although the commentary in the prologue assures the spectator that
order, law and social discipline are not in danger, the accompanying pictures immediately comically "verify" this official outlook.
The heroine of this sympathetic, sentimental comedy by Stevens (or
rather by Russell and Ross, since the director's role did not go be-
yong the filming of the script) is a Washington clerk who, as she
has a rather roomy flat, shares it with two lodgers. One of them
is an industrious, jovial gadabout, delightfully portrayed by Charles
Coburn; the other--a young aircraft mechanic, a handsome penniless
soul. Of course, all will end with a wedding, just as in Capra's
prewar films, to which in fact The More the Merrier refers.

1944

IVAN THE TERRIBLE (Ivan Grozny) Sergei Eisenstein

Script: Eisenstein. Photography: Andrei Moskvin (interiors) and
Eduard Tissé (exteriors). Music: Sergei Prokofiev. Art Direc-
tion: Iosif Shpinel, from sketches by Eisenstein. Cast: Nikolai
Cherkasov (Tsar Ivan IV), Serafima Birman (Yefrosinya Staritskaya,
Tsar's aunt), Ludmila Tselikovskaya (Anastasiya, the Tsarina),
Mikhail Nazvanov (Prince Andrei Kurbsky), Pavel Kadochnikov
(Vladimir Staritsky), Mikhail Zharov (Malyuta Skuratov), Amvrosi
Buchma (Alexei Basmanov), Andrei Abrikosov (Boyar Fyodor Koly-
chev), Alexandr Mgebrov (Archbishop Pimen), Vsevolod Pudovkin
(Nikola, a beggar simpleton), Maxim Mikhailov (Archdeacon), Mik-
hail Kuznetsov (Fyodor Basmanov).

Tsentralnaya Obiedinyonnaya Kinostudiya, Alma-Ata, U.S.S.R.
9006 ft., 100 mins.

Soon after the triumph of Alexander Nevsky, Eisenstein conceived
the idea of making a tripartite fresco based on the life of one of
the most fascinating personalities in the history of Russia--that of
its founder, Ivan the Terrible, the 16th-century Grand Duke of
Moscow who at the age of 17 was crowned the first Tsar of All the
Russias. After the outbreak of the war the project acquired an additional propaganda urgency; the film crew were evacuated to Alma-
Ata in Kazakhstan and work proceeded on the first two parts of the
triptych, Ivan the Terrible and The Boyars' Plot; the third part
was to be made later.

    The story starts in 1547 with the coronation of Ivan who then
pledges to consolidate his power against external enemies and to
defy the selfish and disruptive designs of the boyars (noblemen).
On his victorious return from the war against the Tartars for ac-

cess to the Azov Sea, the Tsar falls gravely ill; his aunt, the
sinister symbol of the power-thirsty boyars, poisons the Tsarina.
After a miraculous recovery Ivan chooses voluntary exile, until a
deputation of his subjects begs him to return to the throne.

Each part is different in mood and character but the complete
story of Ivan's reign is an organic, captivating whole. As in
Alexander Nevsky, Eisenstein only partly intended to make an historically accurate chronicle and injected into the film a good deal
of imagination. But on the other hand, unlike Alexander Nevsky,
the main attention was this time paid to the psychological motivation
of the characters. Eisenstein saw in his hero more than the traditional stereotype--the "Tsar who was a wild beast"--and concentrated on him as a brilliant architect of the greatness of Russia
and on the human aspect of the enigma of power.

Never before had the cinema achieved such a unison of its
elements: music, images, settings and acting are all blended with
absolute mastery. The script was written, in blank verse, in a
stylized Old Russian and the dialogues resemble incantations: rhythmical like a chorale and often confluent with the music. For the
first time the basically musical character of Eisenstein's style is
displayed with clarity. The music itself does not, as before in
Alexander Nevsky, illustrate the images; it rather acts as their
counterpoint. It is the striking visual beauty of Ivan the Terrible
that creates the overpowering mood, with its extraordinary sweeping contrasts of black and white and the changes of location from
the shadow-haunted dusky interiors of the Kremlin to snowbound
landscapes. Interesting here is the final shot of an endless procession of people on the snow, which Eisenstein borrowed from
Stiller's Sir Arne's Treasure.

This visual beauty is as much the contribution of Moskvin
and Tissé as of the exceptional taste of Eisenstein himself in the
plastic media. His designs for Ivan the Terrible, published as a
separate book of drawings, are a work of art in their own right.
The overall effect of Ivan the Terrible is that of a grandiose Wag-
nerian opera. Slow-moving, it is true, but fascinating. As in
Wagner, it was played in the highest emotional note throughout.
Nikolai Cherkasov, solemn and emphatic, succeeded in reconciling
the operatic convention with the demands of psychological cinema,
and the film relies on his performance to an unusually great extent.

Ivan the Terrible is more vivid and brighter in mood than
The Boyars' Plot. It is also more varied and relies more on
imaginative cutting; the slowness and ecstasy of the coronation
scene gives way to the rapid movement of the assault on Kazan.
Its dramatic composition is rather unorthodox: the climax, contrary to all rules, is at the very beginning of the film.

HENRY V   Laurence Olivier

Co-direction and editing: Reginald Beck. Script: Alan Dent, from
the play, "The Life of King Henry V," by William Shakespeare.
Photography: Robert Krasker. Music: William Walton. Art Direction: Paul Sheriff. Costumes: Roger Furse. Cast: Laurence
Olivier (King Henry V of England), Felix Aylmer (Archbishop of
Canterbury), Robert Newton (Ancient Pistol), Esmond Knight (Fluel-
len), Leslie Banks (Chorus), Harcourt Williams (King Charles VI of
France), Renée Asherson (Princess Katharine, his daughter), Ivy St.
Helier (Lady in Waiting, Katharine's teacher), Francis Lister (Duke
of Orleans), Ralph Truman (Montjoy, French Herald), Ernest Thesi-
ger (Duke of Berri, the French Ambassador), Max Adrian (The
Dauphin), George Robey (Falstaff).

Two Cities Films, G.B. 12,296 ft., 137 mins. Technicolor.

Olivier's Henry V is quite simply the first successful screen adaptation of any Shakespearean play; it is also the first example of
really creative use of color in the cinema. In his first attempt at
putting Shakespeare on the screen, Olivier understood that to succeed in translating theatre into cinema one should not fully escape
from the theatre, as had become an obsession with film directors--
he realized that these two media are fundamentally different, but
that the two realities, theatrical and cinematic, can simply be
blended instead of distorted.

     The film starts at the Globe Theatre in London during the
first performance of "Henry V": only after the prologue exhorts
the spectator "to let his imaginary forces work" does the film move
into the open. It seems the recipe had been found: the theatricality
of Shakespeare was dismissed simply by being acknowledged. After
that Olivier could go ahead with bringing out the cinematic qualities
of the drama, and it has since become a cliché that Shakespeare is
very cinematic. The visual aspect of Henry V is deliberately styled
after Paolo Ucello's paintings, a trifle simplified in design, decorative and without excessive realism. This was a very lucky choice
of visual convention: it provided not only a perfect key to the period and to the mood of the work (in the theatre one would call it
"suitable stage design") but also served as an excuse for some of
the deficiencies inevitable with the wartime shortages of materials.
In this way Olivier could unashamedly use the backdrops obviously
present in many scenes in the film and still preserve charm and
good taste.

     Otherwise Henry V is full of examples of Olivier's individual
style of bringing Shakespeare to the screen, the style which he
would later use, with modifications, in his other two films made

from the Great Bard's plays. To these techniques belong the presentation of monologues on the soundtrack without the corresponding lip movement and the sweeping and often ingenious camera movements which convey messages of which the spectator is not even aware--in one scene the camera draws back instead of closing in on the King in order to stress his unity with the host of soldiers whom he exhorts to battle and who gradually appear in the frame.

It was incidentally these very sentiments of patriotism and the need for unity which motivated the making of Henry V, a situation similar to that at the roots of Ivan the Terrible (which Eisenstein was just shooting in Russia); both films were also the theretofore most expensive ventures of the film industries in their respective countries. Olivier had wonderful costumes made for his film and it is hard to credit the fact that they were often makeshift efforts. The final impression is splendid: medieval in tone, mellow in color, full of imagination and scope. The brilliant, full, and fluid scene of the Battle of Agincourt remains a classical cinematic battle piece and weighs heavily in the final judgment accorded the film. One need mention only as a matter of course the class of the acting, not only by the director/star himself but by the whole team.

FRENZY (Hets) Alf Sjöberg

Script: Ingmar Bergman. Photography: Martin Bodin. Music: Hilding Rosenberg. Cast: Stig Järrel ("Caligula"), Alf Kjellin (Jan-Erik Widgren), Mai Zetterling (Bertha Olsson), Olof Winnerstrand (Headmaster), Gösta Cederlund (Pippi), Stig Olin (Sandman), Olav Riego (Mr. Widgren), Märta Arbin (Mrs. Widgren), Jan Molander (Pettersson), Hugo Björne (Doctor), Gunnar Björnstrand (Teacher).

Aktiebologel Svensk Filmindustri, Sweden. 9112 ft., 101 mins.

Sjöberg's next success after The Road to Heaven was a further proof of the renaissance in Swedish cinema. His work always gives prominence to disputes about man's road through life; this time he chose the path to maturity as his theme. Bergman's excellent script (he was here debuting as a film writer) gave the director the fullest opportunity for precise delineation of the characters in the social context of Sweden; but Sjöberg went further. He did not limit himself to creating a psychological drama analyzing the actions, impulses and contradictions of man in a conflict situation, but introduced into the tissue of the work an interesting allegory of the situation in Europe. Namely, Fascism, understood as a psychopathological moral evil and represented in the film by a sadistic Latin master, cast strikingly to resemble Himmler.

This teacher, hated by the whole class, derives particular
pleasure from terrorizing one of the final year pupils, a sensitive
boy, unable to form a psychological barrier in himself. The young
man regains peace and poise through his friendship with a young female shop assistant whom he once met drunk in the street and
walked home. The girl fell into alcoholism and depression because
of an individual who persecutes her, but she would not reveal who
the tyrant is. Sympathy towards the boy helps her to regain her
emotional balance. But evil does not sleep; the tormentor returns, the girl is again in crisis. The boy leaves, the setback
drives him into illness. When he returns to her room after some
time, he finds her dead.

The teacher is hiding behind the door. Caligula (as he is
called by the pupils) is suspected of murder but is cleared by the
facts (the girl died from a heart attack). But the boy is defeated
once again when the vengeful psychopath causes his expulsion from
school. The only moral victory of the hero is the confrontation
with Caligula in the presence of the headmaster. The headmaster
privately takes the boy's side; but the would-be graduate will have
to fend for himself in future after this brutal showdown with the
cruelty of life.

Previously in the cinema, studies of a psychopath who under-
mines society achieved even in the most ambitious cases only a social dimension; this applies particularly to the films of Fritz Lang.
Frenzy is not only a conscious, dramatic and topical treatment, but
seems to work also on the political level: in the finale the hero
brings to mind associations with nations liberated from the stifling
threat of Fascism. But did Sjöberg really want to give his film
such ideological overtones? There is no conclusive proof of this,
but the obvious parallel between the psychopathic teacher and Himmler gives Caligula, in the context of the film, the character of a
key to a hidden psychological structure--even if this occurred spontaneously. Perhaps the associations with Fascism stem from the
very atmosphere of the picture, from its somber, post-expressionist
visual aspect, from the symbols which bring to mind the German
silent school.

From this angle Sjöberg's film is a consistent and excellently
directed work; other technical details also, like the staging, use of
the soundtrack, editing, and direction of actors prove the high class
of the director. On the other hand, he did not do so well with his
dialogues, which often overstate obvious things, with his symbols,
which are obtrusive, and with the finale. The colorless ending is
in sharp contrast with the intensity of the earlier parts of the film,
and closes the picture on a note of undecided melancholy, as if the
director did not want to be unrelieved in reiterating the grim facts
of life, yet still tried to shun any optimistic touch.

THE WOMAN IN THE WINDOW   Fritz Lang

Script: Nunnally Johnson, from the novel, "Once Off Guard," by
J. H. Wallis. Photography: Milton Krasner. Music: Arthur
Lang. Cast: Edward G. Robinson (Prof. Richard Wanley), Joan
Bennett (Alice Reed), Raymond Massey (District Attorney Frank
Lalor), Dan Duryea (Heidt, bodyguard), Edmond Breon (Dr. Bark-
stone), Thomas E. Jackson (Inspector Jackson), Dorothy Paterson
(Mrs. Wanley), Arthur Loft (Mazard), Frank Dawson (Steward).

Christie Corporation/International Pictures/RKO Radio Pictures,
U.S.A. 8922 ft., 99 mins.

This film is one of the most spectacular thrillers of the 40's with
its classical motifs and its ruthless look at life. Man a woman's
victim: a college psychology professor, infatuated with a picture of
a beautiful girl, meets the portrait's model by chance, follows her
to her apartment and is forced to kill a jealous thug in self-defense.
They hide the body; carelessly the professor gets involved in the
police search, forces himself into a tight spot, and is blackmailed
to boot. It seems that nothing will save him ... until the build-up
of suspense is suddenly dispersed by a completely unexpected ending
which brings us back to the world of The Cabinet of Dr. Caligari.

    The really méchant sequence of the removal of the corpse
from the apartment to the woods is the best in the film. The cau-
tious conclusion is that the roots of evil and the potential for violence exist in everyone (the professor attempts to kill the blackmailer). But Lang would not say more. While in his M of 13
years earlier there was genuine human tragedy and suffering behind
the killer's whine, and the story was supported by penetrating psychological observation, The Woman in the Window is only an excellent melodrama and does not venture beyond the brilliant manipulation of plot.

IT HAPPENED TOMORROW   René Clair

Script: Dudley Nichols and Clair, based on stories by Lord Dun-
sany, Hugh Wedlock and Howard Snyder and ideas of Lewis R.
Foster. Photography: Archie Stout and Eugen Schüftan. Music:
Robert Stolz. Cast: Dick Powell (Larry Stevens), Linda Darnell
(Sylvia), Jack Oakie (Cigolini), Edgar Kennedy (Inspector Mulrooney),
John Philliber (Pop Benson), Edward Brophy (Jake Schomberg),

George Cleveland (Mr. Gordon), Sig Ruman (Mr. Beckstein), Paul Guilfoyle (Shep), George Chandler (Bob).

Arnold Pressburger, United Artists, U.S.A.   7651 ft., 85 mins.

René Clair is probably the director who introduced the most light-hearted fantasy into films in the mature period of cinema--comic ghosts and cinematic wonders as in the early films of Méliès. It Happened Tomorrow, the second of his American successes, continued the witty legerdemain which gave so much charm to I Married a Witch: this time there are no ghosts but only a toying with time and some unassuming variations on the theme of the fickleness of fate.

The concept of the plot is as simple as it is rich in splendid possibilities for piling up coincidences: a certain young journalist receives tomorrow's papers through the post every morning. Of course he is always first with the news and does not miss the occasion to line his pockets with money won on the pools. He has the world on a string but only up to a point. One day the wondrous newspaper announces to the lucky dog his own death....

It Happened Tomorrow is notable above all for its brisk pace; probably not since The Italian Straw Hat was Clair so versatile. He was also no less witty than in his best comedies; and since he knew how to retail the humor in a whole series of situational gags and skillfully rounded off the whole structure, he proved that he had caught his second wind after so many lean years. Indeed, even though Clair's last Hollywood venture, an adaptation of Agatha Christie, was to misfire, after his return to France he would make a number of refined and charming films.

THE WAY AHEAD   Carol Reed

Script: Eric Ambler and Peter Ustinov, from a story by Ambler. Photography: Guy Green. Music: William Alwyn. Cast: David Niven (Jim Perry), Raymond Huntley (Davenport), Billy Hartnell (Sgt. Fletcher), Stanley Holloway (Brewer), James Donald (Lloyd), John Laurie (Luke), Leslie Dwyer (Beck), Hugh Burden (Parsons).

Two Cities Films, G.B.   10,378 ft., 115 mins.

When the war broke out, Reed, already an established director, at first handled neutral themes: Kipps (1941) made from the novel by H. G. Wells, Young Mr. Pitt (1942) is a story of the life of the British prime minister. But one cannot shun the present forever,

and especially could not at a time when common effort meant everything and even the King, because of fuel restrictions, had a line
painted inside his bath to indicate the maximum amount of hot water
allowed. The origins of The Way Ahead are broadly similar to
those of Dickinson's Next of Kin: it was to be an instructive film
for the army about the training of recruits (first title "The New
Lot") and it grew into a feature.

      Reed was still not interested in battles; again the real war
is beyond the horizon. It is a film about how people become soldiers. Seven civilians are called up just after Dunkirk: they are
not enthusiastic about it all, they resent military discipline and,
frankly, are a bit afraid. Very, very gradually the barriers between being a civilian and being a soldier are brought down and they
grow to form a closely-knit combat unit of men ready to meet death
in the North African campaign.

      Clearly, for such a theme veracity is everything: and Reed
provided it. He captured the essence of incipient antagonism between people and their growth of understanding, he ensured natural,
credible acting, and arranged for good dialogue and from these elements composed a skillful and technically imaginative film with good
editing, fast pace and just enough suspense to add a non-documentary
touch. The Way Ahead is a classic among British films about the
infantry, in the same way as Coward's In Which We Serve is about
the Navy and Asquith's The Way to the Stars, about the RAF.

DOUBLE INDEMNITY Billy Wilder

Script: Wilder and Raymond Chandler, based on the story by James
M. Cain. Photography: John F. Seitz. Music: Miklos Rozsa,
with Symphony in D minor by César Franck. Cast: Fred MacMur-
ray (Walter Neff), Barbara Stanwyck (Phyllis Dietrichson), Edward
G. Robinson (Barton Keyes), Porter Hall (Mr. Jackson), Jean
Heather (Lola Dietrichson), Tom Powers (Mr. Dietrichson), Byron
Barr (Nino Zachette), Richard Gaines (Mr. Norton), Fortunio Bona-
nova (Sam Gorlopis), John Philliber (Joe Pete).

Paramount, U.S.A. 9663 ft., 107 mins.

Double Indemnity, Wilder's first outstanding film, counts among the
classics of film noir, the characteristic product of the 40's. The
film noir is American by birth but European by descent. It revels
in the Germanic tradition of romanticized horror; recalls the decadent mood of the films of the French Poetic Realism; and uses
some typical situations and accessories (for instance the concept of
a femme fatale) which are firmly European. Only the idiom of ur-

ban crime is unmistakably American. All this is not accidental; the principal creators of the genre (directors Lang, Hitchcock, Preminger, and Wilder, and composer Rozsa, who wrote the ominous score for Double Indemnity), all came from the other side of the Atlantic.

The starting point of most of their films is second-rate literature. Double Indemnity is no exception although its script is precise and dramatically tight. The story (somewhat melodramatically presented as the recorded confession of a villain) is thrilling, Hitchcockian and cynical. A wife, aided by her insurance agent lover disposes of her rich husband for the insurance premium, doubled as is the case for railway accidents. The claims inspector smells a rat; the lover discovers that he was double-crossed and kills the woman.

Double Indemnity is excellently directed: Wilder knew how to cash in on the menacing poetry of Californian roads in twilight, dusky railway depots, shuttered rooms and furtive meetings in supermarkets; he could instantly conjure up the wicked air of decay and seediness, and splendidly caught the mood of the 40's in the urban America of double-breasted suits and obsolete automobiles. The result is an intelligent, gripping thriller (note the celebrated scene when the car stalls after the murder); wry, without a trace of compassion for anybody--a clinical record of a case of greed and ruthlessness.

LAURA   Otto Preminger

Script: Jay Dratler, Betty Reinhardt and Samuel Hoffenstein, from the novel by Vera Caspary. Photography: Joseph La Shelle. Music: David Raksin. Cast: Gene Tierney (Laura Hunt), Dana Andrews (Mark McPherson), Clifton Webb (Waldo Lydecker), Vincent Price (Shelby Carpenter), Judith Anderson (Anne Treadwell), Dorothy Adams (Bessie Clary), Ralph Dunn (Fred Callahan), Cy Kendall (Inspector).

20th Century-Fox, U.S.A. 7921 ft., 88 mins.

Laura, another significant contribution to the tradition of film noir is Preminger's first important work. This film is not a drama of dusky suburban streets and sinister motives, but develops inside brightly-lit expensive New York apartments. The motives, however, are as wicked as in Double Indemnity. Thus Preminger contributed a new element to the genre: the elegance, theatrical in origin, of the parlor melodrama; a comedy of evil-minded manners, which largely relies on atmosphere and the subtle undertones of a clever dialogue.

Such is <u>Laura</u>, a detective story with an exceedingly complex plot complete with the wrong person murdered and the gun concealed in an antique clock. The assortment of black characters reminds one of the corpse-in-the-library thrillers of Agatha Christie: the insanely jealous poseur of a columnist; a character living off rich women; his cynical mistress; the idealized heroine of the title. Direction is quiet and seemingly disinterested, the dialogue smart, acting (particularly Clifton Webb's) expert, photography bright and high-key which, paradoxically, turns the glamor magazine story into a poignant and threatening study of highlife greed.

ARSENIC AND OLD LACE   Frank Capra

Script: Julius J. Epstein and Philip G. Epstein, from the play by Joseph Kesselring. Photography: Sol Polito. Music: Max Steiner. Cast: Cary Grant (Mortimer Brewster), Priscilla Lane (Elaine Harper), Raymond Massey (Jonathan Brewster), Jack Carson (O'Hara), Edward Everett Horton (Mr. Witherspoon), Peter Lorre (Dr. Einstein), James Gleason (Lieut. Rooney), Josephine Hull (Abby Brewster), Jean Adair (Martha Brewster).

Warner Bros., U.S.A. 10,610 ft., 118 mins.

The last famous Capra comedy: this time it would not be a sentimental story sustained in the spirit of the New Deal, with a profusion of social connotations, but a macabre farce according to the best British "horror in the suburbs" recipe, and made from a phenomenally popular stage play. Capra did not stand on his head to try to make the play more cinematic; he limited himself to an excellent choice of actors, vivid handling of the plot, and full use of the plethora of situational gags. The gags fall in places into forcible exaggeration, but this is surely forgivable in view of the logic and internal consistency of the whole.

The fun of <u>Arsenic and Old Lace</u> consists of following the adventures of a chap who finds it difficult to reconcile family obligations and personal happiness. After graduation the hero returns with his refined fiancée to the house of the aunts who brought him up, and finds with horror that the aunts entertain themselves by quietly killing off their elderly tenants. The bodies are buried in the cellar by a subnormal cousin. Having gotten wind of what is happening, another relative, a professional thug, turns up with yet another corpse, wanting, naturally enough, to contribute to the collection in the cellar. But the aunts object to burying "an alien body."

How can one hide the shocking truth from the fiancée and at

the same time quietly move the aunts to a mental hospital? Quite
a problem. If the hero had not solved it the film would not be a
comedy. But it is, and one of the most amusing of its zany kind.

THE SEVENTH CROSS   Fred Zinnemann

Script: Helen Deutsch, from the novel by Anna Seghers. Photog-
raphy: Karl Freund. Music: Roy Webb. Cast: Spencer Tracy
(George Heisler), Signe Hasso (Toni), Hume Cronyn (Paul Roeder),
Jessica Tandy (Liesel Roeder), Agnes Moorehead (Mme. Marelli),
Herbert Rudley (Franz Marnet), Felix Bressart (Poldi Schlamm),
Ray Collins (Ernst Wallau), Alexander Granach (Zillich), Kurt Katch
(Leo Hermann).

MGM, U.S.A. 10,057 ft., 112 mins.

In a Nazi concentration camp there are seven crosses intended for
the escaped prisoners. Six of them are caught, but one cross will
not be required--the seventh prisoner manages to flee his oppres-
sors. Anna Seghers' novel tells of his odyssey through Germany
in the shadow of the swastika and about the solidarity of the honest
people who risk their lives to help him. The American screen
adaptation was meant to convey the truth of a situation about which
Zinnemann (an Austrian by birth) and his collaborators felt strongly.
The United States still knows very little about Hitler's Third Reich:
things such as this are both distant and not easy to understand in
a democratic society.

Thus The Seventh Cross came, almost inevitably, to skate
on the verge of propaganda, excess factual information and mysti-
cism, as Zinnemann tried to reach his audience. But the director
emerged creditably from the difficult task he had undertaken out of
deep conviction, and the resulting success of the film is due to the
restraint and probity of the imagery, from which it never departed
for the sake of external appeal. Of course, the method adopted by
Zinnemann condemned him from the very start to a defensive artistic position: if someone wants to be honest, he risks the accusation of bleakness.

But Zinnemann did not look for an artistic alibi. On the
contrary, he made his position even worse through sentimental support of human honesty; this would later be the weakness most often
singled out in his films, and it was here aggravated by the disastrous musical score. Besides this, the middle part of the film
contains lengthy patches, loses much of its potential impact and reflects all the imperfections of the not yet fully crystalized style of
the director--in particular the lack of proportion between the main

plot and the background.   Yet this generally faithful screen adaptation of the novel of a German anti-Fascist writer has some really
beautiful moments, finely brought out by Freund's camera work and
tangibly recreating everyday life in the country of the Brown Shirts.

GASLIGHT   George Cukor

Script: John Van Druten, Walter Reisch and John L. Balderston,
from the play, "Angel Street," by Patrick Hamilton and the 1940
film Gaslight by Thorold Dickinson. Photography: Joseph Ruttenberg. Music: Bronislau Kaper. Cast: Charles Boyer (Gregory
Anton), Ingrid Bergman (Paula Alquist), Joseph Cotten (Brian
Cameron), Angela Lansbury (Nancy Oliver), Dame May Whitty (Miss
Thwaites), Barbara Everest (Elizabeth Tompkins), Emil Rameau
(Mario Guardi), Eustace Wyatt (Budge), Edmund Breon (General Hud-
delston), Halliwell Hobbes (Mr. Mufflin).

MGM, U.S.A. 10,229 ft., 114 mins.

Gaslight is a typical example of Cukor's society melodramas. The
director's most famous films, The Philadelphia Story and Adam's
Rib (1949), were elegant, sunlit affairs full of easy living and clever
talk, somewhat theatrical in their polished, well-balanced plot and
their reliance on dialogue. Gaslight, made after the British film of
the same title, was given treatment along similar lines; the details
of the plot were tailored to suit the cutter. The murderer of Alice
Alquist, a singer, was never found. Her niece marries a handsome
stranger who seems to be more interested in the attic of the house
of murder, which she inherited, than in his young wife. Later he
tries to drive her mad so that he can search the house at leisure
for the jewels he missed when he murdered her aunt.

Gaslight, although one of Cukor's best films, does not match
the British original. It is, on the other hand, an amiable period
melodrama in a Victorian setting, dominated by soft lighting and
elaborate camera movements, a film of moods and undertones.
Cukor knows how to create atmosphere; an eerie effect of the dead
woman's presence in the house is obtained by often drawing the
camera's attention to objects which belonged to her. Likewise
Cukor conjures up the romantic mood of a pre-Raphaelite painting
during the couple's sunny Italian honeymoon and suggestively evokes
the claustrophobic feel of the Victorian household where gas lights
dim menacingly when the husband searches the attic.

In the absence of particular brilliance on the part of the director, the film is distinguished by the acting in the three main
roles. Ingrid Bergman gives a particularly radiant performance as

the wife--a role which is among the best in her career and which
helps one to understand why Cukor is regarded as a "director of
women."

HAIL THE CONQUERING HERO   Preston Sturges

Script: Sturges. Photography: John Seitz. Music: Werner Hey-
mann. Cast: Eddie Bracken (Woodrow Truesmith), Ella Raines
(Libby), Bill Edwards (Forrest Noble), Raymond Walburn (Mr.
Noble, the Mayor), Franklin Pangborn (Chairman of the Reception
Committee), William Demarest (Sergeant), Georgia Caine (Mrs.
Truesmith), Freddie Steele (Bugsy).

Paramount, U.S.A. 9053 ft., 101 mins.

Sturges' reputation as a vitriolic satirist of American society is
based, apart from the earlier Sullivan's Travels, on two riotous
comedies deriding small-town America: The Miracle of Morgan
Creek (1944) and Hail the Conquering Hero. The latter is his best
satirical film and his last important one. Imagine a marine who is
discharged from the Navy on medical grounds but is very shy of returning to his home town. When he phones his mom, "hay fever"
becomes "jungle fever" on the unclear line and everyone in town
comes to the station to welcome the hero of Guadalcanal. He is
invited to run in the mayoral election as the most distinguished citizen; but he suddenly confesses the truth to the populace. They do
not mind at all, but praise him all the more for his honesty!

Anyone who saw Sullivan's Travels will rightly expect Sturges
to squeeze every potentiality out of such a story; and as that film
contemplated the unbridgable rift between the poor and the well-to-
do liberals, Hail the Conquering Hero investigates the relationship
between heroism and humiliation, in the vein of a no-holds-barred
spoof. The prevailing mood of the movie is coldly cynical. Sturges
aims at exposing the naiveté of the electorate and the real motive
hidden behind a vote for this or that candidate. The edge of satire
seems leveled also at the American electoral system when we hear
that at one point the hero is tipped for the White House.

The major flaw of the film is the sudden collapse of the satirical tone. When the hero confesses, the picture suddenly becomes
a sentimental melodrama. But the small-town scenes are excellent:
a frenetic, scrambling, myopic canvas populated with hilarious
characters (but less funny if you think about it). Andrew Sarris'
description of Sturges as "the Breughel of the American cinema"
appears very apt. Crowd scenes, shot with a static camera, are
the best and still allow, as does the rest of the picture, room for

accurate characterization.   The really fine split-second cutting
makes one think of the editing in the mature silent films.   And the
whole picture, with its episodic narrative, does indeed go back to
slapstick comedy.

1945

LES ENFANTS DU PARADIS   Marcel Carné

Script: Jacques Prévert.   Photography: Roger Hubert.   Music: Joseph Kosma and Maurice Thiriet.   Art Direction: Alexandre Trauner, Léon Barsacq and Raymond Gabutti.   Cast: Pierre Brasseur (Frédérick Lemaître), Arletty (Garance), Jean-Louis Barrault (Baptiste Debureau), Maria Cesarès (Nathalie), Marcel Herrand (Pierre Lacenaire), Louis Salou (Count Edouard de Montray), Pierre Renoir (Jéricho), Jane Marken (Madame Hermine), Fabien Loris (Avril), Etienne Decroux (Anselme Debureau), Marcel Pérès (Director of Funambules Theatre), Gaston Modot (Blind Man), Paul Frankeur (Police Inspector).

Pathé Cinéma, France.   Part I: Le Boulevard du Crime, 9066 ft., 100 mins.; Part II: L'Homme blanc, 7762 ft., 86 mins.

When, soon after making Les Visiteurs du soir, the actor Jean-Louis Barrault told Prévert and Carné the life story of Baptiste Debureau, the famous 19th-century mimic actor, the idea emerged of making it into a film.   This was a more difficult task; even despite the refuge of peaceful Nice the wartime conditions were not inviting.   There was also a regulation limiting the length of new feature films to 90 minutes, a clever way out of which was to split Les Enfants du paradis into two parts.   Carné's second excursion into the past turns out to be one of the highlights of the French cinema, an immensely suggestive poetic vision of a bygone epoch. Mid-19th-century France of rapid social changes: the bourgeoisie grow in strength and challenge the royalist ancien régime; a new social class, the urban proletariat, appears.

The story is set in the milieu of the actors of a boulevard theatre de Funambules; the many plots all center around the great

love of Bapiste and Garance. Baptiste fascinates Garance, a beautiful courtesan, by indicating, in mime, the real culprit when she is
accused of theft. They will never be together: Baptiste will marry
Nathalie, the elusive Garance will hover between the anarchist letter writer Lacenaire, the actor Lamaître and the decadent Count de
Montray. A few years later Lamaître is a great actor, Baptiste a
great mime and Garance the mysterious lady in black who comes to
the theatre every night to watch him. Jealous Lacenaire murders
de Montray, her lover, while Baptiste and Garance are briefly reunited only to be separated again by Nathalie who pledges never to
give up Baptiste. Garance silently leaves and Baptiste tries in vain
to find her in the carnival crowds.

This complex plot gives an idea of the literary manner of the
film--as if transplanted from the 19th-century romantic novels of
Alexandre Dumas and Honoré de Balzac. The film resembles a
flowing river of which only one current can be seen at a time--a
tiny episode of a constantly changing life. A fitting comparison,
since the message of the film is: You cannot step twice into the
same river. The past magic is irretrievable, and no one can reverse the course of life--a typically French fatalistic philosophy, in
which chance is the dominant force. Yet Carné did not allow his
film to be overwhelmed by literature. He is saved by the power
and freshness of his vision.

Les Enfants du paradis emerges as a parable of the relationship of life and art, a dispute about the sense of existence, "a gigantic philosophical ballet," and a panorama of styles in French
theatre (represented by the different styles of acting of each of main
protagonists). Yet it would be wrong to think that this film was an
unexpected development in Carné's work. It is only its logical culmination, using familiar motifs (hopeless love), "typical" characters,
and characteristic symbols (vagrant Jéricho symbolizes destiny and
Baptiste, the union of life and art).

At the same time one feels that the real heroes, the "Children of Paradise" of the title, are the mobs filling the galleries of
the theatre, and that the film is the ultimate in Carné's populist
cinema. Les Enfants du paradis was the most ambitious French
production to date, it gathered the cream of French actors and film-
makers. Shown only after the Liberation, it became a triumphant
proof of the vitality of the national cinema.

THEY WHO STEP ON THE TIGER'S TAIL (Tora no O-o Fumu
    Otokotachi) Akira Kurosawa

Script: Kurosawa, from the Kabuki play, "Kanjincho." Photography:
Takeo Ito. Music: Tadashi Hattori. Cast: Denjiro Okochi (Ben-

kei), Susumu Fujita (Togashi), Masayuki Mori (Kamei), Takashi
Shimura (Kataoka), Aritake Kono (Ise), Yoshio Kosugi (Suruga),
Dekao Yoko (Hidachibo), Hanshiro Iwai (Yoshitsune), Kenichi Eno-
moto (Porter).

Toho, Japan.   Released in 1952.   5167 ft., 57 mins.

Kurosawa's first masterpiece, the shortest of his films, is an illustration of a famous historical episode.   General Yoshitsune is fleeing with his entourage from the anger of his brother.   All are disguised as traveling monks.   They arrive at a border crossing point;
the problem is to convince the guards that they are genuine monks.
The achievement of this takes almost the entire length of the film.
The controversy is between four people: the commander of the
post, the general, one of his retainers called Benkei and a porter
traveling with the party.   The roles are changed and the general
masquerades as a porter.

Kurosawa shows himself in this sketch to be a master of
dramatic narrative.   Unperturbed by the basically static quality of
the story he employs dynamic and imaginative film techniques and
gives it life, power and suspense.   The uneasy, volatile camera ob-
serves the action from surprising angles; the development of the
narrative is speeded up and punctuated by fast dissolves and com-
mented upon by the original, disturbing music.   The film works on
two different levels.   First, as a parody, a near-operatic farce in
which the dignity of the officials is contrasted with the basically
ludicrous situation they are in.   The key personality is the comic
figure of the shrewd porter.

Secondly, it is an allegory, in the style of Rousseau on the
meaning of authority.   The battle of wits with the border guards is
won when the "general" cleverly strikes the "porter"; it is thus in-
conceivable for their social positions to be fake--at that time in
Japan servants did not strike masters even in pantomine.   Thus the
film has an unexpected social aspect.   Kurosawa's resurrection of
the use of wipes is an interesting technical touch, obsolete since the
introduction of sound cinema.

LA BATAILLE DU RAIL   René Clément

Script: Clément and Colette Audry. Photography: Henri Alekan.
Music: Yves Baudrier. Cast: Antoine Laurent (Camargue),
Desagneux (Maquis Chief), Leroy (Station Master), Redon (Mechan-
ic), Pauléon (Station Master at St. André), Rauzena (Shunter), Jean
Clarieux (Lampin), Barnault and Kronegger (Germans) and the
French Railwaymen.

Coopérative Générale du Cinéma Français, France. 7800 ft., 87 mins.

The first report of the fight of the French against the Nazi occupation; a short film commissioned by the Resistance Movement grew in size to reflect a panorama of activities aimed at deflecting the Nazi war supplies on their way to the Normandy front. The material shot by the thus-far unknown amateur film-maker simply turned out to be too good a chance to miss to make a definitive work documenting the French contribution towards the liberation of Europe. Although La Bataille du rail is certainly uneven, largely through the circumstances of production and despite its obvious lack of professional fluency, it is at the same time moving and deeply authentic. Its dynamism and boldness are impressive.

The director of this epic tale of the struggle of the French railwaymen indisputably achieved by his debut a prominent place in the vanguard of French cinema. A number of episodes use editing and significant detail with remarkable aptness: for instance the scene of the shooting of the hostages, when Clément shows, in a close-up, one of them watching a spider descending on its thread, or the culminating moment of the derailment of the train, in which the final chord of the dying motion is the accordion rolling down the embankment. The latter scene was filmed using six cameras simultaneously, which shows that Clément well understood the essence of cinema and the power pent up in the adventurous use of detail.

This understanding applied itself equally not only to the décor but also to the staging of situations. One of the episodes mercilessly shows the defeat of the Maquis in a battle with an armored train: this is the best proof that La Bataille du rail was not peddling easy, optimistic assurances of the success of the French partisans. The fight against the enemy was not waged in the style of a folk ballad; it was desperate and tragic--and it is shown just in this spirit. The documentary values of Clément's film are augmented by the use of non-professional actors, who often really participated in the actual events. This was of course quite natural in view of the intentions of the film's creators and it is worth noting that this coincided with the general tendency towards greater realism on the screen; the tendency to portray situations the experiences of war had brought nearer to everyone.

In Italy these tendencies gave rise to a powerful procession of Neorealist films, but in France La Bataille du rail was not followed by other similar pictures. Clément himself would not use this particular creative method again. In the years to come he would be making films revolving around outstanding acting performances; only Le Mura di Malapaga would be a relative exception.

THE STORY OF G. I. JOE   William A. Wellman

Script: Leopold Atlas, Guy Endore and Philip Stevenson, from war reports by Ernie Pyle. Photography: Russell Metty. Music: Ann Ronell and Louise Applebaum. Cast: Burgess Meredith (Ernie Pyle), Robert Mitchum (Lt. Walker), Freddie Steele (Sgt. Warnicki), Wally Cassell (Private Dondaro), Jimmy Lloyd (Private Spencer), Jack Reilly (Private Murphy), Bill Murphy (Private Mew).

United Artists, U.S.A.   9838 ft., 109 mins.

The portrayal of war in literature and films went through a significant evolution--at first it was an adventure, later a demonic vision of hell. But Wellman shows its real face: war as a dangerous task, a tragic everyday duty. The film is based on the reports of the greatest American war correspondent, who was killed during the invasion of Okinawa. Pyle did not rely on stylistic finesse, nor did he impress with exotic details; he transferred onto the pages of his notebook what he saw directly before his eyes, supplementing it only with reflections which sprang spontaneously from the everyday life of the soldiers. This tone is preserved in Wellman's film, an outstanding blend of restraint and authenticity, the crowning work of his best period, which started with the concentrated reflection of The Ox-Bow Incident.

The story begins with episodes from the battles in North Africa in 1943, when the American forces joined the Allies, and ends during the period of the March on Rome, following the breach of the German defenses at Monte Cassino. During this period Pyle accompanied one of the infantry battalions and followed the wartime fortunes of the young Americans: the acquisition of experience in battle, the everyday hassle with military duties, the large and small joys, the encounters with death. The recorded events are not arranged on the screen according to any dramatic construction. They are simply equivalent to the pages of a reporter's notebook; their order is chronological and their choice is a measure of their commonness.

The dominating feature of Wellman's film is the realism, supported by the texture of photography and the convincing, subtle acting. For a different theme, a similar style would have resulted in sterility, but in this picture the drama is generated by the subject matter itself. Wellman did not limit his efforts to matter-of-fact reporting; he steeped The Story of G. I. Joe in an aura of weariness, indifference and sadness for those who depart. This film is a prime example of the achievement of the desired perfection--and the best memorial for every ordinary soldier who fought in the war.

THE LOST WEEKEND   Billy Wilder

Script: Charles Brackett and Wilder, based on the novel by Charles
R. Jackson.   Photography: John F. Seitz.   Music: Miklos Rozsa,
with overture and opening aria of Verdi's "La Traviata." Cast:
Ray Milland (Don Birnam), Jane Wyman (Helen St. James), Howard
Da Silva (Nat), Philip Terry (Wick Birnam), Doris Dowling (Gloria),
Frank Faylen (Bim), Mary Young (Mrs. Deveridge), Lillian Fon-
taine (Mrs. St. James), Anita Bolster (Mrs. Foley), Lewis L.
Russell (Charles St. James).

Paramount, U.S.A.   8912 ft., 99 mins.

Although Jackson's book about an alcoholic cannot match the much
more subtle contemporary study, the novel "Under the Volcano" by
Malcolm Lowry, the film made from it is the most celebrated, and
the best, American "problem picture" of the 40's.   The Lost Weekend is the chronicle of the four-day drinking spell of an alcoholic
failed writer.   In the first shot the camera, diving into the flat
through the window, discovers Birnam concealing a whisky bottle
outside while his brother, off whom Birnam lives, prepares to leave
for the weekend.   Left alone Birnam starts to drink heavily; to raise
funds he appropriates money left for the housemaid, tries to pawn a
typewriter, then to steal a lady's bag.   He ends up at the infernal
Alcoholic Ward, but manages to escape.

     The theme itself was bold from the point of view of the Mo-
tion Picture Production Code.   Wilder approached it without a trace
of sensationalism.   He conceded the fact that the camera was perhaps not the most appropriate instrument for medical diagnosis, dispensed with Freudian explanations and pop psychology, and instead
simply observed the protagonist.   Milland gives an intelligent portrayal of a weak-willed drunk--charming, cunning, pathetic.   Visually, Wilder gave the film great dramatic power by the restrained use
of para-documentary techniques, without falling into the pitfalls other
American directors found hard to avoid.

     The picture of sultry New York is startlingly realistic: when
the hero goes on his desperate search for a pawnshop he is followed
by a hidden camera.   The nightmare world of an alcoholic is visually
approached through low-key photography, frequent use of unusual camera angles and striking compositions; significant objects are often
given prominence (whisky glasses, the menacing liquor bottle concealed inside a lampshade); deep-focus photography stresses the disturbed dimensions of the hero's world.   The slow pace of the opening is suddenly discharged in the scenes of delirium tremens, where
Wilder uses real animals as the hero's fantasies.   The power and
vicious quality of these sequences are strongly reminiscent of Buñuel

(Los Olvidados) and Surrealist art. The neurotic music is a good
exponent of the mood of the picture. It is only the final renuncia-
tion of drink by Birnam which is unconvincing.

BRIEF ENCOUNTER   David Lean

Script: Noël Coward, Lean and Anthony Havelock-Allan, from the
play, "Still Life," by Coward. Photography: Robert Krasker.
Music: Second Piano Concerto in C minor, Op. 8, by Sergei Vas-
silievich Rachmaninov, played by Eileen Joyce (National Symphony
Orchestra conducted by Muir Mathieson). Cast: Celia Johnson
(Laura Jesson), Trevor Howard (Alec Harvey), Cyril Raymond (Fred
Jesson), Everley Gregg (Dolly Messiter), Stanley Holloway (Albert
Godby, ticket collector), Joyce Carey (Myrtle Bagot, barmaid),
Margaret Barton (Beryl Walters, bar assistant), Dennis Harkin
(Stanley, chocolate seller).

Cineguild, G.B.   7750 ft., 86 mins.

One of the finest portrayals in cinema of a certain unfulfilled feeling between two decent people, suddenly dazzled by their unexpected
encounter. The meeting, at the railway station, is the result of
pure chance; they are both attached to their families, do not seek
adventure, nor are they driven by the restlessness of youth. Yet
they allow themselves to be engulfed by the unleashed emotion, but
not to the end. They entrusted their fate to chance when they met
and that chance makes them part. Lean told the brief story of the
shy romance with an extraordinary, pastel freshness without impressive cinematic effects and without the build-up of dramatic conflicts.

Coward's excellent script was transferred to the screen in a
manner it deserved; the result is an intimate psychological study,
which not only amounts to a revelation in the cinema of the 40's,
but also in the wider context of cinema history. The uncommonness
of Brief Encounter when it was made rested mainly in its turn towards everyday life, in setting the plot in a strongly delineated
background of provincial England--the railway waiting room, the
streets of the town--and not in the coziness of parlors, previously
the unbreakable rule. The concreteness of the scenery was in fact
used by Lean somewhat too ostentatiously: the background episodes, intended to enhance realism, were often overdone and
obtrusive.

The authenticity of Brief Encounter was achieved through the
very choice of the scenery and above all through the characterization of the protagonists. Celia Johnson and Trevor Howard are lit-

erally inseparable from the parts they play, they fascinate the spectator with the intimate and candid quality of their acting and make
the complex relationship of the heroes wholly credible. Among
other values which put the seal on the success of Brief Encounter
two should be mentioned: an excellent feel for the narrative rhythm
and the use of the internal monologue of the heroine, which in many
scenes strikes a very interesting relationship with the accompanying
images. The monologue, while occasionally pushing the film into
verbal exaggeration, sometimes gives it the curious aura of the nostalgic thought spared from the passing of time to survive only in the
memory. Lean, who for the first time proved himself to be a director of considerable importance, would often use the subjective
narrative in the future. He realized that this is one of the most
valuable ways to create mood on the screen.

ROME, OPEN CITY (Roma, Città Aperta) Roberto Rossellini

Script: Sergio Amidei, Federico Fellini and Rossellini, from a
story by Amidei and Alberto Consiglio. Photography: Ubaldo Arata.
Music: Renzo Rossellini. Cast: Anna Magnani (Pina), Aldo Fa-
brizi (Don Pietro Pellegrini), Marcello Pagliero (Giorgio Manfredi),
Maria Michi (Marina), Harry Feist (Major Bergmann), Francesco
Grandjacquet (Francesco), Giovanna Galletti (Ingrid), Vito Annichia-
rico (Marcello, Pina's son), Carla Revere (Lauretta), Nando
Bruno (Agostino), Carlo Sindici (Police Superintendent), Joop van
Hulzen (Hartmann), Akos Tolnay (Austrian deserter), Eduardo Pas-
sarelli (Policeman), Amalia Pelegrini (Landlady).

Excelsa Film, Italy. 9586 ft., 106 mins.

Rome, Open City, generally considered the most typical work of
Italian Neorealism, is one of the most interesting examples of a
situation in which a number of more or less deliberate circumstances lead to a result everyone was awaiting but which was not
fully understood by the authors themselves. This epic of the underground fight of the Italians against the Nazi occupation was not made
to illustrate any theoretical concepts: Rome, Open City responded
to the needs of the moment, it was a natural reaction to the terror
and indignity of 1944. The creative method itself stemmed not so
much from a deliberate choice of cinematic tools as from limitations forced by the war. Of course, Rossellini, Amidei and Arata
wanted to soak their film in authenticity, but the real reason why
the texture of the photography in Rome, Open City is so reminiscent
of a hasty documentary is the fact that the material was shot with
rather primitive equipment and irregular supplies of raw stock.

It is true that the makers wanted to get closer to real life,

but they took the camera into the streets and into real interiors not
for the reasons professed by the new generation of Italian directors,
but simply because in 1944 and 1945 the film studios were in ruins.
The film was started when the Germans were actually still in Rome,
so one can hardly call the use of hidden camera a deliberate choice.
The picture uses a number of non-professional actors; again, this
was not dictated by artistic trendiness but rather by the desire to
use their spontaneous behavior as a means of achieving credibility.
Rossellini himself, for several years previously a professional documentary maker, described this creative method as a semi-intuitive
search.   The result was hailed--though not immediately--as the rule-
book of the new film school.

One cannot say the recognition was unjustified: externally
Rome, Open City is an exponent of the Neorealist doctrine, but the
fact remains that what was not an artistic intention but a mere necessity seriously weakened the formal aspect of the film.   The specific gravity of Rossellini's picture, if one disregards its great historical importance, resides in something else: in the fervor of the
population of a city throttled by the Nazi terror, in the actions of
many people of different backgrounds and different beliefs united in
resistance to the enemy.   Among the heroes of the film we find a
worker and a Catholic priest (excellently portrayed by Aldo Fabrizi),
an engineer-resistance leader and a Roman working-class woman.
Everyone cooperates to help those hunted by the Gestapo, no one refuses shelter to strangers, even to the Austrian deserter.

These characters are portrayed without any emphasis and are
equipped with positive features of character as well as faults and
funny vices: in short, they are ordinary people.   When the time of
trial comes they are ready to pay the highest price for their ideals
and the Germans will not succeed in antagonizing even the priest and
the Communist engineer, who will both die in full awareness of the
reason for their sacrifice. Rossellini took no political stand: he
simply praised all people of good will.   He could not avoid exaggeration, which is augmented by the musical score; propaganda and melodramatic effects are sometimes in evidence.   But what remains in
the spectator's memory is a noble sincerity, a passionately suggestive vision of a city, an emotive consciousness of the moral strength
of man.

THE WAY TO THE STARS   Anthony Asquith

Script: Terence Rattigan. Photography: Derek Williams. Music:
Nicholas Brodszky. Cast: Michael Redgrave (David Archdale),
John Mills (Peter Penrose), Rosamund John (Miss Todd), Douglas
Montgomery (Johnny Hollis), Renée Asherson (Iris Winterton), Bonar
Colleano, Jr. (Joe Friselly), Stanley Holloway (Mr. Palmer), Basil

Radford (Tiny Williams), Felix Aylmer (the Rev. Charles Moss), Joyce
Carey (Miss Winterton).

Two Cities Films, G.B. 9777 ft., 109 mins.

By 1945 the Battle of Britain is already history; only abandoned air
fields overgrown with grass on which sheep graze and forgotten pin-
ups stirred by the wind in deserted barracks remain--such is the
nostalgic first tracking shot of The Way to the Stars, a story of the
ground crew of a small air base in the Midlands. The film, which
takes us back to the heroic days of 1940, remains totally unheroic--
it can hardly even be described as a war film. For war is not
shown at all; it rages beyond the horizon, in distant Germany, and
its presence is felt by the protagonists only when their friends do
not come home from a mission. The Way to the Stars is a film of
attitudes: two pilots share a room; one of them gets married only
to be killed soon after, leaving wife and child; his friend breaks his
own engagement, not wanting to be unfair to his girl. It is only
after American pilots arrive at the airfield that Peter thinks it all
over and decides to marry after all.

        Much credit for the quality of this film is owed to the script.
But the direction was also good: Asquith handled with restraint and
dignity the problem of responsibility to close relatives which faces
people with dangerous occupations. Tragedy never looms too large,
but can be sensed in the background--muted and understated in the
traditional British fashion. A lot has changed since the war: social divisions in England have become much less acute and nowadays
the film may seen a bit too piously heartening and naively optimistic
for our violent times. But despite minor faults (a certain episodic
quality resulting from following many threads at once and excessive
length) it remains an exceptionally subtle document of the attitudes
and sentiments of the war years.

LES DAMES DU BOIS DE BOULOGNE   Robert Bresson

Script: Bresson and Jean Cocteau, from an episode in Diderot's
"Jacques le Fataliste." Photography: Philippe Agostini. Music:
Jean-Jacques Grunenwald. Cast: Maria Cesarès (Hélène), Elina
Labourdette (Agnès), Lucienne Bogaërt (Madame D.), Paul Bernard
(Jean), Jean Marchat (Jacques).

Les Films Raoul Ploquin, France. 90 mins.

When considered in the context of Les Anges du péché, a subtle
spiritual study situated in a convent, the choice of theme for Bres-

son's second work must be regarded as surprising. Les Dames du Bois de Boulogne, an updated version of one of the episodes of Diderot's classic "Jacques le Fataliste," is a polished society melodrama, a story of the revenge of a rejected woman. As before, this is a film of intricate psychological interactions. There are only four people involved: when Hélène learns that Jean does not love her any more, she shrewdly arranges for him to meet Agnès and her mother. Jean falls in love with the girl, marries her and learns--too late--that he has married a whore.

Although the film moves in a sophisticated and painstakingly polished world of elegant apartments and refined conversations, its visual appearance can be traced back to the American gangster dramas of the early 30's. It is interesting that Bresson's style of direction was at this time still the exact opposite of what his later films made known as his personal touch: here he used lush contrasts of black and white and ornamental camera work with a multitude of tracking and panning shots. In the scene when Jean leaves Hélène's apartment, the camera follows him from the upper floor to street level in one uninterrupted shot. Moreover, the drama develops almost entirely in interiors.

The by-product of this creative method is the distinct sentimentality of the picture; the elegant form is jarring, especially in conjunction with the overly emotional music. All this is quite astonishing for anyone familiar with Bresson's later work. Yet Les Dames du Bois de Boulogne bears clear marks of brilliance. In the final scene Bresson provided one of his magnetic touches when the apparently dead bride opens her eyes: this moment contains the essence of his craft. The highlight of the film is 21-year-old Maria Cesarès, who gives a mesmerizing performance in the difficult role of a mature woman.

Les Dames du Bois de Boulogne was to be Bresson's last film with professional actors and his only excursion into the haute monde. His future works would all be restrained studies of sacrifice and suffering.

THE GREAT TURNING POINT (Veliky Perelom) Friedrich Ermler

Script: Boris Chirskov. Photography: Arkadi Koltsaty. Music: Gavriil Popov. Cast: Alexandr Zrazhevsky (Gen. Panteleyev), Mikhail Derzhavin (Gen.-Lt. Muravyov, Commander of the Front), P. Andriyevsky (Gen. Vinogradov, Chief of Staff), Yuri Tolubeyev (Gen.-Maj. Lavrov), Andrei Abrikosov (Gen. Krivenko), Mark Bernes (Minutka), Pavel Volkov (Stepan, a scout).

Lenfilm, U.S.S.R. 9551 ft., 106 mins.

The war films of the 1940's usually showed the direct struggle against the enemy, dealing with single individuals or groups faced with the urgency of combat. When the narrative embraced a wider horizon and spoke of whole battles it was only through the direct involvement in them of chosen individual characters. Several years after the war ended cinematic epics began to appear which took an overall view of the struggle, and whose protagonists were not individual soldiers but whole armies. The Russians led here, but they cheapened their bold vision with the monumental brashness of Stalinist propaganda (which is what flawed the first classical giant of the genre, Petrov's The Stalingrad Battle, 1949).

The characteristic feature of most films made during the war was the fact that there was no room in them for a more penetrating moral or psychological analysis; the situation demanded an unhesitatingly singular view of the content and the admixture of an ideological message. This feature was strongest in the Soviet cinema, where almost all war films were basically political posters animated by simple fictional devices. In this context The Great Turning Point is an extraordinary exception in both Soviet and foreign film production. Instead of the everyday combat and battle scenes we are given detailed studies of the character and actions of the men in generals' uniforms, and the war effort is shown from the point of view of those who decide the fate of campaigns.

The script, based on documentary materials collected over several years and mostly related to the Stalingrad Operation, tells the story of a Great Game, in which the Soviet Command attempts to lure the pressing Nazi armies into the midst of their positions and then begin a carefully timed counteroffensive to trap them. Success depends on everyone--on the stamina of the staff officers as well as on the absolute discipline of the ordinary soldiers. The dramatic quality of this game, in which the element of a gamble has an important role, was used by Ermler with consistency and a great economy of means of expression. Technical brilliance would have been superfluous here, when the subject itself bestows such an underlying tension on the plot.

The director of The Great Turning Point, who repeatedly proved to be an expert in psychological drama, concentrated above all on the authenticity of the behavior of the main characters and on highlighting the factors that bring victory. This story, which avoids slogans, became the most interesting attempt in cinema at showing war at the top command level.

THE LAST CHANCE (Die letzte Chance)   Leopold Lindtberg

Script: Richard Schweizer, from his own novel. Photography: Émile

Berna. Music: R. Blum. Cast: E. G. Morrison (Major Telford),
John Hoy (Lt. Halliday), Ray Reagan (Sgt. Braddock), Luisa Rossi
(Tonina), Edoardo Masini (Innkeeper), Giuseppe Galeati (Carrier),
Leopold Biberti (Swiss lieutenant), Therese Giehse (Frau Wittels),
Robert Schwarz (Bernard, her son).

Praesens Film, Switzerland. 9435 ft., 105 mins.

Autumn 1943: after the Nazis occupied Italy, many groups of
refugees--anti-Fascists, Jews, escaped prisoners from labor and
POW camps, shot-down Allied flyers--tried to slip across the Swiss
border. The Last Chance tells of the journey of one group, people
for whom reaching Switzerland means not only regaining freedom,
but simply saving their lives. The passage is extremely difficult,
especially for the less strong. The Germans doggedly hunt the es-
capees and try with bloody repressions to force the inhabitants of
the sub-Alpine villages to stop aiding them. But it is hard to fence
off the road to freedom: the Swiss haven is reached, although not
by all, and at a terrible price.

The fact that this beautiful film about the comradeship of
people of different nations, about sacrifice and heroism in the battle
against oppression, was made in neutral Switzerland has an almost
symbolic meaning. The movie itself has acquired a symbolic dimension through the universal quality of its humanist message, its
objectivity and restraint: not the personalities of the film's makers
but their total dedication to the dramatic strength of their theme
was of decisive importance.

This does not mean that The Last Chance is the result of an
indifferent registration of events; on the contrary, care and commitment are very much in evidence. In certain respects the film-
makers reached genuine mastery; certainly in the dramatic structure of the script, in the acting, and in the precise editing (especially in the scenes of high dramatic tension). To be credited
most of all are the painterly photographic compositions drawn with
Émile Berna's camera.

A TREE GROWS IN BROOKLYN   Elia Kazan

Script: Tess Slesinger and Frank Davis, from the novel by Betty
Smith. Photography: Leon Shamroy. Music: Alfred Newman.
Cast: Dorothy McGuire (Kathy Nolan), Joan Blondell (Aunt Sissy),
James Dunn (Johnny Nolan), Lloyd Nolan (Detective McShane), Peggy
Ann Garner (Francie Nolan), Ted Donaldson (Neely Nolan), James
Gleason (McGarrity), Ruth Nelson (Miss McDonough), John Alexander
(Steve Edwards), J. Farrell McDonald (Garney).

20th Century-Fox, U.S.A. 11,569 ft., 129 mins.

A sensitive film about a poor Brooklyn family, adapted from the bestseller chronicle "of life and death among the poor of the city"-- a drunken but kindly singing-waiter father, a puritanical mother, a young son and a bright adolescent daughter. She is Kazan's main center of interest: her striving for knowledge, her tender relationship with her father, her disarming naiveté. The father dies just before another child is born and life becomes even more difficult. But, of course, even the darkest cloud has a silver lining for the Irish family.

      Some of the novel's sentimentality and studious simplicity found its way into the picture. This was inevitable; it is simply that melodramatic storytelling always rings a patronizing note in films about the poor (compare John Ford's How Green was My Valley). In both cases even the setting of the plot in the past (around 1900) did not help. It seems that such a theme comes out best with semi-documentary treatment and even then not always. Yet fortunately Kazan did not want to undertake a definitive sociological discussion of urban poverty. Instead, the picture should be treated on its own terms and its sentimentality considered a stylized artistic convention. Its intensity gives the impression that Kazan is talking about his own childhood; there are touches of genuine poetry and the pathos is never obtrusive. Although some scenes are too long at the expense of others (the tree of the title is almost absent in the film) and the dialogue often seems "typical," Kazan's first feature is pleasant and sincere.

THE HOUSE ON 92ND STREET   Henry Hathaway

Script: Barre Lyndon, from a story by Charles G. Booth and John Monks. Photography: Norbert Brodine. Music: David Buttolph. Cast: William Eythe (Bill Dietrich), Lloyd Nolan (Inspector George A. Briggs), Signe Hasso (Elsa Gebhardt), Gene Lockhart (Charles Ogden Roper), Leo G. Carroll (Col. Hammersohn), Lydia St. Clair (Johanna Schmedt), Harry Bellaver (Max Coburg), Harro Meller (Conrad Arnulf), William Post, Jr. (Walker), Salo Douday (Franz Von Wirt), Alfred Zeisler (Col. Strassen).

Louis de Rochemont, 20th Century-Fox, U.S.A. 7892 ft., 88 mins.

During the war documentaries were of considerable importance for propaganda and information. The key man in United States wartime documentaries was Louis de Rochemont, producer of the "March of Time" newsreel which appeared regularly from 1935. Even Holly-

wood had to take notice of the new influence of documentaries.
After the war de Rochemont became interested in the commercial
cinema and produced a series of films which while dealing with
quite orthodox themes blended solid professionality with semi-documentary technique.   The first of them was The House on 92nd
Street; later came Boomerang! and Call Northside 777.   These three
titles are enough to illustrate the thematic evolution: the earliest
is a spy thriller still preoccupied with the war, the other two are
sensational dramas with very strong social overtones.

Nazi intelligence attempts to get hold of American nuclear
secrets, code-named "Process 97." They recruit a young German-
American who, on FBI advice, goes to Germany to an espionage
course and is later sent to the U.S. with a microfilmed message inside his watch.   The FBI net tightens and their attention is finally
centered around a house on 92nd Street which is the spy headquarters.   In handling this theme Hathaway made use of the "March of
Time" newsreel techniques: the style of the narrative is factual and
objective and the shooting was done almost entirely on location,
even including telephoto shots of the activities outside a real German Consulate somewhere in the U.S.

Appropriately, the picture used rather little-known actors--
a contemporary critic remarked that "for once the absence of
Messrs. Greenstreet and Bogart has a salutary influence on a spy
drama." Hathaway simply showed the ways of spies and the methods the FBI use in tracking them down; the camera enters labora-
tories, wanders among files.   The film has a clear stamp of genuineness and firmly holds the spectators' attention.   To use the
cliché phrase, Hathaway showed that real life can be more fascinating than fiction.   Although the "realist" trend in the American cinema turned out to be little more than a passing fancy, it still produced several gripping films.   This is one of them.

BOULE DE SUIF   Christian-Jaque

Script: Henri Jeanson and Louis d'Hée, from "Boule de Suif" and
"Mademoiselle Fifi, " short stories by Guy de Maupassant. Pho-
tography: Christian Matras. Music: Maurice-Paul Guillot. Cast:
Micheline Presle (Elisabeth Rousset, "Boule de Suif"), Louis Salou
(Lt. d'Eyrick, "Fifi"), Berthe Bovy (The Woman), Louise Conte
(The Countess), Mona Doll (The Nun), Suzet Maïs (Mme. Loiseau),
Alfred Adam (Cornudet), Jean Brochard (Loiseau), Denis d'Inès
(Curé), Gabrielle Fontan (Mme. Follenvie).

Artis-Films, France. 9000 ft., 100 mins.

The third screen adaptation of de Maupassant's story of a prostitute from Rouen who during the Franco-Prussian war demonstrates the superiority of her character over a whole gallery of bourgeois philistines. More strictly, this is not an adaptation of one short story but of two, and the film ingeniously and precisely ties them into the whole. In this combination, the story "Boule de Suif" plays a superior role so far as the story goes, but the spiritual intentions of the picture are determined by the second story, "Mademoiselle Fifi." "Boule de Suif" is an ironic confrontation of moral attitudes; "Mademoiselle Fifi," a dramatic judgment of patriotic attitudes in which a working-class girl and bourgeois types are juxtaposed.

In the outcome the heroine triumphs not only on the private, but also on the political level. Thus Christian-Jaque and his scriptwriters imaginatively transgressed strict fidelity to de Maupassant, since they not only respected his point of view, but even developed it. The war of 1870 should not be understood too literally from the film even though the climate of those years was meticulously recreated. In fact the film was designed as an allegory of the attitudes of the French during the German occupation.

In this version and in the previous film by Romm, the formal values are most fully in evidence in the sequence of the ride in the carriage. In the first adaptation it was inseparably tied to the aesthetics of the silent cinema and built on the excellent montage of close shots. Christian-Jaque, aware of Ford's adaptation of the story (Stagecoach), showed it not less impressively: for a quarter of an hour the camera watches in long shots the faces of the stagecoach passengers and expertly characterizes them. This is in turn complemented by Jeanson's expert dialogues. Christian Matras' photography reached considerable heights in this sequence as it did indeed in the other parts of the story, both in the interiors and in the portrayal of landscape. The acting is another strength of the film: at least two roles--those of Micheline Presle and Louis Salou --must surely be called outstanding. Care in casting and directing the actors would in fact be typical of all Christian-Jaque's later films.

THE SOUTHERNER   Jean Renoir

Script: Renoir and Hugo Butler, from the novel, "Hold Autumn in Your Hand," by George Sessions Perry. Photography: Lucien Andriot. Music: Werner Janssen. Cast: Zachary Scott (Sam Tucker), Betty Field (Nora Tucker), J. Carroll Naish (Devers), Beulah Bondi (Granny), Bunny Sunshine (Daisy), Jay Gilpin (Jot), Percy Kilbride (Harmie), Blanche Yurka (Ma), Charles Kemper (Tim), Norman Lloyd (Finlay).

Loew-Hakim for United Artists, U.S.A.   8359 ft., 93 mins.

Renoir left France upon the outbreak of the war. After a brief
spell in Italy where he co-directed Tosca (1941), based on the story
of the operatic heroine, he came to America. The films he made
during his seven-year stay here very much sustained his life-long
tradition of social interests. The beginning was not promising:
Swamp Water (1941) can claim authentic portrayal of social conditions as its only worthwhile aspect, but The Southerner, Renoir's
third and best American film, is much more important.

It is a simple chronicle of one year's events in the life of a
Texas cotton grower's family who take over an abandoned farm and
are determined to make it self-supporting despite the unfriendly
weather conditions, the hostile neighbors and the illnesses of the
children. It is not only that Renoir displayed a perfect feel for the
social conditions in Texas; he also steeped the film in an aura of
passionate involvement, this inimitable touch that makes Renoir's
films what they are: the portrayals of the battle of man against his
environment. The Southerner, a film made mostly on location, is
most strongly related to Toni, although one can also cite Le Crime
de M. Lange with its idea of a workers' cooperative.

Renoir's film plays a similar role as a classic of the rural
South as The Grapes of Wrath plays for the other part of the country. This is not a coincidence: Ford is probably the only director
whose treatment of such a theme could survive unharmed. The message of The Southerner is as a matter of fact similar to Ford's,
praising perseverance and the American pioneering spirit. It has
been said that the actors look like impostors in their roles but it is
almost inevitable that with hindsight some actors will appear in "unusual" parts in their earlier films, for instance Zachary Scott never
plays a poor farmer again.

A WALK IN THE SUN   Lewis Milestone

Script: Robert Rossen, from the novel by Harry Brown. Photog-
raphy: Russell Harlan. Music: Fredric Efrem Rich. Cast: Dana
Andrews (Sgt. Tyne), Richard Conte (Rivera), John Ireland (Windy),
George Tyne (Friedman), Lloyd Bridges (Sgt. Ward), Sterling Hollo-
way (McWilliams), Herbert Rudley (Sgt. Porter), Norman Lloyd
(Archimbeau).

20th Century-Fox, U.S.A.   10,520 ft., 117 mins.

A Walk in the Sun was planned by Milestone to be in a sense a re-

make of his First World War classic, All Quiet on the Western
Front. In accordance with the new developments in film-making he
wanted this time to make rather than a pacifist address a semi-
documentary account of the war as seen through the soldiers' eyes.
He tried to show the war not as a carnage but above all as an in-
exorably boring and demanding duty.

The action spans only a few hours between the landing of the
Lee Platoon (of the Texas Division) on an Italian beach near Salerno
until midday when they have achieved their objective, a farmhouse
six miles from shore. The lieutenant is killed during the landing,
a sergeant dies ashore and the brave Sergeant Tyne takes over.
With heavy casualties the men blow up an armored car and, having
diverted the attention of the Nazis, capture the farmhouse.

A Walk in the Sun is a film made with great directorial sensitivity showing the soldier's task with insight: his impatient waiting for the opportune moment to attack, the helplessness in face of
enemy aircraft, the fear of death, the cracking up under the pressure of events. Milestone's restraint is praiseworthy: there are
no flashbacks, no sentimentality, no large-scale battle scenes and
not even any enemy soldiers. The fact that the film is only a partial success must be blamed on the script's providing for too profuse
and too literary dialogues. Also the film's idea of the emotions of
soldiers at war is sometimes a little unconvincing. The action however never moves too slowly. A Walk in the Sun is still a classic
among war films even though it suffered the considerable disadvantage of release soon after The Story of G. I. Joe, the best of them
all.

THE OVERLANDERS   Harry Watt

Script: Watt. Photography: Osmond Borradaile. Music: John
Ireland. Cast: Chips Rafferty (Dan McAlpine), John Nugent Hay-
ward (Bill Parsons), Daphne Campbell (Mary Parsons), Jean Blue
(Mrs. Parsons), Helen Grieve (Helen Parsons), John Fernside
(Corky), Peter Pagan (Sinbad), Frank Ransome (Charlie), Henry
Murdock (Aborigine Nipper).

Ealing Studios, Australia/G.B.   8198 ft., 91 mins.

When in 1942 a Japanese invasion threatened Northern Australia, the
government decided to adopt a scorched earth policy; cattle were to
be killed, people evacuated. But one defiant drover decided with a
handful of helpers to take 1000 head of cattle to Queensland across
2000 miles of desert country. The obstacles are formidable: some
water holes are dry, some muddy; there are river crossings, dan-

gerous mountain passes, the constant threat of a stampede. The
pioneers even have to catch wild horses after their own have died
from eating poisoned grass. The adventurous journey is a success
and an encouragement to other cattle-breeders.

The Overlanders was an Australian assignment for Harry
Watt, a young English documentarist, a pupil of Grierson and maker
of Target for Tonight (1941) and Night Mail (1942). It was shot in
the extremely difficult conditions of a country without a film industry; the negative had to be sent to England aboard a Navy destroyer.
Watt avoided the temptation to make an Australian western; instead
the film derives strength from its documentary style--its genuineness and authentic drama have not often been matched even by the
films of John Ford. The director captured what is most characteristic of Australia: wide spaces, rough people, unique slang, dry
humor. This style of film-making coincided with the general return
to realism in the cinema, which is probably why the film was received as a revelation.

This reception is not fully justified by the intrinsic qualities
of the film: the fictional elements of The Overlanders are an alien
intrusion; the romantic subplot, a story from a different film; the
beginning is stiff and the ending, disappointing--in short it contained
some of the tawdry, wooden touches present in many films of the
40's. But the freshness and directness still win by a long way: the
lasting impression of the picture is that of a fascinating drama of
adventure, the discovery of an unknown land.

BLITHE SPIRIT   David Lean

Script: Noël Coward, from his own play. Photography: Ronald
Neame. Music: Muir Mathieson. Cast: Rex Harrison (Charles
Condomine), Constance Cummings (Ruth, his second wife), Kay Ham-
mond (Elvira, his first wife), Margaret Rutherford (Madame Arcati),
Hugh Wakefield (Dr. Bradman), Joyce Carey (Mrs. Bradman), Jac-
queline Clarke (Edith, the maid).

Two Cities Films, G.B.   8609 ft., 96 mins. Technicolor.

The collaboration between Lean and the playwright Coward, begun
with In Which We Serve, went on to This Happy Breed (1944)--a
condescending, if well acted and photographed melodrama about a
middle-class London family. Blithe Spirit is for a change a grotesque comedy: a novelist who lives in a chic country home with
his second wife and is interested in spiritualism finds the inter-
ference in their life of the ghost of his first wife a bit of a problem
--until it turns out that the psychic gifts of the maid were responsi-

ble for the imbroglio.

The movie is not more than an efficient illustration of the
play with color pictures, and it is as well that Lean was not over-
ambitious. In fact, considering the arch-theatrical character of the
play (the stage action is limited to one room) he did not do too badly. He preserved the chief Coward virtues of the apparently effort-
less but still precise characterization and elegant if over-abundant
dialogue, and while doing all this with a perhaps excessive respect
for the author, left the picture--especially the acting--within ear-
shot of the theatre.

On equal terms with the series of Ealing comedies, this film
is a specimen of British humor in the cinema: it all starts from
an absurd situation, which is subsequently treated accordingly to
most strict requirements of logic. The basic supernatural situation
has plenty of comic potential, and Lean uses it with restraint and
taste, although the color conception of the ghost is rather unhappy.
René Clair did somewhat better in his comedies The Ghost Goes
West and I Married a Witch, both very similar in tone and character.

MILDRED PIERCE   Michael Curtiz

Script: Ranald MacDougall and Catherine Turney, from the novel by
James M. Cain. Photography: Ernest Haller. Music: Max Stein-
er. Cast: Joan Crawford (Mildred Pierce), Ann Blyth (Veda
Pierce), Jack Carson (Wally Fay), Zachary Scott (Monty Beragon),
Eve Arden (Ida), Bruce Bennett (Bert Pierce), Jo Ann Marlowe (Kay
Pierce), Lee Patrick (Maggie Binderhof), Goerge Tobias (Mr. Chris).

Warner Bros., U.S.A.   9961 ft., 111 mins.

Voracious parental love: a housewife mother sacrifices everything
in order to give her daughter what she never had herself. She becomes a waitress to earn enough for the daughter's dancing lessons;
thanks to her business abilities she soon owns first one, and later a
chain of restaurants and marries a layabout aristocrat for prestige
reasons. In the end she attempts to incriminate an innocent man in
a murder committed by her daughter, only to realize, too late, that
she has created a selfish monster.

Curtiz makes this typical rage-to-riches story, with its
inevitable clichés (the other daughter, a darling, dies) into a film
which casts a powerful spell. Told in the convention of a detective
story, starting with the murder scene, the semi-sensational tone is
related to the director's earlier legendary Casablanca. The mood-

creating elements are the same: deserted roads, twilit suburbs,
glistening fur coats, chiaroscuro photography and tight construction
(although some scenes could do with cutting).   The principal appeal
of this shadow-ridden story of moral decay is the superb Oscar-
winning performance of Joan Crawford as the mother.   It is still
difficult to understand the extent of her doting intoxication, but once
we take this literary inheritance of the film for granted, the actress
performs with complete conviction.

1946

THE BOYARS' PLOT (Boyarski Zagovor) [Ivan the Terrible--Part II] Sergei Eisenstein

---

Script: Eisenstein. Photography: Andrei Moskvin (interiors) and Eduard Tissé (exteriors). Music: Sergei Prokofiev. Art Direction: Iosif Shpinel, from sketches by Eisenstein. Cast: Nikolai Cherkasov (Tsar Ivan IV), Serafima Birman (Yefrosinya Staritskaya, Tsar's aunt), Pavel Kadochnikov (Vladimir Staritsky, her son), Amvrosi Buchma (Alexei Basmanov), Mikhail Kuznetsov (Fyodor Basmanov), Andrei Abrikosov (Boyar Fyodor Kolychev), Mikhail Zharov (Malyuta Skuratov), Erik Pyriev (Tsar Ivan as a child), Mikhail Nazvanov (Prince Andrei Kurbsky), Vladimir Balashov (Pyotr Volynets), Pavel Massalsky (King Zygmunt August of Poland), Ada Voitsik (Yelena Glinskaya).

Mosfilm, U.S.S.R. 7792 ft., 87 mins. (Not released until September 1958). Black and white with one sequence in color (Agfacolor).

By the time Ivan the Terrible was released (in 1945), Eisenstein had nearly finished the second part of the planned trilogy. The Boyars' Plot is a classical tragedy of destructive passions, sustained in the Shakespearean tradition. The film is more concentrated than its predecessor and the treatment and development of characters, deeper and more mature. The Russian people implore the Tsar to return to the throne from self-imposed exile. Back in Moscow, Ivan meets with the sedition and conspiracy of the boyars led by his aunt, Yefrosinya Staritskaya. Solitary and suspicious, he surrounds himself with bodyguards and institutes a reign of terror against his enemies. A passing justification for this is given in a flashback from Ivan's childhood in which he watches the boyars murder his mother. Two of his former friends join the enemy ranks; the conspiracy culminates in an assassination plot which the Tsar

thwarts by disguising his dim-witted cousin-cum-possible-successor
Vladimir in the royal robes: a fanatic stabs the youth to death in
the cathedral.

The mood of The Boyars' Plot is one of treachery and near-
paranoid suspicion; shadowy figures linger in colonnaded interiors
and there are very few exterior scenes. Even more completely
than in Ivan the Terrible, Eisenstein dissected dictatorship in general and the personality of Stalin in particular. The film becomes
a study of the corrupting influence of absolute power, an in-depth
analysis of the dramatic dilemma of a dictator--alone, tottering under the burden of his own cruelty. Among many obvious political
allusions, Eisenstein seems to have suggested a parallel between
Ivan the Terrible's manipulation by the oprichniki (his personal bodyguard) and Stalin's manipulation by Beria, his chief of police.

Admittedly, the film lacks historical objectivity and not only
in portraying its central characters; note, for instance, the grossly
caricatured presentation of the Polish court. These "distortions"
became the pretext for the seizure of the film by the censors.
Stalin's own words were: "Ivan the Terrible, a man of strong will
and character is here weak and indecisive, somewhat like Hamlet;
the oprichniki are like the Ku-Klux Klan, while in fact they were a
progressive people's guard and Malyuta Skuratov, their leader, was
a great Russian soldier."

The pace of The Boyars' Plot is even more slow and ponderous than that of the first part of the trilogy, save for the frenetic
banquet scene of the dance of the imperial bodyguards. This sequence, shot in color on stock captured during the war, is a wonderful summary of Eisenstein's theoretical beliefs regarding color as a
means of expression. The overall result is nothing if not monumental and the film's dramatic intensity, brought almost to the
breaking point, creates an apotheosis of Russia and the Russian
spirit. The photography, which contains many unforgettable compositions, employs low camera positions designed to elevate the characters and turn them into statues rather than living people; the
close-ups of faces reveal larger-than-life passions; enormous shadows on the walls generate an atmosphere of threat (an interesting
reference to Warning Shadows); the score also is predominantly
minor in mood. So is Cherkasov's portrayal of the hero: grandiose,
menacing, perfect.

Although the script was completed, Eisenstein would never
make the third part of the trilogy, which was to be shot entirely in
color. It was to show the Tsar's defeat of the Livonians and the
Russian breakthrough to the shores of the Baltic Sea. During the
party to celebrate the award of the Stalin Prize to Ivan the Terrible
Eisenstein collapsed with a brain hemorrhage. Some hours later he
learned that The Boyars' Plot had been banned. He died in Moscow
in February 1948, at the age of 50. Dictatorship was too touchy a
subject to be discussed in any detail during Stalin's life, although
Stalin is said to have seen the film many many times in his private

viewing room in the Kremlin. The Boyars' Plot emerged from cold
storage only after 12 years.

PAISÀ   Roberto Rossellini

Script: Federico Fellini and Rossellini, from stories by Victor
Haines, Marcello Pagliero, Sergio Amidei, Fellini, Klaus Mann,
Rossellini and Vasco Pratolini (Florence episode). Photography:
Otello Martelli. Music: Renzo Rossellini. Cast: (i) Sicily;
Carmela Sazio (Carmela), Robert Van Loon (Robert), Carlo Pisa-
cane (Peasant); (ii) Naples; Dots M. Johnson (Negro M.P.), Alfon-
sino Pasca (Little boy); (iii) Rome; Maria Michi (Francesca), Gar
Moore (Fred, an American soldier); (iv) Florence; Harriet White
(Harriet), Renzo Avanzo (Massimo), Gigi Gori (Partisan); (v)
Romagna; Bill Tubbs (American chaplain); (vi) Po Valley; Dale Ed-
monds (Dale, O.S.S. man), Cigolani (Partisan).

Organizzazione Films Internazionali/Capitani Film, Italy. 124 mins.

For Rossellini, Rome, Open City was a search for a style. Paisà
however was a completely thought-out, planned and consistent film,
typical both of its creator and of the Italian national cinema after
the Second World War: "Improvisation in conditions of direct communion with real life," as the director himself said of the film.
The concept of the story is similar to that of the previous work,
but wider and much more ambitious; this time it is not the picture
of one city, but a panorama of Italy during the crucial liberation
period.

These sentiments are emphasized by the film's title (paisà
is the Anglo-Saxon corruption of the Italian word paese meaning
homeland). Six chronologically arranged episodes from the liberat-
ing progress of the Allied armies were designed to give a general
view of the fortunes of Rossellini's compatriots in the period between the summer of 1943 and the end of the war. A Sicilian girl
guiding an American patrol; orphans of liberated Naples; a Roman
prostitute; insurgents in Florence; Franciscan monks confronted by
American army chaplains; partisans besieged in the Comacchio
marshes--these are the representatives of the nation of which Paisà
speaks.

Each episode is sustained in a different tone. The Neopolitan
story is a realistic generic picture rich in reflection; the melancholy Roman story is melodramatic, but it is a melodrama drawn
straight from life; the battles in Florence are shown in the manner
of a chronicle (in which Rossellini in fact made use of authentic
documentary footage); the visit to the monastery is inlaid with some

excellently photographed portrait studies of the monks; and the final
story, the broadest in treatment and also the greatest, is a virtuoso
study of atmosphere, landscape and dramatic tension and at the
same time constitutes the tragic and emotional dominating force of
the film.   Such different components assembled in one picture should,
it would seem, pull the structure apart. Yet Paisà is strikingly coherent. The mood is perfectly measured and the film is convincing
and full. This creative approach resulted in the greatest Neorealist
works, and Paisà, Rossellini's best film, has an unassailable place
among them.

NOTORIOUS   Alfred Hitchcock

Script: Ben Hecht, from a theme by Hitchcock.   Photography:
Ted Tetzlaff. Music: Roy Webb. Cast: Ingrid Bergman (Alicia
Huberman), Cary Grant (Devlin), Claude Rains (Alexander Sebas-
tian), Louis Calhern (Paul Prescott), Leopoldine Konstantin (Mrs.
Sebastian), Reinhold Schünzel (Dr. Anderson).

RKO Radio Pictures, U.S.A.   103 mins.

A spy melodrama: an American girl, Alicia, whose father has
been imprisoned in the U.S.A. for spying, agrees to cooperate with
a government agent in investigating a Nazi gang in South America.
Its leading member, a former friend of her father, falls in love
with her. She marries him and discovers his secret: uranium
samples concealed in wine bottles. When her new husband and his
ruthless mother find out she knows, they slowly begin to poison
her....

Often dismissed as a "women's magazine story," Notorious
is in fact one of the high points in Hitchcock's cinema, a work of
great simplicity and considerable sophistication. The story line is
surprisingly straight, containing fewer scenes than usual, and the
locale is little-varied. It is a modern, dramatically perfect script.
The central problem is the love of two men for the same girl and
her resulting dilemma between duty and personal choice. It is the
more praiseworthy that with all these limitations the director
achieved a maximum effect: an almost tangible sense of unreality,
an electrifying suspense which seems to be derived from nowhere.

The photography, clear and noble, gives the film an inner
dramatic structure by focusing tension around two objects: a key
and a wine bottle. In the party scene, in a stunning technical display, the camera closes from a great distance on a key held in the
hand. Hitchcock's uranium gimmick does not now seem extraordinary, but as the film was being prepared in the pre-atom-bomb

days, this inspired guess put the director briefly under FBI scrutiny. The lion's share of the success of the film is due however to the fascinating, sensitive performance of Ingrid Bergman, maybe the best in her career.

LE DIABLE AU CORPS   Claude Autant-Lara

Script: Jean Aurenche and Pierre Bost, from the novel by Raymond Radiguet. Photography: Michel Kelber. Music: René Cloërec. Cast: Micheline Presle (Marthe Grangier), Gérard Philipe (François Jaubert), Jean Debucourt (His father), Germaine Ledoyen (His mother), Denise Grey (Marthe's mother), Palau (M. Marin), Jean Varas (Jacques Lacombe).

Transcontinental-Film, France. 10,043 ft., 112 mins.

The 11th of November, 1918, which brought the end of the Great War, was a day of rejoicing in all Europe. The prologue of Le Diable au corps evokes those moments: flags in the street, gun salutes, the tolling of bells. But this is only in the background; in the foreground the camera selects a high school student whose despair becomes all the more glaring in contrast with the mood all around. The boy is saying farewell to his love: he accompanies, from a distance, the funeral cortège of a young woman. She was his mistress--but he had no right to her as she was married to a man fighting at the front. What a disgrace, to seduce the wife of a man defending his Country! How inappropriate this death seems to be on the eve of victory!

Or does it? Do the lovers indeed deserve to be condemned? The flashbacks, which take up nearly the whole of the film, reveal the truth about the affair whose tragic end was predetermined by its beginning: it could last only as long as the war. But in Le Diable au corps the war is not a factor aggravating the moral charges against the lovers. On the contrary, it is the war, the faith in Duty to the Motherland and the pressure of circumstances which brought about the drama. For it was not the husband, but the spontaneous 16-year-old who awoke passion in the inexperienced Marthe; it was not her wish but obedience to her mother's ambition for her daughter's bourgeois happiness that brought about her marriage.

Autant-Lara passionately declared himself against all false standards, against the hypocrisy which vitiates individual happiness, and especially against any wartime moral reevaluation. Later, in Tu ne tueras point (1960), a passionate if peremptory work, and abstractly pacifist, he declared himself the enemy of any uniform and

any army; here he was only against their being glorified.   This was
enough, however, for Le Diable au corps to meet with the same
protests Radiguet's book had encountered when it was first published
a quarter of a century earlier.   In fact in the literary prototype the
accents were differently distributed: the hero, demoniac in his
youthful insouciance (thus the title, meaning "The Devil in the
Flesh") thumbed his nose at the bourgeois and the book did not sym-
pathize with his rationale and his cynical experiments carried out
on everybody, including even his mistress.

But in the film, both Gérard Philipe (who was appearing in
his second screen part after his debut as Prince Myshkin in L'Idiot,
1946) and the woman he loves are free from guilt.   The story of
"Le Diable au corps," even when taken with all its overtones, does
not appear to be a particularly valuable material for an adaptation.
Yet the film is excellent without a doubt, and not only because of
the expert film-making.   The director's commitment to the theme
gave the picture an exceptional narrative subtlety and a striking
conviction in describing the emotional states of the protagonists.
The power of the screen vision was predetermined by the innovative
narrative structure of the film itself.   The use of flashbacks gives
the story a peculiar, intimate feel, and the twofold return to the
present, done with dissolves accompanied by the increasing peal of
the out-of-tune bells on the soundtrack, is finely suited to the character of past events.   The flashbacks start when the hero in his
memories reaches the moment of parting with his beloved.

The fine editing, the free camera movement and the muslin-
like texture of the photography give the narrative a great fluency,
and the delicately thrown-in visual metaphors breathe pure poetry;
for instance before the first night of the lovers the balletic camera
pans around the bed ends on the shot of the fireplace.   But Le
Diable au corps would not be what it is if it were not for Philipe
and Micheline Presle: it is their charm which gives the story of
outcast lovers most of its special character.

GREAT EXPECTATIONS   David Lean

Script: Lean and Ronald Neame, from the novel by Charles Dickens.
Photography: Guy Green.   Music: Walter Goehr.   Editing: Jack
Harris.   Cast: John Mills (Pip), Valerie Hobson (Estella), Bernard
Miles (Joe Gargery), Francis L. Sullivan (Jaggers), Finlay Currie
(Magwitch), Martita Hunt (Miss Havisham), Anthony Wager (Pip as
a child), Jean Simmons (Estella as a girl), Alec Guinness (Herbert
Pocket), Ivor Barnard (Wemmick), Freda Jackson (Mrs. Gargery),
Torin Thatcher (Bentley Drummle).

Cineguild, G.B.   10,624 ft., 118 mins.

Among the series of outstanding films made in Britain during and immediately after the Second World War--the golden age of the national cinema--there were several adaptations of literary classics of which the best are Olivier's <u>Henry V</u> and <u>Hamlet</u> and Lean's <u>Great Expectations</u>. This film has been described as a childhood book vividly brought to life. As a matter of fact the novel is not one of Dickens' greatest achievements, covering its profusion of improbabilities and strange coincidences with a coat of melodrama.

The story, set in the 1830's, follows Pip, a blacksmith's apprentice, through childhood and adolescence. When a child, Pip befriends Estella and her eccentric rich lady guardian. One day Pip helps an escaped convict. In his teens he receives a fortune from an anonymous benefactor which allows him to embark upon fashionable London life. The godsend is from the convict who became rich in Australia and returns in disguise; Pip tries to help him avoid arrest and later saves his beloved Estella (the convict's daughter, it turns out) from becoming the prey of her crazy guardian.

A number of scenes are notable either because of evocative atmosphere or striking camera work (or both): the brilliantly edited opening sequence of Pip's encounter with the convict in a country cemetery with the bare branches hanging low over the gravestones and the wind playing uneasily in the grass; the scenes of Pip's arrival in London in which the landmarks of the capital are shown with the camera looking upward from the coach. In the latter sequence, the things which were in fact dictated by the practical necessity of not showing modern vehicles in a period film become a revealing visual touch which draws the spectator's attention to objects so often shown on postcards and elsewhere, but which now unexpectedly appear new and unusual.

This fairy-tale story obeys a logic of its own and its moralistic and allegorical meaning is easy to decipher. The fact that the most effective way of making a dream credible is to treat it in a realistic manner has been known since Murnau's <u>Nosferatu</u>. Lean told his story in a matter-of-fact manner, firmly grasping the Dickensian idiom and placing emphasis--as he did before with Coward's script--on fidelity to the literary material and relative avoidance of formal experiments. The film is a tasteful illustration of the book with pictures, academic in the best sense of the word.

This would, however, not have been sufficient to outweigh the faults of the script if it were not for the acting. Excellent characterization is the forte of Dickensian prose and, appropriately, the type casting of the film is perfect--virtually every acting performance is outstanding. Dramatic suspense and charming humor combine to give the film a unique flavor and help to preserve the entire atmosphere of the original. The outcome is not only the first outstanding adaptation of Dickens, but the best so far.

THE BEST YEARS OF OUR LIVES   William Wyler

Script: Robert E. Sherwood, from the novel, "Glory for Me," by
MacKinlay Kantor. Photography: Gregg Toland. Music: Hugo
Friedhofer. Cast: Myrna Loy (Milly Stephenson), Fredric March
(Al Stephenson), Dana Andrews (Fred Derry), Teresa Wright (Peggy
Stephenson), Virginia Mayo (Marie Derry), Cathy O'Donnell (Wilma
Cameron), Hoagy Carmichael (Butch Engle), Harold Russell (Homer
Parrish), Gladys George (Hortense Derry), Roman Bohnen (Pat Der-
ry), Marlene Aames (Luella Parrish).

Samuel Goldwyn Productions, U.S.A. 16,020 ft., 178 mins., later
cut to 15,378 ft., 171 mins.

The end of the war did not put an end to all conflicts. The demobilized soldiers became civilians and reclaimed their place in
ordinary life--but life had changed and they had changed too.
William Faulkner cast a particularly penetrating light on the problem
in his short stories. Now Wyler, himself a discharged officer,
tackled it. After the British middle-class respectability of Mrs.
Miniver, the director felt much more himself on the familiar ground
of The Best Years of Our Lives.

    Three ex-flyers return to their home town. Al, a success-
ful banker, to his safe existence; Fred, a former soda jerk whom
the war made an air force captain, to an anxious meeting with his
wartime bride, whom he does not know well; Homer, a former student crippled in the war, to the doubts of how his sweetheart will
react to his mutilation. Two will succeed in coming back: Al will
again speak at dinner parties, though he will now give an unsecured
loan to a young farmer; Homer's sweetheart will not fail him; Fred,
rejected by everybody, will remain an outsider; the best years of
his life are gone. The parade's gone by, and he will be left to
melancholy reflection in the cockpit of a plane in a scrapyard.

    Wyler's film is an example of the persistence of the aca-
demic respectability of Hollywood in the face of changing conditions.
When the film was made, postwar tendencies toward realism were
already felt in America. Their partial acceptance by Wyler is the
main reason for the inflated fame the film achieved. The once-
respected social criticism was never there and the picture in fact
praises the American way of life in the everything-has-its-faults
tone. On the other hand the film does, at least partly, reflect the
spirit of that time of sudden hopes, dashed dreams and hidden anxieties. This is summed up in one of the early scenes when the
three friends hitch a lift home in a bomber; their discussion reflects their latent anxiety and uncertainty about the future.

This complex, detailed epic finds an interesting visual key:
the ultra-clear photography (through stopped-down lenses) conveys
the feel of the unpleasant reality which has to be faced, the too-
tangible, too-bright light in the eyes. Realism in the interiors was,
interestingly, achieved by scaling the studio sets to normal size,
instead of making them larger, as is usual. In the absence of
startling discoveries, Wyler's film deserves credit for at least
acknowledging a painful real situation.

SHOESHINE (Sciuscià) Vittorio De Sica

Script: Cesare Zavattini, Sergio Amidei, Adolfo Franci, Cesare
Giulio Viola and De Sica, from a story by Zavattini. Photography:
Anchise Brizzi. Music: Alessandro Cicognini. Cast: Rinaldo
Smordoni (Giuseppe Filippucci), Franco Interlenghi (Pasquale Mag-
gi), Aniello Mele (Raffaele), Bruno Ortensi (Arcangeli), Pacifico
Astrologo (Vittorio), Francesco de Nicola (Ciriola), Antonio Carlino
(L'Abruzzese), Enrico de Silva (Giorgio).

Alfa Cinematografica, Italy. 8340 ft., 93 mins.

A curious similarity links the titles of the two most outstanding
Italian films made just after the war: Paisà is an Anglo-Saxon
corruption of the Italian paese (homeland), Sciuscià is derived from
"Shoe shine!," the cry of boys whose clients were mostly American
soldiers; the neologism soon came to be identified with those who
coined it--boys from the streets of postwar Italy. The similarity of the two titles is not a coincidence, but a measure of
how closely the film-makers followed real life in those years, of
what weight they gave to what happened and what was heard in the
crowd in the streets.

They considered it their artistic duty to watch and to listen:
the tragic events of the newly overcome cataclysm had left deep
material traces and had carved profound scars on the human psyche.
To show that on the screen, to shake consciences with an appeal
for the improvement of the social system and a renaissance of
moral values--such was the manifesto of authors of which the foremost were Zavattini and De Sica. Their particular concern lay
with the youngsters, war orphans, teenage drop-outs growing up in
the demoralizing conditions of life in a destroyed country. The
children are watching us: the catchword of De Sica's first important film applies with equal strength to his two later films, Shoeshine and Bicycle Thieves. In the first of these Zavattini and De
Sica presented an uncompromising, bitter protest against a society
that cynically ignored past experiences and neglected its duty toward future generations.

The action of the film takes place in 1945 in Rome: the two young protagonists, making do as shoe-shine boys, dream about buying a particular white horse. Not missing any opportunity for collecting the required money, they get involuntarily entangled in a criminal affair and are sent to a reform school. The institution which was meant to promote re-education, turns out to be disseminating evil and is the cause of the tragic failure of the two friends: during their escape the younger perishes, and the other is condemned to live with the memory of this death. The expressive cruel drama of the wronged child constitutes the most pessimistic moment in the work of Zavattini and De Sica. The picture shows all honest intentions wasted in the face of the indifference of people and the blind mechanisms of social order.

Shoeshine makes all the stronger an impression as De Sica contrasted his uncompromisingly critical attitude with true stylistic poetry and with heart-rending metaphor. The spiritual strength of this film by far transcends its technical aspects. Shoeshine has technical imperfections--non-rhythmical, sometimes chaotic editing and photographic faults reminiscent of Rome, Open City--but also a feel of spontaneity, the simplicity of a chronicle, a profusion of location photography and non-professional actors. It was mainly through these assets that in two years the Italian film school grew to become the most important trend in the world in cinematic art.

THE BIG SLEEP   Howard Hawks

Script: William Faulkner, Leigh Brackett and Jules Furthman, from the novel by Raymond Chandler. Photography: Sidney Hickox. Music: Max Steiner. Cast: Humphrey Bogart (Philip Marlowe), Lauren Bacall (Vivian), John Ridgely (Eddie Mars), Martha Vickers (Carmen), Dorothy Malone (Bookshop girl), Peggy Knudsen (Mona Mars), Regis Toomey (Bernie Ohls), Charles Waldren (General Sternwood), Charles D. Brown (Norris), Bob Steele (Canino), Elisha Cook Jr. (Jones), Louis Jean Heydt (Joe Brody), Sonia Darrin (Agnes), Theodore von Eltz (Geiger), Tom Rafferty (Carol Lundgren).

Warner Bros., U.S.A.   10,238 ft., 114 mins.

Gangster cinema had been through a considerable evolution since the early days of Public Enemy and Scarface which, while showing crime from the criminals' point of view, laid the blame at society's door and carried the inevitable message that crime does not pay. In the disenchanted 40's, starting with The Maltese Falcon, directors began to adopt a cynical view of the gangster free-for-all. The protagonists could no longer claim our sympathy and the reason for their eventual failure was now ironic fate and not the inherent invincibility of good.

This is the case with The Big Sleep, one of a number of films made from Raymond Chandler's thrillers. A private detective is summoned to the suburban residence of rich General Sternwood and his two beautiful but spoiled daughters, to solve a blackmail mystery. The plot lacks the clarity of The Maltese Falcon and is virtually impossible to understand (Hawks himself reputedly still does not know who committed one of the murders); what can be understood seems highly improbable. The film has other assets though: fast, intelligent direction, good acting, a sympathetic portrayal of the detective's relationship with one of the daughters.

In most aspects this is a typical film noir with its matter-of-factness, cynical black humor, heavy dependence on dialogue, and significant choice of morally objectionable characters (one of the girls is an alcoholic nymphomaniac, the other a roulette addict); the detective too is no saint. The Big Sleep is the second film of the Bogart-Bacall team inaugurated with To Have and Have Not (1944); it contains the characteristic blend of luxury, sleaziness, sophistication and vulgarity; the precious artificial, sheltered life of the thrillers of the period.

BEAUTY AND THE BEAST (La Belle et la bête) Jean Cocteau

Co-direction: René Clément. Script: Cocteau, from a fairy tale by Mme. Leprince de Beaumont. Photography: Henri Alekan. Music: Georges Auric. Cast: Jean Marais (The Beast/Avenant/Ardent), Josette Day (Beauty), Marcel André (Merchant), Mila Parély (Adélaide), Nane Germon (Félicie), Michel Auclair (Ludovic).

André Paulvé, France. 8983 ft., 100 mins., cut to 8301 ft., 92 mins.

Jean Cocteau's single-handed endeavors in the cinema generally headed towards artistic disaster. They were pushed in that direction by pseudo-avant-gardism (Le Sang d'un poète, 1930), a scribbler's lack of feel for the natural, and the exaltation which, in the context of the personal message of these films gave the impression of outright narcissism. It is true that Cocteau defended himself here and there with ironic humor, but this was not enough. The author, without coming to terms with the conventions of cinematic fantasy, ambitiously tried to marry imagination and the realistic use of modern detail (Orphée). He invariably found himself, however, on the borderline of embarrassing ridicule and only occasionally offered in his work crumbs of genuine art.

Beauty and the Beast is an exception to this. With Clément's cooperation, the French poet created a film at once very characteristic of his personal style and at the same time fine and full of charm. The reason for this success lies probably in the fact that Cocteau did not present in the film products of his own imagination but merely a visual interpretation of an old French legend. A beautiful girl, who for the sake of her sick father goes to live in the castle of a repulsive monster, through the power of her love makes this beast (who is an enchanted prince) return to his true noble self.

The original and strongly emphasized designs of the film blend the historical tradition with a whole range of typically Surrealist visual symbols. The way that these symbols were used shows their lack of connection with the imagery of the followers of André Breton, and they should be seen as only the projection of Cocteau's own, post-Surrealist fancies. All the same these interesting symbols give the picture a considerable visual appeal, further enhanced by the camera work. Alekan's photography--dusky in the interiors, luminous in the open--was as crucial for creating the suggestive mood of a fairy tale as the balanced, dreamy, balletic quality of the narrative rhythm.

Cocteau and Clément's formal methods are undoubtedly on the very verge of academicism, but the skill with which they are employed, and their reference to the story make what would in different circumstances be the artificial to appear justified and stylish.

LA SYMPHONIE PASTORALE   Jean Delannoy

Script: Pierre Bost, Jean Aurenche and Delannoy, from the short story by André Gide. Photography: Armand Thirard. Music: Georges Auric. Cast: Michèle Morgan (Gertrude), Pierre Blanchar (The Pastor), Line Noro (Amélie, his wife), Louvigny (Casteran), Jean Desailly (Jacques), Andrée Clément (Piette Casteran), Rosine Luguet (Charlotte).

Les Films Gibé, France. 9450 ft., 105 mins.

A film adaption of André Gide's tragic and famous short story about the destructive powers of love. A middle-aged pastor falls in love with the beautiful blind girl he has adopted; his wife begins to hate the girl and his son the father, because he also loves her. When Gertrude regains her sight after a successful operation, the conflicts come into the open and tragedy is unavoidable. Torn between contradictory feelings of love, respect and gratitude, the girl kills herself.

Gide's story is an allegory about man's eternal pursuit of the unreachable ideal and the inevitability of failure. Delannoy's film loses most of this spiritual message and moves towards a record of jealousy and animosity within a family; the tissue of the film becomes impoverished and sentimentality grows more difficult to avert. The tension is mechanical and there is a certain predictability in the finale, the race to save Gertrude from the water, which is obviously derived from Griffith's classic Way Down East. Pierre Blanchar's acting in the role of the pastor seems overdone and dated.

Delannoy specialized in pictures with a philosophical-literary background and had some success, at least in the 40's, in popularizing intellectual ideas through the medium of cinema. Let us state at once that he was never a really outstanding director, but a technically skilled craftsman and a good stylist. Yet one cannot dismiss La Symphonie pastorale: its fine visual key to the story, the snowbound landscapes, create a mood of spiritual elevation, of pure feelings, and convey the austere simplicity of the life of a French Protestant family--a background which Gide knew well from his childhood.

The film's greatest asset is the unforgettable performance of Michèle Morgan as the heroine. No other actress could better express the animal-like, instinctive sensitivity of a blind girl and her gradual awakening to the world after the operation. Morgan's sublimity is only matched by the haughty majesty of the mountains that surround the village where the tragedy develops.

VIVERE IN PACE   Luigi Zampa

Script: Suso Cecchi D'Amico, Aldo Fabrizi, Piero Tellini and Zampa. Photography: Carlo Montuori. Music: Nino Rota. Cast: Aldo Fabrizi (Uncle Tigna), Gar Moore (Ronald), Mirella Monti (Silvia), John Kitzmiller (Joe), Heinrich Bode (Hans), Ave Ninchi (Corinna), Ernesto Almirante (Grandfather), Nando Bruno (Party Secretary), Aldo Silvani (Doctor), Gino Cavalieri (Priest).

Lux-Pao, Italy. 90 mins.

Vivere in Pace is located somewhere in the center of the evolutionary chain linking Four Steps in the Clouds, that ancestor of Neorealism, to the style which was later to be typical of the commercial Italian cinema. Full of movement, animated gesticulation and generic gags, it seems to grow directly from the popular traditions of the nation which created Commedia dell'arte. This is of course that familiar turn towards realism, towards everyday life;

but a film composed simply of the above elements would have been merely skilled entertainment if it had not been for the theme and the overriding plans of the director.

Zampa, despite his ambitions to social criticism, which he indulged in satirical films, was generally no more than an efficient craftsman. This time however he came across a motif which had hidden uncommonness and he used its possibilities to the full. He chose the same method Kádar and Klos were to use 19 years later in The Shop in the High Street: he arrived at a similar conclusion (one cannot live carelessly and indifferently in a time of historical cataclysm) in a similar manner, namely by moving on from a comedy of manners to a moving drama. Events, personalities, moods are expressed quite simply, but with a mastery: the message of Vivere in Pace is not only direct and easily assimilable; it is also penetrating.

The events of the film develop in a small village in the Apenines, far from the beaten track. Tigna, a good-humored peasant, discovers two escaped American POW's in his barn. One of them, the Negro Joe, is wounded. Tigna would prefer to be rid of such trouble, but on the other hand he cannot throw out men in need: so he hides the refugees in a cellar. Everything goes more or less smoothly, but unfortunately only up to a point: Joe gets hold of the stock of wine kept near his hiding place just on the evening when Tigna is visited by a German policeman--the only local representative of the occupation authorities. In vain are the dramatic efforts of the family who attempt to drown the noises coming from under the floor and pour drink into the German: in the end the tipsy Joe enters the room.

A moment of horror, but the German, also mightily drunk, reacts quite unexpectedly: he takes the appearance of the American for a sign of the end of the war and, arm in arm with his former enemy, noisily sets out into the streets. The shots fired in celebration wake the inhabitants, euphoria breaks out. When the misunderstanding is sorted out, a total evacuation takes place. The mood of the story rapidly changes, a premonition of tragedy sets in, and indeed Tigna and the German, escaping with him in civilian clothes, die from the bullets of a passing SS patrol. War leaves no one in peace; one cannot count on staying out of the way.

MY DARLING CLEMENTINE   John Ford

Script: Samuel G. Engel and Winston Miller, from a story by Sam Hellman, based on the book, "Wyatt Earp, Frontier Marshal," by Stuart N. Lake. Photography: Joseph MacDonald. Music: Cyril J. Mockridge. Cast: Henry Fonda (Wyatt Earp), Linda Darnell

(Chihuahua), Victor Mature (Doc John Holliday), Walter Brennan
(Old Man Clanton), Tim Holt (Virgil Earp), Ward Bond (Morgan
Earp), Cathy Downs (Clementine Carter), Alan Mowbray (Granville
Thorndyke), John Ireland (Billy Clanton), Grant Withers (Ike Clan-
ton), Roy Roberts (Mayor), Jane Darwell (Kate Nelson).

20th Century-Fox, U.S.A.   8760 ft., 97 mins.

My Darling Clementine is the film that most clearly demonstrates
the mythology and situational patterns of classical stories of the
pioneering West. It is the film that most distinctly reveals the
principal features of Ford's style: his narrative simplicity, careful dramatic structure, technical restraint and moral unequivocality
of content. In fact the theme itself is exceptionally typical of the
genre: a version of one of the most celebrated episodes in the history of the Arizona territory, the 1880 conflict between the Earp
and Clanton clans concluded with the gunfight in the O.K. Corral in
Tombstone.

     On the background of these events Ford projected his idealis-
tic, romantic vision of an epoch in which, it is true, force had the
upper hand, but a just force, applied with honesty and bravery by
men such as Sheriff Wyatt Earp, who although historically a rather
controversial personality, appears here in Henry Fonda's interpretation as a character full of dignity. The story of the introduction
of law and order in Tombstone develops with great sense of rhythm,
but rather calmly. In the studio scenes the direction even seems
somewhat too heavy, but when Ford goes out into the open spaces
he can enthrall the spectator with the feel of their wideness. He
was greatly assisted by Joe MacDonald: My Darling Clementine is
one of the best photographed westerns.

DEAD AMONG THE LIVING (Mrtvý Mezi Živými) Bořivoj Zeman

Script: Elmar Klos and Zeman, from the novel, "To Levende og
En Død" (Two Living and One Dead) by Sigurd Christiansen. Pho-
tography: Petr Rovný. Music: Jiří Šust. Cast: Karel Höger
(Valta), Eduard Dubský (Munk), Václav Irmanov (Popov), Zdenka
Procházková (Helena), Lída Matoušková (Klecková), Jana Hridličková
(Jana), Vladimír Řepa (Inspector), František Klika (Manager), Miloš
Hájek (Klečka), František Slégr (Fejfar).

Československa filmová společnost, Czechoslovakia.   8140 ft., 90
mins.

A post office robbery: the bandits kill one clerk, wound a second,

and the third, in terror, allows them to get hold of the money.
During the investigation he is freed from responsibility but in the
eyes of the local populace he still remains a coward. The pressure
of the situation forces the hero to undergo a deep moral self-ap-
praisal: no, he is not at fault. He then starts a fight to clear his
name, all the more so since the analysis of the tragic event brings
to his mind material doubts as to the value of his colleagues'
heroic gestures. His strivings to rehabilitate himself are successful.

It is a pity though, that for Zeman's film success appears
somewhat one-dimensional and was brought about by luck, and not
by an analysis of personal attitudes on the part of the director.
All the same Dead Among the Living has acquired the status of a
debate about responsibility for action taken in the face of mortal
danger. Immediately after the war such a theme was rather topical
in Czechoslovakia, and it is not impossible that in the background
of the film lie the complexes of 1938 when, abandoned by its allies,
the country surrendered to Nazi aggression without a single shot.
Still, analogies of this kind might be a little too far-fetched; Dead
Among the Living is above all a drama of atmosphere, of inner psychological tensions and carefully observed detail.

Although this was the director's feature film debut, the film-
making is marred only by insignificant stumbles--this is all the
more creditable as the narrative is very quiet in pace and tends to
give prominence to feelings rather than dramatic situations.

THE SUN RISES AGAIN (Il Sole Sorge Ancora)   Aldo Vergano

Script: Guido Aristarco, Giuseppe De Santis, Carlo Lizzani, Rug-
gero Jacobbi and Vergano, from a story by Giuseppe Gorgerino.
Photography: Aldo Tonti. Music: Giuseppe Rosati. Cast: Vit-
torio Duse (Cesare), Elli Parvo (Matilde), Carlo Lizzani (Priest),
Lea Padovani (Laura), Massimo Serato, Checco Rissone, Marco
Levi.

A.N.P.I., Italy. 95 mins.

An Italian provincial backwater in 1943-44. On 8 September 1943
Italy was divided into two parts; the Northern part was occupied by
German forces. The action of the picture is set on a large farm
somewhere near Milan. Cesare, a Fascist soldier, deserts his
unit on the day armistice is announced and goes home. He becomes
involved with the daughter of a Resistance fighter, and later with a
rich lady factory owner. He finally joins the partisans and takes
part in a sabotage action. He is caught by the Germans and tor-

tured, but the partisans save him.

The attitudes of people from different social groups; the
growth of resistance to the occupation forces; the liberation--Ver-
gano's film must be considered equally as full a national chronicle
of the last period of the war as Rossellini's Paisà. It is a panorama of events recorded almost hot and, as opposed to Paisà, interpreted from a clearly defined leftist standpoint. The richness
and variety of observation tend to overwhelm the dramatic tissue of
the picture, and the incoherence of the narrative is a further fault,
but all the same The Sun Rises Again stands out just because of its
great power of expression.

Wherever the sincere and tragic pathos and ardor of the eyewitness's account comes to the fore, Vergano's socio-political document is strengthened by the moving humanist touch. This is especially true of the dramatic episode of the execution of the priest,
who is led to death by the local inhabitants to the choral, "Ora pro
nobis," or the night scene of partisans tied to posts and murdered
by torchlight as target practice for a drunken German officer.

THE MURDERERS ARE AMONGST US (Die Mörder sind unter uns)
   Wolfgang Staudte

Script: Staudte. Photography: Friedl Behn-Grund and Eugen
Klagemann. Music: Ernst Roters. Cast: Hildegard Knef (Susanna
Wallner), Ernst Fischer (Dr. Mertens), Arno Paulsen (Captain
Brückner), Erna Sellmer (Frau Brückner), Robert Forsch (Herr
Mondschein), Albert Johannes (Herr Timm).

DEFA, Germany. 7850 ft., 87 mins.

The fact that the first postwar German film chose confrontation with
the Nazi past as its theme should be treated as a matter of course.
Considering the conditions in a defeated, occupied country, one could
hardly expect such an attempt to rise above the average standards
and simplifications of a custom-made condemnation. Yet this look
at German affairs was taken by a director whose deep commitment
to the moral regeneration of German society was not a spur-of-the-
moment whim, but a long-term project which he also debated in his
later films that discuss the causes and legacies of the Third Reich.
Staudte was a gifted heir to the traditions of the German cinema.

In this film, steeped in a catastrophic mood, a major role is
played by the stylistic motifs of Expressionism--in the designs, in
the obtrusively hammered-out symbols and in the nervous, restless
narrative style. Of the three leading characters, the first repre-

sents the evil of Nazism; the second, the moral defeat of a nation conscious of its guilt; and the third, advocacy of the idea of national rebirth through hard work and observance of the law. A former army physician meets an officer responsible for the mass murder of Polish civilians, who has already adapted excellently to the new way of life. Sunk in depression, convinced of the final bankruptcy of humanist ideals, the doctor wants to kill the criminal, but is dissuaded by a girl who has faith in the future. The decision as to the fate of the mass murderer will be placed in the hands of the law.

It is worth mentioning that the scenario provided for a different ending: the doctor's plan was carried out. But this solution was not accepted by the Allied administration. Staudte later accepted that this decision was right, since it was not the ending which was the main exponent of the film's philosophy, but the title-- a title of which the Nazis were already afraid in 1931. "Murderers Are Amongst Us" was the original title of Fritz Lang's M and had to be abandoned because of political pressure. Fifteen years later Staudte, surely not by accident, used this very title. As his future films were to witness, the anxiety he voices was justified. The Germans were haunted by the ghosts of the past for a long time to come.

THE KILLERS   Robert Siodmak

Script: Anthony Veiller, inspired by the short story by Ernest Hemingway. Photography: Woody Bredell. Music: Miklos Rozsa. Cast: Edmond O'Brien (Jim Reardon), Ava Gardner (Kitty Collins), Burt Lancaster (Swede), Albert Dekker (Jim Colfax), Sam Levene (Sam Lubinsky), Charles D. Brown (Packy Robinson), Donald MacBride (Kenyon), Phil Brown (Nick Adams), Charles McGraw (Al).

Universal, U.S.A.   105 mins.

This gangster drama was inspired by Hemingway's miniature short story; the film is a cross between the moral atmosphere of film noir and the documentary texture of a Hathaway police documentary. Only the introductory ten-minute sequence in the bar comes from Hemingway, but it is the climate of this very sequence, the excellent rendering of Hemingway's matter-of-factness and penetrating observation, which gives character to the whole picture. Two professional killers murder an ex-fighter. The police are not acting with great vigor and an insurance company claim agant takes up the investigation, having found a clue--a green handkerchief with an embossed harp in the dead man's effects.

The script develops the thread of intrigue with great finesse

and gives both Siodmak and the young (but later to be famous)
actors a chance to reveal their talents. The vivid staging gives the
events a mark of credibility, and is supported by the full-blooded
acting of Edmond O'Brien, Ava Gardner and the debuting Burt Lancaster.

NO REGRETS FOR MY YOUTH (Waga Seishun-ni Kuinashi) Akira
   Kurosawa

Script: Eijiro Hisaita and Kurosawa. Photography: Asaichi Nakai.
Music: Tadashi Hattori. Cast: Denjiro Okochi (Professor Yagi-
hara), Setsuko Hara (Yukie, his daughter), Susumu Fujita (Noge),
Eiko Miyoshi (Yagihara's wife), Kuninori Kodo (Noge's father),
Haruko Sugimura (Noge's mother), Akitate Kono (Itokawa), Tadashi
Shimura (Police Commissioner).

Toho, Japan. 9921 ft., 110 mins.

After its military collapse and the resulting national tragedy, Japan
began a reassessment of the moral values which had been in force.
Kurosawa was one of the first directors to take on the problem of
reckoning with the past. He did this in an unusual manner: the
scenario which attracted his interest diverges quite substantially
from the crusading course of a dispute on things past, because it
offers not a panorama of life in Japan, but rather an account of the
personal experiences of a girl only indirectly (not to say insubstan-
tially) involved in the political events of the years 1933-1945.

    Because of his views the heroine's father, a liberal profes-
sor, loses his post at Kyoto University. She herself is emotionally
involved with one of her father's students; current events make her
even more committed to the cause of her fiancé who becomes a
revolutionary and later takes up work for Allied intelligence. They
get married; but their life together is very brief. He perishes in
prison; she goes to the country to her husband's parents, determined
to find her place in life herself, and through working for others to
fulfill the ideals she believes in. She does not succeed; but it is
not success that matters. What matters is the personal integrity,
the moral sense of working for others.

    The heroine of No Regrets for My Youth, a character typical
of Kurosawa's philosophy, is recalled in fine roles in his later famous films, To Live and Red Beard. But she herself did not meet
with applause: although No Regrets took second place among the
best Japanese films of 1946, it was received with some reluctance.
For one thing, the protagonist is a woman--at that time a rather unusual circumstance. Secondly, her activities were directed against

the onetime official dogmas and placed individualism above communal action. This did not agree either with the aims of postwar propaganda or with the Japanese traditions, which strongly advocate community action.

A third reason Kurosawa's first personal film was not enthusiastically accepted is that it proposed a cinematic language widely different from that with which he had made his name in Judo Saga: the narrative is lilting and the rhythm pointed by the recurrent visual refrains. The film is permeated with the sensitivity which Kurosawa bestowed on his heroine and the poetic reflectiveness with which he presented her courageous choice. Feeling and commitment to the theme took priority over technique; it would be so in the majority of the films Kurosawa regards as his very own (which, interestingly, are among his least perfect works from the point of view of balance and narrative skill).

THE BANDIT (Il Bandito) Alberto Lattuada

Script: Lattuada, Oreste Biancoli, Mino Caudana, Ettore M. Margadonna, Tullio Pinelli and Piero Tellini, from a story by Lattuada. Photography: Aldo Tonti. Music: Felice Lattuada. Cast: Anna Magnani (Lydia), Amedeo Nazzarri (Ernesto), Carla Del Poggio (Maria), Carlo Campanini (Carlo), Eliana Banducci (Rosetta), Mino Doro (Mirko), Folco Lulli (Andrea), Mario Perrone (The Hunchback).

Lux-Film, Italy.

The stigma of Fascism and the war in a panorama of postwar Italy: a desert of ruins amidst drifting crowds and an atmosphere of temporariness and anxiety. Some people, demoralized by the past and disorientated by the wrongly understood present, challenge society and resort to acts of terror, seeking revenge for suffering and humiliation. The Bandit is the story of a prisoner of war who returns from Russia to Turin to find his house destroyed, his family either dead or dispersed, no prospects of employment and no hope. He gets involved with a criminal gang, takes part in several robberies and is killed after a pursuit in the hills near Turin.

Lattuada was one of the directors who rejected the formalistic heritage of the national Italian cinema to search for new narrative methods based on reality and not on conventions, and thus was better suited to express the anxieties of the time. He has given in The Bandit one of the most bitter visions of a country at the crossroads. It is true that he allowed himself, particularly in the second of the two distinct parts of the film, to be carried away on a wave of sentimentality and second-rate sensationalism, but the sincere and spontaneous character of his picture gives it considerable rank and a position as one of the most interesting works of Italian Neorealism.

1947

ODD MAN OUT Carol Reed

Script: F. L. Green and R. C. Sherriff, from the novel by Green.
Photography: Robert Krasker. Music: William Alwyn. Cast:
James Mason (Johnny MacQueen), Robert Newton (Lukey), Robert
Beatty (Dennis), Fay Compton (Rosie), Cyril Cusack (Pat), F. J.
McCormick (Shell), Kathleen Ryan (Kathleen), Dan O'Herlihy (Nolan),
W. G. Fay (Father Tom), Denis O'Dea (Head Constable).

Two Cities Films, G.B. 10,488 ft., 116 mins.

Towards the close of the golden period of the British cinema Reed
made its greatest achievement, a picture which combines psychological profundity with exceptional technical mastery. Odd Man Out
can be described as "Crime and Punishment" in a Belfast setting.
Johnny, a political leader on the run, takes part in a robbery to
gain funds for the Organization. A man is killed; during the frantic
escape the wounded Johnny suffers an attack of dizziness and is left
behind. The film follows him as he wanders through the city, weak
and delirious, trying to hide from the police and to contact friends
who could help.

Despite its quasi-gangster-movie plot Odd Man Out is little
concerned with the actual action. Also the moral considerations are
completely by-passed. In a film which claims the spectators' sympathy for its outlaw hero, the director's main interests were the
psychological implications of a situation in which the protagonist has
to escape, besieged by his own inner problems, from police informers, false friends, and inexorable Time. The film spans eight
hours--from the raid at 4 p.m. until Johnny's death at midnight;
continuity of action is most important and Reed's painstaking efforts
to keep the spectator informed of the exact time of day (by making

him look at clocks, listen to the chime of church bells, and by inserting chronology into casual background conversations) reminds
one of James Joyce's novel, "Ulysses," where an identical practice
was adopted with the same purpose of aiding psychological scrutiny.
In Odd Man Out this additionally produces a unique feeling of "living
on borrowed time."

It is both interesting and inevitable to compare Odd Man Out
with two earlier pictures: John Ford's The Informer and Marcel
Carné's Quai des Brumes. Both have escape as their theme and
the former was also set in Ireland. Yet Odd Man Out overshadows
them both by its genuinely intellectual content. One feels that creating atmosphere was here no longer an aim in itself. This is not
to say that atmosphere is unimportant. Rarely in fact has awareness of the vulnerability of man's freedom been obtained more acutely or with that foreboding which casts a spell almost as strong as
in an ancient tragedy.

Despite several overlong sequences and an unsatisfactory finale the picture is expert on all levels. Aside from the distinguished part of James Mason, who with hardly ten lines of dialogue
spoken created a complex screen personality, there is the splendid
F. J. McCormick as Shell--sly, ambiguous and incomparably Irish,
he appears as a kind of conscience haunting the hero. In fact all
supporting roles, played by character actors from Irish theatres,
are excellent. Robert Krasker's photography is among the best in
the world's films of the 40's.

While the visual rendering of the hero's hallucinations seems
rather dated, Krasker, who after Henry V and Brief Encounter was
already considered the best British cinematographer, knew how to
find poetry in the ugly city streets, little shops, glistening alleys,
patterns of roofs, streetcar cables, shadows on walls and the children's graffiti. This is accompanied by inventive use of sound,
exaggerated to stress the isolation and helplessness of a wounded
man. The murmur of the city, the chiming of clocks, the shouts of
children playing in narrow passages, the desperate sound of a ship's
siren all have a dramatic justification. Odd Man Out remains one
of not so many "moments of truth" in the cinema.

GERMANY YEAR ZERO (Germania Anno Zero) Roberto Rossellini

Script: Rossellini, Carlo Lizzani and Max Colpet. Photography:
Robert Juillard. Music: Renzo Rossellini. Cast: Edmund Meschke
(Edmund), Ernest Pittschau (His father), Ingetraud Hinze (Eva),
Franz Grüger (Karl-Heinz), Erich Gühne (Herr Henning, the school-
master).

Teverfilm, Italy/Germany. 6661 ft., 74 mins.

Germany Year Zero: the pride of the defeated country lies in ashes; moral corruption accompanies material destitution; the people live in overcrowded flats and are hungry, disenchanted and bitter. There is a family: the sick father tells of the good pre-Hitler days and constantly quarrels with his elder son, a deserter who hides from the occupation forces; the daughter goes with American soldiers. The younger son, 15-year-old Edmund is their main supporter; he knows how to make a few pennies here and there, sometimes by playing records of Hitler's speeches to the laughing Allied soldiers in the ruins of the Chancellery.

All of Rossellini's great films of the 40's portray human tragedies brought about by the war. When soon after the armistice the director went to Berlin to make Germany Year Zero, he retained the tone and the style of Rome, Open City and Paisà, but limited himself to showing a smaller section of reality than in those composite Italian films. But even Germany Year Zero does not have a real story or an ordered narrative. It tells of the tragedy of a youngster with the responsibilities of an adult but a child's emotions. Edmund is tough but also deprived and bewildered and he finally resolves to kill his father whom he believes to be the source of the family's difficulties.

Whether or not the film is the greatest of Rossellini's works, it certainly constitutes the apex of the director's anti-romantic style. The events are told using a semi-documentary technique, with the desperate urgency of an eye witness who is afraid of forgetting. All actors in the film, except the father, were non-professionals and the film emanates the faint aura of amateurism present in all Rossellini's works. The vertiginous camera movements are accompanied by a realistic soundtrack incorporating the ocean of outside noises: in the final scene of Edmund's suicide the sound memento is the scream of a passing tram.

The director has no apparent sympathy for his heroes; he does not commiserate with the fallen nation. This acute clinical chronicle does however contain elements of an impassioned psychological account steeped in lyricism, which contributes to making the picture a memorable apocalyptic vision of the disintegration of a universe.

LE SILENCE EST D'OR   René Clair

Script: Clair. Photography: Armand Thirard. Music: Georges Van Parys. Cast: Maurice Chevalier (Émile), François Périer

(Jacques), Marcelle Derrien (Madeleine), Dany Robin (Lucette), Robert Pizani (Duperrier), Raymond Cordy (Le Frise), Paul Olivier (Cashier), Roland Armontel (Celestin), Gaston Modot (Cameraman), Bernard La Jarrige (Paulo), Paul Demange (Sultan).

RKO Radio Pictures/Pathé Cinéma, France.   8906 ft., 99 mins.

After many years of absence Clair returned to France. He also returned to his youth, to the easy-going Parisian world of Le Million and Quatorze Juillet and to the wonders of the cinema which were the director's starting point on his way to fame. These miracles of the first twenty years of the existence of the cinema, these firstlings and illusions of its fairground period, are presented this time from the inside. The plot is situated in a pre-First World War film studio and some of the gags are based on the film-making technique of the pioneers of the cinema.

The axis of the plot is the rivalry of two men for the favors of a young actress; the rivals are a crafty old studio manager who falls into the trap of his own advice, and his assistant whom he treats with patronizing indulgence. Seemingly the story is a vaudeville fiddle-faddle, but indeed under the polish of a smooth smile it touches on real basics. It is, among other things, a film about the sadness of the passing of time and of mature reconciliation with fate. The Clairian subtlety, the pastel quality of his way of story-telling, gave the film notes of poetry and sincere emotion. Still, the film deals with psychological reality rather than everyday reality. For the most part Le Silence est d'or is like Clair's erstwhile theatre of shadows: lacy, old-fashionedly charming and without rancor.

One cannot be against Clair for all his mastery, and one should be grateful for the smile and exhortation to good humor, whose messenger here is the finely lyrical Maurice Chevalier. It is interesting that Le Silence est d'or had harmful effects on the French cinema. Clair's comeback, with all his renown, became in the context of the traditionally apolitical cinema in France an indirect but powerful impulse to keep on praising the French national charm and cultural traditions. Thus celluloid confectionery, although sometimes brilliant, would reign in the French cinema until the rebellion of the Nouvelle Vague.

QUAI DES ORFÈVRES   Henri-Georges Clouzot

Script: Clouzot and Jean Ferry, from the novel, "Légitime défense," by Stanislas-André Steeman. Photography: Armand Thirard. Music: Francis Lopez. Cast: Louis Jouvet (Inspector An-

toine), Suzy Delair (Jenny Lamour), Bernard Blier (Maurice Mar-
tineau), Simone Renant (Dora), Charles Dullin (Brignon, industrial-
ist), Pierre Larquey (Taxi driver), René Blancard (Police Commissioner), Jean Daurand (Picard), Robert Dalban (Paulo, a vagrant).

Majestic Films, France. 9480 ft., 105 mins.

A second-rate intrigue based on the traditional ploy of a search for
a murderer becomes the starting point of one of the most excellent
French thrillers, a picture which recalls Hitchcock at his best.
The jealous husband of an ambitious music-hall singer wants to kill
the man who he thinks is his wife's lover but finds him already
dead. He thinks the wife is the murderer, and has a childhood
friend cover up incriminating clues (the wife did hit the dead man).
The police suspicions are directed against the husband, but the real
murderer turns out to be someone quite different.

Clouzot exploited to the full all the possibilities latent in the
plot, staged it excellently and played out the tension in every inch
of the film. But the greatest value of Quai des Orfèvres lies in the
richness of psychological and moral observation and in its links with
current trends in the cinema and current intellectual moods. The
picture does not contain anything directly borrowed, although it might
appear to some a sign of Clouzot's accession to the American film
noir or to police documentary. This is however only the result of
the combination of this particular choice of plot with the Stroheimian
interests of Clouzot who, as before in The Crow, observed human
littleness under particularly dramatic circumstances.

The aura of the inherent sadness of the lives of the film's
protagonists corresponded to the postwar Existentialist philosophy,
but it does not seem to have been particularly encouraged by the director. The picture simply offers realistic observation of the milieu
of second-rate revue theatres--not without irony in the approach to
a whodunit plot whose individual elements are treated with the same
ambivalence as are the moral attitudes of the protagonists. Previous models become rejected, sometimes even reversed, and from
behind clichés peers a living man--such for instance is the police
inspector (as performed excellently by Jouvet). The inspector knows
the law well, but he knows people even better, and he performs his
duties for a living and not to fulfill any abstract ideals. He prefers
efficiency to strict ethical principles and is prepossessing despite
his gruffness and grumbling.

Throughout the first part of the film Clouzot brilliantly outlined his own world of moral values and achieved a stifling atmosphere of evil. Wickedness comes out of everyone under the pressure of events, and justice is seen to rest with the one who distrusted longest--for everybody was lying.

MONSIEUR VERDOUX   Charles Chaplin

Script: Chaplin, from an idea by Orson Welles (scenario, "The
Ladykiller"). Photography: Rollie Totheroh, Curt Courant and
Wallace Chewing. Music: Chaplin. Cast: Charles Chaplin (Henri
Verdoux alias Varney alias Bonheur alias Floray), Mady Correll
(Mona, his wife), Allison Roddan (Peter, their son), Martha Raye
(Annabella Bonheur), Ada-May (Annette, her maid), Isobel Elsom
(Marie Grosnay), Marjorie Bennett (Her maid), Margaret Hoffman
(Lydia Floray), Marilyn Nash (The Girl), Helen Heigh (Yvonne),
Irving Bacon (Pierre Couvais), Almira Sessions (Lena Couvais),
Charles Evans (Morris, the detective), William Frawley (Police in-
spector), Bernard J. Nedell (Police superintendent).

United Artists, U.S.A. 11,157 ft., 125 mins.

Von Clausewitz said that war is the logical continuation of diplomacy.
Chaplin put into the mouth of his hero the remark that murder is
the logical continuation of business, and made one of the most provocative works in the history of cinema, supplying logical proof that
it is simply quantity which sanctifies the means. A single crime
makes a man a public enemy, someone who must be eliminated;
war, in which millions are murdered and which often constitutes an
extension of the interests of capital, is tolerated by civilization and
those who kill best in war become heroes. Is the line of argument
of Chaplin's Monsieur Verdoux really all that cynical?

     The plot of the film was inspired by the notorious Landru
Affair. Landru was a seducer and murderer of lonely rich women,
who operated during the First World War and was executed soon
after. It is worth noting that Landru's activities were only made
possible by the war conditions, among other things, by the scarcity
of men at home. Chaplin moves the plot to the 30's; his Landru-
Verdoux becomes a murderer under the pressure of adverse circumstances. He used to be a bank clerk, but in the difficult years of
the Great Crisis he has to take any occupation which provides the
means to support his family.

     The most effective seems to be the idea of killing rich
elderly spinsters; of course this way of earning money does not
quite agree with the rules of society, but Verdoux himself is the
product of that society. His occupation is neither easy nor safe.
But it brings in much-needed money--until the ferment in Europe
at the close of the 30's finally ruins Chaplin's hero: Verdoux loses
all, even his wife and son, and soon after he is caught and charged.
At the same time he metamorphoses into the accuser, the reminder
that modern civilization would like to turn everybody into murderers like himself.

This most pessimistic film from the maker of The Gold Rush
is very, very far from the previous sentimentality, warmth, well-
intentioned accusations and pointed satire toned down with the fireworks of situational humor. Of course, Chaplin also appears here
as a master of humor, but of a black and bitter variety--in the
scene, for instance, of one of the murderous attempts when Verdoux
falls into the water and the victim-to-be saves him from drowning,
or when the hero who notices his son pull a cat's tail wonders from
whom the cruel traits were inherited. Still, there are not many
gags in the film; pace and structural coherence are also lacking.

Chaplin, who wanted among other things to use Monsieur
Verdoux as a platform to protest against the Bomb, often struck
tones of gravity, but with a sarcastic ring. He wanted to be well
understood, so he attached great weight to the spoken word and as
a result overchanged the film with dialogue. But it is not directorial merits which determine the importance of Monsieur Verdoux:
Chaplin, who predictably was violently attacked after this film, made
his impact through uncompromising condemnation of the moral hypocrisy of power politics.

KISS OF DEATH   Henry Hathaway

Script: Ben Hecht and Charles Lederer, based on a story by
Eleazar Lipsky. Photography: Norbert Brodine. Music: David
Buttolph. Cast: Victor Mature (Nick Bianco), Brian Donlevy
(D'Angelo), Coleen Gray (Nettie), Richard Widmark (Tom Udo),
Taylor Holmes (Earl Howser), Howard Smith (Warden), Robert
Keith (Judge), Karl Malden (Sgt. William Cullen).

20th Century-Fox, U.S.A. 8857 ft., 99 mins.

A gangster who cannot go straight because of his criminal past
commits a daring robbery and is caught. In prison he learns that
his wife has committed suicide after an affair with a criminal and
that his two children are now in an orphanage. He accepts the
authorities' offer of freedom in exchange for collaboration and
agrees to inform on his old gang; he can now settle his accounts.
With its brutal and ironic view of life, Hathaway's picture is part
of the same film noir tradition that produced The Maltese Falcon,
Double Indemnity and The Big Sleep.

The director's moralizing ambitions are manifest: Hathaway
was trying to erase some of the glamor which the underworld had
acquired in the cinema over the years. Here it appears as desperate and sordid; its member breaks the code and turns squealer.
But, says Hathaway, the intentions of the law are often also of

doubtful purity and, after all, it is the rejection by society which
pushed the hero onto the path of crime in the first place.   These
moralizing intentions of Kiss of Death are half-powered; an additional disadvantage is that illustrating a thesis tends to turn characters
into archetypes and make their fate too easily predictable.   But* we
do not have to consider Kiss of Death a "social evil" type of film.
It can be appreciated also as a stylish entertaining thriller.

        Not only the sentiments, but also the style of the picture are
close to the semi-documentary "newsreel" style of Hathaway's previous Call Northside 777 and The House on 92nd Street.   Kiss of
Death sometimes resorts even to the use of a narrator; all the
scenes were shot on location, with the beginning in Sing-Sing prison.
The cold-blooded Christmas robbery is shown with a detached matter-of-factness, not far from Dassin's in future Du Rififi chez les
hommes.   It is just this sense of unadulterated genuineness which
is the film's main strength.   The acting is very convincing; Richard
Widmark is particularly effective as a psychopathic murderer--the
role which made his name.

MACBETH   Orson Welles

Script: William Alland and Welles, from the play, "The Tragedie
of Macbeth" (c. 1606), by William Shakespeare.   Photography:
John L. Russell.   Music: Jacques Ibert.   Cast: Orson Welles
(Macbeth), Jeanette Nolan (Lady Macbeth), Dan O'Herlihy (Macduff),
Roddy McDowall (Malcolm), Edgar Barrier (Banquo), Alan Napier
(A Holy father), Erskine Sanford (Duncan), John Dierkes (Ross),
Kenne Curtis (Lennox), Peggy Webber (Lady Macduff), Lionel
Braham (Siward), Archie Heugly (Young Siward), Jerry Farber
(Fleance), Christopher Welles (Macduff child), Morgan Farley
(Doctor), Lurene Tuttle (Gentlewoman), Brainerd Duffield (First
Murderer), William Alland (Second Murderer), George Chirello
(Seyton), Gus Schilling (Porter).

Republic Pictures, U.S.A.   9642 ft., 107 mins.

Welles' genius is full of contradictions: brilliance merged with
mediocrity, impressive display accompanied by shoddiness.
Macbeth is the prime example of this: almost all aspects of the
film are doubtful to say the least, yet the whole is remarkable.
Welles had always been an admirer of Shakespeare, but Macbeth
was only his first (of several) Shakespearian productions.   The idea
was to make a low-cost picture in a naturalistic manner which would
popularize the tragedy.   There were only eight exceptionally artificial sets and the shooting schedule took an incredible 23 days.

All this shows in the film: the grey and monotonous sets provide little variation in the oppressive mood, the accent is sometimes Scottish, sometimes American and rarely in agreement with lip movements; even the acting (except Welles' of course) is dull. Yet this grim, theatrical study of the corrupting influence of power has a strange fascination. It is unusual--but it does preserve the essence of Shakespeare. Welles' extravagant performance creates its own laws and makes the vision of a Scotland inhabited by savages almost convincing; there are a number of imaginative visual effects and as usual brilliant camera work; Duncan's murder is shown in one eight-minute shot.

The character of the theme magnifies the affinities with Eisenstein's Ivan the Terrible, while the circumstances of shooting create striking parallels with the German Expressionist films (but apparently unconsciously on Welles' part). A hostile reception from the critics made him withdraw the film and do some more work on it before the release. This convinced nobody, but still, Macbeth is an interesting example of how the whole can be greater than the sum of its parts.

LES JEUX SONT FAITS   Jean Delannoy

Script: Jean-Paul Sartre, Delannoy and Jacques-Laurent Bost. Photography: Christian Matras. Music: Georges Auric. Cast: Micheline Presle (Eve Charlier), Charles Dullin (Marquis), Jacques Erwin (Dictator Aguerra), Edmond Beauchamp (Dixonne), Marcel Mouloudji (Lucien), Howard Vernon (Chief Militiaman), Renaud Mary (Militiaman), Jean Daurand (Paulo), Marcel Pagliero (Pierre), Fernand Fabre (André Charlier), Colette Ripert (Lucette), Marguerite Moreno (The Lady), Guy Decomble (Poulain), Jim Gérald (Renaudel), Paul Olivier (Eve's father).

Les Films Gibé, France.   8200 ft., 91 mins.

The screen manifesto of Existentialism in the form of a poetic tale about the futility of a man's efforts to change his fate. The guides through the Sartrian world are a proletarian revolutionary and a married woman waiting to be loved, a classical personality for the French cinema and theatre. They meet in the Beyond; their meeting was impossible on earth since they were separated by social barriers. Now they discover they are created for each other and are given the grace of returning to the world for one day to test their choice.

The attempt ends in failure, even though they are both aware of the situation and know the mechanisms which govern their

temporal affairs. In his absorbtion in work for the common good
he will not find time for himself; she cannot reject completely her
class prejudice nor find the strength to oppose her cynical murderer husband. There is no way out of the impasse: man is condemned to be defeated. One cannot decide one's fate when the inertia of events gives chance the upper hand and the psychological
barriers do not even allow one to communicate fully with others.
The struggle, though hopeless, has to be taken up in the name of
human dignity.

The theses of the intellectuals searching for a foothold on the
ruins of the old ethical structures destroyed by the war do not appear in Les Jeux sont faits with the brusque ruthlessness usually
characteristic of the literary work of the late 40's. Certainly, one
of the reasons was the wish to make the professed philosophy more
assimilable--but not only that; of great importance was the artistic
convention in which Delannoy presented Sartre's concepts. His fan-
tastic-romantic vision drives the brutal realities of life into the
shade; although it drew inspiration from the prewar school of Poetic
Realism, it does not even for a moment approach a social document, but rather escapes towards the balladic convention. One of
the reasons for this is the fact that the director's incisiveness did
not allow him any other way of cutting across certain a priori qualities of the script. In dozens of cases this could come out oppor-
tunistic, false, or empty; here it is surprisingly purposeful, maybe
because the film has a lot of genuine warmth.

The academic Delannoy, who with his imagery often ended up
on the reefs of naiveté, in Les Jeux sont faits achieved the effect
of extratemporal elegance. This was possible only with a precise
formal balance; but the maker of La Symphonie pastorale had already proved to be a stylist of some standing.

BRUTE FORCE Jules Dassin

Script: Richard Brooks, from a story by Robert Patterson. Pho-
tography: William Daniels. Music: Miklos Rozsa. Cast: Hume
Cronyn (Captain Munsey), Burt Lancaster (Joe Collins), Charles
Bickford (Gallagher), Whitner Bissell (Tom Lister), Sam Levene
(Louie), John Hoyt (Spencer), Art Smith (Dr. Walters), Howard
Duff (Soldier), Yvonne DeCarlo (Gina).

Universal-International, U.S.A. 8721 ft., 97 mins.

A study of a Nazi-like subclimate in an American jail: a decent
but weak warden looks on while an ambitious and sinister guard
tortures prisoners to the sounds of Wagner and incites them

to rebellion hoping thereby to gain promotion. A jailbreak is
planned by the inhabitants of the R-17 cell. Each of the men is
driven by powerful motifs: one had his parole canceled, another
wants to be at the bedside of his girl who is preparing to undergo
an operation. The guard knows of the escape plan and all
the men are killed; but he himself also falls victim to his
wickedness.

    The jailbreak subplot is not particuarly original and has often
been surpassed (take for instance Becker's Le Trou); prison life
seems to modern eyes a worn-out subject. Yet Brute Force remains
relevant not because of its melodramatic story, but as a powerful
and incisive examination of the origins and escalation of violence in
a microcosm inhabited by a handful of well-drawn characters: a
sadistic guard, a drunken philosophizing prison doctor and a prisoner's leader. This last, the most interesting part in the film, ensured the future career of Burt Lancaster. Brute Force is therefore very much a part of the postwar series of "socially conscious"
American pictures of which the most outstanding directors, apart
from Dassin, were Kazan, Litvak and Wilder. This film established Dassin's style for the rest of the 40's and remains one of
his very best works, although the follow-ups, The Naked City and
Thieves' Highway, achieved much wider popularity.

CALL NORTHSIDE 777   Henry Hathaway

Script: Jerome Cady, Jay Dratler and Quentin Reynolds, from arti-
cles by James P. McGuire. Photography: Joseph MacDonald.
Music: Alfred Newman. Cast: James Stewart (McNeal), Richard
Conte (Frank Wiecek), Lee J. Cobb (Brian Kelly), Helen Walker
(Laura McNeal), Betty Garde (Wanda Skutnik), Kasia Orzazewski
(Tillie), Joanne de Bergh (Helen Wiecek-Rayska), Howard Smith
(Palmer), Moroni Olsen (Parole Board Chairman), George Tyne
(Tomek Zaleska), Michael Chapin (Frank Wiecek's son).

20th Century-Fox, U.S.A. 9981 ft., 111 mins.

In 1944, thirteen years after Joseph Mojczek of Chicago was sent
to prison for practically all his life for the alleged murder of a
policeman, a mysterious advertisement appeared in the press: it
offered $5000 to anyone who would expose the real criminal. The
intrigued James McGuire of the "Chicago Tribune" found the adver-
tiser, the prisoner's mother. She was unshakenly convinced of her
son's innocence and had for many years collected the money needed
to buy the information to have his case reviewed. McGuire undertook a private investigation during the course of which he became
convinced that a judicial mistake was indeed a possibility; he com-

mitted himself to finding the truth and eventually achieved a re-
opening of the case and an annulment of the sentence after a clue
was found to prove Mojczek's innocence.

This authentic and fascinating story was Hathaway's starting
point in making the last of his famous police documentaries. The
script limits itself to relating the real events, and the film was
shot where the events actually took place--in the houses and streets
of Chicago, in the grim tenements of its Polish district. The scenery, excellently recorded by MacDonald's camera, breathes authenticity; the journalistic direction with its purposeful restraint and
stress on the tangible gives the feel of direct participation in the
drama; the acting of James Stewart and Lee J. Cobb is no less authentic.

As a result, Call Northside 777 is not only one of the closest
portrayals of the American reality of its time. It is also convincing, with its frank criticism of the police and the judiciary, its
faith in the positive features of man and the importance of the fight
to uphold democratic principles. This is not achieved by way of
wordy tirades: Hathaway's picture, deprived equally of showiness
and annalistic dryness, speaks with the tangibility of the scenery in
which the reporter moves and with the intensity of his search for
the truth.

THE TRAGIC PURSUIT (Caccia Tragica)   Giuseppe De Santis

Script: Carlo Lizzani, Umberto Barbaro, Corrado Alvaro, Cesare
Zavattini, De Santis, Ennio De Concini and Michelangelo Antonioni.
Photography: Otello Martelli. Music: Giuseppe Rosati. Cast:
Vivi Gioi (Daniela), Andrea Checchi (Alberto), Carla Del Poggio
(Giovanna), Vittorio Duse (Giuseppe), Massimo Girotti (Michele),
Checco Rissone (Mimi), Guido Della Valle (German).

Libertas Film/A.N.P.I./Dante Film, Italy.   8010 ft., 89 mins.

The debut of the leader of militant Neorealism, a violent story of
conflicts in rural Italy just after the war. Landowners try to boost
the price of corn artificially by not cultivating parts of their land.
The government gives grants to cooperatives wanting to cultivate
this land. The landowners' reply is terror spread by mercenary
gangs. The tragic pursuit of the title is after one of such gangs
and is undertaken by a group of cooperative workers from Emilia,
robbed of the money which was to be an installment on a lease.

De Santis tells his tale with an excellent feel for the rhythm,
passion and technical bravura--but at the same time with a lack of

moderation. He floods the film with technical effects, over-con-
trasts the situations and personalities, confuses the narrative by introducing obtrusive symbols, and forgets about stylistic homogeneity.
The final result is much closer to a sensational fireworks drama
than to a consciously attractive social statement. These features,
which so glaringly appear in The Tragic Pursuit, represent the later
imagery of the director rather well: De Santis was never faultless
or original, although he was at times great.

The period of his splendor significantly coincided with the
triumphs of Neorealism: when the trend began to decline, De
Santis also had nothing new to offer. His career in films is an excellent illustration of the principle that a commitment to the burning
problems of contemporary life combined with an ability to take advantage of existing examples might suffice to make fascinating works
for the screen.

SOMEWHERE IN EUROPE (Valahol Európában...) Géza Radványi

Script: Radványi and Béla Balázs. Photography: Barnabás Hegyi.
Music: Dénes Buday. Cast: Arthur Somlay (Simon Tamás),
Zsuzsa Bánki (Eva), Miklós Gábor (Hosszú), György Bárdy, Laci
Horváth (Kuksi), István Rozsos, students of the Drama School and
25 children.

Mafirt-Radványi, Hungary. 10,000 ft., 111 mins.

One of the cruelest aspects of war is that it leaves behind homeless
orphaned children. The heroes of Radványi and Balázs' film are
some of the creatures which Central Europe inherited from the years
1939 to 1945--children from one of the countries on the Danube, as
the commentary puts it. They came out of the conflagration by different paths; now they wander in search of the means to live--first
singly, then in bigger groups. In the end they form bands and act
with all the more aggression the more intolerance they encounter.

The first part of the film, made in the manner of a brutally
frank report, reaches the heights of an excellent work of art syn-
thetically portraying the times. Later, however, Somewhere in
Europe veers towards an individual, symbolic and semi-fantastic
tale; the uncompromising realism turns into rhetorical and melodramatic didacticism--moving, it is true, but artistically of a much
lower standard. The story goes as follows: the adolescent gang
meets an elderly virtuoso pianist in an apparently deserted castle.
The artist, who has separated himself from the cruelty of the outside world, offers the drifting children a roof and food and decides,
in the name of the responsibilities of his generation, to take up the

battle to rule the young souls.

He succeeds easily--and this is the weakness of the concept of the film. Although the selfish and intolerant local people oppose the benefactor and the ensuing confrontation even claims a victim, the children allow themselves to be guided too easily. They hardly resemble individuals coming out of a cataclysm and poisoned with the bacillus of war. The truth, unfortunately, was less optimistic. But this still does not invalidate the humanist message of the first important film from Communist Hungary: the principal method of ennobling a human being is to make him subject to the influence of beauty.

Of the two co-authors of the film, Béla Balázs is probably more responsible for the form it took than the newly-independent Radványi. One of the most outstanding theoreticians of the cinema, he was abroad throughout the inter-war period and returned to Hungary after 1945. During the last years of his life Balázs took an active part in building the national cinema. It is probably he who was responsible for the formal aspect of the first part of the film, dominated by reminiscences of the silent cinema, such as the rapid editing and the elements of Expressionist aesthetics (the wax effigy of Hitler, the tilted camera, the shadow of a German in the scene of rape). The whole of the film, with its spontaneity, definitely rises far above any borrowings and much of its atmosphere is owed not only to the direction and the very good photography, but also to the adolescent actors, especially Laci Horváth.

THE TREASURE OF SIERRA MADRE   John Huston

Script: Huston, from the novel by Bruno Traven. Photography: Ted McCord. Music: Max Steiner. Cast: Humphrey Bogart (Dobbs), Walter Huston (Howard), Tim Holt (Curtin), Bruce Bennett (Cody), Barton MacLane (McCormick), Alfonso Bedoya ("Gold Hat"), A. Soto Rangel (Presidente), Manuel Donde (El Jefe), John Huston (White Suit).

Warner Bros., U.S.A.   11,324 ft., 126 mins.

The story goes that Huston was born in a house that his grandfather won at poker and was thus under the sign of the wheel of fortune. There is in this a certain wry symbol of the interests of the director, who elevated the doggedly chased Adventure to the rank of a great metaphor of the aspirations of man. The Treasure of Sierra Madre, which made the name of its director legendary, is one of the clearest expositions of the Huston world: adventure is here seen to polarize human attitudes. It becomes a testing ground; peo-

ple succumb to the demon of evil or to the impulses of sublimity,
but are in no case earthbound.

Adventure brings defeat, but is at the same time enriching.
When, in the film's finale, the survivors of the group of gold prospectors find that the spiteful breath of fate has blown their treasure
over the desert sands, they burst out laughing. Their laughter is
not a sign of madness but of a mature acceptance of the changea-
bility of fate. Their defeat is thus a heroic defeat and it signifies
an inner victory: Huston's men are the last troubadours of the era
of the great recluses, spending their lives in search of fullness and
rejecting the uniformity of the world. They find their ancestors in
Antiquity, as does the hero of Cacoyannis's Zorba the Greek.

In the years 1947-1955, Huston's great years, the protagonists still preserved an authentic quality; in the period following, adventure would become trivialized, turning into an exotic surrogate,
and the star of its creator would wane. One of the reasons for this
is the fact that the films of Huston--that screen counterpart of Joseph Conrad and Hemingway--speak above all through the intensity
of experience and not through fascinating form. Indeed, some parts
of The Treasure of Sierra Madre make visually ravishing cinema
and some of Huston's later films would show signs of external
brilliance, but the daily bread of the director is the simplicity of
the staging--sometimes even awkward, but almost always literal.
One should not look for riches on the surface of the screen, but in
the human soul. This message is convincingly transmitted by the
cast. Walter Huston, the director's father, and Humphrey Bogart
can be described as expressing the model Huston characters to the
fullest.

BOOMERANG!   Elia Kazan

Script: Richard Murphy, from "The Perfect Case," an article by
Anthony Abbott. Photography: Norbert Brodine. Music: David
Buttolph. Cast: Dana Andrews (Henry L. Harvey), Jane Wyatt
(Mrs. Harvey), Lee J. Cobb (Chief Robinson), Cara Williams (Irene
Nelson), Arthur Kennedy (John Waldron), Sam Levene (Woods),
Robert Keith (McCreery), Taylor Holmes (Wade), Lester Lonergan
(Cary), Lewis Leverett (Whitney).

20th Century-Fox, U.S.A.   88 mins.

In a small town in Connecticut an Episcopalian minister, a generally
respected citizen, is shot dead in the street. The investigation,
conducted on the brink of an election, is long without result. In
the end the police find a suspect, the politicians of the party in of-

fice can breathe more easily. The guilt of the accused seems to
be indisputable, both in the light of the evidence and in the unani-
mous testimonies of the witnesses, but the public prosecutor who
conducts the case works very conscientiously and will not be unduly
influenced by anything.

He does not discover the truth but he claims a moral victory; he is the first of those Kazan heroes who fight uncompromisingly for the ideals of justice and democratic humanism.   The director was always a verbal advocate of these ideals but their un-
shaken defense was expressed better by the situations and personalities of his pictures, in the years 1947-1952, than by his oppor-
tunistic and loyalist attitudes. (Four years after Gentleman's Agreement (1947), a debate on racial intolerance, and Boomerang!, dis-
closing the machinations in the local apparatus of power, Kazan
gave his unequivocal support to the House Un-American Activities
Committee.) The style of the soon to be leading Hollywood formal
master was not yet completely formed: a roughness of staging
in Boomerang! is often in evidence and results in a certain re-
moteness and artificiality. The picture, based on authentic events,
was in fact intended as a direct reflection of reality and belongs to
that de Rochemont-inspired trend which became known as police
documentary.

The films de Rochemont produced were intended to counter
the film noir. Hathaway understood how to achieve this, but Kazan
did not: the journalistic triviality of certain fragments of Boomerang! alternates with the outright intrusiveness of such scenes as the
proof of the suspect's innocence during the court case. But at the
same time Kazan saturated the story with his sharply focused outlook on the characters and motives, provoked the spectator's reflection and committed him on the side of his hero. This sufficed
to make Boomerang!, dominated by the excellent, deeply moving
acting of Lee J. Cobb, one of the most valuable statements of the
American cinema of the late 40's.

LE SILENCE DE LA MER   Jean-Pierre Melville

Script: Melville, from the novel by Vercors (Jean Bruller). Pho-
tography: Henri Decaë. Music: Edgar Bischoff. Cast: Howard
Vernon (Werner von Ebrennac), Nicole Stéphane (The niece), Jean-
Marie Robain (The uncle), Ami Aroe (Werner's fiancée), Denis
Sadier (SS officer), Heim, Fromm, Rudelle, Vernier, Max Her-
mann (German officers).

O.G.C., France. 86 mins.

This debut of the director whose later films would pay homage to
the American gangster drama, but who was then interested in something quite different, is an adaptation of a subtle and muted psychological novel, the title of which refers to the French nation, that
was written in 1942 and soon after became a legend.   Melville made
it into a film in 27 days in primitive conditions and using 19 different kinds of film stock.   The author of the book was won over by
the result, although Melville had not acquired the screen rights previously.

The film was made with utter respect for the novel and was
even shot in the same house.   The story of the wordless love of a
German officer and the French girl in whose house he is billeted is
told in the first person singular by the girl's uncle.   This is an impossible love; von Ebrennac joins the old man and his niece every
evening at the fireside and indulges in long monologues full of subtle
and refined admiration for French culture.   But silence is the only
way to protest the presence of the enemy.   One might say that the
success of the film was already latent in the narrative method of
the book.   Melville abided by this and made a picture which is an
example of how a faithful adaptation of intrinsically literary material can have a curious cinematic quality.

Nearly the whole film takes place in one room where the
camera, with silent patience, watches a succession of winter eve-
nings.   Melville established a sparing personal style which know-
ingly limited the range of means of expression and gave prominence
to inanimate objects--in fact, this style is now considered the invention and hallmark of the great French director, Robert Bresson.
This is not so--it was Melville who influenced Bresson, who had directed two films thus far, neither of which showed trace of his later style.   It is simply that the styles of Bresson and Melville
evolved in opposite directions.

Le Silence de la mer can be interestingly compared to one
of Bresson's films, Diary of a Country Priest, which is similar in
literary origin and sparing style.   In both films tension mounts almost unnoticed and for no apparent reason: when towards the end
of Le Silence de la mer the answer to von Ebrennac's respectful
knocking is "come in," this comes almost as a dramatic release.
The simple use of the camera and soundtrack and the straight style
of the narrative caused Melville to be hailed 12 years later as a
pioneer of the Nouvelle Vague.   This was probably justified, although Melville's only direct link with the later movement (which he
incidentally did not join) was Henri Decaë (here discovered by Melville), who became its leading cameraman.

DITTA, CHILD OF MAN (Ditte Menneskebarn) Bjarne and Astrid Henning-Jensen

Script: the Henning-Jensens, from the first part of the novel by Martin Andersen Nexø. Photography: Verner Jensen. Music: Herman D. Koppel. Cast: Töve Maës (Ditte), Karen Poulsen (Old Maren "Bedste"), Rasmus Ottesen (Søren), Karen Lykkehus (Sorine), Jette Kehlet (Little Ditte), Edvin Tiemroth (Lars Peter), Ebbe Rode (Johannes), Kai Holm (Innkeeper), Maria Garland (Karen Bakkedaard), Preben Neergaard (Karl, her son).

Nordisk Films Kampagni, Denmark. 9150 ft., 102 mins.

This account of the life story of a country girl, the illegitimate child of a rural charwoman, was written with great sense of style and social sensitivity by Nexø, and suggestively and lyrically transferred to the screen by the Henning-Jensens. Social circumstances did not give Ditta's mother a chance: the worlds of the poor and of the rich remain separated by an ever-palpable barrier, the underprivileged are left jaundiced, bitter and powerless to improve their status.

Ditta is also doomed: her charm and inner serenity do not count and the girl's fate is a mirror image of her mother's. The directors disclosed this sad repetition with typically Scandinavian restraint—without obtrusiveness, without orthodoxy, but with full conviction and warm compassion. At moments the film resorts to old-fashioned imagery and excessive sentimentality, but the direct appeal of both the photography and acting is striking. Töve Maës is particularly sympathetic, very faithful to the screen character she portrays.

ANTOINE ET ANTOINETTE Jacques Becker

Script: Becker, François Giroud and Maurice Griffe. Photography: Pierre Montazel. Music: Jean-Jacques Grunenwald. Cast: Roger Pigaut (Antoine Moulin), Claire Mafféi (Antoinette Moulin), Annette Poivre (Juliette), Noël Roquevert (M. Roland), Jacques Meyrand (M. Barbolot), Gaston Modot (Cashier).

Société Nouvelle des Établissements Gaumont, France. 7852 ft., 87 mins.

During his search for the characteristic features of life in different
social milieux Becker found himself among Parisian laborers. He
wanted to show that their life was no less interesting and worthy of
study than life under more exotic circumstances. The French critics,
with their tendency to exaggeration, immediately acclaimed Antoine
et Antoinette as the first French film about the working class, while
in fact Becker's picture only very narrowly finds a place among realistic descriptions of life, not to mention socially critical films.

It is true that the shooting was done on genuine locations,
which was something rather exceptional in French conditions. It is
also true that the first part of the film really is an interesting description of the everyday life of a suburban tenement house. But
the final result turns out to be nothing more than a modernized version of populism à la René Clair as seen in Quatorze Juillet. Becker has merely poured the very old wine into a new bottle: the plot
is based on the worn-out situation of the chase after the lottery
ticket which will give the young printer and his shop assistant wife
a chance to buy their dream motorcycle.

This smooth and conflictless film makes up for its lack of
social commitment with other values: the subtlety of the psychological description of the protagonists, the vividness with which the
supporting characters are sketched, and the self-contained beauty
which the film discovers in the greyness of everyday life. These
are no small achievements, and are enough to make Antoine et
Antoinette one of the most likeable pictures of its time.

LES MAUDITS   René Clément

Script: Jacques Rémy, Clément and Henri Jeanson, from a story
by Jacques Companeez and Victor Alexandrov. Photography: Henri
Alekan. Music: Yves Baudrier. Cast: Marcel Dalio (Larga),
Paul Bernard (Couturier), Henri Vidal (Dr. Guilbert), Michel Auclair
(Willy), Florence Marly (Hilde), Jo Dest (Forster), Jean Didier (Submarine captain), Anne Campion (Ingrid), Andréas von Halberstadt (General von Hauser), Karl Munch (Adjutant), Fosco Giachetti (Garosi).

Speva Films, France.   105 mins.

The ease with which Clément moved between diametrically different
themes and with which he employed extremes of cinematic style distinguishes him not only in the French cinema. After making La
Bataille du rail, sustained in the style of a documentary reconstruction, Clément collaborated with Cocteau on the poetic fairy tale
Beauty and the Beast, and later with Noël-Noël on the cabaret-
comedy Le Père tranquille (1946). Now in Les Maudits the turn

came for naturalistic, metaphoric drama about the self-annihilation
of Nazi evil.

Clément's future undertakings would be no less varied--as if
the director wanted to tackle the full range of themes and styles
available in the cinema. This might even give grounds for calling
him a director without an artistic personality, a flashy executive,
but on reflection this seems too hasty a judgment. In every case
Clément gave the convention chosen his own imprint, employing each
of them consciously and purposefully. In the contents he always
took individual stands, although these cannot be arranged in a logical
line of interests. Les Maudits is in fact quite close to Clément's
previous independent film, La Bataille du rail, and the director did
not abandon the topicality that characterized his debut or the passion
with which he handled it. He merely moved into the entirely different world of fiction.

The action of the film takes place aboard a German submarine carrying all kinds of Nazi survivors to South America. It
is spring 1945 and the mission of 13 people aboard the U-boat is to
prepare the ground for the Nazism which hopes to be reborn in the
neutral bases across the Atlantic. The unity of these people is
quite illusory and discipline is kept entirely through terror of a
bestial fanatic. A French doctor, forced to cooperate with the refugees, triggers off fear of an epidemic. When the first opportunity
appears to slip out of the power of the one most terrifying Nazi, a
ruthless struggle results which ends with the death of all the participants. Only the doctor, the observer, stays alive and the film is
told as his story, to be preserved for posterity.

Clément was probably hoping to be able to show his
anti-Nazi message in the form of a realistic drama of facts, but it
is doubtful whether such an undertaking was at all possible. The
characters, despite all their precise and complex delineation, are
too archetypal, the plot too breakneck. Also, the fact that the dialogues were conducted in French makes the whole less credible.

All the same, Les Maudits impresses with its suggestive reconstruction of the interior of a submarine; a stifling atmosphere of
depression, fear and psychological and moral disintegration which
thickens with the incoming news of the Führer's fall. Impressive
direction is supported by the dusky, depressing texture of Alekan's
excellent photography. If the film lacks strength of conviction in
the details of the plot and the personalities of actors, this is to a
great extent compensated for by its formal appearance.

DARK PASSAGE   Delmer Daves

Script: Daves, from the novel by David Goodis. Photography: Sid
Hickox. Music: Franz Waxman. Cast: Humphrey Bogart (Vincent
Parry), Lauren Bacall (Irene Jansen), Bruce Bennett (Bob), Agnes
Moorehead (Madge Rapf), Tom D'Andrea (Sam, the cab driver),
Rory Mallinson (George Fellsinger), Houseley Stevenson (Plastic
surgeon).

Warner Bros., U.S.A.   9544 ft., 106 mins.

One of the most memorable crime melodramas of the 40's, a film
which could also be one of the best if it were not for the far-fetched
plot. A prisoner escapes from San Quentin; he is first given a lift
by a crooked cabdriver, then saved by a girl artist who lets him
stay in her flat. He wants to prove his innocence, but the witnesses
of the crime of which he was found guilty die one after another.

Dark Passage is notable for several reasons: first because
the jail-breaker will get off (but, of course, he was not guilty),
and second because of the novel method of narration. The first
half-hour of the film is seen entirely through the hero's eyes, and
we are only shown his face after he has gone through plastic surgery. When we do see him, he looks remarkably like Humphrey
Bogart, the protagonist-in-chief of gangster melodramas of the 40's.
This narrative style is an interesting reference to Robert Montgomery's entirely subjective film, Lady in the Lake (1946), and it
was probably just the restraint in the use of the subjective narrative
that saved Dark Passage from the failure of that film.

Dark Passage is also remarkable for its sense of style: the
fine opening sequence of the escape in a barrel, the sound of fog-
horns in the girl's apartment (which introduce a nostalgic touch not
unlike the prewar films of Marcel Carné), the plush luxury of the
apartment opposed to the hostility of the outside world. Agnes
Moorehead gives a good portrait of the vicious woman whose false
testimony sent a man to jail for life for murder. The illogicalities
of the film did not prevent Bogart and Bacall from achieving perfect
understanding of their screen parts and in the final reckoning Dark
Passage is an example of how maximum style can accompany minimum message.

LA CHARTREUSE DE PARME   Christian-Jaque

Script: Pierre Véry, Pierre Jarry and Christian-Jaque, from the novel by Stendhal. Photography: Nicolas Hayer. Music: Renzo Rossellini. Cast: Renée Faure (Clelia Conti), Gérard Philipe (Fabrice Del Dongo), Louis Salou (Ernest IV of Parma), Maria Cesarès (Duchess Sanseverina), Lucien Coëdel (Rassi, chief of police), Louis Seigner (Grillo, the jailer), Tullio Carminati (Comte Mosca), Tina Lattanzi (Paolina), Aldo Silvani (Fabio Conti), Sonia Salinas (Marietta).

André Paulvé/Scaléra Film, France. 170 mins.

La Chartreuse de Parme is one of the few screen transpositions of famous literary works which can in certain aspects stand comparison with the original and yet live a life of their own. The complex action takes place in post-Napoleonic times when Italy consisted of many small sovereign states. One of them, the Principality of Parma, was in the power of the tyrannical Ernest IV. The book traces the adventures of a young man, his unhappy love and the awakening of political awareness which leads him to association with the Carbonarians in their struggle for liberty which will eventually bring about the unification of Italy.

Despite impoverishing the Stendhalian psychological and social description with the magnification of the adventure aspect of the story, despite the loss of the historio-philosophic undertones, the spirit of the novel (in English, "The Charterhouse of Parma"), stemming directly from the plot, has been preserved on the screen. Christian-Jaque achieved this mainly through precise building of mood, atmospheric staging of the romantic trysts, careful design, fine manipulation of lighting and the composition of the frame, dynamic skill in conducting mass scenes, and the choice of an excellent quartet of main actors with Gérard Philipe in the lead.

The role of Fabrice Del Dongo, which with its complexity seems to exceed the scope of any one conceivable screen personality, was one of the most perfect in the career of Philipe, the most famous French film actor, and was of cardinal importance to the screen appearance of La Chartreuse de Parme. The nuances and ambivalences of the literary original, omitted in the adaptation, were replaced by the fascination with the personality of the main protagonist of this romantic drama of feelings.

THEY LIVE BY NIGHT   Nicholas Ray

Script: Charles Schnee, from the novel, "Thieves Like Us," by
Edward Anderson. Photography: George E. Diskant. Music:
Leigh Harline. Cast: Cathy O'Donnell (Keechie), Farley Granger
(Bowie), Howard Da Silva (Chicamaw), Jay C. Flippen (T-Dub),
Helen Craig (Mattie), Will Wright (Mobley), Harry Harvey (Hagen-
heimer), Ian Wolfe (Hawkings).

RKO Radio Pictures, U.S.A.   8597 ft., 96 mins.

They Live by Night, an intended B-movie, has become something of
a cult film. Three escaped prisoners hide at a highway service station after a desperate flight. Two are hardened criminals; they have
taken along Bowie, a sensitive youngster, only because a successful
bank hold-up requires three men. Bowie loves Keechie, the niece
of one of his companions, and marries her secretly. They want to
live an ordinary life, but Bowie needs money to fight his unjust
prison sentence and is forced by the other two to take part in a
raid. This seals his fate: the robbery fails and Bowie is betrayed
and shot in a police ambush.

      This is only one of many films which present a criminal's
eye view of crime, but--despite a quite un-surprising story--one of
the most convincing. They Live by Night is at once a realistic
gangster drama made in the true somber style (and the title gives
a good idea of the mood of the film) and a tender love story. Ray
dispensed with the cynicism inherent in a picture of this type and
made his film a subtle tale of two young people's fight for some
happiness. The visual style of the film is striking. Right from the
first shot, when the camera, from a height, follows and closes in
on a fast-moving car, through the excellent scene of the bank robbery, the picture is full of life and rapid movement; and yet it conveys the anguish of first love.

      Ray's first film called the tune which was to re-echo in all
his best films, the problem of rebellion against authority and the
problem of relative morality. The director argued that there is no
general, immutable morality which can be applied in all environments and in all situations--society should not condemn a rebel outright. "To understand is to forgive," say the French and Ray has
made his point: the spectator discovers to his surprise that he was
on the side of the criminals all along. The sentiments voiced by
They Live by Night and subsequent films were in harmony with the
spiritual anxiety of the young of the 1950's and made Ray's name
synonymous with their rebellion. This is best shown by the reception accorded to Rebel Without a Cause, Ray's most famous film,
although not his best.

THE LADY FROM SHANGHAI   Orson Welles

Script: Welles, based on the Inner Sanctum mystery, "If I Die Before I Wake," by (Raymond) Sherwood King. Photography: Charles Lawton Jr. Music: Heinz Roemheld. Cast: Rita Hayworth (Elsa Bannister), Orson Welles (Michael O'Hara), Everett Sloane (Arthur Bannister), Glenn Anders (George Grisby), Ted De Corsia (Sidney Broome), Erskine Sanford (The Judge), Gus Schilling (Goldie), Carl Frank (District Attorney), Louis Merrill (Jake), Sam Nelson (Yacht captain).

Columbia, U.S.A.   7758 ft., 86 mins.

Welles' remark about film being the most magnificent electric toy for a little boy can perhaps be best understood in the context of The Lady from Shanghai. A young Irish adventurer is enticed by the beautiful wife of a rich lawyer into joining the crew of her husband's yacht. The lawyer's partner, who is also in the party, offers the young man a large sum to frame a disappearance which would look like murder. But when the partner is really killed the Irishman has to face trial. Somehow he manages to escape....

     The openly tawdry sensational story of this film noir seems to serve above all for directorial frolics among which the most prominent is doubtless the legendary culmination in the hall of mirrors. This in fact is yet another example of Welles' virtuoso use of precedents from the past; its prototype can easily be found in Chaplin's The Circus. The dramatic shoot-out between the protagonists in the hall of mirrors is at once the fulcrum of the development of the plot and the summing up of the misogynist attitude of the director towards the heroine.

     In The Lady from Shanghai Welles constructs one of the most extreme portrayals of the femme fatale, whose myth runs throughout Hollywood from the times of The Blue Angel to glow with full color in the period of film noir. It is said that the director's intentions were personal: The Lady from Shanghai was to be his sour divorce gift to Rita Hayworth....

THE STRIKE (Siréna)   Karel Steklý

Script: Steklý and Jiří Weiss, from the novel by Marie Majerová. Photography: Jaroslav Tuzar. Music: E. F. Burian. Cast: Marie

Vášová (Mrs. Hudec), Ladislav Boháč (Mr. Hudec), Oleg Reif (Rudolf), Nadĕžda Maurová (Růžena), Pavla Sucha (Emča), Josef Bek (Karel Hampl), Bedřich Karen (Bacher), Bohumil Machník (Roth), Lída Matoušková (Mrs. Kazda), Anna Houdková (Mrs. Zeithaml).

Československa filmová společnost, Czechoslovakia. 7451 ft., 83 mins.

The first Czech strike--a primitive, violent eruption against the capitalists which took place in 1889 in the Prague suburb of Kladno, a center of mining and metallurgical industries. Simple in structure, full of drama and expressiveness, the film is like a banner carried on a workers' march, but it constitutes an internal rather than an external description of the events. On the other hand there is no impulsiveness here but a coherent multilayered narrative and realistic objectivity. Nor is there any triviality; the film has expressive characters and a well thought-out pictorial conception. Siréna became the first postwar success of the Czechoslovak cinema and received the Grand Prix at the Venice Film Festival in 1947.

JOUR DE FÊTE   Jacques Tati

Script: Tati, Henri Marquet and René Wheeler. Photography: Jacques Mercanton. Music: Jean Yatove. Cast: Jacques Tati (François, the postman), Guy Decomble (Roger, the showman), Paul Frankeur (Marcel, his partner), Santa Relli (Roger's wife), Roger Rafal (Hairdresser), Beauvais (Café proprietor), Delcassan (Old gossip), Maine Vallée (Jeannette).

Cady Films, France. 7830 ft., 87 mins. One sequence in color (Thomsoncolor).

A lonely and independent continuer of the wonderful silent cinema of situational gags, which interpreted the world in terms of a conflict between man and matter, walked onto the screen. To be more exact, he rode in on a bicycle. It is only in the film following that Tati metamorphosed into the heron-gaited Monsieur Hulot and started to observe the ridiculous facets of what we know as normal human behavior. Here he is one of the defective characters who populate a little provincial town--a pole-like postman in a shrunken uniform, with too large shoes and completely incomprehensible speech.

A traveling fair comes to the village of Sainte-Sévère, surrounded by children and animals. The villagers see a short film about American postal services in the cinema tent and exhort the local postman to imitate them. A hilarious slapstick part of the film shows how he attempts to do this. But it is soon all over:

the fun fair leaves and the village returns to its former dormant
state. The flimsy intrigue of Jour de fête consists of pantomime
microscenes connected by the place of action. Probably the
division of the film into several shorts (an act that was pending
after unsuccessful attempts to find a distributor) would present no
difficulties; one can still easily find the common denominator running throughout. It is the vision of reality as conglomeration of
maladjustment, inefficiency and failure.

At moments Tati seems to be as close to Surrealism as Keaton was; but while Keaton built up absurd situations on clashes with
matter, Tati discovered absurdity in matter itself. Keaton obtained
gags from the dynamic quality of situations, but Tati exploited the
comic potential dormant in basically static deformity or unnatural-
ness. Sometimes he did this with disarming clumsiness, sometimes
he lacked imagination in arranging the situations, and occasionally
he happened to include comic ideas of rather doubtful quality, but
even in his debut Tati impressed the spectator with his exceptional
sense of humor, with his ability to observe and to employ dramatically contrasts and contradictions and with his independence. When
he would put the results of his observations of the peculiarity of the
world into the coherent and logical Monsieur Hulot's Holiday, he
would be rightly acclaimed as the best comic of the sound cinema.

PURSUED   Raoul Walsh

Script: Niven Busch. Photography: James Wong Howe. Music:
Max Steiner. Cast: Robert Mitchum (Jeb Rand), Teresa Wright
(Thorley Callum), Judith Anderson (Mrs. Medora Callum), Dean
Jagger (Grant Callum), John Rodney (Adam Callum), Alan Hale
(Jake Dingle), Harry Carey Jr. (Prentice McComber), Ernest
Severn (Jeb as child), Charles Bates (Adam as child), Peggy Miller
(Thorley as child), Clifton Young (The Sergeant).

United States Pictures for Warner Bros., U.S.A. 9095 ft., 101
mins.

During his film career, which started in 1912, Walsh was responsible for the formation of a very definite type of Western hero.
Not a happy-go-lucky cowboy or a ruthless avenger, his was a man
of complex personality and ambiguous relationship to reality, an
outsider often baffled by the world and often full of moral doubts.
This type of hero is well illustrated in Pursued, one of the classical psychological Westerns--a drama of ruthless fate in a Western
setting, or at least of what Jeb Rand considers to be fate.

Jeb, an orphan, was brought up together with Adam Callum

and Adam's sister Thor, by their mother. But everything turns inexplicably against him; he loses a draw with Adam for draft to the
army; later Adam turns against him and Jeb has to kill him in self-
defense; Thor agrees to marry Jeb but only so that she can kill him.
But she finds herself unable to harm the man she loves and the
whole mystery turns out to be the family feud started by the erstwhile affair between Jeb's father and Mrs. Callum.   Even in ancient dramas and Biblical stories the supposed fate turns out to be
simply the workings of human beings.

The theme of Pursued has, indeed, a definite Biblical element, and it may be interesting to note that a similar Cain-Abel
relationship was the theme of Kazan's East of Eden a few years
later.   It can be argued that the solution on screen of the conflict
between the symbolic elements of good and evil constitutes optimistic
humanism.   It is not fate but people who spread hatred in the world.
The director certainly gave the picture a very evocative visual form:
the hero is haunted by sudden flashes of light, memories of the
boots with spurs which he saw as a hidden witness of his parents'
death.   The whole of this subtle and somber film is told in a flashback.   It has excellent acting and, most importantly, truly great
photography.

ONE WONDERFUL SUNDAY (Subarashiki Nichiyobi) Akira Kurosawa

Script: Keinosuke Uegusa and Kurosawa. Photography: Asaichi
Nakai. Music: Tadashi Hattori. Cast: Isao Numasaki (Yuzo),
Chieko Nakakita (Masako), Ichiro Sugai (Yamiya, the black-marke-
teer), Midori Ariyama (Sono, his mistress), Masao Shimizu (Bar
owner), Zeko Nakamura (Merchant), Atsushi Watanabe (Guttersnipe).

Toho, Japan. 9678 ft., 108 mins.

A picture which is very Western in character and can be traced
back to French populist films (Clair, Duvivier) as well as to Fejös's
Lonesome and to Capra's laughter-through-tears comedies.   Kurosawa traces a young couple, a factory worker and his fiancée,
through a spring Sunday together.   They have only 35 yen between
them.   They play baseball with some boys in the street and accidentally smash some cakes in a shop window, go to the zoo, shelter
from the rain.   Then they want to go to a concert, but the touts
have bought all the cheap seats.   So they indulge in fantasy: first
by playing at having their own café, then he "conducts" an invisible
orchestra in an empty sports stadium.   Then it is time to part, so
they go to the railway station and make a date for the next Sunday.

Kurosawa avoided most of the pitfalls following from the

scarcity of dramatic scenes in this limited plot. The situations are
never far-fetched or artificial but stem from everyday life. The
film is played on a lyrical string, but still the melodramatic potential of the story is a little too pronounced especially in the fantasy-
laden part. The whole is quite charming: Kurosawa is an acute
observer of the joys and disappointments of the ordinary life of ordinary people and knows how to give his picture warmth and poetry.
The quiet style he achieved is, despite the use of Schubert's music,
not distant from that of the more traditionally Japanese directors,
Ozu and Mizoguchi. This style was not to last; Kurosawa's next
films would be dramas full of sound and fury.

LES DERNIÈRES VACANCES   Roger Leenhardt

Script: Leenhardt and Roger Breuil, from an idea by Maurice
Junod. Photography: Philippe Agostini. Music: Guy Bernard.
Cast: Odile Versois (Juliette), Michael François (Jacques), Pierre
Dux (Valentin Simonet), Renée Devillers (Cécile), Berthe Bovy
(Aunt Délie), Christiane Barry (Odette), Jean Varas (Pierre Ga-
bard), Jean d'Yd (Old uncle).

Les Productions Cinématographiques-Pierre Gerin, France. 95
mins.

It was the French who gave the most sensitive artistic portrayals
of l'age ingrat, the period between childhood and adulthood--a time
of anxiety, mixed emotions, idealism and sentimentality. In literature it appears in Alain-Fournier's novel, "Le Grand Meaulnes";
in the cinema, in a modest film called Les Dernières vacances.
A boy and a girl spend a sunny summer with their families in a
large country house in the French Midi. The house is too expensive and is going to be sold. Juliette is attracted by a prospective
buyer, a Paris architect, and Jacques becomes doubly antagonistic.
He wants to save the house and he cares for Juliette. When the
visitor leaves, they find their mutual sympathy undiminished. The
holiday is at an end, the young people have to part. They will
never come back to the house and who knows what the future has
in store for them?

The only notable film directed by Leenhardt, a film critic
and sometime documentarian, has a definite literary background.
It is not only that it resembles a novel in structure and narrative
style but also that it is steeped in the French literary tradition of
nostalgic fascination with childhood memories. Les Dernières
vacances is an example of a film-roman and has something of the
retrospective quality of Marcel Proust's novels. It seems that it
is in these terms that the film should be considered. One would

look in vain for new contributions to the cinematic language; the
technique is unsophisticated to say the least. Leenhardt offers
other qualities instead: a quite original, fine personal style, the
genuineness and sensitivity of an autobiographical account, and a
typically Gallic harmonious-optimistic view of life.

PRESENTIMENT (Předtucha) Otakar Vávra

Script: Vávra, from a novel by Marie Pujmanová. Photography:
Jan Stallich. Music: Jiří Srnka. Cast: František Smolík (Mr.
Jelínek), Marie Brožová (His wife), Nataša Tanská (Jarmila),
Terezie Brzková (Cilka), Josef Vinklář (Václav Jelínek), Antonín
Mikulič (Ivan Jelínek), Jaroslav Mareš (Karel), Rudolf Hrušínský
(Toufar).

Vávra-Feix, Czechoslovakia. 8379 ft., 93 mins.

Among the films about the conflicts and disappointments inherent in
passing from childhood to maturity, Presentiment has a modest position but one worthy of attention. Vávra's subtle drama distinguishes
itself both by its formal elegance and its frank but unobtrusive critical observation of the morality and way of life of the petty bourgeoisie. The central character is a small-town schoolmaster's
daughter, who with youthful defiance opposes everything that appears
to her unstraightforward and hypocritical. The style of camera
movement anticipates in a way the films of the early 60's; a fluid
variation of point of view is accompanied by a meticulous scrutiny
of events. The editing and the methods of building up the mood belong entirely to traditionalist cinema: each scene is balanced and
played out to the full. Vávra creates the poetic aura of anxiety by
making use of beautiful exteriors and by inserting symbolic shots of
trains rushing through bridges into the distance.

NO ONE KNOWS A THING (Nikdo Nic Neví) Josef Mach

Script: Mach and Petr Nedoma, from a story by Jan Schmitt.
Photography: Josef Střecha. Music: Josef Stelibský. Cast:
Jaroslav Marvan (Martin Plechatý), František Filipovský (Petr
Nový), Eduard Linkers (Fritz Heinecke, Gestapo man), Jana
Dítětová (Věra Budínová), Stanislav Neumann (Koula), Ota Motyčka
(Vrátný), Jaroslav Seník (Kulisák Beran), Robert Vrchota (Karel
Bureš, engineer).

Československá filmova společnost, Czechoslovakia.   6827 ft., 76 mins.

There were very few people in Europe who could bring themselves to make fun of Nazism immediately after the end of the war. Ironically, in the occupied countries the Germans were being derided even before the war was over--usually in street songs and political jokes and parodies, which all amounted to a sort of psychological self-defense.   Soon after 1945, however, wartime topics came to be treated with increased seriousness in these countries and recollections of the past were accompanied by tragic accents; these times would begin being discussed in a comic vein only in the late 50's.   The Czechs alone dared to make an occupation farce barely two years after Potsdam.

Their film, No One Knows a Thing, which transferred to the screen the street wisecracks about the German supermen, tells of the adventures of two Prague street-car conductors who are forced by circumstances to remove a drunken Nazi soldier from the city. They strive towards strictest secrecy and in their naiveté believe that no one knows a thing, while in reality all the birds are cackling about the whole operation.   The reason for the success of Mach's film lies mainly in the right choice of situations and characters and in the folkloristic tone of observation, in which aspect No One Knows a Thing successfully refers to the prewar tradition of the films of Frič.   Admittedly, the picture has little intellectual finesse to offer, but instead a lot of all-out clowning.   All the same, this is very ingenious clownery, and even the best directors of the genre would not be ashamed of such scenes as the backstage adventures or the concert.

1948

BICYCLE THIEVES (Ladri di Biciclette) Vittorio De Sica

Script: Cesare Zavattini, from a novel by Luigi Bartolini. Photography: Carlo Montuori. Music: Alessandro Cicognini. Cast: Lamberto Maggiorani (Antonio), Enzo Staiola (Bruno, his son), Lianella Carell (Maria), Gino Saltamerenda (Baiocco, dustman), Vittorio Antonucci (Thief), Giulio Chiari (Pauper).

Produzioni De Sica, Italy. 8100 ft., 90 mins.

Zavattini, the spiritual leader of the Neorealists, professed a rigorous fidelity to actual facts. This principle he adhered to in Bicycle Thieves, probably the most classical work of the Italian school. De Sica completely abandoned the ornamentation and poetic metaphors of his previous Shoeshine. He became severe, sparing, logical. He believed that the most effective weapon of a crusading film-maker was didactics and particularly didactics conveyed through the eyes of a small boy. As a matter of fact, De Sica had already made children his spokesman in earlier films--but now he did it with exceptional consistency.

His appointed guide to the problems of everyday postwar Italy is a 10-year-old boy. His father is unemployed but after trying hard at the labor exchange, finally obtains a job as a bill-poster. He needs his bicycle for work, so the family retrieve it from the pawnshop and pawn the bed linen instead. Alas, the bicycle is soon stolen. Prolonged searched through the streets and back lanes of Rome are fruitless; the desperate man tells his son to go home and then tries to steal a bicycle. But the boy has not gone away and witnesses his father's double defeat: his attempt to take someone else's property and his getting beaten up by the passers-by. In tears, casting furtive glances at each other, they go home, mingling with the crowd.

De Sica did not have to make Zavattini's script any more
credible: the tangible reality of the events shown in the film cannot
be disputed.   The makers of the film however not only wanted the
content to be documentary in character but attached equal importance
to pictorial verisimilitude.   Rather than attractively, the story is
shown truthfully, with urban exteriors, a natural style of direction
and choice of actors, who correspond both in appearance and characters to the parts they play.   The roles were therefore entrusted
to non-professionals.   Lamberto Maggiorani, who plays the father,
indeed came from a working-class background.   The results of this
approach cannot be questioned.

Even if Bicycle Thieves can be accused of excessive formal
restraint, this complaint fades away in confrontation with the truth
and clarity of the images.   Visually the film has a universal power
of appeal.   Authenticity was only a material from which De Sica
sculpted his original logical structure: his mastery consisted not of
registering but of organizing actual facts.

The hopeless economic situation of the hero and those like
him is revealed step by step, the social institutions become gradually
devalued and the rules of society undermined: the police are busy
fighting demonstrators and not chasing thieves, the workers become
degraded by committing at first slight, but later serious, offenses
against the property code.   It is true that De Sica and Zavattini end
with registration and do not suggest a solution, but it seems that the
solution logically following from their proof is obvious: a clenched
fist.   Showing it would be only dotting the "i."

LOUISIANA STORY   Robert Flaherty

Script: Frances and Robert Flaherty.   Photography: Richard Lea-
cock.   Music: Virgil Thomson.   Cast: Joseph Boudreaux (Alexander, the boy), Lionel Le Blanc (His father), E. Bienvenu (His
mother), Frank Hardy (Driller), C. T. Guedry (Boilerman).

Robert Flaherty Productions, Inc., U.S.A.   6998 ft., 78 mins.

After Man of Aran Flaherty made a film called Elephant Boy (1937)
in cooperation with Zoltan Korda, and was then silent for ten years.
His next film, Louisiana Story is not only his last it is also his
finest.   It is the quintessence of Flaherty's cinema, another explora-
tion of man's links with nature, another image of a remaining fragment of an earthly paradise.   This lyrical fairy tale is set in the
Bayou country of the swamps of the Mississippi delta inhabited by

Acadians, the French-speaking people expelled in 1755 from Nova
Scotia. The players are the people themselves. The hero of the
film is a 13-year-old boy, a child of nature, totally absorbed in
canoeing, fishing, hunting and playing with his pet raccoon in the
subtropical waterways.

Flaherty's camera identifies with him, adopting his naive,
wondering view of the world. For the first 30 minutes the camera
follows Alexander in his boat through the overgrown waterways
where the sun glistens through the luxuriant vegetation hanging
above the water. These minutes of pure visual magic are among
the most mesmerizing moments in cinema history. Flaherty's
greatness and originality can be said to be due to the purely visual
emotion which his films generate. He did not observe, he created
and objects acquired new significance just because his camera was
looking at them.

When the oil people arrive to start drilling in the neighborhood, Alexander's attention is naturally attracted. Flaherty did not
comment on this clash between the world of nature and modern
technology and did not discuss its social significance. His seemingly dispassionate observation is the best description of the antagonism
between the old and the new and it explains all. The idle camera
gives the film a delicate albeit sensuous quality rightly compared
with Debussy's music; it provides the essence, with few words, of
a pure, timeless world. In Greek mythology Arcadia, part of
Greece, was a sort of pastoral earthly paradise, and Flaherty's
Acadians might aptly be called Arcadians.

THE FALLEN IDOL   Carol Reed

Script: Graham Greene. Photography: Georges Périnal. Music:
William Alwyn. Cast: Ralph Richardson (Baines), Michèle Morgan
(Julie), Bobby Henrey (Felipe), Sonia Dresdel (Mrs. Baines), Denis
O'Dea (Det. Insp. Crowe), Walter Fitzgerald (Dr. Fenton), Karel
Stepanek (First Secretary), Jean Young (Mrs. Barrow).

London Films, G.B. 8562 ft., 95 mins.

The second of Reed's trio of big pictures that started with Odd Man
Out. The ambition of the script was to combine a suspense story,
a psychological study and a picture of the world of adults as seen
through the eyes of a sensitive eight-year-old. The children are
watching us: Felipe, a son of an ambassador, idolizes Baines, his
father's butler, who impresses him with his imaginary past adventures. The parents leave Felipe for a weekend in the charge of
Baines and his wife. The boy unknowingly betrays the butler's af-

fair with an embassy typist and the unsympathetic Mrs. Baines pretends to go away but secretly stays in the embassy and falls to her death while spying on the lovers. Felipe, thinking that Baines has killed her, tries to save his hero.

With a few touches of the camera, Reed created a complex pattern of psychological relationships and captured the magic and loneliness of the world of childhood: the treasured grass snake in an attic room, the reverberating eerie atmosphere of a foreign embassy. Apart from the leading performance, which is beyond praise (and it is one of the best child performances in the cinema), Ralph Richardson and Michèle Morgan gave excellent studies of a gentleman's gentleman and a shy French girl. While The Fallen Idol now seems to be burdened with a certain stiff academic touch characteristic of the 40's (of which Odd Man Out and The Third Man are surprisingly free), it is an enchanting film, equally memorable for its charming picture of the London of the past and the languorous pace of an English Sunday afternoon.

HAMLET   Laurence Olivier

Script: Olivier and Alan Dent, from the play by William Shakespeare. Photography: Desmond Dickinson. Music: William Walton. Sets: Roger Furse. Cast: Laurence Olivier (Hamlet), Eileen Herlie (Queen Gertrude), Basil Sydney (King Claudius), Norman Wooland (Horatio), Felix Aylmer (Polonius), Terence Morgan (Laertes), Jean Simmons (Ophelia), Stanley Holloway (Gravedigger), Harcourt Williams (Chief player), Russell Thorndike (Priest).

Two Cities Films, G.B. 13,926 ft., 155 mins.

The second Shakespearean adaptation by the actor-director who pioneered the bringing of the great playwright's works to the screen. This time Olivier went a little further than in Henry V, but still he realized that Shakespeare's most famous tragedy is too strongly tied to the theatre to attempt full "cinematization." He preserved the conventional character of the sets--but maximally simplified--and decided to fill the space thus created with atmosphere and psychological tension. He preserved the original dialogue, bringing out its full splendor, and used the rhythm of the verse somewhat like editing in organizing the drama.

This treatment gave the screen Hamlet an unusual fluency and a magnetic fascination. The impressive lightness of the film is magnified by the veritably balletic style of the camera work, with the camera assuming the role of a narrator. Desmond Dickinson's pans, close-ups and tracking shots were probably meant to be an

antidote to the threat of the "tinned theatre" effect which appears in
Pagnol's films. If this was the case, Olivier achieved his aim: the
film does impress with its reliance on the visual, but one cannot
unreservedly applaud the treatment accorded to the literary content
of the tragedy.

Admittedly, the play had to be substantially shortened for the
screen; the problem however is that Olivier, while omitting among
other things, Fortinbras, chose the plots so as to be left almost
exclusively with a psychological drama with certain psychoanalytical
overtones. This directed Hamlet's tragedy onto the lines of the
personal drama of a hesitant recluse, which amounts to a most superficial interpretation of the sense of the play. This concept of
the drama acquired its own raison d'être thanks to Olivier's performance in the main role which went, as it were, against the line
he adopted with the text.

Olivier's Hamlet is not an undecided neurotic, but a dynamic
and clear-sighted man, a man who knows the consequences of his
actions. The director, fascinating in his own personality, moving
among excellently chosen partners, averted the perils simply with
his acting. The way the lines are given by the whole acting team
in fact can surely be described as unsurpassed.

THE LAST STAGE (Ostatni Etap) Wanda Jakubowska

Script: Jakubowska and Gerda Schneider. Photography: Boris
Monastirsky. Music: Roman Palester. Cast: Barbara Drapińska
(Marta), Zofia Mrozowska (Gypsy), Alina Janowska (Dessa), Barbara
Fijewska (Anielka), Halina Drochocka (Lalunia), Aleksandra Śląska
(Head guard), Antonina Górecka (Anna), Maria Vinogradova (Nadia),
Tatiana Goretskaya (Yevgenya), Edward Dziewoński (Camp doctor),
Kazimierz Pawłowski (Gestapo chief), Władysław Brochowicz (Camp
commandant), Huguette Faget (Michèle), Stanisław Zaczyk (Tadek),
Stefan Śródka (Bronek), Janina Maris (Guard).

Film Polski, Poland. 9900 ft., 110 mins.

An indictment of Fascism; the first cinematic testimony of genocide
in the concentration camps. The report from Auschwitz, the greatest Nazi factory of death and the cemetery of over three million
people is given by an eyewitness, Wanda Jakubowska, formerly a
prisoner both in this camp and in Ravensbrück. Before the war she
had connections with the cinema and her debut in feature films was
in 1939. She had already decided to tell the truth about the fate
humans had prepared for humans during her imprisonment in
Auschwitz--on the assumption she would survive. She did and with

the cooperation of her camp companions gave a conscience-shaking
picture of life beyond the barbed wire.

In the context of the contemporary climate of spontaneous
reckoning with the past, The Last Stage, a film made in a surge
of emotion and with exceptional intuition, is a perfect work. It
does not fall into the emphases of a public prosecutor's speech and
does not dissolve into vague sentimentality. The film's matter-of-
fact description of the inhuman situation is terrifying. It stresses
details which are in fact ordinary, but which take on a particularly
poignant expression in the context in which they are used. The
dramatic construction can be described as a loose mosaic which refuses to constrict reality with fictional clichés and traditional dramatic constructions (whenever such fictionalization does occur, the
film immediately lowers its standards).

The problem was to reach the audience, which at first could
not comprehend the madness of the Nazis. This was indeed what
determined the narrative method of the film as well as its simple
imagery and the factual texture of the photography. One of the consequences was the relinquishment of individual heroes--but even
despite this the narrative is not all on one level. Most of the
events presented concern a clearly defined group: the women from
many countries who work in the camp hospital. Through them
Jakubowska presents the fortunes of the prisoners: the suffering
and mental crises, the desperate egotism of some and the solidarity
of the majority, the struggle for the preservation of dignity and
above all the touching eruptions of compassion. The Last Stage, a
passionate protest against the Nazi methods of debasing human beings, is at the same time a hymn in praise of human indestructi-
bility.

THE NAKED CITY   Jules Dassin

Script: Albert Maltz and Malvin Wald, from a story by the latter.
Photography: William Daniels. Music: Miklos Rozsa and Frank
Skinner. Cast: Barry Fitzgerald (Lt. Dan Muldoon), Howard Duff
(Frank Niles), Dorothy Hart (Ruth Morrison), Don Taylor (Jimmy
Halloran), Ted De Corsia (Garzah), House Jameson (Dr. Stoneman),
Anne Sargent (Mrs. Halloran), Adelaide Klein (Mrs. Batory), Jean
Adair (Little old lady).

Universal, U.S.A.   8599 ft., 96 mins.

The crowning work of the American police documentary school.
The trend that was inspired by the producer, de Rochemont, found
especially in The Naked City many points of contact with the imagery

of the Italian Neorealists. Daniels' camera, traveling through a
labyrinth of walls, above roofs and across bridges and slipping into
rooms through the windows, gives one of the most competent images
of New York in feature cinema. Also the commentary which accompanies the action is documentary in style.

Dassin's striving for intimate contact with the spectator can
be seen in his concessions to generic cinema and his frequent use
of humor to give color to the plot; Barry Fitzgerald's performance
comes out very well in this tonality. The intrigue itself is rather
common but one of the aims was exactly this commonness. Two
Homicide Bureau detectives are shown in the process of solving the
murder of a young woman. They discover that she led a gang of
jewel thieves whose victims were members of New York society.
The murderer turns out to be one of the dead woman's companions.
The camera follows them through underworld haunts and New York
sidewalks during a heat-wave.

The film was shot almost entirely in the streets and uses in
all 107 different locations. The climax was enacted with the spectacular scenery of the Brooklyn Bridge in the background and is
reminiscent of the exciting endings of Hitchcock's films. The Naked
City was to make its impact through its portrayal of the colorful
aspects of everyday life and its accumulation of striking elements
normally unnoticed and even unsuspected in the stream of urban life.
The postscript is significant: "There are eight million stories in
the naked city. This has been one of them." Dassin knew how to
tell it well; apart from Du Rififi chez les hommes this is his best
film.

RED RIVER Howard Hawks

Script: Borden Chase and Charles Schnee, from the novel, "The
Chisholm Trail," by the former. Photography: Russell Harlan.
Music: Dmitri Tiomkin. Cast: John Wayne (Tom Dunson), Mont-
gomery Clift (Matthew Garth), Joanne Dru (Tess Millay), Walter
Brennan (Groot), Coleen Gray (Fen), John Ireland (Cherry), Noah
Berry Jr. (Buster), Chief Yowlachie (Quo), Harry Carey Sr. (Mel-
ville), Harry Carey Jr. (Dan Latimer), Mickey Kuhn (Matthew as
a boy).

Monterey Productions, U.S.A. 11,406 ft., 127 mins.

A classic pioneering tale based on an authentic episode from the
history of the West, the first attempt at getting a herd of cattle
along the Chisholm trail from Texas across the Red River to Kansas. The events took place in 1865 when, after the Civil War, the

importance of the traditional markets in the South was greatly reduced. The leading character in Hawks' film is a ruthless Texan
rancher, a man who once abandoned his fiancée for money and on
whom fate took revenge by removing her forever. He is thus not
so much a hero, but a severely portrayed anti-hero, who suffers
defeat in Hawks's world of noble and unassailable moral principles.

But his fall is not final: the egotistical and iron-fisted self-
made man finds a chance of salvation in a situation which results
from the rebellion of his adopted son. The youth, having frustrated
his protector's plans, shows him the way to live in harmony with
other people. One of the proudest classics of the traditional western, Red River embraces within its archetypal construction an exceptional richness of psychological observation. The world of the
West is here a legendary world, yet populated by living characters,
characters which do not need the alibi of a convention--and the familiar prairie landscapes and herd of cattle become organic components of the picture, helping to complete its dramatic scope.

LETTER FROM AN UNKNOWN WOMAN   Max Ophüls

Script: Howard Koch, based on the short story, "Brief einer Unbe-
kannten, " by Stefan Zweig. Photography: Franz Planer. Music:
Daniele Amfitheatrof. Cast: Joan Fontaine (Lisa Berndle), Louis
Jourdan (Stefan Brand), Mady Christians (Frau Berndle), Marcel
Journet (Johann Stauffer), Art Smith (John), Howard Freeman (Herr
Kastner), John Good (Lt. Leopold von Kaltnegger), Leo P. Pessin
(Stefan, junior), Otto Waldis (Concierge), Erskine Sanford (Porter),
Sonia Bryden (Frau Spitzer).

Universal-International, U.S.A. 8100 ft., 90 mins., cut to 87 mins.
for release in the U.S.A.

After Ophüls the screen melodrama was never the same: he ennobled it, gave it genuine feeling and a restrained tenderness and
elevated it to the rank of poetry. He also occupied an exceptional
position among expatriate film directors and it was only Erich von
Stroheim who could, like Ophüls, recreate the atmosphere of a
European country in America. For Letter from an Unknown Woman
is a Viennese film made in Hollywood. As previously in Liebelei,
the director returned to the vanished imperial capital and perfectly
captured its atmosphere, its passé charm.

The story is told in a flashback as a letter from a mortally
ill woman to a man she loved. Fifteen-year-old Lisa met Stefan, a
famous pianist, when they lived in the same apartment house. She
silently admired him; then she moved away with her parents. Eight

years later they had a brief affair; Stefan promises to return after
a concert tour, but when they meet again he cannot even remember
her. Zweig's short story was more realistic and tragic, but Ophüls
toned it down. The contemptible sounding plot did not turn to trea-
cle and Letter from an Unknown Woman is a tender, deeply moving
film.

From the point of view of acting it is very much a concerto
for two fine actors, and the supporting cast are a little too "typical"
and less credible. Ophüls has often been compared with Mozart;
his work conceals storms of emotion under an elegant, unruffled surface. Curiously, this time it turned into a commercial disadvantage: the magically fluid camera movement and the incomparable
softness of Planer's photography were taken at the time of the film's
release, especially in view of Ophüls' rather conservative style, for
yet another display of a Hollywood sentimentality. Ophüls would
have to wait four years until La Ronde gains him wide popularity.

MANON   Henri-Georges Clouzot

Script: Clouzot and Jean Ferry, from the novel by L'Abbé Antoine-
François Prévost, "L'Histoire du Chevalier des Grieux et de Manon
Lescaut." Photography: Armand Thirard. Music: Paul Misraki.
Cast: Cécile Aubry (Manon Lescaut), Michel Auclair (Robert Des-
grieux), Serge Reggiani (Léon Lescaut), Gabrielle Dorziat (Madame
Agnès), Raymond Souplex (M. Paul), André Valmy (Bandit chief),
Henri Vilbert (Ship's captain), Héléna Manson (Normandy peasant),
Andrex (Marseille black marketeer), Daniel Ivernel (American offi-
cer).

Alcina, France. 8652 ft., 96 mins.

The first postwar years in France were pervaded by a definite
spiritual mood. The end of the war brought liberation, but also
terminated the moral obligation to fight the common enemy. The
general collapse of moral values which followed coincided with the
period of the prominence of Existentialist philosophy, which saw
man as helpless in the labyrinth of the world, defenseless against
omnipotent Fate (or, more correctly, Chance).

The air of escapism and desperation was to leave deep
traces in French culture. This includes French films, thus far
rather by-passed by the realist tendencies dominating the cinema
elsewhere in the world. Only the American film noir made a certain impact, probably on the wave of Existentialist sentiment. The
films of Clouzot are spiritually related to those of Huston, Hawks
and Hathaway, the common denominator being the passion for wide-

eyed cynical scrutiny. Clouzot had already started exploring the
baseness of human nature in The Crow and Quai des Orfèvres.

Manon is a modernized version of the romantic 18th-century
novel of passion and corruption, rather unexpectedly set in France
during the Nazi occupation and immediately afterwards. Cavalier
Robert Desgrieux is now a resistance fighter who saves Manon, accused of collaboration, from lynching. They fall in love and go to
live in Paris with Manon's brother Léon. Robert is soon forced by
Manon's insatiable desire for luxury to join with Léon in black market speculations, but when he discovers Manon making good money
by prostitution he kills Léon as the imagined root of all the trouble.
Robert has to flee and Manon joins him aboard a ship bound for
Palestine. After landing, the whole party of illegal immigrants are
massacred by a Bedouin detachment, Manon dies and Robert, unhurt, drags her body towards an oasis, a symbol of perished hope.

Manon is an unusual film. Its faults are many: Clouzot repeatedly succumbed to melodramatic and sensationalist temptations;
several scenes (particularly the astonishing finale) are not entirely
convincing. The narrative is rather fragmentary and Cécile Aubry--
though excellent--simply looks too young for the part. The strong
point of Manon is the excellence of the cinematic craft. The un-
faltering precision of the camera in exploring vice and destitution
leaves nothing to the imagination.

Because of this the film was received with mixed feelings
and while the technical expertise and narrative skill (most of the
film is told in flashback as Robert and Manon tell their story to the
captain) were acknowledged, everyone (including the censor) was
shocked by this quaint mixture of brilliance (Léon's murder) and
bad taste--the final scene of Robert bumping Manon's body along
the stones was the last straw. Nowadays things appear in a somewhat different perspective, and what was considered bad taste before, now has become almost a means of expression. The shoddiness of life in the early postwar years has rarely been expressed
more acutely.

YELLOW SKY   William A. Wellman

Script: Lamar Trotti, from a story by W. R. Burnett. Photog-
raphy: Joseph MacDonald. Music: Alfred Newman. Cast: Gregory
Peck (Jim Stretch), Anne Baxter (Mike), Richard Widmark (Dude),
Robert Arthur (Bull Run), John Russell (Lengthy), Henry Morgan
(Half Pint), James Barton (Grandpa), Charles Kemper (Walrus),
Robert Adler (Jed).

20th Century-Fox, U.S.A.   8717 ft., 97 mins.

Yellow Sky is a western, dazzlingly photographed in deep contrasts and narrated with vigorous consistency, a film in which an uncomplicated plot becomes a canvas for some original psychological analyses. Wellman performed dramatic surgery on the plot in quite a surprising way. Seven outlaws led by Stretch rob a bank and to escape the pursuit of the U.S. cavalry force their way through the Arizona saltflats. They find a ghost town whose only inhabitants are a girl and her grandfather, gold prospectors. Under the influence of the girl (and gold) their attitudes go through a process of mutual confrontation and reevaluation. Greed becomes an overpowering instinct and Dude, one of the party, planning to make off with the gold, unsuccessfully challenges Stretch's leadership. In the somewhat unconvincing ending Stretch holds up the bank again, but only in order to repay the money he once stole.

The tale is told without any ornamentation at all. On the contrary, it shows a cool, severe simplicity of direction. Yellow Sky is a classical parable about how little separates good and evil, tenderness and brutality in man. It is these undertones, supported by the convincing portrayal of the protagonists' reactions and by the vivacious detail, which assure Yellow Sky its place as an outstanding picture. Joe MacDonald's excellent use of the visual potential of the scenery makes the film truly ravishing.

DRUNKEN ANGEL (Yoidore Tenshi) Akira Kurosawa

Script: Keinosuke Uegusa and Kurosawa. Photography: Takeo Ito. Music: Fumio Hayasaka. Cast: Takashi Shimura (Sanada, the doctor), Toshiro Mifune (Matsunaga, the gangster), Reisaburo Yamamoto (Okada, the gang boss), Chieko Nakakita (Miyo, the nurse), Michiyo Kogure (Nanae, Matsunaga's mistress), Noriko Sengoku (Gin, the bar girl), Eitaro Shindo (Takahama, doctor's friend), Choko Iida (Old servant), Yoshiko Kuga (Schoolgirl).

Toho, Japan. 13,468 ft., 150 mins.; released version 8825 ft., 98 mins.

The Japanese Neorealism (which can be discussed in the context of Kurosawa's films of the period 1947-1950) went through an evolution similar to that of Italian Neorealism: from the recording of events in the lives of ordinary people (which was the theme of One Wonderful Sunday), through the saturation of the background with touchy topical social problems in Drunken Angel, to the socio-psychological analyses of Stray Dog. The similarities between the texture of Kurosawa's films and the Italian films are not, as a matter of fact, familial, since the Japanese had at that time no contacts at all with European film-makers. The coincidences stem simply from the new spiritual tendencies that developed simultaneously in many countries just after the war and which used transformed everyday reality as their starting point.

Yet it would be a serious misunderstanding of Drunken Angel to consider it only from the point of view of fidelity in reflecting topical problems. This film was indeed of great importance for the Japanese cinema as a signpost to reality, but for its creator it really meant something quite different: it was his first intellectually full statement, and at the same time, in its formal aspect, a film quite representative of his whole oeuvre. This representativeness is not synonymous with perfection. Although the film has at least one brilliant scene (the climactic ruthless knife fight between two gangsters, in which the wonderful inventiveness of setting is supported by the no less excellent photography steeped in the white paint spilled during the struggle), there are many moments when the direction is heavy and the dramatic climaxes are obtained forcibly and melodramatically.

There is the whole of Kurosawa in the style of Drunken Angel, with his dynamism and lyricism, contrasts of calm and violence, poetic subtlety and severe naturalism--but this is Kurosawa without either his later formal virtuosity or the clarity of the earlier Judo Saga. The story of an alcoholic doctor who attempts to bring a ray of light into a district of poverty and crime and his repeated and useless attempts at the spiritual and physical salvation of a tubercular gangster, is important for its generalizing content, its interpretation of the world and its appreciation of the value of positive human activity. Kurosawa's attitude--if not in the thesis itself, at least in the mood--brings to one's mind associations with Existentialist philosophy: the fortunes of man are determined by the all-prevading evil; the rescue afforded by discretion is unobtainable for most people since reason is too weak a weapon compared with instinct. Defeat is unavoidable but one must not surrender since it is only through action that one preserves the superior treasure of human dignity.

The circle of interest and the psychological ambivalence of the characters of Drunken Angel have one more affinity--to the writings of Dostoyevsky. Starting from this film the Russian writer who so fascinated Kurosawa would be increasingly markedly present. Drunken Angel also marked the rise of Toshiro Mifune, an excellent actor who, together with Takashi Shimura, would be Kurosawa's constant collaborator.

LA TERRA TREMA Luchino Visconti

Script: Visconti. Photography: G. R. Aldo (Aldo Graziati).

Music: Willi Ferrero. Filmed on locations in Acitrezza, Sicily,
with a cast of non-professionals.

Salvo d'Angelo, Universalia, Italy.   160 mins.

Acitrezza, a fishing village in Catania: Visconti, aristocrat by
birth, Communist by conviction, chose it as the location of the first
part of his planned film triptych about the social problems of Sicily.
The remaining episodes, which were to show people of mining and
agricultural backgrounds, were never made for financial and cen-
sorial reasons, but the first part grew to feature size and turned
out to be his only fully Neorealist film. In his later undertakings
Visconti would not limit himself to photographing social actuality,
but would decisively lean toward reproducing psychological reality.

La Terra Trema belongs to the classics of Neorealism, and
even in the heyday of the trend was considered to be its masterpiece; altogether it occupies an exceptional position among the works
of the period. It is not a vivid portrayal of society, but a semi-
authentic report, visually refined and somewhat heavy in staging.
Visconti endorsed neither the grey, coarse texture of the Neorealist
"chronicles of current events, " nor the narrative refinements of
Zavattini. He was here as provocatively independent as he was in
the Ossessione with which he devastated the Italian cinema, and as
he was in the series of famous performances of Tennessee Williams,
Arthur Miller, Anouilh and Cocteau with which in the years 1946
and 1947 he in turn devastated the Italian theatre.

He did not care about the rules of dramatic structure: the
leading idea of the film is the unhampered observation of facts and
behavior. The substructure of this observation, however, betrays
manipulation of reality, its skillful reorganization, to suit the requirements of the narrative rhythm and the needs of the incisive,
matter-of-fact debate on the mechanisms of capitalism. Although
the narrative is seemingly spontaneous (even incoherent, in its juxtaposition of the non-professional actors' coarseness and the high-
contrast photography that beautifies the severity of the exteriors),
deep within there is an elaborateness of style and a fictional organization of the recorded details.

The story about the exploitation of Sicilian fishermen, and
the challenging response by their most class-conscious representatives seems dispassionate--but these are also only appearances.
The pictorial aspect, the strength of the title (meaning "the earth
trembles") and the power of the intellectual references of the key
sequences make this film the most radical pronouncement of the
Italian cinema at that period.

88

THE STREET HAS MANY DREAMS (Molti Sogni per le Strade)
[U.S. title: Woman Trouble] Mario Camerini

Script: Piero Tellini. Photography: Aldo Tonti. Music: Nino
Rota. Cast: Anna Magnani (Linda), Massimo Girotti (Paolo),
Checco Rissone (Donato), Dante Maggio (Emilio), Checco Durante
(Parish priest), Manlio Busoni (Police inspector), Giorgio Nimmo
(Romoletto).

Lux-Film, Italy. 7984 ft., 88 mins.

The old master of the Italian generic comedy caught the new wind
of Neorealism in his sails and created a surprisingly fresh, toned-
down and rich film--his best, if an underestimated work. The plot
of The Street Has Many Dreams was based, as in his older films,
on the comic potential of appearances. But this is comedy with a
tragic lining, far from the previous warmly sentimental trifles. Instead, unobstrusively and unconventionally the humor was related to
the social context. The fact that the Neorealist method of presentation and evaluation of reality was not used as a background, but constitutes an organic whole with the contents of the film is particularly
remarkable. These are not the tragicomical elements in life but life
as a tragicomedy--and there is no background to speak of.

On Camerini's intimate screen the plot develops among single
individuals: an unemployed car mechanic, his common-looking wife
and their small son. The man steals a car, a little out of revenge
for the contemptuous treatment he received from the owner, and a
little because he wants to give pleasure to his family and take them
for an excursion. He claims, of course, that he borrowed it. A
multitude of complications follow, but all ends comparatively well--
mainly through the shrewdness of the hero's wife, in the interpretation of whom, Anna Magnani, discovered by Rossellini, proved also
to be a talented comedy actress.

THE SOIL UNDER YOUR FEET (Talpalatnyi Föld) Frigyes Bán

Script: Pál Szabó. Photography: Árpád Makay. Music: Sándor
Veres. Cast: Ádám Szirtes (Jóska Góz), Ági Mészáros (Mari
Juhos), Viola Orbán (Old Mrs. Góz), Ferike Vidor (Mrs. Juhos),
Benő Tamás (Mr. Juhos), Árpád Lehotay (Mihály Zsiros Tóth),
Mariska Vizvári (His wife), István Egri (Ferke, their son), Tibor
Molnár (Jani Tarcali), Zoltán Maklári (Imre Hegyi), László Bánhidy

(András Szilasi), Lajos Garday (Mihály Bologh).

Magyar Filmgyártó, Hungary.   9478 ft., 105 mins.

Before the official propagandist pomposity of the years 1948-1955
invalidated the achievements of the cinema industry in the Communist
countries, a handful of intensive and authentic films emerged.   In
the case of Hungary there were two, one of which is Somewhere in
Europe.   The other, The Soil Under Your Feet, is an angry and intimate song of the land, of injustice and of the beauty of the feelings
of free people, set in provincial Hungary in the interwar period with
its sharp contrasts and vivid, traditional way of life.   The central
characters are a peasant girl whose parents are forced by poverty
to give her in marriage to a wealthy landowner's son, and her lover
who rescues her from the wedding.   Although they are together the
couple have to live through years of poverty and hardship--this is all
prewar Hungary had in store for the peasants.

The ordinary life of the village is portrayed with care and
sensitivity: the wedding feast, the work in the fields.   The style of
the film resembles a blend of a czardas and a folk sonata and gives
the story about the stubborn struggle of the poor against the adver-
sities of existence and the dull doggedness of the rich, a mark of
originality and directness, while the directorial talent of Bán liberated the picture from certain clichés concealed in the script.

BORDER STREET (Ulica Graniczna)   Aleksander Ford

Script: Ludwik Starski, Ford and Jan Fethke.   Photography:
Jaroslav Tuzar.   Music: Roman Palester.   Cast: Maria Broniew-
ska (Jadzia), Tadeusz Fijewski (Bronek), Jerzy Złotnicki (Dawidek),
Dionizy Ilczenko (Władek), Władysław Godik (Liberman), Mieczysława
Ćwiklińska (Klara), Eugeniusz Kruk (Fredek), Jerzy Pichelski (Woj-
tan), Jerzy Leszczyński (Dr. Białek), Władysław Walter (Cieplikow-
ski), Stefan Śródka (Natan), Josef Munclingr (Kuśmierak).

Film Polski, Poland.   11,316 ft., 126 mins.

The Nazi occupation of Warsaw seen through the eyes of Polish
Jews: a terror which in some cases led to collaboration but, for
the overwhelming majority, to unity in the face of oppression, to
the abolition of erstwhile social barriers and to the organization of
passive and active resistance.   The central scene is the penetrating,
pathetic image of the elimination of the Jewish ghetto (which includes
some documentary footage).   The protagonists of Ford's film are the
youngsters of a typical city tenement: their attitudes are a high-

contrast reflection of the attitudes of the adults and a proof of the
director's hope for the integration of a nation bitterly experienced
in the tragedies of the war.

The evident propagandist intention of Border Street, the exhortation to common action within the mutilated social organism and
to liquidate the mutual prejudice between Jews and Poles, fortunately
gave way to the desire to create a cinematic memorial to the memory of those who were deported or murdered by the invaders, and
above all to honor those who put up a heroic resistance. In comparison with other postwar protests against the war, Ford's film
distinguishes itself by its far-reaching transformation of reality:
this is not a documentary registration but a cinematic canvas, dignified and well set in the traditional dramatic structures.

The narrative of Border Street is old-fashioned and theatrical
and the over-stressing of editing and symbolism then fashionable
seems obtrusive. There are both infantilism and clichés in the
plot and the pedantic intellectual references jar. The visual compositions are academic as well. To boot, there is some trivial
local color traceable back to the prewar Polish cinema, in which--
interestingly--Ford was considered a nonconformist and in which he
made films much closer to reality than this. Yet all these faults
vanish in the overall strength of expression of Border Street. The
truth about people is here perhaps a little schematic in detail, but
still real when considered in its entirety. Jaroslav Tuzar's photography reconstructs the atmosphere of occupied Warsaw with great
fidelity, the ardor of the young actors commits the spectator to the
side of the director's message. Border Street is a sincere film
about the nobility of people who do not surrender.

SORRY, WRONG NUMBER   Anatole Litvak

Script: Lucille Fletcher, from her radio play. Photography: Sol
Polito. Music: Franz Waxman. Cast: Barbara Stanwyck (Leona
Stevenson), Burt Lancaster (Henry Stevenson), Ann Richards (Sally
Hunt Lord), Wendell Corey (Dr. Alexander), Harold Vermilyea
(Waldo Evans), Ed Begley (James Cotterell), Leif Erickson (Fred
Lord), William Conrad (Morano), John Bromfield (Joe, detective).

Paramount, U.S.A.   8004 ft., 89 mins.

In The Snake Pit Litvak showed his fascination with the human mind
at the end of its tether. In Sorry, Wrong Number a neurotic bed-
ridden woman, alone in her luxurious apartment, accidentally over-
hears on the telephone a plan to murder her. The telephone is her
only link with the outside world; she desperately rings for help, but

the police are incredulous, her doctor does not treat her story
seriously. A conversation with a former friend discloses startling
facts about her husband and it slowly becomes clear that it was he
who hired the killers.

Untroubled by the limited space (most of the film takes place
in one room) Litvak's cold and precise direction is impressive.
The camera circles ceaselessly, changes its pace, pauses on objects. Sounds are significant: the telephone bells, the deafening
noise of the nearby subway train. The director expertly builds the
sense of captivity, steps up the tension and with a sure hand leads
the story to its inevitable tragic end. In the final effect Sorry,
Wrong Number is a rhapsody in fear for which the plot is only an
excuse. The highly complex narrative structure of the film, a
series of flashbacks, sometimes even nested, can be confusing.

Perhaps the fact that the film was made from an expert
radio play explains its great dramatic consistency, but on the other
hand it was rightly said that, paradoxically, the fact that the audience can not only hear but see the story lessens the tension compared to the broadcast, by "spreading" its impact onto two senses.
The much-praised performance of Barbara Stanwyck is basically
theatrical-operatic and could have been more convincing.

CRISS CROSS   Robert Siodmak

Script: Daniel Fuchs, from the novel by Don Tracy. Photography:
Franz Planer. Music: Miklos Rozsa. Cast: Burt Lancaster
(Steve Thompson), Yvonne DeCarlo (Anna), Dan Duryea (Slim Dun-
dee), Stephen McNally (Pete Ramirez), Richard Long (Slade Thompson), Esy Morales (Orchestra leader).

Gold Film, U.S.A. 7869 ft., 87 mins.

The most interesting of the films noirs made by Siodmak, a director
who had the chance to reach for the laurels of a Hitchcock but who,
apparently, frittered his abilities away in 13 thematically similar
films, all made in the period 1944-1949. To start with, Siodmak
seemed no worse than the maker of Strangers on a Train and Shadow of a Doubt as an observer of human littleness, deviation and
falls. His high technical skill was also very impressive as was the
ease with which he complemented the suggestive handling of the narrative with his favorite dusky aura of pessimism and crime.

Criss Cross is sustained in just this tonality. The plot is
based on the in-fighting among the participants in an excellently
planned daylight robbery. The man who works as a guard on an

armored car offers to help the gang in a robbery, in a desperate
bid to save his ex-wife Anna from their bad influence. During the
raid he realizes that he is being double-crossed, fires back at the
robbers and saves most of the money. Anna's attempt to make off
with the loot fails and Slim, the leader of the gang, shoots both her
and her ex-husband.

The moral implications of the plot are very characteristic of
the genre. The robbery fails not because crime does not pay, but
exclusively because Steve Thompson changed his mind. There is in
fact not much dynamic action in the film, although the robbery sequence is a fine example of bravura film-making for its time. An
important aspect of the picture is psychological penetration, in the
achievement of which Siodmak received great help from Burt Lancaster and Yvonne DeCarlo. The heroine is one of the classic examples of a femme fatale in the cinema and even more convincing
in her psychology than Barbara Stanwyck in Double Indemnity or Rita
Hayworth's immoral angel in The Lady from Shanghai.

UNE SI JOLIE PETITE PLAGE   Yves Allégret

Script: Jacques Sigurd. Photography: Henri Alekan. Music:
Maurice Thiriet. Cast: Gérard Philipe (Pierre), Madeleine Robin-
son (Marthe), Jane Marken (Landlady), Jean Servais (Composer),
Julien Carette (Traveling salesman), Gabriel Govin (Foundling), Mona
Dol (Mme. Cullier), André Valmy (Garage owner).

C.I.C.C., France. 7950 ft., 88 mins.

The French postwar film noir, developed from the commingling of
the indigenous tradition of Poetic Realism, Existentialism as preached
in the literary cafés of Paris, and the influences of the American
thriller, and reinforced with a measure of naturalism, found its most
characteristic representative in Yves Allégret. Clouzot is too great
to be considered typical; but Allégret was entirely contained within
the trend and made all his best films in its principal period, 1947-
1955. The first of them is Dédée d'Anvers (1947), and the second
and best, Une si jolie petite plage.

The story takes place during the dead holiday season in a
small seaside town: a young man arrives at one of the little hotels.
It turns out that he spent a grim childhood there as a poor orphan.
He left as the lover of an aging but rich singer--and was apparently
rescued. But in this love affair he also started to descend to his
previous degradation and he killed; now he returns in a useless attempt to liberate himself from the past, besieged by memories, by
a blackmailer and by the law. He has lost hope for himself, but at

least he wants to save his successor whom he meets on an almost
identical path, from a similar fate.

The most important role in this rain-sodden drama is played
by the atmosphere of a deserted provincial town, very suggestively
created by Allégret through the soundtrack and the dusky photography,
which emanates condensed fatalism. There is also Gérard Philipe,
excellent as usual. It is surely thanks to him that a deeply penetrating human element appears in this finely turned if cold picture.
The part was, as a matter of fact, specially written by Sigurd with
him in mind.

WITHOUT PITY (Senza Pietà) Alberto Lattuada

Script: Federico Fellini and Tullio Pinelli, from an idea by Ettore
M. Margadonna. Photography: Aldo Tonti. Music: Nino Rota.
Cast: Carla Del Poggio (Angela), John Kitzmiller (Jerry), Pierre
Claude (Pierre Luigi), Giulietta Masina (Marcella), Lando Muzio
(South American Captain), Daniel Jones (Richard), Otello Fava
(Dumb man), Folco Lulli (Bandit), Enza Giovine (Sister Gertrude).

Lux-Film, Italy. 8277 ft., 92 mins.

Livorno soon after the war: a huge American base, in whose orbit
flourishes a black market run by a gang which also takes care of
smuggling and prostitution. They ensnare a girl who has come to
town in search of her missing brother. There is no room for happiness in this ruthless world enclosed on one side by poverty and
on the other by violence: even the unexpected ray of light cast on
the heroine by the love of a black sergeant from the base will not
avert her fate. The Negro's desertion results in blackmail by the
gangsters and an attempt to escape in a truck brings death to both.
She is killed during the chase and he suicidally drives the truck into
a cliff.

Lattuada's grim film is one of the most pessimistic works of
Neorealism. The exposition did not resort here to easy generalizations and to seeing evil only in social unbalance. Psychological
reality is laid bare and a thesis suggested that defective social circumstances enhance man's inborn ruthlessness, and are principally
responsible for his selfishness, intolerance and racism. Without
Pity is not a didactic exhortation to honesty, but the bitter conclusions of a humanist.

The formal aspect of the film clearly suits its message:
photography saturated with deep shadows, whose high contrasts carry the weight of the dramatic expressiveness. With its rough docu-

mentary texture the camera work refers to the style of <u>Rome, Open City</u>, but is at the same time an independent compositionally balanced visual statement: Aldo Tonti, the photographer of <u>Ossessione</u>, showed his great ability once more.

THE WINSLOW BOY   Anthony Asquith

<u>Script</u>: Terence Rattigan and Anatole de Grunwald, from the former's play. <u>Photography</u>: Frederick Young. <u>Music</u>: William Alwyn. <u>Cast</u>: Cedric Hardwicke (Arthur Winslow), Neil North (Cadet Ronnie Winslow), Margaret Leighton (Catherine Winslow), Francis L. Sullivan (Attorney General), Robert Donat (Sir Robert Morton), Marie Lohr (Grace Winslow), Basil Radford (Desmond Curry), Jack Watling (Dickie Winslow).

London Films, G.B. 10,642 ft., 118 mins.

The play, "The Winslow Boy," set in Edwardian England, was based on the Archer-Shee affair of 1912, which achieved national notoriety. A 14-year-old cadet is dismissed from college for the alleged theft of a five-shilling postal order. The boy's father, a retired bank official, is determined to clear his name. The fight is not easy; the cogs of officialdom move slowly, if at all, the complacent lethargy of the bureaucrats is present at all levels. It is only through exceptional perseverence and sacrifice that brings near ruin upon the family, and with the help of a famous lawyer, that the dramatic battle is won.

Asquith's film works mainly on the level of a moralizing dispute about justice, an impassioned plea for the most treasured British freedom, the right to be regarded as innocent until proved guilty by a fair trial. <u>The Winslow Boy</u> is a solid British film of the period when solidity was the strongest feature of the national cinema; it is worthwhile because of good acting and an interesting portrayal of the social scene in an England which was slowly emerging from its Victorian limbo.

THE SNAKE PIT   Anatole Litvak

<u>Script</u>: Frank Partos and Millen Brand, based on the novel by Mary Jane Ward. <u>Photography</u>: Leo Tover. <u>Music</u>: Alfred Newman. <u>Cast</u>: Olivia de Havilland (Virginia Cunningham), Mark Stevens

(Robert Cunningham), Leo Genn (Dr. Kik), Celeste Holm (Grace),
Glenn Langan (Dr. Terry), Helen Craig (Miss Davis), Leif Erickson
(Gordon), Beulah Bondi (Mrs. Greer), Lee Patrick (Asylum inmate).

20th Century-Fox, U.S.A. 108 mins.

Hollywood investigating social evils: as Wilder's The Lost Weekend
examined the problem of alcoholism, The Snake Pit centers on the
agony of mental patients in state-run institutions. The film follows
the case history of a young woman who becomes mentally ill and is
treated with an orthodox mixture of electric shocks and drugs. The
shortage of beds prevents systematic treatment, but a doctor having
diagnosed a guilt complex after the death of the patient's friend,
achieves a cure through prolonged frank discussions. The difficulties inherent in the theme of mental disease forced Litvak to choose
a basically sensational approach in which brutal scenes (shock treatment) accompany melodramatic ones (the dance at the asylum). The
resulting popular view of psychiatry is not far from Hitchcock's
Spellbound (1945).

        All the same, what is now a film on a trite subject once had
enough impact to influence state legislatures. While The Snake Pit
cannot pretend to be a serious study of mental illness as such, it
succeeds in the psychological portrayal of the unhappy central character.   Olivia de Havilland's role is a disciplined blend of sensitivity, intuition and inner intelligence. Further, the photography is
outstanding. Much of the film was shot from the patient's point of
view; the alternation of objective and subjective shots creates the
sensation of the use of first and third person in book narrative; the
torment of madness is expressed through unusual camera angles
and the nonsynchronous sound track.

L'ÉCOLE BUISSONNIÈRE   Jean-Paul Le Chanois

Script: Le Chanois and Élise Freinet. Photography: André Du-
maître, Marc Fossard and Maurice Pecqueux. Music: Joseph
Kosma. Cast: Bernard Blier (Pascal Laurent), Juliette Faber
(Lise Arnaud), Edouard Delmont (Arnaud), Pierre Coste (Albert),
Jean-Louis Allibert (Innovator), Arius (Mayor), Aquistapace (An-
tique dealer), Ardisson (Hairdresser), Maupi (Chemist), Danny
Caron (Cécile).

Union Générale Cinématographique/Cooperative Générale du Ciné-
matographie Français, France. 8426 ft., 94 mins.

The first success of the leading director of the populist, leftist

trend in the French cinema. A young teacher comes to take over
a school in a stagnant little provincial town where the majority of
the local notables consider learning a worthless distraction and
where children were tamed rather than taught.   The problem of a
teacher's struggle against backwardness, not new in the cinema,
was presented by Le Chanois with conviction and freshness, and
without haughty declarations and obtrusive conclusions.   He sketched
the milieu and the characters--children and adults--well, developed
situations with quiet realism and seasoned the film with warmth and
humor.   Bernard Blier, who created one of his best roles here, is
an impressive exponent of the director's intentions.

LE MURA DI MALAPAGA (Beyond the Gates) [French title: Au-
    delà des grilles] René Clément

Script: Cesare Zavattini, Suso Cecchi D'Amico, Alfredo Guarini,
Jean Aurenche and Pierre Bost. Photography: Louis Page. Music:
Roman Vlad.   Cast: Jean Gabin (Pierre), Isa Miranda (Marta),
Vera Talchi (Cecchina), Andrea Cecchi (Joseph), Robert Dalban
(Bosco), Ave Ninchi (Maria), Carlo Tamberlani (Police inspector).

Italia Produzione/Francinex, France/Italy. 7920 ft., 88 mins.

In the course of his journeys through cinematic styles and conventions, Clément reached the stage of Italian Neorealism, which in
the scenery of the narrow streets of Genoa brings to mind the
French traditions of psychological cinema.   Le Mura di Malapaga
is the drama of three people: a fugitive Frenchman wanted for killing his wife, the Italian woman separated from her husband who
takes him to her house, and her 12-year-old daughter.   The atmosphere created results partly from the background description in Zavattini's script which Clément was not only able to imbue with authenticity, but even to make into the actual flesh of the film.

        The vivid episodes staged with warmth and wit use non-pro-
fessional actors and functionally employ the traditional Italian
densely built-up cities.   This results in the film's being more a
realistic description of the milieu than a map of psychological interactions.   All the same, the observation of the relationships of
the protagonists turns out to be quite interesting; this is the un-
deniable achievement of the convincing acting of Jean Gabin and
Vera Talchi.

ROPE   Alfred Hitchcock

Script: Arthur Laurents, from the play by Patrick Hamilton adapted
by Hume Cronyn. Photography: Joseph Valentine and William V.
Skall. Music: Leo F. Forbstein, based on a theme by Poulenc.
Cast: James Stewart (Rupert Cadell), Farley Granger (Philip), John
Dall (Shaw Brandon), Joan Chandler (Janet Walker), Cedric
Hardwicke (Mr. Kentley), Constance Collier (Mrs. Atwater), Edith
Evanson (Mrs. Wilson), Douglas Dick (Kenneth Lawrence), Dick
Hogan (David Kentley).

Transatlantic Pictures, U.S.A.   7253 ft., 81 mins. Technicolor.

An exercise in the usual Hitchcockian dry sense of humor: two
homosexual students strangle their friend and hide the corpse in a
chest on which a buffet for their guests is arranged soon later. For
not quite an hour and a half (the screen time is strictly identical
with real time) Hitchcock doubly intrigues his audience: firstly with
the problem of whether the murder will be discovered and secondly
with how the discovery will be achieved by the boys' former college
professor.

    The very attractive idea of shooting the entire feature in one
take is practically achieved by eight TMTs (ten-minute-takes) joined
together by close-ups of characters' backs. Inevitably the source
of a certain artificiality, this slows down the action and puts in
danger the essence of cinema, to which editing and variety of camera angles are vital. But it all works out to Hitchcock's advantage:
the close-ups and turns of the restless camera create the mood of
uncertainty, threat and claustrophobia and have a large share in
making Rope a film of innuendoes and hidden cues, a study of the
breakdown of confidence.

    The method forces unusual demands on the cameraman, not
only because of the difficult (at the time) use of color in the studio,
but also because of the constant need for stressing and pointing by
means of close-ups. The technical experiment is partly successful
but only in the context of Rope; in the director's next film, Under
Capricorn, long takes were to turn into a disadvantage. Hitchcock's
own comment is, "Films must be cut." The difficult parts of Dall
and Granger exceeded their acting abilities, but this is compensated
for by a very good performance from James Stewart.

AS OTHERS SEE US (Les Casse-pieds) Jean Dréville

Script and co-direction: Noël-Noël. Photography: Léonce-Henry Burel. Music: René Cloërec. Cast: Noël-Noël, Bernard Blier, Marion Tourres, Jean Tissier, Paul Frankeur, René Blancard, Claire Olivier, Henri Crémieux, Marguerite Deval, Clérouc.

Cinéphonic, France. 7500 ft., 83 mins.

A comedy in a way unique, a cabaret-style lecture about bores, particularly about a certain species of homo sapiens, which the authors describe as "leg-breakers." A leg-breaker is an individual who, when encountering an acquaintance or a client makes any movement and the performance of any function quite impossible through his incessant talk. In other words a quintessential bore. Although this lecture is richly illustrated with factual evidence in the form of sketches, a concoction of this kind might still be expected, witty or not, to be in effect mighty boring.

In fact, it is not only not boring, but indeed quite admirable, with its skill in blending individual elements, its intelligence and Gallic lightness. Noël-Noël, the driving force behind the whole undertaking, did not even for one moment forget that while talking about bores one can easily find oneself a pot calling the kettle black. Dréville on the other hand did not miss any conceivable trick and created cinema within cinema, a review of the methods of screen entertaining.

THE QUIET ONE Sidney Meyers

Script: Helen Levitt, Janice Loeb and Meyers. Photography: Richard Bagley and Helen Levitt. Music: Ulysses Kay. Commentator: James Agee. Cast: Donald Thompson (Donald Peters, "The Quiet One"), Clarence Cooper (Institute teacher), Sadie Stockton (Grandmother), Estelle Evans (Mother), Paul Baucum (Stepfather).

Film Documents Inc., U.S.A. 67 mins.

A 16 mm. psychological study of a delinquent colored child. When his father dies, little Donald Peters' mother leaves him and goes with another man. Lonely and bewildered the boy soon gets into trouble with the law and is eventually sent to a school for delinquent children.   There, while learning arts and crafts, with the help and understanding of the teachers, the first glimmers of communication appear and although the newly discovered emotions erupt with great force, Donald will be saved for society.

This semi-documentary contains an excellent clinical study of maladjustment, accurate and free from the sensationalism usual with such themes (vide The Snake Pit).   To a spectator it appears as a tangibly real drama of frustration and loneliness in the crowd, similar in class and scope to Cassavetes' Shadows which would be welcomed some years later as a revelation.   While semi-amateur efforts are, regardless of their intrinsic value, usually spoiled by un-professional film-making, The Quiet One had no such problems. The story develops slowly but with no unnecessary effects and hardly any dialogue.   There are some well-conceived, imaginative scenes: for example the pottery class episode, when the boy makes a half-formed bowl into a sea-shell and listening to its sound wordlessly intimates lost childhood memories.

THE MILL ON THE PO (Il Mulino del Po)   Alberto Lattuada

Script: Federico Fellini, Tullio Pinelli, M. Bonfantini, Carlo Musso, Lattuada and S. Romano, from the novel by Riccardo Bacchelli. Photography: Aldo Tonti.   Music: Ildebrando Pizzetti.   Cast: Carla Del Poggio (Berta), Jacques Sernas (Orbino), Mario Besesti (Il Clapasson), Giulio Cali (Smarazzacucco), Anna Carena (L'Argia), Giacomo Giuradei (Princivalle), Leda Gloria (La Spiza), Nino Pavese (Raibolini).

Lux-Film, Italy.   9695 ft., 108 mins.

The close of the 19th century; the beginning of the process of concentration of capital.   This is reflected in the film in the demise of floating water mills, a local speciality on the banks of the river Po, and in the first murmerings of the growing class conflicts, the strikes by exploited peasants against the landowners.   The protagonists of Bacchelli's novel, which Lattuada adapted to the screen, are a girl who lives in one of the last remaining floating mills and her fiancé, a leader of those hired laborers who oppose the exploitation.   Love against a stormy social background: a similar marriage of themes is often encountered later and not only in the literature-inspired Italian cinema.

But The Mill on the Po was first; it is also probably qualitatively the most consistent example of a Neorealist treatment of a historical situation and its maker's clearest social statement.   The

social aspect is responsible for a certain exaggeration in the verbal
stressing of the class context--as if Lattuada wanted to compensate
for talking about the past and not about the present. At the same
time the film has a painterly visual treatment and creates a poetic
mood of intimate narrative. As in most of Lattuada's films, the
tendencies to emphatic exaggerations were controlled and balanced
by the aesthetically conscious attention to form.

OLIVER TWIST   David Lean

Script: Lean and Stanley Haynes, from the novel by Charles
Dickens. Photography: Guy Green. Music: Arnold Bax. Cast:
Alec Guinness (Fagin), Robert Newton (Bill Sikes), John Howard
Davies (Oliver Twist), Henry Stephenson (Mr. Brownlow), Francis
L. Sullivan (Mr. Bumble), Kay Walsh (Nancy), Anthony Newley (Art-
ful Dodger), Mary Clare (Mrs. Corney), Josephine Stuart (Oliver's
mother).

Cineguild, G.B. 10,436 ft., 116 mins.

The resounding success of Great Expectations distinctly confirmed
the existence of cinematic potential in Dickens' witty, imaginative
and edifying novels. Lean was encouraged to adapt to the screen
the most famous of them, "Oliver Twist," the story of an orphan
brought up by the parish who escapes from an apprenticeship to a
coffinmaker and gets involved with a London gang of juvenile delinquents run by the sinister Fagin, until he is finally traced by his
rich grandfather.

The film is a gloomy look at Dickens, in which the deep
shadow-ridden photography stresses the squalor and desperation of
the life of the 19th-century poor. There is only a trace of the
optimism of Great Expectations and for good measure only a part
of its brilliance; Oliver Twist has none of the fast expert editing
and impressive sets of the other film. It is conservative, solid
and a trifle theatrical, relying more on acting than on the film-
making (which is unnoticeable--to say so in this case is a compli-
ment). The fragile, open-eyed Oliver, the splendid Mr. Bumble
and the burlesque Alec Guinness as Fagin are classical Dickensian
screen characters. The latter performance caused serious censor
trouble: it was at the time, mainly because of the size of Fagin's
nose, considered anti-Semitic.

KEY LARGO   John Huston

Script: Richard Brooks and Huston, from the play by Maxwell An-
derson. Photography: Karl Freund. Music: Max Steiner. Cast:
Humphrey Bogart (Frank McCloud), Lauren Bacall (Nora Temple),
Edward G. Robinson (Johnny Rocco), Lionel Barrymore (Temple),
Claire Trevor (Gaye Dawn), Thomas Gomez (Curly), Harry Lewis
(Edward "Toots" Bass), John Rodney (Clyde Sawyer), Marc Lawrence
(Ziggy), Monte Blue (Ben Wade), Dan Seymour ("Angel" Garcia), Jay
Silverheels (Johnny), Rodric Redwing (Tom).

Warner Bros., U.S.A.   102 mins.

Kay Largo, a tiny island off the Florida coast, is the southernmost
place in the United States. A group of gangsters hold up a hotel
proprietor, his daughter-in-law, and a guest, a veteran army officer
who has come to tell the proprietor about his son's last moments
during the Italian campaign. A hurricane rages outside while the
bandits threaten and wait for a getaway boat to take them to Cuba;
the gables of the house creak in the gale while the gangsters sweat.
The powerful atmosphere of decadence and claustrophobia in a subtropical enclosure has something of the menacing, theatrical character of Tennessee Williams' plays. The film's impact is largely
due to Karl Freund's atmospheric photography: the constantly moving
camera anxiously circles like a tropical bird and suddenly swoops
into close-ups.

Humphrey Bogart was one of the very few actors who are
the real creators of the atmosphere of films in which they appear;
the mood he transplanted into Key Largo is a mixture of Curtiz's
Casablanca and Huston's The Maltese Falcon. Yet the film does
not match the coherence and impact of either of these; Huston found
the sentimental touch, so typical of many American gangster films
of the 40's, too difficult to avoid. Neither did he give Key Largo
the quality of a universal philosophical parable, as he did with The
Treasure of Sierra Madre. Instead, the film works on the level of
the confrontation of psychologies. Bogart was this time firmly on
the side of the law; Edward G. Robinson was for a change cast as
a crook and gave a splendid performance as a cynical and vicious
gangster on the run, which brings to mind his best role of the kind
in Little Caesar. Of course, Bogart's weary gallantry has the last
word.

SCOTT OF THE ANTARCTIC   Charles Frend

Script: Walter Meade and Ivor Montague. Photography: Jack
Cardiff, Osmond Borradaile and Geoffrey Unsworth. Music: Ralph
Vaughan Williams. Cast: John Mills (Capt. R. F. Scott, R.N.),
Harold Warrender (Dr. E. A. Wilson), Derek Bond (Capt. L. E. G.
Oates), James Robertson Justice (P. O. "Taff" Evans), Reginald
Beckwith (Lieut. H. R. "Birdie" Bowers), Diana Churchill (Kath-
leen Scott), Anne Firth (Oriana Wilson), Kenneth More (Lieut.
"Teddy" Evans).

Ealing Studios, G.B.   9886 ft., 110 mins. Technicolor.

Scott of the Antarctic is a semi-documentary reconstruction of the
tragic expedition to the South Pole led by the legendary British explorer. After months of preparation, Captain Scott sailed toward
the Antarctic and after a long overland trek reached the Pole on 18
January 1912, only to find that he had been preceded by the Norwegian discoverer Amundsen. On the return journey Scott and his
four companions died from exhaustion and hunger.

The film was made by the man who seemed best qualified
for the task among British directors. Frend carefully avoided the
temptations of sensationalism and spectacle (even when actual facts
would justify it) and chose a simple, rough and restrained narrative
framed by beautiful color images of polar landscapes and wild life,
some taken on location in the Antarctic. The English sequences at
the start, hesitant and incongruous, are a weakness but the director
then continued with a reticent clarity, resorting to images rather
than dialogue. Thus he created a convincing chronicle of "the gallant failure," although (through no fault of the acting) obviously he
could not fully develop the complex and controversial personality of
Scott as he appears from his own diary on which the film is based.

The explorer was a man who went to the Antarctic ostensibly
for reasons of science but who was carried away by personal vanity
and the spirit of competition with Amundsen. The present opinion
is that Scott's party could have survived the last 11 miles of the
trek were it not for their gentlemanly attitude which stopped them--in
contrast to Amundsen--from eating their dogs. Scott of the Antarctic
is a success within its self-imposed limits and a worthy tribute to
the heroism which Frend praised earlier in San Demetrio, London
and later in The Cruel Sea.

FORT APACHE   John Ford

Script: Frank S. Nugent, from the story, "Massacre," by James
Warner Bellah. Photography: Archie Stout. Music: Richard Hage-
man. Cast: John Wayne (Capt. Kirby York), Henry Fonda (Lt. Col.
Owen Thursday), Shirley Temple (Philadelphia Thursday), John Agar
(Lt. Michael O'Rourke), Ward Bond (Sgt. Major O'Rourke), George
O'Brien (Capt. Sam Collingwood), Victor McLaglen (Sgt. Mulcahy),
Pedro Armendariz (Sgt. Beaufort), Anna Lee (Mrs. Collingwood),
Irene Rich (Mrs. O'Rourke).

Argosy Pictures/RKO Radio Pictures, U.S.A. 11,505 ft., 128 mins.

The first part of Ford's "cavalry trilogy," a document of the director's nostalgic longing for the bygone free frontier days. The further parts would be She Wore a Yellow Ribbon and Rio Grande
(1950). Fort Apache is the most cheerful of them and the most dynamic, the later parts being bitter recriminations of defeat. Incidentally, in none of these films is Ford at his best. The disci-
plinarian Lt. Col. Thursday, bitter at the loss of his Civil War
rank of General, takes command of the remote Fort Apache garrison in Arizona. The Colonel resents the idea of his daughter's
marrying one of his officers, whom she loves, because of his humble background. He contemptuously underestimates the Indians and
when an Apache tribe crosses into Mexico, driven out by the corruption of local agents, Thursday tricks them and orders them back.
The confrontation with the Indians ends in the massacre of the cavalry.

      Fort Apache is a clear reference to the Custer legend, which
Ford sets out to destroy. This is a film of defeat, although John
Wayne in the end hid the truth about Thursday's Last Stand from inquisitive journalists. The film is an interesting chronicle of life in
a remote military outpost and a voice in the discussion on the meaning of authority (the Yankee colonel among Southern officers). One
feels however that it lacks pace and it would not be mentioned here
if it were not for the acting. John Wayne and Victor McLaglen appear throughout the trilogy in practically unchanged roles; Fonda is
good as the absurdly proud colonel. Only Shirley Temple, with her
angelic innocence, seems a character from a different film. The
photography gives prominence to the wide spaces of the Arizona
desert and employs, although somewhat too self-consciously, the
usual Fordian motifs.

LES PARENTS TERRIBLES   Jean Cocteau

Script: Cocteau, from his own play. Photography: Michel Kelber.
Music: Georges Auric. Cast: Yvonne de Bray (Sophie), Jean
Marais (Michel), Gabrielle Dorziat (Léonie), Josette Day (Made-
leine), Marcel André (Georges).

Films Ariane/Films Sirius, France.   8902 ft., 98 mins.

It is probably true that Cocteau's name remains in cinema history
largely because he gave most of his scripts to someone else to direct.   After the precious Le Sang d'un poète (1930), Cocteau took
a long break from directing and concentrated on writing stage plays,
composing music, and drawing his admirable graphic designs.   It
was only in 1946 that he made Beauty and the Beast, probably relying extensively on René Clément, the co-director.   Two years
later, while Melville was shooting Les Enfants terribles, Cocteau
himself transferred to the screen his own exceptionally popular 1938
play, "Les Parents terribles."

   Both films trace unusual relationships, both tell of people
who never seem to go out and both mark Cocteau's temporary abandonment of mythological subjects and stylized décor in favor of modern, but by no means ordinary, life.   The hysterical mother shows
excessive possessiveness towards her adolescent son and resents
his desire to marry the girl he loves.   The situation becomes further complicated when it turns out that the girl is the father's mistress.   The intrigue involving the diplomatic talents of an aunt ends
with the mother's suicide which re-unites the young couple.   This
strange plot, half-tragic, half-vaudeville, and exceedingly theatrical,
has little physical movement.

   The cerebral, literary quality of scripts such as this one always jars one on the screen and it must be said to the director's
credit that, fully aware of this, he made a full circle and not only
did not conceal but studiously preserved the theatrical character of
the story.   This turns into an unusual trump and results in a film
which, although not free from the self-consciousness characteristic
of Cocteau's work, has a special place among screen adaptations.
The total exclusion of exteriors and the display of the action on two
sets of contrasting character (the gloomy family flat and the bright,
gay flat of the girl) are preserved.

   At the same time the director used a whole assortment of
purely cinematic effects.   With little conspicuous camera movement,
the force of expression was vested in excellent editing, in the dramatic use of close-ups, and in the varied camera angles.   The
scene in which Michel tells his mother about his love for Madeleine

contains the famous shot showing only her eyes and his mouth above.
The sounds from the outside (the distant fire engine heard during a
quarrel, the neighbors knocking on the wall) are a clever sound
commentary on the dramatic situations inside the flat.   All five
actors perfectly fulfilled the great demands imposed on them by this
penetrating study of madness.

CLOCHEMERLE   Pierre Chenal

Script: Gabriel Chevallier, from his own novel.   Photography:
Robert Le Febvre. Music: Henri Sauguet. Cast: Brochard
(Piechut, the Mayor), Simone Michels (Judith), Maximilienne
(Justine Putet), Jane Marken (Baroness Courtbiche), Paul Demange
(François Toumignon), Félix Oudart (Curé Ponosse), Cri Cri Mul-
ler (Adèle Torbayon), Armontel (Tafardel), Saturnin Fabre (Alexan-
dre Bourdillat).

Cinéma-Productions, France. 8397 ft., 93 mins.

It seems hard to find a more archetypal bourgeois than a French
one.   It follows that the French bourgeois is the best object of
critical treatment.   If one does it in the field of comedy it is sufficient to add a few drops of rose water to the ocean of vituperation
and the wolf will be fed and the sheep unharmed.   This is what Chenal,
a former director of grim psychological dramas, did in adopting the
onetime shocking book by Chevallier.

The crux of the intrigue is the public urinal, inaugurated with
civic pomp in the main square of the town, opposite the church.
Some consider it a provocation, others a triumph of progress; in
any case, every single citizen of the permanently wine-tipsy population of a little town in Beaujolais takes a stand in the controversy.
And all will be flogged with the whip of satire.

In Chevallier's novel the satire was ruthless; in Chenal's
version, which limited itself to the first part of the book (which
made the plot smoother and more flowing), it is a little milder and
based on the reflection that people are people.   This in fact did not
harm the bumptious farce, which blended Gallic ribaldry with slapstick fracases and seasoned the lot with splendid dialogue.   If one
can find fault in Clochermerle it would be in the breathless chase
after effects.   It is though, in view of the briskness of this chase,
a small sin.

CONSCIENCE (Svědomí) Jiří Krejčík

Script: Vladimír Valenta, Jiří Fried and J. A. Novotný. Photography: Rudolf Stahl. Music: Jiří Šust. Cast: Marie Vášová (Mrs. Doležal), Miloš Nedbal (Mr. Doležal), Jan Prokeš (Jirka), Irena Kačírková (Vlasta), Bohuš Zahorský (Commisar Mautner), Eduard Dubský (Verbl), František Kovářík (Headmaster), Vladimír Hlavatý (Professor).

Československý státni film, Czechoslovakia.   9055 ft., 101 mins.

After Zeman's Dead Among the Living this is the best achievement of the Czech school of psychological drama, which though active only in the short period 1946-1948, still succeeded in producing several mature and original films. In Conscience, Krejčik, interested in the inner human dilemmas, presented the case of a comfortable man who tries to live a decent life, but is led by a coincidence to choose between moral principles and a peaceful existence for himself and his family. During a casual extramarital escapade the hero is involved in a road accident in which a child is killed. To reveal himself to the law means to lose everything. Such a decision cannot be taken lightly by a respected citizen and director of a loan society. It is only the shock of his son's finding out the truth that turns the opportunist who tried to buy peace toward the police station.

While keeping a certain distance from the details of contemporary life, Krejčik gave the film the tone of a modest morality play. If he allowed himself a certain overstressing, it was done only in revealing the problem of the upbringing of the young generation and in contrasting reality and the need to create awareness of the principles of justice. The film is factual, concentrated and painstaking. The stressing of the mental drama does not however signify that the formal aspect is dull. As in the majority of Czech films, the photography is characterized by visual clarity and effective imagery--in spite of the fact that this was the debut of the cameraman.

PASSPORT TO PIMLICO   Henry Cornelius

Script: T. E. B. Clarke. Photography: Lionel Banes. Music: Georges Auric. Cast: Stanley Holloway (Arthur Pemberton), Betty Warren (Connie Pemberton), Barbara Murray (Shirley Pemberton),

Paul Dupuis (Duke of Burgundy), Margaret Rutherford (Prof. Hatton-
Jones), John Slater (Frank Huggins), Jane Hylton (Molly), Raymond
Huntley (Mr. Wix).

Ealing Studios, G.B.   7575 ft., 84 mins.

English law abounds in old statutes which have never been repealed
and a comedy based on this had long been overdue. When a be-
lated bomb explosion shakes Pimlico, at that time a poor quarter
of London, an ancient Royal Charter is found decreeing Pimlico to
be in perpetuity part of the Duchy of Burgundy. A local shopkeeper
assumes power, the neighbors become ministers, even a descendant
of the Dukes of Burgundy is found. Starting from this absurd prem-
ise the film further develops with immaculate logic and consequence:
Pimlico becomes a separate state where English war-time food ra-
tioning and licensing are not in force; customs barriers are set up.

      The opportunities for deriding government bureaucracy, di-
plomacy and the law become innumerable (Basil Radford and Naunton
Wayne are two government officials in dispute over responsibility for
the Pimlico operation). So, the social picture of England lends itself to hilarious distortions, without the film's becoming anything
approaching social criticism.

      One of the archetypal Ealing Comedies and a huge commer-
cial success, Passport to Pimlico is not free from faults: the
documentary news chronicle is far too long, comical situations are
squeezed dry and some obvious opportunities were not taken up.
But it remains a pleasant joke, full of the disarming Cockney humor of bygone times.

MACLOVIA   Emilio Fernández

Script: Mauricio Magdaleno. Photography: Gabriel Figueroa.
Music: Antonio Diaz Conde. Cast: Maria Félix (Maclovia), Pedro
Armendariz (José Maria), Carlos Moctezuma, Columba Cominguez,
Arturo Soto Rangel, Miguel Inclán, Eduardo Arozamena.

Filmex S.A., Mexico. 9320 ft., 104 mins.

A fishing village somewhere in a remote corner of Mexico. A
straightforward, good-hearted peasant loves a beautiful girl. The
feeling is reciprocal but what's the use, as her rich father is not
eager to give his daughter to any upstart. So the proud Maclovia
falls into the hands of a lusty and cruel sergeant, who on account
of his position as a local military commander seems to be the best

match in the vicinity. A melodrama? By all means a melodrama,
but an organically folk-inspired one, a melodrama which defends its
convention with the source of its inspiration, with an unadulterated
naiveté of simple moral conclusions. But this applies only to the
contents; the aesthetic standard rests, as in other films of Fernández and Figueroa, almost entirely in the stylized, decorative photography.

Maclovia is one of the best photographed films of this outstanding team of Mexican film-makers, a work which ennobles the
simple-hearted romanticism of the story with its visual appeal.
Perhaps it is too ennobling: Figueroa's compositions imperiously
subordinated the narrative rhythm to their own needs and reduced
the actor to the role of a photographer's model. Still this did not
result in an internal stylistic discord, and the whole--despite the
controversial character of the method--is an acceptable reflection
of the spirit of Mexican cultural traditions.

1949

BITTER RICE (Riso Amaro) Giuseppe De Santis

Script: Corrado Alvaro, De Santis, Carlo Lizzani, Carlo Musso, Ivo Perilli and Gianni Puccini. Photography: Otello Martelli. Music: Goffredo Petrassi. Cast: Vittorio Gassman (Walter), Silvana Mangano (Silvana), Doris Dowling (Francesca), Raf Vallone (Marco), Checco Rissone (Aristide), Nico Pepe (Beppe), Adriana Sivieri (Celeste), Lia Corelli (Amelia), Maria Grazia Francia (Gabriella).

Lux-Film, Italy. 9300 ft., 103 mins.

An explosive blend of topical social drama and a condensed sensational situation; that which in The Tragic Pursuit was still feverish and unbalanced became in Bitter Rice thought-out and refined, although not uncontroversial. The film bears some signs of drastic ornamentation, for instance in the culminating scene of the shootout in the slaughter-house, and some provocative eroticism. There are also some motifs which are doubtful, not because they were borrowed from "thriller noir, " but because they were forcibly transplanted into an Italian film without the necessary modification.

Since however De Santis states that he made his film as a strip cartoon because the time had come to hit the audience on their nerves, rather than on their heads, one has to forgive him for some of his sins. This initial intention did not become a smoke screen for thin content, but brought about an excellent film, in which the attractive plot and expert staging carry an abundance of psychological and sociological observation, convincing social conclusions and meditation on the fickleness of human nature. The plot of the film develops in the rice planting season in the Po valley, when whole regiments of young women come from all over the country to work in the fields.

In the first part of the film De Santis concentrates on their
interests and environment, showing the difficult work in the rice
fields and the exploitation of the cheap labor. These passages of
Bitter Rice are severe, authentic and 100 per cent Neorealist.
Later still, the documentary quality of the narrative becomes a
kaleidoscopic tale of passion, crime and punishment. In the camp
where the rice girls live a scoundrel appears with a woman accomplice. One of the girls, whose head is full of sentimental literature,
discovers their secret; she dreams of improving her status and gets
involved in an intrigue which ends with a dramatic conflict and a
harvest of death. At the funeral the comrades of the dead heroine
throws handfuls of rice on her body.

De Santis contained a sizeable charge of poetry in this fascinating picture. The style which he displays has been described
as Baroque, and this is probably not a bad description. The diapa-
son of cinematic effects employed give a full and magnetic cinema
experience, especially through the dynamic visuality and rhythm.
Also excellent are the newly discovered actors: Silvana Mangano,
a 19-year-old model, and Raf Vallone, who had previously dabbled
in journalism.

LATE SPRING (Banshun)   Yasujiro Ozu

Script: Ozu and Kogo Noda, from the novel by Kazuro Hirotsu.
Photography: Yushun Atsuta. Music: Senji Ito. Cast: Chishu
Ryu (Shukichi Somiya, a university professor), Setsuko Hara
(Noriko, his daughter), Haruko Sugimura (Masa Taguchi, his sis-
ter), Hohi Aoki (Katsuyoshi, her son), Jun Usami (Shoichi Hattori,
Shukichi's assistant), Yumeji Tsukioka (Aya Kitagawa, Noriko's
classmate), Kuniko Miyake (Akiko Miwa, a widow), Masao Mishima
(Yuzuru Onodera, university professor, Shukichi's friend), Yoshiko
Tsubouchi (Kiku, his wife), Yoko Katsuragi (Misae, his daughter).

Shochiku, Japan. 9724 ft., 108 mins.

In the silent days Yasujiro Ozu became the greatest shomin-geki
film-maker in Japanese cinema. Soon after the war, when the director reached his middle forties, his art went through a transformation. The first sign of this was the different social status
of his heroes: they were no longer urban proletarians or of the
lower middle-class, now they enjoy a fairly comfortable financial
position. But the main motif of Ozu's art--relationships within a
family, and particularly the rift between parents and children--re-
mains unchanged.

A college professor lives with his 27-year-old unmarried daughter. He thinks she is wasting her life looking after him and introduces a young man to her. Although reluctant at first, the girl finally agrees to marry when she hears her father himself intends to take a wife. So they part and the father sits alone in his room.

The director's style became even more restrained and elegiac than before; his films even more Japanese in character. Ozu was the philosopher of Japanese cinema, his message is one of reconciliation. He became more aware of the transience of human existence and began to look at life as a river which flows slowly but never stops. Late Spring is a nostalgic acknowledgment of inevitability: children and parents must part sometime--such is the order of things. A variation of an almost identical story became the theme of Ozu's last film, An Autumn Afternoon, a Buddhist philosophy of meditation, whose perfect balance is a characteristic feature of Japanese literature, as is the idea of achieving inner peace only in unison with Nature.

Ozu stresses this unison even in the titles of his films, · which are curiously monotonous permutations of the names of seasons: Early Summer, Early Spring, Early Autumn, Late Autumn; a sort of parallel commentary on the fate of Ozu's portagonists. Thus Late Spring: a period of stillness, of waiting for summer. Feelings are never brought to the surface in this masterpiece of understatement and the economy of style is likewise extreme. The virtually immobile camera was placed at floor level; long shots with little apparent movement within the frame were established with takes of buildings and monuments and joined together with simple cuts, rejecting fade-outs or dissolves. Images of nature appear as a sort of interlude: the sequence of the father and daughter's visit to Kyoto is memorable, inset with almost immobile shots of hills, trees and buildings, a wordless testimony that the road to wisdom leads through contemplation.

LA BEAUTÉ DU DIABLE   René Clair

Script: Clair and Armand Salacrou. Photography: Michel Kelber. Music: Roman Vlad. Cast: Michel Simon (Professor Faust and Mephistopheles), Gérard Philipe (Henri, Faust as a young man), Nicole Besnard (Marguerite), Simone Valère (The Princess), Carlo Ninchi (The Prince), Paolo Stoppa (The Prosecutor), Raymond Cordy (Valet), Tullio Carminati (Chamberlain), Gaston Modot (Circus proprietor).

Universalia/Ente Nazionale Industrie Cinematografiche/Franco-London-Films, France/Italy. 8637 ft., 96 mins.

Let us love one another, the world is too full of dark forces for us
to try to frolic with them. Perhaps these are not quite Clair's
words in La Beauté du diable--but that is the final conclusion of
this uncommon attempt at sizing up the Faust myth. Clair is not
concerned with a game or a theatre of shadows: the interpretation
of the old German folk legend leans towards a philosophical parable
about human needs and aspirations. It was meant to be a challenge
to those who waste the fruits of the progress of civilization by
plunging the world into chaos and uncertainty; it was as well a protest against misuse of such scientific discoveries as nuclear energy.
In all of this, the film refers to the tradition of French humanist
thought and to Rousseau in particular. Thus the transfer of the
story to the early 19th century--a period crucial to scientific progress; thus the abandonment of the abstract fantasies and the trifling
plots that Clair cultivated with such ardor during previous 15 years;
thus finally the tragic tones, which, incidentally, the director later
regretfully considered not sufficiently pronounced.

It is difficult to consider La Beauté du diable a fully successful work, but to be fair it was very difficult to achieve the
ideal. That which was offered by Clair adds up--with all its intellectual pretentiousness and immaturity--to an intelligent, original
and rich film. This is neither Marlowe nor Goethe transformed onto the screen, but a romanesque Faust--unsymbolic, human (thanks
to the warmth of the humor and the important emotional subplot),
and a little of Jekyll and Hyde-ish in the light mood.

If the story of Marguerite is banal, and the sets of the
quasi-Italian principality are only to be described as studio-post-
card, the psychological subplot of Faust is very precise and the ingenuity shown in arranging the episodes most impressive. The
best moment in this old-fashioned but most charming film is the
sequence in which the drunken Mephistopheles imprudently shows
his victim a diabolical mirror in which images of the future can be
seen.

Clair's earlier mainly descriptive visual style, which used
long shots only occasionally broken up by fast editing, was transformed here into a staccato of nervous, dramatically rugged takes
of explosive dynamism, while the camera performed an excited
series of shots closing on and drawing back from objects. Throughout the film Clair invariably maintained a fast narrative pace, excellently conducting the profuse but condensed dialogue and season-
ing all situations with ironic wit--he did not want to be boring at
any cost. In this aspect the great trumps of the director were
Michel Simon and Gérard Philipe: the direct humanism of La Beauté
du diable and the fact that with all its spiritual dilemmas the film
did not turn into a cool pseudo-philosophical treatise, is to a great
extent thanks to the Gallic lightness of the leading actors.

STRAY DOG (Nora Inu)   Akira Kurosawa

Script: Ryuzo Kikushima and Kurosawa. Photography: Asaichi
Nakai. Music: Fumio Hayasaka. Cast: Toshiro Mifune (Mura-
kami, the detective), Takashi Shimura (Sato, the head detective),
Ko Kimura (Yuro, the criminal), Keiko Awaji (Harumi, his girl),
Reisaburo Yamamoto (Hondo, the suspect), Noriko Sengoku (Girl).

Shintoho, Japan. 10,965 ft., 122 mins.

It is not difficult to understand why Simenon was Kurosawa's favorite
thriller writer. The deep and warm human interest stories displayed by the French author upon a background of police investigations are quite close to the outlook of this searching humanist of
the Japanese cinema. Stray Dog, the first Kurosawa thriller (one
would be reluctant to count the earlier Drunken Angel as a thriller)
was intended to be an exact counterpart to the style of the creator
of Inspector Maigret. This idea later underwent considerable
modifications, and the director himself has nowadays been somewhat
critical of the excessive display of technical skill which, in his opinion, was inappropriate for such a work. All the same one can find
in the film a lot more than brilliantly handled sensational intrigue.

A young Tokyo detective has his gun stolen in a crowded bus.
The desperation with which he searches for the weapon is on one
hand motivated by fear of losing his job and on the other by the
awareness that the stolen pistol can kill; thus the problem of the
moral responsibility for a careless act is involved. The wandering
through the back streets of Tokyo, through boulevards and night
clubs, during which the camera in a series of dissolves and/or long
descriptive scenes penetratingly characterizes the city, is at first
fruitless. The desperate Murakami finds a lead in the end and after
a dramatic chase catches the villain, fights a lonely, exhausting
struggle, looks closely at him--and sees that his opponent is a man
whose life is a negative reflection of his own and that it is only
through a lucky turn of fate that he is not like that himself.

In the extremely tense culminating scene, Kurosawa showed
how little separates the good and evil features of man and how unjust an unequivocal condemnation generally is. Evil abounds everywhere and the author of Stray Dog accepted this resignedly. But he
inveighed in this film against all the catalysts that result in evil and
against social conditions that increase the chance of being pushed
onto the path of crime by accident. As in Drunken Angel, here also the characteristic traits of Kurosawa's philosophy of life are revealed: pity for those whom fate condemns to failure and exhortation to understanding of the brittleness of the human character.
Kurosawa does not incite hate: he is the defense counsel of human-

ity, not its prosecutor.

INTRUDER IN THE DUST   Clarence Brown

Script: Ben Maddow, from the novel by William Faulkner. Pho-
tography: Robert Surtees. Music: Adolph Deutsch. Cast: David
Brian (John Gavin Stevens), Claude Jarman Jr. (Chick Mallison),
Juano Hernandez (Lucas Beauchamp), Porter Hall (Nub Gowrie),
Elizabeth Patterson (Miss Habersham), Charles Kemper (Crawford
Gowrie), Will Geer (Sheriff Hampton), David Clarke (Vinson Gowrie).

MGM, U.S.A. 7773 ft., 86 mins.

Intruder in the Dust is the fullest screen equivalent of Faulkner's
writing, an adaptation of the novel written a year earlier whose
central character is an old Negro unjustly accused of the cowardly
murder of a white man.   The central character of Intruder in the
Dust, full of grave dignity and immutable in his lone stand in the
face of a threat of lynching by the townspeople is, after Hallelujah!,
probably the number one black human being in the American cinema.
Instead of giving a more or less infantile treatment of the black
problem, Clarence Brown, a Hollywood veteran, cast this character
against a perfectly charted landscape of provincial Southern attitudes.

    The whole Faulknerian world is contained here with amazing
fidelity as is the Faulknerian style, with its psychological finesse,
restrained but tangible imagery, sour severity of outlook and inseparable aura of reflection on the complexity of people and events.
The great writer was very unfortunate with the film adaptations of
his works, despite having been a Hollywood scriptwriter himself, but
in the year of his Nobel prize for literature he scored a real screen
success.   Perhaps a significant circumstance is that most of the
open-air shooting was done in Faulkner's native Oxford, Mississippi,
where he was in close touch with the crew.

THIEVES' HIGHWAY   Jules Dassin

Script: Z. I. Bezzerides, from his novel, "Thieves' Market."
Photography: Norbert Brodine. Music: Alfred Newman. Cast:
Richard Conte (Nick Garcos), Valentina Cortese (Rica Martino), Lee
J. Cobb (Figlia), Barbara Lawrence (Polly), Jack Oakie (Siob),
Millard Mitchell (Ed Kennedy), Joseph Pevney (Pete Bailey), Morris

Carnovsky (Yanko).

20th Century-Fox, U.S.A.   8335 ft., 93 mins.

Jules Dassin doubtless has a prominent place among the film-
makers who took an interest in the social problems of the America
of the 40's. As a matter of fact, his unorthodox views got him into trouble with the House Un-American Activities Committee and as a
result he moved to Europe. Besides being absorbed in social questions, Dassin was equally involved in a passion for powerful cinema,
searching for an aggressive, explosive style with which to document
his fascination with violence and ruthlessness. This preoccupation
is the reason why Thieves' Highway, a film which could have become a powerful study of the conflicts convulsing America, reached
only the level of an impressive sensational drama.

     Many of the features with which, for instance, De Santis
equipped his Bitter Rice are absent here: Thieves' Highway is a
solo played by a virtuoso but only on one string--devoid of psychological penetration, and deprived of poetry or of deeper meaning.
This superficiality can partly be explained by the difficulties with the
censors Dassin had earlier with Brute Force and The Naked City.
But the principal reason for it is his voluntary departure from the
documentary style of film-making in favor of the seemingly more
communicative (and certainly more attractive) condensed dramatic
situations. The plot of Thieves' Highway is rather reminiscent of
the mythology of the pioneers of the West, and it has more affinity
with the convention of film noir than with a story about the exploitation of labor.

     The main protagonist is the son of a truck driver who trans-
ported vegetables and fruit to the San Francisco market and was
mutilated in an "accident" caused by the Mafia. Now Nick sets out
to provoke the gang that is exploiting and terrorizing the truck
drivers and to take vengeance on its leader. Although he does not
actually break the gang, he achieves moral satisfaction and as a
bonus gains the leader's girl. His action is thus that of a strong
man in a world dominated by violence; his success is the success of
calculation and determination in an encounter with evil blindly confident of its might.

     So, while there is a great distance between the victory of a
lonely hero and any concrete social conclusions, Thieves' Highway
must still be considered one of the most interesting films noir.
Dassin invested his film with a lot of truth about the rapaciousness
of the world of commerce. He also directed the actors well (Lee
J. Cobb and Jack Oakie distinguished themselves), but deserves
most credit for making a film of fascinating dynamic visuality.
Two scenes shot with skill and bravura--the night drive to San
Francisco and the truck crash--are classics of sensational cinema.

LOS OLVIDADOS (The Young and the Damned) Luis Buñuel

Script: Buñuel, Luis Alcoriza and Oscar Dancigers. Photography:
Gabriel Figueroa. Music: Rodolfo Halffter, from themes by Gus-
tavo Pittaluga. Cast: Estela Inda (Marta), Miguel Inclán (Don Car-
melo), Alfonso Mejía (Pedro), Roberto Cobo (Jaibo), Alma Delia
Fuentes (Meche), Francisco Jambrina (Farm School Director), Ef-
rain Arauz (Pockface), Javier Amezcua (Julian), Mario Ramirez
(Occhito).

Ultramar Films, Mexico. 8020 ft., 88 mins.

Negative elements lie dormant in everyone, inborn and eternal, but
they would not come to the surface during childhood, were it not
for poverty, the indifference of parents and the cruelty of the world.
It is these factors which stimulate evil in the receptive but unre-
sistant characters. Adolescents already on a social margin soon
turn into delinquents and, in disadvantageous social conditions, their
re-education, as Los Olvidados ironically demonstrates, is a joust
against windmills. This film, about the forgotten children of Mexico
City, remains one of the most convincing and honest registrations
of the problem of difficult youth.

This is how Luis Buñuel made his presence felt again in the
cinema. An anarchistic surrealist of the late 20's and early 30's,
Buñuel, with his Un Chien andalou (1928) and L'Age d'or (1930),
challenged the fossilized conventions of the bourgeoisie in the name
of respect for nature and the vital forces of man. After 1932 he
ceased independent creative work for a lengthy period, returning to
it only at the close of the 40's. After two insignificant melodramas
he made Los Olvidados, which although under the patronage of the
Mexican educational authorities, is considered equally as provocative
as the early films of his French period. But one really has to
count this notion among the innumerable legends surrounding the
Spanish master of the screen: his picture is simply consistently
true in its brutal frankness and this puts it in contrast with the
cinema of the time.

Buñuel's alleged total pessimism should be regarded with no
less skepticism: the mood of the film is not determined by any
programmatic despondence but simply by a sober analysis of the
rules of the cruel world he depicts. It is thus a pessimism justified
by concrete social conditions, a despondency which offers a program
of changes to be enacted through a change of political system. Buñuel's spokesman in the film is the sensible director of the approved
school, acutely aware of his powerlessness: "If we could only lock
up poverty here and not the children!"

But not all problems can be settled by changing the social
system. Buñuel talks also about individual ethics: he shows the
disastrous results of the "eye for an eye" philosophy of life, ad-
vocating mutual understanding and the abandonment of opportunism,
selfishness and fear. In its final effect, with all the unorthodoxy
that caused so many misunderstandings, Los Olvidados is a factual,
straightforward and wise film. Unfortunately, when leading up to
his conclusions, Buñuel used obtrusive and melodramatic devices;
the cardinal turns of the plot are forced by fatalistic chance and
psychological logic gives way to ominous coincidence. Their almost
symbolic frequency led the film in a direction quite different from
that intended by the director and substantially weakened the suggestiveness of Buñuel's message. This was however counterbalanced
by the texture of the images, the rough authenticity of the staging,
and the cool reportage quality of the photography, which never escaped into sentiment and which displays the full talent of Figueroa
(so different here from Fernández' films, but at the same time so
successful in fulfilling the director's intentions).

If Buñuel allows himself poetry, it is the poetry of abstract
symbols, the poetry of the subjective imagery of the protagonists
(Pedro's Freudian dream, Jaibo's delirium before death). This remains in full accord with his youthful Surrealist manifesto: the
world of beauty is incompatible with the grim concreteness of the
prison of civilization.

THE THIRD MAN Carol Reed

Script: Graham Greene, from his own story. Photography: Robert
Krasker. Music: composed and played on the zither by Anton
Karas. Cast: Joseph Cotten (Holly Martins), Trevor Howard (Ma-
jor Calloway), Alida Valli (Anna), Orson Welles (Harry Lime),
Bernard Lee (Sgt. Paine), Paul Hörbiger (Porter), Ernst Deutsch
("Baron" Kurtz), Siegfried Breuer (Popescu), Erich Ponto (Dr.
Winkel).

London Film Productions, G.B. 9428 ft., 105 mins.

Carol Reed has a deserved reputation for creating films with unusual atmosphere and The Third Man is par excellence an atmospheric film. Like The Fallen Idol it was made from a Graham
Greene script and, as before, it merges the qualities of a melodrama and a mild thriller. Holly Martins, a third-rate journalist,
arrives in postwar Vienna to work as publicity agent for a certain
Harry Lime, said to be running a voluntary hospital. He learns
that Lime has been killed in a road accident; the police tell him
he was a racketeer. Martins sets out to find the truth for himself.

The story is not particularly interesting anyway, but the
form it acquired on the screen is unexpected and made the film
Reed's stylistically most interesting work. The Third Man is composed of a greater than usual number of shots, usually short (with
the exception, of course, of the famous final tracking shot at the
cemetery), and was edited in the temperamental staccato of an
Italian opera, giving the film a wry and ironic appearance. It is
a sinister portrayal of a shell of a city with nearly-empty streets,
deserted cafés, a black market and an atmosphere of suspicion and
uncertainty.

The Third Man is also a political statement; while accurately
portraying the typical postwar corruption and cosmopolitanism, it
contains a message: "war breaks people." Although the picture
seems to amount to a clear triumph of style over content, it has
some memorable elements: Martins' pursuit of Lime in the huge
reverberating sewers, Welles' impressive performance as the corrupted wreck. Reed made frequent use of the tilted camera--but
the thing which is decisive for the mood is the music, played entirely on the zither with a strumming, ironic abandon. The Third
Man is Reed's last outstanding film; his later work seems slight
and disappointing when compared to his suggestive pictures of the
40's.

ALL THE KING'S MEN   Robert Rossen

Script: Rossen, from the novel by Robert Penn Warren. Pho-
tography: Burnett Guffey. Music: Louis Gruenberg. Cast:
Broderick Crawford (Willie Stark), Joanne Dru (Anne Stanton), John
Ireland (Jack Burden), John Derek (Tom Stark), Mercedes McCam-
bridge (Sadie Burke), Shepperd Strudwick (Adam Stanton), Ralph
Dumke (Tiny Duffy), Anne Seymour (Lucy Stark), Katharine Warren
(Mrs. Burden), Raymond Greenleaf (Judge Stanton), Walter Burke
(Sugar Boy).

Columbia, U.S.A. 9860 ft., 110 mins.

A screen adaptation, full of political conviction, of the famous novel
written three years earlier about the destructive influence of power,
the fatal two-edgedness of total war in the name of higher causes.
Robert Penn Warren used the personality of Huey Long, governor of
Louisiana in the years 1928-1935 as the prototype; the novel traces
the path of an un-self-critical political leader who, from being an
authentic, straightforward defender of the interests of the underprivileged, is transformed under the demoralizing influence of the
intrigues of the electoral machinery, into a dictator corroded by
hatred, whose most important aim is the destruction of all his op-

ponents.

Although Rossen did not fully exploit the possibilities offered
by the novel, and treated the hero with an excessive, precipitate
onesidedness, especially in the latter parts of the picture, he gave
an important film, warning and disquieting with its vehement imagery. All the King's Men is not only the story of a spineless individual in a world of machinations and hypocrisy, but also a grim
panorama of the political market of provincial America, where the
formlessness of the electoral mob becomes fodder for the dema-
goguery of the leaders and where honesty is the most naive and
least effective principle.

Rossen attached much more attention to the strength of the
communication of this very message than to the dramatic balance,
aesthetic homogeneity or psychological subleties of the film itself.
It is true that he gave Crawford an excellent chance to prove himself (from which the actor gained an Oscar), but most of the director's care was lavished upon the expressiveness of the individual
episodes. This led to a certain incoherence of the narrative (which
also results from the massive cutting of the first version of the
film), and thus a certain superficiality. These faults are compensated for by the journalistic passion and the suggestive density of
images, which Rossen achieved to a great extent thanks to his use
of the Wellesian concepts of deep focus.

THE SET-UP   Robert Wise

Script: Art Cohn, based on the poem by Joseph Moncure March.
Photography: Milton Krasner. Music: C. Bakalesnikoff. Cast:
Robert Ryan (Stoker), Audrey Totter (Julie), George Tobias (Tiny),
Alan Baxter (Little boy), Wallace Ford (Gus), Percy Helton (Red),
Hal Fieberling (Tiger Nelson), Darryl Hickman (Shanley), Kenny
O'Morrison (Moore), James Edwards (Luther Hawkins), David Clarke
(Gunboat Johnson).

RKO Radio Pictures, U.S.A.   6464 ft., 72 mins.

The world of American professional boxing is doubtless one of the
most tempting themes ever put on the screen. It is difficult to find
another milieu that to a greater extent combines visual attraction
with social observation; it seems equally difficult to get hold of a
better motif for deliberations about the psychology of a man strug-
gling for position. Thus it is not an accident that among film-
makers hovering around the ropes of the ring were the realists--
members of the postwar trend of film noir--who, like Rossen in
Body and Soul (1947) or Robson in Champion, looked back-stage and

showed bitter pictures of a world corroded by corruption, of the
destruction of the people involved and of the predatory exploitation
of the ambitious pretenders to fame.

Wise did the same in The Set-Up, but he offered much more.
His vision is not limited to one-sided journalistic criticism, but
sums up the whole truth about the brutality of boxing.   From behind the sometimes primitive staging, the melodramatic shoals of
the plot and the stereotyped situations, the director glimpsed a
generalizing principle which he used to transform this modest story
into praise for a man who challenges fate in order to preserve his
dignity.   One should not regard this transformation as accidental.
The script, based on a poem, has the action take place in a town
with the meaningful name of Paradise City; its dramatic construction recalls ancient principles.   The classical form of The Set-Up
is also stressed in the microstructure--through Wise's precise editing and stylistic homogeneity.

The director's hero is a 35-year-old professional boxer de-
terminedly trying to stay on the surface and to climb higher in his
career, already coming to a close.   He gravely prepares for a four-
round fight to which he attaches certain hopes; not knowing that the
fight has been set up.   Told about it at the last moment he rejects
his manager's orders.   After a dramatic struggle he wins, although
he is aware of the probable price of this victory.   The Syndicate are
waiting outside the door of the hall.   The lonely Stoker will not win
this struggle.   Bestially beaten and with a broken wrist, he drags
himself to his hotel to the wife who so many times before had tried
to persuade him to put his gloves away.   Now it is done: this is
the end of his career, but a proud one.

THE HEIRESS   William Wyler

Script: Ruth and Augustus Goetz, from their own play suggested by
the novel, "Washington Square," by Henry James.   Photography:
Leo Tover.   Music: Aaron Copland.   Cast: Olivia De Havilland
(Catherine Sloper), Montgomery Clift (Morris Townsend), Ralph
Richardson (Dr. Austin Sloper), Miriam Hopkins (Lavinia Penniman),
Vanessa Brown (Maria), Mona Freeman (Marian Almond), Ray Col-
lins (Jefferson Almond), Betty Linley (Mrs. Montgomery), Selena
Royle (Elizabeth Almond).

Paramount, U.S.A.   10,348 ft., 115 mins.

Wyler returned once more to the female psychological portraits
which made him famous in the late 30's and early 40's--and for the
third time he brought his leading lady an Oscar.   The successor of

Bette Davis in Jezebel and Greer Garson in Mrs. Miniver is Olivia
De Havilland. The heroine which she subtly reproduces from the
pages of Henry James is a girl who, even with an attractive dowry
is unpopular with men; then she invests all her feelings in the first
young man to take a serious interest in her. Unfortunately, the
interest has a purely financial motivation and this is detected by her
stern father. He gives her the choice of disinheritance or a break
with the gold-digger. The ill-starred girl, whose supplications are
of no use, chooses the first alternative: a dissipated husband is
better than loneliness. She agrees to elope, but the young man
does not turn up and returns only after many years, when the fortune's guardian can no longer stand in his way. He is apparently accepted, but when only the door separates him from the goal he finds this
door locked. This is revenge, and his knocking is unanswered.
The proud heiress chooses loneliness.

The turn-of-the-century melodrama which constitutes the plot
was directed by Wyler with most impressive skill: it is hard to
find, even in his career, another film with a similar density of
imagery, fluent narrative and suggestive mood. The original, multi-
dimensional kind of photographic composition of The Little Foxes
and The Best Years of Our Lives reached in The Heiress a muted
maturity. The picture is homogeneous, pure despite its complexity,
and finely communicative. Although this cinematic chamber piece
was not written with very resonant motifs, it is not merely a fine
bagatelle. Wyler's inquisitiveness in probing his heroine's personality resulted in excellent portrayals that contain much severe truth
about the cruelty of human selfishness.

GIVE US THIS DAY   Edward Dmytryk

Script: Ben Barzman, from the novel, "Christ in Concrete," by
Pietro Di Donato. Photography: C. Pennington Richards. Music:
Benjamin Frankel. Cast: Sam Wanamaker (Geremio), Lea Padovani
(Annunziata), Kathleen Ryan (Kathleen), Charles Goldner (Luigi),
Bonar Colleano (Julio), Bill Sylvester (Giovanni), Karel Stepanek
(Jaroslav), Sydney James (Murdin).

Plantagenet (Geiger-Bronstein), G.B.   Approx. 10,792 ft., 120 mins.

In New York, in the 1920's, an Italian immigrant bricklayer sets out
to bring home a bride from the old country. The girl, whom he
knows only from a photograph, has made a condition: ownership of
their own home. He does not yet have sufficient money, but does
not intend to wait, so he summons his fiancée and pretends he has
fulfilled the condition, hoping that everything will somehow sort itself out. It does in fact so far as the marriage itself is concerned,

but there are difficult years of sacrifice and financial trouble; there is an addition to the family, but the dream house is still out of reach.   Difficulties in finding employment make the hero take dangerous jobs and in the end disaster strikes.   The sum needed for building the house is obtained through the life insurance payment received by the widow.   A shattering finale, full of pathos, striking in its social accusation--and cheap.

Such indeed is the entire film, oscillating between the nobility of its human concern and a pretentious symbolism; compressing within itself a whole panorama of stylistic devices--from Italian Neorealism to Dreiserian naturalism, from melodrama to mystic exaltation.   Dmytryk, one of the Hollywood Ten who were accused in 1947 of pro-Communist sympathies by the Un-American Activities Committee and were sent to prison, tried in this manner to introduce into American cinema (although through the medium of a film made in Great Britain) the new European tendencies to profess interest in the topical and touchy problems of the day.

Dmytryk's social convictions are obvious--he had already made them clear in Crossfire (1947)--but the method by which they are expressed does not carry the intended force.   The fault lies partly in the literary material, but only Dmytryk himself is to blame for such effects as the juxtaposition of sentimental lyricism and drastic brutality or the shallow psychoanalytical and philosophical accents.   And if Give Us This Day, despite its unevenness, is in the end something more than a trifle, this is brought about mainly by the realistic description, the photographic expression of which is consonant with the director's authentic imagery.

IN THE NAME OF THE LAW (In Nome della Legge)   Pietro Germi

Script: Federico Fellini, Germi, Giuseppe Mangione, Mario Monicelli, Tullio Pinelli and Aldo Bizzarri, from the novel, "Piccola Pretura" (The Magistrates Court), by Giuseppe Guido Loschiavo. Photography: Leonida Barboni.   Music: Carlo Rustichelli.   Cast: Massimo Girotti (Magistrate Guido Schiavi), Charles Vanel (Massaro Turi Passalacqua), Jone Salinas (Baroness Teresa Lo Vasto), Camillo Mastrocinque (Baron Lo Vasto), Turi Pandolfini (Don Fifi), Peppino Spadaro (Lawyer Faraglia), Saro Urzi (Police sergeant), Ignazio Balsamo (Ciccio Messana).

Lux-Film, Italy. 9338 ft., 104 mins.

A sensational drama with social interests, in which the Italian cinema touched the burning problem of the Sicilian Mafia for the first time.   If one is to believe the makers of the film, this happened

rather by accident: Germi arrived in Sicily simply to make a
thriller in an attractive locale; only after becoming acquainted with
the local facts of life did he change his intentions regarding the
character of the planned film, and tried to reflect on the screen
the real conflicts of this sun-scorched, impoverished land. It is
said that one of the director's most significant Sicilian experiences
was the meeting with the local Mafia boss, who is supposed to have
demanded, with threats, that the ending of the film be changed.

The fact remains that Germi refers to the Mafia in a tone of
no more than gentle remonstrance (and he is talking about the times
when the bloody excesses of Salvatore Giuliano took place!), but it
cannot be denied that the film contains a richness of vivid social
and local observation. As in the thematically similar The Day of
the Owl of 20 years later, the representative of the law who has
arrived to solve a crime crashes against the wall of fear and indifference. Like the later critics of Sicilian conditions, Germi discloses the fine network of mutual dependence between the terrorists
and the wealthy.

The ending of the film is, however, the product of the action
of four forces: the investigating magistrate, the Mafia, the landowners, and the peasants. The magistrate wins because he acts
effectively and understands the greater importance of the spirit of
the law than the letter and because he manages to enlist the support
of the peasants, whom the outrageous crime has liberated from intimidation. The Mafia has to resign itself to handing over the
murderer to the law, a man who tried to exploit the might of his
organization with too much insolence. So, Germi found a solution;
Damiani, Petri and Rosi were not to have similar illusions in the
60's. In their films it is the terror which has the upper hand.

CHAMPION   Mark Robson

Script: Carl Foreman, from the story by Ring Lardner. Photog-
raphy: Franz Planer. Music: Dmitri Tiomkin. Cast: Kirk
Douglas (Midge Kelly), Marilyn Maxwell (Grace Diamond), Arthur
Kennedy (Connie Kelly), Paul Stewart (Tommy Haley), Ruth Roman
(Emma Bryce), Lola Albright (Mrs. Harris), Luis Van Rooten
(Jerome Harris), John Day (Johnny Dunne).

United Artists, U.S.A. 8848 ft., 98 mins.

This brutal drama which uncovers the back stage of professional
boxing is akin to The Set-Up made in the same year. It is an excellent psychological portrayal of an individual formed by the world
of power and money. The other film, by Wise, grew into an au-

thentic morality play; the basic problem of Champion (deficient virtue in victorious confrontation with greed) is no less ambitious--
but the conclusions are too easy and too predictable. It is true that
Foreman tried to tone this aspect down by introducing into the plot
twists designed to motivate the ending, but in the final count something else has the greatest value in the film: the critical portrayal
of the world in and around the ring, reflections on the postwar atmosphere in America, and above all the description of the hero's
psychological development.

As his boxing career develops, this former soldier, whom
life had disposed to use his elbows, replaces recklessness with ir-
responsibility, force with brutality and self-assurance with blind
egocentrism. He feels stronger not only than all his opponents but
also than the bosses of the sporting business. He cannot lose, and
he does not lose to the end--but there death is awaiting him. The
personality of the ill-starred titan of the ring appears on the screen
as full and entirely credible: he is more than a director's spokesman, he is a living man whom Kirk Douglas in his first great role
presents with direct and balanced intensity. The authenticity of this
performance is reinforced by Robson's directorial approach, a concrete, laconic equivalent of reality, and by the severe, chronicle
quality of the photography.

LES ENFANTS TERRIBLES   Jean-Pierre Melville

Script: Jean Cocteau and Melville, from the novel by Cocteau.
Photography: Henri Decaë. Music: J. S. Bach's Arrangement in
A Minor for four pianos of Antonio Vivaldi's Concerto in B Minor
for four violins; Antonio Vivaldi's Concerto Grosso in A Minor.
Cast: Nicole Stéphane (Elisabeth), Edouard Dermithe (Paul), Renée
Cosima (Agathe/Dargélos), Adeline Aucoc (Mariette), Jacques Ber-
nard (Gérard), Roger Gaillard (His uncle), Mel Martin (Michaël),
Maria Cyliakus (The mother), Maurice Revel (Doctor), Jean-Marie
Robain (School bursar), Annabel Buffet (The mannequin).

O.G.C., France. 10,600 ft., 118 mins., later cut to 9540 ft.,
106 mins.

The novel, "Les Enfants terribles," together with Alain-Fournier's
"Le Grand Meaulnes" and Radiguet's "Le Diable au corps," is one
of those inimitably French books which paint the melancholy world
of adolescence. Partly biographical, it describes a quaint brother-
sister relationship full of adolescent myths, the decadent nihilism
of youth, its feverish devotions, clandestine rituals and secret
games. It is significant that the novel was written (in 1929) when
Cocteau was undergoing an opium cure.

Elisabeth and her brother Paul live in their private dream
world full of coveted memories and rites which only they can understand.   When their mother dies and Elisabeth marries a millionaire
(who quickly dies) they continue with their secret game in new surroundings until the communion of souls is violated by a stranger--
a girl in love with Paul. The balance is disturbed once and for all
and death remains the only solace.

When Cocteau, having just seen Le Silence de la mer, asked
Melville to undertake the adaptation (he himself was busy shooting
Orphée), the director well understood the problems involved. Although Melville did not avoid a somewhat pretentious bookishness,
the picture was saved by his sense of proportion, although he preserved fidelity to the book. In spite (or perhaps because) of that,
the result was a completely cinematic, visual film. Much credit
for this is due to the camera work--fluent, full of striking compositions and elaborate movements (like the unexpected closing crane
shot). The hand-held camera gives the feeling of genuineness and
immediacy.

It is Melville who was responsible for forming the visual
style of Henri Decaë, later principal cameraman of the Nouvelle
Vague (of which Melville is considered a precursor). Les Enfants
terribles is a haunting, but flawed film: Edouard Dermithe could
not cope with the difficult role of Paul, and there are other imperfections, mostly due to Cocteau's influence. Much of the mood is
owed to the wonderful Bach score, at once triumphant and melancholy.

KIND HEARTS AND CORONETS Robert Hamer

Script: Hamer and John Dighton, from the novel, "Israel Rank" (1907),
by Roy Horniman. Photography: Douglas Slocombe. Music: the aria,
"Il Mio Tesoro Intanto," by Wolfgang Amadeus Mozart. Cast: Alec
Guinness (The Duke of Chalfont/Lord Ascoyne D'Ascoyne, the banker/
the Rev. Henry D'Ascoyne/General Lord Rufus D'Ascoyne/Admiral
Horatio D'Ascoyne/Young Ascoyne D'Ascoyne/Young Henry D'Ascoyne/
Lady Agatha), Dennis Price (Louis D'Ascoyne Mazzini), Valerie Hob-
son (Edith D'Ascoyne), Joan Greenwood (Sibella Holland), Audrey
Fildes (Mama), Miles Malleson (Hangman), Clive Morton (Prison
governor), John Penrose (Lionel Holland).

Ealing Studios, G.B. 9529 ft., 106 mins.

Kind Hearts and Coronets is a classic in the series of Ealing Comedies which hilariously exploited the comic potential in the British
way of life and which marked one of the happiest spells in British
film-making. The Cockney Passport of Pimlico was the first; later

came the Scottish Whisky Galore! (1948), Kind Hearts and Coronets
--a spoof on the aristocracy--and the middle-class The Lavender
Hill Mob.

　　　　Kind Hearts and Coronets is a story of the successful, if
somewhat unusual, efforts of a young man to reclaim his rights to
a dukedom. His mother was the daughter of the seventh Duke of
Chalfont, the title which can, as a special privilege, be passed on
in the female line. But when Louis's mother eloped with a handsome Italian singer, the family rejected her son's rights to the title.
The last straw, as far as Louis is concerned, is the family's re-
fusal of a place in the family vault to his mother's body. So, the
only way out is clearly to liquidate the entire family tree. Everything goes smoothly, but when the coronet is already the hero's,
things take an unexpected turn: a false accusation by a spurned
mistress causes the eight-fold murderer to land in prison and be
convicted of a crime he actually had nothing to do with.

　　　　The script which Hamer prepared for himself is undeniably
excellent. Less praiseworthy is the lack of coherence of the picture, which is broken up into a series of retrospective episodes in
which the cumbersome relatives are disposed of by the charming
hero by means of ingenuously devised "accidents." Particularly at
fault are the slow beginning and the overly long scenes of the hero's
trial by the House of Lords. On the other hand, all is done with a
satirical anti-aristocratic touch, witty dialogue and a wonderful
sense of humor--enough to ensure an appropriate dessert, for the
story. As dessert, there are eight roles (seven male and one female) played by the splendidly adaptable Alec Guinness.

SHE WORE A YELLOW RIBBON   John Ford

Script: Frank S. Nugent and Laurence Stallings, from the story,
"War Party," by James Warner Bellah. Photography: Winton C.
Hoch and Charles P. Boyle. Music: Richard Hageman. Cast:
John Wayne (Capt. Nathan Brittles), Joanne Dru (Olivia), John Agar
(Lt. Flint Cohill), Ben Johnson (Sgt. Tyree), Harry Carey (Lt.
Pennell), Victor McLaglen (Sgt. Quincannon), Mildred Natwick (Mrs.
Allshard), George O'Brien (Maj. Allshard).

Argosy Pictures/RKO Radio Pictures, U.S.A. 103 mins.

This is the second part (Fort Apache was made the year before) of
Ford's "cavalry trilogy," and similar to the first part in more ways
than one. The time for reflection had come, and She Wore a Yellow Ribbon is Ford's lament for the universe that exploded with
Custer's defeat--a film of autumnal melancholy and trumpet calls

for the dead.   Not an Injuns vs. Pale Faces story, this is a document about a polluted world where neither side wins and the cavalry
has to steal surreptitiously through the once-free land.

     She Wore a Yellow Ribbon, unlike Fort Apache, is centered
around one character, and reflects on old age and a man's fight for
his principles.   The aging Captain Nathan Brittles escorts his commanding officer's family to a stagecoach in a remote town; the party
has to turn back after a confrontation with the Indians.   The cavalry
is not the same; only the land itself hasn't changed and Ford stressed
this with Oscar-winning photography, styled to evoke the paintings of
the frontier artist Frederick Remington, predominantly using pure,
strong color.   The use of colored lighting is interesting and in several scenes created the feel of less-than-real solemnity.   But even
here there is humor, provided mainly by a pair of old soldiers
nearing retirement (Wayne's gallant captain, McLaglen's Irish NCO).

UNDER CAPRICORN   Alfred Hitchcock

Script: James Bridie, from the novel by Helen Simpson adapted by
Hume Cronyn. Photography: Jack Cardiff. Music: Richard Adin-
sell. Cast: Ingrid Bergman (Lady Henrietta Flusky), Joseph Cotten
(Sam Flusky), Michael Wilding (Charles Adare), Margaret Leighton
(Milly), Jack Watling (Winter), Cecil Parker (The Governor), Denis
O'Dea (Corrigan).

Transatlantic Pictures, G.B.   10,526 ft., 116 mins.   Technicolor.

Sydney 1830: the Governor's nephew, newly arrived from England,
recognizes his cousin in the alcoholic wife of a now rich ex-convict,
and falls in love with her.   The jealous husband wounds the young
man during an argument; not wanting her husband to be tried for
assault, Henrietta admits responsibility for the crime for which he
had been transported.

     It would be impossible to guess, without the screen credits,
that Under Capricorn was directed by Alfred Hitchcock.   The director was of course conversant with romantic costume melodramas--
he proved this with his Jamaica Inn (1939), even though that picture
was at heart a traditional near-thriller and was shot in a fast and
efficient style.   None of this here: Under Capricorn is a rambling
and stylistically sophisticated adaptation of an average romantic novel,
and is extremely sparing with thrills.   This is probably why it was
a commercial disaster, but the blame for the incomplete artistic
success must ultimately be put on the literary original.

     Furthermore, the fluid camera movement with complex track-

ing shots, some of them switching from one floor to another, and
in several cases up to eight minutes long, slows down the action
and surrounds the film with an aura of dreamy fantasy. This style
of directing is clearly a hangover from Hitchcock's earlier Rope.
What little action there is tends to get lost in the bouts of (good)
dialogue, and the last 15 minutes are less than satisfactory.

     Yet Under Capricorn is by any standard an interesting twist
in Hitchcock's development and remains most worthwhile for his admirers. The director included several very good scenes (one of
them is of course Henrietta's discovery of a shrunken head in her
bed) and excellently evoked the oppressive mood of a brooding mansion ruled by a sinister housekeeper in love with her master, turning the film into a study of a woman's fight to preserve her sanity,
strongly reminiscent of Notorious. Under Capricorn is a thoroughly
professionally made color movie, with several outstanding acting
performances. It was in fact scripted with Ingrid Bergman in mind.

MANÈGES   Yves Allégret

Script: Jacques Sigurd. Photography: Jean Bourgoin. Cast:
Simone Signoret (Dora), Bernard Blier (Robert), Jane Marken
(Mother), Frank Villard (François), Jacques Baumer (Louis).

Films Modernes/Discina, France. 7990 ft., 88 mins.

With his earlier Une si jolie petite plage, Allégret established himself as the leading exponent of the pessimistic, "Existentialist" trend
in postwar French cinema. Manèges reinforced this reputation so
far as the mood is concerned, but has only a part of the other
film's power of persuasion. A predatory little tart ensnares the
middle-aged owner of a riding school, marries him and proceeds,
with the help of her jolly mother, to suck him dry. The gullible
husband permits all up to a point: when a car accident paralyzes
Dora, he leaves her to her mother.

     The grim tonality of the story brings to mind some of the
films of Jean Renoir (such as La Bête humaine) and indeed it seems
that Renoir would have been capable of handling the subject with
more consistency. Starting in the hospital, the story is told in a
series of perhaps excessively complex flashbacks. Also, Allégret
did not put enough psychological motivation in the film (the deeper
reasons behind Dora's voracious greed are not given, nor is Robert's
gullibility explained). The appeal of Manèges lies less in the directing (although there are a number of really good méchant scenes in
the later part of the film) than in the powerful mood and the fine
performances from the leading actors, which all but redeem the lit-

erary weaknesses of the structure.

OCCUPE-TOI D'AMÉLIE (Keep an Eye on Amelia) Claude Autant-Lara

---

Script: Jean Aurenche and Pierre Bost, from a play by Georges Feydeau. Photography: André Bac. Music: René Cloërec. Cast: Danielle Darrieux (Amélie d'Avranches), Julien Carette (Pochet), Coco Aslan (Prince de Palestrie), André Bervil (Etienne), Jean Desailly (Marcel Courbois), Victor Guyau (Van Putzeboum), Armontel (General Koschnadieff), Charles Deschamps (The Mayor).

Lux-Film, France. 8605 ft., 96 mins.

As René Clair once, in The Italian Straw Hat, removed the dust from the vaudeville of the Labiche-Michel team, so did Autant-Lara later with Feydeau's turn-of-the-century farce. Although he did not transpose it in time, and remained faithful to the stage original (which he even openly stressed with the theatrical frames of the prologue and the epilogue), he did give the film a vertiginous pace and dynamic vivacity. And despite all this acceleration he still made the turns with subtlety and precision.

A man has to marry in order to benefit from a sizeable inheritance. Amélie, a Parisian coquette entrusted to his care by a hussar friend, agrees to go through a mock marriage to satisfy the uncle who is the trustee of the fortune. The shrewd uncle however finds out and arranges with the mayor for the marriage to be real. But by now the young couple do not mind....

In accordance with his habits, the director proceeded with an all-out bombardment of bourgeois hypocrisy, but this time, unlike the earlier Douce and Le Diable au corps, in a comedy mood. As for the acting, Danielle Darrieux and Jean Desailly gave performances of vigor and charm.

KNOCK ON ANY DOOR Nicholas Ray

Script: Daniel Taradash and John Monks Jr., from the novel by Willard Motley. Photography: Burnett Guffey. Music: George Anthell. Cast: Humphrey Bogart (Andrew Morton), John Derek (Nick Romano), George Macready (District Attorney Kerman), Ellene

Roberts (Emma), Susan Perry (Adele Morton), Mickey Knox (Vito),
Barry Kelley (Judge Drake).

Santana, U.S.A. 8964 ft., 100 mins.

In 1952, in France, André Cayatte made Nous sommes tous les
assassins ("We are all murderers"), one of the most outstanding
reckonings with the judicial system in the cinema. It is represented as society's cover-up for its own insensitivity to the forces
pushing some individuals onto the path of crime. The "We Are All
Murderers" of the American cinema was in fact made, by Nicholas
Ray, three years before its French counterpart.

The accused before the majesty of the law is the killer of a
policeman, a boy grown up in slums and marked by their criminal
subculture. But morally, the accused is society as a whole. The
charge against it is that of being responsible for the fate of the accused. "Until we liquidate slums, one can knock on any door and
find Tony Camonte": such is the defending attorney's closing statement and such is also the conclusion of the film.

Done with fluency and technical skill, Knock on Any Door is
composed of two distinct parts: in the first, tracing the life story
of the hero in a flashback, Ray repeatedly slipped into a melodrama
and schematism far from the severity of true socially-conscious
cinema. Sometimes the director appears to have addressed his film
to our sentiments, just as Humphrey Bogart directs the burden of
the defense argument to the women members of the jury, hoping
that they will be moved by the plight of the handsome boy. But in
the second part the film becomes a real courtroom drama, a genre
with a tradition in the American cinema, albeit without the customary
light relief. One feels then that Twelve Angry Men is not far away.

There is an interesting glance behind the scenes, at the behavior of the defense attorney and the prosecutor in the judge's
chambers, where animosities (unlike in the courtroom) are for real
and not just for show. There is also a timid attempt at touching
upon irregularities inherent in the administration of justice: while
Bogart hunts for the votes of women jury members who outnumber
the men 7 to 5, the prosecutor extracts the truth from the accused
by dint of mental cruelty. This, the most controversial aspect of
Knock on Any Door, is a typically Ray-esque excursion into the
realm of psychoneurotic psychology and seems an interesting parallel
to the French Justice est faite. So, it is in the finale that the picture gains momentum; the accusation, justified and important in its
own right, becomes convincing, even though the means used were
sometimes of doubtful quality.

PUEBLERINA   Emilio Fernández

Script: Fernández. Photography: Gabriel Figueroa. Cast:
Columba Domínguez (Paloma), Roberto Cañedo (Aurelio), Ismael
Perez (Felipe).

Mexico.

The last famous film of the Fernández-Figueroa team. As before,
the pair of leading characters invariably follow the ritual of folk
heroes: she is quiet and wronged, he, brave and honest, and in the
background rich villains are lying in wait. One of them raped the
heroine and is now afraid of the vengeance of the peasant, who spent
six years in jail for defending the girl and became involved with her
after his return. Although the peasant does not look dangerous, it
is still better to render him harmless. Aurelio has to fight in self-
defense when assaulted, and has to escape as a result: there is no
justice for the poor.

Pueblerina is perhaps the most socially radical of Fernández'
works and it would appear, perhaps unexpectedly, that his films belong in a way to militant art. The picture distinguishes itself by
its ultimate degree of photographic stylization. The black-and-white
quality of the plot and the lack of depth of the characters are complemented by Figueroa's high-contrast, monumental photography. It
was to be cinematic equivalent of the traditions of Mexican art--and
it has indeed become so, although this time it would appear definitely to be overdone.

While in Maria Candelaria the role of photography was generally descriptive, here the composition of the frame often dictated
the arrangement of situations; the rhythm of the story becomes too
majestic and the landscapes assume an almost exclusively ornamental
role. And yet there is something great in this folk poem: its convention requires acceptance of a highly atypical aesthetic key, but
in exchange offers a contact with an original artistic statement, dignified and straightforward.

ON THE TOWN   Gene Kelly and Stanley Donen

Script: Adolph Green and Betty Comden, based on their musical
(with music by Leonard Bernstein), from an idea by Jerome Robbins
(his ballet "Fancy Free"). Photography: Harold Rosson. Choreog-

raphy: Kelly and Donen. Art Direction: Cedric Gibbons and Jack
Martin Smith. Music: Roger Edens and Lennie Hayton. Cast:
Gene Kelly (Gabey), Frank Sinatra (Chip), Jules Munshin (Ozzie),
Betty Garrett (Brunhilde Esterhazy), Ann Miller (Claire Huddesen),
Vera-Ellen (Ivy Smith), Florence Bates (Madame Dilyovska), Alice
Pearce (Lucy Shmeeler), George Meader (Professor).

MGM, U.S.A. 8803 ft., 98 mins. Technicolor.

It would not be right to say that the musical was born with the appearance of The Jazz Singer (1927), the legendary Al Jolson vehicle.
That film, hailed as the first talkie, was in fact silent save for the
singing sequences and pictures built on music were for a long time
after merely filmed cabaret acts consisting of separate "numbers"
(thus their poor fluency) and they dated very quickly. The road
from the music-hall to the musical was a long one and only on the
threshold of the 50's did the cinema develop its own style of dealing
with music on the screen.

On the Town is virtually the first formally successful musical.
The film accompanies three sailors in New York on a 24-hour leave
from their battleship. Kelly finds the girl he saw on a poster,
Sinatra fancies a lady taxi-driver, Munshin a pretty archeology student. On the Town was made on real New York City locations; the
numbers are perfectly blended and stem naturally and spontaneously
from the situations; fast tempo and pleasant colors (slightly garish,
which reinforces the 40's touch) complete the picture. The best
songs are "We're Going on the Town," "New York, New York," and
"Prehistoric Joe."

INDEX OF DIRECTORS

This index lists the names of all directors appearing in this volume ("Journey One, " through 1949) whose films are (or will be in a subsequent volume) discussed as separate entries. Directors whose films are only mentioned in passing are not included.

The chronological list of films after the page reference(s) under each director's name contains all relevant films in the period covered by the text. If a film is discussed in the book as a separate entry, it is marked with an asterisk * and if the original title of such a film is in a language other than English, it is given in parentheses following the English title.

For a film merely mentioned, only the English title--or the title used in English-speaking countries-- is given (without an asterisk). (Note that for some films, e.g. Yves Allégret's three, the original, or foreign-language, title is also the one used in English-speaking countries.)

Alexandrov, Grigori 100, 110, 129, 200, 231-2, 291-2
  (1934) *Jolly Fellows (Vesyolye Rebyata)
  (1936) Circus
  (1938) *Volga-Volga

Allégret, Marc 212-3
  (1932) *Fanny

Allégret, Yves 482-3, 518
  (1947) Dédée d'Anvers
  (1948) *Une si jolie petite plage
  (1949) *Manèges

Antonioni, Michelangelo 446

Asquith, Anthony 198-9, 288-9, 387, 402-3, 484
  (1929) A Cottage on Dartmoor
  (1931) *Tell England
  (1938) *Pygmalion
  (1945) *The Way to the Stars

  (1948) *The Winslow Boy

Autant-Lara, Claude 355, 371, 419, 519
  (1927) Construire un feu
  (1941) Mariage de Chiffon
  (1942) Lettres d'amour
  (1943) *Douce
  (1946) *Le Diable au corps
  (1949) *Occupe-toi d'Amelie

Bacon, Lloyd 377-8
  (1943) *Action in the North Atlantic

Bán, Frigyes 478-9
  (1948) *The Soil Under Your Feet (Talpalatnyi Föld)

Barkas, Geoffrey 198
  (1931) *Tell England

Barnet, Boris 158
(1928) *The House in
    Trubnaya Street (Dom
    na Trubnoy)

Becker, Jacques 355, 445,
    452-3
(1942) Dernier atout
(1942) *Goupi Mains Rouges
(1947) *Antoine et Antoinette

Bergman, Ingmar 67, 113, 142,
    365, 383

Blasetti, Alessandro 168, 170,
    217-8, 356
(1929) *Sun (Sole)
(1933) *1860
(1942) *Four Steps in the
    Clouds (Quattro Passi fra
    le Nuvole)

Blystone, Jack G. 88
(1923) *Our Hospitality

Boese, Carl 60
(1920) *The Golem (Der
    Golem, wie er in die
    Welt kam)

Borzage, Frank 140
(1927) *Seventh Heaven

Bresson, Robert 126, 355,
    364, 367-8, 403-4, 451
(1943) *Les Anges du péché
(1945) *Les Dames du Bois
    de Boulogne

Brooks, Richard 491

Brown, Clarence 504
(1949) *Intruder in the Dust

Bruckman, Clyde 88, 101-2,
    115, 119
(1926) *The General

Buñuel, Luis 72, 131, 151,
    244, 399, 506-7
(1928) Un Chien andalou
(1930) L'Age d'or
(1949) *Los Olvidados

Cacoyannis, Michael 449

Camerini, Mario 169, 170, 212,
    248-9, 283, 369, 478
(1929) *Rails (Rotaie)
(1932) *What Rascals Men Are!
    (Gli Uomini, Che Mascal-
    zoni!)
(1935) *I'll Give a Million
    (Darò un Milione)
(1937) *Il Signor Max
(1948) *The Street Has Many
    Dreams (Molti Sogni per le
    Strade)

Capra, Frank 225, 249, 254-5,
    264, 283, 295, 338, 357, 379,
    389, 461
(1934) *It Happened One Night
(1936) *Mr. Deeds Goes to
    Town
(1938) *You Can't Take It With
    You
(1939) Mr. Smith Goes to
    Washington
(1944) *Arsenic and Old Lace

Carné, Marcel 34, 135, 240,
    273-4, 287, 302-3, 347-8,
    394-5, 436, 455
(1936) Jenny
(1937) *Drôle de drame
(1938) *Quai des Brumes
(1939) *Le Jour se lève
(1942) *Les Visiteurs du soir
(1945) *Les Enfants du paradis

Cassavetes, John 489

Cavalcanti, Alberto 139
(1927) *En Rade

Cayatte, André 180, 360, 520

Chaplin, Charles 30, 32-3, 50-1,
    67-8, 74, 77-8, 88, 90-2, 98,
    102, 111-3, 120, 137-8, 146-7,
    149, 158, 172-3, 175-6, 194,
    202, 207, 249-51, 255, 260,
    265, 317, 322-4, 354, 369,
    440-1, 458
(1918) *Shoulder Arms
(1921) *The Kid

(1921) The Idle Class
(1922) Pay Day
(1922) *The Pilgrim
(1923) *A Woman of Paris
(1925) *The Gold Rush
(1927) *The Circus
(1930) *City Lights
(1936) *Modern Times
(1940) *The Great Dictator
(1947) *Monsieur Verdoux

Charell, Erik 188-9
(1931) *The Congress Dances
     (Der Kongress tantzt)

Chenal, Pierre 235, 495
(1934) *Crime and Punish-
     ment (Crime et châtiment)
(1948) *Clochemerle

Christensen, Benjamin 71-2, 364
(1921) *Witchcraft Through
     the Ages (Häxan)
(1929) Seven Footprints to
     Satan

Christian-Jaque 234, 290-1,
     339, 408-9, 456
(1938) *Les Disparus de
     Saint-Agil
(1941) *The Murder of Father
     Christmas (L'Assassinat du
     Père Noël)
(1945) *Boule de Suif
(1947) *La Chartreuse de
     Parme

Chukhrai, Grigori 138

Clair, René 33-4, 74, 102,
     133-4, 146-7, 153, 175-6,
     187, 206-7, 212, 214-5,
     243, 249, 251, 354, 367,
     385-6, 413, 437-8, 453,
     461, 501-2, 519
(1923) Paris qui dort
(1924) Entr'acte
(1927) *The Italian Straw
     Hat (Un Chapeau de
     paille d'Italie)
(1928) La Tour
(1928) *Les Deux timides
(1930) *Sous les toits de
     Paris
(1931) *Le Million
(1932) *À nous la liberté
(1933) *Quatorze Juillet
(1934) Le Dernier milliardaire
(1935) *The Ghost Goes West
(1941) The Flame of New
     Orleans
(1942) *I Married a Witch
(1944) *It Happened Tomorrow
(1947) *Le Silence est d'or
(1949) *La Beauté du diable

Clément, René 105, 396-7, 425-
     6, 453-4, 486, 494
(1945) *La Bataille du rail
(1946) *Beauty and the Beast
     (La Belle et la bête)
(1946) Le Père tranquille
(1947) *Les Maudits
(1948) *Le Mura di Malapaga

Clouzot, Henri-Georges 355, 360,
     362-3, 438-9, 473-4, 482
(1942) L'Assassin habite au 21
(1943) *The Crow (Le Corbeau)
(1947) *Quai des Orfèvres
(1948) *Manon

Cocteau, Jean 403, 425-6, 453,
     494, 514-5
(1930) Le Sang d'un poète
(1946) *Beauty and the Beast
     (La Belle et la bête)
(1948) *Les Parents terribles

Cornelius, Henry 496
(1948) *Passport to Pimlico

Coward, Noël 352-3, 387, 400,
     412-3, 421
(1942) *In Which We Serve

Crisp, Donald 42, 55, 102
(1924) *The Navigator

Cruze, James 32, 89-90
(1923) *The Covered Wagon

Cukor, George 329, 391-2
(1940) *The Philadelphia Story
(1944) *Gaslight
(1949) Adam's Rib

Curtiz, Michael xxii, 245, 300-
1, 342-3, 361, 413
  (1935) *Captain Blood
  (1938) *The Adventures of
    Robin Hood
  (1941) *The Sea Wolf
  (1942) *Casablanca
  (1945) *Mildred Pierce

Damiani, Damiano 513

Daquin, Louis 335-6, 377
  (1941) *Us Kids (Nous, les
    gosses)

Dassin, Jules 442, 444-5,
470-1, 504-5
  (1947) *Brute Force
  (1948) *The Naked City
  (1949) *Thieves' Highway

Daves, Delmer 455
  (1947) *Dark Passage

Decoin, Henri 360
  (1942) *Strangers in the
    House (Les Inconnus dans
    la maison)

Delannoy, Jean 358-9, 426-7,
443-4
  (1942) *Pontcarral
  (1945) *La Symphonie pas-
    torale
  (1947) *Les Jeux sont faits

De Santis, Giuseppe 350, 430,
446-7, 499-500, 505
  (1947) *The Tragic Pursuit
    (Caccia Tragica)
  (1949) *Bitter Rice (Riso
    Amaro)

De Sica, Vittorio 37, 212, 248-
9, 283, 369-70, 423-4, 465-6
  (1943) *The Children Are
    Watching Us (I Bambini
    Ci Guardano)
  (1946) *Shoeshine (Sciuscià)
  (1948) *Bicycle Thieves
    (Ladri di Biciclette)

Dickinson, Thorold 330-1, 357-
8, 387, 391
  (1940) *Gaslight
  (1942) *Next of Kin

Dieterle, William 75, 107, 265-
6, 282, 327, 378
  (1936) *The Story of Louis
    Pasteur
  (1937) *The Life of Émile
    Zola
  (1940) *Dr. Ehrlich's Magic
    Bullet

Disney, Walt 34, 275-6, 319
  (1928) Steamboat Willie
  (1937) *Snow White and The
    Seven Dwarfs
  (1940) *Fantasia

Dmytryk, Edward 511-2
  (1947) Crossfire
  (1949) *Give Us This Day

Donen, Stanley 521-2
  (1949) *On the Town

Donskoy, Mark 286, 295-6
  (1938) *The Childhood of
    Maxim Gorky (Detstvo
    Gorkovo)
  (1938) *Among People (V
    Lyudyakh)
  (1939) My Universities

Dovzhenko, Olexandr 32, 171-2,
252, 309
  (1930) *Earth (Zemla)

Dréville, Jean 488
  (1948) *As Others See Us
    (Les Casse-pieds)

Dreyer, Carl Theodor 61-2, 106,
114-5, 126-7, 190, 194-5, 233,
363-5
  (1919) The President
  (1920) Leaves from Satan's
    Book
  (1920) *The Parson's Widow
    (Prästänkan)
  (1924) Mikaël
  (1925) *Master of the House

(Du Skal Aere Din
Hustru)
(1927) *The Passion of Joan
of Arc (La Passion de
Jeanne d'Arc)
(1931) *Vampyr, ou l'étrange
aventure de David Gray
(1943) *Day of Wrath
(Vredens Dag)

Dupont, Ewald André 99, 112-
3, 116
(1925) *Vaudeville (Varieté)

Duvivier, Julien 203-4, 262-
4, 276-7, 291, 312, 461
(1932) *Poil de carotte
(1936) *Pépé le Moko
(1936) *La Belle équipe
(1937) *Un Carnet de bal
(1939) *La Fin du jour

Dzigan, Yefim 253
(1936) *We from Kronstadt
(My iz Kronshtata)

Eisenstein, Sergei 32, 35,
94, 100-1, 105, 110-1,
118-9, 125, 128-30, 156,
163, 165, 171-2, 197,
200-1, 231-2, 236, 253-
4, 259, 271-3, 284-5, 334,
373, 380-1, 383, 415-6,
443
(1924) *Strike (Stachka)
(1925) *Battleship Potemkin
(Bronenosets "Potyom-
kin")
(1927) *October (Oktyabr)
(1929) The Old and the New
(1932) * ¡Que Viva Mexico!
(1937) *Bezhin Meadow
(Bezhin Lug)
(1938) *Alexander Nevsky
(Alexandr Nevsky)
(1944) *Ivan the Terrible
(Ivan Grozny)
(1946) *The Boyars' Plot
(Boyarski Zagovor)

Ekk, Nikolai 189-90

(1931) *A Pass to Life
(Putyovka v Zhizn)

Epstein, Jean 31, 82, 87-8,
92, 139, 144, 152, 194, 198,
222
(1922) Pasteur
(1922) *L'Auberge rouge
(1923) *Coeur fidèle
(1923) *La Belle Nivernaise
(1928) *The Fall of the House
of Usher (La Chute de la
maison Usher)
(1928) *Finis Terrae
(1930) Mor-Vran
(1931) *L'Or des mers

Ermler, Friedrich 164, 209,
247-8, 307, 313-4, 404-5
(1929) *Fragment of an Empire (Oblomok Imperii)
(1932) *Counterplan (Vstrechnyi)
(1935) *Peasants (Krestyaniye)
(1939) *A Great Citizen
(Veliky Grazhdanin)
(1945) *The Great Turning
Point (Veliky Perelom)

Etaix, Pierre 74

Fejös, Pál 145, 211, 461
(1928) *Lonesome
(1932) *Marie, a Hungarian
Legend (Tavaszi Zápor)

Fellini, Federico 71, 401, 417,
483, 489, 512

Fernández, Emilio 373-4, 497-
8, 507, 521
(1943) *Maria Candelaria
(Xochimilco)
(1948) *Maclovia
(1949) *Pueblerina

Feyder, Jacques 34, 81-2, 105-
6, 132, 152-3, 215-6, 228-9,
241-2, 260, 287, 290, 294
(1922) *Crainquebille
(1924) *Visages d'enfants

(1927) *Thérèse Raquin (Du
    sollst nicht ehebrechen)
(1928) *Les Nouveaux
    messieurs
(1929) The Kiss
(1933) *Le Grand jeu
(1934) *Pension Mimosas
(1935) *Carnival in Flanders
    (La Kermesse héroïque)
(1939) La Piste du Nord

Flaherty, Robert 36, 157,
185-6, 224-5, 236, 466-7
(1921) Nanook of the North
(1925) Moana
(1931) *Tabu
(1931) Industrial Britain
(1934) *Man of Aran
(1937) Elephant Boy
(1948) *Louisiana Story

Fleischer, Dave 34, 319
(1939) *Gulliver's Travels

Ford, Aleksander 479-80
(1948) *Border Street
    (Ulica Graniczna)

Ford, John 32, 34, 106,
210, 234, 237-9, 263, 279,
303-5, 314, 316, 321-2, 341-
2, 407, 409-10, 412, 428-9,
436, 493, 516-7
(1924) *The Iron Horse
(1932) *Arrowsmith
(1934) *The Lost Patrol
(1935) *The Informer
(1939) *Stagecoach
(1939) *Young Mr. Lincoln
(1940) *The Grapes of Wrath
(1941) *How Green Was My
    Valley
(1946) *My Darling Clemen-
    tine
(1948) *Fort Apache
(1949) *She Wore a Yellow
    Ribbon

Forst, Willi 234-5
(1933) Unfinished Symphony
(1934) *Maskerade

Franju, Georges 229

Frend, Charles 370, 492
(1943) *San Demetrio, London
(1948) *Scott of the Antarctic

Frič, Martin 240, 464
(1934) Heave-ho!
(1935) *Jánošík

Gance, Abel 31, 87, 92-4, 297
(1919) J'accuse
(1923) *La Roue
(1927) Napoléon

Germi, Pietro 512-3
(1949) *In the Name of the
    Law (In Nome della Legge)

Gosho, Heinosuke 35, 202
(1931) The Neighbour's Wife
    and Mine

Grangier, Gilles 374
(1943) *Adémaï, bandit
    d'honneur

Grémillion, Jean 376-7
(1943) *Le Ciel est à vous

Griffith, D. W. 30, 41-6, 55-6,
62-3, 67, 69-71, 82, 87, 89-
90, 94, 135, 290, 334, 427
(1915) *The Birth of a Nation
(1916) *Intolerance
(1918) Hearts of the World
(1919) *Broken Blossoms
(1920) *Way Down East

Hamer, Robert 370, 515-6
(1949) *Kind Hearts and
    Coronets

Hathaway, Henry 244, 407-8,
441-2, 445-6, 473
(1935) *Peter Ibbetson
(1936) The Trail of the Lone-
    some Pine
(1945) *The House on 92nd
    Street
(1947) *Kiss of Death

(1947) *Call Northside 777

Hawks, Howard 32, 192, 207-
8, 310-1, 340-1, 366-7,
424-5, 471-3
(1932) *Scarface
(1939) *His Girl Friday
(1941) *Sergeant York
(1943) *Air Force
(1944) To Have and Have
Not
(1946) *The Big Sleep
(1948) *Red River

Henning-Jensen, Astrid &
Björne 452
(1947) *Ditta, Child of Man
(Ditte Menneskebarn)

Hill, George 180
(1930) *The Big House

Hitchcock, Alfred 34, 121,
166-7, 181, 195, 199, 216,
224, 229-30, 249, 260-1,
268, 280, 292-3, 299, 317,
320, 326-7, 344-5, 368-9,
372, 388, 418, 439, 471,
487, 517-8
(1925) The Pleasure Garden
(1926) *The Lodger
(1929) *Blackmail
(1930) *Murder
(1934) *The Man Who Knew
Too Much
(1935) *The Thirty-Nine
Steps
(1936) *The Secret Agent
(1936) Sabotage
(1937) *Young and Innocent
(1938) *The Lady Vanishes
(1939) Jamaica Inn
(1940) *Foreign Corres-
pondent
(1941) *Suspicion
(1943) *Shadow of a Doubt
(1943) *Lifeboat
(1945) Spellbound
(1946) *Notorious
(1948) *Rope
(1949) *Under Capricorn

Howard, Leslie 288-9

(1938) *Pygmalion

Huston, John 327, 336-7, 448-
9, 473, 491
(1941) *The Maltese Falcon
(1947) *The Treasure of
Sierra Madre
(1948) *Key Largo

Imamura, Shohei 258

Innemann, Svatopluk 210
(1932) *Before Matriculation
(Před Maturitou)

Jakubowska, Wanda 469-70
(1948) *The Last Stage
(Ostatni Etap)

Jessner, Leopold 75-6, 108,
113
(1921) *Backstairs (Hintertreppe)

Junghans, Karl 162-3
(1929) *Such Is Life (Takový
Je Život)

Jutzi, Phil 165
(1929) *Mother Krause's
Journey to Happiness
(Mutter Krausens Fahrt
ins Glück)

Kádar, Ján 428

Kazan, Elia 406-7, 445, 449-
50, 461
(1945) *A Tree Grows in
Brooklyn
(1947) Gentleman's Agree-
ment
(1947) *Boomerang!

Keaton, Buster 30, 32, 67-8,
74, 88-9, 101-3, 115, 117,
119, 120-1, 123-4, 149-50,

154-5, 167-8, 307, 460
(1921) Cops
(1923) The Three Ages
(1923) *Our Hospitality
(1924) *Sherlock Junior
(1924) *The Navigator
(1925) *Seven Chances
(1925) *Go West
(1926) *Battling Butler
(1926) *The General
(1927) College

Keighley, William 300
(1938) *The Adventures of
Robin Hood

Kelly, Gene 521-2
(1949) *On the Town

Kheifits, Yosif 258-9
(1936) *Baltic Deputy
(Deputat Baltiki)

Kinugasa, Teinosuke 147-8
(1926) A Page of Madness
(1928) *Crossways (Jūji-ro)

Klos, Elmar 428-9

Korda, Alexander 34, 193,
213, 219-20, 259-60, 266-
7, 299, 323
(1931) *Marius
(1933) *The Private Life of
Henry VIII
(1936) *Rembrandt

Korda, Zoltan 376, 466
(1937) Elephant Boy
(1943) *Sahara

Kozintsev, Grigori 226-7,
271, 294
(1924) Adventures of Ok-
tyabrina
(1926) The Cloak
(1931) Alone
(1934) *The Youth of Maxim
(Yunost Maksima)
(1937) *The Return of
Maxim (Vozvrashcheniye
Maksima)
(1938) *The Vyborg Side

(Vyborgskaya Storona)

Krejčík, Jiří 496
(1948) *Conscience (Svědomí)

Kurosawa, Akira 36-7, 343-4,
360, 365-6, 395-6, 433-4,
461-2, 475-6, 503
(1943) *Judo Saga (Sugata
Sanshiro)
(1945) *They Who Step on the
Tiger's Tail (Tora no O-o
Fumu Otokotachi)
(1946) *No Regrets for My
Youth (Waga Seishun ni
Kuinashi)
(1947) *One Wonderful Sunday
(Subarashiki Nichiyobi)
(1948) *Drunken Angel
(Yoidore Tenshi)
(1949) *Stray Dog (Nora Inu)

Lamprecht, Gerhard 196
(1931) *Emil and the Detectives (Emil und die Detektive)

Lang, Fritz 31, 65-6, 69, 78-
9, 103-5, 110, 122-3, 125,
153-4, 183-4, 218-9, 230,
256-7, 274, 325-6, 345-6,
385, 388, 432
(1919) The Spiders
(1921) *Destiny (Der müde
Tod)
(1922) *Dr. Mabuse, the
Gambler (Dr. Mabuse, der
Spieler)
(1924) *Nibelungen (Die
Nibelungen)
(1926) *Metropolis
(1928) *The Spies (Spione)
(1931) *M
(1933) *The Testament of Dr.
Mabuse (Das Testament des
Dr. Mabuse)
(1934) Liliom
(1936) *Fury
(1940) *The Return of Frank
James
(1941) *Western Union

(1944) *The Woman in the
    Window

Lattuada, Alberto 434, 483,
    489-90
(1946) *The Bandit (Il
    Bandito)
(1948) *Without Pity (Senza
    Pietà)
(1948) *The Mill on the Po
    (Il Mulino del Po)

Lean, David 36, 352, 400-1,
    412-3, 420-1, 490
(1942) *In Which We Serve
(1945) *Blithe Spirit
(1945) *Brief Encounter
(1946) *Great Expectations
(1947) This Happy Breed
(1948) *Oliver Twist

Le Chanois, Jean-Paul 485-6
(1948) *L'École buissonnière

Leenhardt, Roger 462-3
(1947) *Les Dernières
    vacances

Lejtes, Józef 238
(1934) *The Young Trees
    (Młody Las)

Leni, Paul 31, 75, 107-8,
    266
(1921) *Backstairs (Hinter-
    treppe)
(1924) *Waxworks (Das
    Wachsfigurenkabinett)

Le Roy, Mervyn 32, 179,
    204-5, 274-5, 378
(1930) *Little Caesar
(1932) *I Am a Fugitive
    from a Chain Gang
(1937) *They Won't Forget
(1943) *Madame Curie

L'Herbier, Marcel 31, 59,
    74-5, 87
(1920) *L'Homme du large
(1921) *Eldorado

Linder, Max 30, 73-4, 84-5,

146
(1921) *Seven Years' Bad Luck
(1922) Be My Wife
(1922) *The Three Must-Get-
    Theres

Lindtberg, Leopold 405
(1945) *The Last Chance (Die
    letzte Chance)

Litvak, Anatole 317, 445, 480-
    1, 484-5
(1939) *Confessions of a Nazi
    Spy
(1948) *The Snake Pit
(1948) *Sorry, Wrong Number

Lizzani, Carlo 430, 436, 446,
    499

Lubitsch, Ernst 64, 320
(1939) *Ninotchka

Mach, Josef 463-4
(1947) *No One Knows a Thing
    (Nikdo Nic Neví)

Malle, Louis 229

Mamoulian, Rouben 195-6, 247
(1931) *City Streets
(1931) Dr. Jekyll and Mr.
    Hyde
(1933) Queen Christina
(1935) Becky Sharp

Melville, Jean-Pierre 450-1,
    494, 514-5
(1947) *Le Silence de la mer
(1949) *Les Enfants terribles

Meyers, Sidney 488
(1948) *The Quiet One

Milestone, Lewis 177-8, 192,
    310-1, 314-5, 410-1
(1930) *All Quiet on the
    Western Front
(1931) *The Front Page
(1939) *Of Mice and Men
(1945) *A Walk in the Sun

Mizoguchi, Kenji 35, 246,
   255-8, 307-8, 462
   (1926) Paper Doll's Whis-
      per of Spring
   (1936) *Osaka Elegy (Na-
      niwa Erejī)
   (1936) *Sisters of the Gion
      (Gion no Shimai)
   (1939) *The Story of the
      Last Chrysanthemum
      (Zangiku Monogatari)

Monicelli, Mario 512

Murata, Minoru 69-70
   (1921) *Souls on the Road
      (Rojō no Reikon)

Murnau, Friedrich Wilhelm
   31, 79-80, 98-9, 128-9,
   140, 158-9, 174, 185-6,
   421
   (1922) *Nosferatu (Nosferatu
      --Eine Symphonie des
      Grauens)
   (1924) *The Last Laugh
      (Der letzte Mann)
   (1927) *Sunrise
   (1928) Four Devils
   (1928) *Our Daily Bread
   (1931) *Tabu

Naruse, Mikio 35, 245-6
   (1935) *Wife, Be Like a
      Rose (Tsuma Yō Bara
      no Yoni)

Olivier, Laurence 36, 38,
   318-9, 382-3, 421, 468-9
   (1944) *Henry V
   (1948) *Hamlet

Ophüls, Max 151, 205-6,
   234, 472-3
   (1932) *Liebelei
   (1948) *Letter from an
      Unknown Woman

Ozu, Yasujiro 35, 202-3,
216-7, 265, 359-60, 462,
500-1
   (1931) Chorus of Tokyo
   (1932) *I Was Born, but...
      (Umarete-wā Mita Keredo)
   (1933) *Passing Fancy
      (Dekigokoro)
   (1936) *The Only Son (Hitori
      Musuko)
   (1941) The Toda Brother
      and His Sisters
   (1942) *There Was a Father
      (Chichi Ariki)
   (1949) *Late Spring (Banshun)

Pabst, G. W. 31, 116, 136-7,
   144-5, 148, 161-2, 165, 176-
   8, 182-5, 220, 231, 311
   (1925) *The Joyless Street
      (Die freudlose Gasse)
   (1926) Secrets of a Soul
   (1927) *The Love of Jeanne
      Ney (Die Liebe der Jeanne
      Ney)
   (1928) *Pandora's Box (Die
      Büchse der Pandora)
   (1929) *Diary of a Lost Girl
      (Das Tagebuch einer
      Verlorenen)
   (1930) *Westfront 1918
   (1931) *The Threepenny Opera
      (Die Dreigroschenoper)
   (1931) *Kameradschaft
   (1933) *Don Quixote (Don
      Quichotte)

Pagnol, Marcel 193-4, 212-3,
   236-7, 261-2, 315-6, 469
   (1934) *Angèle
   (1936) *César
   (1939) *The Baker's Wife (La
      Femme du boulanger)

Panfilov, Gleb 126

Pascal, Gabriel 328-9
   (1940) *Major Barbara

Pastrone, Giovanni 40-1
   (1913) *Cabiria

Penn, Arthur 353

Petri, Elio 513

Petrov, Vladimir 300, 405
(1938) *Peter the First
(Pyotr Pervyi)
(1949) The Stalingrad Battle

Pick, Lupu 31, 72-3, 95,
113, 153-4, 231, 303
(1921) *Shattered (Scherben)
(1923) *New Year's Eve
(Sylvester--Tragödie
einer Nacht)

Piscator, Erwin 230-1
(1934) *Revolt of the Fishermen (Vosstaniye Ry-
bakov)

Powell, Michael 345
(1941) *49th Parallel

Preminger, Otto 388-9
(1944) *Laura

Protazanov, Yakov 56, 138
(1927) *The Forty-First
(Sorok Pervyi)

Pudovkin, Vsevolod 32, 118-
9, 124, 127-8, 137, 141-2,
162, 165, 271, 380
(1925) Chess Fever
(1926) *Mother (Mat)
(1927) *The End of St. Petersburg (Konyets Sankt-
Peterburga)
(1928) *Storm Over Asia
(Potomok Chingiskhana)

Radványi, Géza 447-8
(1947) *Somewhere in Europe
(Valahol Európában...)

Ray, Nicholas 457, 519-20
(1947) *They Live by Night
(1949) *Knock on Any Door

Reed, Carol 36, 299, 311-2,

386-7, 435-6, 467-8, 507-8
(1938) *Bank Holiday
(1939) *The Stars Look Down
(1941) Kipps
(1942) Young Mr. Pitt
(1944) *The Way Ahead
(1947) *Odd Man Out
(1948) *The Fallen Idol
(1949) *The Third Man

Reisner, Charles F. 67, 149
(1928) *Steamboat Bill Jr.

Renoir, Jean 33-4, 151, 182,
227-8, 242-3, 251-2, 263,
269-70, 291, 296-7, 305-7,
350-1, 371, 409-10, 518
(1931) La Chienne
(1932) Boudu Saved from
Drowning
(1934) *Toni
(1935) *Le Crime de M. Lange
(1936) La Vie est à nous
(1936) *Partie de campagne
(1937) *La Grande illusion
(1937) La Marseillaise
(1938) *La Bête humaine
(1939) *La Règle du jeu
(1941) Tosca
(1941) Swamp Water
(1945) *The Southerner

Resnais, Alain 164

Richardson, Tony 199

Robison, Arthur 83-4
(1922) *Warning Shadows
(Schatten--Eine nächtliche
Halluzination)

Robson, Mark 332, 509, 513-4
(1949) *Champion

Romm, Mikhail 233-4, 263-4,
281, 409
(1934) *Boule de Suif (Pyshka)
(1936) *The Thirteen
(Trinadtsat)
(1937) *Lenin in October
(Lenin v Oktyabre)
(1939) Lenin in 1918

Room, Abram 125, 135-6, 158, 163
(1926) *Death Bay (Bukhta Smerti)
(1927) *Bed and Sofa (Tretya Meshchanskaya)
(1929) *The Ghost That Will Not Return (Privideniye, Kotoroye Ne Vozvrash-chayetsya)

Rosi, Francesco 513

Rossellini, Roberto 37, 170, 401-2, 417-8, 431, 436-7
(1945) *Rome, Open City (Roma, Città Aperta)
(1946) *Paisà
(1947) *Germany Year Zero (Germania Anno Zero)

Rossen, Robert 342, 508-9
(1947) Body and Soul
(1949) *All the King's Men

Rovenský, Josef 221, 246-7
(1933) *The River (Reka)
(1935) *Maryša

Rye, Stellan 39
(1913) *The Student of Prague (Der Student von Prag)

Sagan, Leontine 187
(1931) *Girls in Uniforms (Mädchen in Uniform)

Sanin, Alexandr 56
(1919) *Polikushka

Schnéevoigt, George 61, 114, 190
(1931) *Hotel Paradis

Sedgwick, Edward 154-5, 167
(1928) *The Cameraman
(1929) *Spite Marriage

Shengelaya, Nikolai 155-6
(1928) *Eliso

Siodmak, Robert 197, 432-3, 481-2
(1930) People on Sunday
(1946) *The Killers
(1949) *Criss Cross

Sjöberg, Alf 351-2, 383-4
(1942) *The Road to Heaven (Himlaspelet)
(1944) *Frenzy (Hets)

Sjöström, Victor xxii, 31, 46-9, 54, 58-9, 71, 83, 108-9, 113, 123, 142, 163, 174, 352
(1913) Ingeborg Holm
(1916) *A Man There Was (Terje Vigen)
(1917) *The Outlaw and His Wife (Berg-Ejvind och Hans Hustru)
(1920) *The Phantom Carriage (Körkarlen)
(1924) *He Who Gets Slapped
(1926) *The Scarlet Letter
(1928) *The Wind

Staudte, Wolfgang 431-2
(1946) *The Murderers Are Among Us (Die Mörder sind unter uns)

Steklý, Karel 458
(1947) *The Strike (Siréna)

Stevens, George 379
(1943) *The More the Merrier

Stevenson, Robert 224, 267-8
(1936) *Tudor Rose

Stiller, Mauritz 31, 46, 53-4, 58, 108, 174, 352, 381
(1919) *Sir Arne's Treasure (Herr Arnes Pengar)
(1920) *Erotikon
(1924) The Saga of Gösta Berling

Sturges, Preston 338-9, 392
(1940) The Great McGinty
(1941) *Sullivan's Travels
(1944) The Miracle of Morgan Creek

(1944) *Hail the Conquering
    Hero

Tarich, Yuri 124
(1926) *Wings of a Serf
    (Krylya Kholopa)

Tati, Jacques 459-60
(1947) *Jour de fête

Trauberg, Ilya 164-5, 170
(1929) *The Blue Express
    (Goluboi Ekspress)

Trauberg, Leonid 226, 271,
    294
(1924) Adventures of Oktya-
    brina
(1926) The Cloak
(1931) Alone
(1934) *The Youth of Maxim
    (Yunost Maksima)
(1937) *The Return of Maxim
    (Vozvrashcheniye Mak-
    sima)
(1938) *The Vyborg Side
    (Vyborgskaya Storona)

Truffaut, François 176, 229

Uchida, Tomu 266-7, 308-9,
    344
(1936) *Theatre of Life
    (Jinsei Gekijō)
(1937) The Naked Town
(1939) *Earth (Tsuchi)

Ustinov, Peter 386

Vančura, Vladislav 210-1
(1932) *Before Matriculation
    (Před Maturitou)

Van Dyke, Woodbridge S. 157
(1928) *White Shadows on
    the South Seas

Vasiliev, Sergei & Georgy 223
(1934) *Chapayev

Vávra, Otakar 293, 463
(1938) *The Guild of the
    Kutná Hora Maidens
    (Cech Panen Kutnohorských)
(1947) *Presentiment
    (Předtucha)

Vergano, Aldo 168, 430-1
(1946) *The Sun Rises Again
    (Il Sole Sorge Ancora)

Vidor, King 33, 113-4, 143,
    146, 160-1, 232-3, 298, 328
(1925) *The Big Parade
(1928) *The Crowd
(1929) *Hallelujah!
(1934) *Our Daily Bread
(1938) *The Citadel
(1940) *Northwest Passage

Vigo, Jean 92, 222-3
(1929) À propos de Nice
(1933) Zéro de conduite
(1934) *L'Atalante

Visconti, Luchino 37, 218, 350-
    1, 356, 476-7
(1942) *Ossessione
(1948) *La Terra Trema

Von Gerlach, Arthur 85
(1922) *Vanina (Vanina oder
    die Galgenhochzeit)

Von Sternberg, Josef 32, 109,
    134-5, 140, 148-9, 151, 157,
    161, 169, 173-5, 179, 188,
    197-8, 288
(1925) Salvation Hunters
(1927) *Underworld
(1928) The Drag Net
(1928) *The Docks of New York
(1930) *The Blue Angel (Der
    blaue Engel)
(1931) *An American Tragedy

Von Stroheim, Erich 44, 68-9,
    91, 96-8, 130-2, 150-1, 156-7,
    162, 174, 228, 269, 290-1,
    306, 371, 439

(1918) Blind Husbands
(1919) The Devil's Passkey
(1921) *Foolish Wives
(1924) *Greed
(1925) Merry Widow
(1927) *The Wedding March
(1928) *The Honeymoon
(1928) *Queen Kelly
(1933) Walking Down
        Broadway

Walsh, Raoul 460
(1947) *Pursued

Watt, Harry 375, 411-2
(1941) Target for Tonight
(1942) Night Mail
(1943) *Nine Men
(1945) *The Overlanders

Wegener, Paul 31, 39, 60-1, 86
(1920) *The Golem (Der
        Golem, wie er in die
        Welt kam)

Weiss, Jiří 458

Welles, Orson 37-8, 138,
  272, 279, 317, 332-5, 348-
  50, 440, 442-3
(1938) Too Much Johnson
(1941) *Citizen Kane
(1942) *The Magnificent
        Ambersons
(1947) *The Lady from
        Shanghai
(1947) *Macbeth

Wellman, William A. 32, 179,
  191, 353, 376, 398, 474-5
(1931) *Public Enemy
(1937) A Star Is Born
(1937) Nothing Sacred
(1942) *The Ox-Bow Incident
(1945) *The Story of G.I. Joe
(1948) *Yellow Sky

Wiene, Robert 31, 52, 108
(1919) *The Cabinet of Dr.
        Caligari (Das Kabinett
        des Dr. Caligari)

Wilder, Billy 151, 168, 196-7,
  387-8, 399, 445, 485
(1944) *Double Indemnity
(1945) *The Lost Weekend

Wise, Robert 332, 509-10, 513
(1949) *The Set-Up

Wyler, William 278, 289-90,
  307, 318-9, 339-40, 356-7,
  442-3, 510-1
(1937) *Dead End
(1938) *Jezebel
(1939) *Wuthering Heights
(1941) *The Little Foxes
(1942) *Mrs. Miniver
(1946) *The Best Years of
        Our Lives
(1949) *The Heiress

Yamamoto, Kajiro 343, 365
(1941) *Horse (Uma)

Yamanaka, Sadao 279-80, 360
(1937) *Humanity Like a Paper
        Balloon (Ninjō Kami Fusen)

Yutkevich, Sergei 209
(1932) *Counterplan
        (Vstrechnyi)

Zampa, Luigi 427-8
(1946) *Vivere in Pace

Zarkhi, Alexandr 258-9
(1936) *Baltic Deputy
        (Deputat Baltiki)

Zeman, Bořivoj 429-30, 496
(1946) *Dead Among the Living
        (Mrtvý Mezi Živými)

Zinnemann, Fred 236, 390
(1934) *The Wave (Redes)
(1944) *The Seventh Cross

INDEX OF FILMS

This index lists the titles of all films appearing
in the text of this volume.

If a film is (or will be in a subsequent volume)
discussed in an entry of its own, it is marked with
an asterisk * and if the original title of such a film
is in a language other than English, it is given in
parentheses following the entry under the English
title; it is also entered in the index under the original title with the English version in parentheses.

For a film merely mentioned in the text, only the
one title used in English-speaking countries is given
(without an asterisk). (Note that for some films,
e.g. "Ademaï, bandit d'honneur" and "L'Age d'or,"
the original, or foreign language, title is also the
one used in English-speaking countries.)

Alphabetization is without regard to initial definite
or indefinite articles in any language.

Pages constituting an entire entry devoted to a
particular film are underscored.

Films whose titles are similar to others are further identified by the director's name in brackets.

*Action in the North
  Atlantic 36, 353, 377-8
Adam's Rib 391
*Ademaï, bandit d'honneur
  374
Adventures of Oktyabrina 227
*The Adventures of Robin
  Hood 300-1
L'Age d'or 506
*Air Force 36, 366-7, 376
*Akahige (Red Beard) 433
*Akasen Chitai (Street of
  Shame) 255
*Alexander Nevsky (Alexandr
  Nevsky) 35, 105, 254,
  284-5, 380-1
*Alexis Zorbas (Zorba the
  Greek) 449
*Alibi 169

*All Quiet on the Western
  Front 33, 177-8, 270, 411
*All the King's Men 37, 508-9
Alone 227
*An American Tragedy 197-8
*Among People (V Lyudyakh)
  295-6
*Angèle 236-7
*Les Anges du péché 36, 364,
  367-8, 403
*À nous la liberté 34, 206-7,
  214, 251
*Antoine et Antoinette 452-3
À propos de Nice 222
L'Arroseur arrosé 29
*Arrowsmith 210
*Arsenic and Old Lace 389-90
*As Others See Us (Les Casse-
  pieds) 488

*L'Assassinat du Père Noël
  (The Murder of Father
  Christmas) 291, 339
L'Assassin habite au 21 362
*L'Atalante 92, 222-3
Atlantis 62
*L'Auberge rouge [Epstein]
  82-3
Au-delà des grilles SEE
  Le Mura di Malapaga
*An Autumn Afternoon (Sama
  no Aji) 501
*Avant le déluge 360

*Backstairs (Hintertreppe)
  75-6
*Baisers volés 176
*The Baker's Wife (La Femme
  du boulanger) 193, 262,
  315-6
*Baltic Deputy (Deputat
  Baltiki) 258-9
*I Bambini Ci Guardano (The
  Children Are Watching Us)
  369-70
*The Bandit (Il Bandito) 434
*Il Bandito (The Bandit) 434
*Bank Holiday 299, 311
*Banshun (Late Spring) 500-1
*La Bataille du rail 36, 396-
  7, 453-4
*Battleship Potemkin
  (Bronenosets "Potyomkin")
  xx, 32, 110-1, 129-30,
  156
*Battling Butler 120, 123-4
*La Beauté du diable 501-2
*Beauty and the Beast (La
  Belle et la bête) 425-6,
  453, 494
Becky Sharp 195, 247
*Bed and Sofa (Tretya
  Meshchanskaya) 135-6,
  158
*Before Matriculation (Před
  Maturitou) 210-1
*La Belle équipe 264
*La Belle et la bête (Beauty
  and the Beast) 425-6,
  453, 494
*La Belle Nivernaise 92,
  222

Be My Wife 84
*Berg-Ejvind och Hans Hustru
  (The Outlaw and His Wife)
  31, 48-9, 54, 59
*The Best Years of Our Lives
  37, 422-3, 511
*La Bête humaine 296-7, 518
Between Showers 50
Between Worlds SEE Destiny
Beyond the Gates SEE Le
  Mura di Malapaga
*Bezhin Lug (Bezhin Meadow)
  271-3, 284
*Bezhin Meadow (Bezhin Lug)
  271-3, 284
*Bicycle Thieves (Ladri di
  Biciclette) 202, 370, 423,
  465-6
*The Big House 180
*The Big Parade 33, 113-4,
  143, 232
*The Big Sleep 37, 424-5, 441
*The Birth of a Nation xx, 30,
  42-3, 45, 56, 70
*Bitter Rice (Riso Amaro) 499-
  500, 505
*Blackmail 166-7
The Black Pirate 247
*Der blaue Engel (The Blue
  Angel) 67, 109, 149, 161,
  173-5, 188, 197, 458
Blind Husbands 69
*Blithe Spirit 412-3
*The Blue Angel (Der blaue
  Engel) 67, 109, 149, 161,
  173-5, 188, 197, 458
*The Blue Express (Goluboi
  Ekspress) 164-5, 170
Body and Soul 509
*Boomerang! 408, 449-50
*Border Street (Ulica Graniczna)
  37, 479-80
Boudu Saved from Drowning 307
*Boule de Suif (Pyshka) [Romm]
  233-4, 263
*Boule de Suif [Christian-Jaque]
  408-9
Le Boulevard du Crime SEE
  Les Enfants du paradis
*Boyarski Zagovor (The Boyars'
  Plot) 35, 380-1, 415-7
*The Boyars' Plot (Boyarski
  Zagovor) 35, 380-1, 415-7

*Brief Encounter 400-1, 436
*Broken Blossoms 55-6, 63,
   67
*Bronenosets "Potyomkin"
   (Battleship Potemkin) xx,
   32, 110-1, 129-30, 156
*Brute Force 37, 444-5, 505
*Die Büchse der Pandora
   (Pandora's Box) 144-5,
   161-2, 183
*Bukhta Smerti (Death Bay)
   125, 136

*The Cabinet of Dr. Caligari
   (Das Kabinett des Dr.
   Caligari) 31, 52-3, 72,
   78, 80, 84-5, 99, 108,
   385
*Cabiria 40-1
*Caccia Tragica (The Tragic
   Pursuit) 446-7, 499
*The Caine Mutiny 378
*Call Northside 777 38, 408,
   442, 445-6
*The Cameraman 154-5
A Caprice SEE Passing
   Fancy
*Captain Blood 245, 301
*Un Carnet de bal 276-7
*Carnival in Flanders (La
   Kermesse héroïque)
   229, 241-2, 260, 294
*Casablanca 36, 361, 413,
   491
*Les Casse-pieds (As Others
   See Us) 488
*Cech Panen Kutnohorských
   (The Guild of the Kutná
   Hora Maidens) 293-4
*César 193, 213, 237, 261-2
*Champion 37, 509, 513-4
*Chapayev 35, 223-4, 227,
   253
*Un Chapeau de paille d'Italie
   (The Italian Straw Hat)
   64, 133-4, 146, 187,
   354, 386, 519
*The Charge of the Light
   Brigade 199
*La Chartreuse de Parme 456
*The Chase 353
Chess Fever 118

*Chichi Ariki (There Was a
   Father) 359-60
Un Chien andalou 506
La Chienne 227, 297
*The Childhood of Maxim Gorky
   (Detstvo Gorkovo) 286-7, 296
*The Children Are Watching Us
   (I Bambini Ci Guardano) 369-
   70
Chorus of Tokyo 202
*La Chute de la maison Usher
   (The Fall of the House of
   Usher) 144, 152, 194
*Le Ciel est à vous 376-7
Cinderella [Méliès] 29
*The Circus [Chaplin] 113,
   137-8, 458
Circus [Alexandrov] 291
*The Citadel 298
*Citizen Kane 37, 98, 124,
   307, 317, 332-5, 349-50
City Girl SEE Our Daily
   Bread [Murnau]
*City Lights 34, 172-3, 194,
   207, 249, 255
*City Streets 195-6
The Cloak 227
*Clochemerle 495
*Coeur fidèle 87-8, 139
College 120
*Confessions of a Nazi Spy 36,
   317-8
*The Congress Dances (Der
   Kongress tantzt) 188-9
*Conscience (Svědomí) 496
Construire un feu 371
Cops 117
*Le Corbeau (The Crow) 36,
   362-3, 439, 474
The Coronation of Edward VII
   29
A Cottage on Dartmoor 199
*Counterplan (Vstrechnyi) 209-
   10
*The Covered Wagon 32, 89-90
*Crainquebille 81-2, 105-6, 205,
   229
*Crime and Punishment (Crime
   et châtiment) [Chenal] 235-6
*Le Crime de M. Lange 242-3,
   410
*Crime et châtiment (Crime and
   Punishment) [Chenal] 235-6

*Criss Cross 481-2
Crossfire 512
*Crossways (Jūji-ro) 35,
    147-8
*The Crow (Le Corbeau) 36,
    362-3, 439, 474
*The Crowd 143, 146, 232
*The Cruel Sea 492

*Les Dames du Bois de
    Boulogne 403-4
*Dark Passage 455
*Daró un Milione (I'll Give
    a Million) 248-9
*Day of the Owl (Il Giorno
    della Civetta) 513
*Day of Wrath (Vredens Dag)
    36, 363-5
*Dead Among the Living
    (Mrtvy Mezi Živými) 429-
    30, 496
*Dead End 278-9, 319, 340
*Death Bay (Bukhta Smerti)
    125, 136
Dédée d'Anvers 482
*Dekigokoro (Passing Fancy)
    216-7
*Deputat Baltiki (Baltic Deputy)
    258-9
Dernier atout 355
*Les Dernières vacances
    462-3
Le Dernier milliardaire 207,
    243
*Destiny (Der Müde Tod) 65-
    7, 104
*Detstvo Gorkovo (The Child-
    hood of Maxim Gorky)
    286-7, 296
*Les Deux timides 146-7,
    176
The Devil's Passkey 69
*Le Diable au corps 371,
    419-20, 519
*Diary of a Country Priest
    (Le Journal d'un curé de
    campagne) 451
*Diary of a Lost Girl (Das
    Tagebuch einer Verlorenen)
    161-2
*Les Disparus de Saint-Agil
    290-1, 339

*Ditta, Child of Man (Ditte
    Menneskebarn) 452
*Ditte Menneskebarn (Ditta,
    Child of Man) 452
*The Docks of New York 32,
    140, 148-9, 288
*Dr. Ehrlich's Magic Bullet
    327-8
Dr. Jekyll and Mr. Hyde 195
*Dr. Mabuse, the Gambler (Dr.
    Mabuse, der Spieler) 31, 69,
    78-9, 104, 107, 154, 219
*Dr. Mabuse, der Spieler (Dr.
    Mabuse, the Gambler) 31, 69,
    78-9, 104, 107, 154, 219
*Dom na Trubnoy (The House in
    Trubnaya Street) 158
*Don Quichotte (Don Quixote)
    220-1
*Don Quixote (Don Quichotte)
    220-1
*Double Indemnity 37, 387-8,
    441, 482
*Douce 36, 371, 519
The Drag Net 148
*Die Dreigroschenoper (The
    Threepenny Opera) 184-5
*Drôle de drame 273-4, 287
*Drunken Angel (Yoidore Tenshi)
    37, 475-6, 503
*Du Skal Aere Din Hustru
    (Master of the House) 114-5
*Du sollst nicht ehebrechen
    (Thérèse Raquin) [Feyder]
    132, 153

*Earth (Tsuchi) [Uchida] 308-9,
    344
*Earth (Zemla) [Dovzhenko] 32,
    171-2, 252
The Earth Sings 221
The Earth Thirsts 233
*East of Eden 461
*L'École buissonnière 485-6
Ecstasy 221
*1860 217-8
Eisenstein's Mexican Project
    201
*Eldorado 74-5
Elephant Boy 466
*Eliso 155-6
*Emil and the Detectives (Emil

und die Detektive) 196-7
*Emil und die Detektive (Emil
  and the Detectives) 196-7
*The End of St. Petersburg
  (Konyets Sankt-Peterburga)
  127-8, 141
*Les Enfants du paradis 36,
  394-5
*Les Enfants terribles 494,
  514-5
*En Rade 139-40
Entr'acte 134
*Erotikon 63-4

*The Fallen Idol 467-8, 507
*The Fall of the House of
  Usher (La Chute de la
  maison Usher) 144, 152,
  194
*Fanny 193, 212-3, 261
*Fantasia 324-5
Farrébique 309
La Femme de nulle part 59
*La Femme du boulanger
  (The Baker's Wife) 193,
  262, 315-6
*Le Feu follet 229
Fièvre 59, 87, 139
*La Fin du jour 264, 312-3
*Finis Terrae 152, 198
The Flame of New Orleans
  354
*Foolish Wives 68-9, 131,
  174, 228
*Foreign Correspondent 36,
  326-7
*Fort Apache 493, 516-7
*The Forty-First (Sorok Pervyi)
  [Protazanov] 138-9
*The Forty-First (Sorok Pervyi)
  [Chukhrai] 138
*49th Parallel 345
Four Devils 159
*Four Steps in the Clouds
  (Quattro Passi fra le
  Nuvole) 350, 356, 427
The Fourth Marriage of Dame
  Margaret SEE The Par-
  son's Widow
*Fragment of an Empire
  (Oblomok Imperii) 164,
  209, 248

*Frenzy (Hets) [Sjöberg] 383-4
*Die freudlose Gasse (The
  Joyless Street) 116, 136,
  165, 320
*The Front Page 34, 192, 310-
  1
*Fury 34, 256-7, 274-5

*Gaslight [Dickinson] 330-1,
  358, 391
*Gaslight [Cukor] 391-2
Gate of Hell 148
*The General 89, 103, 119-21,
  155
Gentleman's Agreement 450
*Germania Anno Zero (Germany
  Year Zero) 37, 436-7
*Germany Year Zero (Germania
  Anno Zero) 37, 436-7
*Girls in Uniforms (Mädchen in
  Uniform) [Sagan] 187-8
*Give Us This Day 511-2
*The Ghost Goes West 243-4,
  354, 413
*The Ghost That Will Not Re-
  turn (Privideniye, Kotoroye
  Ne Vozvrashchayetsya) 163
*Gion no Shimai (Sisters of the
  Gion) 257-8, 307
*Il Giorno della Civetta (The
  Day of the Owl) 513
*The Gold Rush 51, 68, 92,
  98, 111-2, 137, 146, 173,
  441
*The Golem (Der Golem, wie
  er in die Welt kam) 60-1,
  86
*Der Golem, wie er in die Welt
  kam (The Golem) 60-1, 86
*Goluboi Ekspress (The Blue
  Express) 164-5, 170
*Goupi Mains Rouges 355
*Go West 117
*La Grande illusion 33-4, 151,
  182, 269-71, 291
*Le Grand jeu 34, 215-6, 227,
  229, 263, 287, 290
*The Grapes of Wrath 233,
  237, 314-5, 321-2, 342, 410
*A Great Citizen (Veliky
  Grazhdanin) 226, 307, 313-
  4

*The Great Dictator 36, 51,
  173, 251, 317, 322-4, 357
*Great Expectations 420-1,
  490
The Great McGinty 338
The Great Train Robbery
  30, 32
*The Great Turning Point
  (Veliky Perelom) 37,
  404-5
*Greed 96, 97-8, 131, 195
Der grosse Spieler SEE
  Dr. Mabuse, der Spieler
Guadalcanal Diary 378
*The Guild of the Kutná Hora
  Maidens (Cech Panen Kutno-
  horských) 293-4
*Gulliver's Travels 319
*Gycklàrnas Afton (Sawdust
  and Tinsel) 113

*Hail the Conquering Hero
  392-3
*Hallelujah! 160-1, 504
*Hamlet [Olivier] 421, 468-9
*Häxan (Witchcraft Through
  the Ages) 71-2, 364
Hearts of the World 56
Heave-ho! 240
*The Heiress 510-1
The Heir to Genghis-Khan
  SEE Storm Over Asia
*Henry V 382-3, 421, 436,
  468
*Herr Arnes Pengar (Sir
  Arne's Treasure) 31, 53-
  4, 58, 381
*Hets (Frenzy) [Sjöberg] 383-4
*He Who Gets Slapped 108-9,
  113
*High Noon 304
*Himlaspelet (The Road to
  Heaven) 351-2, 383
*Hintertreppe (Backstairs)
  75-6
*His Girl Friday 192, 310-1
*Hitori Musuko (The Only Son)
  265
L'Homme blanc SEE Les
  Enfants du paradis
*L'Homme du large 59-60,
  74

*The Honeymoon 156-7
*Horse (Uma) 343-4
*Hotel Paradis 190-1
*The House in Trubnaya Street
  (Dom na Trubnoy) 158
*The House on 92nd Street
  407-8, 442
*How Green Was My Valley
  341-2, 407
*Humanity Like a Paper
  Balloon (Ninjō Kami Fusen)
  279-80

*I Am a Fugitive from a Chain
  Gang 34, 204-5
I Confess 121
L'Idiot 420
The Idle Class 77
*Ikiru! (To Live) 433
*I'll Give a Million (Daró un
  Milione) 248-9
*I Married a Witch 354, 386,
  413
*Les Inconnus dans la maison
  (Strangers in the House)
  262, 360-1
Industrial Britain 224
Inferno SEE Dr. Mabuse, der
  Spieler
*The Informer 239-40, 436
*In Nome della Legge (In the
  Name of the Law) 512-3
*The Insect Woman (Nippon
  Konchuki) 258
*In the Name of the Law (In
  Nome della Legge) 512-3
*Intolerance 30, 41, 44-6,
  55, 62, 70, 82, 89
*Intruder in the Dust 504
*In Which We Serve 36, 352-3,
  370, 375, 387, 412
*The Iron Horse 32, 106, 328
*The Italian Straw Hat (Un
  Chapeau de paille d'Italie)
  64, 133-4, 146, 187, 354,
  386, 519
*It Happened One Night 225-6,
  254
*It Happened Tomorrow 385-6
*Ivan Grozny (Ivan the Ter-
  rible) 35, 54, 105, 125,
  380-1, 383, 415-6, 443

*Ivan the Terrible (Ivan
  Grozny) 35, 54, 105, 380-
  1, 383, 415-6, 443
Ivan the Terrible--Part II
  SEE The Boyars' Plot
Ivan the Terrible [Tarich]
  SEE Wings of a Serf
*I Was Born, but...
  (Umarete-wā Mita Keredo)
  202-3, 217

J'accuse 93
Jamaica Inn 517
*Jánošík 240-1, 294
Jazz Comedy SEE Jolly
  Fellows
The Jazz Singer 32, 522
Jenny 287
Jesse James 325
*Les Jeux interdits 105
*Les Jeux sont faits 443-4
*Jezebel 289-90, 511
*Jinsei Gekijo (Theatre of
  Life) 266-7
*Jolly Fellows (Vesyolye
  Rebyata) 231-2, 291
*Jour de fête 459-60
*Le Journal d'un curé de
  campagne (Diary of a
  Country Priest) 451
*Le Jour se lève 35, 302-3,
  347
*The Joyless Street (Die
  freudlose Gasse) 116, 136,
  165, 320
*Judo Saga (Sugata Sanshiro)
  [Kurosawa] 365-6, 434,
  476
*Jūji-ro (Crossways) 35,
  147-8
*Justice est faite 520

*Das Kabinett des Dr. Caligari
  (The Cabinet of Dr. Cali-
  gari) 31, 52-3, 72, 78,
  80, 84-5, 99, 108, 385
*Kameradschaft 182-3, 185,
  220, 311
Keep an Eye on Amelia
  SEE Occupe toi d'Amélie
*La Kermesse héroïque (Car-

nival in Flanders) 229, 241-2,
  260, 294
*Key Largo 37, 491
*The Kid 67-8, 77
Kid Auto Races at Venice 50
*The Killers [Siodmak] 432-3
Kimiko SEE Wife, Be Like a
  Rose
*Kind Hearts and Coronets 515-
  6
Kipps 386
The Kiss 153
*Kiss of Death 441-2
*Knock on Any Door 519-20
*Der Kongress tantzt (The
  Congress Dances) 188-9
*Konyets Sankt Peterburga (The
  End of St. Petersburg) 127-8,
  141
*Körkarlen (The Phantom Car-
  riage) 58-9, 71, 83
*Krestyaniye (Peasants) 247-8,
  313
Kriemhilds Rache SEE
  Nibelungen
Kriemhild's Revenge SEE
  Nibelungen
*Krylya Kholopa (Wings of a
  Serf) 124-5

*Ladri di Biciclette (Bicycle
  Thieves) 202, 370, 423,
  465-6
*The Lady from Shanghai 138,
  458, 482
Lady in the Lake 455
*The Lady Vanishes 34, 292-3
*The Last Chance (Die letzte
  Chance) 36-7, 405-6
*The Last Laugh (Der letzte
  Mann) 31, 95, 98-9, 113,
  143
*The Last Stage (Ostatni Etap)
  37, 469-70
*Late Spring (Banshun) 500-1
*Laura 37, 388-9
*The Lavender Hill Mob 516
Leaves from Satan's Book 62
Lenin in 1918 281
*Lenin in October (Lenin v
  Oktyabre) 281
*Lenin v Oktyabre (Lenin in

October) 281
*Letter from an Unknown
Woman 244, 472-3
Lettres d'amour 371
*Die letzte Chance (The Last
Chance) 36-7, 405-6
*Der letzte Mann (The Last
Laugh) 31, 95, 98-9, 113,
143
*Die Liebe der Jeanne Ney
(The Love of Jeanne Ney)
136-7
*Liebelei 205-6, 234
*Lifeboat 368-9
*The Life of Émile Zola 282
Liliom 256
*Little Caesar 32, 135, 169,
179, 204, 208
*The Little Foxes 339-40,
357, 511
*The Lodger 121-2
*Lonesome 145-6, 211, 461
*Los Olvidados 400, 506-7
*The Lost Patrol 237-8, 263,
304
*The Lost Weekend 37, 399-
400, 485
*Louisiana Story 466-7
*The Love of Jeanne Ney (Die
Liebe der Jeanne Ney) 136-
7

*M 183-4, 219, 385, 432
*Macbeth [Welles] 442-3
*Maclovia 374, 497-8
*Madame Curie 378-9
*Mädchen in Uniform (Girls in
Uniforms) [Sagan] 187-8
*The Magnificent Ambersons
348-50
*Major Barbara 328-9
Making a Living 50
*The Maltese Falcon 37,
336-8, 424-5, 441, 491
*Manèges 518-9
*Man of Aran 224-5, 466
*Manon 473-4
*A Man There Was (Terje
Vigen) 31, 46-7, 142
*The Man Who Knew Too
Much [1934] 34, 229-30,
261, 268

*Maria Candeleria
(Xochimilco) 36, 373-4,
521
Mariage de Chiffon 371
*Marie, a Hungarian Legend
(Tavaszi Zápor) 211-2
*Marius 193-4, 212, 261
La Marseillaise 297
*Maryša 246-7
*Maskerade 234-5
*Master of the House (Du Skal
Aere Din Hustru) 114-5
*Mat (Mother) 32, 118-9,
127-8, 141
*Les Maudits 453-4
Merry Widow 69
*Metropolis 31, 121, 122-3,
153, 183
Mikaël 114
*Mildred Pierce 413-4
*1860 217-8
*Le Million 34, 176, 187, 438
*The Mill on the Po (Il Mulino
del Po) 489-90
The Miracle of Morgan Creek
392
*Mr. Deeds Goes to Town 34,
254-5, 283, 295
Mr. Smith Goes to Washington
255
*Mrs. Miniver 36, 356-7, 422,
511
*Młody Las (The Young Trees)
238
Moana 157, 186
*Modern Times 34, 207, 250-1,
323
*Molti Sogni per le Strade (The
Street Has Many Dreams)
478
*Monsieur Hulot's Holiday (Les
Vacances de M. Hulot) 460
*Monsieur Verdoux 37, 440-1
*The More the Merrier 36, 379
Mor-Vran 198
*Mother (Mat) 32, 118-9, 127-8,
141
*Mother Krause's Journey to
Happiness (Mutter Krausens
Fahrt ins Glück) 165-6
*Die Mörder sind unter uns
(The Murderers Are Among
Us) 37, 431-2

*Mrtvy Mezi Živými (Dead Among the Living) 429-30, 496
*Der Müde Tod (Destiny) 65-7, 104
*Il Mulino del Po (The Mill on the Po) 489-90
*Le Mura di Malapaga 397, 486
*Murder 181, 230
*The Murderers Are Among Us (Die Mörder sind unter uns) 37, 431-2
*The Murder of Father Christmas (L'Assassinat du Père Noël) 291, 339
*Mutter Krausens Fahrt ins Glück (Mother Krause's Journey to Happiness) 165-6
*My Darling Clementine 428-9
*My iz Kronshtata (We from Kronstadt) 35, 253-4, 259
My Universities 296

*The Naked City 445, 470-1, 505
The Naked Town 267
*Naniwa Erejī (Osaka Elegy) 255-6, 258, 307
Naniwa Hika SEE Osaka Elegy
Nanook of the North 157
Napoléon 93
*The Navigator 102-3
The Neighbour's Wife and Mine 202
*Next of Kin 36, 357-8, 387
*New Year's Eve (Sylvester-- Tragödie einer Nacht) 31, 73, 95-6, 303
*Die Nibelungen (Nibelungen) 31, 103-5, 110, 122, 125
Night Mail 412
*Nikdo Nic Neví (No One Knows a Thing) 463-4
Nine Days a Queen SEE Tudor Rose
*Nine Men 375, 376
*Ninjō Kami Fusen (Humanity Like a Paper Balloon) 279-80
*Ninotchka 320

*Nippon Konchuki (The Insect Woman) 258
*No One Knows a Thing (Nikdo Nic Neví) 463-4
*Nora Inu (Stray Dog) 37, 475, 503-4
*No Regrets for My Youth (Waga Seishun ni Kuinashi) 37, 433-4
*Northwest Passage 328
*Nosferatu (Nosferatu--Eine Symphonie des Grauens) 79-80, 99, 107, 129, 159, 421
Not Against the Flesh SEE Vampyr, ou l'étrange aventure de David Gray
Nothing Sacred 353
*Notorious 280, 418-9, 518
*Nous, les gosses (Us Kids) 335-6, 377
*Nous sommes tous les assassins 520
*Les Nouveaux messieurs 152-3
Une Nuit sur le Mont Chauve 325

*Obchod na Korze (The Shop in the High Street) 428
*Oblomok Imperii (Fragment of an Empire) 164, 209, 248
*Occupe-toi d'Amélie 519
*October (Oktyabr) 32, 129-30, 156, 165
*Odd Man Out 435-6, 467-8
*Of Mice and Men 314-5
*Oktyabr (October) 32, 129-30, 156, 165
The Old and the New 130, 172
*Oliver Twist 490
*Los Olvidados 400, 506-7
*One Wonderful Sunday (Subarashiki Nichiyobi) 37, 461-2, 475
*The Only Son (Hitori Musuko) 265
*On the Town 521-2
*L'Or des mers 198
Orphée 425, 515
*Osaka Elegy (Naniwa Erejī) 255-6, 258, 307
*Ossessione 37, 350-1, 356, 477, 484

*Ostatni Etap (The Last Stage) 37, 469-70
*Our Daily Bread [Murnau] 158-9
*Our Daily Bread [Vidor] 232-3
*Our Hospitality 88-9, 124
Out in the World SEE Among People
*The Outlaw and His Wife (Berg-Ejvind och Hans Hustru) 31, 48-9, 54, 59
*The Overlanders 411-2
*The Ox-Bow Incident 326, 353-4, 398

A Page of Madness 147
*Paisà 37, 417-8, 423, 431, 437
*Pandora's Box (Die Büchse der Pandora) 144-5, 161-2, 183
Paper Doll's Whisper of Spring 246, 255
*Les Parents terribles 494-5
Paris qui dort 133
*The Parson's Widow (Prästänkan) 61-2
*Partie de campagne 251-3
*Passing Fancy (Dekigokoro) 216-7
*La Passion de Jeanne d'Arc (The Passion of Joan of Arc) 106, 115, 126-7, 194, 233
*The Passion of Joan of Arc (La Passion de Jeanne d'Arc) 106, 115, 126-7, 194, 233
*Passport to Pimlico 496-7, 515
*A Pass to Life (Putyovka v Zhizn) 189-90
Pasteur 82
Pay Day 77
*Peasants (Krestyaniye) 247-8, 313
*Pension Mimosas 34, 228-9, 287
People on Sunday 197
*Pépé le Moko 262-3, 331
Le Père tranquille 453

Pescados SEE The Wave
*Peter Ibbetson 244-5
*Peter the First (Pyotr Pervyi) 300
*The Phantom Carriage (Körkarlen) 58-9, 71, 83
*The Philadelphia Story 329-30, 391
*The Pilgrim 77-8, 324
La Piste du Nord 242
The Pleasure Garden 121
*Poil de carotte 203-4
*Polikushka 56-7
*Pontcarral 358-9
*Porte des Lilas 207
*Potomok Chingiskhana (Storm Over Asia) 32, 127, 141-2, 165
*Prästänkan (The Parson's Widow) 61-2
*Presentiment (Předtucha) 463
The President 62
*The Private Life of Henry VIII 34, 219-20, 260, 267, 299
*Privideniye, Kotoroye Ne Vozvrashchayetsya (The Ghost That Will Not Return) 163
*Pred Maturitou (Before Matriculation) 210-1
*Předtucha (Presentiment) 463
*Public Enemy 32, 179, 191-2, 424
*Pueblerina 374, 521
*Pursued 460-1
*Putyovka v Zhizn (A Pass to Life) 189-90
*Pygmalion 288-9, 329
*Pyotr Pervyi (Peter the First) 300
*Pyshka (Boule de Suif) [Romm] 233-4, 263

*Quai des Brumes 35, 139, 287-8, 302-3, 347, 436
*Quai des Orfèvres 438-9, 474
*Quatorze Juillet 212, 214-5, 438, 453
*Quattro Passi fra le Nuvole (Four Steps in the Clouds) 350, 356, 427
Queen Christina 195
*Queen Kelly 150-1

The Queen of Hearts 29
*¡Que Viva Mexico! 200-1,
  236, 272, 373
*The Quiet One 488-9

*Rails (Rotaie) 169-70
*Rashomon (Rashō-mon) 148,
  366
*Rebel Without a Cause 457
*Red Beard (Akahige) 433
*Redes (The Wave) 236
*Red River 471-2
*La Règle du jeu 34, 243,
  305-7, 316
*Rembrandt 259-60
*The Return of Frank James
  325-6, 346
*Return of Maxim (Vozvrash-
  cheniye Maksima) 227, 271,
  294
*Revolt of the Fishermen
  (Vosstaniye Rybakov) 230-1
*Du Rififi chez les hommes
  442, 471
Rio Grande 493
*Riso Amaro (Bitter Rice)
  499-500, 505
*The River (Reka) 221
*The Road to Heaven
  (Himlaspelet) 351-2, 383
Road to Life SEE A Pass to
  Life
*Rojō no Reikon (Souls on the
  Road) 35, 69-71
*Roma, Città Aperta (Rome,
  Open City) 37, 170, 401-2,
  417, 424, 437, 484
*Rome, Open City (Roma,
  Città Aperta) 37, 170, 401-2,
  417, 424, 437, 484
*La Ronde 473
*Rope 280, 487, 518
*Rotaie (Rails) 169-70
*La Roue 92-4, 297
*Reka (The River) 221

Sabotage 195
The Saga of Gösta Berling 58
*Sahara 376
Salvation Hunters 134
*Sama no Aji (An Autumn

Afternoon) 501
*San Demetrio, London 36,
  352, 370, 375, 378, 492
Le Sang d'un poète 425, 494
*Sawdust and Tinsel (Gycklàrnas
  Afton) 113
*Scarface 32, 179, 196, 205,
  207-8, 337, 424
*The Scarlet Letter 123
*Schatten--Eine nächtliche
  Halluzination (Warning
  Shadows) 31, 75, 83-4, 416
*Scherben (Shattered) 31, 72-3,
  95, 154
*Sciuscià (Shoeshine) 423-4, 465
*Scott of the Antarctic 492
*The Sea Wolf 342-3
*The Secret Agent 167, 260-1
Secrets of a Soul 136, 148
*Senza Pietà (Without Pity) 483-4
*Sergeant York 340-1
*The Set-Up 37, 509-10, 513
*Seven Chances 115
Seven Footprints to Satan 71
*The Seventh Cross 37, 390-1
*Seventh Heaven 140
*The Seventh Seal (Det Sjunde
  Inseglet) 67, 365
*Seven Years' Bad Luck 73-4,
  84
*Shadow of a Doubt 372, 481
*Shadows 489
*Shattered (Scherben) 31, 72-3,
  95, 154
*Sherlock Junior 101-2, 155
*She Wore a Yellow Ribbon
  493, 516-7
*Shirasagi (The White Heron)
  148
*Shoeshine (Sciuscià) 423-4,
  465
*The Shop in the High Street
  (Obchod na Korze) 428
*Shoulder Arms 50-1, 324
Siegfried SEE Nibelungen
*Siegfrieds Tod SEE Nibelungen
*Il Signor Max 283
*Une si jolie petite plage 482-3,
  518
*Le Silence de la mer 450-1,
  515
*Le Silence est d'or 437-8
*Sir Arne's Treasure (Herr

Arnes Pengar) 31, 53-4, 58, 381
*Siréna (The Strike) [Steklý] 458-9
*Sisters of the Gion (Gion no Shimai) 257-8, 307
*Det Sjunde Inseglet (The Seventh Seal) 67, 365
*Smultronstället (Wild Strawberries) 142
*The Snake Pit 37, 480, 484-5, 489
*Snow White and the Seven Dwarfs 275-6, 319
*The Soil Under Your Feet (Talpalatnyi Föld) 478-9
*Sole (Sun) 168, 170, 218
*Il Sole Sorge Ancora (The Sun Rises Again) 430-1
*Somewhere in Europe (Valahol Európában...) 37, 447-8, 479
*Sorok Pervyi (The Forty-First) [Protazanov] 138-9
*Sorok Pervyi (The Forty-First) [Chukhrai] 138
*Sorry, Wrong Number 37, 480-1
*Souls on the Road (Rojō no Reikon) 35, 69-71
*Sous les toits de Paris 33, 175-6, 212, 214
*The Southerner 409-10
Spellbound 485
The Spiders 79
*The Spies (Spione) 153-4
*Spione (The Spies) 153-4
*Spite Marriage 155, 167-8
*Stachka (Strike) [Eisenstein] 100-1, 232
*Stagecoach 234, 237, 303-5, 326, 409
The Stalingrad Battle 409
A Star Is Born [Wellman] 353
*The Stars Look Down 311-2
*Steamboat Bill Jr. 149-50
Steamboat Willie 275
*Storm Over Asia (Potomok Chingiskhana) 32, 127, 141-2, 165
*The Story of G.I. Joe 36, 376, 398, 411
*The Story of Louis Pasteur 265-6
*The Story of the Last Chrysanthemum (Zangiku Monogatari) 307-8
A Story of the London Fog SEE The Lodger
*La Strada 71
Strange Incident SEE The Ox-Bow Incident
*Strangers in the House (Les Inconnus dans la maison) 262, 360-1
*Strangers on a Train 481
*Stray Dog (Nora Inu) 37, 475, 503-4
*The Street Has Many Dreams (Molti Sogni per le Strade) 478
*Street of Shame (Akasen Chitai) 255
*Strike (Stachka) [Eisenstein] 100-1, 232
*The Strike (Siréna) [Steklý] 458-9
*The Student of Prague (Der Student von Prag) 39-40, 60-1, 86
*Der Student von Prag (The Student of Prague) 39-40, 60-1, 86
*Subarashiki Nichiyobi (One Wonderful Sunday) 37, 461-2, 475
*Such Is Life (Takový Je Život) 162-3
*Sugata Sanshiro (Judo Saga) [Kurosawa] 365-6, 434, 476
*Sullivan's Travels 338-9, 392
*Sun (Sole) 168, 170, 218
*Sunrise 128-9, 140, 159
*The Sun Rises Again (Il Sole Sorge Ancora) 430-1
*Sunset Boulevard 151, 168
*Suspicion 344-5
*Svědomí (Conscience) 496
Swamp Water 410
*Sylvester--Tragödie einer Nacht (New Year's Eve) 31, 73, 95-6, 303
*La Symphonie pastorale 359, 426-7, 444

*Tabu 159, 185-6, 224
*Das Tagebuch einer Verlorenen
   (Diary of a Lost Girl) 161-2
*Takový Je Život (Such Is Life)
   162-3
*Talpalatnyi Föld (The Soil
   Under Your Feet) 478-9
Target for Tonight 412
*Tavaszi Zápor (Marie, a
   Hungarian Legend) 211-2
*Tell England 198-9
Ten Days That Shook the
   World SEE October
*Terje Vigen (A Man There
   Was) 31, 46-7, 142
*La Terra Trema 476-7
*Das Testament des Dr.
   Mabuse (The Testament of
   Dr. Mabuse) 218-9
*The Testament of Dr. Mabuse
   (Das Testament des Dr.
   Mabuse) 218-9
*La Tête contre les murs 229
*Theatre of Life (Jinsei
   Gekijō) 266-7
*Thérèse Raquin (Du sollst
   nicht ehebrechen)
   [Feyder] 132, 153
*There Was a Father (Chichi
   Ariki) 359-60
*They Live by Night 37,
   196, 457
*They Who Step on the Tiger's
   Tail (Tora no O-o Fumu
   Otokotachi) 395-6
*They Won't Forget 34, 204,
   274-5
*Thieves' Highway 37, 445,
   504-5
*The Third Man 468, 507-8
*The Thirteen (Trinadtsat)
   263-4
*The Thirty-Nine Steps 34,
   249, 280
This Happy Breed 412
Thou Shalt Honor Thy Wife
   SEE Master of the House
The Three Ages 89
*The Three Must-Get-Theres
   84-5
The Three Lights SEE
   Destiny
*The Threepenny Opera (Die

Dreigroschenoper) 184-5
Three Sharing SEE Bed and
   Sofa
Thy Soul Shall Bear Witness
   SEE The Phantom Carriage
Time in the Sun 200
The Toda Brother and His
   Sisters 360
To Have and Have Not 425
*To Live (Ikiru!) 433
*Toni 227-8, 242, 270, 297,
   307, 410
Too Much Johnson 333
*Tora no O-o Fumu Otokotachi
   (They Who Step on the
   Tiger's Tail) 395-6
Torn Curtain 320
Tosca 410
La Tour 214
*The Tragic Pursuit (Caccia
   Tragica) 446-7, 499
The Trail of the Lonesome
   Pine 247
*The Treasure of Sierra Madre
   37, 448-9, 491
*A Tree Grows in Brooklyn
   406-7
*Tretya Meshchanskaya (Bed
   and Sofa) 135-6, 158
*Trinadtsat (The Thirteen)
   263-4
A Trip to the Moon 29
*Tsuchi (Earth) [Uchida] 308-9,
   344
*Tsuma Yō Bara no Yoni (Wife,
   Be Like a Rose) 245-6
*Tudor Rose 267-8
Tu ne tueras point 419
Turbine 50,000 SEE Counter-
   plan
*Twelve Angry Men 520

*Ulica Graniczna (Border Street)
   37, 479-80
*Uma (Horse) 343-4
*Umarete-wa Mita Keredo
   (I Was Born, but...) 202-3,
   217
*Umberto D. 37
*Under Capricorn 487, 517-8
*Underworld 32, 134-5, 148-9,
   179, 196

Unfinished Symphony 234
*Gli Uomini, Che Mascalzoni!
  (What Rascals Men Are!)
  212, 249
*Us Kids (Nous, les gosses)
  335-6, 377

*Les Vacances de M. Hulot
  (Monsieur Hulot's Holiday)
  460
*Valahol Európában... (Some-
  where in Europe) 37, 447-8,
  479
*Vampyr, ou l'étrange aven-
  ture de David Gray 194-5,
  364
*Vanina (Vanina oder die
  Galgenhochzeit) 31, 84,
  85-6, 107
*Varieté (Vaudeville) 99,
  112-3, 114, 116
*Vaudeville (Varieté) 99,
  112-3, 114, 116
*Veliky Grazhdanin (A Great
  Citizen) 226, 307, 313-4
*Vesyolye Rebyata (Jolly
  Fellows) 231-2, 291
*Veliky Perelom (The Great
  Turning Point) 37, 404-5
*Vertigo 216
La Vie est à nous 243
*Visages d'enfants 105-6
*Les Visiteurs du soir 36,
  303, 347-8, 394
*Vivere in pace 37, 427-8
*V Lyudyakh (Among People)
  295-6
*Volga-Volga 291-2
*Vosstaniye Rybakov (Revolt
  of the Fishermen) 230-1
*Vozvrashcheniye Maksima
  (The Return of Maxim)
  227, 271, 294
*Vredens Dag (Day of Wrath)
  36, 363-5
*Vstrechnyi (Counterplan)
  209-10
*The Vyborg Side (Vyborgskaya
  Storona) 227, 294-5
*Vyborgskaya Storona (The
  Vyborg Side) 227, 294-5

*Das Wachsfigurenkabinett
  (Waxworks) 107-8, 113, 266
*Waga Seishun ni Kuinashi (No
  Regrets for My Youth) 37,
  433-4
Walking Down Broadway 151
*A Walk in the Sun 410-1
*Warning Shadows (Schatten--
  Eine nächtliche Halluzination)
  31, 75, 83-4, 416
*The Wave (Redes) 236
*Waxworks (Das Wachsfiguren-
  kabinett) 107-8, 113, 266
*The Way Ahead 352, 386-7
*Way Down East 62-3, 427
*The Way to the Stars 352, 387,
  402-3
*The Wedding March xx, 130-1,
  132, 156
*We From Kronstadt (My iz
  Kronshtata) 35, 253-4, 259
*Western Union 345-6
*Westfront 1918 33, 176-7, 178
*What Rascals Men Are!
  (Gli Uomini, Che Mascalzoni!)
  212, 249
Whisky Galore! 516
*The White Heron (Shirasagi)
  148
*White Shadows on the South
  Seas 157
*Wife, Be Like a Rose (Tsuma
  Yō Bara no Yoni) 245-6
*Wild Strawberries (Smultron-
  stället) 142
*The Wind 123, 142-3
*Wings of a Serf (Krylya
  Kholopa) 124-5
*The Winslow Boy 484
*Witchcraft Through the Ages
  (Häxan) 71-2, 364
*Without Pity (Senza Pietà)
  483-4
*The Woman in the Window 37,
  385
*A Woman of Paris 90-2
Woman Trouble SEE The
  Street Has Many Dreams
The Wrong Man 121
*Wuthering Heights 318-9

*Xochimilco (Maria Candelaria)

36, 373-4, 521

*Yellow Sky 474-5
*Yoidore Tenshi (Drunken
    Angel) 37, 475-6, 503
*You Can't Take It With You
    34, 295
*Young and Innocent 280
*Young Mr. Lincoln 316-7
Young Mr. Pitt 386
*The Young Trees (Młody Las)
    238
*The Youth of Maxim (Yunost
    Maksima) 226-7, 271, 294
*Yunost Maksima (The Youth
    of Maxim) 226-7, 271,
    294

*Zangiku Monogatari (The
    Story of the Last
    Chrysanthemum) 307-8
*Zemla (Earth) [Dovzhenko]
    32, 171-2, 252
Zéro de conduite 222
*Zorba the Greek (Alexis
    Zorbas) 449